THE INVISIBLE CONSTITUTION IN COMPARATIVE PERSPECTIVE

Constitutions worldwide inevitably have 'invisible' features: they have silences and lacunae, unwritten or conventional underpinnings, and social and political dimensions not apparent to certain observers. *The Invisible Constitution in Comparative Perspective* helps us understand these dimensions to contemporary constitutions, and their role in the interpretation, legitimacy and stability of different constitutional systems. This volume provides a nuanced theoretical discussion of the idea of 'invisibility' in a constitutional context, and its relationship to more traditional understandings of written versus unwritten constitutionalism. Containing a rich array of case studies, including discussions of constitutional practice in Australia, Canada, China, Germany, Hong Kong, Israel, Italy, Indonesia, Ireland and Malaysia, this book will look at how this aspect of 'invisible constitutions' is manifested across different jurisdictions.

Rosalind Dixon is Professor of Law at UNSW Sydney, whose work focuses on comparative constitutional law and constitutional design, theories of constitutional dialogue and amendment, socio-economic rights, and constitutional law and gender. She is co-president elect of the International Society of Public Law, and on the Editorial Board of its associated journal, the International Journal of Constitutional Law. She is also advisor to the Public Law Review and Journal of Institutional Studies. Her work has been published in leading journals in the United States, Canada, the United Kingdom and Australia. She is co-editor, with Tom Ginsburg, of *Comparative Constitutional Law* (2011) and *Comparative Constitutional Law in Asia* (2014). She is also co-editor, with Mark Tushnet and Susan Rose-Ackermann, of the Edward Elgar series on Constitutional and Administrative Law and editor of the Constitutions of the World series.

Adrienne Stone is Redmond Barry Distinguished Professor, Director of the Centre for Comparative Constitutional Studies and Kathleen Fitzpatrick Australian Laureate Fellow at Melbourne Law School. She is First Vice President of the International Association of Constitutional Law and is a Fellow of the Academy of Social Sciences in Australia. She writes on constitutional law and theory, with particular attention to freedom of expression. Her work has published widely in international journals on these questions. She is co-editor, with Cheryl Saunders, of the *Oxford Handbook on the Australian Constitution* (2018) as well as co-editor with Frederick Schauer of the forthcoming *Oxford Handbook in Freedom of Speech* (2018).

Comparative Constitutional Law and Policy

SERIES EDITORS

Tom Ginsburg *University of Chicago*
Zachary Elkins *University of Texas at Austin*
Ran Hirschl *University of Toronto*

Comparative constitutional law is an intellectually vibrant field that encompasses an increasingly broad array of approaches and methodologies. This series collects analytically innovative and empirically grounded work from scholars of comparative constitutionalism across academic disciplines. Books in the series include theoretically informed studies of single constitutional jurisdictions, comparative studies of constitutional law and institutions, and edited collections of original essays that respond to challenging theoretical and empirical questions in the field.

BOOKS IN THE SERIES

Constituent Assemblies edited by Jon Elster, Roberto Gargarella, Vatsal Naresh, and Bjorn Erik Rasch

Judicial Review in Norway Anine Kierulf

The DNA of Constitutional Justice in Latin America: Politics, Governance, and Judicial Design Daniel M. Brinks and Abby Blass

The Adventures of the Constituent Power: Beyond Revolutions? Andrew Arato

Constitutions, Religion and Politics in Asia: Indonesia, Malaysia and Sri Lanka Dian A. H. Shah

Canada in the World: Comparative Perspectives on the Canadian Constitution edited by Richard Albert and David R. Cameron

Courts and Democracies in Asia Po Jen Yap

Proportionality: New Frontiers, New Challenges edited by Vicki C. Jackson and Mark Tushnet

Constituents Before Assembly: Participation, Deliberation, and Representation in the Crafting of New Constitutions Todd A. Eisenstadt, A. Carl LeVan, and Tofigh Maboudi

Assessing Constitutional Performance edited by Tom Ginsburg and Aziz Huq
Buddhism, Politics and the Limits of Law: The Pyrrhic Constitutionalism of Sri Lanka Benjamin Schonthal
Engaging with Social Rights: Procedure, Participation and Democracy in South Africa's Second Wave Brian Ray
Constitutional Courts as Mediators: Armed Conflict, Civil–Military Relations, and the Rule of Law in Latin America Julio Ríos-Figueroa
Perils of Judicial Self-Government in Transitional Societies David Kosař
Making We the People: Democratic Constitutional Founding in Postwar Japan and South Korea Chaihark Hahm and Sung Ho Kim
Radical Deprivation on Trial: The Impact of Judicial Activism on Socioeconomic Rights in the Global South César Rodríguez-Garavito and Diana Rodríguez-Franco
Unstable Constitutionalism: Law and Politics in South Asia edited by Mark Tushnet and Madhav Khosla
Magna Carta and its Modern Legacy edited by Robert Hazell and James Melton
Constitutions and Religious Freedom Frank B. Cross
International Courts and the Performance of International Agreements: A General Theory with Evidence from the European Union Clifford J. Carrubba and Matthew J. Gabel
Reputation and Judicial Tactics: A Theory of National and International Courts Shai Dothan
Social Difference and Constitutionalism in Pan-Asia edited by Susan H. Williams
Constitutionalism in Asia in the Early Twenty-First Century edited by Albert H. Y. Chen
Constitutions in Authoritarian Regimes edited by Tom Ginsburg and Alberto Simpser
Presidential Legislation in India: The Law and Practice of Ordinances Shubhankar Dam
Social and Political Foundations of Constitutions edited by Denis J. Galligan and Mila Versteeg
Consequential Courts: Judicial Roles in Global Perspective edited by Diana Kapiszewski, Gordon Silverstein, and Robert A. Kagan
Comparative Constitutional Design edited by Tom Ginsburg

The Invisible Constitution in Comparative Perspective

Edited by

ROSALIND DIXON
University of New South Wales

ADRIENNE STONE
University of Melbourne

CAMBRIDGE UNIVERSITY PRESS

CAMBRIDGE
UNIVERSITY PRESS

University Printing House, Cambridge CB2 8BS, United Kingdom

One Liberty Plaza, 20th Floor, New York, NY 10006, USA

477 Williamstown Road, Port Melbourne, VIC 3207, Australia

314-321, 3rd Floor, Plot 3, Splendor Forum, Jasola District Centre, New Delhi - 110025, India

79 Anson Road, #06-04/06, Singapore 079906

Cambridge University Press is part of the University of Cambridge.

It furthers the University's mission by disseminating knowledge in the pursuit of education, learning and research at the highest international levels of excellence.

www.cambridge.org
Information on this title: www.cambridge.org/9781108405478
DOI: 10.1017/9781108277914

© Rosalind Dixon and Adrienne Stone 2018

This publication is in copyright. Subject to statutory exception and to the provisions of relevant collective licensing agreements, no reproduction of any part may take place without the written permission of Cambridge University Press.

First published 2018
First paperback edition 2019

A catalogue record for this publication is available from the British Library

Library of Congress Cataloging in Publication data
Names: Dixon, Rosalind, editor. | Stone, Adrienne (Adrienne Sarah Ackary), editor.
Title: The invisible constitution in comparative perspective / edited by Rosalind Dixon, University of New South Wales, Sydney; Adrienne Stone, University of Melbourne.
Description: Cambridge, United Kingdom ; New York, NY, USA : Cambridge University Press, 2018. | Series: Comparative constitutional law and policy
Identifiers: LCCN 2018009841 | ISBN 9781108417570 (hardback)
Subjects: LCSH: Constitutional law.
Classification: LCC K3165 .I585 2018 | DDC 342—dc23 LC record available at https://lccn.loc.gov/2018009841

ISBN 978-1-108-41757-0 Hardback
ISBN 978-1-108-40547-8 Paperback

Cambridge University Press has no responsibility for the persistence or accuracy of URLs for external or third-party internet websites referred to in this publication, and does not guarantee that any content on such websites is, or will remain, accurate or appropriate.

Contents

Contributors		*page* ix
PART I	CONCEPTUALISING THE INVISIBLE CONSTITUTION	
1	The Invisible Constitution in Comparative Perspective *Rosalind Dixon and Adrienne Stone*	3
2	Soundings and Silences *Laurence H. Tribe*	21
3	Originalism and the Invisible Constitution *Lawrence B. Solum*	61
4	The Implicit and the Implied in a Written Constitution *Jeffrey Goldsworthy*	109
5	The Centrality and Diversity of the Invisible Constitution *Patrick Emerton*	146
6	Interim Constitutions and the Invisible Constitution *Caitlin Goss*	167
PART II	THE VIEW FROM ASIA PACIFIC AND THE MIDDLE EAST	
7	Behind the Text of the Basic Law: Some Constitutional Fundamentals *Johannes M. M. Chan*	193
8	The Constitutional Orders of 'One Country, Two Systems': A Comparative Study of the Visible and Invisible Bases of Constitutional Review and Proportionality Analysis in the Chinese Special Administrative Regions of Hong Kong and Macau *Albert H. Y. Chen and P. Y. Lo*	230

9	The Platonic Conception of the Israeli Constitution *Iddo Porat*	268
10	The Indonesian Constitutional Court: Implying Rights from the 'Rule of Law' *Simon Butt*	298
11	Is the Invisible Constitution Really Invisible? Some Reflections in the Context of Korean Constitutional Adjudication *Jongcheol Kim*	320
12	Constitutional Implications in Australia: Explaining the Structure – Rights Dualism *Rosalind Dixon and Gabrielle Appleby*	343
13	Malaysia's Invisible Constitution *Yvonne Tew*	376
14	The 'Invisible Constitution' seen Realistically: Visualising China's Unitary System *Han Zhai*	401

PART III   THE VIEW FROM EUROPE AND NORTH AMERICA

15	The Evolution of Natural Law in Ireland *Eoin Carolan*	431
16	"Additive Judgments": A Way to Make the Invisible Content of the Italian Constitution Visible *Irene Spigno*	457
17	Germany's German Constitution *Russell A. Miller*	482
18	Unwritten Constitutional Principles in Canada: Genuine or Strategic? *David Schneiderman*	517
19	Lost in Transition: Invisible Constitutionalism in Hungary *Gábor Attila Tóth*	541
Index		563

Contributors

Gabrielle Appleby is Associate Professor and Associate Dean (International and External Engagement) at the University of New South Wales, Faculty of Law.

Simon Butt is Professor of Indonesian Law and Associate Director of the Centre for Asian and Pacific Law at the University of Sydney Law School.

Eoin Carolan is Professor and Director of the Centre for Constitutional Studies at University College Dublin.

Johannes M. M. Chan is Professor of Law and former Dean of the University of Hong Kong, Faculty of Law.

Albert H. Y. Chen is Cheng Chan Lan Yue Professor of Constitutional Law at the University of Hong Kong, Faculty of Law.

Patrick Emerton is Associate Professor at Monash University, Faculty of Law.

Jeffrey Goldsworthy is Emeritus Professor of Law, Monash University; Adjunct Professor of Law, The University of Adelaide; and Professorial Fellow, University of Melbourne Law School.

Caitlin Goss is Lecturer at the University of Queensland, TC Beirne School of Law.

Jongcheol Kim is Professor at Yonsei Law School.

P. Y. Lo is Barrister and visiting fellow of the Centre for Comparative and Public Law, Faculty of Law, University of Hong Kong.

Russell A. Miller is the J. B. Stombock Professor of Law at the Washington and Lee University School of Law.

Iddo Porat is Associate Professor of Law at the College of Law and Business, Israel.

David Schneiderman is Professor of Law and Political Science at the University of Toronto, Faculty of Law.

Lawrence B. Solum is the Carmack Waterhouse Professor of Law at the Georgetown University Law Center.

Irene Spigno is Professor of Comparative Constitutional Law and Human Rights at the Inter-American Academy of Human Rights of the Autonomous University of Coahuila, Mexico.

Yvonne Tew is Associate Professor of Law at the Georgetown University Law Center.

Gábor Attila Tóth is Alexander von Humboldt Fellow at the Humboldt University, Berlin and an associate professor of Law at the University of Debrecen.

Laurence H. Tribe is the Carl M. Loeb University Professor and Professor of Constitutional Law at Harvard Law School.

Han Zhai is an associate research fellow at the Research Institute of Law and Policy, School of Law and Policy, School of Law, Wuhan University.

PART I
CONCEPTUALISING THE INVISIBLE CONSTITUTION

1

The Invisible Constitution in Comparative Perspective

Rosalind Dixon and Adrienne Stone[*]

In the 'Invisible Constitution', Laurence Tribe invites us to reflect on the idea of the 'invisible' Constitution as 'the ocean of ideas propositions, recovered memories and imagined experience' in which the text of the United States Constitution floats or operates.[1] The idea is a rich and captivating one which has commanded the attention of readers worldwide. But what do we mean when we refer to constitutional 'invisibility'? Invisibility, as Larry Solum notes in his chapter, is an evocative concept; yet it is also an ambiguous one.

1.1. CONCEPTUAL UNDERSTANDINGS: EXTRA-TEXTUAL CONSTITUTIONAL SOURCES AND INFLUENCES

One understanding of constitutional 'invisibility' (the 'unwritten' understanding) is closely connected to ideas about small 'c' or unwritten constitutionalism: invisible constitutions might be understood to be those that lack canonical legal status or formal status as an instrument labelled 'constitutional' in character. In this sense, the idea of the invisible constitution could also be understood as linked to traditions of political rather than legal constitutionalism.[2]

Another, related approach to the idea of 'invisibility', however, is more closely connected to written constitutional traditions (the 'extra-constitutional'

---

[*] We wish to acknowledge the support of the Melbourne Law School, the Faculty of Law at the University of New South Wales and the Australian Research Council through Adrienne Stone's Kathleen Fitzpatrick Australian Laureate Fellowship. The chapters in the volume were first presented at an International Association of Constitutional Law (IACL-AIDC) Roundtable, The Invisible Constitution in Comparative Perspective, held at Melbourne on May 2-3, 2016 and we thank the IACL-AIDC and all the participants in that Roundtable for their contributions. We also thank Marcus Roberts, Elizabeth Brumby and Melissa Voigt for their editorial and research assistance.

[1] Laurence H. Tribe, *The Invisible Constitution* (Oxford: Oxford University Press, 2008), 9.

[2] Janet McLean, 'The Unwritten Political Constitution and Its Enemies' (2016) 14 *International Journal of Constitutional Law* 119; J. A. G. Griffith, 'The Political Constitution' (1979) 42 *Modern Law Review* 1.

understanding). Any written constitution must be interpreted – or 'implemented'[3] – by government officials in ways that mean that the actual constitutional *law* of a particular jurisdiction is made up of what Tribe describes as 'a complex superstructure of rules, doctrines, standards, legal tests, judicial precedents, legislative and executive practices, and cultural and social traditions' or values.[4] Similarly, Larry Solum, in his contribution to this book, identifies six categories of extra-textual sources that can and do regularly influence the actual constitutional law of various countries – i.e., other foundational documents outside the scope of the capital 'C' constitution, documents and records relating to the framing and ratification of the constitution, moral and political philosophical understandings or values, social norms and values, institutional practices (including judicial decisions, statutes and executive actions) and various discretionary decisions by different constitutional actors.

In this sense, all constitutions comprise a mix of visible and invisible elements or elements that are, more or less, explicitly *reflected* in the text of a written constitution. This understanding of the term constitutional 'invisibility' more readily lends itself to broad comparative inquiry than notions of the 'unwritten' constitution.[5]

The sphere of 'invisibility' in this context is, of course, inevitably bound up with what the text of a particular constitution actually says and how we understand notions of constitutional meaning and interpretation. In some constitutions, how courts structure and approach the balancing of competing constitutional and legislative demands necessarily involves the development and application of extra-textual or 'common law'-style constitutional principles, whereas in others the text itself spells out a quite explicit constitutional framework within which the process of balancing must take place.[6] In many constitutional systems, the text of the constitution is likewise quite sparse when it comes to articulating a country's basic constitutional identity, or core constitutional 'values'. Any reliance by a court on such values will thus necessarily involve some form of resort to extra-constitutional sources. In other constitutional systems, however, the text of the constitution itself is quite explicit in stating the country's founding commitments and values. The resort to such

---

[3] Richard H. Fallon, Jr., 'The Rule of Law as a Concept in Constitutional Discourse' (1997) 97 *Columbia Law Review* 1.
[4] Tribe, Supra note 1, 10.
[5] We are indebted to Dr Lulu Weis her insightful commentary delivered at the IACL–AIDC Roundtable, *The Invisible Constitution in Comparative Perspective* at Melbourne Law School in May 2016, framing the distinction in these terms.
[6] Compare e.g., South African Constitution s 36; Canadian Charter of Rights and Freedoms s 1; Hong Kong Bill of Rights Ordinance Arts 8, 10, 15–18; Macau Basic Law Art 32.

values by courts will thus itself involve a form of express *textual* rather than extra-textual constitutional influence.[7]

Similarly, how we understand the sphere of invisibility, in this context, will be connected to long-standing debates about the proper approach to ascertaining the *meaning* of particular provisions of a constitutional text. Larry Solum and Jeffrey Goldsworthy, for instance, in their contributions to the volume argue that constitutional meaning is a matter of 'communicative meaning' fixed at the time the text was framed and ratified. For both Solum and Goldsworthy, this means that resort to *certain* non-textual constitutional sources (e.g., sources that go to historical understandings of language or elucidate certain logical assumptions on the part of drafters) will be a legitimate part of the process of constitutional construction itself, whereas most such sources will be truly external or extrinsic to such a process.

Other theories of constitutional interpretation, in contrast, take an approach to constitutional meaning that is more accommodating of non-textual sources. Johannes Chan, in Chapter 7, describes constitutional interpretation as 'guided by various fundamental values in our constitutional system ... shaped by the social, political and historical contexts of the society in which the constitution operates'. Patrick Emerton, in Chapter 5, suggests that the best understanding of constitutional 'meaning' necessarily invites – indeed requires – attention to broader social and political context. In this view, many fewer sources will also properly be understood as extra-textual in nature: they will be embedded within practices of textual interpretation and thus logically *internal* rather than external or outside of the text itself. Similarly, many adherents to a 'dynamic' or living approach to constitutional interpretation will see attention to various non-textual sources (such as evolving community values) as *internal* to the process of constitutional interpretation, where more 'originalist' scholars would see such a process as entirely external to a proper approach to constitutional construction.[8]

The basic idea of various legal sources as *non*-explicit in the text of a written constitution, however, is still one that is readily understandable and has

---

[7] See e.g., South African Constitution s 1. Reliance on section 1 for interpretation of other provisions of the SA Constitution, as Kate O'Regan has noted, involves a form of triangulation by the Constitutional Court of South Africa among different express textual constitutional sources: Kate O'Regan, IACL–AIDC Roundtable, Melbourne Law School, 2–3 May 2016.

[8] Compare e.g., Lawrence B. Solum, 'Originalism and the Unwritten Constitution' (2013) *University of Illinois Law Review* 1935; Jeffrey Goldsworthy, 'Interpreting the Constitution in its Second Century' (2000) 24 *Melbourne University Law Review* 677; Richard H. Fallon, 'A Constructivist Coherence Theory of Constitutional Interpretation' (1987) 100 *Harvard Law Review* 1189; Vicki C. Jackson, 'Constitutions as "Living Trees"? Comparative Constitutional Law and Interpretive Metaphors' (2006) 75 *Fordham Law Review* 921; Jack M. Balkin, 'The Roots of the Living Constitution' (2012) 92 *Boston University Law Review* 1129.

intuitive appeal. The outer boundaries of such an understanding will inevitably be contested – in part because of differences in constitutional interpretive methodology and in part due to important and largely unanswered questions about what is necessary for a practice to count as sufficiently legal to amount to an invisible constitutional rather than non- or even anti-constitutional influence. (Carolan, in Chapter 15, provides an important acknowledgement of the centrality of such questions, but does not attempt to provide any complete answer to them.) But the basic idea of the invisible constitution as the *extra-textual* constitution nonetheless retains broad conceptual and comparative utility.

1.1.1. Sociological Understandings – or the 'Hidden' Constitution

A second understanding of 'invisibility' is largely sociological in nature: it refers to ordinary notions of what is obvious or apparent to the 'naked' eye. Invisibility, in this view, does not denote any stable conceptual category or set of categories. Rather, it corresponds to what is hidden or non-observable to ordinary readers of a constitution – i.e., aspects of a constitutional tradition that are sufficiently deep or outside the confines of what is understood as constitutional within a given system, that they are often overlooked as elements of actual constitutional practice. If constitutions, for instance, ultimately depend on a set of social practices for their authority as constitutional documents, then these practices themselves are in some sense a critical – but largely invisible – part of a constitutional system.

Similarly, some forms of constitutional practice may be so far removed from any deliberate or conscious set of institutional actions or choices that they are often invisible to those who study the constitutional role of particular institutions. Constitutional invisibility in this sense could be understood as similar to Adam Smith,[9] or Frederik Hayek's notion,[10] of the invisible hand or role of price-signals and markets in the achievement of allocative efficiency in markets: no visible human agent or agency, is involved in the overall workings of the market in this context and yet markets perform an extremely wide-ranging role in aggregating information and resources.[11] While often focused on the far more visible role of individual agents – i.e., courts, legislators or executive actors, constitutional law could also be understood to have a similar set of invisible

---

[9] Adam Smith, *The Theory of Moral Sentiments* (London: A. Milar, 1759); Adam Smith, *An Inquiry into the Nature and Causes of the Wealth of Nations* (London: Methuen & Co., 1776).
[10] F. A. Hayek, *The Road to Serfdom* (Chicago, IL: University of Chicago Press, 1944).
[11] Compare also Humean understandings: David Hume, *A Treatise of Human Nature* (Oxford: Oxford University Press, 1739); David Hume, *Essays: Moral, Political, and Literary* (Indianapolis, IN: Liberty Fund, rev. edn 1985).

elements. It often depends on political dynamics and interactions over which no individual actor is fully master or in control, or even fully cognisant of.[12]

What is the relationship between sociological understandings of invisibility of this kind and more conceptual understandings of the role of extra-constitutional sources or practices? In large part the answer depends on the particular constitutional context. In some countries, the extra-textual nature of particular constitutional influences will mean they are overlooked as aspects of actual constitutional practice: in the United States, for example, scholars such as Amar,[13] Ackerman,[14] Strauss[15] and Tribe[16] have argued that a range of extra-textual constitutional sources play a crucial but *under-appreciated* role in American constitutional practice – i.e., they point to the important but previously under-theorised role of intra-textual relationships, informal constitutional 'moments' or change, common law interpretive influences and structural and political values in actual constitutional practice in the United States. In other jurisdictions, in contrast, the mere fact that particular constitutional sources are unwritten or extra-textual in origin will not necessarily render them 'invisible' to an ordinary observer. In countries such as the United Kingdom and New Zealand, constitutions are broadly understood to be unwritten in nature and thus the unwritten constitution is quite clearly visible to most legal audiences and informed citizens. Thus, in countries of this kind something more will generally be required for unwritten or extra-textual sources to be truly 'hidden' in nature: such influences must be so deep, strategic or implicit rather than explicit, in nature, to make them non-observable to ordinary constitutional actors.

Invisibility in this more sociological sense is also inherently *time*-sensitive: the very process of scholars identifying various legal practices as part of constitutional practice in a particular jurisdiction tends to render those practices more visible, in ways that ultimately reduce the claim that they have to be included in any definition of 'the invisible constitution'. Indeed, this is one of the values of comparative constitutional scholarship on the invisible constitution: it offers the potential to render more visible constitutional practices in various countries in ways that then allow constitutional 'insiders' and 'outsiders' better to appreciate their centrality to a particular country's legal and constitutional arrangements, and insiders in particular to more critically engage

---

[12] See e.g., Sanford Levinson, *Our Undemocratic Constitution: Where the Constitution Goes Wrong (And How We the People Can Correct It)* (Oxford: Oxford University Press, 2008).
[13] Akhil Reed Amar, *America's Unwritten Constitution: The Precedents and Principles We Live By* (New York, NY: Basic Books, 2012).
[14] Bruce Ackerman, *We the People, Volume 1: Foundations* (Cambridge: Harvard University Press, 1993).
[15] David A. Strauss, 'Common Law Constitutional Interpretation' (1996) 63 *University of Chicago Law Review* 877.
[16] Tribe, Supra note 1.

with those practices.[17] Invisibility in this sense, however, is also inevitably an ever-decreasing phenomenon in a world of increasingly rich comparative constitutional scholarship. The more we, as scholars, identify particular constitutional norms as part of the invisible constitution, the more visible they become in ways that progressively render them outside the scope of our inquiry on the invisible constitution.

1.2. CONTRIBUTORS' UNDERSTANDINGS

Contributors to the volume also, at various points, take both of these approaches to the idea of indivisibility. Iddo Porat, in Chapter 9 on Israel, identifies the Israeli constitution as engaging two distinct notions of invisibility – the idea of constitutions as in large part unwritten or found outside a canonical capital 'C' constitutional document *and* the idea of constitutions as hidden to a range of actors. It is a fundamental matter of political disagreement within Israel, he suggests, as to whether the thirteen Basic Laws enacted by the Knesset in fact amount to a constitution. The argument that there is a constitution in Israel critically depends on contested ideas about what it means for a court to create a constitution, via the interpretation of 'ordinary' statutes. Given that controversy, if one does believe that Israel has a constitution, one might also argue that the Israeli constitution is one that is largely invisible to many observers – both within the polity and elsewhere.

A number of chapters understand the idea of invisibility as more directly connected to written constitutional traditions or as referring to a variety of extra-constitutional influences on the practice of written constitutions, or practices not directly bounded by constitutional text. Simon Butt, in writing about the Indonesian Constitution (Chapter 10), focuses on extra-textual constitutional sources in the broad sense – i.e., the making of certain rights-based 'implications'; as well as the legislative practices underpinning those judicial decisions. In the Korean context (Chapter 11), Jongcheol Kim examines both a range of judicial doctrines and longstanding executive practices, which have helped create the idea of a 'customary constitution' in Korea. In Australia, Rosalind Dixon and Gabrielle Appleby focus on various judicial doctrines, involving the 'implication' of various principles under the Australian Constitution as the basis for analysing the Australian constitutional experience. And in Italy (Chapter 16), Irene Spigno likewise focuses on certain forms of judicial doctrine which involve the reading in of statutory language

---

[17] Cf Rosalind Dixon and Vicki Jackson, 'Constitutions Inside Out: Outsider Interventions in Domestic Constitutional Contests' (2013) 48 *Wake Forest Law Review* 149.

or forms of 'additive remedy' as implicitly creating an extra-textual dimension to constitutional practice in Italy.

Albert Chen and P. Y. Lo (Chapter 8) focus on proportionality doctrine and its variable application across cases, as an important extra-textual – or common law aspect – of constitutional practice in Hong Kong and Macau. Yvonne Tew (Chapter 13) also focuses specifically in this context on the competition between Islamic constitutional ideals and more secular constitutional principles, while Kim analyses doctrines of proportionality as devices for mediating conflicts within the invisible constitution in Korea: he notes doctrines of proportionality have allowed the Korean Constitutional Court both to sanction wrongdoing by President Roh *and* prevent disruption to the democratic process, by preventing relatively minor wrongdoing providing grounds for impeachment.[18]

Russell Miller (Chapter 17) also focuses on legal traditions, or 'families' or systems, as an aspect of extra-textual constitutional influence or practice in Germany; while Iddo Porat focuses on various substantive normative ideals both of constitutional and political morality and the judges' own role in realising that moral vision, as potentially implicit in the kind of progressive judicial expansion of the scope and entrenchment of the rights guaranteed by the 1992 Basic Laws in Israel. Eoin Carolan also takes a similar deep view of extra-textual constitutional influence and considers the role of natural law traditions and ideas as a potential source of extra-textual influence on the interpretation of the Irish Constitution.

A smaller number of chapters adopt a more distinctly sociological understanding of the invisible constitution or focus on various 'hidden' aspects of constitutional practice in a particular jurisdiction. Emerton, for instance, focuses on the ultimate rule of recognition for a constitution, *qua* constitution, as an important aspect of the invisible constitution in this 'deep' or sociological sense. This is also an understanding that might be associated with the contribution of Chen and Lo: one important aspect of the difference between Hong Kong and Macau they analyse in this context concerns the degree to which the Basic Law in each jurisdiction is understood to authorise weaker versus stronger levels of judicial scrutiny. In China, Han Zhai (Chapter 14) likewise suggests that a variety of localised practices and political dynamics contribute to a far more complex, decentralised system of government in China than is suggested by the formal text of the 1982 Constitution of China.

Other chapters focus on aspects of constitutional practice that are more invisible in the Smithian sense – or 'self-realising'. Caitlin Goss (Chapter 6),

---

[18] Kim (Chapter 11) at 26–7.

for example, examines the role of prior constitutions – specifically constitutions explicitly styled as 'interim' in nature – in the drafting and interpretation of later, more 'final' constitutions. She also suggests that while some aspects of this form of invisible constitutional overhang might be understood as quite deliberate and self-conscious on the part of drafters and judges, others might be more unconscious psychological pressures or influence or systemic pressures emanating from particular regional political or institutional forces (e.g., in Europe) or domestic political sources.

David Schneiderman (Chapter 18) and Johannes Chan also both take a distinctly sociological view of the invisible constitution in Canada and Hong Kong. In the Canadian context, Schneiderman focuses on various 'unwritten' or extra-textual constitutional principles that are a well-known part of Canadian constitutional practice. But he also goes on to analyse the deeper *strategic* judicial calculus that he sees as underlying the development of these unwritten principles, as a potentially under-appreciated or hidden aspect of well-known Canadian constitutional decisions such as the *Reference Re Secession of Quebec Case*.[19] In analysing the jurisprudence of the Hong Kong Court of Final Appeal (CFA), Chan likewise identifies potential strategic, and thus also largely non-observable, dynamics underpinning decisions such as the *Congo Case*, in which the Hong Kong CFA decided to refer a question for interpretation to the Standing Committee of the National Peoples' Congress (NPCSC) in Beijing.[20] Schneiderman, in this context, also provides a useful methodological contribution for scholars seeking to identify this more strategic dimension to the invisible constitution: he suggests that by a form of 'Occam's razor' logic that strategic explanations are most persuasive where reliance on unwritten constitutional principles seems unnecessary to justify the result reached by a court, because textual sources are sufficient to justify a similar result.[21]

Gabor Toth's contribution (Chapter 19) on Hungary is in this vein as well. He shows how the retention in form of the pre-1989 *Constitution* and the subsequent development of a rich jurisprudence based on 'invisible' commitments to 'equality' and 'dignity' ultimately failed to secure liberal democracy and progressive constitutionalism in Hungary. This failure he attributes, in part, to the deeper underlying sociological facts of Hungarian politics and culture attention which reveals that the constitutionalism of the Constitutional Court could not prevent the emergence of a new form of authoritarianism.

---

[19] [1998] 2 SCR 217.
[20] *Democratic Republic of the Congo v. FG Hemisphere Associates LLC*, FACV No 5/2010, 8 June 2011.
[21] Compare Rosalind Dixon, 'Toward a Realistic Comparative Constitutional Studies? (2016) 64 *American Journal of Comparative Law* 193.

We regard this as part of the value and richness of the volume, though where possible we ask contributors to make clear their particular understanding of 'invisibility' within the context of each chapter. For ease of reference and understanding, we also invite contributors at various points to label their understanding of 'invisibility' as more or less conceptual versus sociological; and unwritten versus extra-textual, as well broad versus narrow (deep/normative or shallow/formal) and agency-freighted versus self-realising in nature.

1.2.1. The Invisible Constitution in Comparative Context

Beyond these important definitional and conceptual differences, the contributions to the volume can be divided into three broad categories.

1.2.1.1. Normative Legitimacy of the Invisible Constitution

One set of contributions focuses on the invisible constitution through a normative or theoretical lens. Goldsworthy (Chapter 4), for instance, offers an important clarification of what we mean by the idea of 'implication' in a constitutional context. Genuine implications, Goldsworthy suggests, are not 'made' by judges: they are embedded within the existing communicative meaning of constitutional language and are not explicit in that language simply because they are obvious to any ordinary or reasonable observer. Another way of describing such implications might thus be seen as purely 'linguistic' in nature. Other implications, Goldsworthy suggests, are more freestanding or 'fabricated' in nature: they are 'made' or created by judges as a matter of either logical or practical necessity, based on other textual or structural features of the constitution. Another way of viewing this distinction, as Solum (Chapter 3) notes, is in terms of a distinction between constitutional implications in the broadest sense and a narrower set of implications that simply involve the 'contextual enrichment' of language. Solum points, for example, to four categories of contextual enrichment of language: 'implicatures', which convey communicative content that differs from the semantic content of an utterance or text; 'implicitures', which involve situations in which what he said implicitly includes something else that is closely related; 'presuppositions', where the community of content of particular language is provided by an unstated assumption or background belief that is conveyed by what is said; and 'modulation', whereby the conventional semantic meaning can be adjusted or modulated to fit a particular context.

Secondly, while defending implications in the narrower sense, both Goldsworthy and Solum provide a clear normative argument against implications in a broader sense. Goldsworthy argues that written constitutions should be interpreted by reference to both the original public meaning of the text and a principle or presumption of *expressio unius* – i.e., a principle that no other norms are to be inferred under the constitution that do not find express textual recognition in the text of the constitution. This means that all freestanding or 'fabricated' implications must in some way be *logically* necessary to give effect to the text of the constitution itself, not simply practically useful or conducive to the effective operation of the structures created by the text. Solum takes a similar view, and endorses implications that are *logically* necessary to the text, as consistent with an originalist methodology. But he also goes somewhat further than Goldsworthy, in allowing for the possibility of legitimate forms of implication as part of the process of constructional choice. From an originalist standpoint, he suggests, even reference to contemporary extra-constitutional sources may be legitimate in contexts where the original communicative meaning of the constitution is indeterminate or where the text 'underdetermines the content of constitutional law'. Extra-territorial influences of this kind may be *unbounded* by the text of the constitution, but it may still be sufficiently consistent with the text to be accepted by many originalists.

In a Korean context, Kim provides a more outcome-specific critique of the reliance by the Constitutional Court of Korea (KCC) on the notion of an invisible or 'customary' constitution.[22] The KCC, in the *Capital Relocation Case*, held that the longstanding status of Seoul as the national capital created a 'customary' constitutional norm regarding the capital's location which could only be altered by way of a national referendum.[23] This, Kim argues, was also problematic in a number of respects: it involved the KCC intervening in a highly contentious political case or entering the 'political thicket' without clear textual or other justification and in ways that arguably impeded rather than advanced the cause of democratic reform in Korea. Further, in relying on such a principle, Kim argues that the KCC did not articulate a persuasive account of what kinds of practices were sufficient to create a customary constitutional norm of this kind or of why it was appropriate to treat informal customary constitutional norms as fully equivalent to formally entrenched, written norms for the purposes of processes of constitutional change. In other cases, in contrast, Kim argues that reliance by the KCC on extra-textual constitutional sources arguably helped advance democracy: it allowed the KCC to avoid the threat to democracy posed by

---

[22] Kim (Chapter 11) at 15–24.
[23] Case NO.: 2004Hun-Ma554, KCCR : 16-2(B) KCCR 1, http://english.ccourt.go.kr/cckhome/eng/decisions/social/socialDetail.do

the potential impeachment of President Roh[24] and to increase pressure on the electoral system to give greater respect to principles of one person, one vote or equality of voting power.[25] In the Indonesian context, Butt (Chapter 10) offers a more modest normative critique of the Indonesian Court's approach to constitutional implications. He criticises the *reasoning* of the Indonesian Constitutional Court in its series of decisions implying various criminal due process rights as implicit in the concept of '*Negara Hokum*' (rule of law) found in the founding values of the Constitution. He suggests that norms of transparency and public reason-giving are important requirements of judicial legitimacy in all cases, but particularly strong demands on courts in an Indonesian context: he notes the long history of deliberate ideological manipulation of the idea of '*Negara Hokum*' in Indonesia and the argument this provides for a more principled, non-ideological elaboration of the ideal by the current court. He also notes the pervasive history of judicial corruption which arguably places the onus on the court to articulate a principled justification for its decisions in ways that rebut any appearance of corruption as an influence on constitutional decision-making.

Conversely, other contributors offer a partial or qualified normative defence of aspects of extra-textual constitutional influence on practices of constitutional decision-making or practice in various jurisdictions. Spigno, for example, defends the practice of reading-in or 'additive judgments' in the jurisprudence of the Italian Constitutional Court as normatively legitimate, based on the indirect textual authorisation for such a practice in the guarantee of equality in Art 3 of the Italian Constitution *and* limits she identifies as implicit in the actual practice or implementation of the doctrine – i.e., the unwillingness of the court to deploy the doctrine where there are multiple different ways of remedying a constitutional equality violation, where it would be contrary to the relevant legislative purpose or context (or what she describes as certain set legislative 'rhymes') or where it is inconsistent with the relevant subject-matter (e.g., the criminal nature of proceedings).

Carolan, in turn, defends the relationship between the visible and invisible constitution in Ireland as a valuable source of constitutional stability: 'connecting the Constitution to broad normative principles, the content of which are not made explicit', Carolan argues, 'provides a means of publicly declaring the systems goodness will nonetheless preserving a politically necessary space for moral contestation'. Where the Constitution was originally a quite direct bridge between natural law ideas about compassion and charity,

---

[24] Kim (Chapter 11) at 25–30.
[25] Kim (Chapter 11) at 30–4.

those ideas are now often mediated in Ireland via express constitutional commitments, such as commitments to dignity and justice. This, Carolan notes, also allows the natural law dimension of the Irish Constitution to adapt to an increasingly diverse and secular society, in ways that allow it to serve as a site of identification both for religious Catholics or natural law adherents and those committed to more plural religious traditions.

Han Zhai, in exploring the relationship between the visible and invisible constitution in China, suggests that de facto forms of decentralisation create 'effective local laboratories' for governmental experimentation which contribute to a more legitimate form of government in China than is often suggested by comparative constitutional studies that focus solely on the formal, visible aspects of the 1982 Chinese Constitution.

1.2.1.2. The Content and Contours of the Invisible Constitution

Another set of contributions focus more directly on the content and development of the invisible constitution in various constitutional systems and what that trajectory might tell us about the nature of the invisible constitution more generally. Iddo Porat and Caitlin Goss, for instance, identify 'human dignity' as an important express constitutional norm or commitment that has served as a locus for the incorporation of extra-textual constitutional ideas or values under the Israeli Basic Law and various 'final' constitutions that succeed earlier, 'interim' constitutional documents. Carolan likewise notes how express constitutional values such as 'dignity', 'autonomy' and 'justice' have provided a way in which natural law influences – as a form of 'shadow' or invisible constitutional influence – have gradually been positivized under the Irish Constitution. Butt holds up the 'the rule of law' (or in Indonesia, the idea of '*Negara Hokum*') as another constitutional ideal which, at least if sufficiently expressed in the text of the constitution, can provide a basis for a range of constitutional implications (such as those relating to minimum requirements of due process and a fair trial). Johannes Chan, in writing on Hong Kong's constitutional jurisprudence, likewise notes a principle of non-arbitrary government or the 'integrity of the common law system' is an important extra-textual principle guiding the approach of the Hong Kong Court of Final Appeal (CFA) to the scope of its duty to refer questions of interpretation to the NPCSC.[26]

---

[26] For the link between the rule of law notions of non-arbitrary government and the rule of law, see e.g., Martin Krygier, 'Four Puzzles about the Rule of Law: Why, What, Where? And Who Cares?' in James E. Fleming (ed.), *Getting to the Rule of Law*: NOMOS L (New York, NY: New York University Press, 2011) 64–106; Fallon, Jr., Supra note 3.

Tew, in describing Malaysian constitutional experience, points to the long-standing contest in Malaysia between liberal-secular and Islamic constitutional ideas and the clear 'victory' for religious ideas in a range of key constitutional contexts – including in cases involving the reasonableness of limiting rights of religious conversion for the purposes of inter-faith marriage,[27] the unilateral decision by one parent to convert a child's religion without the knowledge or consent or another parent[28] and various civil law cases interpreting secular statues. In doing so, she also highlights an important additional dimension to the idea of the 'invisible constitution': as comprising relatively settled or predictable patterns in how courts resolve constitutional conflicts in the context of questions of constitutional proportionality.

Chan, Chen and Lo, in writing on Hong Kong and Macau, also focus on similar aspects of the invisible constitution – i.e., consistent patterns in the application of a doctrine of proportionality in the two jurisdictions. Not every decision by a court to give priority to one constitutional norm, or value or legal interest, over another, will necessarily be part of the invisible constitution in an enduring sense. But consistent patterns of priority given to one value over another *will* be candidates for inclusion in our understanding of the invisible constitution. In Hong Kong, Chen and Lo suggest, for instance, the doctrine of proportionality is generally applied in a quite searching and robust way. The only exception, as Chan notes in his separate chapter, is in the context of cases involving socio-economic rights. In Macau, in contrast, Chen and Lo argue that the doctrine is applied in a far more deferential and curtailed way, which more closely approximates a form of rationality or reasonableness-based review.

Both Chan and Miller, in their respective chapters, also analyse the invisible constitution through the lens of different *legal systems* or *traditions*. In the Hong Kong context, Chan notes the degree to which the Hong Kong CFA's constitutional jurisprudence reflects an ongoing tension or dialogue, between common law and mainland constitutional ideas and how this tension is mediated or informed by notions of continuity versus change in constitutional interpretation in Hong Kong. In a German context, Miller describes the ways in which the German Basic Law and jurisprudence of the Constitutional Court is shaped both by common law traditions of evaluative judgment and relatively unbounded judicial discretion and adherence to a doctrine of precedent *and* more distinctly 'civilian' traditions. In many contexts, Miller notes, the Basic Law is quite specific and code-like in nature and delegates the task

[27] Lina Joy [2007] 3 All. Malay. Rep. 693; [2005] 5 All Malay. Rep. 663.
[28] *Pathmanathan a/l Krishnan v. Indira Gandhi a/p Mutho* [2016] Current Law Journal 911 (C.A.).

of implementing or concretizing constitutional meaning to legislatures rather than courts.[29] He also notes the degree to which the Federal Constitutional Court of Germany avoids reliance on dissent, attempts to systemize its decisions through structured forms of proportionality reasoning and other doctrines. Ultimately, he acknowledges the clear traffic or dialogue between civil and common law traditions within the German constitutional context, but in doing so also points to legal tradition as a critical dimension to our understanding of the invisible constitution. We cannot, he suggests, properly understand a written constitutional system without attention to the background legal context and traditions within which it operates.

1.2.1.3. An External Viewpoint: Explaining the Invisible Constitution

Another set of contributions are more positive or empirical in nature. Caitlin Goss, in her chapter on interim constitutions, suggests that as a positive, political matter, interim constitutions will often create political dynamics or interests that will push for the retention of institutional features found in previous supposedly 'interim' constitutions. Butt, in his chapter on Indonesia, notes what he regards as a surprising absence of controversy surrounding the implication of criminal due process rights in the Indonesian Constitution and connects that observation to a range of important context-specific factors. At the same time, Butt suggests that another explanation for the *non*-controversy surrounding the making of constitutional implications in Indonesia may lie in their very invisibility to broader constitutional actors – i.e., the non-salience for citizens and elected political officials of relevant constitutional decisions. He also points to the relatively clear connection between those rights and prior statutory entitlements in Indonesia and a trajectory of judicial decisions involving at least partial retreat, rather than simply ongoing expansion of such implications. The implication of various criminal due process rights, Butt notes, continued steadily under the Chief Justiceships of both Asshidique (2003–8) and Mahfud (2008–13), but has seemingly come to a halt under the subsequent three Chief Justices.

Tew and Chan, in writing about Malaysia and Hong Kong respectively, note the relationship between debates over originalist versus evolving approaches to interpretation or continuity versus change in constitutional practice, as an important factor shaping the substantive content of the invisible constitution.

---

[29] Compare Rosalind Dixon and Tom Ginsburg, 'Deciding Not to Decide: Deferral in Constitutional Design' (2011) 9 *International Journal of Constitutional Law* 636–72 (distinguishing by law clauses from more abstract delegations to courts).

Tew notes that in the Malaysian context, evolving approaches to interpretation have often favoured the priority given to Islamic constitutional ideals, whereas a more strictly originalist or purposive approach has tended to support a stronger emphasis on liberal-secular constitutional values. Chan likewise notes that, in Hong Kong, a commitment to legal continuity tends to favour common law legal principles and thus also a commitment to 'liberty and freedom under the common law system', where an emphasis on constitutional change will often favour mainland constitutional principles.

In analysing the quite different approach to proportionality doctrine in Hong Kong and Macau, Chen and Lo identify a number of potential contributing factors: the greater role of foreign law in the drafting of the Hong Kong Basic Law compared to that in Macau, the role of judges who are foreign nationals (and often prominent judges from other common law or constitutional jurisdictions) on the Hong Kong CFA and the greater linguistic challenges to ongoing foreign influence, in the form of a robust doctrine of proportionality, in Macau (where the legal system operates in Chinese and Portuguese) compared to Hong Kong (with a legal system operating in English). They also note that differences in the size of the two jurisdictions is a factor contributing to the relative number of opportunities for the development of a robust proportionality-based constitutional jurisprudence and the relatively conservative nature of the legal and judicial elite in Macau, compared to Hong Kong.

Similarly, in analysing the trajectory of constitutional implications in Australia, Dixon and Appleby identify a complex range of structural *and* socio-cultural factors as underpinning this trajectory. At the outset, they note a marked contrast between the approach of the High Court of Australia (HCA) to structural and rights-based constitutional implications: in a structural context, they suggest, the HCA has been quite willing to recognise a range of implications (such as those relating to federalism, the separation of powers and even political democracy), whereas in the context of individual rights, the court has consistently declined to recognise various implications. They further argue that this reflects a complex, intersecting set of influences – i.e., the limited express recognition of rights under the Australian Constitution or weak support in the text and structure of the Australian Constitution for individual rights-based protections; the 'slippery slope' argument this creates in individual cases in which the HCA is asked to recognise a rights-based implication; and the specific historical and legal-cultural influences in Australia, which make it important for the HCA closely to anchor judicially enforced implications *in* the text and structure itself.

Chan and Schneiderman also make interesting observations as to the kinds of dynamics underpinning the kind of strategic judicial calculus they observe, but is often over-looked, in decisions such as the *Secession Reference Case* and *Congo Case*. In the *Secession Reference Case*, Schneiderman suggests, the SCC was under clear institutional stress: it faced a constitutional challenge of tremendous significance and a direct challenge to its legitimacy. The government of Quebec refused to recognise the Court's jurisdiction to hear the case, even though it directly implicated the status of Quebec as a province of Canada. The Supreme Court's decision to identify various well-accepted constitutional principles – such as federalism, democracy, constitutionalism and the rule of law – as *unwritten* provided an important means of legitimising its reliance on other, far less well accepted principles (i.e., a duty to negotiate) as also unwritten in nature. And in the *Congo Case*, Chan suggests that the Hong Kong CFA was responding to a desire to preserve its own perceived integrity and effectiveness by avoiding a repeat of an earlier decision in *Ng Ka Ling* v. *Director of Immigration* (the right of abode case) in which it was immediately overruled by the committee, without any clear or open consideration of its reasoning.[30]

1.2.2. *The Invisible Constitution: Unanswered Questions and Future Directions*

When we set out to investigate the idea of the invisible constitution in a comparative context we were unsure as to how far the metaphor would take us: as the excellent contributions to this book attest to, the answer is very far indeed. We are also particularly pleased that in their combined focus on the Asia-Pacific region, the various contributions to the volume help de-centre many of our prevailing habits in comparative constitutional scholarship. It may be somewhat overstated to say that comparative constitutional scholarship systematically *overlooks* the experiences of the 'Global South',[31] but there is still a clear tendency in comparative scholarship to privilege the experiences of Europe and North America or the Anglo-American world, at the expense of a deeper and richer engagement with the experiences of Asia, Africa and Latin America. We are thus extremely pleased that both in the genesis of this volume, and its final layout, we are able to contribute to a form of comparative

---

[30] (2001) 4 HKCFAR 211.
[31] Ran Hirschl, *Comparative Matters: The Renaissance of Comparative Constitutional Law* (Oxford: Oxford University Press, 2014). Cf Daniel Bonilla Maldonado (ed.), *Constitutionalism of the Global South: The Activist Tribunals on India, South Africa and Colombia* (Cambridge: Cambridge University Press, 2013).

constitutional law scholarship that is truly global in nature, but that also begins – rather than ends – with the experiences of countries in the Global South.[32]

We also acknowledge, however, that there remain important outstanding questions about the idea of the 'invisible constitution' in comparative perspective, which the book does not fully address. The book clearly does not cover all or even nearly all relevant comparative case studies nor does it systematically address at least two important questions: one, how the scope or desirability of the invisible constitution may be shaped by the relative age, specificity and flexibility of a written constitution; and second, how various national constitutions interact with each other in the domain of the invisible constitution.

It seems quite plausible, for instance, that both the likelihood and legitimacy of various extra-textual constitutional influences may depend in part on the relative age, specificity and flexibility of a constitutional text. The more specific a constitutional document, the weaker the case will often be for wide-ranging extra-textual constitutional reference; whereas the more open-textured it is, the more legitimate it will be. Similarly, the more recent a constitutional document, the less persuasive the case may be for such influence; whereas the older a written instrument, the more legitimate such influences may be. The same pattern or argument could also apply to the difficulty of amending a written constitution: formal procedures for constitutional amendment allow a means of updating a constitutional text in ways that reduce the pressure for extra-textual constitutional influence or 'implication' by a court.[33] They may also offer a potential mechanism for overriding a court decision.[34] Thus, while judicial interpretation and amendment may not be perfect substitutes, either normatively or empirically, the scope of legitimate judicial decision-making may still be conditioned to some degree on the formal and practical availability of powers of constitutional amendment.[35]

These are issues that contributors touch on at various points: Iddo Porat, for example, notes the recent and quite deliberate nature of constitutional choices

---

[32] We wish to acknowledge in this context the extremely valuable support of the IACL, Melbourne Law School and the UNSW Faculty of Law, in making possible the IACL Roundtable at Melbourne Law School (2–3 May 2016) that preceded this collection.

[33] Rosalind Dixon, 'Constitutional Amendment Rules: A Comparative Perspective' in Tom Ginsburg and Rosalind Dixon (eds.), *Comparative Constitutional Law* (Cheltenham: Edward Elgar, 2011) 96–111.

[34] We do not to date have an adequate understanding of the complex nature of the relationship between the implied or extra-textual nature of various constitutional norms or practices, and their susceptibility to formal constitutional override by way of amendment: cf. Rosalind Dixon and Adrienne Stone 'Constitutional Amendment and Political Constitutionalism: A Philosophical and Comparative Reflection', David Dyzenhaus and Malcolm Thorburn (eds.), *Philosophical Foundations of Constitutional Law* (Oxford: Oxford University Press, 2016) 95–118.

[35] Dixon, Supra note 21, 193.

in Israel as a potential objection to the judicial development of unwritten constitutional understandings in Israel. Schneiderman also notes the degree to which in Canada, many scholars might regard the 'age, rigidity or prolixity of the Constitution' as factors influencing the degree to which the Supreme Court of Canada has tended to rely on unwritten constitutional principles.

Similarly, the task of comparing the content of invisible constitutions across different countries itself invites attention to the way in which constitutions may serve as extra-textual constitutional influences across borders: one constitution's written *or* unwritten constitution may be an important extra-textual influence on the interpretation of another country's written constitution, in ways that create a complex interaction of visible and invisible comparative constitutional engagement. This form of comparative influence may also be more or less apparent, or hidden, to informed observers in a particular country: in some countries, comparative influence is routinely accompanied by explicit citation to foreign judgments and practices, whereas in others (particularly those within or influenced by the civilian tradition) comparative influence is more unstated or implicit. In that sense, it may also be more hidden, absent informed and careful scholarship designed to uncover these previously hidden comparative or transnational influences.

Various contributors to the volume at times acknowledge the importance of these questions: Chen and Lo, for instance, note the importance of comparative and international law as an influence on the drafting of the Hong Kong Basic Law, in shaping the approach of the CFA in various contexts, and the role of foreign judges in shaping the CFA's jurisprudence and thus also as an important factor explaining the quite different experience of Macau, which has operated in the shadow of a far weaker, less direct form of comparative constitutional influence. Again, however, few contributors begin to address the idea of a set of invisible transnational constitutional influences, or how we might best understand both the visible and invisible traffic in ideas – themselves both textual and extra-textual – across borders.

One of the hallmarks of a great academic conversation is that it often raises as many important questions as it answers, and by that criterion we know that you will join us in judging this collection a great success. We also hope that others in the future will take up the challenge laid out in this section and help further broaden our understanding of the invisible constitution in comparative perspective.

2

Soundings and Silences

Laurence H. Tribe*

It was 1964. I was in my second year of law school when Simon and Garfunkel released the early version of their first and maybe greatest musical masterpiece, "The Sounds of Silence," a commercial failure that temporarily broke the duo apart until the piece was remixed in 1965 and re-released in 1966.[1] As revised, it has had a lasting legacy as art. And it quickly became my favorite song from the 1960s. As the song's own lyrics put it,

> a vision softly creeping
> Left its seeds while I was sleeping
> And the vision that was planted in my brain
> Still remains
> Within the sound of silence.[2]

I still recall how those lyrics echoed in my mind during a class I was taking in the fall of 1965 called *Advanced Constitutional Law* taught by the former Solicitor General and Watergate Special Prosecutor, Professor Archibald Cox. The professor came into the classroom carrying the slip opinion the Supreme Court had released that June in the now-famous case of *Griswold* v. *Connecticut*, which held that a married couple's use of contraceptives to enjoy sex without risking pregnancy could not be made a crime.[3] The right of reproductive freedom, later extended to unmarried individuals[4] and eventually

---

* This chapter was originally published as 'Soundings and Silences' (2016) 115 *Michigan Law Review* Online 26. The original format has been retained even where this result in deviations from the format used elsewhere in this volume.

[1] Geoffrey Himes, *How* "The Sound of Silence" *Became a Surprise Hit*, Smithsonian (January 2016), www.smithsonianmag.com/arts-culture/sound-silence-surprise-hit-180957672/?no-ist [https://perma.cc/LEZ3-LTF7].

[2] Simon and Garfunkel, "The Sounds of Silence," on Wednesday *Morning, 3 A.M.* (Columbia Records 1964).

[3] 381 U.S. 479 (1965).

[4] *Eisenstadt v. Baird*, 405 U.S. 438, 454–5 (1972).

extended from contraception to abortion,[5] hadn't been mentioned in the Constitution. But the Court's majority had concluded it was there just the same: the Constitution's silence on the subject wasn't to be construed as denying constitutional protection to "a right of privacy older than the Bill of Rights."[6]

I didn't know it at the time, but that same vision would come to structure much of what I learned and have since taught about the law. During my clerkship for Justice Potter Stewart in 1967–8, for example, I was proud to have had an opportunity to play a role in the Supreme Court's holding, in a case called *Katz v. United States*,[7] that electronically eavesdropping on phone conversations that someone expected would not be overheard by Big Brother constituted a "search or seizure" within the meaning of the Fourth Amendment's ban on "unreasonable searches and seizures."[8] The Court's justification for this landmark holding was that, although government agents had not physically trespassed on or into any property occupied by the person on whom it was spying, the Constitution "protects people, not places,"[9] and the government's electronic overhearing and recording of the defendant's conversations conflicted with his justifiable "expectation of privacy."[10]

The Fourth Amendment, as Justice Hugo Black insisted in dissent, was *silent* with respect to eavesdropping, whether by private citizens or by government agents.[11] And the Framers had certainly been well aware of the practice of government eavesdropping when the Bill of Rights was drafted in 1789 and ratified in 1791 (although they of course had no idea that *electronic* eavesdropping might someday be possible).[12] Moreover, as Justice Black emphasized, the *entire Constitution* was silent with respect to a right of "privacy."[13] The majority's response, in the opinion I helped draft, was that *implicit*

---

[5] *Roe v. Wade*, 410 U.S. 113, 165–6 (1973).
[6] *Griswold*, 381 U.S. at 486.
[7] 389 U.S. 347 (1967).
[8] *Katz*, 389 U.S. at 353, 369. Almost forty years earlier, the Court had handed down *Olmstead v. United States*, 277 U.S. 438 (1928), *overruled in part by Katz*, 389 U.S. at 352–3, which held that the government could violate the Fourth Amendment only by trespassing on people's property. In *Katz*, the Court was going to vote 4-4 (with Justice Marshall recusing himself) to leave standing the decision below, which had relied on *Olmstead*, but the arguments I helped persuade Justice Stewart to adopt changed the result to a 7-1 ruling in the other direction. Stephen Reinhardt, "Tribute to Professor Laurence Tribe" (2007) 42 *Tulsa Law Review* 939, 940–1.
[9] *Katz*, 389 U.S. at 351.
[10] Ibid., at 361 (Harlan, J., concurring).
[11] See ibid., at 365–6 (Black, J., dissenting).
[12] Ibid., at 366 (Black, J., dissenting).
[13] Ibid., at 373–4 (Black, J., dissenting).

in the Constitution was a right to expect that certain conversations would indeed remain private, even if the government made it known that it might be listening in. To reach that conclusion, the majority necessarily looked outside the four corners of the Fourth Amendment's text to formulate what it deemed a tacit postulate of the freedom of expression, a freedom expressly protected by the First Amendment. As the Court saw it, the *system of free expression* could not survive the chilling effect that would result from requiring all phone users to assume that they might be broadcasting their words to the uninvited ears of the FBI just because they hadn't taken measures to block out the uninvited eyes of passers-by.[14] The fact that the defendant in *Katz* made his call from inside a glass telephone booth was not dispositive of his right to informational privacy against the government.[15]

It would be a stretch to attribute that treatment of the Constitution's silence with respect to informational privacy to the song Paul Simon had written a few years earlier. But that song played in my mind's eye, and I must say that Justice Stewart was a Simon and Garfunkel fan as well.

Flash forward a dozen years or so to the first edition of the treatise I published in 1978, entitled *American Constitutional Law*.[16] That book's final chapter, entitled "The Problem of State Action," grappled with one of the most perplexing aspects in the law of the United States Constitution: its character as a body of law addressing not ordinary private conduct, but only *government conduct*.[17] Because government is responsible not only for the discrete acts of public officials and agents acting on its authority, but also for the body of laws and rules promulgated by government, it follows that the law of the Constitution is a kind of *meta-law*.[18] Among its rules are some that address the things that government actors have an affirmative constitutional obligation to do, so that many instances of what might be regarded as *government inaction* pose troubling constitutional questions.[19]

---

[14] Ibid., at 352.
[15] Ibid.
[16] Laurence H. Tribe, *American Constitutional Law* (1st edn 1978).
[17] Ibid., at 1147.
[18] See Laurence H. Tribe, "The Curvature of Constitutional Space: What Lawyers Can Learn from Modern Physics" (1989) 103 *Harv. L. Rev.* 1.
[19] See e.g., *Town of Castle Rock v. Gonzales*, 545 U.S. 748, 766–8 (2005) (holding that a woman did not have a property interest under the Due Process Clause in the town's enforcement of her restraining order against her estranged husband, who later killed their three children); *DeShaney v. Winnebago County Department of Social Services*, 489 U.S. 189, 194–7 (1989) (holding that the Due Process Clause does not impose affirmative obligations on local officials to protect an infant from his abusive father, even after local officials receive reports of possible abuse).

But to prevent the Constitution from becoming just another ordinary law – and to create breathing space for choices that government is either constitutionally obliged or at least free to permit or prohibit as it sees fit – the Supreme Court has generally interpreted constitutional provisions as having nothing at all to say about *non*governmental choices. That is so even if those constitutional provisions (like the Eighth Amendment's ban on "cruel and unusual punishments")[20] whose text does not expressly *say* they are limited to the acts of some level of government – in contrast with, for example, the First Amendment[21] and the Fourteenth,[22] which are limited by their very terms to government action. One might accordingly say that the constitutional principle limiting the Constitution's reach to "state action" is an unwritten command derived from the Constitution as a whole – a command that the Court has essentially "heard" in the sounds of constitutional silence.

So, for example, however cruel and extraordinary a parent's punishment of a supposedly misbehaving child might be, even a parent clearly guilty of child abuse in violation of state or local law could not be deemed to have violated the Eighth Amendment's prohibition against inflicting "cruel and unusual punishments" – despite the fact that the Amendment is literally silent as to whether its prohibition restricts only government actors. So too, a terrorist guilty of mass murder in violation of federal law would not have deprived anyone of life "without due process of law," which the Fifth Amendment requires the Federal Government to provide before it executes someone. And that is the case even though the Fifth Amendment's text, unlike that of the Fourteenth, contains no explicit limitation on government action.[23]

Of course, even though the Fourteenth Amendment by its terms prevents only *states* from depriving people of life (or liberty or property) without due process of law, and bans only *state* deprivation of "the equal protection of the laws,"[24] it would be entirely possible and indeed proper to hold a state government that knowingly, and while looking the other way, permits the beating or killing of an individual responsible for indirectly depriving that person of life or liberty without "due process of law," in violation of the Fourteenth Amendment.[25] And if the practice of "looking the other way" targets members

---

[20] U.S. Const. amend. VIII.
[21] Ibid., amend. I.
[22] Ibid., amend. XIV.
[23] Ibid., amend. V.
[24] Ibid., amend. XIV.
[25] Cf. Tribe, Supra note 16, at 8–12 (discussing the dissents in *DeShaney v. Winnebago County Department of Social Services*, 489 U.S. 189, 203–13 [1989]).

of a racial or religious minority, then that selective "inaction" by a state could well amount to a denial of equal protection of the laws.[26]

Developing and understanding the constitutional doctrines that determine when the requisite "state action" is present and when it is absent turns out to be particularly challenging. My treatise ended by summing up the final chapter – the one analyzing those doctrines – as a chapter about "what we do not want particular constitutional provisions to control."[27] And I closed the book with the question: "[I]s it not fitting that a book about the Constitution should close by studying what the Constitution is not about?"[28]

Needless to say, there are plenty of things beside private action that the Constitution is "not about." As Chief Justice John Marshall emphasized in *Marbury* v. *Madison*,[29] decided in 1803, the Constitution is *not* about what Marshall called purely discretionary choices left to the political branches,[30] like the president's choice of whom to nominate to the Court,[31] or Congress' choice of how best to regulate interstate or foreign commerce, or whether to facilitate commercial and fiscal activity by chartering a national bank.[32]

The Constitution *is* about certain *limits* on permissible political choices. Sometimes, the Supreme Court holds that a particular constitutional limit has been exceeded – as it held in *Marbury* with respect to Congress' attempt to expand the Court's own jurisdiction beyond the limits set by Article III.[33] In doing so, the Court exercises a power of "judicial review" that *Marbury* proclaimed was part, even if a silent part, of the entire constitutional plan.[34]

But many of the most important Supreme Court decisions take the form of holding that a particular limit either has not been exceeded or, more fundamentally, that the asserted limit is *not* in fact part of the Constitution at all. The holding of Marshall's 1819 opinion in *McCulloch* v. *Maryland*,[35] for instance, was that – unlike the Articles of Confederation, which had limited federal authority to the powers the Articles "expressly delegated" to the national

---

[26] See *DeShaney*, 489 U.S. at 197 n. 3 ("The State may not, of course, selectively deny its protective services to certain disfavored minorities without violating the Equal Protection Clause.") (citing *Yick Wo* v. *Hopkins*, 118 U.S. 356 [1886]).
[27] Tribe, Supra note 16, at 1174.
[28] Ibid.
[29] 5 U.S. (1 Cranch) 137 (1803).
[30] *Marbury*, 5 U.S. (1 Cranch) at 170.
[31] See ibid., at 167.
[32] *McCulloch* v. *Maryland*, 17 U.S. 316, 422–3 (1819).
[33] Ibid., at 175–6.
[34] See ibid., at 179–80.
[35] 17 U.S. (4 Wheat.) 316 (1819).

government[36] – the 1787 Constitution, in deliberately *omitting* the word "expressly," entrusted to the national government certain non-enumerated powers reasonably related to its delegated missions of regulating commerce and the like.[37] In upholding congressional power to charter a national bank in *McCulloch*, Marshall thus heard a message in the sound of silence that he detected when comparing the Constitution with the Articles that had preceded it.

As students of American constitutional history know well, there was a period from the late nineteenth century until 1937 during which the Supreme Court heard a very different message, one less tolerant of centralized federal power and more protective of so-called states' rights.[38] When the Court in 1918 struck down congressional legislation banning the interstate shipment of the products of child labor, for instance, in *Hammer v. Dagenhart*,[39] it went so far as to reinsert the key word "expressly" into its stingier summary of national legislative power![40]

The point of this largely autobiographical introduction is to motivate the discussion that follows by setting out some concrete examples of what I mean by "constitutional silence" and how it pervades all of constitutional law.

It is a commonplace that much of what our Supreme Court does involves filling in the "great silences of the Constitution," as Justice Robert Jackson put it when striking down the protectionist dairy regulation that New York State enacted without congressional authorization in 1949 in *H.P. Hood & Sons, Inc. v. Du Mond*.[41] That decision was one of many implementing what has come to be called the "dormant Commerce Clause," a set of unwritten constitutional principles limiting state commercial regulation in the face of congressional silence coupled with the Constitution's delegation to Congress of the power to regulate interstate commerce.[42] Although the silence of the Constitution's text with respect to such state regulation has not been construed to forbid or abolish it altogether, it has been understood to limit it considerably. Alexander Hamilton's *Federalist 83*, dedicated to the relationship between the state and federal courts in the plan of the new Constitution, spoke of such limiting silences, noting "the wide difference between *silence* and *abolition*."[43]

---

[36] Articles of Confederation of 1781, art. II.
[37] See *McCulloch*, 17 U.S. (4 Wheat.) at 406.
[38] See generally Robert L. Stern, "The Commerce Clause and the National Economy, 1933–1946" (1946) 59 Harv. L. Rev 645.
[39] 247 U.S. 251 (1918) (overruled by *United States v. Darby*, 312 U.S. 100 [1941]).
[40] *Hammer*, 247 U.S. at 275.
[41] 336 U.S. 525, 535 (1949).
[42] See Laurence H. Tribe, *American Constitutional Law*, at 1029–43 (3rd edn 2000).
[43] Alexander Hamilton, *The Federalist No. 83*, at 441 (J. R. Pole ed., 2005).

What may be more commonplace is the proposition that constitutional silences, like silences of other kinds, aren't just occasional gaps or omissions in an otherwise seamless design. They are everywhere and come in as many flavors and varieties as sounds. Ambiguity and multiplicity of meanings are in a sense manifestations of silence. There are as many reasons to be silent as there are to speak, and as many ways to hear meaning in the sounds of silence.

But *words* are partly silent too. In his book *Gardens: An Essay on the Human Condition*, Robert Pogue Harrison recalls the portion of *Phaedrus* in which Socrates compares the obvious silence of paintings to the subtler silence of written words.[44] Socrates says "you might suppose that they understand what they are saying, but if you ask [written words] what they mean by anything they simply return the same answer over and over again."[45] Every sentence, every phrase, is in part silent with respect to how a reader or listener is to go about attributing meaning to it – how narrowly or literally it is to be taken; what significance is to be attributed to what it excludes along with what it includes; how its context, both elsewhere in the same text and in preceding and comparable texts, ought to figure in what it conveys.[46]

Two Supreme Court decisions, *Bush v. Gore*[47] in 2000 and *Arizona State Legislature v. Arizona Independent Redistricting Commission*[48] in 2015, both decided by the narrowest of margins, dramatically illustrate the enormous leeway justices perceive in the answers they hear when they ask either somewhat general language, like "equal protection of the laws," or seemingly specific terms, like "the Legislature" of "each State," what those words, in Socrates's terms, "mean" to be communicating.

In *Bush*, a case in which I played the role of an advocate,[49] the key concurring opinion by then–Chief Justice Rehnquist understood the word "Legislature" (as applied to Florida) to convey a single federal meaning.[50] The Chief deemed this meaning independent of the Florida Supreme Court's holding that the State's Constitution must be consulted in order to decide *what the Florida Legislature must be understood to have prescribed* as the State's method

---

[44] Robert Pogue Harrison, *Gardens: An Essay on the Human Condition* 61 (2008).
[45] Ibid. (quoting Plato, Phaedrus and the Seventh and Eighth Letters 97 [Walter Hamilton trans., 1973]).
[46] See 2 Charles Hartshorne and Paul Weiss *The Collected Papers of Charles Sanders Peirce* 135 (4th prtg. 1978) ("A sign, or *representamen*, is something which stands to somebody for something in some respect or capacity").
[47] 531 U.S. 98 (2000).
[48] 135 S. Ct. 2652 (2015).
[49] See Laurence H. Tribe, "eroG .v hsuB and Its Disguises: Freeing *Bush v. Gore* from Its Hall of Mirrors," (2001) 115 *Harv. L. Rev* 170.
[50] *Bush*, 531 U.S. at 112 (Rehnquist, C.J., concurring).

for selecting presidential electors.[51] The four justices dissenting on that basic point would have held, I think rightly, that it is up to each state to decide in its own constitution (subject only to federal constitutional protections for the state's residents) not only how that State's "Legislature" is to be composed, but also what counts as a permissible method for that "Legislature" to "appoint ... Electors" for purposes of casting that State's votes in the Electoral College.[52]

In *Arizona Legislature*, the majority opinion by Justice Ginsburg understood the word "Legislature" (as applied to Arizona) to encompass the State's entire electorate, voting in a state-wide referendum.[53] This interpretation led to the conclusion that Arizona had complied with the Constitution's requirement that each State's "Legislature" make legislative apportionment decisions by adopting, in that State's constitution, a referendum mechanism for delegating that lawmaking power to the people as a whole.[54] Appealing as I found the majority's idea that a State's constitution could provide that its electorate would share lawmaking authority on an equal footing with the State's Legislature – an approach that creatively addressed the problem of partisan gerrymandering by an incumbent-protecting legislative body – I found the dissenting opinions of Chief Justice Roberts,[55] joined by Justices Scalia, Thomas, and Alito, and of Justice Scalia,[56] joined by Justice Thomas, difficult to fault analytically.

Whatever conclusion one reaches in such cases, the important lesson I draw from them for purposes of an inquiry into silence is that we should beware of "hearing" silences where nearly all readers, setting aside how they would *like* a particular controversy to end, identify determinative text that fills up the relevant field. "The heart has its reasons," as Pascal famously said, "that reason does not know." Good enough. And those heartfelt reasons deserve a hearing. But when they defy reason, the meaning of living by the rule of law is that reason should prevail.

My work over the years has included both studying existing constitutions, particularly that of the United States, and assisting others with the drafting of new constitutions – from the Marshall Islands to the Czech Republic to South Africa. Among the things I noticed was that those undertakings, although distinct, were related – and related most significantly in the way that formative

---

[51] Compare ibid., at 115, *with Gore v. Harris*, 772 So. 2d 1243, 1254 (Fla.), *rev'd sub nom. Bush v. Gore*, 531 U.S. 98 (2000).
[52] *Bush*, 531 U.S. at 123 (Stevens, J., dissenting).
[53] *Arizona Legislature*, 135 S. Ct. at 2671.
[54] Ibid.
[55] Ibid., at 2677–94 (Roberts, C.J., dissenting).
[56] Ibid., at 2694–9 (Scalia, J., dissenting).

decisions about *what to say and what not to say* in a new constitution have bearing on later decisions about *how to interpret* what a constitution says or fails to say.

My decision to pay special attention to the various roles of silence in the distinct but related projects of constitution-making and constitution-interpreting was underscored by an observation a law student of mine (Louis Fisher, J.D. 2016) once made about how he had been struck by the "presence of absence" in Berlin's modern urban landscape.[57] My student was moved by the way Berlin harnessed the "power of negative space in framing the public memory of World War II, from skeletal monuments outlining former churches to negative-space sculptures of murdered Jewish families."

I was born in Shanghai to Russian Jewish refugees, many of whose closest relatives had perished in the pogroms of Russia or had been silenced in the ultimate sense at the hands of the Nazis. That made this image of absence particularly vivid and meaningful to me. As I look back at where I came from and what I have done over the course of my professional life, it strikes me that attempting to organize and give structure to the study of legal silence has been a primary purpose of much of what I have written and taught over the past half-century. In recent years, I decided to focus more systematically on that attempt in an advanced seminar I have been teaching at Harvard Law School and, to a lesser degree, in courses I have taught as a University Professor to Harvard College undergraduates. This chapter is an outgrowth of that effort – an outline of how I hope to pursue it in the years that remain, and how I hope others will pursue it as well.

2.1. DOOR-CLOSING SILENCES VERSUS DOOR-OPENING SILENCES

The introduction to this chapter discussed both: (1) the absence of the qualifying word "expressly" from the description of the powers "delegated" to the national government in the 1787 Constitution; and (2) the absence of any reference to nontrespassory "eavesdropping," whether aided or unaided by technology, from the Fourth Amendment's ban on "unreasonable searches and seizures." Both were offered as examples of constitutional silences that have required interpretation by the Supreme Court.

The difference between those two silences is at least as important as the similarities. The Court in *McCulloch* treated the first silence as strongly suggestive of a *binding decision* in the Constitution to entrust the United States

---

[57] See generally Cass R. Sunstein, "There Is Nothing That Interpretation Just Is" (2015) 30 *Const. Comment.* 193.

Government – in that case, the newly established Congress – with less tightly constrained powers vis-à-vis the States than the unsuccessful Articles of Confederation had entrusted to the Continental Congress.[58]

That silence, understood in light of what Chief Justice Marshall argued were the purposes of the Constitution, *closed* the door to a decentralizing approach that had been deemed inadequate at the Constitution's founding. When the Court in *Hammer* later *reopened* that door by essentially *reinserting a constraining term that had been deliberately erased*, it did so without any persuasive argument that changed circumstances (or a better understanding of our founding history) justified the turnabout.[59] That step simply substituted the constitutional vision of the justices who sat in 1918 for that reflected in the 1787 Constitution as ratified in 1789. The fact that this substitution, and the dramatically narrower view of national authority it represented, lasted for less than half a century and was announced more as an ipse dixit than with a plausible explanation doesn't in itself prove that the majority in 1918 was wrong. It does, however, reinforce a conclusion that that era's attempted reversal of the trajectory on which the founding generation set the nation was misguided.[60]

The Court in *Katz* treated the Constitution's silence with respect to electronic eavesdropping as reflective of *no decision either way* on whether a requirement of reasonableness (and a presumption that the absence of a warrant normally triggers a conclusion of unreasonableness) should be imposed on invisible privacy intrusions – intrusions involving no tangible entrance into a physical area occupied by the target of the government's surveillance.[61] Government eavesdropping of the only kind that would have been possible in 1789–91 may well have been thought at the time of the Framing, as Justice Black's dissent insisted, to fall entirely outside the category of banned

---

[58] *McCulloch v. Maryland*, 17 U.S. (4 Wheat.) 316, 406 (1819).

[59] *Hammer v. Dagenhart*, 247 U.S. 251, 276 (1918) (*overruled by United States v. Darby*, 312 U.S. 100 [1941]).

[60] The period from 1890 to 1937, when the *Hammer v. Dagenhart* era came to an abrupt end with the decision in *West Coast Hotel v. Parrish*, 300 U.S. 379, 395 (1937) (upholding a state's minimum wage law), is often described as the "*Lochner* era," named after the 1905 decision in *Lochner v. New York*, 198 U.S. 45, 62 (1905) (striking down a state's maximum hours law). The complex jurisprudential currents – and the politics of judicial appointments – that led to the simultaneous turnaround in the narrow vision of both *congressional* economic power (a shift usually associated with the decision in *NLRB v. Jones & Laughlin Steel Corp.*, 301 U.S. 1, 43 (1937) (upholding key provisions of the National Labor Relations Act), and *state* economic power during that roughly half-century – long era is beyond the scope of this chapter. For competing views on this period of doctrinal history, compare Edward S. Corwin, *The Commerce Power Versus States Rights* (1936), with Randy E. Barnett, *Restoring the Lost Constitution* (2004).

[61] *Katz v. United States*, 389 U.S. 347, 353 (1967).

government intrusions into the "right of the people to be secure in their persons, houses, papers, and effects" – the right that the Fourth Amendment expressly protects from "unreasonable searches and seizures."[62] As the dissent said, citing Blackstone's famous eighteenth-century *Commentaries*, "eavesdropping ... was ... 'an ancient practice which at common law was condemned as a nuisance'."[63] "In those days," Justice Black observed, "the eavesdropper listened by naked ear under the eaves of houses or their windows, or beyond their walls seeking out private discourse,"[64] and enhancing the ear's listening power technologically, Black insisted, made no difference as a matter of principle: because "the Framers were aware of [physical eavesdropping]" and could easily have "used the appropriate language" to subject *all* eavesdropping to the Constitution's constraints (of having to obtain a warrant and the like), Justice Black treated the *silence* the Framers chose on the matter as decisive.[65] In so doing, he overlooked the far-greater threat to freedom of undeterred "private communication"[66] posed by potentially ubiquitous and undiscoverable electronic surveillance than by occasional government agents lurking under the "eaves of houses or their windows" where observant occupants might detect their presence.[67] At least, with respect to such forms of surveillance, treating the silence of those who made the Constitution and its amendments the law of the land as preclusive punishes all of us for the fact that the Framers were not endowed with the gift of prophecy. It is indefensible to treat all constitutional silences as though they reflected strategic choices with respect to something different in kind from what could have been anticipated. Sometimes, as the saying goes, a cigar is just a cigar.

Justice Black was certainly smart enough to understand all that. The driving force behind his approach was not a misguided belief that his insistence on a narrow and time-bound reading of the protective words of the Bill of Rights would best capture the Constitution's underlying purposes notwithstanding changed scientific or social conditions. Rather, the driving force behind Black's approach was institutional in character. It was a long-standing hostility to *judicial* extrapolation from a constitutional provision's underlying purposes as translated to "keep the Constitution up to date" or "to bring it into harmony with the times."[68] That view, reflective of Black's deep belief that the

---

[62] Ibid., at 365 (Black, J., dissenting) (quoting U.S. Const. amend. IV).
[63] Ibid., at 366 (quoting *Berger v. New York* 388 U.S. 41, 45 [1967]).
[64] Ibid. (quoting *Berger*, 388 U.S. at 45).
[65] Ibid.
[66] Ibid., at 352.
[67] Ibid., at 366 (Black, J., dissenting).
[68] Ibid., at 373.

"history of governments proves that it is dangerous to freedom to repose such powers in courts," was a staple of his jurisprudence.[69] He famously equated entrusting politically unaccountable justices with that kind of "translating" authority with making the Court "a continuously functioning constitutional convention."[70]

This is not the place to engage in the ongoing "originalism" debate over whether fidelity to the Constitution requires (or even permits) an approach as literal as that of Justice Black.[71] Despite the colorful rebirth of that approach in the jurisprudence of the late Justice Antonin Scalia and its persistence in the opinions of Justice Clarence Thomas, it has *not* been the approach followed by other justices in the Court's history, including any (other than Justice Thomas) who serve today.[72] My purpose in this chapter is not to pursue that debate by rehearsing the arguments that I and many others have made against that approach. Suffice it to say here that only an approach paying much closer attention to the *underlying purposes of constitutional structures and rights-protecting provisions* can account for the bulk of the Supreme Court's interpretive work over the last seventy-five years or so.[73]

To account for decisions like *Katz* (and a plethora of others, including *Griswold*), it is necessary to avoid a door-closing approach to the Constitution's silences in the absence of the kind of analysis that Marshall employed in *McCulloch* when evaluating the Constitution's demonstrably deliberate omission of limiting language that the Articles had contained in describing national lawmaking authority.[74] If one is determined to preserve the underlying point of a constitutional provision, it is essential to keep in mind Marshall's admonition in *McCulloch* that "it is a *constitution* we are expounding" – one

---

[69] Ibid., at 374.
[70] Ibid., at 373; see also Howard Ball, *Hugo L. Black: Cold Steel Warrior*, 109–12 (1996).
[71] Plenty has been written on this debate already. Compare, e.g., David A. Strauss, *The Living Constitution* (Geoffrey R. Stone ed., 2010); Laurence H. Tribe, *The Invisible Constitution* (2008); and H. Jefferson Powell, "The Original Understanding of Original Intent" (1985) 98 *Harv. L. Rev* 885 with, e.g., Frank H. Easterbrook, "Alternatives to Originalism?" (1996) 19 *Harv. J. L. & Pub. Pol'y* 479; Michael W. McConnell, "Textualism and the Dead Hand of the Past" (1998)_66 *Geo. Wash. L. Rev.* 1127; William H. Rehnquist, "The Notion of a Living Constitution" (1976) 54 *Tex. L. Rev.* 693; Antonin Scalia, "Common-Law Courts in a Civil-Law System: The Role of United States Federal Courts in Interpreting the Constitution and Laws," in *A Matter of Interpretation: Federal Courts and the Law*, 3 (Amy Gutmann ed., 1997); Antonin Scalia, "Originalism: The Lesser Evil" (1989) 57 *U. Cin. L. Rev.* 849.
[72] Laurence Tribe and Joshua Matz, *Uncertain Justice: The Roberts Court and the Constitution* 8–13, 141, 142 (2014).
[73] See Richard H. Fallon, Jr., *The Dynamic Constitution* (2nd edn 2013).
[74] *Griswold v. Connecticut*, 381 U.S. 479 (1965).

designed to "endure for ages."[75] An approach that would demand updating the text itself through frequent invocation of the deliberately difficult amendment process of Article V to account for changes wrought by time and technology would generate a document far more prolix and detailed than many of those to whom the Constitution is addressed could plausibly absorb, or would be likely to cherish as the nation's founding document.

Among the features of the Constitution that seem to me crucial to its success over the centuries is the widespread recognition of its character not as a set of disconnected points, but as a connected structure that, despite its gaps – some deliberate and others unintended – invites understanding as a coherent, if not always internally consistent, whole. So, for example, the Fourth Amendment's promises as elaborated in *Katz* are separated in space if not by time from the First Amendment's simultaneously ratified prohibition on laws "abridging the freedom of speech."[76] But the Court in *Katz* recognized, without having to *cite* the First Amendment that it had to read the Fourth Amendment broadly enough to avoid unjustifiably undermining the system of open and undeterred communication that the First Amendment was dedicated to protecting.[77]

Two years after *Katz*, when the Court in *Stanley v. Georgia*[78] held that government cannot criminalize someone for the mere private possession or observation of books or films whose "obscene" content stripped them of First Amendment protection in the course of commercial distribution or display, it was clear that neither the First Amendment nor the Fourth, taken alone, could explain the Court's conclusion.[79] Much that occurs inside a "private" living space, from spousal or child abuse to bomb-making, and even the solitary consumption of prohibited substances, may be investigated and prosecuted so long as the Fourth Amendment's procedural requirements are satisfied; and the private possession of the products of sexual exploitation of actual children, for instance, can be criminalized consistent with the First Amendment – as a narrowly tailored means of drying up the market for such material.[80] Government power deployed in service of that end is wholly unlike government power exercised to prevent some unwanted impact on the psyche of the private beholder. To prosecute someone simply for finding satisfaction or excitement in widely deplored visual stimuli or ideas would, the *Stanley* Court held, impinge on the "freedom of the mind," a concept that – although

---

[75] *McCulloch v. Maryland*, 17 U.S. (4 Wheat.) 316, 407, 415 (1819).
[76] U.S. Const. amend. I.
[77] See *Katz v. United States*, 389 U.S. 347, 352 (1967).
[78] 394 U.S. 557 (1969).
[79] See *Stanley*, 394 U.S. at 564–8; ibid., at 569–72 (Stewart, J., concurring in the result).
[80] *Osborne v. Ohio*, 495 U.S. 103, 108–10 (1990).

nowhere mentioned in the Constitution's text – was part of the connective tissue that linked the First Amendment's underlying purposes and postulates to those of the Fourth.[81]

So too with government information-gathering that could not, by any linguistic stretch, be seen as entailing conduct within the ambit of the Fourth Amendment's restraints on "searches and seizures," even as that notion was expanded in *Katz*.

Consider, for instance, wide-ranging and deeply probing background investigations into, and interrogations of, individuals seeking various government benefits, like employment with NASA.[82] The issue presented in such cases is *not* the legitimacy of giving a broader definition to constitutional terms reaching us from centuries earlier – as with stretching the terms "search" and "seizure" to encompass high-tech variants (for example, electronic surveillance or, as in *Kyllo v. United States* in 2001, thermal imaging enabling government to "see" through the walls of a private home)[83] unimaginable when the words were first used in the Constitution.[84] The issue is rather the legitimacy of drawing lines to link disparate constitutional provisions like the First and Fourth Amendments, as the Court implicitly did in *Katz*, in order to treat forms of government intrusion into personal control over private information as potentially outlawed by the Constitution, even though clearly beyond the reach of any particular prohibition.

Specifically, the puzzle in cases like *NASA v. Nelson*[85] in 2011 is whether to treat the Constitution's verbal isolation of several distinct points (like the First and Fourth Amendments) along a broader spectrum that implicates the same general set of values (there, values of "informational privacy")[86] as though the silence between those points represents a *negation* of any constitutional right

---

[81] See *Stanley*, 394 U.S. at 560, 565–6. And yet, as recently as August 2016, the Eleventh Circuit upheld a municipal ordinance banning the sale or rental of sex toys against a Fourteenth Amendment challenge made by a woman suffering from multiple sclerosis who sought to use sex toys to "facilitate intimacy" with her husband and by an artist who used sexual devices in his artwork. *Flanigan's Enterprises, Inc. of Georgia v. City of Sandy Springs*, No. 14-15499, 2016 WL 4088731, at *1–*2 (11th Cir. Aug. 2, 2016). Although the case didn't involve prosecuting mere private possession and use – and thus the court had no occasion to compare or contrast *Stanley* – it makes little sense to limit *Stanley*'s logic to protect one's right to create and use a sex toy at home, but not one's right to acquire such a toy elsewhere.
[82] E.g., *NASA v. Nelson*, 562 U.S. 134, 140–2 (2011).
[83] *Kyllo v. United States*, 533 U.S. 27 (2001).
[84] See ibid., at 31–2; see also Lawrence Lessig, "Fidelity in Translation" (1993) 71 *Tex. L. Rev.* 1165.
[85] 562 U.S. 134 (2011).
[86] *NASA*, 562 U.S. at 146.

that falls outside the points isolated.[87] Doing so would entail unjustifiably treating the absence of language expressly connecting the distinct constitutional provisions as a "door-closing" silence, in the parlance of this chapter. The alternative would be to treat the absence of connecting language linking the provisions in question as a "door-opening" silence; an open invitation to bring within constitutional control *other* kinds of government action that impinge on the same set of overlapping values, even though falling outside the points expressly isolated in the Constitution's text.

As we will see in the section of this chapter dealing with *rules of construction or interpretation bearing on textual gaps or omissions*, the text is in fact *not* entirely silent on that choice of approaches. But even if it were, it is important to note that one option open to constitutional interpreters is *to remain silent about how to read the Constitution's silence on the existence of a general right to informational privacy beyond either the First Amendment or the Fourth*. That is exactly what the Supreme Court did in the NASA case, where the majority opinion written by Justice Alito held that the government's nonphysical "probes" into the personal backgrounds of people seeking government employment to work on improving the Hubble Telescope's ability to conduct deep space probes were not too invasive to comply with whatever unwritten constitutional right of "informational privacy" might exist.[88] Concurring in the result but dissenting from the majority's approach, Justice Thomas and the late Justice Scalia all but tore their hair out over the Court's insistence on leaving that question unanswered. To them, it seemed obvious that the silence of the Constitution's text on the existence of a right of informational privacy had a door-closing character, given the fact that distinctive dimensions of what such a right might be designed to protect were indeed picked out and protected by a specific constitutional provision.[89]

The place of silences in judicial opinions *about* the Constitution – a matter on which the majority and the concurring justices in NASA strongly disagreed – will be taken up in a later section of this chapter, distinguishing silences

---

[87] See *Poe v. Ullman*, 367 U.S. 497, 543 (1961) (Harlan, J., dissenting; citations omitted "[L]iberty is not a series of isolated points ... It is a rational continuum which, broadly speaking, includes a freedom from all substantial arbitrary impositions and purposeless restraints."
[88] *NASA*, 562 U.S. at 159; see also ibid., at 161 (Scalia, J., concurring in the judgment).
[89] Ibid., at 161–2 (Scalia, J., dissenting). But right-leaning jurists are not the only ones who fall into this trap. See e.g., *Atwater v. City of Lago Vista*, 532 U.S. 318, 336–40 (2001) (opinion for the Court by Souter, J.; rejecting the view that the Due Process Clause "forbade peace officers to arrest without a warrant for misdemeanors" on the ground that founders were not concerned enough about the practice to prohibit it in the most relevant specific provision, the Fourth Amendment.

about *what the Constitution commands, permits, or prohibits* from silences in what courts *say* about the Constitution. But first it is important to focus on the substantive issue that divided the Alito majority from the Scalia/Thomas concurrence. That is the issue of whether the existence of a broad right of informational privacy should be deemed precluded by the *juxtaposition* of the Constitution's silence about such a wide-ranging right with its *textual protection of more narrowly defined rights* that are, in a sense, subspecies of that broad right. The alternative is to regard the silence as to the existence of such a right as potentially leaving the matter open.

That the specially concurring justices in NASA focused solely on the Fourth Amendment as the relevant narrower right and paid no attention to the First is not of particular significance for present purposes; what counts is their assertion that, whenever the Constitution narrowly protects a particular value from one or another species of invasion, its failure to protect that value from *other* invasions as well (and, indeed, from the broad genus of invasions of which the species isolated is but one example) should be taken to slam the door on the possibility that such other invasions might be constitutionally foreclosed.[90] That canon of construction, beyond being incompatible with how the Constitution itself tells readers to treat certain kinds of gaps or silences (as we will see below), makes sense only in a constitution conceived as a set of isolated and self-contained points rather than a constitution regarded as a coherent whole. And that is certainly not the way Chief Justice Marshall conceived it in the seminal *McCulloch* case.

To return briefly to Marshall's analysis in *McCulloch*, its method – which Professor Akhil Amar has aptly termed "intertextual" – proceeded in significant part by comparing the words of the Constitution with the words of the text it replaced.[91] Rounding out the summary of Marshall's method, it is noteworthy that he also employed "intratextual" comparisons when considering constitutional silences and the significance they should be accorded.[92] For instance, Marshall contrasted the Constitution's clause empowering Congress "To make all Laws which shall be *necessary and proper* for carrying into Execution the foregoing Powers, and all other Powers vested by this Constitution in the Government of the United States,"[93] with the Constitution's ban on state actions that, without congressional consent, "lay any Imposts or Duties on Imports or Exports, except what may be *absolutely necessary* for executing

---

[90] See NASA, 562 U.S. at 161.
[91] Akhil Reed Amar, "Intratextualism" (1999) 112 *Harv. L. Rev.* 747, 799–800.
[92] See ibid., at 756–7.
[93] U.S. Const. art. I, § 8 (emphasis added).

Soundings and Silences

[the state's] inspection Laws."[94] The Constitution's silence with respect to the *degree* of "necessity" required to comply with the Necessary and Proper Clause rightly reinforced Marshall's conclusion that this silence underscored the degree of deference courts owed to Congress in its judgment of just *how essential* a measure was for "carrying into execution" various delegated powers.[95]

Nor are textual comparisons, whether "inter" *or* "intra," the only relevant ways of distinguishing deliberate (and thus presumptively door-closing) silences or omissions from unintended (and thus presumptively door-opening) silences or omissions. Consider, to address a truly fundamental example, the topic of *secession from the Union*. Unlike the Articles of Confederation, which expressly said that the States ratifying the Articles in 1781 had entered into a "perpetual Union,"[96] the Constitution ratified in 1791 said nothing at all about the possibility of dissolving the "more perfect Union" described in the Preamble.[97]

We all know how tensions over *slavery* among the thirteen states that entered into the new Union required referring to that "peculiar institution" only euphemistically – with code words like "*such Persons* as any of the States now existing shall think proper to admit,"[98] and "all *other Persons*" (as contrasted with "*free Persons*") in the infamous three-fifths clause,[99] as well as in Article V's explicit carve-out for any constitutional amendments that might end the slave trade (again identified only obliquely and without ever mentioning the dreaded word) before 1808.[100]

Less often foregrounded was the way tensions at the Founding over possible secession by any State that wished to exit evidently required no mention of the Union's indissolubility, which the Court in its 1869 decision in *Texas* v. *White* treated as so self-evidently axiomatic as to go without saying.[101] In my 2008 book, *The Invisible Constitution*, I treated that antisecession axiom as now firmly a part of our "unwritten Constitution."[102] But whether one agrees or disagrees, any such axiom is certainly not written in ink on parchment. Rather, it was inscribed in blood on the killing fields of the Civil War when

---

[94] Ibid., art. I, § 10 (emphasis added).
[95] See *McCulloch v. Maryland*, 17 U.S. (4 Wheat.) 316, 387–8 (1819).
[96] Articles of Confederation of 1781, pmbl.
[97] U.S. Const. pmbl.
[98] Ibid., art. I., § 9 (emphasis added).
[99] Ibid., art. I., § 2 (emphasis added).
[100] Ibid., art. V.
[101] See *Texas v. White*, 74 U.S. (7 Wall.) 700, 700 (1868).
[102] Tribe, Supra note 71, at 28–9.

the Union prevailed over the Confederacy – before the axiom had been given the Court's doctrinal blessing in the *Texas* case.

The same issue arises on the international stage in the modern era. I think back to working in Prague in the early 1990s with Pierre Trudeau, who had served several years earlier (1968–79 and 1980–4) as Canada's Prime Minister. We were part of a group assisting Vaclav Havel in drafting a new constitution for Czechoslovakia after it broke in late 1989 from the USSR (in the so-called "Velvet Revolution"), but before it eventually split into two nations in 1993, Slovakia and the Czech Republic. One especially difficult issue was whether to include a provision expressly addressing the possible secession of what later became Slovakia. Trudeau had grappled with similar questions with respect to Quebec long before Canada's highest court, in *Reference Re Secession of Quebec*, held unilateral secession by Quebec to be unlawful.[103] Trudeau recognized that remaining silent in the Czech/Slovak situation about the secession issue might not hold off the centrifugal forces pulling Czechoslovakia apart, but he nonetheless advised, I think wisely, that those forces not be encouraged by providing a clear path to national dissolution in the newly independent country's written constitution.

In other historic circumstances, such as the formation of the EU in the Maastricht Treaty of 1992[104] as amended by the Lisbon Treaty of 2009, which included Article 50, regularizing the secession process that Great Britain voted to initiate when "leave" prevailed over "stay" in Brexit, the formation and widely accepted legitimacy of a founding document for a nation or for a confederation of nations might preclude leaving such matters unspoken.[105] In such instances, the matter of unilateral exit might have to be squarely addressed in advance, despite the prospect that doing so might make the entire effort fall apart prior to its launch, or might make future exit, and the early collapse of the constitutional project, more likely. The pros and cons of addressing the secession issue at the outset in any particular setting, as my Harvard colleague Vicki Jackson has carefully shown, are complex and contextually dependent.[106]

---

[103] Reference Re Secession of Quebec, [1998] 2 S.C.R. 217, para. 104 (Can.).
[104] Treaty on European Union, February 7, 1992, 1992 O.J. (C 224) 1, 1 C.M.L.R. 719.
[105] Treaty of Lisbon Amending the Treaty on European Union and the Treaty Establishing the European Community, art. 50, December 17, 2007, 2007 O.J. (C 306) 1.
[106] Vicki C. Jackson, "Comparative Constitutional Federalism and Transnational Judicial Discourse" (2004) 2 *Int'l J. Const. L.* 91, 121–3; see also Vicki C. Jackson, "Secession, Transnational Precedents, and Constitutional Silences," in *Nullification and Secession in Modern Constitutional Thought*, 314–42 (Sanford Levinson ed., 2016).

Deeply related both to slavery and to national unity is the Constitution's all but complete silence on the profoundly significant topic of *race*, a subject that no history of the United States purporting to explain anything of importance can afford to ignore. Only the Fifteenth Amendment so much as *mentions* race, and it does so only in the context of the right of United States citizens to vote in state or federal elections.[107] (Interestingly, the Constitution is also silent on the existence of any general "right to vote,"[108] confining itself to the prohibition of disenfranchisement on account of "race, color, or previous condition of servitude" (Fifteenth Amendment);[109] the guarantee that United States Senators shall be "elected by the people" of their respective States (Seventeenth Amendment);[110] the prohibition of disenfranchisement on account of "sex" (Nineteenth Amendment);[111] the prohibition of disenfranchisement for "failure to pay any poll tax or other tax" (Twenty-fourth Amendment);[112] and the prohibition of disenfranchisement "on account of age" for "citizens ... eighteen years of age or older" (Twenty-Sixth Amendment).[113])

Although Justice Scalia once wrote – incorrectly, as it turns out – that the Fourteenth Amendment expressly bars states from making distinctions among individuals on the basis of their race,[114] it does no such thing. Rather, it is *conspicuously silent* on the degree to which, and the circumstances in which, government may use racial classifications to decide whom it may reward with particular opportunities, employ for particular purposes, target for particular burdens, or otherwise single out for other than purely data-gathering purposes. In fact, *Fisher v. University of Texas*,[115] decided in 2016, was the first case in thirteen years[116] (and only the third case ever)[117] in which the Court upheld

[107] U.S. Const. amend. XV.
[108] Heather K. Gerken, "The Right to Vote: Is the Amendment Game Worth the Candle?" (2014) 23 *Wm. & Mary Bill Rts. J.* 11, 11; see generally Pamela S. Karlan, "Ballots and Bullets: The Exceptional History of the Right to Vote" (2003) 71 *U. Cin. L. Rev.* 1345.
[109] U.S. Const. amend. XV.
[110] Ibid., amend. XVII.
[111] Ibid., amend. XIX.
[112] Ibid., amend. XXIV.
[113] Ibid., amend. XXVI.
[114] *Schuette v. Coalition to Defend Affirmative Action*, 134 S. Ct. 1623, 1639 (2014) (Scalia, J., concurring in the judgment; "Does the Equal Protection Clause of the Fourteenth Amendment *forbid* what its *text plainly requires*?" Needless to say (except that this case obliges us to say it), the question answers itself. "The Constitution *proscribes government discrimination on the basis of race*, and state-provided education is no exception" quoting *Grutter v. Bollinger*, 539 U.S. 306, 349 (2003) Scalia, J., concurring in part and dissenting in part (second emphasis added).
[115] *Fisher v. University of Texas at Austin*, 136 S. Ct. 2198 (2016).
[116] See *Grutter v. Bollinger*, 539 U.S. 306 (2003) (decided thirteen years earlier).
[117] See ibid. (upholding race-conscious law school admissions program); *Metro Broad., Inc. v. FCC*, 497 U.S. 547 (1990) (upholding race-conscious programs to promote minority ownership

a government affirmative action program expressly taking the race of individuals into account in allocating benefits or burdens – there, admission slots in a state's universities, allocated to achieve educational diversity.

In this chapter, I will not address the merits of that decision, which I have elsewhere applauded,[118] but I will note that, particularly in the context of characterizing the decision as: (1) going out of its way to decide large constitutional questions that might better have been left open; (2) being suitably modest and admirably minimal about how much to resolve; or (3) not going far enough to button down the constitutional issues left up in the air; it turns out, unsurprisingly, that how observers characterize what the Court did or failed to do seems more a function of their preferred style of adjudication and degree of judicial intervention than any intrinsic characteristic of the Court's ruling.[119]

The same can be said of the sequence of Supreme Court decisions along the path to marriage equality and toward a strong constitutional norm of nondiscrimination with respect to sexual orientation and/or gender identity – the decisions from *Romer v. Evans*[120] in 1996, to *Lawrence v. Texas*[121] in 2003, to *United States v. Windsor*[122] in 2013, to *Obergefell v. Hodges*[123] in 2015, to whatever future case extends the principles of those holdings to discrimination between transgender and cisgender individuals. All of those decisions, of course, hung their constitutional protections on the textual hooks of due process and equal protection. But they did so by invoking and elaborating underlying principles of personal liberty, privacy, and equal dignity not to be found anywhere in the Constitution's express terms.[124] In that sense, all were children of *Griswold v.*

---

and control in the broadcasting industry), *overruled by Adarand Constructors, Inc. v. Pena*, 515 U.S. 200 (1995).

[118] E.g., Adam Liptak, "Supreme Court Upholds Affirmative Action Program at University of Texas," *New York Times* (June 23, 2016), www.nytimes.com/2016/06/24/us/politics/supreme-court-affirmative-action-university-of-texas.html [https://perma.cc/LLW8-PFPZ].

[119] Compare, e.g., Richard Primus, "Affirmative Action in College Admissions, Here to Stay," *New York Times* (June 23, 2016), www.nytimes.com/2016/06/23/opinion/affirmative-action-in-college-admissions-here-to-stay.html [https://perma.cc/TCU7-BG36] (celebrating *Fisher* as a "huge victory for supporters of affirmative action") with, e.g., Cass R. Sunstein, "On Affirmative Action, Supreme Court Rules for Humility," *Bloomberg View* (June 23, 2016), www.bloomberg.com/view/articles/2016-06-23/on-affirmative-action-supreme-court-rules-for-humility [https://perma.cc/N33A-9KPB] (praising *Fisher* for its "judicial modesty").

[120] 517 U.S. 620 (1996).
[121] 539 U.S. 558 (2003).
[122] 133 S. Ct. 2675 (2013).
[123] 135 S. Ct. 2584 (2015).
[124] See Laurence H. Tribe, "Equal Dignity: Speaking Its Name," (2015) 129 *Harv. L. Rev. F.* 16, 19–23.

Connecticut[125] and its abortion-related progeny, *Roe* v. *Wade*[126] and *Planned Parenthood of Southeastern Pennsylvania* v. *Casey*.[127]

From the perspective of either constitutional silence or silence in decisions construing the Constitution, this arc of rulings is a treasure trove of insights too far-reaching to be elaborated here. Suffice it to say that the engine driving those decisions was as much external to both the Constitution's text and the legal process as internal to either. Chief Justice Roberts was surely incorrect when he wrote in his bitter *Obergefell* dissent that the post-*Obergefell* celebrations of marriage equality were not celebrations of the Constitution because, in his words, "[the Constitution] had nothing to do with it."[128] The Constitution, in all its moving parts both legal and cultural, had *everything* to do with it.

Especially notable, from the perspective of silence, is how the majority opinion in *Obergefell*, written by Justice Kennedy, treated the dissenting justices' insistence that the Court was illegitimately redefining the institution of "marriage" without proof that the traditional, "one man + one woman" definition had been intentionally designed to denigrate or stigmatize same-sex couples.[129] But the dissenters missed the point. As the majority saw the matter, the exclusion of same-sex marriage from what the dissenters described as the traditional definition, while almost certainly *not* expressive at the time of homophobia or hatred of gays or lesbians, was reflective of unexamined assumptions that evolving understandings of liberty, equality, and dignity have rightly led succeeding generations to question.[130] The Constitution's text says nothing about marriage, let alone about same-sex marriage. But those silences were rightly treated by the Court as invitations to fill in the gaps, gaps not left in the document out of any deliberate design to treat that singularly important form of state-sanctioned relationship as unentitled to special constitutional solicitude, or out of any deliberate design to treat same-sex couples as less worthy than their opposite-sex counterparts. In the terms used in this text, these were silences that allowed doors to open rather than force them to close.

---

[125] 381 U.S. 479 (1965).
[126] 410 U.S. 113 (1973).
[127] 505 U.S. 833 (1992). *Casey* was also notable in that it finally identified the gender equality strand underlying the Court's reproductive rights line of cases, 505 U.S. at 852–3 (plurality opinion), something that *Griswold* and *Roe* conspicuously failed to do.
[128] *Obergefell*, 135 S. Ct. at 2626 (Roberts, J., dissenting).
[129] See ibid.; ibid., at 2642 (Alito, J., dissenting).
[130] Ibid., at 2598 (majority opinion).

2.2. STRUCTURAL SILENCES VERSUS SILENCES ABOUT RIGHTS

The preceding section cut one major slice through the topic of silences, distinguishing those that effectively *open* a constitutional conversation by leaving a number of options on the table from those that shut such conversation down by essentially limiting the options to one. But of course that "one" remaining option – for instance, reading the Constitution's delegations of power to the national government more broadly than those contained in the Articles of Confederation, or recognizing rights of informational privacy beyond those protected by the Fourth Amendment from unreasonable physical invasions of private property – typically leaves numerous *sub-options* open. As with Robert Frost's "[t]wo roads [that] diverged in a yellow wood," each road turns out to lead to numerous further paths at succeeding forks, just as do the capillaries that branch out from the circulatory system's arteries.[131]

This section cuts a different slice through the same topic, dividing silences along a distinct axis. This division separates those silences that bear on the structure created by the Constitution from those that bear on the individual rights the Constitution protects against either a particular level or branch of government, or against government as a whole.

This is not to say that these two topics are entirely distinct. Many justices have been fond of pointing out that the *structural checks and balances and divisions of governmental authority* created by the Constitution – including both the *horizontal* divisions among the three federal branches elaborated by "separation of powers" doctrines, and the *vertical* divisions between the federal government and the states elaborated by "federalism" doctrines – exist in no small part to shield individuals from overbearing, oppressive, or unaccountable government power.[132] It remains useful nonetheless to distinguish: (1) gaps

---

[131] Robert Frost, "The Road Not Taken," in *Mountain Interval* 9, 9 (1916).

[132] See e.g., *Free Enterprise Fund v. Public Company Accounting Oversight Board*, 561 U.S. 477, 501 (2010) ("[T]he Framers recognized that, in the long term, structural protections against abuse of power were critical to preserving liberty.") (quoting *Bowsher v. Synar*, 478 U.S. 714, 730 [1986]); *Clinton v. City of New York*, 524 U.S. 417, 450 (1998) (Kennedy, J., concurring) "Liberty is always at stake when one or more of the branches seek to transgress the separation of powers. Separation of powers was designed to implement a fundamental insight: Concentration of power in the hands of a single branch is a threat to liberty."; *New York v. United States*, 505 U.S. 144, 181 (1992) "Just as the separation and independence of the coordinate branches of the Federal Government serves to prevent the accumulation of excessive power in any one branch, a healthy balance of power between the States and the Federal Government will reduce the risk of tyranny and abuse from either front." quoting *Gregory v. Ashcroft*, 501 U.S. 452, 458 (1991); *Morrison v. Olson*, 487 U.S. 654, 710 (1988) Scalia, J., dissenting; "While the separation of powers may prevent us from righting every wrong, it does so in order to ensure that we do not lose liberty."

or silences in the Constitution's description of how the federal branches relate to one another and to the states; from (2) gaps or silences in the Constitution's description of the rights protected against each level or branch of government.

It is arguably less important that the lines the Court ends up drawing provide clear guidance to the relevant government bodies when the Court identifies new categories of "unenumerated" rights – like the right to reproductive freedom or nondiscrimination based on sex-related or gender-related characteristics – than when the Supreme Court undertakes to decide, in the face of what appears to be constitutional silence, whether:

1. an action by the federal executive branch unconstitutionally intrudes upon congressional authority and thereby impermissibly aggrandizes unilateral presidential power, as the Court did in striking down President Truman's nationalization of the steel industry without prior authority from Congress in *Youngstown Sheet & Tube Co. v. Sawyer*;[133] or
2. an action by Congress unconstitutionally intrudes upon executive authority and thereby impermissibly aggrandizes legislative power, as the Court did in *Zivotofsky v. Kerry* in 2015;[134] or
3. a law enacted by Congress unconstitutionally invades state prerogatives, as the Court did in part of its ruling about the Affordable Care Act in *NFIB v. Sebelius* in 2012;[135] or
4. a state statute enters an area it is forbidden to enter without congressional permission by virtue of the so-called dormant Commerce Clause, as the Court has done on countless occasions;[136] or
5. the federal executive branch can require state compliance with executive action, as the Court did in *Medellin v. Texas*;[137] or
6. states impermissibly intrude on exclusively federal executive or legislative authority, as the Court did in *Arizona v. United States*.[138]

In a paper I recently published in the online Forum of the *Yale Law Journal*, "Transcending the Youngstown Triptych: A Multidimensional Reappraisal of Separation of Powers Doctrine," after exploring a problem closely related to that of *constitutional* silence – the problem of *congressional* silence – I argue that concern for the individual-rights consequences of resolving

---

[133] 343 U.S. 579 (1952).
[134] 135 S. Ct. 2076 (2015).
[135] 132 S. Ct. 2566 (2012).
[136] E.g., *Hunt v. Washington State Apple Advertisement Commission*, 432 U.S. 333 (1977).
[137] 552 U.S. 491 (2008).
[138] 132 S. Ct. 2492 (2012).

congressional-executive disputes one way rather than another has been a long-neglected dimension of the separation-of-powers puzzle.[139]

I illustrate the point by taking a close look at the decision in *Zivotofsky* v. *Kerry*, where none of the justices paid any attention to the consequences for the Zivotofsky family of how the Court resolved the dispute between the US State Department and Congress.[140] Congress had enacted a law specifying that when a US citizen is born in Jerusalem to an American family living there, that family is entitled upon request to have its baby's United States passport stamped so as to identify *Israel* as the nation of the baby's birth.[141] The State Department, acting on the direction of a series of US presidents, defied that law, denying the Zivotofsky family's religiously motivated request on the theory that for US passports to proclaim a view by the Executive Branch that Jerusalem is the capital of Israel would interfere with the policy of the Executive that the United States should remain neutral on the ongoing dispute over whether the government of Israel is indeed sovereign over all of Jerusalem.[142]

A closely divided Supreme Court ruled for the Executive. Regardless of whether one agrees or disagrees with that unusual ruling – the second ever in which the Court upheld the authority of the Executive to defy a duly enacted federal statute[143] – I think that it was wrong for the Court to be silent on, and seemingly not even to consider, the individual rights arguments on the family's side of the scale.[144]

I will return in the third section of this paper to the broader question of when the Court *should* be silent on a constitutional matter, and when it should instead address the matter squarely. For now, I turn to the extent to which the Constitution is or is not silent on the proper *method of construing* both structural and individual rights issues posed by constitutional cases and controversies.

---

[139] Laurence H. Tribe, "Transcending the Youngstown Triptych: A Multidimensional Reappraisal of Separation of Powers Doctrine" (2016) 126 *Yale L. J. F.* 86, 100.
[140] Ibid., at 103–4.
[141] Foreign Relations Authorization Act Fiscal Year 2003, Pub. L. No. 107–228 § 214(d), 116 Stat. 1350, 1366 (2002).
[142] *Zivotofsky* v. *Kerry*, 135 S. Ct. 2076, 2082 (2015).
[143] See *Myers* v. *United States*, 272 U.S. 52 (1926) (upholding the authority of the President to defy the Tenure of Office Act of 1867 and to remove an executive officer without consent of the Senate).
[144] Conceptualizing the scope of the individual rights at issue in Zivotofsky is admittedly challenging and would affect how the Court weighs those rights. A sufficiently wider lens may have also considered the rights of classes of people beyond those in the same situation as little Menachem Zivotofsky – for example, people who wanted to visit Israel but might have been unable to do so if the Court had upheld the law and relations with Middle Eastern nations had deteriorated as a result of the Court's decision.

2.3. SILENCES IN THE CONSTITUTION GENERALLY VERSUS SILENCES IN THE CONSTITUTION'S RULES OF INTERPRETATION

I begin this part of the chapter by returning to one of the decisions I described briefly in the autobiographical introduction, explaining what first led me to use the "sounds of silence" as a frame through which to view the largest constitutional questions: *Griswold v. Connecticut*, the Supreme Court's 1965 invalidation of a state law criminalizing the use of contraceptives by married couples.[145] Nothing in the Constitution's text could be invoked to explain fully why such a law could not withstand constitutional scrutiny.

In an early draft of the Court's opinion striking the law down, Justice Douglas sought to describe the conduct of a married couple to have unprotected sexual intercourse as an exercise of the First Amendment right "peaceably to assemble," but Justice Black deftly responded that what he regularly did with his wife of many years didn't seem to either of them to be an instance of peaceable assembly.[146]

After abandoning that somewhat silly effort, Douglas settled on putting the entire Bill of Rights into a jurisprudential Cuisinart, and emerged with a mélange that treated a "right of marital privacy" as a mix of various "penumbras" of the First, Third, Fourth, Fifth, and Ninth Amendments.[147] Although that Douglas effort was understandably derided by commentators as singularly undisciplined to the point of being opaque, if not altogether incoherent, a valid and indeed profound point lurked within the famed libertarian's slapdash opinion.[148] The point was that those disparate amendments were not just a sequence of unconnected limits on government authority over intimate personal choices. They were instead parts of a broader shield against totalitarian government, a shield whose shape could not be specified with precision at any given time, but whose existence could not be denied or even denigrated simply because it was not spelled out in detail anywhere in the Constitution's text.

Douglas included the Ninth Amendment along with the others that he poured into his verbal blender,[149] not pausing to recognize that he was making a category error: the other amendments Douglas included each had a substantive ambit referring to a particular kind of individual decision, or a procedural ambit dealing with a specific sort of governmental practice. Unlike the first eight amendments, the Ninth is a *rule of construction*, an overarching

---

[145] 381 U.S. 479, 485–6 (1965).
[146] Bernard Schwartz, *The Unpublished Opinions of the Warren Court*, 231–7 (1985).
[147] *Griswold*, 381 U.S. at 482–6.
[148] E.g., Robert H. Bork, *The Tempting of America* 98 (1990).
[149] 381 U.S. at 484.

meta-principle directing the Federal Government and all its branches, including the Judiciary, never to regard the piecemeal and incomplete character of the enumerated substantive and procedural rights as preclusive of other rights, depending on the circumstances. That Amendment states: "[t]he enumeration in the Constitution of certain rights *shall not be construed* to deny or disparage others retained by the people."[150]

Griswold thus constituted an instance in which the Constitution's own text did *not* in fact silently leave the Court free to choose between Douglas's approach and that of the dissenting justices, each of whom treated the Constitution's silence on the existence of a right to intimate personal, sexual, or marital privacy – its failure to "enumerate" that right in the Bill of Rights or anywhere else in the Constitution – as though that silence represented a constitutional prohibition on the recognition of any such a right and on its federal judicial enforcement.[151] Properly understood, the Ninth Amendment is a command, directed to all federal officials (including, of course, Supreme Court Justices), about how *not* to construe the rest of the Constitution's text.

Although Justice Goldberg, concurring separately, invoked the Ninth Amendment in just the right way (for the first time ever in any Justice's opinion, whether for the Court or in a concurrence)[152] – a tribute, I think, to my friend and former Harvard colleague Stephen Breyer, the Justice who had been Goldberg's law clerk at the time – the truth is that the Ninth Amendment's meta-rule had never before been treated as a serious source of, or constraint on, constitutional doctrine. Indeed, although his having done so may in significant part help to explain Judge Robert Bork's lopsided rejection by the Senate when President Reagan nominated him to the Court, Bork had casually dismissed the Ninth Amendment's rule of construction as an incomprehensible, and therefore judicially unenforceable, "ink blot" during his confirmation hearings roughly two decades after *Griswold*, which he famously went out on a limb to denounce.[153]

Whatever the most convincing explanation for *Griswold v. Connecticut* might be, that decades-old decision, now part of the firmly settled constitutional

---

[150] U.S. Const. amend. IX (emphasis added).
[151] 381 U.S. at 510 (Black. J., dissenting; "I like my privacy as well as the next one, but I am nevertheless compelled to admit that government has a right to invade it unless prohibited by some specific constitutional provision."); ibid., at 530 (Stewart, J., dissenting; "With all deference, I can find no such general right of privacy in the Bill of Rights ...").
[152] See ibid., at 488–90 (Goldberg, J., concurring).
[153] See Ramesh Ponnuru, "Judge Bork's Ink Blot," *National Review* (December 20, 2012, 4:00 A.M.), www.nationalreview.com/article/336142/judge-borks-ink-blot-ramesh-ponnuru [https://perma.cc/BLY6-UCWS]; Steven F. Hayward, *The Age of Reagan*, 565–6 (2009).

canon, remains to this day the judicial foundation on which any number of more recent holdings rest – holdings that involve interests as disparate as the rights of women to decide, within certain limits, whether or not to continue their pregnancies to term (*Roe v. Wade*,[154] *Planned Parenthood of Southeastern Pennsylvania v. Casey*,[155] and *Whole Woman's Health v. Hellerstedt*[156]); the rights of grandparents to choose which of their grandchildren to welcome into their homes (*Moore v. City of East Cleveland*[157]); the rights of consenting adults to engage in whatever forms of private sexual intimacy and coupling give them pleasure without imposing on any nonconsenting participant or observer (*Lawrence v. Texas*[158]); and the rights of same-sex couples to receive exactly the same official recognition as "married" opposite-sex couples enjoy under the federal or state law (*Obergefell v. Hodges*).[159]

In each of the leading cases establishing these rights, notwithstanding the Constitution's silence as to their existence, the Court was met with dissents that share a common objection. Reduced to their essentials, each of these dissents insisted that the failure of the constitutional text to give verbal expression to the right in question had to be treated as binding on federal courts, unless and until the resulting silence was replaced with text adopted in accord with Article V's process for formally amending the Constitution.[160] That those dissents have regularly, although to be sure not always, been rejected – sometimes in highly controversial rulings but usually in rulings that eventually met with broad public approval, and invariably in rulings that have withstood the test of time – speaks volumes about the importance of not giving undue weight to constitutional gaps and omissions when interpreting that document – one intended, as the great Chief Justice John Marshall put it in 1819, to "endure for ages."[161]

Lamentably, the jurisprudence of the Ninth Amendment is, to say the least, underdeveloped, if only because it remained unmentioned, and perhaps all but forgotten, until 1965. Another possible explanation for the relatively recent emergence of that amendment in the Court's body of precedent is that, until Justice Goldberg's concurring opinion in *Griswold*, people appear to have

---

[154] 410 U.S. 113, 129 (1973).
[155] 505 U.S. 833, 849 (1992).
[156] See 136 S. Ct. 2292, 2309 (2016).
[157] 431 U.S. 494, 499 (1977).
[158] 539 U.S. 558, 564–6 (2003).
[159] 135 S. Ct. 2584, 2599–600 (2015).
[160] See e.g., *Obergefell*, 135 S. Ct. at 2627–9 (Scalia, J., dissenting); *Lawrence*, 539 U.S. at 605–6 (Thomas, J., dissenting); *Moore*, 431 U.S. at 542–4 (White, J., dissenting).
[161] *McCulloch v. Maryland*, 17 U.S. (4 Wheat.) 316, 415 (1819).

assumed that the Ninth Amendment had to be mere window dressing lest it become a completely boundless source of newly invented and even fanciful rights. The more modest prospect of using the Ninth Amendment not as a shapeless and bottomless sea of potential new rights, but solely as a rule of construction seems not to have occurred to anyone, at least not to any federal judge, before the mid-1960s.

Perhaps the most convincing use of the Ninth Amendment is a relatively modest one. I have in mind situations in which the question presented involves a value or set of values *almost but not quite* covered by a constitutional provision, or even by several such provisions. NASA v. Nelson, discussed previously, was a case of just that sort: however intrusive a government's employment questionnaire and the accompanying background inquiries might be, the resulting invasion of what has come to be called "informational privacy" cannot quite be deemed a "search" or a "seizure" without stretching language past the breaking point.[162] Thus it cannot come squarely within the ambit of the Fourth Amendment, at least as most of us read the text of that provision. Nor can it come squarely within the ambit of the First Amendment, although there are some Supreme Court precedents, mostly dating to the late 1950s and early 1960s, in which probes into a person's allegedly far-left (specifically, communist) political affiliations were held to violate the First Amendment.[163] But the inquiries challenged in the NASA case were not even arguably ideological in character, and the right he asked the Court to recognize was not couched in terms that would have been limited to political inquiry.

Yet the position taken by Justices Scalia and Thomas in that case was a radical one, viewed through the lens of the Ninth Amendment (which, sadly, the majority did not invoke when rejecting the Scalia/Thomas position as unreasonably constraining). Their position was that, because a right of informational privacy is *not covered by* – that is, *enumerated in* – the Fourth Amendment, it follows that it *cannot* be found within what might be called the gravitational field of that amendment,[164] perhaps influenced as well by the gravitational

---

[162] See 562 U.S. 134 (2011).
[163] E.g., *Baird v. State Bar of Arizona*, 401 U.S. 1, 8 (1971); *Speiser v. Randall*, 357 U.S. 513, 528–9 (1958).
[164] NASA, 562 U.S. 134, 162 (2011) (Scalia, J., concurring in the judgment; "But the Government's collection of private information is regulated by the Fourth Amendment, and '[w]here a particular Amendment provides an explicit textual source of constitutional protection against a particular sort of government behavior, that Amendment ... must be the guide for analyzing these claims' ... That should have been the end of the matter." quoting *Cty. of Sacramento v. Lewis*, 523 U.S. 833, 842 [1998]).

field of the First Amendment.[165] That cramped interpretation looks like as pure an instance of violating the Ninth Amendment's rule of construction as can be imagined.[166]

Another such instance came before the Supreme Court in 1980, in *Richmond Newspapers, Inc. v. Virginia*.[167] That case, which I argued at the Court against the Commonwealth of Virginia, held that only extraordinary circumstances could ever justify excluding the press and the public from courtrooms trying a criminal case just because neither the trial court, nor the prosecution, nor the defendant (who could not invoke an accused's Sixth Amendment right to a *public* trial in order to *exclude* the public) wants the proceedings to be open for public observation.[168]

It was my view at the time that the First Amendment's freedoms of speech and press, which media lawyers thought sufficient to justify the result we sought in *Richmond Newspapers*, could not in themselves comfortably support a presumptive right of public observation of proceedings like those in that case. The reason was that none of the participants in the trial in question was a "willing speaker."[169] All relevant actors opted to keep the proceedings out of public view, much as an author who chooses not to share her diary with anyone opts to keep that diary to herself – and does so without triggering anyone's First Amendment right to be free of government interference to prevent a willing speaker from communicating with a willing listener. But the "freedom of speech" and "of the press," while plausibly encompassing freedoms to hear and observe and to report, *presuppose* that the source of what one wants to hear or observe *wishes to communicate* that information. As others have observed, the First Amendment is not a Freedom of Information Act.[170]

For that reason, I thought it essential to invoke not just the First Amendment but also the Ninth, identifying its purpose as that of preventing anyone from "construing" the silence of the Constitution's text as to the existence of a

---

[165] 562 U.S. at 164.
[166] See ibid., at 160 ("One who asks us to invent a constitutional right out of whole cloth should spare himself and us the pretense of tying it to some words of the Constitution.").
[167] *Richmond Newspapers, Inc. v. Virginia*, 448 U.S. 555 (1980).
[168] Ibid., at 559–60, 580.
[169] See *Virginia State Board of Pharmacy v. Virginia Citizens Consumer Council, Inc.*, 425 U.S. 748, 756 (1976).
[170] See e.g., Amy Jordan, "The Right of Access: Is There a Better Fit than the First Amendment?" (2004) 57 *Vand. L. Rev.* 1349, 1377; David M. O'Brien, "The First Amendment and the Public's 'Right to Know'" (1980) 7 *Hastings Const. L. Q.* 579, 588–9;Barry Sullivan, "FOIA and the First Amendment: Representative Democracy and the People's Elusive 'Right to Know'" (2012) 72 *Md. L. Rev.* 1, 15.

contested right as a decisive negation of that right.[171] I thought that argument was particularly essential when, as in *Richmond Newspapers*, the contested right protects values close to the heart of rights that the Constitution *does* in fact enumerate. And, to my delight (and to the consternation of those on my side of the case who sought mightily to prevent me from so much as mentioning the all-but-forgotten Ninth Amendment, which they viewed as radioactive), the plurality opinion by Chief Justice Burger upheld our contention that the Constitution presumptively precluded closing the proceedings to the press and public, and centrally invoked the Ninth Amendment, focusing on the reasons for James Madison's decision to include it in the Bill of Rights.[172]

As our brief had detailed and the plurality opinion explained, Madison's principal reason for including that rule of construction in the Bill was to mollify those who feared that, just as a Constitution without *any* listing of specific rights might be invoked (despite the Tenth Amendment) to enable the Federal Government to run roughshod over the rights enumerated, so too a Constitution that *listed* certain rights might be taken by future generations to imply that the list was exhaustive and that no rights *other* than those enumerated were entitled to federal constitutional recognition.[173] To prevent the Bill of Rights from exerting that kind of "repulsive gravitational force" – to prevent it from becoming a kind of "dark energy" – the Ninth Amendment was included as one of the Bill's two final provisions.

The other such provision was the Tenth Amendment, a rule of construction that is, in a sense, the mirror image of the rule embodied in the Ninth. It directs that "[t]he powers not delegated to the United States by the Constitution, nor prohibited by it to the States, are reserved to the States, respectively, or to the people."[174] As with the Ninth Amendment, my courses in constitutional law over the years have addressed the degree to which that rule about "powers not delegated" – again, a textually expressed rule about matters *not* expressed in the text – either has or should have played a role in the way structural principles of federal–state relations, relations sometimes described under the rubric of "vertical federalism," have evolved over time, with the arc of unenumerated federal powers largely ascendant in the early nineteenth century, turning

---

[171] See Laurence H. Tribe, "Public Rights, Private Rites: Reliving Richmond Newspapers for My Father" (2003) 5 *J. App. Prac. & Process* 163, 164–5.
[172] *Richmond Newspapers*, 448 U.S. at 579–80.
[173] Ibid., at 579 n.15.
[174] U.S. Const. amend. IX.

downward from the late nineteenth until roughly 1937,[175] then ascendant again until the 1990s,[176] and on a mostly downward trajectory in the years since.[177]

Without any change in the Constitution's text, the dominant judicial approach to the Constitution's silences with respect to both rights and powers has undergone enormous transformation through the medium of the legal culture, reflected and implemented by the federal judiciary, exercising a power of judicial review that we must recall is itself nowhere enumerated in the Constitution – a vast power extracted from a conspicuous silence.

Noteworthy is the fact that such textual rules about how gaps, absences, or silences are to be understood are *themselves* surrounded by silences: are the Ninth and Tenth Amendment's rules about those gaps, absences, or silences to be enforced by the federal judiciary, or are they merely reminders of postulates entrusted to the political branches or to state courts, not enforceable by federal judges?

Disputes over such choices are unending in our law. And, perhaps this is necessarily so because the tower of rules and meta-rules and meta-meta rules is inevitably unending. The great philosopher Bertrand Russell is said to have asked a woman who told him the Earth rested on the back of a huge turtle, "What holds up the turtle?" – trying to lead her into a logical dead-end. Quickly besting the brilliant logician, she instantly replied: "It's no use, Professor … It's turtles all the way down."[178]

2.4. SILENCES IN THE CONSTITUTION ITSELF VERSUS SILENCES IN WHAT IS SAID ABOUT THE CONSTITUTION

As we saw in connection with *NASA v. Nelson*, the majority's determination *not to say* whether the Constitution contains a generalized right of "informational privacy" infuriated two of the justices, who thought it obvious *both* that

---

[175] Robert L. Stern, "The Commerce Clause and the National Economy, 1933–46: Part One" (1946) 59 *Harv. L. Rev.* 645.

[176] Ibid., at 691–3; Robert L. Stern, "The Commerce Clause and the National Economy, 1933–46: Part Two," (1946) 59 *Harv. L. Rev.* 883, 886–90.

[177] John R. Vile, "Truism, Tautology or Vital Principle? The Tenth Amendment since *United States v. Darby*," (1997) 27 *Cumb. L. Rev.* 445.

[178] In *A Brief History of Time*, first published in 1988, Stephen Hawking said the subject was a "well-known scientist (some say it was Bertrand Russell)." Stephen Hawking, *A Brief History of Time* 1 (1988). In the *Princeton Review* in 1882, William James told the story in the third person and described it as "rocks all the way down." William James, "Rationality, Activity, and Faith" (1882) 2 *Princeton Rev.* 58, 82. Some claim that it was really James who first told the story in the much more memorable "turtles" version. Out of deference to the great physicist Stephen Hawking, I will use his attribution to Russell in this essay.

no such right could possibly exist, *and* that the Court was wrong not to come right out and say so. Any such right, they insisted, would have to be "invent[ed] right out of whole cloth."[179] No less vehemently, those justices accused the majority of needlessly teasing the legal profession and the American public: "Thirty-three years have passed since the Court first suggested that the right may, or may not, exist. It is past time for the Court to abandon this Alfred Hitchcock line of our jurisprudence."[180]

Notwithstanding the protest by Justices Scalia and Thomas, both of them are among the jurists who have frequently said that the Court should avoid constitutional pronouncements when not necessary to the resolution of a concrete case or controversy. Indeed, as every student of the Court's body of decisions knows well, the vast bulk of what the Court does involves deciding what *not* to decide, both about the Constitution and about other matters of federal law. Of the seven to eight thousand petitions asking the Court each year to weigh in on such matters, only six or seven dozen are selected by the Court in granting writs of certiorari to review the questions presented.[181] When the Court denies review, as it nearly always does, it is expressing no view either way on whether the decision it has left untouched was right or wrong, and it is only once in a blue moon that any justice either concurs to explain his or her agreement with the denial of cert, or dissents to protest that the case should have been set down for full briefing and argument on the merits.

Much could be said, and more than enough has already been written, about the factors that enter into decisions about whether to grant cert, and I won't be adding to that voluminous literature here. Rather, I will focus – and then, only briefly – on a narrower set of issues, those presented when the Court is not just leaving a case totally unreviewed but is undertaking to review it, and is then considering whether to dodge some substantive constitutional question that the case might squarely present or might at least reasonably be thought to present. That is the issue of "constitutional avoidance," which some see as a problem[182] and others study as a doctrine.[183] The Court first articulated constitutional avoidance as a matter of doctrine in 1936, in

---

[179] *NASA v. Nelson*, 562 U.S. 134, 160 (2011) (Scalia, J., concurring in the judgment).
[180] Ibid., at 165.
[181] For example, in the 2014–15 term the Court disposed of 7,006 petitions for certiorari and granted certiorari to only seventy-one of those petitions. *October Term 2014*, J. S. Ct. II (June 30, 2015), www.supremecourt.gov/orders/journal/jnl14.pdf [https://perma.cc/5DWL-KRTW].
[182] E.g., Richard A. Posner, "Statutory Interpretation – in the Classroom and in the Courtroom," (1983) 50 *U. Chi. L. Rev.* 800, 815–16.
[183] E.g., Gilbert Lee, "How Many Avoidance Canons Are There After *Clark v. Martinez*?," (2007) 10 *U. Pa. J. Const. L.* 193.

a famous concurring opinion by Justice Brandeis in *Ashwander* v. *Tennessee Valley Authority*.[184] Refusing to address the claim that the entire TVA Act – a federal statute designed to promote rural electrification as part of FDR's "first" New Deal – was unconstitutional, Justice Brandeis memorably articulated a set of considerations that he said ought to lead federal courts to avoid deciding difficult constitutional questions that might dispose of a case when it would be possible to decide the case on narrower grounds – grounds leaving those difficult questions unanswered at least for the time being.[185]

There are more than a few occasions when the Court has all but tortured the words of a federal statute in order to avoid resolving a particularly perplexing constitutional issue. One particularly egregious example involved *Bond* v. *United States*, a 2014 Supreme Court decision stemming from a US attorney's seemingly bizarre and at the very least unwise decision to charge a woman with violating the law Congress had enacted to implement the Chemical Weapons Convention, even though all the distraught woman did was conspicuously spread toxic substances on the car, mailbox, and door knob of a rival for her husband's affection in the hope that her rival would develop an uncomfortable rash.[186] Although the terms of the law literally covered what the woman had done, the Court, in an opinion written by Chief Justice Roberts, managed to cobble together six justices to hold that, because of uncertainty about whether Congress *really meant what it said* as applied to circumstances like those presented in that case, respect for "basic principles of federalism" supported holding that the accused woman's "local criminal activity" could not be punished under the *Act to Implement the International Convention on the Prohibition of the Development, Production, Stockpiling and Use of Chemical Weapons and on Their Destruction*.[187] The Court's majority wrote that, just as it would have had a duty to interpret an *ambiguous* federal law so as to avoid difficult constitutional questions about the reach of the treaty power and of Congress's power to implement a duly ratified treaty, so too it had a duty to find some way to hold even an *unambiguous* federal law inapplicable if holding it applicable in accord with its manifestly applicable terms would have made such avoidance impossible.[188]

---

[184] 297 U.S. 288, 346 (1936) (Brandeis, J., concurring; "The Court developed, for its own governance in the cases confessedly within its jurisdiction, a series of rules under which it has avoided passing upon a large part of all the constitutional questions pressed upon it for decision.").
[185] *Ashwander*, 297 U.S. at 344–8, 355–6.
[186] 134 S. Ct. 2077, 2085–6 (2014).
[187] Ibid., at 2088–90.
[188] See ibid., at 2090.

Unsurprisingly, the four dissenters, led by Justice Scalia, made mincemeat of that reasoning: "Somewhere in Norristown, Pennsylvania, a husband's paramour suffered a minor thumb burn at the hands of a betrayed wife. The United States Congress – 'everywhere extending the sphere of its activity, and drawing all power into its impetuous vortex' – has made a federal case out of it. What are we to do?"[189] His answer was straightforward: "As sweeping and unsettling as the Chemical Weapons Convention Implementation Act of 1998 may be, it is clear beyond doubt that it covers what Bond did; and we have no authority to amend it. So we are forced to decide – there is no way around it – whether the Act's application to what Bond did was constitutional."[190] Scalia would have held that it was not, and he forcefully accused the Court of exceeding its authority by contriving *not* to do so.[191] (Oh how I miss the late Justice Scalia's clarity – much as I often disagreed with him.)

Many and one hopes most, instances of constitutional avoidance are far easier to justify than that presented in *Bond*. Federal laws are often written in genuinely ambiguous ways that can be construed narrowly enough to spare those laws from facial invalidation (and, at the same time, sufficiently narrowly to avoid effectively accusing Members of Congress of having violated their oath to uphold the Constitution). When laws are drafted with sufficient facial ambiguity, that kind of narrowing construction can be performed without twisting statutory words beyond recognition or, even worse, leaving those words standing but stubbornly refusing to apply them in particular circumstances where federal enforcement authorities foolishly failed to exercise their discretion not to prosecute.

The Court decides a number of clearly defensible constitutional avoidance cases on a regular basis. Those that are most controversial involve raising barriers to individuals and businesses seeking to bring federal constitutional challenges before Article III courts, barriers either very narrowly defining the class of those with "standing" to invoke federal judicial power or treating certain matters, such as the constitutionality of actions by the Commander in Chief in pursuing undeclared wars, as posing nonjusticiable political questions and thereby leaving individual victims without any possibility of obtaining judicial redress.[192]

---

[189] *Bond*, 134 S. Ct. at 2094 (2014) (Scalia, J., dissenting; quoting *The Federalist No. 48*, at 333 (James Madison) (J. Cooke ed., [1961]).
[190] Ibid.
[191] Ibid., at 2102.
[192] E.g., Louis Henkin, "Is There a 'Political Question' Doctrine?" (1976) 85 *Yale L. J.* 597, 623 n.74 (collecting cases in which federal courts used standing and political questions doctrines to avoid ruling on the constitutionality of the Vietnam War).

There is a veritable cottage industry of books and articles about the so-called passive virtues of abstaining from a decision, as well as counter-books and articles delineating the "subtle vices of the passive virtues."[193] This chapter is not a useful place to sum up that literature or to build on it, but it is worth noting at least one particular form of "constitutional avoidance" that entails the very opposite of remaining silent about what is *in* the Constitution. That form of avoidance turns out to be more frequently invoked than one might suppose.

The most consequential example in recent years was the approach taken by Chief Justice Roberts to provide a fifth vote to reject a sweeping constitutional attack on President Obama's most significant domestic achievement, the passage of the Affordable Care Act (ACA). In *NFIB* v. *Sebelius*, decided in 2012, the Chief joined four justices in concluding that Congress had exceeded its power under the Commerce Clause and the Necessary and Proper Clause in undertaking to require virtually all businesses and citizens to purchase federally approved health insurance[194] – but he joined another four justices in concluding that Congress acted within the taxing power in imposing federal tax penalties on those who failed to purchase such insurance in accord with the ACA.[195] Congress had, as far as the naked eye could see, done more than impose taxes on nonpurchasers: it had in essence purported to make nonpurchasers into outlaws.[196] But the Chief Justice, alone among the justices in that respect, asserted the authority in essence to *rewrite* the ACA, abetted by the administration's promise, offered obligingly during oral argument,[197] to refrain from criminally prosecuting any nonpurchasers, so that the ACA could masquerade (at least for the duration of the Obama administration) as a mere tax, which the Chief Justice insisted – with a clear if not altogether convincing explanation – was a less drastic and invasive form of power than a free-standing regulation.[198]

I don't mean to be as critical of the chief as this may sound. On the contrary, in the 2014 book I coauthored with Joshua Matz, *Uncertain Justice*, I *defend* the Chief's unusual way of sustaining the heart of the ACA,[199] following

---

[193] Compare, e.g., Alexander Bickel, *The Least Dangerous Branch: The Supreme Court at the Bar of Politics*, 111–98 (1962), with, e.g., Gerald Gunther, "The Subtle Vices of the 'Passive Virtues' – A Comment on Principle and Expediency in Judicial Review" (1964) 64 *Colum. L. Rev.* 1.
[194] 132 S. Ct. 2566, 2593 (2012).
[195] *NFIB*, 132 S. Ct. at 2600.
[196] Ibid., at 2651–5 (Scalia, J., dissenting).
[197] See Transcript of Oral Argument at 44–50, *Department of Health and Human Services v. Florida* 132 S. Ct. 1618 (2012) (No. 11–398).
[198] See *NFIB*, 132 S. Ct. at 2596–7 (opinion of Roberts, C.J.).
[199] Tribe and Matz, *Uncertain Justice*, 66–8.

a path I had publicly predicted he would take (and had argued he *should* take) months before the decision was announced.[200]

What I *do* mean to be saying is simply that, although presented as an instance of constitutional avoidance, the Roberts opinion didn't actually *avoid* any constitutional question, but instead *resolved it against what Congress quite plainly wrote*. The Chief Justice conceded that "reading" the congressional mandate to purchase insurance as though it offered individuals and employers the *option* of *either* purchasing insurance or *paying a federal tax penalty for not doing so* required rejecting by far the most natural reading of the ACA and replacing it with a version of the law that Congress had not actually crafted. But he said that he *had* to adopt that reading in order to avoid the more drastic step of striking down the ACA altogether. Thus, the Chief Justice essentially *rewrote* Congress' handiwork so as to avoid the politically unpalatable and institutionally injurious result of dooming the entire ACA. In doing so, he was taking two significant and controversial steps.

One was a step that four dissenting justices criticized as a usurpation of Congress' exclusive *power to raise and collect taxes* under Article I[201] – while four concurring justices defended it as entirely legitimate in as much as it did not entail subjecting anyone to a tax liability that Congress had not in fact authorized, albeit under a regulatory rubric.[202]

The other was a step that the four dissenters praised as a proper application of prior Commerce Clause jurisprudence[203] – while the four concurring justices attacked it as unprecedented and unjustifiable.[204] To those four, the Chief had imposed a substantial and analytically incoherent new constraint on Congress' Article I power to regulate interstate commerce when he insisted that Congress had exceeded its power to *regulate* commercial activity when it sought to *create* such activity by compelling supposedly "inactive" individuals to *enter* the stream of commerce.[205] It was an instance of using faux-avoidance not as a genuinely interpretive technique but, rather, as a more modest remedy for a constitutional violation than out-and-out rejection of Congress'

---

[200] Josh Blackman, *Unprecedented: The Constitutional Challenge to Obamacare*, 183–4 (2013); Laurence Tribe, *Chief Justice Roberts Comes into His Own and Saves the Court While Preventing a Constitutional Debacle*, SCOTUSblog (June 28, 2012, 3:41 P.M.), www.scotusblog.com/2012/06/chief-justice-roberts-comes-into-his-own-and-saves-the-court-while-preventing-a-constitutional-debacle/ [https://perma.cc/52DM-A64R].
[201] See *NFIB*, 132 S. Ct. at 2651 (Scalia, J., dissenting).
[202] See ibid., at 2612–13 (Ginsburg, J. concurring).
[203] Ibid., at 2645–7 (Scalia, J., dissenting).
[204] Ibid., at 2621–3 (Ginsburg, J. concurring).
[205] Ibid.

entire enactment would have been.[206] But what seemed more modest vis-à-vis the ACA was anything but modest vis-à-vis the Constitution.[207]

That observation leads to a final note: whenever the Supreme Court either issues a formal constitutional condemnation (even if in the course of upholding an exercise of power on other grounds, as in *NFIB*), or gives its formal constitutional blessing to a contested exercise of state or federal power, evaluating the long-term impact of what the Court has done requires a comparison with the impact of what *would have happened* had the Court simply refrained from speaking to the constitutional question at hand. The evaluation requires, to be clear, a comparison with the impact of silence.

Perhaps the best example of what I have in mind is *Korematsu v. United States*, the infamous – indeed, anticanonical – case in which the Court in 1944 deferred to government assertions that the forced relocation of Japanese Americans (all United States citizens of Japanese ancestry living along major stretches of the West Coast) was essential to America's national security.[208] Among the many reasons *Korematsu* was a blot on the Court's and the nation's history was that the Court displayed uncritical faith in factual claims by government lawyers about the threat posed by persons described as Japanese–American spies and saboteurs, even though these claims directly contradicted confidential reports by high-level military and intelligence officials that, as it turns out, the Justice Department had deliberately misrepresented to the Supreme Court – an inexcusable lapse for which the Solicitor General formally apologized decades later.[209]

The Court stopped short of ever actually *upholding* the internment – in "so-called Relocation Centers," which dissenting Justice Owen Roberts rightly said was but "a euphemism for concentration camps"[210] – of loyal Americans of Japanese descent, purportedly upholding "only" the orders imposing a curfew

---

[206] See Eric S. Fish, "Constitutional Avoidance as Interpretation and as Remedy," (2016) 114 *Mich. L. Rev.* 1275 (developing a helpful distinction between avoidance as interpretation and avoidance as remedy).

[207] See Neal Kumar Katyal and Thomas P. Schmidt, "Active Avoidance: The Modern Supreme Court and Legal Change," (2015) 128 *Harv. L. Rev.* 2109, 2138 ("[*NFIB*] required, as a logical matter, establishing *two* separate constitutional propositions: that a mandate cannot be constitutional as a tax and that a mandate cannot be passed under the commerce power. That's an awful lot of constitutional law to make in a decision that turns finally on the interpretation of a statute.").

[208] 323 U.S. 214, 219–20 (1944).

[209] Neal Katyal, *Confession of Error: The Solicitor General's Mistakes during the Japanese-American Internment Cases*, Department of Justice (May 20, 2011), www.justice.gov/opa/blog/confession-error-solicitor-generals-mistakes-during-japanese-american-internment-cases [https://perma.cc/D25U-CW6Q].

[210] *Korematsu*, 323 U.S. at 230 (Roberts, J., dissenting).

on those Americans and requiring them to leave their homes and the areas in which they had lived for years to report to designated "Assembly Centers."[211] Indeed, in a much-overlooked decision issued the same day as *Korematsu*, in a case called *Ex parte Endo*, the Court ruled in an opinion by Justice Douglas that the *forcible internment* of US citizens merely by virtue of their Japanese ancestry was *not* in fact authorized by federal law.[212] The Court thus avoided having to decide whether, *if* federally authorized, such race-based internment would, under the circumstances existing at the time, comport with the Fifth Amendment's Due Process Clause.[213]

The Court's *Korematsu* opinion contained a slim silver lining: it voiced the first dictum in our constitutional history stating that the principles of "equal protection of the laws" applicable to racial discrimination by *state* authorities under the Fourteenth Amendment, enacted in 1868, apply as well to racial discrimination (and presumably to other forms of discrimination also) by *federal* authorities under the Fifth Amendment, enacted in 1791 – despite the Fifth Amendment's self-conscious silence as to any equality principle and the obvious incompatibility of its history with that principle, at least with respect to the paradigm case of race. Specifically, the Court in *Korematsu* said that "all legal restrictions which curtail the civil rights of a single racial group are immediately suspect," and must be "subject[ed] to the most rigid scrutiny" to ensure that they are in fact justified by "[p]ressing public necessity" and do not reflect "racial antagonism."[214] But the Court then shamefully proceeded to find the requisite justification by deferring uncritically to the merely asserted judgment of the President and of military authorities in the perilous circumstances confronting our nation in the wake of Japan's attack on our naval forces at Pearl Harbor.

One of the three dissenters, Justice Robert Jackson, issued a passionate condemnation not just of the Court's finding but, more fundamentally, of the Court's decision *not to remain silent*:

It would be impracticable and dangerous idealism to expect or insist that each specific military command in an area of probable operations will

---

[211] Ibid., at 221–2.
[212] 323 U.S. 283, 303–05 (1944).
[213] *Endo*, 323 U.S. at 299–300; see also Patrick O. Gudridge, "Remember Endo?," (2003) 116 *Harv. L. Rev.* 1933.
[214] *Korematsu* 323 U.S. at 216 (emphasis added). Notably, the possible differences between legal restrictions curtailing "civil rights" along expressly racial lines and those affecting "only" the distribution of positive, government-created entitlements along such lines, have yet to be fully explored. Equally unresolved are arguments about what violations, if any, depend on the mental state with which government actors either curtail a group's "civil rights" or affect its access to government benefits, entitlements, or privileges. See Richard H. Fallon, "Constitutionally Forbidden Legislative Intent," (2016) 130 *Harv. L. Rev.* 523.

conform to conventional tests of constitutionality. When an area is so beset that it must be put under military control at all, the paramount consideration is that its measures be successful, rather than legal. The armed services must protect a society, not merely its Constitution ... No court can require such a commander in such circumstances to act as a reasonable man; he may be unreasonably cautious and exacting. Perhaps he should be. But a commander, in temporarily focusing the life of a community on defense, is carrying out a military program; he is not making law in the sense the courts know the term. He issues orders, and they may have a certain authority as military commands, although they may be very bad as constitutional law.

But if we cannot confine military expedients by the Constitution, neither would I distort the Constitution to approve all that the military may deem expedient. That is what the Court appears to be doing, whether consciously or not. I cannot say, from any evidence before me, that the orders of General DeWitt were not reasonably expedient military precautions, nor could I say that they were. But even if they were permissible military procedures, I deny that it follows that they are constitutional. If, as the Court holds, it does follow, then we may as well say that any military order will be constitutional, and have done with it ...

Much is said of the danger to liberty from the Army program for deporting and detaining these citizens of Japanese extraction. But a judicial construction of the due process clause that will sustain this order is a far more subtle blow to liberty than the promulgation of the order itself. A military order, however unconstitutional, is not apt to last longer than the military emergency. Even during that period, a succeeding commander may revoke it all. But once a judicial opinion rationalizes such an order to show that it conforms to the Constitution, or rather *rationalizes the Constitution to show that the Constitution sanctions such an order*, the Court for all time has validated the principle of racial discrimination in criminal procedure and of transplanting American citizens. The principle then lies about like a loaded weapon ready for the hand of any authority that can bring forward a plausible claim of an urgent need. Every repetition embeds that principle more deeply in our law and thinking, and expands it to new purposes. All who observe the work of courts are familiar with what Judge Cardozo described as "the tendency of a principle to expand itself to the limit of its logic." A military commander may overstep the bounds of constitutionality, and it is an incident. But if we review and approve, that passing incident becomes the doctrine of the Constitution. There it has a generative power of its own, and all that it creates will be in its own image.[215]

---

[215] *Korematsu*, 323 U.S. at 244–7 (Jackson, J., dissenting; emphasis added, footnote omitted).

It is by no means clear what Jackson would have had the Court *do* with the conviction of Fred Korematsu, "born on our soil, of parents born in Japan," for "merely ... being present in the state whereof he is a citizen, near the place where he was born, and where all his life he has lived," in violation of a "series of military orders which made [his] conduct a crime" by forbidding him to remain – and at the same time forbidding him to leave.[216] This surreal and untenable Catch 22 required him, if he wished to avoid violation, "to give himself up to the military authority" to submit to "custody, examination, and transportation out of the territory, to be followed by indeterminate confinement in detention camps."[217]

Would Jackson have let Korematsu's conviction stand *without any judicial review at all*? Could he have held that the conviction should have been reviewed, but somehow *upheld* that same conviction while not addressing in any way the constitutionality of the orders he had been convicted of violating?

My purpose here is not to explore the intricacies of the extraordinary sort of "judicial silence" that Justice Jackson seemed to favor in the singular circumstances of Fred Korematsu's case. My only purpose is to illustrate, in the dramatic form the subject demands, the importance of evaluating every instance of a pronouncement about what the Constitution says – or what it fails to say – against the background alternative of somehow contriving to remain silent.

Silences, whether in the Constitution itself or in authoritative judicial pronouncements about what the Constitution requires, allows, or forbids, cannot be meaningfully evaluated without comparing them to the array of alternatives – comparing them to the background of soundings that those silences interrupt or replace. The question is always: silence ... compared to *what*?

The reciprocal relationship between soundings and silences, the topic of this chapter, is ultimately shrouded in mystery. That brings me to my final observation: few fortune cookies reveal messages worth saving. A possible exception turned up in a cookie a friend was served at a popular Chinese restaurant in Cambridge: "Everything that we see is a shadow cast by that which we do not see."[218]

I would add only: "Everything that we do *not* see is a shadow cast by that which we might have seen."

---

[216] Ibid., at 242–3.
[217] Ibid., at 243.
[218] For several years, I had simply assumed that the author of this haunting image would remain hidden from view, laboring away in some obscure fortune cookie factory. But my resourceful research assistant Colin Doyle, a 3L at Harvard Law School – finding that scenario as unlikely as it was romantic – pursued the matter assiduously and recently informed me that the source of the message in question was none other than an early sermon by Dr. Martin Luther King Jr., reprinted in his 1958 book, *The Measure of a Man*. Martin Luther King, Jr., *The Measure of a Man* 32 (1959).

3

Originalism and the Invisible Constitution

Lawrence B. Solum

3.1. INTRODUCTION: THE PROBLEM FOR ORIGINALISTS OF AN INVISIBLE CONSTITUTION

The notion of an "invisible constitution" contrasts to that of a written, explicit, and visible constitution.[1] This chapter explores the relationship between the idea of an unwritten or invisible constitution and originalism as a constitutional theory with emphasis on the constitutional practice of the United States. In the American context, Thomas Grey's 1975 article "Do We Have an Unwritten Constitution?"[2] was the focal point for a debate that continues today and was taken up by Laurence Tribe in *The Invisible Constitution*.[3]

---

[1] The phrase "invisible constitution" has been used in various ways. Contemporary usage includes the following: Judgment of October 31, 1990 (The Death Penalty Case), Alkotmánybíroság Határozatai [Constitutional Law Court], 1990/107 MK. 88 (Hung.) (translated in Ethan Klingsberg, "Judicial Review and Hungary's Transition from Communism to Democracy: The Constitutional Court, the Continuity of Law, and the Redefinition of Property Rights" (1992) *Brigham Young University Law Review* 41 ("[t]he concurrence of the President of the Court in The Death Penalty Case described the decision's reliance on the right to human dignity as a utilization of the "invisible constitution" – [which is] beyond the [control of both the] Constitution, which is often amended ... [, and] future Constitutions"); Vicki C. Jackson, "*Cook v. Gralike*: Easy Cases and Structural Reasoning" (2001) 2001 *Supreme Court Review* 299, 313–14 ("[statutes prohibiting] the use of government monies or resources for the purpose of supporting a particular candidate for election or reelection ... may be thought of as a kind of "invisible constitution,' reflecting, and supporting, constitutional values though not in their specific terms necessarily constitutionally required"); Laurence H. Tribe, *The Invisible Constitution* (Oxford: Oxford University Press, 2008).
[2] Thomas C. Grey, "Do We Have an Unwritten Constitution?" (1975) 27 *Stanford Law Review* 703.
[3] See Tribe, Supra note 1.

Grey's question has been echoed by Michael Moore,[4] Antonin Scalia,[5] Akhil Amar,[6] and others.[7] One of the motivations for Grey's essay was the early stirrings of originalism. Descendants of the interpretivism and textualism that Grey interrogated now occupy center stage in contemporary debates about constitutional theory. But since Grey wrote, originalism and textualism have evolved. This chapter addresses the idea of an unwritten or invisible constitution from the perspective of contemporary originalist theory. Is the notion of an unwritten or invisible constitution consistent with the originalist claim that constitutional practice should be constrained by the original public meaning of the constitutional text?

"Originalism" is a family of contemporary theories of constitutional interpretation and construction that share two core ideas. First, the communicative content of the constitutional text is fixed at the time each provision is framed and ratified – the "Fixation Thesis."[8] Second, constitutional practice should be constrained by that communicative content of the text, which we can call the "original public meaning" – the "Constraint Principle."[9] Other matters (such as original intent versus original public meaning) are debated by contemporary originalists.

We can begin with a three-step argument that highlights the problematic relationship between originalism and an invisible or unwritten constitution: (1) the predominant form of contemporary originalism is public meaning originalism, a form of textualism. (2) An unwritten or invisible constitution is not a text. (3) Therefore, public meaning originalists should reject the notion of an unwritten or invisible constitution.

This simple syllogism[10] is misleading, in part because the phrases "invisible constitution" and "unwritten constitution" provide an unfortunate frame

[4] Michael S. Moore, "Do We Have an Unwritten Constitution?" (1989) 63 *Southern California Law Review* 107.
[5] Antonin Scalia, "Is There an Unwritten Constitution?" (1989) 12 *Harvard Journal of Law and Public Policy* 1.
[6] Akhil Reed Amar, *America's Unwritten Constitution* (New York, NY: Basic Books, 2012).
[7] The literature on unwritten constitutions, unenumerated constitutional rights, the Ninth Amendment, and related topics is vast. The work that influenced the writing of this chapter includes: Jed Rubenfeld, "The New Unwritten Constitution" (2001) 51 *Duke Law Journal* 289; Suzanna Sherry, "The Founders' Unwritten Constitution" (1987) 54 *University of Chicago Law Review* 1127; Adrian Vermeule, "The Facts about Unwritten Constitutionalism: A Response to Professor Rubenfeld" (2001) 51 *Duke Law Journal* 473.
[8] Lawrence B. Solum, "The Fixation Thesis: The Original Meaning of the Constitutional Text" (2015) 91 *Notre Dame Law Review*, 1.
[9] Lawrence B. Solum, *"The Constraint Principle: Original Meaning and Constitutional Practice"* (unpublished manuscript on file with the author, 2017).
[10] The word "syllogism" is used loosely: as stated, the argument is enthymematic, although a valid syllogistic version could easily be stated.

for the real issues at hand. The United States does not have an unwritten constitution in the same sense that the United Kingdom does; no one seriously disputes that claim (if it is understood narrowly). And even the United Kingdom has a constitution comprised largely of writings, although the writings are not an integrated document but are instead a collection of statutes, royal proclamations, and many other texts. Opponents of the idea of an unwritten or invisible constitution in the American context do not dispute the existence of judicial decisions that create or articulate rules of constitutional law. In one sense, the United States obviously has an "unwritten" constitution: not all of the content of constitutional law is explicitly stated in the constitutional text. In another sense, the United States does not have an "unwritten" constitution: there is an integrated writing that is conventionally called "the Constitution of the United States of America." Framing the issues in terms of the notion of an "unwritten constitution" or "invisible constitution" obscures rather than illuminates the questions that are at stake.

In this chapter, I will use an alternative vocabulary to describe the set of issues raised by the evocative phrases "invisible constitution" and "unwritten constitution." The phrase "extra-textual sources" will be used to designate sources of constitutional law that are outside the text of the United States Constitution (as amended).[11] One incomplete version of the written text is under glass in the National Archives; complete versions with the amendments can be found in the United States Code and on the Internet. Extra-textual sources include judicial opinions, the Articles of Confederation, the Declaration of Independence, the ethos of the framing era, theories of justice, the Northwest Ordinance, the historical practices of the institutions of government and the American people, and many other things as well.

Here is the plan. In Section 3.1, I will attempt to concisely formulate the core of originalism as a constitutional theory. Section 3.2 will address extra-constitutional sources, laying out a typology of the sources themselves and the roles that they can play in constitutional interpretation and construction. Section 3.3 will then examine several categories of extra-textual sources from an originalist perspective. The conclusion articulates the thesis that textual sources of constitutional law should have primacy in constitutional interpretation and construction.

---

[11] See Tribe, Supra note 1, 6 (discussing the relationship between "invisible constitution" and extra-textual sources).

3.2. ORIGINALIST CONSTITUTIONAL THEORY IN THE UNITED STATES

Our topic is the relationship between originalism and extra-textual sources of constitutional law. We can begin by asking the general question, "What is originalism?" And in particular, "How has originalist constitutional theory developed in the United States?"[12] In brief, the answer to the first question is that originalism is a family of constitutional theories that agree on the Fixation Thesis and the Constraint Principle, with one member of the family, Public Meaning Originalism, playing a central role in contemporary debates.

3.2.1. *Communicative Content and Legal Content*

Let me begin with a very general distinction in legal theory – the distinction between "legal content" and "communicative content."[13] As applied to a constitution, this distinction marks the difference between the legal content of constitutional doctrine and norms, on the one hand, and the communicative content (linguistic meaning in context) of the constitutional text, on the other hand. This distinction is fundamental to our investigation of the relationship between originalism and extra-textual sources of constitutional norms, and we need to be clear and precise about these foundational ideas before we proceed further.

What is "communicative content?" The communicative content of a legal text is its meaning. But the word "meaning" standing alone is ambiguous. When we ask the question, "What does this clause of the Constitution *mean?*," we might be asking about the linguistic meaning of the words – but we also might be asking about the effect that provision will have, or about the content of the doctrines of constitutional law that implement the clause. "Communicative content" refers to the linguistic meaning of the text in the context in which it was framed and ratified. This notion of communicative content is good enough for many purposes, but we can be a bit more precise.

It is important to distinguish communicative content with the related but distinct idea of legal content. The communicative content of the constitutional text can be more or less identical to the legal content. That is, the legal content of constitutional doctrine (whether explicit in judicial decisions or implicit in the practice of officials) may simply translate the communicative content of the text into legal effect. But this is not necessarily the case. The gap between communicative

---

[12] Much of the theoretical apparatus developed by originalists in the American context was anticipated by the work of Professor Jeffrey Goldsworthy in Australia. See Jeffrey Goldsworthy, "Originalism in Constitutional Interpretation" (1997) 25 *Federal Law Review* 1.

[13] See Lawrence B. Solum, "Communicative Content and Legal Content" (2013) 89 *Notre Dame Law Review* 480.

content and legal content can be seen in several ways. Most obviously, some legal texts have no legal content at all: the Constitution of the Confederate States of America has communicative content, but there are no associated doctrines of constitutional law in the actual world. Other legal texts have legal content that contradicts the communicative content: for example, I believe that the legal effect given to the Privileges or Immunities Clause of the Fourteenth Amendment is inconsistent with the legal content of the constitutional doctrines promulgated by the Supreme Court as an "interpretation" of that Clause. Finally, many constitutional provisions have legal content that is richer than the communicative content of the text itself: for example, free speech doctrine is a complex body of law containing dozens or hundreds of legal norms that cannot be found in the communicative content of the phrase "freedom of speech."

How does a legal text (e.g., the United States Constitution) communicate? One part of the answer to that question focuses on the semantic meaning of the words and phrases that make up the text. If we want to know the meaning of the Commerce Clause, we need to know the meaning of the words: for example, the Commerce Clause includes the words "regulate," "commerce," "among," "several," and "states." These words have conventional semantic meanings – meanings that are determined by patterns of usage that produce shared linguistic conventions.

But the meaning of a clause is not determined by the meaning of the words alone. There are further conventions – regularities in usage that determine the way words combine to produce meanings. We sometimes call these regularities "rules" of grammar and syntax, but the term "rule" is somewhat misleading because it suggests that authors and speakers must conform to a set of prescriptive rules. Failure to conform would then constitute a violation – what we sometimes call a "grammatical error." Syntax and grammar enable meaning because of regularities in usage; communication can take advantage of the regularities in various ways (not just by strict adherence to a "rule"), and the regularities are not necessarily fully captured by the idea of a rule. There may be clusters and variations that are comprehended by competent speakers of the language but would violate the rules formulated by prescriptive grammarians.

The principle of compositionality expresses the idea that part of the meaning of an utterance (e.g., a clause in the Constitution) is the product of the conventional semantic meaning of the words, and the regularities of syntax and grammar that combine them.[14] The contribution made by conventional

---

[14] Richard Grandy, "Understanding and the Principle of Compositionality" (1990) 4 *Philosophical Perspectives* 557; Donald Davidson, "Theories of Meaning and Learnable Languages", in *Inquiries into Truth and Interpretation* (Oxford: Clarendon Press, 2001) 3.

semantic meanings, syntax, and grammar to the full communicative content of an utterance can be called its "semantic content." Lawyers sometimes call the semantic content of a statute its "literal meaning." In theoretical linguistics and the philosophy of language, the terms "syntax" and "semantics" are used to refer to the investigation of this component of meaning.

But the semantic content of an utterance does not do all the work. The meaning of a sentence is not always its "literal meaning." Written sentences occur in contexts, and the meaning of a sentence will depend on that context.

Consider the following sentence:

"This sentence (in this chapter) provides a trivial example of the contribution made by context to meaning."

The sentence in quotation marks uses the word "this" in two places ("this sentence" and "this chapter"). The word "this" is an indexical. Indexicals have conventional semantic meanings. Competent speakers of English understand words like "this," "here," "now," and so forth. But you don't know what "this" is, or where "here" is, or when "now" is, unless you have information about the context in which these words were uttered. Thus, the first use of "this" modifies the word "sentence" and points to the sentence in which it occurs. And the second use of "this" refers to this "chapter" – the one you are reading now. Used in a different context, the word "this" would refer to other things.

Or take the word "Senate" as that word is used in the United States Constitution. Acontextually, "senate" might mean "an assembly of citizens," or "the building in which a legislative assembly meets," or "the deliberative body of a college or university faculty." But in context, the word "Senate" refers to a particular legislative body created by the Constitution itself – the Senate of the United States that is part of the United States Congress created by the Constitution of 1789.

These examples of the contribution that context makes to meaning may seem trivial. There is nothing complex or counterintuitive about the examples – they are easy cases! But the intuitively obvious nature of these examples is what makes them so powerful. They show beyond doubt that the communicative content of an utterance is not necessarily identical to its semantic content.

When it comes to the contribution that context makes to meaning, the case of legal texts is complex. For example, the clauses of the United States Constitution are embedded in multiple layers of context. Take the Constitution of 1789 (as it existed before amendment). Each clause is embedded in a surrounding Article, and the Articles are embedded in the whole Constitution, which has a Preamble. The Constitution was framed and then ratified in a historical context. This historical context includes surrounding texts, including the predecessor Articles of Confederation, but it also includes actions and events – the Revolutionary War, the failure of the Continental Congress to raise revenues, and so forth.

Some portion of the total context in which the Constitution of 1789 was framed and ratified is context that was shared. By "shared," I mean that it was generally available to framers, ratifiers, and citizens during the period of drafting and ratification. Call this common source of contextual meaning "the publicly available context of constitutional communication" (or "the publicly available context" for short). This publicly available context combines with the semantic meaning of the words and phrases to produce the "communicative content" of the constitutional text.

Philosophy of language and theoretical linguistics use the word "pragmatics" to designate the study of the effect of context on communicative content. The contribution that context makes to communicative content can be called "pragmatic enrichment," but for our purposes we can use the phrase "contextual enrichment" to refer to this idea, avoiding possible confusion with other meanings of the word "pragmatic" in legal discourse.

We can illustrate the idea of communicative content with an example. Take the free speech provision of the First Amendment to the United States Constitution. The semantic content (or "literal meaning") is sparse: "Congress shall make no law ...abridging the freedom of speech." Pace Justice Black, the literal meaning of the clause is both vague and ambiguous.[15] What is the "freedom of speech?" What constitutes an "abridging" of the freedom of speech? Read acontextually, these phrases could mean many things. The phrase "freedom of speech" in the United States Constitution might have a different meaning than the same phrase used in a campus speech code or in the Constitution of South Africa.

Context enriches this vague and ambiguous content of the Free Speech Clause in various ways. The clause itself contrasts speech with press, assembly, and petition. The First Amendment is structurally related to the original Constitution, which includes a scheme of limited and enumerated

---

[15] Jeffrey D. Hockett, *New Deal Justice: The Constitutional Jurisprudence of Hugo L. Black, Felix Frankfurter, and Robert H. Jackson* (Lanham, MD: Rowman & Littlefield Publishers, 1996), 3; "Justice Black and the Bill of Rights" (1977) 9 *Southwestern University Law Review* 937, 938 (transcript of CBS News Special, broadcast December 3, 1968, quoting Justice Black: "[w]ell, I'll read you the part of the First Amendment that caused me to say there are absolutes in our Bill of Rights ... Now, if a man were to say this to me out on the street, 'Congress shall make no law respecting an establishment of religion' – that's the First Amendment – I would think: Amen, Congress should pass no law.").

congressional powers, and to the Ninth Amendment (proposed and ratified at the same time as the First) that forbids constructions of the Constitution that deny or disparage rights retained by the people on the basis that other rights (including the freedom of speech) are enumerated. And the First Amendment was framed and ratified in a particular historical context, some of which was publicly shared by those who attended the Philadelphia convention, some by the state ratifying conventions, and some by "We the People," the citizenry of the United States. This publicly available context of constitutional communication may have enriched the meaning of the phrase "freedom of speech" – giving relatively more clarity and determinacy to a phrase that would be highly underdeterminate considered out of context. This enriched meaning is the communicative content of the Free Speech Clause.

Now consider the legal content that is associated with the Free Speech Clause. Consider the example mentioned above: free speech doctrine is substantially more complex and rich than the communicative content conveyed by the text of the First Amendment – even taking contextual enrichment into account. The legal content of free speech doctrine includes a variety of complex legal rules governing a wide variety of topics ranging from the regulation of billboards to campaign finance to child pornography on the Internet. Take billboard regulation as an example: the Supreme Court has articulated what it calls "the law of billboards"[16] as a subset of free speech doctrine, but it is clearly the case that the full legal content of this body of rules is not contained in the communicative content of the Free Speech Clause. Obviously, the law of billboards is not in the semantic content of the First Amendment; neither the word billboard nor a synonym appears in the text. Almost as obviously, the precise content of the law of billboards is not a logical implication of the semantic content. And when we add the contribution made by the publicly available context of constitutional utterance, it is also obvious that the law of billboards was not *in* the communicative content of the First Amendment: competent speakers of English who were aware of the publicly available context would not have thereby been able to predict the precise contours of the Supreme Court's billboard doctrines.

The point is that context contributes to communicative content. So far, I have illustrated this point using judicially crafted constitutional doctrine, but the same phenomenon can occur in the political branches with constitutional constructions articulated explicitly (e.g., in opinion letters or preambles) or assumed implicitly, in both individual actions and settled practices.

---

[16] *Metromedia Inc. v. City of San Diego*, 453 U.S. 490, 501 (1981).

More generally, the legal content of constitutional doctrine is far richer (contains more information) than does the communicative content of the constitutional text. In theory, one might imagine a regime of "super strict construction" – in which the content of constitutional doctrine is required to have a one-to-one correspondence with the communicative content of the constitutional text. In practice, the enormous complexity of constitutional practice has produced a set of constitutional doctrines that far outruns the linguistic meaning of the constitutional text.

3.2.2. The Core of Originalism

With the distinction between communicative content and legal content in place, we are now able to give a relatively precise statement of the core of originalist constitutional theory. We shall focus on the core, because originalism is itself multifarious and complex. Originalism has evolved both as a mode of judicial practice and as an academic theory. During that evolution, the originalist family of constitutional theories has included versions that emphasized the original intentions of the framers, the original understandings of the ratifiers, and original public meaning.[17] Despite these variations, the originalist family is united by agreement on two core principles, which I have named the "Fixation Thesis" and the "Constraint Principle."

3.2.2.1. The Fixation Thesis

The Fixation Thesis can be stated as follows:

> The communicative content of the constitutional text (the linguistic meaning in context) is fixed at the time each constitutional provision is framed and ratified.

The idea expressed by the Fixation Thesis is simple, but its full articulation has two distinct components. The first component is semantic:

> The semantic content of constitutional meaning is fixed by linguistic practices at the time each constitutional provision is framed and ratified.

For example, the phrase "domestic violence" is used today to refer to spousal abuse, child abuse, and elder abuse within a family, but current usage is not

---

[17] Lawrence B. Solum, "What is Originalism? The Evolution of Contemporary Originalist Theory" in Grant Huscroft and Bradley W. Miller (eds.), *The Challenge of Originalism: Theories of Constitutional Interpretation* (Cambridge: Cambridge University Press, 2011), 33.

an accurate guide to the semantic meaning of the same phrase when in Article IV of the United States Constitution; as used in the late eighteenth century, "domestic violence" referred to riots, rebellions, and other forms of harmful physical force within the territory of a political unit – in context, within the boundaries of a state.[18] The first aspect of the Fixation Thesis is important, because meanings change over time; this is the well-known phenomenon of linguistic drift,[19] also known as semantic shift.[20]

The second aspect of the Fixation Thesis goes to contextual enrichment – the contribution of context to communicative content. The context of a particular utterance or writing is fixed in time. This contextual component can be stated as follows:

> The contextually disambiguated and enriched communicative content of constitutional meaning for a given constitutional provision is fixed by the publicly available context of constitutional communication at the time that each provision of the text was framed and ratified.

Before giving examples, we need to note an important clarification. The context is fixed at the time the text is framed and ratified, *but* it includes the entire publicly available context – and that context may itself be composed of events that predate ratification. The Constitution of 1789 was drafted in 1787 and obtained sufficient votes for ratification in 1788. Similarly, each amendment was proposed and ratified during a particular period.[21] For this reason, the publicly available context of each provision of the Constitution is time-bound. The public context will include communications and events that are close in time to the drafting and promulgation of the text, but events in the distant past could be important parts of the context to the extent that framers, ratifiers, and

---

[18] See Jack Balkin, *Living Originalism* (Cambridge: Belknap Press, 2011), 37; Lawrence Solum, "Semantic Originalism," *Illinois Public Law Research Paper No. 07–24* (November 22, 2008), 3 (http://papers.ssrn.com/abstract=1120244). For a clever and utterly implausible argument to the contrary, see Mark S. Stein, "The Domestic Violence Clause in 'New Originalist' Theory," (2009) 37 *Hastings Constitutional Law Quarterly* 129, 133–5. Cf. Jay S. Bybee, "Insuring Domestic Tranquility: Lopez, Federalization of Crime, and the Forgotten Role of the Domestic Violence Clause" (1997) 66 *George Washington Law Review* 1.

[19] Sol Steinmetz, *Semantic Antics: How and Why Words Change Meaning* (New York, NY: Random House, 2008).

[20] John Newman, "Semantic Shift", in Nick Riemer (ed.), *The Routledge Handbook of Semantics* (Abingdon: Routledge, 2016).

[21] The Twenty-Seventh Amendment to the Constitution is a special case: it was proposed by Congress on September 25, 1789, but ratification did not occur until May 7, 1992. See Certification of Amendment to the Constitution of the United States Relating to Compensation of Members of Congress, 57 Fed. Reg. 21, 187–8 (May 19, 1992).

citizens shared the belief they were relevant to the meaning of some constitutional provision.

The public context of constitutional communication can include information that occurs prior to the drafting and promulgation of a constitutional provision, but future events cannot be part of the publicly available context of constitutional communication – not without time travel! Thus, the American Civil War is not part of the public context of constitutional communication for the original Constitution and the first twelve amendments, but the text of those provisions and the Civil War itself were part of the public context of constitutional communication for the Reconstruction Amendments.

In sum, the Fixation Thesis expresses the idea that communicative content is fixed in time. The thesis results from two facts about meaning: (1) semantic content is fixed by linguistic practice at the time of utterance; and (2) the context of an utterance is time-bound.

3.2.2.2. The Constraint Principle

The Fixation Thesis is the first element of the core of contemporary originalism. The second element is the Constraint Principle. The idea of the Constraint Principle is simple and highly intuitive. The following version of the principle is simple and unqualified; a more precise version will be introduced later in this text.

> The communicative content of the constitutional text should constrain the content of constitutional doctrine.

Although it is theoretically possible for an originalist to view originalism as a purely linguistic theory, in practice almost all originalists are concerned with the relationship between original meaning and what constitutional actors do, including the content of constitutional doctrine. At a minimum, originalists believe that the original public meaning of the text should play some role in determining how courts should decide cases, and how other officials (e.g., the President and Congress) should act. The role that communicative content plays in determining legal content and effect can be called its "contribution." Many living constitutionalists would agree that the original meaning of the text (if ascertainable) should play some role in determining the content of contemporary constitutional doctrine – although they may believe that original meaning can be trumped or outweighed by other factors. Living constitutionalists of this sort could be characterized as affirming a very weak form of originalism, but that way of dividing originalists from nonoriginalists risks conceptual confusion by placing many opponents of "originalism" (as they use the word) in the originalist camp.

Theorists who describe themselves as adherents of "originalism" characteristically believe that the contribution of the text to doctrine should be more robust than mere consideration as a factor or modality in a pluralist practice. The Constraint Principle is meant to express this core belief in an abstract way that leaves room for differences among the different members of the originalist family of theories. The general and abstract statement of the Constraint Principle introduced previously can be made more precise by laying out a more precise version, which I shall call "Constraint as Consistency."

3.2.2.3. Constraint as Consistency

Constraint as Consistency can be formulated as the conjunction of three requirements and three qualifications as follows:

> *Requirement One*: The set of operative constitutional doctrines must be consistent with the set that would directly translate the communicative content of the text into doctrine and the logical implications of that set (together the "direct translation set"), and the decision of constitutional cases must be consistent with that set.
>
> *Requirement Two*: All of the communicative content of the constitutional text and its logical implications must be reflected in the legal content of constitutional doctrine.
>
> *Requirement Three*: All of the content of constitutional doctrine must be fairly traceable to the direct translation set, where traceable content includes precisifications, implementation rules, and default rules presupposed (or otherwise supported) by the text.
>
> *Qualification One*: The requirements in (1) and (2) operate only to the extent that the communicative content of the constitutional text is epistemically accessible; they are not violated by departures from unknown communicative content until such time as the content becomes known.
>
> *Qualification Two*: If the requirements of constraint are not satisfied, then constitutional practice should be brought into compliance with constraint over time, giving due regard to the effects of constitutional change, including effects on the rule of law.
>
> *Qualification Three*: The requirements of constraint are defeasible in limited and extraordinary circumstances, as specified by the best theory of defeasibility.[22]

---

[22] The topic of defeasibility is important but, for the most part, I will bracket the question of defeasibility conditions in this chapter.

Constraint as Consistency can be thought of as a minimalist version of the Constraint Principle – the version that almost all originalists can accept and that (by stipulation) "nonoriginalists" reject.[23] Some originalists may affirm more robust versions of constraint: for example, some originalists might require that all the content of constitutional doctrine must be identical to or logically implied by the communicative content of the constitutional text. That version of constraint would be inconsistent with any notion of an invisible or unwritten constitution, because it leaves no room for extra-textual sources to play a role in the articulation of constitutional law.

Together the Fixation Thesis and the Constraint Principle (in the form of "Constraint as Consistency") express the core of contemporary originalist thought. These are the ideas upon which almost all originalists agree as the minimum core of originalism. As the historical evolution of originalist thought demonstrates, there is another topic upon which originalists disagree. We can introduce this topic via a question: what determines original meaning? In this chapter, I will focus on one answer to this question – the version of originalism that is usually called "public meaning originalism."

3.3. PUBLIC MEANING ORIGINALISM

The history of originalism includes a set of variations on the theme of original meaning. Some originalists have emphasized the original intentions of the framers, others the original understanding of the ratifiers, and others the original public meaning of the constitutional text.[24] This chapter will adopt public meaning originalism as the model version of originalism for two reasons. First, public meaning originalism is the dominant form of originalism in contemporary originalist scholarship.[25] Second, for reasons that I have explored at length in other work, I believe that public meaning originalism is the best candidate

---

[23] In the text, I stipulate that "originalism" is a family of theories unified by fixation and constraint and that "nonoriginalism" refers to theories that reject constraint. A more adequate account of the divide between originalists and nonoriginalists would acknowledge the possibility of forms of nonoriginalism that reject the Fixation Thesis but accept the Constraint Principle. Moreover, the word "originalism" is the subject of metalinguistic negotiation or contestation: the meaning of the word is disputed. On the idea of metalinguistic negotiation, see David Plunkett and Timothy Sundell, "Disagreement and the Semantics of Normative and Evaluative Terms" (2013) 13 *Philosophers' Imprint* 23; David Plunkett and Timothy Sundell, "Dworkin's Interpretivism and the Pragmatics of Legal Disputes" (2013) 19 *Legal Theory* >3; David Plunkett and Timothy Sundell, "Antipositivist Arguments from Legal Thought and Talk: The Metalinguistic Response" in Graham Hubb and Douglas Lind (eds.), *Pragmatism, Law, and Language* (Abingdon: Routledge, 2014), 56–75.

[24] See Solum, Supra note 17.

[25] Ibid.

for the correct or true theory of constitutional meaning.[26] In this chapter, we shall simply stipulate that public meaning originalism serves as a model version of contemporary originalist theory.[27]

What is public meaning originalism? Like other originalist theories, public meaning originalism affirms the Fixation Thesis and the Constraint Principle. What is distinctive about public meaning originalism can be expressed (tentatively) as the "public meaning thesis:"

> The communicative content of the Constitution is fixed (1) by the conventional semantic meaning of the text as understood by competent speakers of American English and (2) by the contextual disambiguations and enrichments that were communicated via the publicly available context at the time each provision of the Constitution was framed and ratified.[28]

Thus, the communicative content of the Constitution of 1789 is fixed by linguistic practice and the publicly available context of the founding era. Similarly, the communicative content of the Fourteenth Amendment is fixed by linguistic practice and context in 1866 through 1868.

3.4. THE INTERPRETATION–CONSTRUCTION DISTINCTION

One more idea is required to complete our description of originalism. This idea can be called "the interpretation–construction distinction." This distinction marks the difference between two related activities within constitutional practice. The first activity is the discovery of the communicative content of a legal utterance: I will use the term "interpretation" to name this first activity. The second activity is the determination of the legal content and legal effect produced by a legal text: I will use the term "construction" to name this second and distinct activity. The interpretation–construction distinction is an old one in American legal theory, and it has been much discussed recently in constitutional theory, but the words "interpretation" and "construction" are also used in a broader sense to refer to both activities (discovering meaning and determining legal effect). Nothing hangs on the terminology, since we could

---

[26] See Solum, Supra note 18; Lawrence B. Solum, "Should we be originalists?" in Robert W. Bennett and Lawrence B. Solum (eds.), *Constitutional Originalism* (Ithaca, NY: Cornell University Press, 2011).
[27] The phrase "model version" expresses the idea that public meaning originalism provides a model or exemplary instance of originalism.
[28] This version is offered as an approximate version of the public meaning thesis. A more definitive statement will be developed for "The public meaning thesis" – a work in progress.

describe the interpretation–construction distinction using other words.[29] The idea of the interpretation–construction distinction is implied by the distinction between communicative content and legal content, but it extends that distinction from the realm of content to the realm of constitutional practice.

To understand the significance of the interpretation–construction distinction for constitutional theory, we need to grasp another, related distinction from the philosophy of language and theoretical linguistics – the distinction between "vagueness" and "ambiguity."[30] When we communicate via language (written or oral), we use words and phrases that can be formed into complex expressions using the rules of syntax and grammar. Sometimes, the smallest meaningful unit of expression is a single word. At other times, whole phrases carry meanings that cannot be dissected into the meaning of constituent words. But whatever the relevant unit of meaning might be, both words and phrases can be either vague or ambiguous.

In ordinary speech, the distinction between vagueness and ambiguity is not always observed. The two terms are sometimes used interchangeably, and when this is the case, they both mark a general lack of what we might call "determinacy" (or "clarity" or "certainty") of meaning. But the terms "vague" and "ambiguous" also have technical (or more precise) meanings, such that there is a real difference in their meanings.

In this technical sense, ambiguity refers to the multiplicity of sense: a term is ambiguous if it has more than one sense. A classic example is the word "cool." In one sense "cool" means "low temperature," as in, "the room was so cool we could see our breath." In another sense, "cool" means something like "hip" or "stylish," as in, "Miles Davis was so cool that every young trumpet player imitated him." And cool has several other senses – referring to temperament or self-control, to certain colors, and to a lack of enthusiasm (or the presence of skepticism or mild hostility).

The technical sense of vagueness refers to the existence of borderline cases: a term is vague if there are cases where the term might or might not apply. A classic example is the word "tall." In one sense, "tall" refers to height (of a person or other entity) that is higher (in some way or to some degree) than average. Abraham Lincoln was tall: at almost 6′4″ he was a paradigm of tall for

---

[29] Lawrence B. Solum, "The Interpretation–Construction Distinction" (2010) 27 *Constitutional Commentary* 95. For example, Jeffrey Goldsworthy uses the phrases "clarifying interpretation" and "creative interpretation" to refer to what I call "interpretation" and "construction." See Jeffrey Goldsworthy, "The Implicit and the Implied in a Written Constitution" in Rosalind Dixon and Adrienne Stone *The Invisible Constitution in Comparative Perspective* (Cambridge: Cambridge University Press, 2018), 112.

[30] Ibid.

his time. Napoleon was not tall, although at 5′6″ he was of average height for his time (though British propaganda depicted him as short). There are persons who are clearly tall and clearly not tall, and there are borderline cases: for example, in the United States in the twenty-first century, males who are 5′11″ are neither clearly tall nor clearly not. Finally, a given word or phrase can be both vague and ambiguous. Cool is ambiguous, and in the temperature sense, it is also vague.

In addition to "vagueness" in this strict sense, legal theory is also concerned with a related but distinct linguistic phenomenon, which we can call "open texture." This phrase has a tangled intellectual history that I will not attempt to sort out on this occasion. For our purposes, I will stipulate that "open texture" includes the following: (1) multidimensional vagueness; (2) multiple criteria concepts with incommensurable dimensions; and (3) family resemblance concepts. We could slice and dice the conceptual terrain in various ways, but I will use "open texture" as an "agglomeration" term – that is, as a word that gathers distinct but related concepts together under a single word.[31] In the discussion that follows, I will use "vagueness" for the purposes of illustration; a more complete account would require explicit consideration of open texture as well.

How does the distinction between ambiguity and vagueness relate to the interpretation–construction distinction? Consider the case of ambiguity first. Many words and phrases have the property of semantic ambiguity. That is, when a word or phrase is considered acontextually, it can have more than one meaning. Consider the thought experiment of a message in a bottle. You are at the beach and you find a slip of paper that contains only the word "cool" or the phrase "domestic violence." You can guess at the meaning, but you won't know how the author was using the word because you lack information about context. Consider the same words as they appear in messages that provide additional context: "Hey dude, this message in a bottle thing is totally cool." Or: "I am a victim of domestic violence. Please protect me from my father." The additional context – in these cases provided by the sentence in which the word appears – is sufficient to resolve the semantic ambiguity.

In constitutional interpretation, ambiguity can usually be resolved by resorting to the publicly available context of constitutional communication. For contemporary readers, the phrase "domestic violence" is unambiguous. We know that it refers to things like insurrections, riots, and rebellions – not spousal, child, or elder abuse within a family. But we can imagine another constitution in which the phrase would be understood as referring to violence

---

[31] I am grateful to Brian Slocum for suggesting the phrase "agglomeration term."

within the family, as in the following hypothetical clause: "Every person has a right to personal security, including the right to be free from violence by strangers and from domestic violence." Once again, even a few adjacent words are sufficient to resolve the ambiguity.

We can restate this point more formally:

> Characteristically, ambiguity in the semantic content of a constitutional text is liquidated by context and hence does not appear in the communicative content of the text.

Because "interpretation" in the technical sense in which we are using that word is just the activity that ascertains the communicative content of a text, it follows that ambiguity in semantic content can usually be resolved by interpretation (so long as the interpreter takes context into account).

The qualifying word "characteristically" expresses the notion that there is no guarantee that semantic ambiguity can be resolved by context. For example, it might be the case that complete information about the publicly available context of constitutional communication would resolve the ambiguity, but also that the relevant evidence of that context is no longer available because of the passage of time. Another possibility is that the text is inherently ambiguous; this could occur because the drafters of a legal text were unable to compromise on some issue; in this situation, they might choose language that is deliberately ambiguous and hence cannot be liquidated by resort to context. We can call these special cases "irreducible ambiguity."

Now consider vagueness and open texture. Recall that if a word is vague, the semantic meaning of the word admits of borderline cases. H. L. A. Hart expressed a similar idea with his notion of "core" and "penumbra."[32] In the core of settled meaning, the applicability of the rule to a particular case is clear. In the penumbra, we have borderline cases – where the application of the rule is underdetermined by the legal materials that are its source. Outside the penumbra, the rule clearly does not apply. Open texture poses similar but more complex problems of application. For example, the word "reasonable" (and "unreasonable" which appears in the Fourth Amendment to the United States Constitution) may well be a multiple-criteria concept with incommensurable dimensions: if so, then the decision whether a particular practice is unreasonable may be underdetermined by the concept.

---

[32] See H. L. A. Hart, "Positivism and the Separation of Law and Morals" (1958) 71 *Harvard Law Review* 593, 606–15; see also H. L. A. Hart, in Penelope A. Bulloch and Joseph Raz (eds.), *The Concept of Law*, 2nd edn (Oxford: Oxford University Press, 1994), 125–7.

Of course, we have recognized that there is a distinction between communicative content and legal content. From the fact that the communicative content (linguistic meaning in context) of a constitutional provision is vague or open-textured, it does not necessarily follow that the legal content is also vague – a vague constitutional provision could have received an authoritative construction that resolves the ambiguity.

Vague and open-textured texts characteristically require construction. Of course, there are a variety of ways in which construction can liquidate ambiguity. Here are a few:

Precisification: Vague provisions can be precisified via rules that draw bright lines sorting borderline cases.

Default Rules: Open-textured provisions can be rendered determinate via general default rules, e.g., a default rule of deference to democratic institutions.

Precedent and Historical Practice: Within a construction zone, precedent and historical practice can liquidate the meaning of provisions that are irreducibly ambiguous or vague.

Each of these methods of construction can reduce the degree of underdeterminacy created by vague or open-textured language.

The point we have been developing can be summarized as follows:

Characteristically, vagueness or open texture in the communicative content of a constitutional text is resolved by a legal norm that enables determination of the legal content or legal effect of the text.

Because "construction" in the technical sense in which we are using that word is just the activity that ascertains the legal content and effect of a text, it follows that vagueness in communicative content is usually resolved by construction – although there may be exceptions.[33]

3.5. CONSTITUTIONAL TEXT AND EXTRA-TEXTUAL SOURCES

The question addressed by this chapter concerns the relationship between originalism and an unwritten or invisible constitution. Up to this point, we have been concerned with the preliminary question, "what is originalism?" Having answered that question, we can now return to our problem: can originalism (as we now understand it) embrace a partially unwritten or invisible constitution? Because the phrases "unwritten constitution" and "invisible

---

[33] Here is one possible exception: there may be some cases in which contextual enrichment precisifies a vague word or phrase. That is, there may be cases in which the semantic content contributed by a term is vague, but the communicative content is not vague because the publicly available context adds precisification – reducing the zone of underdetermination.

constitution" are unfortunate for our purposes, we can ask this question more clearly: can originalists embrace extra-textual sources of the legal content of constitutional doctrine and practice? We can address this question in two steps. First, we need to say something about extra-textual sources – what are they? Second, we need to investigate the role that extra-textual sources can play in constitutional interpretation and construction. When we have taken those two steps, we will be able to give an abstract answer to our question about originalism and extra-textual sources of constitutional doctrine and practice. After we state the abstract answer, we will turn to a more particularized inquiry.

3.5.1. Typology: Sources of Constitutional Norms

What are the sources of constitutional norms? That's a big question. To make it more manageable, we can begin by distinguishing between two kinds of sources, which we can call "textual sources" and "extra-textual sources." We might think of the textual sources as divided into two categories. The first category consists of contiguous strings of constitutional text that are marked off as discrete units of constitutional meaning; we can call these text strings "clauses." The second category of textual sources concerns the properties of the text that emerge from the ways in which individual clauses relate to one another. We can call these relationships between clauses "structural features of the constitutional text" or "structure" for short. Thus, textual sources include clauses and structure.

The second kind of source comes from outside the constitutional text – extra-textual sources. At this stage of our investigation, we want to suspend judgment about the legitimacy of these extra-textual sources – we are merely listing some of the possible candidates for the role of plausible sources of constitutional norms. Again, we can categorize the possibilities. One category consists of foundational documents other than the Constitution of the United States; examples include the Declaration of Independence, the Treaty of Paris, and the Articles of Confederation. Another category consists of documents and records that relate to the framing and ratification of the original Constitution and its amendments; examples include *The Federalist Papers*, Madison's notes on the Philadelphia Convention, and the records of the ratifying conventions. A third category of possible sources consists of moral and political values.[34] The fourth category is social norms and values; the content

---

[34] This third category – moral and political values – raises certain worries about the use of the word "source," because some legal positivists may believe that moral facts cannot determine legal content. Let us set aside positivist worries about use of the word "source" to describe the role that political morality could play in determining the content of constitutional norms; if you wish, you can substitute "constitutional actors' beliefs about moral and political values." The third category is described in terms of the values themselves (or the officials' beliefs about them).

of these norms may correspond to true propositions of political morality, but this need not be the case. The fourth category refers to what is sometimes called "ethos" – the positive morality of a particular political culture. The fifth category is institutional practice. One particularly salient member of this category consists of judicial decisions and opinions that establish authoritative precedents. But the practices of nonjudicial actors could also serve as a source of constitutional norms; sometimes the term "historical practice" is used to describe a subset of this category. Finally, the logical space of extra-textual sources includes the idea that constitutional law might simply be "made up" by some official; judges come to mind.

Our typology is summarized in Table 3.1.

TABLE 3.1. *Sources of the Legal Content of Constitutional Doctrine in the United States*

From the Constitutional Text (Textual Sources)	Examples
Clauses	Commerce Clause, the 11th Amendment, the Privileges or Immunities Clause
Structure	The relationship between the grants of power in the first three Articles

Outside the Constitutional Text (Extra-textual Sources)	Examples
Other Foundational Documents	The Treaty of Paris, the Declaration of Independence, the Articles of Confederation, State Constitutions, Superstatutes
Documents and Records Relating to the Framing and Ratification of the Original Constitution or its Amendments	Madison's Notes, the Ratification Debates, the Federalist Papers, the Antifederalist Papers, Drafting and Ratification History of the Amendments
Moral and Political Philosophy (Values)	Consequentialism, Deontology, Virtue Ethics, Social Contract Theory, Justice as Fairness, Popular Sovereignty Theory
Social Norms and Values	Systems of belief and associated behavior, shared beliefs about morality and politics, popular beliefs about the actual or ideal content of constitutional norms
Institutional Practice	Judicial decisions, legislation and statutes, rules, practices, and informal norms of Congress and the Executive branch, also the analogue of these at the state and local levels
Discretion	The discretionary decisions of officials, including judges and executive branch officials

3.5.2. Three Roles for Extra-textual Sources in Constitutional Interpretation and Construction

Our typology provides a categorization of some of the possible sources of constitutional norms. Our next step is to focus on the extra-textual sources, and investigate the roles they might play in the activities of constitutional interpretation and construction. Let's begin with the role that such sources might play in interpretation.

3.5.2.1. Extra-textual Evidence of Communicative Content

Interpretation aims to recover the communicative content of the text in context. In some cases, the interpretive enterprise is easy. We can discern the semantic context of the text because we are competent speakers of the natural language English; in many cases, the semantic content of the constitution is easily accessible, because the words and phrases used at the time the provision was drafted have the same meanings today. Frequently, we know enough about context without investigation. But in other cases, the meaning of the text will be relatively inaccessible. The meaning of the words may be unfamiliar, or we may need to know more about context.

Extra-textual sources can play the role of aids to interpretation. First, extra-textual sources can provide evidence of the conventional semantic meaning of the words and phrases that comprise the constitutional text. Evidence of the meaning of the phrase "legislative power" might be found in the Federalist Papers, or in the institutional practices of the Continental Congress, or the early Congresses of the United States. Understanding the ethos of the founding era might aid in discerning the meaning of the phrase "freedom of speech," or we might look to the legal practice of the founding era for an elucidation of the notion of "freedom of the press." If we are original public meaning originalists, we will be looking for two kinds of evidence – evidence of conventional semantic meanings or evidence of the publicly available context of communication.

3.5.2.2. Extra-textual Contributions to Constitutional Constructions that are Bound to the Text

The Constitution of the United States includes a variety of provisions that are general and abstract; some of these are vague or open-textured. These provisions may have a core of settled meaning, but to the extent that they are vague, they will have a penumbra – the space of possible cases where the communicative content of the text underdetermines legal content and effect. We can call this space "the construction zone." In the construction zone, the linguistic meaning of the text cannot tell us how to decide particular cases.

Constitutional construction will be required. When constitutional construction operates within a construction zone created by the constitutional text, we can say that the construction is "bound to the text."[35]

Theories of constitutional interpretation provide an account of the communicative content of the constitutional text. Theories of constitutional construction are different: they are normative theories about what we ought to do with that content. Characteristically, originalist theories of constitutional construction will respect the Constraint Principle – they will only sanction constructions that are consistent with the communicative content of the text. In easy cases, construction may take place without resort to extra-textual sources; the text may be sufficient to provide the legal content that resolves the cases.[36] But in hard cases, even originalists may resort to extra-textual sources to provide legal content.

Consider the First Amendment freedom of speech. Because the text is general, abstract, and vague, we are in the construction zone. In a particular case, more than one outcome may be consistent with the communicative content of the constitutional text. If we look to free speech doctrine as a whole, there are multiple versions of the doctrine that are consistent with the communicative content of the doctrine. This means that we will need to look outside the four corners of the text to resolve at least some possible cases that could arise under the First Amendment freedom of speech.

Consider two possible approaches to the phrase "freedom of speech." The first approach assumes that "the freedom of speech" was a phrase of legal art that referred to a *preexisting legal doctrine*. The second approach assumes that "the freedom of speech" was a phrase of political philosophy that refers to the *general concept of freedom of speech*. These two approaches are offered

---

[35] The phrase "bound to the text" is being used in a stipulated sense. Constructions that are bound to the text are stipulated to be constructions that operate within the zone of underdetermination created by vague or irreducibly ambiguous terms. A fuller account would require consideration of additional sources of underdetermination: such sources might include open texture, gaps, and contradictions.

[36] In some cases, this will mean that the legal content of constitutional doctrine will be sufficiently determined by the communicative content of the text to determine the outcome of the case. In such cases, the activity of construction consists in translating the communicative content of the text into the equivalent legal content (or constitutional doctrine). These are likely to be "easy cases," and because they are easy, the activity of construction may go unnoticed or seem automatic.

Here is an example: Article One provides that each state shall have two senators. Because senators are human beings, borderline cases do not arise. Senators Boxer and Feinstein are two senators – not one or three. Constitutional construction is at work here – the constitutional practice (which determines legal effect) is to follow the original meaning of the Constitution. It could be otherwise; someone might advocate for an amending construction that reapportioned the Senate by population. But on this issue, living constitutionalists and originalists are united in (tacitly or consciously) endorsing the Constraint Principle.

here for the purposes of illustration; I am not advancing either of these two approaches as the correct interpretation of the constitutional text.

The first approach is based on the hypothesis that the public meaning of "the freedom of speech" involves a division of linguistic labor. On this hypothesis, "the freedom of speech" refers to a preexisting legal doctrine. For example, it might have been the case that "the freedom of speech" referred to a rule against prior restraints. On this interpretation, the determination of the full communicative content of "the freedom of speech" would require the consultation of extra-textual legal sources known to the American lawyers of the late eighteenth century, for example, Blackstone's *Commentaries*.[37]

The second approach is based on the hypothesis that the public meaning of "the freedom of speech" involved a concept of political philosophy, which we might call "the freedom of expression." Hypothetically, let us postulate that the public in 1791 would have understood the freedom of expression as a general concept of political philosophy. Determining the content of the concept might require us to consult extra-textual sources, perhaps the political philosophy of John Locke.

3.5.2.3. The Role of Justifications for Originalism in Constitutional Construction

This chapter does not explore the justifications *for* originalism. Rather, on this occasion, I am simply *assuming* an originalist perspective (with public meaning originalism as the model version). But when it comes to originalist theories of constitutional construction, the underlying justification for originalism will make a difference. Theoretical consistency will demand that the originalist theory of constitutional construction cohere with the underlying normative justification for the Constraint Principle. If the Constraint Principle is justified by an account of popular sovereignty, then the theory of constitutional construction must be consistent with popular sovereignty (considering other relevant political values). If the Constraint Principle is justified by rule-of-law considerations, then the theory of constitutional construction must be consistent with the rule of law (or departures must be justified by other salient political values).

Thus, the requirement of theoretical consistency has implications for the way in which originalist theories treat the various categories of extra-textual sources. If the Constraint Principle is justified by rule of law considerations

---

[37] William Blackstone, *Commentaries on the Laws of England vol. IV* (Boston, MA: Beacon Press, 1962), 158.

and a distrust of the institutional capacity of judges to make objective, morally correct decisions, then the theory of constitutional construction would do well to avoid a reliance on the judges' own beliefs about political morality. If the Constraint Principle is justified by popular sovereignty theory, then it might follow that the social norms and values of "We the People" today should play a role in constitutional construction; for example, a default rule favoring deference to legislative choices might be justified on popular sovereignty grounds.

The point is that something outside the text – the justifications for constraint – will play a role in constitutional construction when the text underdetermines legal content.

3.5.2.4. Extra-textual Sources of Constitutional Norms Not Bound to the Text

We have just considered the possibility that extra-textual sources might be used to flesh out the content of constitutional constructions that are bound to the text. But it is at least theoretically possible that there might be constitutional constructions that are "unbound" – that cannot be connected to the zone of underdetermination created by a particular clause or to the structure of the Constitution as a whole or in part.

To illustrate this idea, we can pursue a counterfactual hypothetical. Suppose that the Constitution had absolutely nothing to say about unenumerated rights. Imagine, for example, that the Ninth Amendment had not been ratified, and that the Fourteenth Amendment did not contain any provision with communicative content that provides a textual basis for unenumerated rights. (Suppose, for example, the Fourteenth Amendment had not included the Privileges or Immunities Clause.) Could originalists nonetheless endorse constitutional constructions that created judicially enforceable unenumerated rights?

The answer to this question will depend on the content of the particular version of originalism. Consider the version of the Constraint Principle formulated previously as part of Constraint as Consistency. Recall the third requirement:

> *Requirement Three*: All of the content of constitutional doctrine must be fairly traceable to the direct translation set, where traceable content includes precisifications, implementation rules, and default rules presupposed by the text.

This third requirement rules out constitutional doctrines that are "unbound." And we can imagine even more stringent versions of the Constraint Principle – for example, a principle of super strict construction that requires each and every judicially enforceable rule of constitutional law be a direct translation of the communicative content of the constitutional text.

But we can imagine a much less restrictive version of the Constraint Principle. For example, some originalists might affirm the view that the judicial branch may supplement the constitutional text with unbound constitutional constructions – so long as those constructions are logically consistent with the text. Such an originalist might allow for the addition of unenumerated constitutional rights that are consistent with the enumerated rights, but go beyond them.

We have now categorized extrajudicial sources and the roles they might play in the activities of constitutional interpretation and construction. This completes our investigation of extra-textual sources at the level of abstraction. The next phase of our investigation will examine particular sources and the role that they should play, from an originalist perspective, in constitutional interpretation and construction.

3.6. ORIGINALISM AND EXTRA-TEXTUAL CONSTITUTIONAL CONTENT

We have now established a theoretical framework that will enable us to examine the role of extra-textual sources in constitutional interpretation and construction from an originalist perspective. Recapitulating briefly, we have: (1) identified the core of contemporary originalist theory; (2) marked the distinction between interpretation and construction; (3) noted the existence of construction zones; (4) categorized extra-textual sources; and (5) specified the different roles that these sources might play in constitutional interpretation or construction. We can now apply this framework to particular types of constitutional argument. In each case, we will examine the type and then consider its relationship to the proper attitude of originalism toward the use of extra-textual sources in constitutional interpretation and construction.

3.6.1. Constitutional Implications

The constitution may "imply" things that it does not say. Let us call the content that is implied but not stated "constitutional implication." Some theorists treat constitutional doctrines that are derived or discovered by "implication" from the constitutional text as examples of an unwritten or invisible constitution. The word "implicit" is the adjectival form of the verb "implied" and the corresponding noun "implication." An "implication" is a conclusion that can be drawn from something, although it is not explicitly stated.

In this section, we are investigating "constitutional implication." Before we proceed further, we should note a terminological difficulty. The term "implication" can be used to refer to a variety of phenomena. For example, "implication" may be used as a synonym for "logical implication" or "entailment." But we might also use the word "implication" to refer to certain forms of contextual enrichment: in the philosophy of language and theoretical linguistics, special terminology is used to distinguish the distinct phenomena covered by the word "implication."[38] Thus, implication can be distinguished from "implicature," "impliciture," "presupposition," "modulation," and so forth. More on the others later, but for now we shall stipulate that the word "implication" will be used hereinafter to refer to logical implication or entailment.

Everyone understands that legal texts have logical implications. We can illustrate these implications in simple syllogisms:

Premise One: "The Senate of the United States shall be composed of two Senators from each State."
Premise Two: Alaska is a state.
Conclusion: Therefore the Senate of the United States shall include two Senators from Alaska.

The text of the Constitution does not mention Alaska, but from what the text does say, and from the true factual premise that Alaska is a state, we can imply that Alaska is entitled to two Senators.[39]

What is clear is that originalism should endorse constitutional implication as a general method of constitutional construction. Constitutional implications are not in the text, but they follow from the text.

3.6.2. Four Forms of Contextual Enrichment

What about contextual enrichment? The mechanisms of contextual enrichment are intuitively accessible to competent language users, but these mechanisms are described by a technical vocabulary in the philosophy of language and linguistics. Consider four forms of contextual enrichment.

---

[38] I am treating "implication" as an agglomeration term when it is used in its broadest sense. See note 31.

[39] This account of constitutional implication is not quite right. The first premise is a quote from the text of Article I and the Seventeenth Amendment. Premise two is a fact. The conclusion is a rule of law. Strictly speaking, the argument needs an additional step or two – which move from the text to the communicative content and then to the associated legal content. We can easily imagine an expanded version of the syllogism that fills in the missing steps.

3.6.2.1. Implicature

Implicature conveys communicative content that differs from the semantic content of an utterance or text.[40] Consider the classic example of a letter of recommendation, written by a law professor, for a student applying for a prestigious judicial clerkship. The entire body of the letter reads as follows: "I recommend Ben. He was always on time to class and his attendance record was perfect." The semantic content of the letter consists of a speech act, recommendation, and two supporting statements regarding punctuality and regularity of attendance. But in the context in which the letter was written, much more than the literal meaning is communicated. If the best that can be said about Ben is that he was on time and did not miss class, the implicature is that Ben is not suitable for the position of judicial clerk.

3.6.2.2. Impliciture

Impliciture involves situations in which what is said implicitly includes something else that is closely related.[41] Kent Bach gives the following examples, in which the impliciture (unstated) has been added in brackets:

- Jack and Jill are married [to each other].
- Bill insulted his boss and [as a result] got fired.
- Nina has had enough [pasta to eat].[42]

Thus, if someone says, "Jack and Jill are married," the [to each other] is unstated but implicit, and so forth for the other examples. Constitutional impliciture is common: Article I, Section 9, of the Constitution explicitly states, "[n]o Bill of Attainder or ex post facto Law shall be passed," with [by Congress] as an impliciture. Obviously, the provision does include implicitures such as [by the Parliament of the United Kingdom] or [by the legislature of any nation]. The particular impliciture is derived from the context.

---

[40] See Wayne Davis, "Implicature," *Stanford Encyclopedia of Philosophy* (last revised September 22, 2010) http://plato.stanford.edu/entries/implicature/.
[41] Kent Bach, "Conversational Impliciture" (1994) 9 *Mind and Language* 124.
[42] Kent Bach, "Impliciture vs. Explicature: What's the Difference?" user www.sfsu.edu/kbach/Bach.ImplExpl.pdf.

3.6.2.3. Presupposition

Presupposition is communicative content provided by an unstated assumption or background belief that is conveyed by what is said.[43] Again, examples are helpful:

- Utterance: "Grant was once a law professor." Presupposition: "Grant is no longer a law professor."
- Utterance: "Jeff should not eat meat." Presupposition: "Jeff does eat meat."
- Utterance: "Lisa's wife is pregnant." Presupposition: "Lisa has a wife."

Philosophers of language distinguish between "conversational presuppositions" (also called "speaker presuppositions" or "pragmatic presuppositions") and "conventional presuppositions" (or "semantic presuppositions") that are triggered by particular words or phrases ("no longer" in the first example above). For our purposes, we can put these technicalities to the side. The constitutional text may have a variety of presuppositions. Famously, the Ninth Amendment may presuppose the existence of "rights retained by the people" even though the explicitly semantic content of the text does not state that such rights exist.

3.6.2.4. Modulation

Finally, consider what is sometimes called modulation. The intuitive idea is that a conventional semantic meaning can be adjusted or modulated to fit the context – essentially a new meaning is created (sometimes on the spot) so that an old word is used in a new way. As Francois Recanati observes,

> Sense modulation is essential to speech, because we use a (more or less) fixed stock of lexemes to talk about an indefinite variety of things, situations and experiences. Through the interaction between the context-independent meanings of our words and the particulars of the situation talked about, contextualised, modulated senses emerge, appropriate to the situation at hand.[44]

---

[43] See e.g., David I. Beaver and Bart Geurts, "Presupposition," *Stanford Encyclopedia of Philosophy* http://plato.stanford.edu/entries/presupposition/ (April 1, 2011); Bas C. van Fraassen, "Presupposition, Implication, and Self-Reference" (1968) 65 *Journal of Philosophy* 136; Philippe Schlenker, "Be Articulate: A Pragmatic Theory of Presupposition" (2008) 34 *Theoretical Linguistics* 157.

[44] Francois Recanati, *Literal Meaning* (Cambridge: Cambridge University Press, 2004), 131.

In ordinary speech, modulations may be "one offs," used on a single occasion. But in the law modulation can create a new technical meaning for a word that also has an ordinary sense.

The text of the United States Constitution contains a variety of modulations – special purpose constitutional meanings that can be understood by paying attention to context. One example is (or hypothetically may be) the Recess Appointments Clause, which uses the word "recess." Read acontextually, a recess might be any break in the business of the Senate – even a lunch break.[45] But in context, "recess" is best read as a modulation, the meaning of which plays off the complimentary term "session." The relevant sense of "recess" is a modulation of the conventional semantic meaning that is limited to the break between sessions of the Senate.

Finally, there is a residual category of "free enrichments" that do not fit into any of these categories. For present purposes, free enrichment is set aside.[46]

3.6.3. Contextual Enrichment and Originalist Theory

Ryan Williams has done pioneering work on the role of contextual enrichment from an originalist perspective. After recognizing the legitimacy of constitutional implicature, Williams suggests the following criterion:[47]

> [I]f the implied content is not semantically encoded in the text, interpreters should inquire whether a reasonable member of the ratifying public at the time of enactment would have recognized the implied content as following obviously and noncontroversially from the choice of the particular language used in the provision and the relevant background context.[48]

Further refinements may be required. The notion of a "reasonable member of the ratifying public" is a legal notion. But the question that we are acting

---

[45] Noah Webster's 1828 dictionary offered the following as the sixth definition of "recess:" "Remission or suspension of business or procedure; as, the house of representatives had a recess of half an hour." See http://webstersdictionary1828.com/Dictionary/recess.
[46] Nicholas Allott, *Key Terms in Pragmatics* (London: Bloomsbury Academic, 2010), 80.
[47] Ryan C. Williams, "The Ninth Amendment as a Rule of Construction" (2011) 111 *Columbia Law Review* 498, 544. Williams' discussion of this point is somewhat misleading. He suggests that constitutional implications should be recognized if "the putatively implied content arises as a matter of logical necessity due to a noncancellable, semantically encoded formulation." This formulation is correct, but Williams characterizes this principle as a component of a test "for recognizing constitutional implicatures." That characterization is inaccurate. The logical consequences of semantic content are implications, not implicatures. See Kent Bach, "The Top Ten Misconceptions about Implicature" 3 http://userwww.sfsu.edu/~kbach/TopTen.pdf.
[48] Williams, Supra note 47.

on is not a legal question – it is a question about meaning. For this reason, we might substitute "competent speaker of American English" for "reasonable member."

Williams uses the phrase "implied content," but this usage runs the risk of conflating implication with implicature, impliciture, and presupposition. We might substitute "contextual enrichment." Williams suggests that contextual enrichment should be limited to content that is obvious and noncontroversial, but it is not clear that this is the way that contextual enrichment always works. Sometimes the communicative content of a text may not be "obvious" – it may be that competent speakers would need to read carefully to *see* the contextual enrichment. Likewise, the existence of controversy does not automatically cancel a contextual enrichment. Interpretation and construction of legal texts, and especially of the Constitution, involves motivated reasoning; vested interested or passionate ideologues may create controversy about implicatures that would be recognized by competent speakers motivated by a desire to understand the text.

With these alterations in mind, we might reformulate Williams' proposed principle as follows:

> Contextual enrichment should be recognized when competent speakers of the language at the time the constitutional provision was framed and ratified would recognize the enrichment of the text given the publicly available context of constitutional communication.

Further questions remain.[49] Contextual enrichment gives rise to special cases of vagueness and ambiguity. When the content of a contextual enrichment is vague, the enrichment creates a construction zone. Another possibility is that competent speakers with knowledge of the publicly available context of constitutional communication would disagree about what the content of the enrichment is. This is a special case of ambiguity, "contextual ambiguity." Usually, semantic ambiguity can be resolved by reference to context; in the case of implicative ambiguity, context creates the ambiguity. Of course, it might be the case that the ambiguity appears when some subset of the publicly available context of constitutional communication is considered but resolves in light of the full context. But it is at least theoretically possible that ambiguity is irreducible, and hence that constitutional construction will be required.

---

[49] For further discussion of these issues, see Goldsworthy, Supra note 29, 27.

We can imagine a variety of possible approaches to construction when an irreducible contextual ambiguity exists. We can explore this problem in the context of its most famous exemplar – the Ninth Amendment.

3.6.4. The Ninth Amendment

The Ninth Amendment to the United States Constitution states "[t]he enumeration in the Constitution, of certain rights, shall not be construed to deny or disparage others retained by the people." We can begin with the word "construed." The Ninth Amendment is a rule of construction in the technical sense. This is not a product of the perhaps fortuitous use of "construed," which is a form of the same root word as "construction." Rather, it follows from the interpretation–construction distinction and the implication–implicature construction.

The Constitution enumerates certain rights, in Sections 9 and 10 of Article I, in Article IV, and in various amendments, including the first eight provisions of the Bill of Rights, and subsequent to the Ninth Amendment in various other amendments, including the Fourteenth Amendment. As a matter of interpretation, the enumeration of these rights could not give rise to a constitutional impliciture that denied or disparaged other rights retained by the people. The semantic content of the enumerated rights consists of positive statements about the right in question – freedom of speech, the right to bear arms, and so forth. The fact of enumeration is a structural feature of the Constitution. Nothing in the semantic content of the rights contains a semantic content that explicitly denies or disparages other rights retained by the people. But it is at least possible that the communicative content of the enumeration of particular rights gives rise to an implicature that denies or disparages other rights. The reasoning would go as follows:

> The Constitution enumerates a list of particular rights of the people. The point of enumerating particular rights (and omitting a more general statement) is to create an exhaustive list. Therefore, there is an impliciture – an unstated provision of the Constitution that says something [and no other rights] after the enumerated rights.

The semantic content of the Ninth Amendment forbids this form of impliciture, and it would forbid this impliciture even if the impliciture best captured the public meaning of the Constitution as it would have been without the Ninth Amendment.

But the semantic content does a second thing. Even if enumeration did not give rise to an impliciture of exclusivity, there could be a constitutional doctrine (legal content) that forbade judicial enforcement of unenumerated rights. The reasoning in favor of such a rule of constitutional construction might have proceeded as follows:

> The Constitution enumerates a list of particular rights of the people. This enumeration could give rise to an inference of exclusivity or it could give rise to an opposing inference that other relevantly similar rights are also protected. This implicitive ambiguity requires constitutional construction. The better construction is that the list is exclusive. Therefore, there should be a rule of constitutional doctrine that limits individual rights to those that are enumerated and those that result by logical implication from the enumerated rights.

The semantic content of the Ninth Amendment forbids this construction, and hence the Ninth Amendment is itself a rule of construction.[50]

So far, we have focused on the semantic content of the Ninth Amendment, but most of the debate about the meaning of the Ninth concerns implicature and other forms of contextual enrichment. Again, consider the text: "The enumeration in the Constitution, of certain rights, shall not be construed to deny or disparage others retained by the people." The text does not state that the people do have retained rights. This can be demonstrated by adding the words "if any" to the text as follows: "The enumeration in the Constitution, of certain rights, shall not be construed to deny or disparage others, if any, retained by the people." The "if any" does not create a logical contradiction. For this same reason, the semantic content of the text does not give rise to a constitutional implication that the people have retained rights – it is not logically required by the semantic content.

But the Ninth Amendment does give rise to a straightforward constitutional presupposition that the people retain other rights. The reasoning is simple. There would be no reason for the Ninth Amendment if there were no rights retained by the people; given what the Ninth Amendment does say and the publicly available context of constitutional communication, a competent speaker of English would recognize the presupposition. And hence the presupposition is part of the communicative content of the Ninth Amendment. Given the Constraint Principle, public meaning originalists ought not endorse constitutional doctrine that is inconsistent with the presupposition – at least *ceteris paribus* (that is, assuming that no defeasibility condition comes into play).

---

[50] See Williams, Supra note 47.

Having gotten this far, there is a further question. What is the content of the retained rights? Immediately, we see a problem. The constitutional presupposition is that there are retained rights, but this presupposition does not tell us what the content of the rights might be. Of course, it is possible that the publicly available context of constitutional communication provides sufficient information to give shape to that content. For example, if that context included widespread public agreement on a theory of natural rights such that competent speakers of American English immersed in the political culture would understand that "retained rights" were natural rights, then the publicly shared theory of natural rights might liquidate a substantial amount of the uncertainty created by the presupposition. Similarly, if the shared culture included agreement on theories of popular sovereignty or of federalism, then one of those theories might provide content to the presupposition. Many of the debates about the meaning of the Ninth Amendment should be understood as debates about the content of the publicly available context of constitutional communication.

Suppose, however, that the publicly available context included competing and only partially articulate views about natural rights, popular sovereignty, and federalism. In that case, the content of the constitutional presupposition from the Ninth Amendment might be irreducibly uncertain. Operationally, this would be the case if significant numbers of competent readers aware of the public context would draw substantially different inferences about the content of the constitutional presupposition; similarly, irreducible uncertainty would result if many competent readers would be undecided about the content of the implicature. Such irreducible ambiguity would require constitutional construction.

But that is not the end of the story. It might be that the irreducible uncertainty is only partial. Consider the following example. The First Amendment begins, "Congress shall pass no law" and hence one might conclude that the "freedom of speech" binds only Congress – leaving the executive and judicial branches unrestrained. But the Ninth Amendment juxtaposed with the First Amendment and publicly available context of constitutional communication may give rise to a presupposition that the freedom of speech constrains action by the executive and judicial branches. Even if there was uncertainty about the full content of the presupposed "retained rights," there might be sufficient clarity with respect to a subset of those rights.

This is simply one example of a more general phenomenon – irreducible uncertainty in the content of constitutional enrichments can be partial or total. If it is partial, then the Constraint Principle suggests that originalists should honor that portion of the enrichment that does have ascertainable content.

3.6.5. Extra-textual Constructions of Written Clauses

The Ninth Amendment is difficult, but there are much easier cases. Some provisions of the Constitution seem to have open-textured communicative content. For example, the clauses that vest "executive," "legislative," and "judicial power" may be open-textured in this way. Of course, open-textured semantic content may become relatively more determinate once context is considered, but for many constitutional provisions, it seems likely that a substantial construction zone will remain after contextual disambiguation.

Different versions of originalism can embrace different theories of constitutional construction so long as those theories are consistent with the Fixation Thesis and the Constraint Principle – the unifying principles (or core) of originalism. Some originalists may adopt theories of construction that maximize the authority of the political branches; for example, they might adopt a general rule of construction that calls for judges to defer to the political branches in the construction zone. Other originalists might look to the judicial practice of the Founding Era; the theory that is called "original methods originalism" could serve this purpose.[51] And another group of originalists might look to multiple modalities of constitutional argument, including text, history, structure, precedent, "ethos" of the American social order, and prudence.[52] The content of any particular originalist theory of construction will depend on the underlying normative justification that theory gives for the Constraint Principle, as well as a variety of other factors.

3.6.6. Holism and Structure

Questions about an invisible or unwritten constitution also arise in connection with constitutional arguments from the structural properties of the constitutional text. In the American context, the principle of separation of powers is the most well-known and widely accepted example of a principle of constitutional law that is not explicitly stated in the text, but which is alleged to flow from the overall structure of the text. Structural arguments are related to another feature of constitutional interpretation which is sometimes called "holism."

For example, Akhil Amar articulates the following description of a general method for determining the content of the invisible or unwritten constitution:

---

[51] See John McGinnis and Michael Rappaport, "Original Methods Originalism: A New Theory of Interpretation and the Case against Construction" (2009) 103 *Northwestern University Law Review* 751.

[52] Philip Bobbitt, *Constitutional Interpretation* (Hoboken: Blackwell Publishing, 1991), 12–13.

A single methodological idea unifies all the foregoing case studies and hypotheticals. On each topic, clause-bound literalism fails. Sometimes the key clause in isolation is simply indeterminate. (The phrase "executive Power" can be read narrowly or broadly on the issue of presidential immunity from prosecution.) Other times, the most salient clause, in isolation, sends a rather misleading message. (The First Amendment speaks only of "Congress," but surely presidents, federal courts, and states must also honor citizens' rights to express political opinions.) On occasion the Constitution's true meaning is very nearly the opposite of what the applicable clause seems to say quite expressly. (The vice president does not properly preside over his own impeachment.) *This chapter's unifying idea is that we must read the Constitution as a whole – between the lines, so to speak.*[53]

Let us use the name "constitutional holism" for the view that the meaning of the Constitution is the meaning of the whole document or the "holistic meaning."[54] We can distinguish "holistic meaning" from "clause meaning" – the meaning that results from a clause-by-clause interpretation that considers each clause in isolation. What should originalists think about constitutional holism?

Public-meaning originalists are committed to the public-meaning thesis. The communicative content of the Constitution is a function of contextually enriched semantic content. But what if individual words and phrases cannot be understood in isolation because the Constitution is an organic whole? For example, the phrase "rights ... retained by the People" in the Ninth Amendment might not be comprehensible without reference to "We the People" in the Preamble, which might suggest that "the People" is a polity and not a collection of individuals. Likewise, the Ninth Amendment uses the phrase "the enumeration of certain rights in this Constitution." Gleaning the meaning of this phrase seems to require reference to what is now called "the Bill of Rights," and once that has been accomplished, the meaning of the phrase "rights ... retained by the People" may be clarified. For example, the "retained rights" which are not to be denied or disparaged may be of the same type or kind as the "enumerated rights" such as the freedom of speech and press, the right to bear arms, the right to due process, and so forth.

Does holistic meaning provide a better account of the communicative content of the Constitution than clause meaning? To get at this question, we

---

[53] Amar, Supra note 6, 47 (emphasis added).
[54] See e.g., Akhil Reed Amar, "A Few Thoughts on Constitutionalism, Textualism, and Populism" (1997) 65 *Fordham Law Review* 1657, 1659 (observing "the importance of looking at the Constitution as a whole because what was ratified was the document, not individual clauses" and "[t]he clause is not the unit, or at least [not] the only unit of analysis").

first need to identify and then deflate a misleading picture of the relationship between the meaning of individual clauses and the whole Constitution. It might be thought that there are only two alternative positions on the relationship of the whole to the parts when it comes to constitutional meaning. The first alternative might be called "clause bound interpretivism," which we can define as follows:

> The meaning of each clause must be determined from within the four corners of the clause.

We can now see that clause-bound interpretivism is inconsistent with the public meaning thesis: the meaning of the Constitution for the public (at the time of framing and ratification) is a function of both semantic content and context. So, public-meaning originalists should reject clause-bound interpretivism.

This brings us to a second theory, which might be called "organic unity holism":

> Meaning only attaches to the whole constitution as an organic unity; therefore, individual clauses are not meaningful units of constitutional communication.

This picture, which suggests we must choose between clause-bound interpretivism and organic-unity holism, might be called the "all-or-nothing picture:" either the Constitution's meaning is *all* (the whole Constitution all at once) or it is *nothing* (no meaning attaches to the individual clauses by virtue of their relationship to the whole document).

The all-or-nothing picture creates a false dilemma. There is an alternative picture of the relationship between the meaning of individual clauses and the whole Constitution; that picture can be expressed via two ideas: (1) the familiar device of the hermeneutic circle and (2) the related notion of intra-textualism.

The idea of a hermeneutic circle figured prominently in Protestant theological hermeneutics as a method for understanding the relationship of the meaning of individual biblical passages to the whole text: the meaning of each individual passage of scripture is gleaned in light of the meaning of the Bible as a whole, and the meaning of the whole is gleaned in light of the meaning of all the individual passages.[55] As Hans-Georg Gadamer puts it, "[f]or it is the whole of scripture that guides the understanding of the individual passage:

---

[55] See Lawrence B. Solum, "Originalism as Transformative Politics" (1989) 63 *Tulane Law Review* 1599, 1608.

and again this whole can be reached only through the cumulative understanding of individual passages."[56] Justice Joseph Story's first recommendation for constitutional construction is based on the same notion: "[i]n construing the constitution of the United States, we are, in the first instance, to consider, what are its nature and objects, its scope and design, as apparent from the structure of the instrument, viewed as a whole, and also viewed in its component parts."[57]

Intra-textualism as articulated by Amar expresses a closely related idea with a different metaphor:[58]

> Textual argument as typically practiced today is blinkered ("clause-bound" in Ely's terminology), focusing intently on the words of a given constitutional provision in splendid isolation. By contrast, intra-textualism always focuses on at least two clauses and highlights the link between them. Clause-bound textualism paradigmatically stresses what is explicit in the Constitution's text: "See here, it says X!" By contrast, intra-textualism paradigmatically stresses what is only implicit in the Constitution's text: "See here, these clauses fit together!" But there is no clause in the Constitution that says, explicitly and in so many words, that the three Vesting Clauses should be construed together, or that the Article III grant of federal question jurisdiction should be read alongside the Article VI Supremacy Clause. Intra-textualism simply reads the Constitution as if these implicit linking clauses existed. Clause-bound textualism reads the words of the Constitution in order, tracking the sequence of clauses as they appear in the document itself. By contrast, intra-textualism often reads the words of the Constitution in a dramatically different order, placing textually nonadjoining clauses side by side for careful analysis. In effect, intra-textualists read a two-dimensional parchment in a three-dimensional way, carefully folding the parchment to bring scattered clauses alongside each other.[59]

Both the idea of the hermeneutic circle and the idea of intra-textualism undermine the all-or-nothing picture. Our choices are not limited to clause-bound interpretivism and organic-unity holism. The excluded middle is to read individual clauses in the context of the whole Constitution. The clause–meaning thesis squarely occupies the excluded middle: it insists that clause meaning is bound by the publicly available context, and the whole of the constitutional text is indisputably part of that! Once the all-or-nothing picture is out of the

---

[56] Hans-Georg Gadamer, *Truth and Method* (London: Bloomsbury Academic, 1975), 264.
[57] Joseph Story, *Commentaries on the Constitution of the United States*, abridged edn (Boston: Hilliard, Gray & Co., 1833), 136.
[58] See Akhil Reed Amar, "Intratextualism" (1998) 112 *Harvard Law Review* 747.
[59] Ibid., 788.

way, it becomes apparent that contextual clause meaning can be reconciled with a plausible version of holistic meaning.

One final point: organic unity holism is utterly implausible as a theory of communicative content. The whole Constitution is not the relevant unit for determining communicative content. It is no accident that when we apply the Constitution to particular cases or problems our focus is on clauses and the interaction between clauses. The Constitution as an organic unit says both too much and too little. Too much because the whole Constitution from top to bottom considered as a single unit of meaning doesn't translate into rules of constitutional law: organic unity holism makes the Constitution unintelligible. Too little, because organic unity prevents us from assigning meaning at the level of particularity required to do the work of constitutional practice.

In sum, if holistic meaning is construed plausibly (as incorporating the ideas of the hermeneutic circle and intra-textualism), then it is absorbed into public meaning originalism. But if construed in accord with organic unity holism, holistic meaning is no meaning at all.

Can originalists embrace modest holism? Modest holism can play at least four distinct roles in constitutional interpretation and construction:

1. Reading parts of the Constitution in light of the whole can resolve semantic and syntactic ambiguities.
2. Reading parts of the Constitution in light of the whole can reveal constitutional implications – the logical consequences of the interactions between various clauses.
3. Reading parts of the Constitution in light of the whole can reveal contextual enrichment – in this regard the whole text acts as context for particular clauses, phrases, or words.
4. Reading parts of the Constitution in light of the whole can guide constitutional construction; for example, the relationship between the grants of legislative, executive, and judicial power in the first three articles could guide construction of each.

Originalists can and should endorse modest holism whenever it plays one of these four roles.

3.6.7. Extra-textual Fundamental Law

Extra-textual sources can play yet another role – as freestanding sources of fundamental law. The word "freestanding" plays an important role here. We can begin to understand the notion of "freestanding fundamental law" by way of contrast with two other ideas: (1) the constitutional constructions that are bound to text; and (2) contextual enrichment of the semantic content of the text. Constructions that are bound to the text are not freestanding – they are attached to text that is vague, open-textured, or irreducibly ambiguous. Contextual enrichments (e.g., constitutional implicatures) provide the communicative content of the text in context; they do not stand free from the text.

But we can imagine constitutional doctrine that is derived from freestanding sources. For example, one might believe that fundamental principles of political morality operate directly to create constitutional doctrine. The strongest version of this idea would give these principles of political morality trumping force – they would have legal force even if directly contrary to the text of the Constitution. Consider an example. Slavery and the slave trade both violate fundamental principles of political morality, but the text of the Constitution arguably prohibited Congress from outlawing the slave trade.[60] A more modest version would allow for fundamental law that supplements but does not contradict the constitutional text. For example, one might believe that there is a principle of political morality that is the source of a constitutional rule forbidding capital punishment – even though the communicative content of the Constitution does not contain or imply such a rule.[61]

We have already discussed the Ninth Amendment. Although the amendment itself does not directly state or logically imply that extra-textual fundamental law is judicially enforceable, it might be that the Ninth Amendment creates a constitutional presupposition to that effect. That argument would not be "freestanding" in the sense in which that term is used here. Constitutional construction that precisifies the content of presupposed "retained rights" is consistent with Constraint as Consistency (as outlined previously).

For the sake of argument, we need to assume that neither the Ninth Amendment nor any other textual source provides a textual basis for the incorporation of extra-textual fundamental law. What should be the stance of originalism toward extra-textual fundamental law as a freestanding source of constitutional law? The Constraint Principle suggests that the strong version of the idea of extra-textual fundamental law is clearly inconsistent with originalism. But what about the modest version? One tempting answer implicitly invokes the idea that the Constitution is an integrated writing, but where

---

[60] US Const. Art. I. Sec. 9 ("[t]he Migration or Importation of such Persons as any of the States now existing shall think proper to admit, shall not be prohibited by the Congress prior to the Year one thousand eight hundred and eight, but a Tax or duty may be imposed on such Importation, not exceeding ten dollars for each Person.").

[61] Of course, some opponents of capital punishment could argue that a rule forbidding the death penalty can be derived from the Eighth Amendment to the Constitution.

would that principle come from? It is not stated in the constitutional text, nor is it logically implied by the text.[62]

However, particular parts of the Constitution may support contextual enrichments that are inconsistent with extra-textual fundamental law. For example, Article I, Section Eight enumerates the powers of Congress. The Necessary and Proper Clause negates the inference that only the enumerated powers may be exercised, but it also suggests that unenumerated powers must bear the right kind of relationship to the powers enumerated in Section Eight or elsewhere in the Constitution. It might be argued that the combination of enumeration with the requirements of necessity and propriety create a presumption that rules out constitutional doctrines based on freestanding legislative power derived from some background theory of the powers that governments ought to have.

However, the Necessary and Proper Clause also refers to the powers of "the government of the United States" – and John Mikhail has argued that this feature presupposes a set of unenumerated powers.[63] Richard Primus has made a different argument against what he calls the "internal-limits canon."[64] From an originalist perspective, the question is whether the unenumerated powers can be connected to the constitutional text via contextual enrichment. If a connection can be made, originalists ought to accept the extra-textual powers, but most originalists will reject powers that are truly freestanding – with no connection to the text at all.

Some originalists may believe that extra-textual fundamental law is obviously contrary to the normative basis for the Constraint Principle. For example, if one affirms the Constraint Principle because one believes that judges are untrustworthy, and hence should be constrained by the constitutional text, one will be likely to adopt a rule that prohibits judicial recognition and enforcement of extra-textual fundamental law. But this rule itself is not stated in the text. It might be a construction derived from the phrase "judicial power," or it might itself be derived from a freestanding principle of political morality.

---

[62] This can easily be demonstrated. Add an extra-textual fundamental law clause to the Constitution. The new provision does not contradict or invalidate any of the communicative content of the constitutional text. It follows that the negation of the imaginary provision is not implied by the communicative content of the actual text.

[63] See John Mikhail, "The Necessary and Proper Clauses" (2014) 102 *Georgetown Law Journal* 1045 ("[u]nless it is treated as surplusage, this second clause indicates that the Constitution vests powers in the Government of the United States that are not merely identical or coextensive with the powers vested in Congress or other Departments or Officers of the United States. Because these additional powers are not specified or enumerated in the Constitution, they must be understood to be implied or unenumerated powers.").

[64] Richard Primus, "The Limits of Enumeration" (2014) 124 *Yale Law Journal* 576.

On the other hand, if one's justification for the Constraint Principle were based on a theory of natural rights combined with an argument that public meaning originalism provided for the best institutional structure for the protection of such rights then one might believe that a natural-rights version of extra-textual fundamental law is consistent with originalism.

The word "originalism" is a neologism coined by Paul Brest to describe a constitutional theory that he opposed.[65] Some originalists may believe that the spirit of originalism is fundamentally inconsistent with the notion of freestanding extra-textual fundamental law, and hence should not be called "originalist." Other originalists may insist, with equal fervor, that natural-rights extra-textual fundamental law is at the core of the original meaning of the Constitution. Once we recognize that "originalism" is a stipulated theory term, it becomes clear that there is no truth of the matter in this debate. The best we can do is to be clear about the meaning of our stipulated theoretical language. My own view is that any constitutional theory that affirms the Fixation Thesis and the Constraint Principle is properly called "originalist."

3.6.8. Nonconstitutional Texts

Should originalists embrace arguments that use nonconstitutional texts as sources of constitutional doctrine? For example, should originalists embrace arguments that derive the legal content of constitutional doctrine from the Declaration of Independence, the Treaty of York, Blackstone's Commentaries, or the Federalist Papers? Various versions of these questions have been the subject of vigorous debate. For example, Lee Strang has argued that the Declaration of Independence should not be viewed as an independent source of constitutional norms,[66] but others, such as Scott Gerber, have argued that the Declaration should play a robust role.[67] For the purposes of this discussion, a "nonconstitutional text" is any text that is not part of the United States Constitution – the Constitution of 1789 plus all of the subsequent amendments (roughly, the version of the Constitution in the United States Code).

Consider, for example, Akhil Amar's argument for a robust role for extraconstitutional texts, which he treats as part of America's "symbolic constitution":

---

[65] See Solum, Supra note 17.
[66] Lee J. Strang, "Originalism, the Declaration of Independence, and the Constitution: a unique role in constitutional interpretation?" (2006) 111 *Penn State Law Review* 413.
[67] Scott Douglas Gerber, *To Secure These Rights: The Declaration of Independence and Constitutional Interpretation* (New York, NY: New York University Press, 1995).

America's symbolic constitution surely includes (but is not limited to) the Declaration of Independence, Publius' *The Federalist*, the Northwest Ordinance, Lincoln's Gettysburg Address, and Warren Court's opinion in *Brown v. Board*, and Dr. King's "I have a dream speech."

These works set forth background principles that powerfully inform American constitutional interpretation. Wherever the written Constitution is fairly susceptible to different interpretations, interpreters would hesitate, and do in fact hesitate, to embrace any reading that would violate the clear letter and spirit of these other canonical texts. In short, these texts are *constitutional* in the sense that they are *constitutive* – adherence to these helps *constitute* Americans as a distinct people among all the peoples on earth.[68]

There is much going on in this passage; examining Amar's case for nonconstitutional texts as sources of constitutional law can help us to untangle the various roles such texts might play.

Once again, our question is how nonconstitutional texts should be viewed from an originalist perspective. We can begin with an easy case for public meaning originalists. Some nonconstitutional texts are clearly part of the publicly available context of constitutional communication. Such documents include *The Federalist* and the Declaration of Independence. Because they are part of the publicly available context, they can play a role in arguments for contextual enrichment of the semantic content of the constitutional text. Such enrichments might include the clarification of ambiguity, constitutional implicatures, or arguments about implicit content.

Originalists should embrace another role for nonconstitutional texts. The semantic component of original meaning is fixed by linguistic facts as they stood at the time each provision of the Constitution was framed and ratified. Linguistic facts are established or known on the basis of evidence. In the case of very recent amendments, there may be audio recordings that could be the source of evidence about relevant linguistic facts, but for the Constitution of 1789 and most of the amendments, the relevant linguistic evidence will be provided by nonconstitutional texts – including publicly available documents like *The Federalist*, but also including nonpublic documents, including diaries, private letters, and even the nonpublic records of the Philadelphia Convention.

There is a third role for nonconstitutional texts that some originalists may embrace. Nonconstitutional texts might serve as evidence of what Philip

---

[68] Amar, Supra note 6, 247.

Bobbitt calls "ethos," the shared values of the American people.[69] Some constitutional theorists may believe that such values may trump the communicative content of the constitutional text, but the Constraint Principle commits originalists to the view that ethos can play only a supplementary role. Deploying the terminology of the interpretation–construction distinction, ethos (as evidenced by canonical nonconstitutional texts) could guide constitutional actors in the construction zone – but would have no direct relevance to constitutional interpretation. This view is close to that expressed by Amar, who writes, "[t]rue, these special texts are not on the same legal level as the written Constitution itself. Where the terse text is clear, it trumps. But often the written Constitution is not crystal clear."[70] To be clear, different originalists have different views about constitutional construction and the Constraint Principle: some originalists may reject the idea that substantive values can play a role in the construction zone; for example, originalists might adopt a Thayerian rule of construction, deferring to elected officials when the communicative content of the constitutional text is vague or irreducibly ambiguous.[71]

In sum, originalists can embrace three roles for nonconstitutional texts: (1) if the text is part of the publicly available context of constitutional communication, the text can serve as part of the basis for contextual enrichment; (2) if the text is contemporaneous with the framing and ratifying of a particular provision, the text can provide evidence of linguistic facts that determine semantic content; and (3) if the text provides evidence of norms relevant to constitutional construction, the text may guide the development of constitutional doctrine in the construction zone.

3.6.9. Precedent

What role should precedent (or judicial opinion) play in constitutional practice? In particular, how should originalism treat precedent? This is a large topic on which much has been written.[72] One useful way into the problem is

---

[69] Bobbitt, Supra note 52, 12–13.
[70] Amar, Supra note 6, 247–8.
[71] James B. Thayer, *The Origin and Scope of the American Doctrine of Constitutional Law* (Boston, MA: Little Brown & Co., 1893).
[72] Originalist writing on this topic includes Randy E. Barnett, "Trumping Precedent with Original Meaning: Not as Radical as It Sounds" (2005) 22 *Constitutional Commentary* 257; Kurt T. Lash, "Originalism, Popular Sovereignty, and Reverse Stare Decisis" (2007) 93 *Virginia Law Review* 1437; John O. McGinnis and Michael B. Rappaport, "Reconciling Originalism and Precedent" (2009) 103 *Northwestern University Law Review* 803; Lawrence B. Solum, "The Supreme Court in Bondage: Constitutional Stare Decisis, Legal Formalism, and the Future of

via the interpretation–construction distinction. Interpretation seeks the linguistic meaning of the text. Construction determines the legal content of constitutional doctrine and the effect of that content in particular cases.

What role should precedent play in interpretation (understood in the stipulated sense as the discovery of communicative content)? Originalists are committed to the Fixation Thesis: the communicative content of the constitutional text is fixed at the time each provision is framed and ratified. Public meaning originalists believe that the communicative content is a function of the conventional semantic meaning of the text and contextual enrichment by the publicly available context of constitutional communication. On the surface, these commitments might lead to the conclusion that precedent should have no effect on constitutional interpretation. If a constitutional precedent correctly identifies and applies original meaning, then it is redundant. And if a constitutional precedent departs from original meaning, then the Constraint Principle would seem to require originalists to disregard the precedent.[73]

But this simple picture is misleading. A regime of constitutional interpretation must answer at least two distinct questions. The first question addresses the substantive content of constitutional meaning; public meaning originalism has a distinctive answer to this question. The second question concerns the institutional structure by which constitutional meaning is determined and implemented.

A fully developed version of originalist constitutional practice must address the second question – specifying which institutions are responsible for determining original meaning and how these interactions will structure the activity of constitutional interpretation. One institutional possibility would be polycentric constitutional interpretation: each individual official could make independent judgments about constitutional meaning. The most extreme version of a polycentric regime would be radically different than the status quo. For example, there would be neither horizontal nor vertical stare decisis: each judge would make independent judgments about the meaning of the Constitution. In a purely polycentric regime, executive and legislative officials would have similar interpretive authority – in the extreme case, disregarding coercive judicial orders that were inconsistent with the individual constitutional judgments of executive or legislative officials.

But polycentric constitutional interpretation is not the only possible originalist regime. For example, originalists might adopt the status quo practice that gives the US Supreme Court the final word on questions of

---

Unenumerated Rights" (2006) 9 *University of Pennsylvania Journal of Constitutional Law* 155, 159; Lee J. Strang, "An Originalist Theory of Precedent: Originalism, Nonoriginalist Precedent, and the Common Good" (2006) 36 *New Mexico Law Review* 419.

[73] Amar, Supra note 6, 237.

federal constitutional law unless the political question doctrine applies. This practice would require lower court judges and other officials to defer to the Court on questions of constitutional interpretation – even if they believed that the Court had erred. Similarly, the current Supreme Court could defer to its prior self; adopting the doctrine of horizontal stare decisis structures constitutional interpretation. So long as this institutional structure is consistent with the original meaning of the Constitution, this option is available to originalists. Whether it is the best option depends on a variety of complex institutional questions – effects on stability, efficacy in maintaining original meaning, and so forth.

Precedent might also play a role in constitutional construction. For originalists who embrace the construction zone, nonoriginalist considerations inevitably play a role in constitutional practice when the communicative content of the constitutional text is vague or irreducibly ambiguous. In the construction zone, both vertical and horizontal stare decisis could structure constitutional doctrine – by definition, the construction zone is the space in which the original meaning of the Constitution underdetermines the legal content of constitutional doctrine.

It should be uncontroversial that originalists can embrace an institutional role for precedent so long as that role is consistent with the Constraint Principle. There is, however, a question about the proper role of precedent that is bound to be controversial. Can originalists accept precedents that are both (1) contrary to original meaning, and (2) decided on the basis of nonoriginalist concerns? Although some originalists have argued that *Brown* v. *Board* can be justified on originalist grounds, suppose that *Brown* is inconsistent with original meaning and that the opinion in *Brown* cannot be fairly read as a good faith attempt to reach a decision consistent with original meaning.[74] Under these circumstances, would originalists be compelled to argue that *Brown* should be reversed? Or consider the New Deal era precedents that expanded national legislative power and provided the constitutional foundations for the exercise of legislative, executive, and judicial powers by administrative agencies. Assuming that these decisions are inconsistent with original meaning and that their reasoning cannot be characterized as a good faith attempt to respect original meaning, must originalists argue that they should be overruled?

Justice Scalia has argued for "faint-hearted originalism" – which reconciles originalism to nonoriginalist precedents on pragmatic grounds.[75] Randy

---

[74] See Michael W. McConnell, "The Originalist Case for *Brown* v. *Board of Education*" (1995–6) 19 *Harvard Journal of Law and Public Policy* 457.

[75] Antonin Scalia, "Originalism: The Lesser Evil" (1988–9) 57 *University of Cincinnati Law Review* 849.

Barnett has forcefully criticized Scalia's argument.[76] This theoretical disagreement can be characterized in terms of the Constraint Principle. Originalists differ about the precise contours of the Constraint Principle. Some, like Scalia, adopt versions of the Constraint Principle with defeasibility conditions that are broad in scope. Others, like Barnett, believe in relatively narrow defeasibility conditions – although every originalist is likely to accept that original meaning must give way in some cases: the Constitution is not a suicide pact.[77] When defeasibility conditions come into play, the resulting doctrines are constitutional constructions: legal content of constitutional doctrine that is inconsistent with the communicative content of the constitutional text. The question whether originalists should adopt broad or narrow defeasibility conditions is a complex one: the answer depends on the underlying justifications for originalism, broader issues in political philosophy, and empirical questions about institutional design. These topics are important, but they cannot be resolved on this occasion and are likely to be the subject of ongoing dispute among originalists.

3.6.10. Historical Practice

The final category of extra-textual sources of constitutional law to be examined here is historical practice by the political branches. How should originalists treat constitutional arguments based on the institutional practices of the President and Congress? Should such practices have special authority if they were close in time to the adoption of a particular constitutional provision? For example, should the actions of the first Congress and George Washington have special authority with respect to interpretation and constructions of the Constitution of 1789? These questions can be made more precise by distinguishing the role of historical practice in interpretation and construction.

Consider first the role of historical practice in constitutional interpretation. In the sense stipulated by the interpretation–construction distinction, interpretation aims to recover the communicative content of the constitutional text. Direct evidence of communicative content comes from two sources: (1) evidence of linguistic facts that establish conventional semantic meaning, syntax, and grammar; and (2) historical evidence of the publicly available context of constitutional communication. Post-ratification practice by the executive and legislative branches does not provide direct evidence. Such practices are

---

[76] Randy E. Barnett, "Scalia's Infidelity: A Critique of Faint-Hearted Originalism" (2006) 75 *University of Cincinnati Law Review* 7–24.
[77] *Terminiello v. City of Chicago*, 337 U.S. 1, 37 (1949) (Jackson, J., dissenting).

not linguistic facts. And post-ratification practice cannot be part of the publicly available context of communication because such practices occur after the communicative acts (framing and ratification) have occurred.

Nonetheless, historical practice can provide indirect evidence of original meaning. Suppose that known linguistic facts underdetermine the meaning of a constitutional provision. A typical case of such underdeterminacy might be ambiguity. A word or phrase in the Constitution could have two (or more) semantic meanings. The first Congress legislates in a way that is consistent with one of the alternatives, but not the other. One might infer that Congress' action provides evidence in favor of the interpretation that is consistent with the constitutionality of the legislation. Of course, this evidence is not decisive – after all, Congress (even the first Congress with members who attended the Philadelphia Convention and various ratifying conventions) could be mistaken – or Congress could have failed to recognize the issue, or deliberately violated the Constitution. Nonetheless, early historical practice provides evidence relevant to the resolution of the ambiguity.

How should originalists regard the use of historical practice in constitutional construction? Originalists are committed to the Constraint Principle. When the meaning of the text is clear and relevant, originalists will adopt a construction that aligns the legal content of constitutional doctrine with the communicative content of the constitutional text. But in the construction zone, there may be more than one constitutional doctrine permitted by a vague or irreducibly ambiguous text. So, originalists can accept the use of historical practice to liquidate constitutional meaning in the construction zone.[78]

Originalists can embrace a role for historical practice in constitutional construction. Should they do so? Once again, this is a complex question and different originalists may approach it differently. Originalists whose normative concerns focus on the rule of law and judicial constraint may welcome historical practice arguments – as they provide a basis for settling constitutional questions. Settlement serves the rule of law values of stability, certainty, and predictability. Settlement also serves the function of constraining judges by providing a basis for decision that does not require judges to make first-order normative judgments about the political morality of the settled institutional arrangements.

Other originalists may argue that historical practices should play a modest role because they envision a greater role for normative concerns in the construction zone. And yet other originalists may believe that judges should generally defer to the political branches in the construction zone: these originalists

---

[78] See Amar, Supra note 6, 335.

may believe that the normative force of historical practice should be assessed by the political branches, and hence that Congress or the President may depart from such practices without judicial interference.

3.7. CONCLUSION: THE CASE FOR THE PRIMACY OF THE VISIBLE CONSTITUTION

From an originalist perspective, we have a visible Constitution – a written text with communicative content that should constrain constitutional practice. When we engage in constitutional interpretation, the communicative content of the written Constitution is the target of our investigation. The meaning of the written Constitution, however, is not limited to the semantic content of the words and phrases. The full communicative content of the Constitution is a function of text and context – and hence of inferences, implicitures, presuppositions, and modulations – that sometimes involve extra-textual sources. When we engage in constitutional construction, originalism endorses a principle of constraint: our constitutional constructions must reflect the communicative content of the text and may not contradict that content. But when the communicative content of the constitutional text underdetermines the content of constitutional doctrine, we are in the construction zone. In that zone, extra-textual sources necessarily play a role.

From an originalist perspective, constitutional interpretation and construction necessarily involve extra-textual sources, but only when they are deployed in a way that is consistent with fidelity to the original public meaning of the United States Constitution. Originalists affirm the constraining force of the communicative content of the written Constitution – even when that content depends in part on context that goes beyond the four corners of the document. Originalists can affirm the use of extra-constitutional sources that shape constitutional law in the construction zone, where the communicative content of the text underdetermines the legal content of constitutional law.

These conclusions lead to other important questions. Why should we take up the originalist perspective? More particularly, why should we affirm the Constraint Principle? A full answer to these questions is a very large task, but the basic ideas are familiar and intuitive. Constraint by the constitutional text serves the rule of law. An invisible constitution is neither public nor transparent. If the invisible constitution licenses the Supreme Court to override the constitutional text, the democratic legitimacy of constitutional law is questionable. Of course, there is much more to be said about these questions: they implicate the deepest issues of normative constitutional theory. The aim of this chapter is to clarify the questions. Answers are for another day.

4

The Implicit and the Implied in a Written Constitution

Jeffrey Goldsworthy*

4.1. CLARIFYING AND CREATIVE INTERPRETATION

'Invisible' constitutional norms deal with constitutional matters – the composition, powers and procedures of the principal organs of government – but are not expressly set out in a nation's written constitution (if it has one).

Many different kinds of norms may do this, including: supposedly fundamental, 'unwritten' principles argued to be superior to, and control, even the written constitution itself;[1] non-legal norms of constitutional practice (called 'constitutional conventions' in the British tradition);[2] statutory and common law norms governing the exercise of governmental power and even the interpretation of the written constitution;[3] and norms regarded as implicit in or implied by the written constitution. This chapter concerns these implicit or implied norms.

My impression is that implied norms have been attributed, with different degrees of plausibility, to virtually all constitutions. Sir Owen Dixon, an eminent Australian Chief Justice, once dismissed the notion that implications are illegitimate on the ground that it 'would defeat the intention of any

---

I thank Patrick Emerton, Tria Gkouvas and Dale Smith for helpful comments on an earlier draft.
* This chapter includes some passages previously published in J. Goldsworthy, 'Implications in Language, Law and the Constitution', in G. Lindell (ed.), *Future Directions in Australian Constitutional Law* (Sydney: Federation Press, 1994), 150, and J. Goldsworthy, 'Constitutional Implications Revisited' (2011) 30 *University of Queensland Law Journal* 1.
[1] See the discussion in J. Goldsworthy, 'Unwritten Constitutional Principles', in G. Huscroft (ed.), *Expounding the Constitution: Essays in Constitutional Theory* (Cambridge: Cambridge University Press, 2008), 277.
[2] See e.g., Keith E. Whittington, 'The Status of Unwritten Constitutional Conventions in the United States' (2013) *University of Illinois Law Review* 1847.
[3] J. Goldsworthy, 'The Constitution and Its Common Law Background' (2014) *Public Law Review* 265; Stephen E. Sachs, 'Constitutional Backdrops' (2012) 80 *George Washington Law Review* 1813.

instrument, but of all instruments a written Constitution seems the last to which it could be applied'.[4] This was no doubt because, in order to provide a framework for government able to endure for generations, a constitution must be 'expressed in general propositions wide enough to be capable of flexible application to changing circumstances'.[5] The method of drafting 'is rather to outline principles than to engrave details'.[6] It is often said to follow that some details are 'taken to be so obvious that detailed specification is unnecessary';[7] they 'go without saying because they are implicit in the structure of the constitutional system'.[8]

But constitutional implications are not all of the same kind, for two reasons. First, implications of different kinds can be identified within ordinary language usage. Insofar as the use of language in legal texts just is ordinary language usage, despite including some technical vocabulary, its interpretation will properly be guided by the same principles and find the same variety of implications within it. Second, some legal systems use terms like 'implied' and 'implication' in ways that depart from ordinary linguistic usage, to refer to norms identified by distinctively legal interpretive principles that may vary from one system to another.[9]

Interpretive principles used to disclose constitutional implications of the same kinds as those found in ordinary language usage are likely to be universal, given that such usage tends to be relevantly similar in most if not all natural languages. These principles are studied by linguists and philosophers of language. Distinctively legal interpretive principles used to disclose, or fabricate, so-called 'implications' that are peculiar to legal texts may (but will not necessarily) vary from one legal system to another.

The distinction between these two general categories of what are called implications is related to another distinction, concerning the nature of legal interpretation. The word 'interpretation' is used in law to denote at least two different processes. The first aims at revealing or clarifying the meanings of a legal text, both express and implied, that even if previously obscured were possessed by the text all along. (Note that a law must have some meaning that pre-exists its interpretation, whose primary object is to recover that meaning;

---

[4] *West v. Commissioner of Taxation* (NSW) (1937) 56 CLR 657, 681–2.
[5] *Australian National Airways v. Commonwealth* (1945) 71 CLR 29, 81 per Dixon CJ.
[6] *Tasmania v. Commonwealth and Victoria* (1904) 1 CLR 329, 348 per Barton J.
[7] *Australian Capital Television Pty Ltd v. Commonwealth* (1992) 108 CLR 577, 650 per Gaudron J.
[8] J. Balkin, *Living Originalism* (Cambridge: Harvard University Press, 2011), 204.
[9] See Section 4.5.

otherwise it would be meaningless, and nothing meaningless could be a law.)[10] The second process is more creative, adding new meanings to the text that it did not previously possess, or changing it in other ways.

To mark this distinction, some American theorists call the second, creative, process 'construction' rather than 'interpretation'.[11] But since popular and professional use of the term 'interpretation' encompasses both processes, I prefer to call the first process 'clarifying', and the second one 'creative', interpretation.[12]

The least contentious kind of creative interpretation involves supplementing the meaning of the text by adding new meanings to it. Clarifying interpretations are sometimes unable to resolve interpretive problems such as stubborn ambiguity, vagueness and gaps.[13] Since judges cannot wash their hands of a dispute and leave the parties to fight it out in the street, they must resolve such problems through this kind of creative interpretation. This is legally legitimate when and insofar as it is necessary.

But occasionally, creative interpretation goes further than this. Judges sometimes change the meaning of the text in order to correct or improve it. Some examples that are often considered legally legitimate in common law jurisdictions include: (1) the correction of obvious drafting errors, including internal inconsistencies; (2) 'reading down' over-broad terms to avoid constitutional invalidity;[14] (3) incremental adjustments to the meanings of provisions to enable them to achieve their intended purposes, which unanticipated social or technological developments may have made otherwise impossible;[15] (4) 'implying into' the text terms deemed necessary for its efficacy; and (5) what used to be called the 'equitable interpretation' of provisions to avoid unintended and undesirable consequences in unusual and unanticipated circumstances.[16]

---

[10] See J. Goldsworthy, 'The Case for Originalism', in G. Huscroft and B. Miller (eds.), *The Challenge of Originalism: Theories of Constitutional Interpretation* (New York, NY: Cambridge University Press, 2011), 42, 44.
[11] Larry Solum, Chapter 3 of this book.
[12] I have drawn this distinction since 1994: see Goldsworthy, chapter note, 162.
[13] Clarifying interpretation can, of course, often resolve problems such as ambiguity, but not always.
[14] Severance (i.e., excision) of terms in order to ensure constitutional validity goes beyond interpretation, and amounts to judicial amendment.
[15] Goldsworthy, chapter note, 42, 62–3; J. Goldsworthy, 'Interpreting the Constitution in Its Second Century' (2000) 24 *Melbourne University Law Review* 677, 699–701.
[16] Both (4) and (5) are discussed in Section 4.5. Creative interpretation licensed by human rights legislation such as the *Human Rights Act 1998* (United Kingdom) includes several of these techniques.

It is therefore useful to distinguish between three different processes that are included in the broad term 'interpretation' when applied to legal texts:

(1) Clarifying Interpretation: revealing or clarifying a law's pre-existing meaning(s), including any implied as well as express meanings;
(2) Creative Interpretation, comprising:
    (a) Supplementing Interpretation: supplementing those pre-existing meanings in order to resolve indeterminacies; and
    (b) Rectifying Interpretation: changing those meanings in order to correct or improve the law.

It should be noted that most judges are reluctant to admit their creative role, which is partly why they use the same word, 'interpretation', without distinguishing between these different processes. But these distinctions can help in analysing the role of different interpretive principles and arguments (such as legal presumptions, maxims and canons of interpretation), including those that concern implications. Consider the first distinction I drew, between implications that are common to both ordinary language usage and legal usage and so-called implications that are peculiar to laws because they are determined by distinctively legal interpretive principles. I will argue that implications of the former kind are revealed by clarifying interpretation, whereas those of the latter kind are really added to legal texts through rectifying interpretation. I will call those of the former kind 'genuine' implications and those of the latter kind 'fabricated' implications. The word 'fabricated' is not used to insinuate illegitimacy; to the contrary, I will argue that some of them are fully justified.[17]

Linguistics and philosophy of language have much to teach us about the nature of linguistic meaning and communication. They have little to say about supplementing or rectifying interpretation, which require legal, moral and political, rather than linguistic, judgments. But they can illuminate clarifying interpretation, which aims at revealing or clarifying the law's pre-existing meaning(s), implied as well as expressed. In this regard, it is necessary to distinguish between 'linguistic meaning' and 'legal meaning'. 'Legal meaning' is the meaning that judges ultimately assign to a provision, after applying all relevant interpretive principles and techniques; it results from clarifying, supplementing and rectifying interpretation. It does not precede but is the consequence of, legal interpretation. But clarifying interpretation is concerned with revealing or clarifying linguistic meaning that necessarily pre-exists legal interpretation.[18]

---

[17] Ibid.
[18] One might ask why pre-existing meaning does not depend on special legal interpretive principles as well as ordinary ones. The answer is that the function of legal interpretive principles

4.2. CLARIFYING INTERPRETATION, CONTEXTUAL ENRICHMENT, EXPRESS AND IMPLIED MEANING

Lawyers need a conception of the nature of the pre-existing meaning that a constitution, like any law, necessarily possesses.[19] One possibility is that it consists of the literal meaning of the composition of numbers, words and punctuation marks that constitute the constitution's text, determined by the linguistic conventions governing both ordinary and legal usage of either: (1) the period when the constitution was drafted and enacted; or (2) contemporary society. But this possibility must be ruled out because it cannot accommodate the inexplicit – the implicit and implied – components of a constitution's meaning. As Felix Frankfurter once remarked, the most fundamental question in legal interpretation is: 'What is below the surface of the words and yet fairly a part of them?'[20] The literalist's answer – 'Nothing' – is untenable.

Linguists and philosophers of language distinguish between 'semantics' and 'pragmatics', although they disagree about precisely how to do so. 'Semantics' concerns aspects of meaning fixed by social conventions: mainly, conventional (dictionary) meanings of words plus rules of grammar (syntax) governing the combination of words in meaningful sentences.[21] 'Pragmatics' concerns aspects of the meanings of the utterances of sentences that are determined by context, including linguistic context and the background to and circumstances surrounding the making of an utterance. It is generally agreed that context is relevant because and insofar as it illuminates the speaker's or author's communicative intentions.[22]

This distinction helps to draw other distinctions, including between:

(1) What a sentence literally means;
(2) What an utterance of the sentence expresses; and
(3) What an utterance of the sentence implies.[23]

---

can be illuminated by the distinction between clarifying, supplementing and rectifying interpretation. Many of these principles are just the legal equivalents of ordinary interpretive principles, and help to clarify pre-existing linguistic meaning. Peculiarly legal interpretive principles will usually concern supplementing or rectifying interpretation. However, insofar as lawmakers, in drafting their laws, may take into account the operation of special legal interpretive principles, those principles may be 'picked up' by ordinary interpretive principles concerned with the author's or speaker's communicative intentions.

[19] Goldsworthy, Supra note 10.
[20] F. Frankfurter, 'Some Reflections on the Reading of Statutes' (1947) 47 *Columbia Law Review* 527, 533.
[21] Note that this is a particular use of the term 'semantic' that is distinct from another use, which is to refer to those aspects of meaning that contribute to truth conditions: see K. Bach, 'Conversational Implicture' (1994) 9 *Mind & Language* 124, 132–3 esp note 8.
[22] It is necessary to distinguish what a speaker/author was intending to communicate from what he or she was intending to achieve by communicating it.
[23] Here I must side-step metaphysical questions about whether the express and implied meanings of an utterance are identical to what the speaker meant to express and imply by uttering it. See

(1) concerns the literal meaning of a sentence abstracted from any context of utterance; it is determined solely by semantics (linguistic conventions). (2) and (3) concern, respectively, the express and implied meanings of a particular utterance of a sentence, and are determined by pragmatics (the context of that utterance) as well as semantics.

It is now generally accepted by linguists and philosophers of language that (1) – literal or sentence meaning – is *much* thinner than (2) and (3). The literal meaning of a context-free sentence usually (and arguably always) underdetermines what its utterance in a particular context expresses and implies.[24] The sentence in itself is just a template, blueprint or skeleton that must be pragmatically (contextually) enriched in order to ascertain what an utterance of the sentence expresses and implies. This process of enrichment involves inferring the speaker's or author's likely communicative intentions from contextual information concerning his or her utterance of the sentence in addition to the literal meaning of the sentence itself.[25]

The underdeterminacy thesis is true by definition in the case of implied meanings which, since they are not expressed in words, cannot be derived solely from the conventional meanings of words. What is perhaps surprising is that the literal meaning of a context-free sentence also underdetermines what an utterance of the sentence expresses. Paradoxically, even express meaning sometimes includes inexplicit content.

4.3. CONTEXTUAL ENRICHMENT AND EXPRESS MEANING

Consider the following examples of how even express meaning can include content that is inferred partly from context rather than solely from semantic conventions.

J. Goldsworthy, 'Moderate versus Strong Intentionalism: Knapp and Michaels Revisited' (2005) 42 *University of San Diego Law Review* 669.

[24] The 'always' argument is that even a sentence that appears to state a proposition could, when actually uttered, be used non-literally, for example, ironically or metaphorically: see K. Bach, 'Context ex Machina', in Z. Szabo (ed.), *Semantics versus Pragmatics* (Oxford: Oxford University Press, 2005), 15, 26–7.

[25] I have frequently emphasised this point in earlier publications, starting with 'Implications in Language, Law and the Constitution', chapter note 1, 151; see also J. Goldsworthy, 'Legislative Intentions, Legislative Supremacy, and Legal Positivism' (2004) 42 *San Diego Law Review* 669. Other legal theorists now agree: see e.g., R. Ekins, *The Nature of Legislative Intent* (Oxford: Oxford University Press, 2012), ch 7, and A. Marmor, *The Language of Law* (Oxford: Oxford University Press, 2014), chs 1 and 2 esp 24–34.

4.3.1. Indexical Terms

'Indexicals' are expressions whose referential content is fixed by context, for example: 'I', 'you', 'he', 'she', 'it', 'this', 'that', 'now', 'then', 'today', 'yesterday', 'here'. If I say 'Yesterday he hid it over there', the words 'yesterday', 'he', 'it' and 'there' all have semantic content, but to know when, who, what and where my utterance refers to, you must infer my referential intentions from contextual information. But my utterance does not refer to these things by implication; it does so expressly.[26]

When a word such as 'he' is used in a statute or constitution – as 'he' frequently is in the Australian Constitution – its reference is almost always fixed by its relationship to preceding words.[27] For example, s. 5 states: 'The Governor-General may appoint such times for holding the sessions of the Parliament as he thinks fit'. Here, words such as 'he' are anaphors: they simply refer back to a term used previously in the text, to avoid repetition. Unless there is some ambiguity, their referential content is fixed by the text, and recourse to extra-textual evidence of the lawmakers' intentions is unnecessary. Statutes and constitutions rarely use indexicals whose references are not fixed in that way, but they do use some.[28]

4.3.2. Relational Terms

Some words – such as citizen, alien, foreign, native, queen, mayor – function somewhat like indexicals. It is part of their meaning that they involve a relation between a person and a place, and when the place is not explicitly specified (as in 'I am a citizen') it must be fixed by context.

Section 51(xix) of the Australian Constitution gives the Commonwealth Parliament power to make laws with respect to 'aliens', but it does not explicitly specify the relevant place. In its context, it is clearly intended to refer to those who are aliens – non-subjects or non-citizens – in relation to the Australian community. Otherwise the Parliament could make laws about anyone, since everyone is an 'alien' in relation to countries of which they are not citizens. Alternatively, the power could be reduced to a practical nullity,

---

[26] Bach, Supra note 21, 132–3.
[27] See Sections 5, 15, 17, 33, 34, 35, 40, 46, 48, 58, 64, 72, 84, 117 and 126. I thank Patrick Emerton for this point.
[28] But see C. Green, '"This Constitution": Constitutional Indexicals as a Basis for Textualist Semi-originalism' (2009) 84 Notre Dame Law Review 1607, who constructs an argument for originalism on the use of indexicals such as 'this Constitution', 'now', 'we' and 'here' in the American Constitution.

if it were confined to 'aliens' in the science fiction sense (beings alien to Planet Earth).

The reference of 'aliens' in this context is obvious. Nevertheless, it is significant that it is not determined solely by semantics; the dictionary definition(s) of 'aliens' is consistent with the absurd alternatives just dismissed. Their absurdity is revealed by contextual evidence of authorial intention, not by semantic convention. The obviously intended meaning is arrived at through pragmatic, or contextual, enrichment, even if unconsciously because it is so obvious.[29]

4.3.3. Ambiguous Terms

A word is ambiguous when it has two or more semantic meanings, in which case the context of its use in an utterance will usually determine which of those meanings was intended. Of many possible examples, consider s. 119 of the Australian Constitution: 'The Commonwealth shall protect every State against invasion and, on the application of the Executive Government of the State, against *domestic violence*'. Today, the usual meaning of 'domestic violence' is (something like) 'violence within the home, especially spousal and partner violence'. But in this case the context – textual and historical – establishes that the words mean (something like) 'local rioting or rebellion'. The textual context consists of the link between 'domestic violence' and 'the protection of every State', as well as the term 'invasion'. The historical context includes the accepted meaning of the words in the late nineteenth century, when the Constitution was enacted, and their derivation from a similar clause in the American Constitution (Article IV, s 4) whose meaning was well known at the time. All this is relevant because it is evidence of authorial intention.

4.3.4. Elliptical Expressions

Constitutional provisions, like other utterances, can include ellipses, a term I use in a non-technical sense to refer to an omission of a word or words in an uttered sentence that the audience 'fills in' through pragmatic enrichment. Ellipses are sometimes called 'implicitures', from the adjective 'implicit'.[30]

Some sentences are inherently elliptical, in that they require pragmatic enrichment to express complete propositions: e.g., 'She is ready' [for what?] or 'I've had enough' [of what?]. Section 92 of the Australian Constitution is an

---

[29] Consider also the meanings of 'foreign power' in s. 44(i) and 'foreign corporation' in s. 51(xx) of the Australian Constitution.
[30] Bach, Supra note 21.

example: it provides that 'trade, commerce, and intercourse among the States ... shall be absolutely free', but fails to specify from what it is to be absolutely free. Judicial attempts to fill in this ellipsis produced more litigation than any other interpretive issue concerning the Constitution. Eventually, in 1988, the High Court authoritatively revived a much earlier interpretation, by inferring the intended meaning from historical contextual evidence. The section was rightly understood to mean 'absolutely free [from discriminatory protectionism]', rather than the absurd 'absolutely free [from all legal constraint]' or the unworkable 'absolutely free [from all unreasonable legal restraint]'.[31]

Another example is Article 1, s 9 of the American Constitution, which states: 'No Bill of Attainder or ex post facto Law shall be passed'. Since this was intended to bind only the national legislature, it is understood as if it concludes with the implicit words 'by Congress'.[32]

Other uttered sentences need completion to avoid absurdity: for example, an utterance of 'Everyone has gone to Paris' would (usually) be understood non-literally to mean 'Everyone [in some contextually defined group, such as a family or group of friends] has gone to Paris'. Section 51(ii) of the Australian Constitution gives the Commonwealth Parliament power to makes laws 'with respect to taxation'. This surely does not refer to all taxation, including State taxation; otherwise, the Commonwealth Parliament could amend and repeal State tax laws. What we naturally understand the section to mean is: 'with respect to [Commonwealth] taxation'. Moreover, I suggest that we would intuitively agree that although this is not its literal meaning, it is its express meaning, rather than that the express meaning is qualified by an unexpressed implication.

Modern theories of pragmatics attempt to explain how we draw on context to 'fill in' ellipses and also how to identify other kinds of implicit and implied content.[33] They argue that even when we do so intuitively, without any conscious process of reasoning, the intuition must result from an unconscious calculation. In essence, we interpret utterances by assuming that speakers and authors have attempted to communicate with us in a co-operative fashion, by respecting principles of communication enjoining 'quality' (speak truthfully based on evidence), 'quantity' (say enough but no more than enough to be informative), 'relevance' (speak relevantly to some interest of the hearer)

---

[31] *Cole v. Whitfield* (1988) 163 CLR 360.
[32] See L. Solum Section 3.6.2.2.
[33] In what follows I will ignore many subtle differences between the competing theories, which are almost all based on or inspired by the pioneering work of the philosopher H. P. Grice, whose key papers are collected in his *Studies in the Way of Words* (Cambridge: Harvard University Press, 1989).

and 'manner' (be clear, unambiguous, brief and orderly).[34] When the literal meaning of an uttered sentence is incomplete, or absurd – as in the previous examples – we nevertheless assume that the speaker or author was attempting to communicate something helpful, and complied with the principle of quantity (say no more than enough to be informative) and manner (be brief) by omitting what in the circumstances was so obvious that we would understand it to be taken for granted.

Some ellipses are apparent not because of logical incompleteness or absurdity, but because of what we infer from contextual evidence of the lawmaker's probable intended meaning. For example, Australian lawyers now understand the intended meaning of s. 71 of the Constitution to be (something like): 'The judicial power of the Commonwealth shall be vested [exclusively] in ... the High Court of Australia, and in such other federal courts as the Parliament creates [etc.]'.[35] Although this is commonly regarded as an implication, it is arguably expressed (as in the previous example) because the omitted word is conveyed by ellipsis. Similarly in the United States, it has been argued that the powers given to Congress by Article 1, Section 8 – and the commerce power in particular – were intended to be exclusive, even though that word was not used.[36]

Other Australian examples of constitutional ellipses could be provided.[37] In statutory interpretation, the presumptions that statutes operate territorially and prospectively, may be regarded as filling ellipses. When these presumptions are applied, 'It shall be an offence to x' is interpreted as meaning 'It shall be an offence [*from now on*] to x [*in this jurisdiction*]'. Such presumptions are, of course, defeasible: they are subject to positive evidence of a contrary legislative intention.

In *R v. Young*, Spigelman CJ said of statutes:

> In order to construe the words actually used by Parliament, it is sometimes necessary to give them an effect *as if* they contained additional words. This is

---

[34] These are Grice's four 'maxims of conversation'; his 'neo-Gricean' successors have proposed refined and simplified versions of his theory. For a brief overview, see R. Carston, 'Legal Texts and Canons of Construction: A View from Current Pragmatic Theory', in M. Freeman and F. Smith (eds.), *Law and Language* (Oxford: Oxford University Press 2013), 8.

[35] *NSW v. Commonwealth* (the *Wheat* case) (1915) 20 CLR 54; *Waterside Workers' Federation of Australia v. JW Alexander* (1918) 25 CLR 434.

[36] See B. Friedman and D. T. Deacon, 'A Course Unbroken: The Constitutional Legitimacy of the Dormant Commerce Clause' (2011) 97 *Virginia Law Review* 1877, 1905–28.

[37] E.g., the phrase 'prevented ... from voting' was interpreted by the High Court, relying on textual and contextual evidence of the lawmakers' communicative intentions, as meaning (something like) 'prevented ... from exercising a right to vote', the right having to be found elsewhere in the Constitution: *R v. Pearson; ex parte Sipka* (1983) 152 CLR 254, 278.

not, however, to introduce words into the Act. This involves the construction of the words actually used.[38]

This is an accurate description of how ellipses are (often unconsciously) 'filled in' by the interpreter. Paradoxically, what we regard as expressed depends partly on content that is inexplicit. But, as noted by the Victorian Court of Appeal in *DPP* v. *Leys*, Australian courts have sometimes 'read words into' statutes in ways going well beyond this.[39] In doing so they have either been ascertaining genuine implications or creating fabricated ones.[40] I now turn to genuine implications.

4.4. CONTEXTUAL ENRICHMENT AND IMPLIED MEANING

4.4.1. *Presuppositions*

Sometimes an utterance refers to something, presupposing that it exists without asserting that it does. An example is an utterance of 'The current King of France is bald', which presupposes that there is a current King of France. Philosophers have debated whether, given that there is no King of France, the statement is false, or pointless (because it is neither true nor false).[41]

Constitutional and other legal provisions do this as well: simply by referring to something, they presuppose that it exists. The Ninth Amendment of the American Constitution provides that: 'The enumeration in the Constitution, of certain rights, shall not be construed to deny or disparage others retained by the people'. The existence of other rights is at most presupposed, not stated. Subject to some possible exceptions it seems that they are also not created or constituted by any other provision or implication of the Constitution: they are presupposed to pre-exist it. But what if – like the King of France – they do not, in fact, exist? For example, what if the Constitution's makers were referring to natural rights, but they do not really exist? (Arguably the Amendment should then be taken to refer to whatever real rights – if any – are most similar to the lawmakers' imaginary rights.)

Moreover, even if such rights do exist, does a mere presupposition to that effect have the consequence that they are enforceable by federal courts under

---

[38] (1999) 46 NSWLR 681, [5]–[6].
[39] (2012) 296 ALR 96 124–6.
[40] See note 17 and Section 4.5.
[41] W. G. Lycan, *Philosophy of Language: A Contemporary Introduction* (London: Routledge, 1999), ch 2, and p. 196. There is also debate about whether such presuppositions are semantic or pragmatic, a question 1 cannot explore here.

the Constitution? Or does the Amendment merely declare that they continue to have whatever force and effect in public opinion or state law they previously had (which may, in itself, be difficult to determine)? The answer to these questions must depend either on the meaning of 'deny or disparage', or on some kind of implication in addition to the presupposition that such rights exist. The historical evidence suggests that, rather than implying that such rights can be judicially enforced, the Amendment merely preempts or cancels a negative implication that its makers feared might be drawn in its absence: that the enumeration of some rights implied the non-existence of other, unenumerated ones.[42] The nature of that kind of implication is explained in the next section.

Section 73(ii) of the Australian Constitution provides that the High Court 'shall have jurisdiction' to hear appeals from 'the Supreme Court of any State'. This presupposes but does not state that State Supreme Courts exist, and they were (and still are) established not by that Constitution but by state constitutions. Does the presupposition require that these courts must continue to exist – that the States cannot abolish their Supreme Courts? The High Court has said that, by implication, it does.[43] But this cannot follow merely from the fact that s. 73(ii) presupposes their existence. Many such presuppositions – like the presupposition that there is a King of France – just render the expressions in which they appear false or pointless if the presupposed object does not or ceases to exist.[44]

Indeed, s. 73(ii) goes on to add that the High Court also has jurisdiction to hear appeals from 'any other court of any State from which at the establishment of the Commonwealth an appeal lies to the Queen in Council'. When the Constitution was enacted in 1900, this referred to a particular court in South Australia that no longer exists today.[45] Yet no one has suggested that its abolition violated an implication inherent in or following directly from the presupposition of its existence. It might be argued that the word 'any' functions like 'if any', suggesting that such courts need not continue to exist. But s. 73(iii) gives the High Court jurisdiction to hear appeals from 'the Inter-State Commission', which has not existed for most of Australia's federal history (notwithstanding the express words in s. 101 that 'There shall be an Inter-State

---

[42] For a good discussion of many of these issues, see R. C. Williams, 'The Ninth Amendment as a Rule of Construction' (2011) 111 *Columbia Law Review* 498. See also notes 52 and 53.
[43] *Kirk v. Industrial Court of New South Wales* (2010) 239 CLR 531, 566, 580.
[44] Pointless rather than false in this case because s. 73, like the Ninth Amendment, is directive rather than an assertion of a proposition.
[45] See S. McDonald, '"Defining Characteristics" and the Forgotten "Court"' (2016) 38 *Sydney Law Review* 207.

Commission ...'). The presupposition in s. 73 (iii) that it exists has not been thought to imply that it must exist.

It therefore seems that any implication that State Supreme Courts must continue to exist must be due either to some other kind of implication, or special legal interpretive principles concerning the purpose of s. 73 (ii) and what is necessary to fulfil it.

4.4.2. Implicatures

'Implicature' is a term famously coined by the philosopher H. P. Grice, building on the verb 'to implicate' (meaning 'to imply'). As an example, Grice described a Philosophy Professor, asked to provide a reference for a student seeking a lectureship in philosophy, replying that 'he writes good English and regularly attends tutorials'.[46] The statement damns with faint praise – it 'implicates' that the student has no philosophical ability worth mentioning.

Grice's explanation of how we identify implicatures relied on the communicative principles mentioned previously, of quantity, quality, relevance and manner.[47] But he argued that there need only be general, rather than universal, compliance with these principles. Speakers and authors can communicate something *sub silentio* by blatantly flouting one of the principles at the level of express meaning. The express meaning of the Professor's reference, which says nothing about the student's philosophical ability, plainly flouts the principles requiring quantity and relevance. But the recipient of the reference, assuming the Professor nevertheless intended to communicate something helpful, understands this to be deliberate and itself pregnant with meaning: the Professor is taken to implicate that the student has no philosophical ability worth mentioning. The Professor *exploited* the communicative principles, conveying an implicature by appearing on the surface to flout them.

Some other suggested examples of such exploitation involve nonliteral but direct speech rather than implicature, which is a form of indirect speech. Consider figurative statements that are metaphorical ('Juliet is the sun') or ironical ('That was clever', said after a foolish mishap). Because their literal meanings would obviously violate the principle requiring truthfulness, they are interpreted as conveying some other meaning.[48] As previously noted, most elliptical expressions can probably be analysed in a similar fashion (consider, again, 'Everyone has gone to Paris').

---

[46] Grice, Supra note 33, 33, 37.
[47] See Supra, text to nn 33 to 34.
[48] But see Bach, Supra note 21, 143–4.

Lawyers usually attempt to be as explicit as possible to avoid any chance of misunderstanding. It is therefore extremely rare to find in constitutions examples of deliberate insinuations or hints, intended to be read 'between the lines', such as the one conveyed by the Professor's reference. One of the rare examples may be the way the American Constitution appears to deal with slavery by carefully using euphemisms, rather than the word itself.[49]

Nevertheless, legal texts may include other kinds of implicatures, which result from the likelihood that the speaker or author has complied with, rather than flouted, Grice's principles of communication.

Consider the following sign: 'Children under 15 years admitted free'. Its express meaning is consistent with children of fifteen years or over also being admitted free: it does not expressly rule that out. But it suggests that *only* children under fifteen will be admitted free, because otherwise it would violate the communicative principle of quantity. Readers presume that such a sign is fully informative as to free admission, rather than disclosing only part of the policy to be applied. If children of fifteen or over, or adults, were also admitted for free, the sign would violate that principle and would be seriously misleading. If everyone were admitted free, it would be worse than pointless. The sign is therefore understood either as elliptical ('[Only] children under fifteen years admitted free'), or as implicating that no one else is admitted free.

The interpretive presumption *expressio unius est exclusio alterius* ('the expression of one thing is the exclusion of another') embodies the legal equivalent of the same kind of inference.[50] It is applied to written constitutions, as well as to statutes, and in both cases to procedures, rights and powers.

As for procedures, consider provisions that authorise constitutional amendments. Section 128 of the Australian Constitution expressly provides that 'This Constitution shall not be altered except in the following manner', which it goes on to prescribe. But even if it had merely said 'This Constitution may be altered in the following manner', that manner would arguably – by an inference of the *expressio unius* kind – be exclusive. The provision would be elliptical, the word 'only' being regarded as implicitly qualifying the words 'may be altered'.

It is interesting to compare Article V in the United States Constitution, which sets out the procedure for constitutional amendment without expressly providing that it is exclusive:

> The Congress, whenever two thirds of both houses shall deem it necessary, shall propose amendments to this Constitution, or, on the application of the

---

[49] See discussion in R. Barnett, 'The Misconceived Assumption about Constitutional Assumptions' (2009) 103 *Northwestern University Law Review* 615, 644–50.

[50] For useful discussion see A. Scalia and B. A. Garner, *Reading Law: The Interpretation of Legal Texts* (St Paul: West, 2012), 107–11.

legislatures of two thirds of the several states, shall call a convention for proposing amendments, which, in either case, shall be valid to all intents and purposes, as part of this Constitution, when ratified by the legislatures of three fourths of the several states ... [etc.].

Evidence of original intent confirms an inference of exclusivity.[51] But this must be implicated, because it is difficult to regard the provision as elliptical: there is no natural space where a qualification such as 'only' or 'exclusively' could be understood as implicit. Rather than such a word completing the express content of the clause, a distinct implicature seems required.

As for rights, the inclusion of the Ninth Amendment in the American Constitution was motivated by the fear that in its absence, the enumeration of certain rights in the proposed new Bill of Rights might imply that 'the people' had no other rights. As James Wilson said,

> If we attempt an enumeration, everything that is not enumerated is presumed to be given [to the federal government]. The consequence is, that an imperfect enumeration would throw all implied power into the scale of the government; and the rights of the people would be rendered incomplete.[52]

In other words, an enumeration might give rise to an implicature of the *expressio unius* kind, which the Ninth Amendment was adopted to preempt or cancel.[53] It is a central feature of pragmatic theory that implications can be cancelled by express words.[54]

As for powers, arguments about the existence of implied limits to Commonwealth legislative powers have often relied on that presumption. Section 51 of the Australian Constitution lists thirty-nine subject matters over which the Commonwealth Parliament is given legislative power; State Parliaments generally retain power over other subject matters. The High Court has had to grapple with the difficult issue of whether or not the carefully limited nature of some of the subject matters granted to the Commonwealth has implications for the interpretation of its other powers. An example is whether or not the grant of power by s. 51(i) only over 'trade and commerce with other countries, and among the states' – conspicuously withholding power over trade and commerce within the states – should, by implication, prevent other

---

[51] E.g., H. P. Monaghan, 'We the People[s], Original Understanding, and Constitutional Amendment' (1996) 96 *Columbia Law Review* 12; D. R. Dow, 'When Words Mean What We Believe They Say: The Case of Article V' (1990) 76 *Iowa Law Review* 1; J. R. Vile, 'Legally amending the United States Constitution: The Exclusivity of Article V's Mechanisms' (1991) 21 *Cumberland Law Review* 271.

[52] J. Wilson, quoted by Barnett, Supra note 49, 624; for full discussion, see Williams, Supra note 42, section II.

[53] L. Solum, Section 3.6.4. See also Section 4.4.1.

[54] Lycan, Supra note 41, 193.

granted powers such as that over 'trading corporations' (s. 51(xx)) being used to regulate intra-state trade and commerce. The High Court has held that it does not. But as Michael Stokes has recently argued to the contrary:

> the law normally draws negative implications from positive grants of power because failure to do so undermines the raison d'etre of limited grants of power. The law assumes that grantors of limited power, including constitutional and legislative power, do not intend to give the recipient of the grant other unlimited powers, because to do so would render the grant of limited power unnecessary and otiose.[55]

It has been argued that the 'necessary and proper clause' in the United States Constitution was inserted to preempt or cancel a possible implication that Congress' enumerated powers were strictly exhaustive.[56]

4.4.3. Implications Extrapolated by Induction

It is sometimes argued that a general principle can be extrapolated from particular provisions that collectively give it only partial express protection, by a process of induction, and then treated as if it were a freestanding constitutional norm.[57] An American example is in the judgment of Douglas J in *Griswold v. Connecticut*, who notoriously reasoned that the Bill of Rights protects a general right to privacy due to the 'penumbras and emanations' of several express rights that can be regarded as protecting particular aspects of privacy.[58] An Australian example is the judgment of Deane and Toohey JJ in *Leeth v. Commonwealth*, who suggested that 'the existence of a number of specific provisions which reflect the doctrine of legal equality serves to

---

[55] M. Stokes, 'The Role of Negative Implications in the Interpretation of Commonwealth Legislative Powers' (2015) 39 *Melbourne University Law Review* 175, 200. Stokes goes on to make a complex and debatable argument that does not reflect current High Court doctrine.

[56] United States Constitution, Article 1, s. 8, cl 18. See John Mikhail, 'The Constitution and the Philosophy of Language: Entailment, Implicature, and Implied Powers' (2015) 101 *Virginia Law Review* 1063, 1084.

[57] For discussion of this kind of argument see Mark Walters, 'Written Constitutions and Unwritten Constitutionalism', in G. Huscroft (ed.), *Expounding the Constitution: Essays in Constitutional Theory* (New York, NY: Cambridge University Press, 2008) 245, 263; Goldsworthy, chapter note, 178–82; W. Sinnott-Armstrong, 'Two Ways to Derive Implied Constitutional Rights', in J. Goldsworthy and T. Campbell (eds.), *Legal Interpretation in Democratic States* (Aldershort: Ashgate, 2002), 234–8.

[58] *Griswold v. Conecticut*, 381 U.S. 479 (1965), 484; discussed by Sinnott-Armstrong, Supra note 57, 234–5.

make manifest ... the status of that doctrine as an underlying principle of the Constitution as a whole'.[59]

The suggestion is that, if a number of specific provisions appear to partially protect a general principle, that may be evidence that the principle as a whole is part of the constitution. Let us assume that this might sometimes be plausible. The question is how we should understand the nature of such inductive arguments, and of the implications they are used to reveal. Inductive arguments are inferences to the best explanation of some observed phenomena: they seek to explain the observed in terms of the unobserved. When used in science, for example, an inductive argument might take some observed regularities to be evidence of an underlying causal relationship that can be expressed by a general physical law. In the legal context, what is the nature of this unobserved (unexpressed) thing, which is the counterpart of the physical law? Legal provisions are the products not of mindless causal processes governed by general physical laws, but of intentional human action. The legal equivalent of the physical law revealed by scientific induction is therefore the lawmaker's intention or purpose.

It follows that an inductive argument is persuasive only if particular provisions that selectively instantiate some general principle are evidence that the framers intended the principle itself, and not just the particular provisions, to be judicially enforceable. An implication is justified when there is sufficient evidence of the existence of such an intention. The catch, of course, is that if this is what the inductive argument points to, then other evidence that such an intention could not have existed will defeat the argument. Inductive arguments are defeasible, not conclusive: although they may include evidence of an implication, they can be defeated by stronger counter-evidence.

A comprehensive review of the evidence will often reveal that the framers intended to pursue some general purpose, or implement some general principle, only by particular means and to a limited extent. As Terrance Sandalow pointed out,

> By wrenching the framers' 'larger purposes' from the particular judgments that revealed them, we incur a loss of perspective, a perspective that might better enable us to see that the particular judgments they made were not imperfect expressions of a larger purpose but a particular accommodation of competing purposes. In freeing ourselves from those judgments we are not serving larger ends determined by the framers but making room for the introduction of contemporary values.[60]

---

[59] *Leeth v. Commonwealth* (1992) 174 CLR 455, 502.
[60] T. Sandalow, 'Constitutional Interpretation' (1981) 79 *Michigan Law Review* 1033, 1046.

Judges are surely bound not only by the framers' ends, but by the means they chose to achieve those ends. That is why it has been said that the framers' decisions about what to omit from the Constitution are entitled to as much respect as their decisions about what to include.[61] Otherwise a constitution is just a set of abstract objectives, which the judges can choose to implement in any way they think fit, with no limit to the implications they can purport to find. All the provisions of the Constitution could, collectively, be claimed to instantiate such abstract principles as 'democracy', 'freedom' or even 'justice', and anything not mentioned that (in the opinion of the judges) helps secure democracy, freedom or justice could then be regarded as impliedly guaranteed.[62]

This is why the quoted suggestion of Deane and Toohey JJ in *Leeth* was utterly implausible.[63] We know that, although the framers of the Constitution deliberately protected specific rights to equality, they did not intend to protect a general principle of equality. This is because they included provisions designed to permit both racial and sexual discrimination,[64] and rejected a proposed clause to guarantee equality in general partly because they did not wish to proscribe racial discrimination.[65]

When the provisions of a legal instrument expressly cover only some instances of a potentially broader class, it is usually more plausible to infer that its limited coverage was deliberate, and to ascribe to it an implicature that excludes other instances of the class not expressly covered. As we have seen, that implicature is expressed by the *expressio unius* presumption.[66]

4.4.4. Implicit Assumptions, Supplementations and Qualifications

There is another kind of implication that I will refer to as an 'implicit assumption'. Consider these examples. A law states that at the conclusion of the evidence for the complainant, 'the defendant may address the court'; it does not

---

[61] The Hon. M. Gleeson, *The Rule of Law and the Constitution* (Sydney: ABC Books, 2000) 70.
[62] See Sinnott-Armstrong, Supra note 57, 241.
[63] See note 59. See also Goldsworthy, chapter note, 181–2. J. Kirk, 'Constitutional Implications (II): Doctrines of Equality and Representative Democracy' (2001) 25 *Melbourne University Law Rev* 24, 31–43.
[64] *The Constitution of the Commonwealth of Australia* s. 25, with respect to race, and s. 30, read in the light of s. 41 and the third paragraph of s. 128, with respect to female suffrage.
[65] L. Zines, *Constitutional Change in the Commonwealth* (Cambridge: Cambridge University Press, 1991), 46.
[66] Section 4.4.2.

state that the court must listen, but that is surely implied.[67] A law dealing with restaurants states that they must have clean and well-maintained inside toilets. It does not state that they must be accessible by the restaurant's customers, but again, that is surely implied.[68] A law confers a power on a government official, but does not expressly require that the power not be exercised capriciously or corruptly. That is surely taken for granted and in that sense is implicit or implied.[69]

In each example, an implication is inferred from the lawmaker's obvious purpose in uttering the express words, what is obviously needed to fulfil that purpose and the likelihood that this is so obvious that the lawmaker took it for granted or expected its intended audience to take it for granted.

There are other examples of implications based on similar inferences. One is the venerable presumption that when a general power is conferred or general duty imposed, whatever particular acts are necessary and incidental to exercising the power or performing the duty are impliedly authorised.[70] An example in constitutional law is the doctrine of implied incidental power, which ever since Marshall CJ's judgment in *McCulloch v. Maryland*[71] has usually been regarded as justified not only by necessity, but by what is 'appropriate and adapted' or 'incidental and ancillary', to the exercise of the general power.[72] Marshall CJ mentioned, for example, that implied powers to transport the mail and to prohibit stealing it had been inferred from Congress' express power 'to establish post-offices and post-roads'.[73]

The same principle applies to everyday requests and instructions, which implicitly extend to many unmentioned actions that are incidental and appropriate in order to comply with them. For example, if I ask my son to 'bring some mustard' to the dinner table, he may have to perform many instrumental actions not mentioned, such as going to the kitchen, turning on the light, opening the refrigerator door, shifting other items on the same shelf out of the way and so on.[74]

---

[67] F. Bennion, *Statutory Interpretation, A Code*, 2nd edn (London: Butterworths, 1992), 30. Today, that obligation would be regarded as part of the implied requirement of natural justice.
[68] Marmor, Supra note 25, 35.
[69] See J. Goldsworthy, *Parliamentary Sovereignty, Contemporary Debates* (Cambridge: Cambridge University Press, 2010), 281–5 esp 283. Of course, this depends on context: in a society where official corruption is routine and tolerated, this might not be implied.
[70] Scalia and Garner, Supra note 50, 192–4.
[71] 4 Wheat 316 (1819), 421.
[72] See J. Stellios, *Zines's The High Court and the Constitution* 6th edn (Sydney: Federation Press, 2015), 48–9.
[73] *McCulloch v. Maryland*, note 71, 417.
[74] Sinnott-Armstrong, Supra note 57, 231.

Similarly, if the vindication of an express right truly depends on the protection of some incidental right, it will often be plausible to construe the former as encompassing the latter. For example, if people have a right to vote in an election but for practical reasons are able to vote only at a particular polling station, the right would surely be construed as forbidding any attempt to prevent them from doing so.

But there is a caveat. Requests, instructions and rules should not be regarded as implicitly authorising any actions at all that might turn out to be necessary to comply with them. To the contrary, they are often subject to implicit qualifications that impose side constraints on efforts at compliance. In the case of my son being asked to bring some mustard to the table, if he were to discover that we had run out of mustard, he should not regard my request as implicitly authorising him to break into our neighbours' house and steal theirs or (if he has no driver's licence) to drive illegally to a shop in order to buy some mustard. In these circumstances, any argument that my request implicitly authorises whatever is necessary to comply with it would be met by a much stronger argument that it is implicitly subject to side constraints inherent in background assumptions prohibiting burglary and other unlawful actions.[75] In principle, the same should be true of efforts to implement laws. If it turns out that a law simply cannot be effectively implemented without violating some side constraint that the lawmaker would undoubtedly not have wanted to be violated, then the lawmaker has unintentionally created a dilemma that must be resolved in some other way, involving rectifying interpretation.

It is easy to multiply examples of instructions and rules whose meaning arguably depends partly on implicit side constraints that are so obvious they may not even be noticed.[76] Consider Wittgenstein's famous example of someone asked to 'play a game with the children'.[77] The meaning of the request is determined partly by conventional notions of what games are suitable for children; the request is therefore not properly complied with if the children are introduced to an adults-only game involving, say, sex or Russian roulette.

---

[75] For this reason, Sinnott-Armstrong – who originated this example – was wrong to discount the relevance of original intent or meaning in resolving it: see Sinnott-Armstrong, Supra note 57, 232. See also MacCallum's ashtray example, Supra note 79.

[76] J. Searle, 'Literal Meaning', in his *Expression and Meaning, Studies in the Theory of Speech Acts* (Cambridge: Cambridge University Press, 1979), 117, 133. See also his J. Searle 'The Background of Meaning', in J. Searle, F. Kiefer and M. Bierwisch (eds.), *Speech Act Theory and Pragmatics* (Holland: Reidel, 1980), 221, and J. Searle *Intentionality: An Essay in the Philosophy of Mind* (Cambridge: Cambridge University Press, 1983), 145–8.

[77] L. Wittgenstein, *Philosophical Investigations*, para. 70.

But that goes without saying.[78] Another somewhat dated example involves an assistant being asked to 'fetch all the ashtrays you can find' for a meeting to be attended by many smokers.[79] The assistant is obviously not supposed to rip ashtrays from walls they are attached to or steal them. The request is understood in a context including implicit side constraints prohibiting damage to property and theft.

In all these examples, expressed requests, directives, rules or permissions are regarded as implicitly including unexpressed supplements or qualifications that seem necessary or at least appropriate in order to carry out the speaker's purposes and are sufficiently obvious that they can be taken for granted. But how far can this form of reasoning be taken?

A perennial problem for judges arises when applying the express meaning of a law would have very undesirable and probably unintended consequences in unusual circumstances that the lawmaker apparently did not anticipate. Judges are reluctant to apply the express meaning, because the consequences seem not only unjust, but unjustified by due deference to the lawmaker's authority, given that, had it anticipated those circumstances, it would almost certainly have taken steps to avoid those consequences. The judges have two alternative methods of avoiding them: (1) interpreting the law, through an act of clarifying interpretation, as subject to an implicit exception covering those circumstances; or (2) in effect amending the law by adding an exception to it through an act of rectifying interpretation.

Judges are somewhat reluctant openly to embrace the second alternative, because they have no constitutional authority to amend statutes or constitutions except in very limited circumstances. But even those who most strongly deny the legitimacy of judge-made exceptions to statutory and constitutional laws concede that such laws may be subject to genuinely implicit exceptions or qualifications.[80] Moreover, the first alternative often seems genuinely plausible, as attested by the many legal theorists who have endorsed it.[81]

Consider the following examples. A rule prohibits talking in a library; is it subject to an implicit exception that permits someone to warn patrons that a fire has broken out? And the problem is not confined to general rules. If

---

[78] Perhaps the request is elliptical, meaning: 'Play a [suitable] game with the children'. Or perhaps, as Emerton suggests, the reference of the word 'game' varies with the context, and is determined partly by implicit assumptions: see P. Emerton, 'Political Freedoms and Entitlements in the Australian Constitution – An Example of Referential Intentions Yielding Unintended Consequences' (2010) 38 *Federal Law Review* 169, 175.

[79] G. MacCallum 'Legislative Intent', in R. Summers (ed.), *Essays in Legal Philosophy* (University of California Press, 1968) 237, 256–7.

[80] Scalia and Garner, Supra note 50, 93–111; the acknowledgement of implicit exceptions is at 96–7.

[81] See notes 82–85.

I instruct my son to stay at home and finish his homework, is this subject to implicit exceptions permitting him to leave the house if a fire starts or if his mother is rushed to hospital having a heart attack?

As to the first case, Larry Alexander and Emily Sherwin argue that to refuse to shout 'Fire!' because of the rule would be to misunderstand it.

> No one could reasonably believe that [the rule-maker] intended silence in such a circumstance. Although his words do not expressly except situations like [this], the context of the rule makes it clear that it is not intended to cover warnings of imminent danger ... In reaching [this conclusion] we inevitably are referring to the purpose of the rule: the reason we believe [this case is] excluded is that [it is] too remote from [the rule-maker's] aim.[82]

They cite several other legal theorists whose intuitions are similar.[83] Kent Greenawalt agrees, arguing that:

> We do not commonly think that instructions framed in general words reach situations in which no one would want or expect them to apply. The instruction 'Go to your room and stay there for fifteen minutes' does not *mean* a girl should stay in her room if a fire breaks out or a bear enters her window.[84]

As Ronald Dworkin put it, 'It is a perfectly familiar speech practice not to include, even in quite specific instructions, all the qualifications one would accept or insist on: all the qualifications, as one might put it, that "go without saying".'[85]

Constitutional provisions can give rise to the same issue. Section 117 of the Australian Constitution provides that a resident in one State 'shall not be subject in any other State to any disability or discrimination' that would not equally apply to him if he were a resident in that other State. But does this require every State to allow temporary interstate visitors to vote in an election of its State Parliament? That would seem to be an absurd consequence. It might be avoided by construing the words 'disability or discrimination' so as not to include any differential treatment that is justified all things considered, but in the case of 'disability' this seems implausible, and so far only one

---

[82] L. Alexander and E. Sherwin, *The Rule of Rules: Morality, Rules and the Dilemmas of Law* (Durham, NC: Duke University Press, 2001), 114–15. See also R. H. Fallon Jr., 'The Meaning of Legal "Meaning" and Its Implications for Theories of Legal Interpretation' (2015) 82 *University of Chicago Law Review* 1235, 1260–1.

[83] Alexander and Sherwin, Supra note 82.

[84] K. Greenawalt, *Statutory and Common Law Interpretation* (New York, NY: Oxford University Press, 2013), 103; see also 308, note 52.

[85] R. Dworkin, 'Reflections on Fidelity' (1997) 65 *Fordham Law Rev* 1799 1816. For discussion see J. Goldsworthy, 'Dworkin as an Originalist' (2000) 17 *Constitutional Commentary* 49.

or possibly two High Court Justices have taken that view.[86] The alternative, apparently favoured by the other judges, is to regard the prohibition as subject to unexpressed, implicit exceptions inherent in the structure of government set out elsewhere in the Constitution.[87]

The High Court has also struggled to explain why the requirement in s. 51(xxxi) of the Constitution, that the Commonwealth Parliament must provide 'just terms' in order to compulsorily acquire property from any person or State, does not apply to some kinds of compulsory acquisitions, such as taxation, fines and forfeitures of illegally obtained property, property used for an illegal purpose or enemy property. The Court could regard the 'just terms' requirement as being satisfied in these circumstances, but that might mean that the Court would always have to evaluate the fairness of taxes, fines and so on. Instead, the Court seems to regard the requirement – and possibly the term 'compulsory acquisition' – as limited by implicit assumptions and therefore inapplicable.[88]

Another example concerns s. 44 of the Constitution, which relevantly provides: "Any person who (1) Is ... a subject or a citizen or entitled to the rights or privileges of a subject or citizen of a foreign power ... shall be incapable of being chosen or of sitting as a senator or a member of the House of Representatives." What if a "foreign power" passed a law conferring its citizenship on all Australians, and made it impossible for them to renounce it? Interpreted literally, s. 44 (1) would then make it also impossible for them ever to be elected or to sit as members of their national Parliament, bringing Australia's system of representative government to a halt. Because that would be too absurd to contemplate, the High Court has accepted that there is an

> implicit qualification in s 44(i) that the foreign law conferring foreign citizenship must be consistent with the constitutional imperative underlying that provision, namely, that an Australian citizen not be prevented by foreign law from participation in representative government where it can be demonstrated that the person has taken all steps that are reasonably required by the foreign law to renounce his or her foreign citizenship.[89]

I have in previous work relied on John Searle's argument that the meaning of every utterance depends on tacit background assumptions that are taken

---

[86] Gaudron J and possibly Deane J in *Street v. Queensland Bar Association* (1989) 168 CLR 461, 570–3 and 528–9 respectively; see A. Simpson, 'The High Court's Conception of Discrimination: Origins, Applications and Implications' (2007) 29 *Sydney Law Review* 263, 284.
[87] *Street* (1989) 168 CLR 461, 491–3 (Mason CJ), 512–14 (Brennan J), 546–8 (Dawson J), 559–60 (Toohey J), and 583–4 (McHugh J).
[88] Stellios, Supra note 72, 620–1.
[89] Re Canavan and others [2017] HCA 45, paras 13 and 43–6.

for granted because they are so obvious they do not need to be mentioned or (sometimes) even consciously taken into account.[90] Searle argued that if background assumptions are not grasped, anything we say is open to being misunderstood in unpredictable and bizarre ways. For example: if I order a hamburger in a restaurant, and carefully list all the ingredients I want, I do not think it necessary to specify that they should be fresh and edible, the meat cooked and so on. If I thought about this at all, I would expect it to be taken for granted. Even if I did specify those requirements, I would not think to add that the hamburger should not be encased in a cube of solid lucite plastic that can only be broken by a jackhammer.[91] My order implicitly requires a hamburger that can be immediately eaten without much difficulty.[92]

Such implicit assumptions may not be consciously adverted to either by the speaker or the hearer. But how can speakers have any intentions about matters that are not consciously in their minds? The answer may be that intentions and many other mental states such as beliefs and desires, depend just as much as meanings on a network of background assumptions. Searle, for example, describes what is necessarily assumed by anyone intending to run for President of the United States: that the United States is a republic, that it has a presidential form of government, that it has periodic elections, that these mainly involve a contest between candidates of two major parties, the Republicans and the Democrats, that these candidates are chosen at nominating conventions and so on, indefinitely. Searle concludes that 'certain fundamental ways of doing things and certain sorts of know-how about the way things work are presupposed by any such form of Intentionality'.[93] Indeed, in his view linguistic meaning depends on background assumptions precisely because language is a means of expressing our intentional states, such as our intentions, beliefs and desires.[94] Because those intentional states depend on a network of background assumptions, their expression in language does too.[95]

But how can we distinguish between assumptions that are implicit in an utterance, without having been in the speaker's conscious mind, and matters that the speaker neglected to address and are neither expressed by nor implicit in the utterance? If the speaker has not consciously thought of

---

[90] See Goldsworthy, chapter note, 150.
[91] Searle 'Literal Meaning', Supra note 76, 127.
[92] Patrick Emerton argues that, in this example, the implicit assumptions help to fix the reference of the word 'hamburger': P. Emerton, Supra note 78, 175. This does not affect the argument here, but if correct, it adds a further reason for regarding even express meaning as depending on pragmatic (contextual) enrichment.
[93] Searle, *Intentionality*, Supra note 76, 20; see also ibid., 141.
[94] Ibid., 5, 176–9.
[95] Searle, 'The Background of Meaning', Supra note 76, 231–2.

either one, what is the difference? The difference must be that in the case of implicit assumptions, it would probably have made no difference if the speaker had consciously thought of the matter: he would still have expressed no view, on the ground that it is too obvious to require expression. This may be why MacKinnon LJ proposed that in the case of contracts, the test for an implication should be whether, if an 'officious bystander' had suggested the inclusion of some express provision, the contracting parties would have 'testily suppress[ed] him with a common "Oh, of course"!'[96]

The phenomenon of implicit assumptions can be accommodated by Gricean pragmatic theory.[97] The communicative principle of quantity requires speakers to say as much as but no more than is required for effective communication. Speakers who say more than that waste their hearers' time and effort as well as their own, and risk boring, patronising or confusing their hearers. It follows that no mention should be made of assumptions so obvious that one's hearer can be relied on to take them for granted. And of course, no mention *can* be made of assumptions so obvious that one takes them for granted oneself.

But I am not sure, and do not have the expertise to determine, whether implicit assumptions are a species of implicature. It might be argued that they are inferred partly from the assumption that speakers have complied with the communicative principles, especially that of quantity, and either did not consciously advert to or did not bother to state, the obvious. But that seems debatable. Implicit assumptions seem to be inferred, instead, directly from the obviousness of the lawmaker's purpose in uttering the express words and what is needed to fulfil it. Assumed compliance with the principle of quantity does not seem to play an essential role in identifying what is so obvious that it was implicitly assumed. If anything, the inference seems to go in the opposite direction: we infer compliance with the principle of quantity from the obviousness of the implicit assumption. In the next sub-section I assume that implicit assumptions are not implicatures. Even if they are a species of implicature, they seem to be a special one.

4.4.5. *Obviousness as a Requirement for Implications*

There has been some disagreement as to whether, in order to be recognised as genuine, implications should have to satisfy a test of 'obviousness'. Ryan Williams, for example, in discussing the Ninth Amendment, proposed such

---

[96] *Shirlaw v. Southern Foundries (1926) Ltd* [1939] 2 KB 206, 227.
[97] Grice, Supra note 33–34.

a test for constitutional implicatures,[98] but is criticised by Larry Solum in this book for doing so.[99] Solum points out that implicatures are not always obvious; sometimes 'competent speakers would need to read carefully to *see* the implicature'.[100] Some linguists regard implicatures as 'always somewhat uncertain', because the communicative principles can conflict with one another, and because doubts can arise at any stage of the complex reasoning process that is involved.[101] Other forms of contextual enrichment such as ellipses are also debatable. For example, s. 92 of the Australian Constitution is clearly elliptical, but there was much disagreement about how the ellipsis should be filled.[102]

On the other hand, to show that utterance meanings are shaped partly by what I have just described as implicit assumptions, a test of obviousness may be appropriate. As I have previously argued:

> implicit assumptions are unstated, or even unnoticed, precisely because they are obvious. If so, there can be no such thing as an implicit assumption that does not comply with the obviousness test, and so the test is necessary.[103]

For other kinds of inexplicit content, including implicatures, 'we do not require obviousness in everyday interpretation. We employ a process of reasoning in which speakers' meanings are inferred from various kinds of evidence, with varying degrees of strength, and we are willing to accept a higher risk of error than are the courts in interpreting legal documents'.[104]

Obviousness, then, is not normally required. But it is open to courts to be more cautious. They may be especially wary of error because they are not generally permitted to rewrite the laws they are charged with interpreting. They might regard attributing a non-existent implication to a law to be worse than failing to identify a genuine one through excessive caution. That would, of course, be debatable, but they might consequently subject themselves to

---

[98] Williams, Supra note 42, 544.
[99] L. Solum Section 3.6.3. See also H. Asgeirrson, 'On the Possibility of Non-literal Legislative Speech', in A. Capone and F. Poggi (eds.), *Pragmatics and Law: Theoretical and Practical Perspectives* (Springer Verlag, 2017), 11 who disagrees with A. Marmor on this point.
[100] Solum, Supra note 99.
[101] C. Potts, 'Presupposition and Implicature', in S. Lappin and C. Fox (eds.), *The Handbook of Contemporary Semantic Theory*, 2nd edn (Wiley Blackwell 2015), 168, 183.
[102] See note 31.
[103] Goldsworthy, chapter note, 170. Note also that Mason CJ in the *ACTV* case did not require 'textual' implications to be 'necessary': see notes 120–122.
[104] Goldsworthy, chapter note, 170. I did not at the time mention implicatures in this regard.

a standard of clarity – a requirement of obviousness – that is higher than expected in everyday discourse, in order to guard against the first kind of error.[105] That might also have the salutary effect of motivating lawmakers and their drafters to think more carefully about what they need to make explicit in order to avoid misunderstanding.

4.5. RECTIFYING INTERPRETATION AND FABRICATED IMPLICATIONS

Relying on the notion of implicit assumptions to avoid the undesirable consequences of express meanings in unusual circumstances has been criticised for unrealistically attributing too much to the meaning, or communicated content, of utterances.[106] If that criticism is sound, then to avoid those consequences judges would have to act creatively, in effect amending statutory and constitutional provisions by inserting into them qualifications that the lawmaker failed to include. This used to be called 'equitable interpretation', and is still advocated today.[107] Judges may sometimes be justified in acting as the lawmaker's 'faithful agents', expanding or contracting the meaning of the law in order to better give effect to the lawmaker's purposes and values.

Because judges are reluctant openly to amend statutes and constitutions, they sometimes speak of 'reading into' or 'implying into' them qualifications that are 'necessary' to fulfil the lawmaker's objectives. This returns us to a distinction drawn at the outset of this chapter. When courts ascribe an implication to a constitution, are they always purporting to discover a genuine one, which ordinary linguistic principles reveal the constitution to already include? Or are they sometimes relying on distinctively legal interpretive principles, which justify the insertion of a fabricated implication – one that is really new – into the constitution?

In common law jurisdictions, lawyers routinely use idiosyncratic legal terminology that describes terms being 'implied into' or 'read into' legal texts,

---

[105] Ibid.
[106] See e.g., S. Soames, 'Interpreting Legal Texts: What Is, and What Is Not, Special about the Law', in *Philosophical Essays, Vol 1, Natural Language: What It Means and How We Use It* (Princeton: Princeton University Press, 2009), 403, 415–18; 'What Vagueness and Inconsistency Tell Us about Interpretation', in A. Marmor and S. Soames (eds.), *Philosophical Foundations of Language in the Law* (New York: Oxford University Press, 2011), 31, 46–51.
[107] See e.g., Ekins, Supra note 25, 275–84; J. Evans, 'A Brief History of Equitable Interpretation in the Common Law System' in T. Campbell and J. Goldsworthy, *Legal Interpretation in Democratic States* (Aldershot: Ashgate, 2002), 67; J. Evans, 'Reading Down Statutes', in R. Bigwood (ed.), *The Statute: Making and Meaning* (Wellington: LexisNexis, 2004), 123.

and judges 'making implications' by 'implying' legal powers or legal limits.[108] This is idiosyncratic because, in ordinary English, terms that are genuinely *implied by* a text are *inferred from* it, and implications are *made* by the author of a text, not by its reader or interpreter. To speak of terms being *implied into* or *read into* a text by an interpreter is to use oxymoronic expressions that, in trying to have it both ways, defy ordinary English.[109]

It might be argued that these peculiar legal expressions are merely convenient lawyers' shorthand to describe the discovery of genuine implications. But this seems implausible, because in ordinary English it is only slightly more convenient (quicker and easier) to say (incorrectly) that a term 'was implied into' a text, rather than (correctly) that it was 'found to be implied by' the text. The best explanation is that these idiosyncratic legal expressions function as euphemisms, blurring the distinction between the discovery of genuine implications and the insertion of fabricated ones.[110] It seems that lawyers are often more or less aware that judges are really inserting terms into legal texts in order to correct or improve them, but are reluctant openly to say so.

Some Australian judges have refused to concede this. Windeyer J disapproved of the expression 'making implications', when he said: 'I would prefer not to say "making implications", because our avowed task is simply the revealing or uncovering of implications that are already there'.[111] In *McGinty*, Brennan CJ agreed: 'Implications are not devised by the judiciary; they exist in the text and structure of the Constitution and are revealed or uncovered by judicial exegesis'.[112] They were insisting that implications must be genuine, not fabricated.

Although legal scholars and judges occasionally question it, a test that has long been commonly used to identify implications in legal instruments is that they must be 'necessary'.[113] But two different kinds of 'necessity' can be found in British and Australian case law on implications, whether statutory or

---

[108] *MZXOT v. Minister for Immigration and Citizenship* (2008) 233 CLR 601, 623 [39] (Gleeson CJ, Gummow and Hayne JJ); 629 [64] (Kirby J).

[109] J Goldsworthy, 'Justice Windeyer on the Engineers' Case' (2009) 37 *Federal Law Review* 363 371–2.

[110] Ibid.

[111] *Victoria v. Commonwealth* (the *Payroll Tax Case*) (1970) 122 CLR 353, 402.

[112] *McGinty v. Western Australia* (1996) 186 CLR 140, 168; approved in *Kruger v Commonwealth* (1997) 190 CLR 520, 567 (Gummow J).

[113] For doubts, see *APLA Ltd v. Legal Services Commissioner* (NSW) (2005) 224 CLR 322, 452–4 [384]–[389] (Hayne J); Goldsworthy, chapter note, 170; J. Kirk, 'Constitutional Implications (I): Nature, Legitimacy, Classification, Examples' (2000) 24 *Melbourne University Law Review* 645, 651–2, 656–7, 676.

contractual.[114] One is practical necessity (or in contract law, business efficacy): it consists of an alleged implication being practically necessary to enable some or all of the provisions of a legal instrument to be efficacious or achieve their intended purposes.[115] This can be called the 'practical necessity test'.

The other kind is decisional necessity: it consists of interpreters being compelled to acknowledge an alleged implication because it is so obvious as not to be reasonably deniable. In contract law, the question has sometimes been said to be whether the court is 'necessarily driven' to the conclusion that some term is implied.[116] Lord Esher used the term in this sense when he said: 'necessary Implication means, not natural Necessity, but so strong a Probability of Intention, that an Intention contrary to that, which is imputed ... cannot be supposed'.[117] The term 'necessary' is used loosely here: what is really required is not that the implication cannot *possibly* be denied, but that it cannot *reasonably* be denied.[118] Since a genuine implication depends on the author or speaker having a certain communicative intention, this amounts to a requirement that such an intention is, in the circumstances, obvious. This might be called the 'obviousness test'.[119]

In *Australian Capital Television* v. *The Commonwealth*, in which the Australian High Court first claimed to discover in the Constitution an implied freedom of political communication, Mason CJ observed that implications may be derived from the actual terms of the Constitution if 'the relevant intention is manifested according to the accepted principles of interpretation', but that 'structural rather than textual' implications 'must be logically or practically necessary for the preservation of the integrity of [some constitutional] structure'.[120] By 'textual' implications 'manifested according to the accepted principles of interpretation', which do not need to be 'necessary', he

---

[114] Discussed in Goldsworthy, chapter note, 168–70. See also E. Peden, *Good Faith in the Interpretation of Contracts* (2003) 60–71.
[115] The version found in contract law is called the 'business efficacy' test: see Starke, Seddon and Ellinghaus, *Cheshire & Fifoot's Law of Contract* (6th Aust'n edn 1992) 212–13. As for statutes, see *Slipper Island Resort Ltd* v. *Minister of Works & Development* [1981] 1 NZLR 136, 139.
[116] *Hamlyn* v. *Wood* (1891) 2 QB 488, 494 per Kay LJ, quoted with approval by Lord Atkinson, speaking for the Judicial Committee of the Privy Council, in *Douglas* v. *Baynes* (1908) AC 477, 482. See also *Nelson* v. *Walker* (1910) 10 CLR 560, 586 *per* Isaacs J; H. Lucke, 'Ad hoc Implications in Written Contracts' (1973) 5 *Adelaide Law Review* 32, 34.
[117] *Wilkinson* v. *Adam* (1813) 1 Ves & B 422, 466; 35 ER 163, 180; quoted by Kirk, Supra note 113, 649.
[118] See *Worrall* v. *Commercial Banking Co of Sydney Ltd* (1917) 24 CLR 28, 32 (Isaacs, Barton and Rich JJ).
[119] Goldsworthy, chapter note, 168; Peden, Supra note 114, 61–3.
[120] *ACTV* v. *Commonwealth* (1992) 177 CLR 106, 135.

was referring to implicatures such as those identified by the *expressio unius* presumption.[121] His perceptive observation that these implicatures do not need to be 'necessary' is consistent with my previous denial that they must be obvious.[122] But he insisted that 'structural' implications do have to be 'practically necessary'. Such an implication is derived from a constitutional 'structure', formed by an interrelated group of provisions with a common purpose such as establishing a particular institution or protecting a general principle. In subsequent constitutional cases dealing with 'structural' implications, the High Court has consistently favoured the 'practical necessity' test.[123]

But as a test for genuine implications, this test is dubious. Since it is possible for a provision that is essential to the practical efficacy of a law to have been omitted due to any number of possible mistakes by the lawmakers, its practical efficacy cannot by itself prove that it was included by implication. For example, if the lawmakers erroneously believed that the provision was not practically necessary to achieve their purposes, it is hardly plausible to regard it as an implicit assumption or any other kind of implication. Surely their error would show that the law needs to be amended to correct a deficiency, not that it already includes something they deliberately excluded from it. When what we have said or written turns out to be deficient, genuine implications do not magically spring up to protect us from our mistakes.[124]

It follows that the obviousness test should be preferred to that of practical efficacy as the test for genuine structural implications. Instead of asking whether the alleged implication is practically necessary for the instrument to operate effectively, we should ask whether it is so obvious as not to be reasonably deniable. A structural implication that passes this test is what I previously called an implicit assumption.[125] Practical necessity may, of course, be part of the evidence that something was so obvious it was taken for granted, as shown by the examples in the first paragraph of Section 4.4.4.

But it does not follow that fabricated implications, which are not really there to be discovered, are necessarily illegitimate (although calling them implications might be criticised as misleading). Elsewhere, I have acknowledged that the difficulty of amending constitutions might be regarded as a reason for judges to be more creative when interpreting them, compared with

---

[121] Personal correspondence on file with the author.
[122] See Section 4.4.5.
[123] See e.g., *Lange v. Australian Broadcasting Corporation* (1997) 189 CLR 520, 567; *MZXOT v. Minister for Immigration and Citizenship* (2008) 233 CLR 601, 623 [39], 635 [83] note 95, and 656 [171], 635 [83] (Kirby J).
[124] Goldsworthy, chapter note, 168–70.
[125] See Section 4.4.4.

other laws.[126] Consider the extent to which judges should remedy failures on the part of the constitution's makers to expressly provide for problems. They may have failed to anticipate a problem, because it was very unlikely to arise, or because they were too busy, or insufficiently astute, to do so.

When interpreting statutes, judges are often reluctant to rectify failures of that kind, preferring to leave it to the legislature to do so. But when dealing with a constitution, it is arguable that they should be more willing to provide a solution. If, because of the framers' oversight, a constitution might fail to achieve one of its main purposes, the potential consequences are grave. They include the danger of constitutional powers being abused, of the democratic process or the federal system being subverted, of human rights being egregiously violated and so on. If the constitution is extremely difficult to amend formally or if amendment requires action by the very politicians who pose the threat that needs to be checked, there may be good reasons for the judges to act. True fidelity to the constitution might justify this.

As the great American jurist Learned Hand observed: 'In construing written documents it has always been thought proper to engraft upon the text such provisions as are necessary to prevent the failure of the undertaking'. But because this is 'a dangerous liberty, not lightly to be resorted to', it is essential that the need be 'compelling' and the interpolated provision be confined 'to the need that evoked it'.[127]

The upshot is this. A genuine structural implication is an implicit assumption that satisfies the obviousness test. This is because, since the lawmakers did not expressly mention it, they must be shown to have taken it for granted, which requires that it was too obvious to need mentioning or perhaps even to be noticed. A structural provision that satisfies the test of practical necessity but not that of obviousness was presumably omitted because of some mistake on the lawmakers' part; they must have failed to appreciate either its necessity, or the need expressly to mention it. The Court may be justified in correcting that mistake, to ensure that the law is efficacious, by in effect inserting the provision into it, provided that it does not violate any side constraint imposed by the lawmakers' other purposes or commitments.[128] But if judges decide to rectify a legal instrument, they should frankly acknowledge what they are

---

[126] The following passage is derived from J. Goldsworthy, 'Conclusions', in J. Goldsworthy (ed.), *Interpreting Constitutions, a Comparative Study* (Oxford: Oxford University Press, 2006) 321, 324.

[127] L. Hand, *The Bill of Rights* (1958), 29; see also ibid., 14 where he uses the term 'interpolate'.

[128] See the 'caveat' in Section 4.4.4, paragraph in which note 75 appears.

doing and not hide behind make-believe implications, unless they are morally justified by extraordinary circumstances in concealing what they are doing.[129]

Arguably, it will often make little difference whether or not an implication is genuine or legitimately fabricated. Consider this example. Section 7 of the Australian Constitution empowers the federal Parliament to increase or decrease the number of Senators for each state, subject to a guarantee that 'equal representation of the several Original States shall be maintained'. This guarantee of equality conspicuously fails to mention new states, which can be established by the federal Parliament under s. 121, subject to 'such terms and conditions, including the extent of [their] representation in either House of Parliament, as it thinks fit'. Does it follow that Parliament could give a new state more Senators than the original states each have? That would obviously violate what we know to be the intended role of the Senate: an undoubted purpose of s. 121, when read with s. 7, was to enable new states to be given fewer – but not more – Senators than the original states.

Is that an implicit assumption that was so obvious it 'went without saying', or – if not – a fabricated implication that may legitimately be inserted into s. 121, to restrict the words 'as it thinks fit', on the ground that this is practically necessary to reconcile the purposes of these provisions? Perhaps it does not matter how it is characterised.

4.6. IMPLICATIONS INFERRED FROM 'OBJECTIVE' PURPOSES

Aharon Barak maintains that constitutional implications can sometimes be inferred from the 'structure' of a constitution, which is 'the architecture underlying the constitutional scheme, the constitutional principles which support this scheme, and their underlying assumptions'.[130] That is uncontroversial: we have just discussed both genuine, and fabricated, structural implications. But Barak also argues that the constitution's underlying architecture, principles and assumptions are best determined by seeking its 'objective purpose', which is independent of the actual purposes of the constitution's makers.[131] This consists of 'the goals, values, and principles that the constitutional text is designed

---

[129] See Goldsworthy, chapter note, 183; J. Goldsworthy 'The Limits of Judicial Fidelity to Law: The Coxford Lecture' (2011) 24 *Canadian Journal of Law and Jurisprudence* 305; J. Goldsworthy 'Should Judges Covertly Disobey the Law to Prevent Injustice?' (2011) 47 *Tulsa Law Review* 133.

[130] A. Barak, 'On Constitutional Implications and Constitutional Structure' in D. Dyzenhaus and M. Thorburn (eds.), *Philosophical Foundations of Constitutional Law* (Oxford: Oxford University Press 2016) 53, 59.

[131] Ibid., 54, 68.

[sic] to achieve in a modern democracy at the time of interpretation ... [In other words] society's basic normative positions at the time of interpretation'.[132]

Strictly speaking, words and texts – like other inanimate objects – do not have intentions or purposes. A purpose is a kind of intention: an intention to achieve something. Only intelligent, reasoning beings can have intentions and purposes. It is true that we casually say things such as: 'The purpose of a hammer is to bang in nails'. Could this be a hammer's 'objective' purpose, independent of the purposes of human beings? Surely not: the purpose of any particular hammer must be the purpose for which it was either designed or acquired in order to be used, or for which it is in fact used, and that must be a purpose of the person or people who either designed, acquired or use it.[133] The purpose of a hammer that has not yet been purchased might differ from that of a hammer that has been purchased for some idiosyncratic purpose, such as to be part of a modern sculpture. The purpose of a law must, similarly, be the purpose of either: (1) the people who made it; or other people who subsequently use it, such as (2) (a majority of) the community as a whole, or perhaps (3) the judiciary, acting on the community's behalf.

Barak appeals to the supposed purposes (or fundamental values) of the community as a whole.[134] But it is surely difficult to attribute purposes or values to the community other than at the most abstract level ('democracy', 'equality', 'justice' and so on), which provides little assistance in resolving concrete constitutional disputes. Given that very few citizens would have any knowledge of the particular constitutional provisions in question or of their functions, to attribute helpful purposes to them would usually be to indulge in blatant fiction.

In descending from the community's unhelpfully abstract basic commitments to more specific 'purposes' that can actually assist in resolving interpretive disputes, the judges would have to rely on their own value judgments, which leads to the third possibility previously mentioned.[135] But to allow the

---

[132] A. Barak, *Purposive Interpretation in Law* (Princeton, NJ: Princeton University Press, 2005), 190, and see also 148, 152–3, 155. 'Sic' is inserted because any constitution was designed by those who made it; even if it is later put to different purposes than theirs, it is not redesigned. Perhaps he meant 'intended'.

[133] In biology, we speak of bodily organs such as the heart having 'functions' that are their contributions to the operation of a larger system (the body), even though neither the body nor its component organs were intelligently designed to serve a purpose (at least, according to evolutionists). But we do not attribute 'purposes' to bodily organs.

[134] He describes purposivism as emphasising 'public understanding at the time of interpretation': 'On Constitutional Implications', note 130, 66.

[135] Hence the common criticism that Ronald Dworkin was almost always able to derive from the abstract clauses of the American Bill of Rights and Fourteenth Amendment legal conclusions that matched his own political predilections.

judges to attribute to laws whatever purposes they deem best would undermine the essential role of elected lawmakers, which is precisely to represent the community in intelligently designing laws (including constitutions) to serve chosen purposes. The purposes the lawmakers choose to pursue on behalf of the community have better credentials than anyone else's to be deemed the purposes of the community itself. But on Barak's approach, democratically elected lawmakers merely provide a 'first draft', which the judges turn into law by deciding what purposes it should serve and reshaping its meanings (especially its implied meanings) accordingly.[136] Moreover, the judges can, in effect, keep redesigning the law as it ages and community values (as the judges see them) evolve.[137] As Richard Ekins once described a somewhat similar approach,

> [t]he courts are enjoined to interpret each statute as a purposive communication – but not a communication from real legislators. Instead the statute should be read as though it were a communication from the judge to himself.[138]

To combine the third possibility with those methods of finding or fabricating implications that we have previously examined would be a particularly potent recipe for constitutional quasi-amendment by the judiciary. This would involve pretending that the contemporary community has re-authored the constitution, and then treating the text as either pragmatically enriched by whatever intentions and purposes the judges attribute to the pretended author or as including whatever fabricated implications are deemed practically necessary to achieve those purposes.

Suppose that the judges held that the community has come to expect the constitution or part of it to serve some new purpose which its actual makers did not intend, and also that applying the constitution's express meaning cannot achieve that purpose. In other words, some content in addition to the constitution's express meaning is deemed necessary to achieve that purpose. According to Barak, that content would not need to be added to the constitution by formal amendment, despite the purpose it is needed to achieve being, *ex hypothesi*, a new one. The judges could hold that it is already implied by the constitution, either because it is a fictional implicature or implicit assumption of the constitutions' new, pretended author or because the clause or provision

---

[136] R. Posner, 'Enlightened Despot' *The New Republic*, 29 April 2007.
[137] See Barak's use of the word 'designed' in note 132.
[138] R. Ekins, 'The Relevance of the Rule of Recognition' (2006) 31 *Australian Journal of Legal Philosophy* 95, 100.

is necessary to enable the constitution to fulfil one of that author's purposes. The constitution would spontaneously sprout whatever new implications are necessary to achieve whatever new purposes the judges attribute to the contemporary community. No formal, democratic amendment procedure would need to be followed. Neither the community nor its elected representatives would need to be asked whether they really want the constitution to achieve that new purpose or whether, on reflection, they really want it to include the new provision that it supposedly requires in order to do so.

This seems a logical consequence, and not a fanciful and unfair caricature, of Barak's theory. It is surely unnecessary to spell out how blatantly it would violate the principles of democracy and the rule of law. It could resemble a method of interpretation criticised previously, where all the provisions of the Constitution are, holistically, regarded as instantiating such abstract principles as 'democracy', 'freedom' or even 'justice' and anything not mentioned that (in the opinion of the judges) helps secure democracy, freedom and justice are regarded as impliedly guaranteed.[139]

In common law jurisdictions, the courts draw a distinction between 'objective' intentions (including purposes) and the 'subjective' intentions of lawmakers. Objective intentions have been described as *expressed* or *outwardly manifested* intentions.[140] The distinction is between the actual mental states of lawmakers, which might be obscure or inaccessible, and evidence of those mental states that was publicly manifested or exhibited by the terms of the law, understood in the context of its enactment. But even if 'objective' intentions are sought, 'subjective' intentions remain relevant. An 'objective' intention amounts to this: what a reasonable audience would conclude was the author's 'subjective' intention, given all the publicly manifested evidence of it. The existence of a subjective intention is a crucial presupposition of our attribution of an objective intention to the author of a text and, consequently, to the text itself. If we knew that the creators of a text were incapable of having a subjective intention – for example, they were monkeys pounding randomly on keyboards – we would have no rational basis for attributing any objective intention to them or their text.[141]

I can make sense of the idea of an 'objective' purpose only by thinking of it in this way, as what publicly manifested evidence suggests was the lawmakers' purpose. It is a purpose that reasonable members of the lawmakers' intended

---

[139] See note 62.
[140] *Byrnes v. Kendall* (2011) 243 CLR 253, 273 [53], 274 [55], 274–5 [57], 275 [59] (Gummow and Hayne JJ); 282 [94] (Heydon and Crennan JJ).
[141] For further discussion, see J. Goldsworthy and R. Ekins, 'The Reality and Indispensability of Legislative Intentions' (2014) 36 *Sydney Law Review* 39.

audience – whether lawyers or citizens – would attribute to the lawmakers, based on textual and contextual evidence available to them, and it might, therefore, differ from the actual subjective motives or purposes of the lawmakers as individuals.

If this theoretical explanation of 'objective' purpose is rejected, some other explanation must be provided. It must somehow explain how legal purposes or values can be both created by acts of lawmaking, yet also objective in the sense of being independent of the lawmakers' intentions or purposes. This is likely to be very difficult. We can at least understand how moral values might be objective even if, after philosophical analysis, we do not accept that they are. But that is because we do not think of moral values as being deliberately created by human beings, although they can be deliberately incorporated into a law by lawmakers. By contrast, laws are deliberately created by human lawmakers. How, then, can those laws have 'objective' purposes or values that are independent of the intentions and purposes of the people who made them? Even if a law incorporates an objective moral value, that can only be because the law in its context objectively manifests or evidences the lawmakers' intention to do so. If the notion of an 'objective purpose' is supposed to have some other meaning, it should be regarded with deep suspicion: it is too metaphysically queer to be believable.

Barak also claims that his interpretive theory may be consistent with some theories of pragmatics, albeit not Gricean or neo-Gricean theories.[142] But instead of proving that claim, he calls for further research to develop such theories.[143] This is unlikely to help him. The non-Gricean theories he mentions are similar to Gricean theories in that all treat pragmatic, or contextual, enrichment as revealing the actual author's or speaker's communicative intentions. No theory of pragmatics of my acquaintance, in the field of linguistics or of philosophy of language, is built on the notion of an imaginary 'ideal' author.

4.7. CONCLUSION: INEXPLICIT CONTENT AND LAWMAKERS' INTENTIONS

The literal meaning of a sentence may have logical implications or entailments. But almost all implicit and implied content depends on some ingredient in addition to the words of the text, and as different theories of pragmatics all agree, this can only be contextual evidence of the author's communicative

---

[142] Barak, Supra note 130, 71.
[143] Ibid., 72–3.

intentions, including evidence of his or her purpose in communicating. We have seen how determining even the express meaning of a written constitution can require contextual enrichment, because (inter alia) of the inclusion of indexicals, relational and ambiguous terms and ellipses. The references of relational and ambiguous terms cannot be determined, and ellipses identified and filled in, other than by contextual evidence of authorial intention. In the case of ellipses, somewhat paradoxically, express meaning includes inexplicit content.

In addition, a constitution's implied meaning can include implicatures and implicit assumptions that can also be revealed only through contextual enrichment. Implicatures depend on evidence of the author's intention to communicate something by implication.[144] To speak of an implicit assumption which was taken for granted, is to speak of what the author took for granted. Texts cannot meaningfully be said to take anything for granted, at least not if their meaning is confined to literal meaning, severed from their authors' intentions. Even fabricated implications, which lawyers oddly describe as being 'read into' or 'implied into' laws, are usually justified in terms of what is necessary to fulfil the lawmakers' intentions or purposes.[145]

For these reasons, a constitution protects by implication 'structural' principles or values, such as representative democracy, federalism, the rule of law and the separation of powers, only if and insofar as contextual as well as textual evidence suggests that its makers had the requisite intention or purpose. This is so whether or not the implication is a genuine one ascertained by clarifying interpretation, or a fabricated one inserted by rectifying interpretation.

A major challenge for anyone who rejects intentionalism or originalism is to provide a plausible alternative analysis of these commonplace aspects of legal meaning and interpretation. I am not aware of any serious attempt to do so. Moreover, if it is true that they can plausibly be explained only in terms of inferences from text and context to the lawmaker's probable communicative intentions, then notwithstanding the difficulties of explaining the nature of collective intentions – a promising philosophical research program that has only recently begun – we have no practicable alternative other than continuing to interpret constitutions on the assumption that such intentions exist.[146]

---

[144] See Section 4.4.2.
[145] See Section 4.5.
[146] See also Carston, Supra note 34, 25, quoting Stephen Neale.

5

The Centrality and Diversity of the Invisible Constitution

Patrick Emerton[*]

A constitution – considered as a visible, written legal text – exists within a broader social and political context. This chapter argues that, to a significant extent, it is this context that gives the constitution and the laws made under it whatever legal force they have; but that this context is not (and cannot be) contained within it. Every constitution, therefore, has a crucial yet invisible aspect.[1]

The argument of the chapter is a philosophical one. Its goal, however, is not purely philosophical. Rather, it is to show that considerations of analytic jurisprudence, and analytic philosophy more generally, suggest a sociological conclusion, namely, that each constitutional order must be its own particular thing, by virtue of its distinctive invisible elements.

5.1. ANTI-POSITIVISM AND THE INVISIBILITY OF THE CONSTITUTION

The claim stated in the opening paragraph of this chapter is easy to make out for an adherent of an anti-positivist, more-or-less Dworkinian account of law that identifies *the law* not primarily with *the content of and requirements stated in certain texts*, but rather with *the moral requirements that flow from*

---

[*] This chapter has benefited from discussing many of the issues raised with Hrafn Asgeirsson, Triantafyllos Gkouvas, Joanna Kyriakakis and Dale Smith; from comments provided by Lulu Weis, Tarunabh Khaitan and the editors of this book; and from the comments and questions of audience members at the International Association for Constitutional Law Roundtable (Melbourne Law School, 2nd May 2016) and the Australian Society of Legal Philosophy Conference (Melbourne Law School, 23rd July 2016). This research was supported by the Australian Government through the Australian Research Council awards DP1092523 and DP140102670.

[1] It is the contribution of these phenomena to the *legal force* of the constitution, and of other legal texts and practices, that leads me to characterise them as *constitutional* phenomena.

the promulgation by certain social institutions of certain texts.[2] On Dworkin's own account, the moral requirements in question are those principles which, in light of the demands that integrity imposes on the exercise of the coercive power of the state, would best justify the promulgated texts (together with other legal practices);[3] on Greenberg's account, the moral requirements are those which are caused by certain texts having been promulgated by legal authorities (together with other practices of those authorities).[4] On either account, it seems obvious that the legal meaning and force of any legal text – including a constitution – will depend upon the social context surrounding its promulgation. Furthermore, this context constitutes an 'invisible' element of the constitution in two distinct senses: (1) it lies outside the text, and yet is crucial in determining the legal significance of the promulgated text; (2) it is not something that would typically be included in a catalogue of the *legal* phenomena that occur within a society.[5]

Nevertheless, in a recent paper Greenberg appears to downplay the potential gap, on his account, between the visible and the invisible constituents of law:

> [T]he legislative enactment of a statute may often have roughly the net effect of adding to the content of the law a norm that is more or less captured by the linguistic content of the legislation. But, when it does so, the explanation will be that the enactment of the statute changed the relevant circumstances,

---

[2] The italicised phrase is an attempt to capture what is common to the conception of law presented by Ronald Dworkin, *Law's Empire* (Cambridge, MA: Harvard University Press, 1986) and by Mark Greenberg, 'The Moral Impact Theory of Law' (2014) 123 *Yale Law Journal* 1288. See also the discussion in Mark Greenberg, 'The standard picture and its discontents', in Leslie Green and Brian Leiter (eds.) *Oxford Studies in Philosophy of Law* (Oxford: Oxford University Press, 2011), 56.

[3] Dworkin, Supra note 1, 90–4, 410–13 ('the law of a community on this account is the scheme of rights and responsibilities that … license coercion because they flow from past [political] decisions of the right sort': 93); see also the discussion in Greenberg, 'The Moral Impact Theory', Supra note 1, 1292–3, 1299–1303.

[4] Greenberg, 'The Moral Impact Theory', Supra note 1, 1293, 1301–3.

[5] The editors, in chapter 1, capture a similar sense of the *invisible* when they refer to 'aspects of a constitutional tradition that are sufficiently deep or outside the confines of what is understood as constitutional within a given system, that they are often overlooked as elements of actual constitutional practice'. Martin Krygier's work on the rule of law has consistently articulated the dependence of law's significance upon extra-legal social phenomena: see e.g., 'Transitional Questions about the Rule of Law: Why, What and How?' (2001) 28 *East Central Europe/L'Europe Du Centre Est*, 1; 'The Rule of Law: Pasts, Presents, and Two Possible Futures' (2016) 12 *Annual Review of Law and Social Science*, 199. What is distinctive about the anti-positivist views discussed above is that they are not simply accounts of the social significance of law, but of the *legal* significance of promulgated legal texts.

thus changing what people are morally required or permitted to do – not that the legal norm obtains simply because it was authoritatively pronounced.[6]

However, little argument is provided for this suggestion, which appears to rest upon relatively strong premises about the moral obligations of individuals, especially those who live in democratic societies, to coordinate their actions around highly salient, authoritatively promulgated texts.[7] And even if those premises are true for some places and times, they are not true in general. There are many societies in which the promulgated legal texts are not particularly salient when it comes to social action; or if they are salient, they nevertheless do not generate any sort of moral obligation upon individuals to coordinate their actions around them (e.g., because of the moral character of the government and its legislative programme).[8] Thus Greenberg's suggestion that, in certain cases, text and law may converge does not contradict the general point that, on an anti-positivist account of law of the sort that he defends, the meaning and legal force of law depends upon a broader context which, of necessity, is not itself expressed within the text: an *invisible constitution* in the manner described above.

5.2. CONSTITUTIONS AND RULES OF RECOGNITION

The remainder of this chapter focuses on a jurisprudential approach quite different from the anti-positivism discussed in the previous section. The chapter argues that, within the framework of Hartian positivism, the legal force of the 'visible' linguistic content of a constitutional text and the laws it validates depends to a significant degree upon 'invisible' elements of the constitution and hence that – as these vary with social and political context – so does that legal force.

Central to Hart's conception of a legal system is the existence of a fundamental validating rule of a legal system – the *rule of recognition*.[9] In a number of passages in *The Concept of Law*, Hart identifies a legal system's rule of

---

[6] Greenberg, 'The Moral Impact Theory', Supra note 1, 1342. See also Greenberg, 'The Standard Picture', Supra note 1, 58–9, for a similar suggestion in relation to Dworkin.

[7] This is suggested by some of Greenberg's remarks about democracy, texts and de facto authorities: 'The Moral Impact Theory', Supra note 1, 1293, 1312–15, 1329, 1338, 1340; and see also 'The Standard Picture', Supra note 1, 57.

[8] Martin Krygier conveys the outlook of such societies by way of 'the Bulgarian saying that law is like a door in the middle of an open field. Of course, you could go through the door, but only a fool would bother': 'The Rule of Law: Legality, Teleology, Sociology' in Gianluggi Palombella and Neil Walker (eds.) *Relocating the Rule of Law* (Portland: Hart Publishing, 2009), 60.

[9] H. L. A. Hart, *The Concept of Law*, 2nd edn (Oxford: Oxford University Press, 1994), 100–10.

recognition with the constitution (or certain constitutional provisions or principles) of that system.[10] However, he makes the point that it cannot be the constitutional text that renders the rule of recognition fundamental. Discussing the rule that *what the Queen in Parliament enacts is law*, Hart observes that:

> Even if it were enacted by statute, this would not reduce it to the level of a statute; for the legal status of such an enactment necessarily would depend on the fact that the rule existed antecedently to and independently of the enactment. Moreover ... its existence, unlike that of a statute, must consist in an actual practice.[11]

The point about *actual practice* is a consequence of Hart's general account of the existence of a legal system. Hart holds there to be two conditions necessary and

---

[10] See e.g., ibid., 100–2, 106–7, 110–11, 113–16.

[11] Ibid., 111. Hart further says (293) that:

> If a constitution specifying the various sources of law is a living reality in the sense that the courts and officials of the system actually identify the law in accordance with the criteria it provides, then the constitution is accepted and actually exists. It seems a needless reduplication to suggest that there is a further rule to the effect that the constitution (or those who 'laid it down') are to be obeyed.

Gardner says of this second passage that:

> The picture that Hart seems to be trying to conjure up is of a constitution containing some law that is both written and unwritten – legislated and customary – at the same time. The only picture he succeeded in conjuring up for me, however, is of written law which was displaced, perhaps one step at a time, by unwritten law, so that the formerly legislated constitution lost its force in favour of customary rules with similar content.

John Gardner, 'Can There Be a Written Constitution', in Leslie Green and Brian Leiter (eds.) *Oxford Studies in Philosophy of Law* (Oxford: Oxford University Press, 2011), 180. As far as the relationship between the rule of recognition and a written constitution is concerned, therefore, Gardner prefers to identify the rule of recognition as an *unwritten* rule that 'imposes a legal duty upon law-applying officials'; the duty it imposes is to apply the constitution, which itself identifies and confers powers upon the fundamental political organs and institutions; and because the rule of recognition must be an actual social practice ('custom'), it is ultimately judicial reception of the constitution that confers upon it its constitutional status: 'Can There Be a Written Constitution' 165–7, 175–80, 186–7. The idea that the rule of recognition is constituted simply by judicial practice is contentious, however: Jeffrey Goldsworthy, for instance, takes the view that the rule of recognition is constituted by the shared practice of all the senior officials within a legal system: *The Sovereignty of Parliament: History and Philosophy* (Oxford: Clarendon Press, 1999), 238–46. On such an understanding, the idea that the content of that shared practice might be written down by the lawmaking officials, so that the law-applying officials have a canonical statement of it to refer to when performing their adjudicative tasks, would seem to make sense. In such a case, the duty to conform to the rule of recognition would be overdetermined, but there would be no contradiction.

In any event, as will be discussed below, an unwritten rule of recognition is not as such invisible, and so even if Gardner was correct that the rule of recognition must be unwritten, that would not in itself show that every constitution necessarily has an invisible aspect.

sufficient for a particular legal system to exist: that its rules of recognition, change and adjudication 'be effectively accepted as common public standards of official behaviour by its officials'; and that the rules which are validated by the rule of recognition – i.e., the laws of the system – be generally obeyed by those whom they purport to govern.[12] The second of these conditions can be put aside for the moment while we focus on the first – that is, on the claim that the rule of recognition must be not simply a rule in some abstract or putative sense, but an actual social, normative practice among the officials of the legal system in question.[13] This requirement that the rule of recognition be an actual practice among the officials of the legal system distinguishes *that* rule from the laws that it validates. As Hart says,

> [I]t is plain that there is no necessary connection between the validity of any particular rule [i.e., a law of the system] and *its* efficacy, unless the rule of recognition of the system includes among its criteria, as some do, the provision (sometimes referred to as a rule of obsolescence) that no rule is to count as a rule of the system if it has long ceased to be efficacious.[14]

Whereas,

> [A] rule of recognition is unlike other rules of the system. The assertion that it exists can only be an external statement of fact. For whereas a subordinate rule of a system [i.e., a law of the system] may be valid and in that sense 'exist' even if it is generally disregarded, the rule of recognition exists only as a complex, but normally concordant, practice of the courts, officials, and private persons in identifying the law by reference to certain criteria. Its existence is a matter of fact.[15]

This picture clearly *allows for* an 'invisible' constitution, in two senses very similar to those identified above in relation to anti-positivism: (1) the rule of recognition *may* lie outside the legal texts, while nevertheless being crucial in validating the promulgated texts as *law*; (2) the social practice that constitutes the rule of recognition *need not* be something that would typically be included in a catalogue of the *legal* phenomena that occur within a society.

When we think of typical instances of contemporary state law, this second mode of invisibility may seem implausible: any introductory account of the United Kingdom's legal system, for instance, will make the point that statutes (i.e., what the Queen in Parliament enacts) are law. However, systems that are plural in their sources of law may include, in their rules of recognition, practices

---

[12] Hart, *The Concept of Law*, 116.
[13] For an argument that the rule of recognition might, at least in some cases, be an institutionalised but non-normative practice among the officials of a system, see Brian Z. Tamanaha, *A General Jurisprudence of Law and Society* (Oxford: Oxford University Press, 2001), 142, 152–5.
[14] Hart, Supra note 9, 103.
[15] Ibid., 110.

of having regard to, or disregarding, phenomena that would not normally be thought of as legal phenomena; and these practices of regard or disregard may likewise not be thought of as *legal* in character. This can be illustrated even by reference to Australian law, which (like the law of the United Kingdom) includes not only statutes but the common law. Thus, in discussing the limits of the declaratory theory of the common law, Gummow J observes that 'there may be an explicit change of direction, where, in the perception of appellate courts, a previously understood principle of the common law has become ill adapted to modern circumstances'.[16] To the extent that such changes in the common law unfold as part of the collective action of the senior judiciary, this must mean – in Hartian terms – that the rule of recognition extends to the acknowledgement of certain social changes (i.e., pertaining to 'modern circumstances') as warranting changes in the judge-made law.[17] However, these practices among the judiciary, of recognising certain social changes as relevant to the way the common law is developed and declared, are not typically included in catalogues of Australian legal phenomena.

However, to show the *possibility* of an invisible constitution on the Hartian picture is not to show its *necessity*. In particular, the dependence of the rule of recognition upon actual social facts is not sufficient to show that it is an *invisible* constitutional element because – as we have already seen Hart discuss – the rule of recognition might itself be written down as part of a written constitution; and as we have also seen, even an unwritten rule of recognition may be a well-understood and acknowledged legal phenomenon within a society. Either possibility would be sufficient to render the rule visible.

If we consider the relationship of *validation* that – on Hart's account – obtains between the rule of recognition and the rest of the laws of the system, however, there are additional considerations that are sufficient to establish the centrality of the invisible to the constitution. That is what the rest of this chapter will show.

5.3. 'THICK' VALIDATION AND INVISIBILITY

There seem to be two main ways of thinking about the way in which validation occurs under a rule of recognition: one relatively thick, the other relatively thin. The 'thick' picture of validation will be explained and analysed in this section; the following section will deal with the 'thin' picture.

---

[16] *Wik Peoples* v. *Queensland* (1996) 187 CLR 1, 179–80.
[17] As opposed to being the choices of individual judges who then impose their wills upon their fellow judges in disregard of the social practice that constitutes the rule of recognition.

On the 'thick' picture of validation, what it is that is validated are the various rules and principles that make up the legal system and determine outcomes and consequences within it. In a legal system of even modest complexity, these will include rules and principles that have not been expressly or self-evidently stated by any authoritative source, but rather are derived – as implications, consequences, interpretations and the like – from those sources. Call this *unexpressed law* (which contrasts with *expressed law*). There also are likely to be rules and principles for generating unexpressed law (e.g., rules for reconciling or integrating prima facie conflicting sources; rules of statutory interpretation; rules for deriving authoritative principles from decided cases; etc.), without which no account can be given of how the unexpressed law is part of the system.[18] Call these *rules of legal inference*.[19] On the 'thick' Hartian conception of law, the rules of legal inference themselves stand in need of validation, if they are to be part of the system.

It might be tempting to think that the rules of legal inference could themselves be part (perhaps the major part) of the rule of recognition. However, Dworkin has advanced a very persuasive argument that these sorts of rules are simply not apt to be exemplified as social rules or practices:[20] rules having this sort of complexity, and hence apt to generate disagreement around their interpretation and application, will simply not generate the convergent behaviour that is characteristic of a social rule.

In any event, there is good reason to think that these rules of legal inference could not be written law and hence either: (a) if part of the rule of recognition would render it impossible to (fully) declare that rule in writing; or (b) if

---

[18] On some occasions (e.g., if in the context of an exposition of some point by a court with appropriate standing in a judicial hierarchy), the ascertainment of unexpressed law may render the hitherto-unexpressed *expressed*.

[19] It is beyond the scope of this chapter to consider in any detail the possible content of rules of legal inferences, which obviously can vary extremely widely across different legal systems. Within the Australian legal system, one important class of such rules is that of rules which determine the consequence for one expressed law of changes in another expressed law that do not directly refer to the first expressed law. One example of such a rule is the principle of legality, which determines the consequences for various expressed rules of the common law of the enactment of a statute that does not expressly address those common law rules but on its face may bear upon them (see e.g., *Lacey* v. *Attorney-General* (*Qld*) (2011) 242 CLR 57). A second (which has no special name) is the rule used by the High Court in *PGA* v. *The Queen* (2012) 245 CLR 355 to determine the consequence of various express laws that changed the legal status of women (e.g., emancipation statutes; divorce statutes; enfranchisement statutes, etc.) for the common law rule governing the possibility of rape in marriage: for the majority's statement of the rule, see (2012) 245 CLR 355, 373 [30] (French CJ, Gummow, Hayne, Crennan and Kiefel JJ).

[20] Ronald Dworkin, 'The Model of Rules II', in *Taking Rights Seriously* (Cambridge: Harvard University Press, 1978), 54–7, 61–3.

not, would be a series of centrally important rules that the rule of recognition must validate and yet that must remain unexpressed. The argument to this conclusion depends upon certain ideas found in the philosophy of logic and mathematics.

5.3.1. Hartian Positivism Compared to the Conventionalist Account of Axiomatic Systems

Hart's conception of a legal system yields a picture that evokes certain central ideas of the analytic philosophy of the latter part of the nineteenth century and the first half of the twentieth century. I want to explain how this is so, in order to then derive consequences concerning the invisible elements of a constitutional order.

A key concern in the analytic tradition just mentioned is understanding the nature of axiomatic systems – that is, systems of propositions constructed via logical or mathematical deduction from a set of axioms that are not themselves proved to be true. One core contention to emerge from this tradition is the idea that what underpins an axiomatic system is *convention*. What is meant by this is that the axioms of (say) a system of geometry or of arithmetic should not be understood as expressing primitive truths that are known to intuition but not capable of further analysis; rather, they should be understood as establishing permissible 'moves' within the system, and as thereby implicitly defining the terms that occur within them (e.g., if the axioms of a certain system of geometry use terms such as *point* and *line*, then those axioms serve to implicitly define the meaning of those terms, which meaning is fully given by the 'moves' that may be made by way of deducing propositions in which those terms occur).[21] From the inside, the axioms and the statements that are deduced from them are necessarily true, in the sense that one cannot reject them while nevertheless working with the system in question. But from the outside, they are not necessary at all. Other axioms might be chosen, from which different consequences would follow.

There is an obvious similarity here to Hart's rule of recognition, which from the external point of view is a mere empirical state of affairs,[22] but which is necessarily 'presupposed'[23] by statements that such-and-such a rule is a valid law. Questions of validity arise within the system, and so treat the rule of recognition analogously to a (necessarily true) axiom; but when considered from

---

[21] For an excellent discussion, see J. Alberto Coffa, *The Semantic Tradition from Kant to Carnap: To the Vienna Station* (Cambridge: Cambridge University Press, 1991), 54–61, 128–40, 312–26.
[22] See e.g., Hart, Supra note 9, 102–3, 107–8, 110–11.
[23] For Hart's use of this word, see e.g., ibid. 108–9.

the outside, the rule of recognition is not necessary and clearly might have been otherwise.

But how, exactly, does a conventional rule establish permissible 'moves'? In a system of mathematics or a system of law, these moves are governed by rules of inference – but where do those rules come from, and how are they related to the other elements of the system? The following two subsections take up these questions.

5.3.2. *The Necessarily Unwritten Character of Rules of Legal Inference*

Lewis Carroll, in his essay 'What the Tortoise said to Achilles',[24] makes the following point: while for every valid argument there is a corresponding conditional statement that (a) takes the conjunction of the premises as its antecedent and the conclusion of the argument as its consequence; (b) is logically true; and (c) states the rule of inference that underpins the argument, we nevertheless *cannot* require that this conditional statement itself be a premise in the argument, on pain of incoherence. For instance, consider the argument:

(1) A;
(2) Either not-A or B;

Therefore:

(3) B.

This argument is valid. And there corresponds to it the following logically true conditional, which takes the conjunction of (1) and (2) as its antecedent and takes (3) as its consequent:

(4) If A and either not-A or B, then B.

The conditional (4) states the rule of inference that underpins the validity of the argument from (1) and (2) to (3). However, it cannot be the case that the validity of that argument depends upon *affirming* (4), as if it were a hitherto-suppressed premise. If validity depended upon including the underpinning rule of inference as a premise in the argument, then it would follow that the new argument – from (1), (2) and (4) to (3) – could not be valid unless the rule of inference that underpins it were also included as a premise, which would then demand the inclusion of a further premise stating the rule of inference underpinning this further argument, and so on in an infinite regress.[25]

---
[24] (1895) 4 *Mind*, 278.
[25] For exposition and discussion of Carroll's argument, see Coffa, Supra note 21, 161–2; Alan Musgrave, 'Wittgensteinian Instrumentalism' (1980) 46 *Theoria*, 65, 88–9; Jan Willem Wieland, 'What Carroll's Tortoise Actually Proves' (2013) 16 *Ethical Theory and Moral Practice*

The lesson that is relevant for present purposes is this: the rules of inference that underpin the validity of arguments are not themselves to be considered among the constituent elements of the argument.

When we turn from formal, logical systems to informal and natural language systems such as legal systems, the notion of a *rule of inference* becomes less clear. Nevertheless, a version of Carroll's point continues to apply. Consider some putative law L which is (at least hitherto) unexpressed, and which has been derived from some relevant legal source by application of rules of legal inference; and let R be the rule of recognition, S the source from which L has been derived, and I the legal rules of inference. On the 'thick' Hartian picture of validation, for L to actually be a law it must be the case that R validates S (as a source of law) and L (as the putative law derived from S). Given that (*ex hypothesi*) L is not expressed by S, validating S will not straightforwardly validate L. Rather, it will have to be the case that L follows via I from the law that is expressed in S.

Can I be written down, as principles of the legal system in question? Presumably yes: just as we can write down the rule of inference that underpins the argument from (1) and (2) to (3) – it is written down, above, as (4) – so there is no reason to suppose that we cannot, at least in principle, write down I. However, it seems that our inference to L from what is expressed in S could not *depend upon* our application of a written I, for the reason that Carroll's essay points us to: this would then require application of some further principle of legal inference (call it X) via which L follows from both I and the law that is expressed in S. And *ex hypothesi* X would be unexpressed.

It might be objected that, in the informal reasoning that is characteristic of a legal system, that the same I should be able to govern both: (a) the inference to L from what is expressed in S; and (b) the inference to L from I and what is expressed in S; in other words, it might be objected that X need not be any different from I. However, this possibility suggests a new consideration

---

983, 984. J. F. Thomson characterises the infinite regress as 'just an infinitely long red herring': 'What Achilles Should Have Said to the Tortoise' (1960) 3 *Ratio* 95. His point is this: suppose an argument to (3) taking (1) and (2) as premises were not valid because, in general, no argument from a finite set of premises to a conclusion could be valid if not supplemented by an additional premise stating the rule of inference for such an argument (call this general principle the *supplementation requirement*). Then the premises as supplemented would equally fail to yield a valid argument, because we would still have nothing more than an argument from a finite set of premises to a conclusion – which fails to satisfy the constraint stated in the supplementation requirement! Hence the supplementation requirement states a constraint on validity that necessarily cannot be satisfied, hence is absurd, and hence is false; and we do not need to appeal to the infinite regress to see that this is so. Nevertheless, the idea of the infinite regress has heuristic utility, and is commonly used to explain the point of Carroll's paper (e.g., both Coffa and Musgrave use the device), and hence I have used it in the text.

in favour of the conclusion that *I* must be unexpressed. If the legal rules of inference are stated with sufficient flexibility and informality that they are able to govern inferences in which they themselves figure (e.g., if they state certain principles of analogical reasoning, or state certain principles for the application of general terms to particular cases, etc.), then it seems that any concrete application of them to validate *L* could not be a case of simply applying expressed rules of legal inference, but rather would require generation (by application of principles of interpretation, principle for reconciling conflicting considerations, etc.) of something unexpressed from the expressed rules of legal inference.

I therefore conclude that there is good, though not definitive, reason to think that – on the 'thick' picture of validation – the rules of legal inference, or at least some of them, must be unexpressed.

5.3.3. *The 'Local' Character of Rules of Legal Inference*

If rules of inference are not premises in our arguments, then how are they known to us so that we may apply them? The answer given within the conventionalist tradition is that grasping the rules for the use of key logical and mathematical concepts – e.g., such concepts as *conjunction, negation, addition*, etc. – includes, or even consists in, grasping the permissible inferences to which they give rise. Coffa explains the idea this way:

> Logic is radically different from every other type of knowledge because its 'justification' [ie the rules of inference that underpin logical argumentation] lies not in how things stand but in the understanding of language. As I understand the language in which A *and* B and *not*-A are formulated, I ipso facto recognize that whatever A and B might be, if those two statements were true, B would also be true ...
>
> The basic point is that ... the focus is not the 'seeing' of a certain very general and a prior truth but on the recognition of certain meanings, on *understanding* ...
>
> These 'truths' emerge not from the acknowledgement of facts ... but through the recognition of meaning.[26]

A. J. Ayer, in *Language Truth and Logic*, puts forward the same idea as an account of the necessary truth of propositions of mathematics and logic:

> [W]e say that a proposition is analytic when its validity depends solely on the definitions of the symbols it contains ... If one knows what is the function

[26] Coffa, Supra note 21, 165–7.

of the words 'either', 'or', and 'not', then one can see that any proposition of the form 'Either p is true or p is not true' is valid ... Accordingly, all such propositions are analytic ...

[A]lthough [analytic propositions] give us no information about any empirical situation, they do enlighten us by illustrating the way in which we use certain symbols ... [I]n saying that if all Bretons are Frenchmen, and all Frenchmen Europeans, then all Bretons are Europeans, I am not describing any matter of fact. But I am showing that in the statement that all Bretons are Frenchmen, and all Frenchmen Europeans, the further statement that all Bretons are Europeans is implicitly contained. And I am thereby indicating the convention which governs our usage of the words 'if' and 'all'.[27]

On the 'thick' Hartian picture of validation, it seems natural to suppose that the rules of legal inference would similarly be implicit in the meanings of key terms occurring in the rule of recognition: this would explain where they come from, and how they come to be validated. Because these key terms are likely to be different across different legal systems (at least in principle – in practice, broader socio-historical processes may produce a degree of homogenisation), that suggests that the relevant rules of legal inference may themselves be different across legal systems, and hence 'local' or 'parochial'. Wittgenstein expresses this sort of idea very forcefully (and generalises it across larger swathes of language than those with which this paper is concerned) when he says that

> to imagine a language is to imagine a form of life ... [T]he *speaking of a language* is part of an activity, or a form of life ...
> 'So you are saying that human agreement decides what is true and what is false?' – It is what human beings *say* that is true and false; and they agree in the *language* they use. That is not agreement in opinions but in form of life ... What has to be accepted, the given, is – so one could say – *forms of life*.[28]

Wittgenstein goes so far as to say that 'If a lion could talk, we could not understand him'.[29] Although somewhat aphoristic, Wittgenstein is presenting the core ideas of the conventionalist picture, but extending it beyond formal axiomatic systems to practices of language use and the following of rules more generally.[30]

---

[27] A. J. Ayer, *Language Truth and Logic* 2nd edn (London: Victor Gollancz, 1946) 105–6.
[28] Ludwig Wittgenstein, *Philosophical Investigations* (Oxford: Blackwell Publishing, 1953), §§ 19, 23, 241, 226 (italics in original).
[29] Ibid., 223.
[30] For a sympathetic discussion of Wittgenstein's approach to rules of inference (referring to his *Remarks on the Foundations of Mathematics* rather than the quoted passages from the

When it comes to logic and mathematics, it is generally accepted that the language (English, French, Japanese, etc.) and broader cultural context in which an axiomatic system is set out, and in which consequences are derived, does not affect the validity of the reasoning. To borrow Wittgenstein's terminology, whatever exactly it is about human 'forms of life' that enables us to establish meaningful logical terms and thereby rules of inference that underpin valid arguments, these forms of life seem to be common across human communities.[31] But logic and mathematics are in some ways very simple and primitive elements of human experience, at least in their foundations (*negation, if ... then ...* reasoning, *counting, measurement*, etc.), and hence it may not be that surprising that they are common across human beings. When it comes to the key terms that figure in a rule of recognition, however, and hence to the rules of legal inference that (on this picture) would be implicit in them, we might expect a greater degree of variation in the relevant forms of life. Thus, in addition to necessarily being unexpressed, there is good reason to think that on the 'thick' picture of validation the rules of legal inference must be, in some sense, 'local' or 'parochial' rather than universal. That is not to say that different constitutional orders must be thought of as mutually incomprehensible Wittgensteinian lions, but on the 'thick' picture we might expect constitutional orders to differ from one another in their legal inferential practices in ways that do not emerge self-evidently from their written constitutional texts, and for reasons that would not figure in a typical catalogue of the elements of that legal order.[32] Hence we have good reason to think that, on the 'thick' Hartian conception of validation, every constitutional order necessarily includes an important invisible aspect.

Philosophical Investigation), which also relates this approach to the resolution of Lewis Carroll's puzzle, see A. B. Levison, 'Wittgenstein and Logical Laws' (1950) 14 *Philosophical Quarterly* 345, 348–51.

[31] For one account of these linguistic capacities in terms of common human cognitive capacities, see Stephen J. Barker, *Renewing Meaning: A Speech-Act Theoretic Approach* (Oxford: Clarendon Press, 2004), chapters 7 and 8.

[32] Brian Bix has rightly cautioned against overzealous use of Wittgensteinian argumentation to address questions that arise in the legal domain, which is quite unlike the mathematical and logical domains with which Wittgenstein was chiefly concerned: 'The Application (and Mis-Application) of Wittgenstein's Rule-Following Considerations to Legal Theory' in *Law, Language and Legal Determinacy* (1993), reprinted in Dennis Paterson *Wittgenstein and Law* (Ashgate, 2004). However, if one doubts that the relationship between the rule of recognition and rules of legal inference might resemble the relationship between logical terminology and logical rules of inference that is posited by the conventionalist tradition, it is not clear what other resources the Hartian has to draw upon to account for the content of the rules of legal inference, and their validation. Rather, the alternative seems to be to adopt the 'thin' picture.

This conclusion may seem commonplace or even trivial, because already well-established by scholarship on comparative law and legal cultures. It may nevertheless be of interest to see how a relatively mainstream analytic jurisprudential approach to the study of constitutional orders leads to the same conclusion.

5.4. 'THIN' VALIDATION AND INVISIBILITY

The 'thick' picture of validation discussed in the previous section is distinguished by the claim that even unexpressed laws – that is to say, laws not expressly or self-evidently stated by an authoritative source – must be validated by the rule of recognition. The 'thin' picture, by contrast, extends the demand for validation only to the authoritative sources themselves. When it comes to working out the laws that are stated by or follow from these sources, on the other hand,

> such argumentation does not itself require a rule of recognition to operate recursively upon its results. All it requires is a way of identifying the texts around which casuistry and interpretive argumentation will revolve.[33]

On the 'thin' picture, identifying the content of the law – including the content of the constitution and the other legal content that follows from it – will depend upon particularities of acceptable method. We can therefore expect that different legal cultures, with differing methodologies for deriving the law from texts, will be apt to draw very different conclusions about the law even if confronted with identical texts. For instance, in some legal cultures it may be considered permissible to reason back from the rules stated in a legal text

---

[33] Waldron, 'Who Needs Rules of Recognition' in Matthew Adler and Kenneth Einar Himma (eds.), *The Rule of Recognition and the U.S. Constitution* (Oxford: Oxford University Press, 2009), 349. Although in this essay Waldron does not use the terminology of 'thick' and 'thin', he clearly draws the distinction, and also expresses a preference for the 'thin' picture, when he asks (336) 'why did Hart think it plausible to talk about a fundamental rule for recognizing *rules* of law, as opposed to a rule for recognizing *sources* of (rules of) law? I know of no good answer'. Waldron also argues (332, 339–45, 348–9) that, once the focus is on *sources*, then rather than a rule of recognition our principle concern should be with the rule of change (i.e., the rule that governs the introduction of new authoritative sources into the system, and the cancellation of existing sources), which in a typical constitutional order will be the rule that governs the enactment of legislation and (at least in common law systems) the production of authoritative reports of decided cases. I think that this argument is a strong one (though Gardner disagrees: 'Can There Be a Written Constitution', Supra note 11, 176–8), but in this chapter I only note it.

to the principles that animate or underpin those rules, and then to treat those principles as self-standing parts of the law. But in others this is not a legitimate mode of determining legal (including constitutional) content.[34]

This already makes it evident that, on the 'thin' picture, the constitution will have a crucial invisible component that depends upon local context. But I want to develop this claim further, by showing how – even if common methodologies are adopted – there is nevertheless good reason to believe that there will be a crucial invisible element to the constitution which will depend upon particular social and political contexts.

Within a broadly positivist framework, the identification of the legal content of a legal text requires ascertaining the meaning and consequences of that text. There are various approaches to doing this; I will consider two, characterised by reference to ideas in the philosophy of language. My aim is for these two approaches to be (between them) sufficiently representative that what is true of them is at least plausible for interpretive methods in general.

5.4.1. *Communicative Approaches to Interpretation*

One relatively popular approach to the interpretation of legal texts, including constitutional ones, is what can be called a *communicative* approach: legal texts are understood as the authoritative communications of lawmakers.[35] One important aspect of this approach is its appeal to lawmakers' communicative intentions, and the context within which those intentions are formed and conveyed, to understand what it is that has been communicated.[36] Goldsworthy, for instance, emphasises the role that background assumptions

---

[34] E.g., in Australia, the impermissibility of such reasoning in the context of constitutional interpretation and application is established by the *Engineers' case* (*Amalgamated Society of Engineers v. Adelaide Steamship Co Ltd* (1920) 28 CLR 129) and *Lange v. Australian Broadcasting Corporation* (1997) 189 CLR 520.

[35] For insightful, though devastatingly critical, discussion of this approach see Greenberg, 'The Moral Impact Theory', Supra note 1; 'The Standard Picture', Supra note 1; Mark Greenberg, 'Legislation as Communication? Legal Interpretation and the Study of Linguistic Communication', in Andrei Marmor and Scott Soames (eds.) *Philosophical Foundations of Language and the Law* (Oxford: Oxford University Press, 2011).

[36] See for instance Larry Alexander, 'Constitutional Theories: A Taxonomy and (Implicit) Critique' (2014) 51 *San Diego Law Review* 623, 638–9; Jeff Goldsworthy, 'Implications in language, law and the constitution', in Geoffrey Lindell (ed.), *Future Directions in Australian Constitutional Law* (Leichardt: Federation Press, 1994). Alexander's exposition relies upon an intuitive notion of communication, while Goldsworthy draws upon Grice and Searle to develop a communicative account of the meaning of legal texts.

may play in establishing what has been communicated, or presupposed, by a legal text and hence what the law permits or requires.[37]

On this sort of approach, a constitutional (or other legal) text may have invisible legal *consequences* – unwritten permissions or requirements – which are the result of invisible elements of the constitution's *promulgation* – the background and assumptions which provided the context for the lawmakers' communication, and which thereby yield these invisible consequences. This context will vary with social and political circumstances in two ways: first, and obviously, differences in such circumstances are themselves differences in background that might therefore contribute in differences in what is communicated though not part of the visible text; second, understandings of what is or is not taken for granted in communication, and hence of what is or is not assumed or presupposed in communication, is itself something which can vary with culture (including particularities of legal culture) and which, when it varies, will lead to differences in the unwritten yet communicated legal content.

5.4.2. 'Realist' Approaches to Interpretation

Not all implications generated by a legal text, including a written constitution, need to be understood as the results of communicative intentions. It is possible to identify a category of implications that arise not as a result of lawmakers' intentions (and the context or background assumptions that shape or inform those intentions), but that arise as a result of the legal text containing terms whose reference is to be understood in what might be called 'objective' or 'realist' terms. I will give two examples of such implication that arise within the Australian constitutional context.

The *Australian Constitution* mandates that the members of the legislature shall be <u>directly chosen</u> by <u>the people</u>.[38] It is understood that the underlined phrases do not refer simply to whatever the lawmakers understood to count as a *direct choice*, and to whomever the lawmakers understood to be *the people*. Hence, if the experiences of social and political life reveal that a certain law, or a certain sort of administrative action, is a burden upon direct choice (e.g., by prohibiting the free communication among the people that is a necessary incident of genuinely choosing one's political representative) then that law or action will be unconstitutional, because it is at odds with the constitutional

---

[37] Ibid. For instance, background assumptions about the role that courts will play in declaring and enforcing the law may establish a constitutional role for judicial review of the validity of legislation, even if this is not expressly stated in the constitutional text.
[38] Sections 7, 24.

mandate.[39] Or, if a certain group of voters are without doubt members of *the people*, then a law which would disenfranchise them will be unconstitutional, because it is at odds with the constitutional mandate.[40] These consequences, which can properly be described as implications – they are constitutional constraints upon government action which are not expressly stated in the text – follow not from the intentions of the lawmakers,[41] but from their production of a text which talks about certain things (direct choices, people) and establishes certain requirements in relation to them.[42]

The second example begins with the mandate in the *Australian Constitution* that there shall exist a federal supreme court (the High Court of Australia) in which shall be vested the judicial power of the Commonwealth (i.e., federal judicial power),[43] and that this court shall have jurisdiction to hear appeals from the Supreme Court of any Australian state.[44] It is understood that when the constitution refers to *the judicial power of the Commonwealth*, and to a federal court that is to wield this power, these are not terms that get their content simply from lawmakers' subjective intentions or understandings in the use of such terms. Rather they refer to real phenomena, whose character must be properly understood in order to establish what the constitutional mandate requires.[45] This in turn generates, by way of implication, constraints upon the sort of functions that legislation may vest in the High Court, or in other bodies: the High Court cannot be vested with functions that would be at odds with its character as a court; and other bodies which are not courts cannot be vested with functions that would be tantamount to the exercise of the judicial power of the Commonwealth.[46]

The establishment of a judicial hierarchy, with the High Court exercising appellate jurisdiction over state courts, generates a further implication in a similar fashion. The vesting of functions in a state court, by way of state

---

[39] See e.g., *Lange v. Australian Broadcasting Corporation* (1997) 189 CLR 520.

[40] See e.g., *Roach v. Electoral Commissioner* (2007) 233 CLR 16.

[41] Other than perhaps their linguistic intentions, to use certain referring terms (namely, *direct choice* and *people*).

[42] For a fuller discussion, see Patrick Emerton, 'Political freedoms and entitlements in the Australian Constitution – An example of referential intentions yielding unexpected legal consequences' (2010) 38 *Federal Law Review* 169.

[43] Section 71.

[44] Section 73.

[45] See e.g., *Waterside Workers' Federation of Australia v. J W Alexander Ltd* (1918) 25 CLR 434, 451 (per Barton J): 'Whether persons were Judges, whether tribunals were Courts, and whether they exercised what is now called judicial power, depended and depends on substance and not on mere name.'

[46] See e.g., *Boilermakers' case* (R v. Kirby; Ex parte Boilermakers' Society of Australia) (1956) 94 CLR 254; affirmed in *Attorney-General (Cth) v. The Queen* (1957) 95 CLR 529.

legislation, engages, in a prospective way, the High Court's exercise of the judicial power of the Commonwealth. This is because either (a) the High Court may be apt to hear appeals in respect of the decisions issuing from the exercise of that function, or (b) the exercise of that function may not be apt for appeal to the High Court (e.g., if the function of the state courts is not an exercise of judicial power), meaning that vesting that function in the state court will shape the scope and character of the relationship between the courts in the constitutionally mandated hierarchy.[47] The constitutional consequence is that state legislatures may not vest functions in their courts which would change those courts in ways that would undermine or distort this judicial hierarchy that has the exercise of the judicial power of the Commonwealth at its apex.[48] This constitutional limitation upon the power of state legislatures is not expressly stated: it arises by way of implication. But the implication is not the result of lawmakers' intentions, but rather the textual mandate that a certain judicial hierarchy shall exist.[49]

This sort of realist approach to the meaning of the language of natural science is well-known.[50] Its application to legal language, which refers to social, political and institutional phenomena such as *direct choice, the people, judicial power, courts, an appellate hierarchy having a certain court exercising a certain sort of power at its apex*, etc., is less commonly discussed by philosophers of language.[51] But as a matter of practice, it is implicit in the methodology that

---

[47] See the remarks of Gummow J in *Kable v. Director of Public Prosecutions (NSW)* (1996) 189 CLR 51, 142–3.

[48] See e.g., *Kable v. Director of Public Prosecutions (NSW)* (1996) 189 CLR 51; *Kirk v. Industrial Court of New South Wales* (2010) 239 CLR 531.

[49] The implication is reinforced by the constitutionally-stated power of the federal legislature to vest state courts with federal jurisdiction (sections 71, 77), which establishes a further connection between state courts and the exercise of the judicial power of the Commonwealth: see e.g., *Kable v. Director of Public Prosecutions (NSW)* (1996) 189 CLR 51.

[50] See in particular Hilary Putnam, 'Dreaming and Depth Grammar' in R. J. Butler (ed.), *Analytical Philosophy* (Oxford: Basil Blackwell, 1962) 218–21; 'The Meaning of "Meaning"', in *Mind, Language and Reality: Philosophical Papers, Volume 2* (Cambridge: Cambridge University Press, 1975).

[51] For the application of such an approach to social and institutional, though not distinctively legal, phenomena see Sally Haslanger, 'What Are We Talking About? The Semantics and Politics of Social Kinds' (2005) 20 *Hypatia*, 10. The rejection of such an approach in the jurisprudential context by Jules Coleman and Ori Simchen, 'Law' (2003) 9 *Legal Theory* 1 rests on a misunderstanding. Central to the realist approach is the drawing of a sharp separation between *meaning* and *knowledge*: it is possible to use words to refer to things which one doesn't fully understand (thus, for instance, the ancient Greeks were able to refer to *water* even though they didn't fully understand its nature, believing it to be an element rather than a compound). It follows from this possibility that some language-users will have greater expertise in identifying what counts as an instance of (say) *water* than others (e.g., chemists may be particularly good at this). Coleman and Simchen infer from this that such experts therefore must have some sort of special

underpins the generation of implications in the manner just illustrated by these Australian examples. The characteristics of the phenomena referred to, from which the implications in question flow, are not facts belonging to the natural world but rather facts about history, politics and the realities of social and institutional life.

Where this sort of methodology is adopted, the invisible constitutional content that it generates will depend upon two factors which are likely to be affected by social and political context and differences of legal cultures. First, even when words are used which are (on their face) the same (or are synonymous, in virtue of etymology, as accepted in standard dictionaries of translation, etc.), they may not be properly understood as having the same reference in the 'objective' or 'realist' sense. When used in different constitutional or legal contexts, by lawmakers coming from different political and legal cultures, the same words may not be literally co-referring but rather may refer to importantly different social/political states of affairs. For instance, the nature of the phenomena referred to by terms such as *judicial power*, or *court*, or *appellate hierarchy* is likely to be different in different constitutional orders – because these are phenomena whose characteristics are shaped by the particularities of the history of law and its institutions – and hence the very same text as occurs in the Australian constitution could be expected to yield quite different invisible consequences if transplanted to another context.[52]

Second, different legal systems or legal cultures may employ or permit differing methodologies (e.g., of leading evidence, of taking judicial notice, of accepting executive certificates, etc.) for determining the nature and characteristics of the phenomena referred to by constitutional texts.[53] These differences of methodology may mean that even when particular words or phrases

---

authority to establish the *meaning* of the word 'water' (18–19), and they go on to argue that the word 'law', and other legal language, is not such that its meaning is fixed by experts, and hence cannot be analysed in realist terms. But this inference is erroneous, resting on the very conflation of knowledge and meaning that the realist approach eschews.

[52] This is a very different point from the contrast often drawn between *concept* and *conception*: it is not a point about different sorts of mental or semantic entities falling under the same word, but rather is a metaphysical point, that words which are from the lexicographic point of view synonyms may nevertheless, in differing context of production, refer to importantly different things, particularly when the 'things' in question are extremely complex social states of affairs to which participants' epistemic access is less than fully transparent.

[53] For instance, in *Roach v. Electoral Commissioner* (2007) 233 CLR 162, the Australian High Court referred to the work of historians to help understand the reference of *the people*: e.g., 194–5 [69] (Gummow, Kirby and Crennan JJ). In *Rowe v. Electoral Commissioner* (2010) 243 CLR 1, the Court relied upon data produced by the Australian Electoral Commission to help ascertain details of the manner in which members of the people ensure they are able to participate in the direct choice by being registered on the electoral roll: e.g., 24 [37] (French CJ); 56 [147] (Gummow and Bell JJ).

are literally co-referring in different constitutions, differing conclusions might legitimately be reached about what the nature and characteristics of those referents are, and hence about the unwritten constitutional content that is generated by reference to them. Thus we once again see the conclusion that the constitution includes elements that are invisible in the sense both of being unwritten, and not being phenomena ordinarily thought of as legal phenomena.

As with the previous section's discussion of 'thick' validation, it may seem commonplace to conclude that differences in methodology and practices of argumentation across political cultures are likely to result in different understandings of the implicated content that arises from a particular constitutional text. But the point of this section has been to show that a conclusion of this sort follows even within a mainstream analytical and positivist framework that attempts to regiment legal interpretation within sophisticated theories of language and linguistic reasoning. The conclusion of this line of argument, therefore, is that we should not expect to see any sort of uniformity or convergence in constitutional outcomes, even if there is convergence in these analytic methodologies, at least as long as different constitutions operate in the context of differing legal cultures with different background assumptions, different political/economic cultures, and different methodologies for taking evidence about or otherwise determining the nature of the referents of the key terms occurring in constitutional texts.

5.5. CONCLUSION: CONSTITUTIONAL DIFFERENCE AND CONSTITUTIONAL HOMOGENISATION

The chapter has considered a variety of analytic jurisprudential accounts of law, both anti-positivist and broadly Hartian. It has shown that, on each such account, we have good reason to think that any constitution necessarily has elements that are invisible both in the sense of being unwritten, and being dependent upon the local social and political context in ways that go beyond any typical catalogue of the legal phenomena within a society.

This leads to a further, somewhat tentative conjecture: to the extent that there is an increasing convergence or uniformity of constitutional outcomes across legal systems, the explanation for this is likely to be that differences of legal or political culture and expectation, and more broadly different forms of social life, are being eroded. On the anti-positivist picture, such erosion of differences would result in the moral consequences of promulgating legal texts becoming increasingly similar across societies; on the 'thick' Hartian picture, it would have the same result for the rules of legal inference which are underpinned in part by forms of social life; and on the 'thin' Hartian picture, it would have the same result for the bases for making inferences about the meaning of legal texts whether understood to be shared background and expectations (in the manner of communicative theories), or the social world as an object of reference (in the manner of realist theories). That is to say, constitutional convergence, on this line of thought, would tend to be better understood as a non-rational process of cultural homogenisation than as a rational process of universalising valid legal methodologies.

6

Interim Constitutions and the Invisible Constitution

Caitlin Goss

6.1. INTRODUCTION

Interim constitutions are adopted as deliberately temporary documents which are to be replaced by constitutional texts that are intended to be permanent. They are typically adopted where there is an agreed need for constitutional change, but a lack of agreement as to what that constitutional change should look like. The theme of the 'invisible constitution' is of particular relevance to interim texts, which tend to respond to and generate invisible or unwritten features not only during the time of their operation, but even after they have been replaced. Interim constitutions can influence the nature of both the visible and invisible constitution that exists not only in the interim era, but also after the interim constitution has been replaced by a successor 'permanent' constitution. This happens in two key ways.

First, the very process of enacting an interim constitution creates the possibility for long-term influences upon constitutional development. It is clear that interim texts may control successor texts through legal requirements about what is to be included, as demonstrated through the use of 'Constitutional Principles' in the South African interim text. However what may be less obvious is that even where the drafters of the second constitutional text are not bound to readopt aspects of the interim text, drafting or procedural provisions and path-dependencies can mean that the interim text has a significant long-term influence on the constitutional law of the state.

Second, interim constitutions may be interpreted, during the period of their operation, in expansive ways that respond to or give rise to non-textual meaning; moreover, these expansive judicial interpretations of interim texts may persist beyond their temporal duration, such that the invisible interim constitution becomes a part of the invisible permanent constitution. In this chapter, I highlight the ways in which courts in interim eras may be particularly responsive to non-textual features and therefore also more likely to create a broader 'invisible' constitution.

There are several reasons for considering the theme of the invisible constitution in connection with interim constitutional texts. I define interim constitutions as those constitutional texts that are deliberately – and explicitly – temporary in duration. That is, they provide for their obsolescence and replacement by a future, theoretically permanent, constitution. The reason for defining the category in this way, rather than looking at short-lived constitutions or transitional constitutions generally, is that the very idea of a supreme constitutional text which is intended to expire disrupts the traditional conception of constitutions as permanent and stable.

In 'On the Authority and Interpretation of Constitutions: Some Preliminaries', Joseph Raz provides a seven-part definition of a constitution in the 'thick sense', according to which a constitution is: constitutive of a legal system; stable, at 'least in aspiration'; written; superior law; justiciable; entrenched, i.e., more difficult to change than other law; and expressive of a common ideology.[1] The conception of constitutions as stable, 'at least in aspiration' and 'entrenched' reflects a widely held belief that however long a national constitution in fact endures, it is typically intended to be permanent or indefinite in duration.[2] For many scholars, part of what makes constitutional law different to ordinary law is the way it claims supremacy and permanency. Interim constitutions, which achieve many of the features of Raz's definition, nonetheless eschew (at least to begin with) aspirations of stability and entrenchment in the ordinary sense. It is this theoretical tension that makes interim constitutions an interesting area for further study. Moreover, the term is used widely in both legal and policy discussions without a clear sense of definition and interim constitutions have recently been adopted or proposed in a number of transitional environments. As such, I believe that the category requires further elucidation and comparative study.

The approach I adopt is explicitly formalistic or *ex ante*; I address those constitutions that are intended to be temporary, regardless of their ultimate duration. Another approach would be to adopt an *ex post* view of temporary constitutions and to study those texts that end up being temporary documents that are replaced after a redrafting process by a second constitution. Variations of this approach have been adopted by scholars such as Andrew Arato, who

---

[1] Joseph Raz, 'On the Authority and Interpretations of Constitutions: Some Preliminaries,' in Larry Alexander (ed.), *Constitutionalism: Philosophical Foundations* (Cambridge: Cambridge University Press, 2001), 153.
[2] 'For if a constitution is to be permanent, all parts of the state must wish that it should exist and the same arrangements be maintained': Aristotle, *Politics* IX 350 BC, cited in Raz, Supra note 1. See also Vicki C. Jackson, 'What's in a Name? Reflections on Timing, Naming, and Constitution-Making' (2007) 49 *William and Mary Law Review* 1249.

writes of two-phased 'post-sovereign constitution-making', and Vicki Jackson.[3] Jackson divides post-conflict constitutions into those involving 'a "quick clean break" from a prior, discredited regime' as in post-war Japan; those that 'emerge from a more incremental process of constitutional change, occurring ... over a period that may be closer to a decade' as in Hungary or Poland; and the 'relatively recent innovation' of transitional or interim constitutions, as in South Africa.[4]

However, for the purposes of this chapter, I believe that the appropriate starting point is to begin with a more formalistic definition: to include within the scope of analysis texts that purport to be interim constitutions and then to analyse the category as a whole. Not all of the constitutions I study meet the requirements of Arato's post-sovereign model, and Jackson's incremental versus interim approach divides some interim cases into different groups. However, I believe there is considerable value in charting the group of *intentionally* temporary interim constitutions and finding not only points of similarity, but of difference amongst the group, even as they develop. It is valuable to note that the 1989 constitution of Hungary began in a similar way to those of Albania and Poland but they charted markedly different courses, as the Hungarian constitution endured until the Fundamental Law of Hungary came into force in 2012.[5] Just as constitutions that are intended to be permanent often falter at an early stage, so interim constitutions may end up becoming permanent or long-lasting. The formalist approach to defining interim constitutions may be of particular relevance in the context of the 'invisible' constitution; in what way do constitutions that are intended to be temporary end up having permanent effects? I argue that interim constitutions cannot be viewed as mere placeholders, whose effects may be temporally contained. Interim texts must be regarded as key decisions taken at critical junctures in a state's constitutional history, capable of creating path dependencies that guide constitutional development on a long-term basis. This understanding, I submit, should influence the way that interim constitutions are drafted and adopted.

Before developing these ideas, it is necessary first to develop a working definition of the 'invisible constitution' and to define and contextualise interim constitutions. In the first section of this chapter, I deal with these preliminary, definitional issues. In the second section, I explore each of the ways in which interim constitutions can generate unwritten or invisible features. In the third,

---

[3] Andrew Arato, 'Post-sovereign Constitution-Making in Hungary: After Success, Partial Failure, Now What?' (2010) 26 *South African Journal on Human Rights* 21.
[4] Jackson, Supra note 2, 1260.
[5] *Fundamental Law of Hungary (Constitution of Hungary)* 2011.

concluding section, I reflect upon what this analysis tells us about the nature of interim constitutions and about the concept of the 'invisible constitution'.

6.2. DEFINING TERMS

6.2.1. Defining the Constitution: Visible and Invisible

The definition of the *invisible* constitution depends upon the already vexed question of defining the *visible* constitution. In turn, the definition of the *visible* constitution is interconnected with deep questions about how to define constitutions and how to interpret constitutions. The definition of such terms is far beyond the scope of this chapter; I do however attempt to raise a series of questions and to advance some thoughts about possible ways of approaching these terms.

In *The Invisible Constitution*, Laurence Tribe describes the 'visible' Constitution as 'the Constitution's text'; with the associated rules and judicial interpretation and practices forming the 'invisible Constitution'.[6] Rosalind Dixon and Adrienne Stone have described this as the 'extra-constitutional' understanding of the invisible constitution, where extra-constitutional sources buttress and expand upon the visible, textual basis of the constitution.[7] The invisible constitution on this 'conceptual' formulation might include, depending on where one draws the boundaries, judicial decisions involving constitutional interpretation, texts of constitutional or quasi-constitutional status and/or unarguable constitutional facts or conventions. As Dixon and Stone have observed, the way that one approaches or defines the invisible constitution will be deeply connected to foundational questions about the proper methods of judicial interpretation of constitutional texts.

Another approach that falls within this conceptual understanding of the invisible constitution is that adopted by Chief Justice Sólyom of the Hungarian Constitutional Court, in a series of decisions in the 1990s. This approach (discussed in Section 6.2.2) posits a kind of ideal or true invisible constitution, which reflects ongoing constitutional values, regardless of the actual text of the constitution.

The second way of conceiving of the invisible constitution is to adopt a more sociological or empirical approach, in which the invisible constitution might be comprised of those things that, without legal status, affect and determine

---

[6] Laurence H. Tribe, *The Invisible Constitution* (Oxford: Oxford University Press, 2008), 2.
[7] Rosalind Dixon and Adrienne Stone (eds.) *The Invisible Constitution in Comparative Perspective* (Cambridge: Cambridge University Press, 2017), 1.

constitutional development. This process is observable through a close study of the working of interim constitutional texts. A study of interim constitutions reveals that they are adopted as deliberately temporary texts, but often have through a variety of invisible means, permanent effects on their successor constitutions and on the long-term development of constitutional law and culture in their jurisdictions. This is the result of both deliberate decision-making and of unintentional, path-dependent consequences.

The precise definition of – and the relationship between – these two sets of approaches is beyond the scope of this chapter. However, I suspect that the two approaches are closely interrelated, and may even be interdependent in some ways. In order to demonstrate this, I will briefly discuss John Gardner's work on a related question.

In his article 'Can There Be a Written Constitution?', John Gardner observes that the Constitution of the United Kingdom contains 'no procedure for its own deliberate amendment ... [and] what determines the status of certain law as constitution is its reception into constitutional law by certain law-applying officials, principally the Courts'.[8] As Gardner contends, this may be true for every legal system; that 'its so-called written parts are only parts of it because of their reception into the unwritten law that is made by the customs and decisions of the courts'.[9] The 'heretical' view he ultimately advances is that constitutions 'cannot be, or be contained in, documents'.[10] There are two aspects to his argument: first, the constitution of a nation is not exhausted by its text. This much seems uncontroversial, and it reflects Dixon and Stone's observation that unwritten aspects of constitutions can nonetheless be highly 'visible'. But the 'heretical' aspect of his argument is that even provisions that are constitutionally enshrined are not truly constitutional unless they have been recognised as such by 'customs and ... courts'. He provides the example of a provision in Article V of the United States Constitution (which appears to allow for the 1787 Constitutional Convention) that has never been used, or adjudicated upon; he argues that its status is uncertain, even though it has never been formally revoked. The degree to which this part of the Constitution remains *constitutional* depends upon its reception and treatment as such.

---

[8] John Gardner, 'Can There Be a Written Constitution?' in Leslie Green and Brian Leiter (eds.) *Oxford Studies in Philosophy of Law*, vol. 1 (Oxford: Oxford University Press, 2011), 165.
[9] Ibid., 170.
[10] Ibid.

To draw this back to the invisible constitution, the question of how to identify which extra-constitutional features are *in fact* part of the 'invisible' constitution must be resolved through Hartian questions about recognition and the treatment of certain features *as* constitutional.[11] Moreover, the more one approaches a broader understanding of constitutional meaning (as in Emerton's approach) and the further away one moves from a textualist or originalist understanding (as per Solum and Goldsworthy), the more the two questions collapse into one. That is, the more that we include in the invisible constitution, the more work that must be done on an empirical basis to define it. Perhaps the key difference between the two groups is one of emphasis or purpose: the conceptual approaches attempt to answer *normative* questions about what should count as part of the invisible constitution; the sociological or empirical approaches attempt to answer *descriptive* questions about what in fact counts as or affects the composition of the invisible constitution and thereby the visible constitution.

Finally, I want to make the point that visibility and invisibility, and indeed inclusion in either constitution so defined, may be a question of degree and as Dixon and Stone have observed, of timing.[12] Certain features of a constitution will become more visible or less visible or more or less *salient*, depending upon their reception by constitutionally relevant actors.[13] Dixon and Stone observe that if we disconnect the visible constitution from the notion of the written constitution, then it may become difficult to see what could be left as 'invisible'. They observe that in countries like New Zealand 'something more will generally be required for unwritten or extra-textual sources to be truly "hidden" in nature: such influences must be so deep, strategic, or implicit ... to make them non-observable to ordinary constitutional actors'.[14]

It might be that the 'invisible constitution' comprises the multifarious factors that *can* influence or determine the visible constitution; once such a factor *does* influence or determine the content of the visible constitution then it too is rendered visible. In this chapter, I attempt to highlight the ways that interim constitutions respond to and create invisible constitutional features that can determine the form and content of both the *visible* (or textual) constitution and the *invisible* constitution.

---

[11] Discussed in Gardner, Supra note 8, 173–5.
[12] Dixon and Stone, Supra note 7, 3.
[13] I am grateful here for the comments of Dr Lael K. Weiss at *The Invisible Constitution: Comparative Perspectives Roundtable* (hosted by the International Association of Constitutional Law, Melbourne Law School, 2–3 May 2016).
[14] Dixon and Stone, Supra note 7, 3.

6.2.2. Defining the Interim Constitution

The idea of a constitution as ordinarily being a permanent document appears as early as in Aristotle's *Politics*, and is evident in the debates surrounding the adoption of the oldest extant constitution, in the USA. Alexander Hamilton argued that 'Constitutions should consist only of general provisions: the reason is, that they must necessarily be permanent, and that they cannot calculate for the possible change of things'.[15] Arguing against the prevailing understanding of constitutions as permanent texts, Thomas Jefferson contended that every nineteen years, each generation should rewrite a nation's constitution, deriding those who 'look at constitutions with sanctimonious reverence, and deem them like the ark of the covenant, too sacred to be touched'.[16] On the basis of their comparative constitutional analysis, Elkins, Ginsburg and Melton observe that nineteen years is the average life expectancy of a national constitution, demonstrating that regardless of the intention of permanency most constitutions are short-lived in duration.[17]

Moving beyond the theoretical, what is meant by the claim that constitutions are intended to last permanently or indefinitely? Classical constitutions do not, after all, typically expressly state that they are intended to be permanent.[18] Rather, to describe ordinary constitutions as being permanent or indefinite is to say that their founders envision, *ceteris paribus*, that they will continue as enacted, unless disrupted by an extra-legal force; no legitimate means is established by or implied in the constitution of effecting wholesale constitutional replacement. Additionally, a number of interim constitutions refer to permanent[19] or final[20] constitutions, signalling the intent that their successor documents be permanent or indefinite in duration. Other interim constitutions simply refer to the adoption 'of the Constitution'[21] or 'of the new

---

[15] Alexander Hamilton, in Jonathan Elliot (ed.) *The Debates in the Several State Conventions on the Adoption of the Federal Constitution, as Recommended by the General Convention at Philadelphia, in 1787*, 2nd edn (Washington, DC: Jonathan Elliot, 1836), Volume II, 344.

[16] Zachary Elkins, Tom Ginsburg, and James Melton, *The Endurance of National Constitutions* (Cambridge: Cambridge University Press, 2009), 1.

[17] Ibid., 2.

[18] Cf *Constitution of Iraq 2005*. In the Preamble, the text describes 'this permanent Constitution'.

[19] *Constitutional Declaration of the National Transitional Council of Libya 2011*, Preamble; *Transitional Constitution of the Republic of South Sudan 2011*, ch. II; *Interim National Constitution of the Republic of the Sudan 2005*, s 226(8); *Constitution of the United Arab Emirates 1971*, Preamble, Article 144(3),(4).

[20] *Interim Constitution of the Republic of South Africa 1993*.

[21] *Law on the Major Constitutional Provisions (Albania) 1991*, Article 44(1).

constitution'[22] arguably implying that the difference between the interim text and the more final text is the very temporariness of the transitional document.

In the course of my analysis of interim constitutions in the modern era,[23] I have studied the temporary constitutions of: Albania,[24] Poland,[25] South Africa,[26] the Democratic Republic of the Congo,[27] Iraq,[28] Sudan, Thailand[29] and Nepal.[30] Additionally, I studied the 'border case' of Hungary: the 1989 text of the Constitution of Hungarian[31] was an amended version of the 1949 Communist Constitution.[32] In its 'Preamble', it is stated that the text is to operate 'for the period before the enactment of the new Constitution of the country'. Thus the Constitution is formally a temporary one, even though it remained in place (in a heavily amended fashion) until the Fundamental Law of 2011. Many, though certainly not all scholars writing on the period, have referred to the 1989 text as having initially been intended to be temporary.[33]

---

[22] *Constitutional Provisions Continued in Force Pursuant to Article 77 of the Constitutional Act of 17th October 1992 on the Mutual Relations Between the Legislative and Executive Institutions of the Republic of Poland and on Local Self-Government, Repealing the Constitution of the Republic of Poland of 22nd July 1952*, 1992, Preamble.

[23] I have attempted to review most of the interim constitutions adopted between 1989 and 2010, and have not included analysis of the more recent interim constitutions adopted in Egypt and Libya due to the recency and fluidity of those transitions. See *Constitutional Declaration (Egypt)* 2011; *Constitutional Declaration of the National Transitional Council of Libya*, note 19.

[24] *Law on Major Constitutional Provisions* 1991.

[25] *Constitutional Act of 17th October 1992, on the Mutual Relations Between the Legislative and Executive Institutions of the Republic of Poland and on Local Self-Government Dziennik Ustaw Nr 84 Poz 426* 1992.

[26] *Interim Constitution of the Republic of South Africa* 1993.

[27] *Constitution de la transition de la République Démocratique du Congo* 2003 ('Constitution of the Transition').

[28] *Law of Administration for the State of Iraq for the Transitional Period* 2004 (Iraqi National Council).

[29] *Interim National Constitution of the Republic of the Sudan*, note 19.

[30] *Constitution of the Kingdom of Thailand (Interim Edition) of BE 2549* 2006.

[31] Act No. XXXI of 1989 (Act No. XX of 1949 (as amended)) (1989 Constitution of Hungary).

[32] Act No. XX of 1949 (1949 Constitution of Hungary).

[33] See e.g., Rudolf L. Tőkés, 'Institution Building in Hungary: Analytical Issues and Constitutional Models, 1989–1990' in András Bozóki (ed.) *The Roundtable Talks of 1989: The Genesis of Hungarian Democracy: Analysis and Documents* (Budapest: Central European University Press, 2002) 123, 124, 126, 128, 130, 132, 133 http://hdl.handle.net/2027/heb.08625.0001.001; Andrew Arato, 'The Roundtables, Democratic Institutions and the Problem of Justice' in András Bozóki (ed.) *The Roundtable Talks of 1989: The Genesis of Hungarian Democracy: Analysis and Documents* (Budapest: Central European University Press, 2002) 230–1. http://hdl.handle.net/2027/heb.08625.0001.001; Catherine Dupré, *Importing the Law in Post-Communist Transitions: The Hungarian Constitutional Court and the Right to Human Dignity* (Oxford: Hart Publishing, 2003) 31–2, 34, 162; Zoltán Miklósi, 'Constitution-Making, Competition and Cooperation' in Gábor Attila Tóth (ed.) *Constitution for a Disunited Nation: On Hungary's 2011 Fundamental*

Dupré argues that

> it was understood that it would be *only an interim constitution* registering the concessions made by the ruling party during the Round Tables negotiations and that it would be *replaced by a new constitution* to be adopted by the parliament due to be elected in spring 1990.[34]

The matter was revived in the early 1990s, and a special parliamentary commission was created with a view to drafting a new constitution. Each of these constitutional review projects failed, however, and the momentum for constitutional replacement fell away; for many, the Hungarian constitution was in no way *viewed* as temporary in the 1990s. However the initial formal inclusion, in addition to the discussion of the 1989 constitution as an interim text is, I believe, sufficient to include it as a kind of border case.[35]

6.2.3. How Interim Constitutions Work: A Few Key Features

Interim constitutions are united by the formal characteristic of stipulating that they will be replaced by another constitution. In some cases, there is little detail as to how this will occur; the Preamble of the 1992 Polish *Small Constitution* states that it was passed '[f]or the purpose of improving the activity of the supreme authorities of the State, pending the passing of a new Constitution of the Republic of Poland ...'.[36] In Nepal, a more structured time

---

Law (Budapest: Central European University Press, 2012) 59; Márta Dezső, A. Vincze and B. Vissy, 'Part I: Sources of Constitutional Law' in Márta Dezső (ed.) *Constitutional Law in Hungary* (The Netherlands: Kluwer Law International, 2010), 59 [82].

[34] Dupré, Supra note 33, 32 (emphasis added).
[35] Note that in contrast, I do not consider the German Basic Law of 1990 (*Basic Law for the Federal Republic of Germany* (*Grundgesetz für die Bundesrepublik Deutschland*) (rev 2012) 1949) the revised version of the 1949 West German Basic Law *The Constitution of the German Democratic Republic* (*Die Verfassung der Deutschen Demokratischen Republik* 1949). This is for several reasons: first, that Article was simply a continuing provision of the 1949 Law. Second, it is arguable that the language of Article 146 of the German Basic Law was permissive of a successor text, rather than stipulating that one would be adopted. Third, language from the 1949 text referring to a 'transitional period' was removed in the 1990 text. See Arthur Benz, 'A Forum of Constitutional Deliberation? A Critical Analysis of the Joint Constitutional Commission' in Klaus H. Goetz and Peter J. Cullen (eds.) *Constitutional Policy in Unified Germany* (London: Routledge, 2013), 104; Donald P. Kommers and Russell A. Miller, *The Constitutional Jurisprudence of the Federal Republic of Germany* 3rd edn (Durham: Duke University Press, 2012) 686.
[36] *Constitutional Act of 17th October 1992, on the Mutual Relations Between the Legislative and Executive Institutions of the Republic of Poland and on Local Self-Government Dziennik Ustaw Nr 84 Poz 426*, Supra note 25, Preamble.

frame was adopted, with a Constitutional Assembly charged with the task of producing the draft of a final constitution by 28 May 2010, a deadline that was not met by the Assembly.

Interim texts may be adopted for a variety of reasons, including the desire to reduce or avoid the decision costs and error costs that could come with drafting a constitution in a potentially volatile context, in a compressed time period, as discussed by Rosalind Dixon and Tom Ginsburg in relation to deferral in constitutional design.[37]

Typically, interim constitutions are adopted by unelected negotiating groups or round tables, and then followed by a longer phase of drafting – often more inclusive of the people – for the permanent constitution. Another feature of interim constitutions is that they are often – as with the constitution of the United Kingdom – not encapsulated in a singular canonical text. It is often the case that a series of constitutional or quasi-constitutional texts comprise the written constitution. This is seen in the Polish transition[38] and in Iraq, through the United Nations Security Council Resolutions that had constitutional effect enabling or supporting the *Transitional Administrative Law* ('*TAL*') of 2004.[39] The 2003 Transitional Constitution of the Democratic Republic of the Congo and the 2005 Interim Constitution of the Republic of Sudan existed alongside peace agreements that enjoyed constitutional status.[40] The multiplicity of texts that exist in these interim periods reflects several factors, including the political upheaval that is often present at the drafting of interim texts and a lack of clarity around amendment or replacement procedures relating to the previous constitution.

---

[37] Rosalind Dixon and Tom Ginsburg, 'Deciding Not to Decide: Deferral in Constitutional Design,' (2011) 9 *International Journal of Constitutional Law* 636.

[38] *Constitutional Provisions Continued in Force Pursuant to Article 77 of the Constitutional Act of 17th October 1992 on the Mutual Relations Between the Legislative and Executive Institutions of the Republic of Poland and on Local Self-Government, Repealing the Constitution of the Republic of Poland of 22nd July 1952*, note 22; *Constitutional Act of 23rd April 1992, on the Procedure for Preparing and Enacting a Constitution for the Republic of Poland Dziennik Ustaw Nr 61 Poz 251 1992.*

[39] UNSC Res 1483 (22 May 2003) UN Doc S/RES/1483; UNSC Res 1511 (16 October 2003) S/RES/1511; UNSC Res 1546 (8 June 2004) S/RES/1546. SCR 1483; 1511; 1546.

[40] *Global and Inclusive Agreement on Transition in The Democratic Republic of the Congo, Inter-Congolese Dialogue, Political Negotiations on the Peace Process and on Transition in the DRC 2002; The Comprehensive Peace Agreement Between The Government of The Republic of The Sudan and the Sudan People's Liberation Movement/Sudan People's Liberation Army 2005.*

6.3. INTERIM CONSTITUTIONS AND LINKS TO THE INVISIBLE CONSTITUTION

In this section I explore the ways in which interim constitutions can generate an 'invisible constitution' or invisible constitutional features. In studying the effects of interim constitutions, I have identified two key ways in which interim constitutions generate unwritten constitutional features: first, interim constitutions can strongly influence their successor constitutions, through methods other than binding (or 'visible') pre-commitments. Second, judicial decisions in the interim period can respond to and generate invisible constitutional features, some of which may persist in the post-interim era.

This argument reflects a straightforward fact: although interim constitutions are (intentionally) temporary, they have permanent effects on ongoing constitutional arrangements. This is not as simple as observing that any law may have enduring effects. Rather I contend that because of the circumstances in which interim constitutions are adopted, and the kinds of claims that interim constitutions make, they are particularly prone to having considerable long-term effects on constitutional law and culture.

Interim constitutions are typically adopted at *critical junctures* in a polity. Critical junctures have been defined by Giovanni Capoccia and R. Daniel Kelemen as '*relatively* short periods of time during which there is a *substantially* heightened probability that agents' choices will affect the outcome of interest'.[41] Capoccia and Kelemen note that in emphasising the 'probability that actors' choices will affect outcomes decreases after the critical juncture, this definition suggests that their choices during the critical juncture trigger a path-dependent process that constrains future choices'.[42] Interim constitutions are typically adopted at times that can easily be described as critical junctures, moments in which 'agents face a broader than typical range of feasible options' and where great change is possible.[43] Many of the observations about the potential for interim texts to lead to longer-term 'invisible' constitutional readings relate to the critical juncture in which such temporary texts were adopted.

6.3.1. The Interim Text Endures through the Permanent Text

In his paper on 'Temporary Constitutions', Ozan Varol advances the idea of 'burden shifting':

---

[41] Giovanni Capoccia and R. Daniel Kelemen, 'The Study of Critical Junctures: Theory, Narrative, and Counterfactuals in Historical Institutionalism,' (2007) 59 *World Politics* 341, 348.
[42] Ibid.
[43] Ibid.

> In a durable constitution, the opponents of a constitutional provision bear the burden of amendment or repeal ... In contrast ... the proponents of a temporary constitution or constitutional provision bear the burden of reenacting it following its sunset. This change in the default rule, and the attendant shift in the burden, generates both benefits and costs for constitutionalism that remain underexplored in the literature.[44]

On this analysis, the burden of re-enactment of a provision falls on those who seek to re-enact unless, as Varol acknowledges, there is no clear sunset clause on the temporary text or provision.[45] In that case, a temporary text may lapse, or 'fail' into permanence. However, I submit that a given provision in a temporary text often sets up a powerful default *position* or assumption about what kind of provision will be enacted on that topic in the permanent text, even if the default *burden* falls on its proponents to re-enact it.

I do not seek to argue that interim constitutions predetermine all or even most of the controversial issues in constitutional transitions; many key decisions will be made during the interim era. However, I believe it is still worthwhile identifying the ways in which features of the interim constitution which are *written*, but whose authority and permanency is *unwritten*, endure into the post-interim era.

First, in addition to content restraints (such as the South African Constitutional Principles, discussed in Section 6.2.2) that textually bind successor permanent constitutions, procedural provisions can increase the odds that aspects of the interim constitution will be replicated in the final constitution.[46] Interestingly, while a high degree of procedural control over the drafting process is often associated with high levels of similarity with the final text (as in South Africa), the converse is sometimes also true. The *Small Constitution* of Poland was not a singular document above all others and did not purport to control the text of its successor. The procedure ultimately adopted in subsequent legislation allowed for a multiplicity of constitutional drafts and drafting processes.[47] However, this very different approach created a result similar to that in South Africa. Multiple drafts were tabled between 1992 and 1997 and the ensuing confusion and proliferation of constitutional approaches led to a coalescing around a document on substantially similar terms as the interim text. Various individual provisions may be identified as being identical or broadly similar to

---

[44] Ozan O. Varol, 'Temporary Constitutions' (2014) 102 *California Law Review* 409, 417–18.
[45] Ibid., 419.
[46] Jackson has referred to these as a 'form of partial, *long-term* entrenchment': Jackson, Supra note 2, 1284.
[47] *Constitutional Act of 23rd April 1992, on the Procedure for Preparing and Enacting a Constitution for the Republic of Poland Dziennik Ustaw Nr 61 Poz 251*, note 38.

the *Small Constitution*: many structural elements were preserved,[48] the new procedure adopted in the *Small Constitution* by which the Sejm can dissolve itself by a vote with a two-thirds majority was preserved[49] and so forth.[50]

Second, interim constitutions may influence permanent constitutions due to the political difficulty of renegotiating hard-won agreements made in preliminary talks, even when nothing in the text of the interim document compels drafters to follow it. In South Africa, the interim or 'founding' Bill of Rights 'remained influential even after the coming into force of the final constitution'; many provisions were retained and even where provisions were altered or abandoned the interim constitution was the starting point for all discussion.[51] Spitz and Chaskalson comment that Etienne Mureinik was right, when he

> advised [the Democratic Party] to aim to get as much as possible into the Bill of Rights at the first stage, predicting that it would be difficult for the Constitutional Assembly to remove rights and freedoms that had appeared in the Interim Constitution... The enduring significance of the interim Bill of Rights ... was ultimately formalized by Constitutional Principle II, which required the final Bill of Rights to be drafted after due consideration of the interim document.[52]

Third, institutions created in the interim era or under the interim constitution often persist after the permanent constitution has been adopted, even though it is not constitutionally required. This effect may be described as the 'constitutional laboratory'. One such example is from the Constitution of the Transition of the DRC[53] which established the Electoral Independent Commission (EIC), an institution that was maintained in the final constitution.[54] André Mbata B Mangu observes that the EIC played a crucial role in bringing about multiparty elections after

---

[48] Varol, Supra note 44, 338, citing Mark Brzezinski, *The Struggle for Constitutionalism in Poland* (New York: St Martin's Press, 1998).
[49] Varol, Supra note 44, 417.
[50] Lech Garlicki and Zofia Garlicka, 'Constitution Making, Peace Building and National Reconciliation: The Experience of Poland', in Laurel E. Miller (ed.) *Framing the State in Times of Transition* (Washington, DC: United States Institute of Peace, 2010), 402. See also Pawel Spiewak, 'The Battle for a Constitution' (1997) 6 *Eastern European Constitutional Review* 89, 89.
[51] Richard Spitz and Matthew Chaskalson, *The Politics of Transition: A Hidden History of South Africa's Negotiated Settlement* (Oxford: Hart Publishing, 2000), 409.
[52] Ibid.
[53] *Constitution de la transition de la République Démocratique du Congo* ('Constitution of the Transition'), note 27, Article 154.
[54] Constitution of the Democratic Republic of Congo 2005, Article 211. Brunilda Bara and Jona Bara, 'Constitutional Court and Constitutional Review in Albania: A Historical and Institutional Overview' (2013) 7 *Vienna Journal on International Constitutional Law* 214, 215.

'decades of undemocratic rule' and a host of obstacles.[55] Although there have been issues with the independence of the EIC, it helped to bring about peaceful elections and is another example of the way in which an interim-era institution can influence the administration of the constitution in the long-term.[56]

6.3.2. *Judicial Decision-making and the Invisible Constitution*

Constitutional courts operating during interim constitutional periods have a tendency to respond to or recognise non-textual features, thereby engaging in the invisible constitution. In many cases this interim-era jurisprudence may persist even after the interim constitution has expired and been replaced by a successor, theoretically permanent text. There are a number of reasons for this tendency.

First, the changed circumstances associated with the end of the past regime often mean that for the first time a constitutional court exists and the political climate permits cases involving fundamental human rights to be brought before it.[57] As such, the courts are presented with novel cases requiring decisions on matters that are not resolved in the constitutional text. Second, given the changed political climate and the lack of faith in previously tarnished political institutions, courts may take an expansive view of their role in the newly democratic state. Third, courts may be forced to deal with constitutional 'bootstraps' questions, ruling on the validity of the interim constitution or the interim drafting process and by necessity going beyond the constitutional text to resolve these questions. Fourth, if an interim constitutional text is rushed, incoherent or incomplete, sometimes as a result of having been the product of repeated amendments to an earlier constitution, rather than a singular text, the court may seek to step in to fill these gaps or to eliminate inconsistencies. Fifth, a court may respond to political factors and dynamics in applying constitutional provisions to legislation in the course of judicial review. In some cases, courts may rely on non-textual features in ways that are *expressly contrary* to the terms of the constitutional text. Finally, as is particularly evident in the case of Hungary, a high rate of constitutional

---

[55] André Mbata B. Mangu and Mpfariseni Budelli, 'Democracy and Elections in Africa in the Democratic Republic of Congo: Lessons for Africa', *The Institute for Democracy, Governance, Peace and Development in Africa* (2006) 26 www.idgpa.org/downloads/IDGPA-English%20 3%20-%20Elections%20in%20the%20DRC.pdf.
[56] See generally ibid.
[57] Or, as with the Polish Constitutional Tribunal, an existing Court is granted new powers and independence.

amendment and instability can lead to the Court attempting to define an invisible constitution that endures beyond the daily fluctuations of parliamentary politics.

In this section, I explore several case studies to demonstrate instances in which courts interpreting interim constitutions have referred to non-textual matters in their reasoning. This analysis necessarily focuses on case studies in which constitutional courts have been created and have in fact heard cases on significant constitutional matters. As such, my focus is on Poland, Albania, Hungary, Nepal and South Africa. In other states, particularly those where a 'sham' constitution prevails, including Sudan, constitutional courts have not played such a great role.[58]

In these decisions, some similar non-textual themes recur. In many instances courts operating in interim periods make explicit reference to non-textual factors, including: the history and politics of the state *prior* to the adoption of the interim constitution; the circumstances and public discourse surrounding the drafting of the interim text; and the nature of the interim constitutional period.

The South African Interim Constitution ('SA-IC') created a Constitutional Court and required that the final constitution would have to be 'certified' by the Court, in accordance with thirty-four binding Constitutional Principles ('CPs').[59] The CPs are crucial to the legal structure[60] and 'solemn pact' of the interim constitution.[61] As Siri Gloppen observes, the interim constitution 'gives no details of the [certification] procedure, [and] only states that the outcome is final and binding'.[62] This method of constitutional certification was 'unprecedented'.[63] The Court took a wide view of its task and powers in the Certification, stating that '[t]o do [the Certification], one must place the undertaking in its proper historical, political and legal context; and, in doing so, the essence of the country's constitutional transition, the respective roles

---

[58] David S. Law and Mila Versteeg, 'Sham Constitutions' (2013) 101 *California Law Review* 863.
[59] The Namibian Constituent Assembly had, in 1989, adopted a set of principles emerging from a UN Security Council Resolution as guidelines in its constitutional drafting, but South Africa was the first to adopt *binding* principles.
[60] *Interim Constitution of the Republic of South Africa*, note 26.
[61] Ibid., Preamble.
[62] Siri Gloppen, *South Africa: The Battle over the Constitution* (Hanover: Dartmouth Publishing Co., 1997), 208.
[63] *Certification of the Constitution of the Republic of South Africa* (1996) 4 SA 744 (Constitutional Court of South Africa) [1].

of the political entities involved and the applicable legal principles and terminology must be identified and described'.[64]

In its judgment, the Court recounted the history of apartheid in South Africa, the 'remarkabl[e]' peaceful transition of power and the role of the Interim text as an 'historic bridge between the past of a deeply divided ... and a future founded on the recognition of human rights, democracy and peaceful co-existence and development opportunities for all South Africans'.[65] However, the precise nature of the Certification task was not elucidated in the Constitution, and so the Court had to define its role.[66] The Court clarified that its role was a judicial not a political one, stating that the 'wisdom or otherwise of any provision of the NT [new text] is not this Court's business'.[67] However, as Ebrahim and Miller have noted, 'the [CPs] were essentially political agreements among parties bringing an end to conflict ... [and] a fair amount of the thirty-four principles could be interpreted in various ways'.[68]

The Court's interpretative approach was expressly purposive and teleological, directed at the constitutional commitment to 'create a new order', based on 'a sovereign and democratic constitutional state' in which 'all citizens' are 'able to enjoy and exercise their fundamental rights and freedoms'.[69] Eschewing an approach of 'technical rigidity',[70] the Court favoured an 'holistic' and 'integrated' interpretation of the CPs.[71] In its ruling, the Court, 'mindful ... not to cast too dark a shadow on the text' emphasised that the vast majority of provisions did comply with the CPs.[72] However, it refused to certify[73] the NT, having found a series of provisions that did not comply with the CPs,[74] with some provisions failing to comply with multiple CPs.

The Constitutional Court's interim-era human rights jurisprudence has also demonstrated a reliance on non-textual features and these 'invisible' constitutional features have endured under the permanent constitution. One prominent example is the South African case of *S* v. *Makwanyane and Another*

---

[64] Ibid.
[65] Ibid., 10.
[66] Ibid., 26.
[67] Ibid., 27.
[68] Hassen Ebrahim and Laurel E. Miller, 'Creating the Birth Certificate of a New South Africa: Constitution Making after Apartheid' in Laurel E. Miller (ed.) *Framing the State in Times of Transition* (Washington, DC: United States Institute of Peace, 2010), 140.
[69] *First Certification Decision*, note 63 [34].
[70] Ibid., 36.
[71] Ibid., 37.
[72] Ebrahim and Miller, Supra note 68, 141.
[73] *First Certification Decision*, note 63 [484].
[74] (Draft) Constitution of the Republic of South Africa 1996 ss 23, 24(1), Sch 6 s22(1)(b), 74m 194, 196, 229.

in which the Constitutional Court ruled that the death penalty violated the rights to life and dignity now guaranteed in the SA-IC.[75] Ackerman J explicitly referred to non-textual factors such as the history of the previous regime:

> We have moved from a past characterised by much which was arbitrary and unequal in the operation of the law to a present and a future in a constitutional state where state action must be such that it is capable of being analysed and justified rationally. The idea of the constitutional state presupposes a system whose operation can be rationally tested against or in terms of the law. Arbitrariness, by its very nature, is dissonant with these core concepts of our new constitutional order. Neither arbitrary action nor laws or rules which are inherently arbitrary or must lead to arbitrary application can, in any real sense, be tested against the precepts or principles of the Constitution.[76]

This interpretation of the SA-IC is particularly interesting given that the death penalty was a highly controversial but unresolved issue in the negotiations at Kempton Park. This position on the death penalty has been maintained by the Constitutional Court in the twenty-one years since *Makwanyane* and it is arguable that the decision was endorsed by the drafters of the 1996 Constitution of the Republic of South Africa, through their enactment of that text.[77]

In this way, the interpretation of the interim constitution of South Africa and the reference to non-textual features, has had an enduring effect on the 'invisible' constitutional law of South Africa. This case and others decided in the interim period according to the provisions of the interim constitution have had a profound impact on South African constitutional law, particularly in relation to human rights issues.[78]

Chief Justice Sólyom of the Hungarian Constitutional Court, in his concurring opinion in a decision that ruled that the death penalty was unconstitutional, stated that

> The Constitutional Court shall continue its work to define the principled foundations of the Constitution and of the rights inherent to it. Its decisions would create a coherent system which serves as a secure standard of constitutionality, as an invisible constitution above the Constitution in force which is still subject to modifications dictated by daily political interest.

---

[75] S v. *Makwanyane and Another* (1995) 3 SA 391.
[76] Ibid., 4.
[77] This point was suggested by Justice Kate O'Regan, formerly of the South African Constitutional Court, at the *Invisible Constitution Roundtable*, note 13.
[78] *Zuma & Ors* (1995) 2 SA 642.

The Constitutional Court enjoys freedom in this process as long as it keeps within the bounds of constitutionality.[79]

In this passage, Sólyom advances a notion of an invisible constitution which exists *above* 'the Constitution in force'. The Hungarian constitution in question was a 1989 Act[80] which heavily amended the 1949, communist-era constitution,[81] and experienced high rates of amendment, including in the early post-communist years.[82]

In the post-transition years, particularly between 1990 and 1993, the Hungarian Constitutional Court made landmark decisions in relation to the separation of church and state, freedom of speech, the death penalty,[83] retroactive criminalisation[84] and other human rights issues.[85]

Schwartz, in his book on *The Struggle for Constitutional Justice in Post-Communist Europe*, puts it as follows:

> The amended constitution was necessarily incomplete and marked by internal inconsistencies. Early on, the Court announced that in order to fill in the gaps and cope with the inconsistencies and contradictions, the Court would develop an 'invisible Constitution', a 'system of dogma' principles and methodology drawn from contemporary constitutional thinking in leading national and international courts around the world.[86]

Sólyom's framing of the invisible constitution as 'above' the constitution but tethered to it appears to demonstrate some conceptual confusion or circularity. However, this tendency to take an expansive approach in constitutional interpretation combined with the broad powers of the Hungarian Constitutional Court contributed to that Court becoming one of the most active Constitutional Courts in Europe.[87]

---

[79] *Decision 23 of 1990: 31 October 1990 On Capital Punishment* (Hungarian Constitutional Court).
[80] See note 31.
[81] See note 32.
[82] Between 1990 and 1994, the 1989 text was amended ten times: Dupré, Supra note 34, 32.
[83] See note 79.
[84] *Decision 11 of 1992: 5 March 1992 On the Retroactive Prosecution of Serious Criminal Offences* (Hungarian Constitutional Court).
[85] Andrew Arato and Zoltán Miklósi, 'Constitution Making and Transitional Politics in Hungary', in Laurel E. Miller (ed.) *Framing the State in Times of Transition: Case Studies in Constitution Making* (Washington, DC: United States Institute of Peace, 2010), 369.
[86] Herman Schwartz, *The Struggle for Constitutional Justice in Post-Communist Europe* (Chicago, IL: University of Chicago Press, 2000), 82.
[87] Georg Brunner, cited in Dupré, Supra note 34, 37.

The Hungarian Fundamental Law, which came into force on 1 January 2012, contained an explicit disavowal of the 1949 Constitution and appeared to reject the post-communist era amendments to that law as well. In spite of this disavowal, the Constitutional Court's rulings in the interim era continued to have a significant influence on the law of Hungary.

An example of the continued application of principles developed in the interim era is seen in a 2013 case where the Court invalidated an Act on Election Procedure on the basis that it was unconstitutional. The Court's ruling included reference to numerous cases heard under the previous constitution. In upholding a particular interpretation of Article 7(1) of the Fundamental Law about Hungary's acceptance of the 'generally recognised rules of international law', the Court made its decision according to the approach 'already established by the Constitutional Court on the basis of the previous Constitution' in a 1993 case and noted that the previous constitution contained the 'same essential content'.[88] In a separate part of the judgment, the Court noted that while the two Constitutions contained provisions that were not identical, they were 'similar' and that 'therefore the Constitutional Court's interpretation of the law as contained in its previous decisions is to be followed in the course of reviewing the present case, too'.[89] Thus, even though the jurisprudence under the 1989 Constitution was not only not binding – but disavowed – by the Fundamental Law, it continued to have ongoing influence in Hungarian constitutional law. This influence has been ended, or severely curtailed, by subsequent amendments to the Fundamental law discussed by Toth in Chapter 19.

The Polish Constitutional Tribunal was established in the communist era and commenced hearing cases in 1986. The only body of its kind in the Soviet bloc, it lacked the political or legal power to challenge the supremacy of the legislature, but even in the communist period the Tribunal was effective in its focus on reviewing administrative decisions.[90] One substantial area of jurisprudence established in the interim era relates to the *Rechtsstaat* principle.

The *Rechtsstaat* principle is embodied in Article 1 of the amended 1952 text and states that Poland is a 'democratic state ruled by law, implementing principles of social justice'. Andrzej Zoll, the Chief Justice of the Constitutional Tribunal from 1993–7, describes the 'great deal of freedom' the Tribunal has in

---

[88] *Decision 1 of 2013: AB on the unconstitutionality of certain provisions of Act on Election Procedure* (Hungarian Constitutional Court) [3.2–3.3].

[89] Ibid., 4.

[90] A. E. Dick Howard, 'Prospects for Constitutional Democracy in Poland', in Marek Jan Chodakiewicz, John Radzilowski and Dariusz Tolczyk (eds.) *Poland's Transformation: A Work in Progress* (Piscataway: Transaction Publishers, 2006), 137. See also Jerry Oniszczuk (ed.) 'Introduction', *Constitutional Tribunal, A Selection of the Polish Constitutional Tribunal's Jurisprudence From 1986 to 1999* (Warsaw: Trybunal Konstytucyjny, 1999), 5.

interpreting the principle,[91] which was used to 'read due process standards into the Constitution, including a prohibition against retroactive laws, the protection of "vested" rights, and access to the courts'.[92] The Tribunal exercised powerful legislative review in the period between 1 January 1990 and 30 June 1995 with forty of fifty-two statutes considered being held to be unconstitutional.[93] The Tribunal's influence during this time is all the more notable because the Tribunal's decisions were not binding until the 1997 Constitution.[94]

Oniszczuk argues that the Tribunal's jurisprudence in relation to a range of issues, including the *Rechtsstaat* principle, has continued on into post-1997 jurisprudence, as well as having had a direct impact on the 1997 Constitution itself.[95] Garlicki and Garlicka also highlight the way in which the Constitutional Tribunal contributed to long-term constitutional law during the interim period, noting that

> judges, particularly in the constitutional court, referred to the new constitutional principles, mainly the *Rechtsstaat* principle, and in some cases, rewrote them using both new constitutional principles and provisions of the European Convention on Human Rights. In this way, the judicial branch civilized and modernized the old constitution and prepared a relatively smooth transition to the post-1997 constitutional order.[96]

Although more recent developments have considerably challenged the independence and authority of the Constitutional Tribunal, decisions of the interim era Tribunal based on non-textual features have continued to have an enduring effect on Polish constitutional law.[97] In one of the decisions relating to the amendment of the *Constitutional Tribunal Act*, the Tribunal referred to its decisions in the interim era on the same topic.[98]

---

[91] Irena Grudzinska-Gross, 'Interview with Professor Andrzej Zoll, Chief Justice of the Polish Constitutional Tribunal' (1997) 6 *Eastern European Constitutional Review* 77, 77.
[92] Howard, Supra note 90, 138.
[93] Ibid.
[94] *Amended Constitution 1952*, Article 33a(2) (judgments of the Constitutional Tribunal on the nonconformity of laws to the Constitution are subject to examination by the Sejm); Grudzinska-Gross, Supra note 91, 77–8.
[95] Oniszczuk, Supra note 90, 11.
[96] Garlicki and Garlicka, Supra note 50, 404.
[97] Paulina Starski, 'Constitutionalism in Times of Extraordinary Developments: Resolving the Polish Constitutional Crisis', *Constitution Net* (13 April 2016) www.constitutionnet.org/news/constitutionalism-times-extraordinary-developments-resolving-polish-constitutional-crisis.
[98] The content of the principle of the autonomy of the Sejm's rules of procedure has been analysed in the Tribunal's jurisprudence before in its ruling of 26 January 1993 (ref. no. U 10/92, OTK in 1993, part I, item 2) – which was issued prior to the entry into force of the Constitution

In Nepal, the 2007 interim constitution outlasted its intended duration by some six years, before finally being replaced in 2015.[99] Repeated extensions for the drafting of the permanent constitution were granted by the Supreme Court, some invoking the doctrine of 'necessity'. Continuing political discord, the inability of the legislature to complete the constitutional drafting required of it by the interim constitution and the willingness of the Supreme Court in many cases to sanction repeated extensions, contributed to the prolonged duration of the interim constitution. The decisions of the Supreme Court have the potential to have a lasting impact upon Nepali constitutional law, including the endorsement of the doctrine of necessity. The doctrine of necessity posits that *'that which is otherwise not lawful is made lawful by necessity'*[100] and was used on several occasions to justify extensions to the temporal jurisdiction of the IC.[101] On other occasions, the Court disallowed similar extensions.[102] Following a 2011 ruling that no further extension would be granted for the Constituent Assembly to complete its task the CA was dismissed and replaced by a second CA, a step which was not provided for in the constitution.[103] The complicated series of events in Nepal demonstrate the way in which an interim constitution that lacks clear solutions in the event of stasis or deadlock opens itself to collapse or to creative interpretation by a court. Further, the case of Nepal shows that where there is political and legal uncertainty during an interim period, courts may play an outsized role or generate a constitution that is broader than – or even contradictory to – its written features. The period may be described as involving a kind of dialogic relationship between the Supreme Court and constitution drafters, involving a 'sequel of implicitly or explicitly shaped communications back and forth between two or more actors characterized by the absence of a dominant actor ... with the

---

of 1997, which is currently binding, [6.9], in Ref. No. K 34/15, 3 XII 2015, available at http://trybunal.gov.pl/en/hearings/judgments/art/8748-ustawa-o-trybunale-konstytucyjnym/.

[99] *Constitution of the Kingdom of Nepal* 2015.

[100] See discussion in Rajib Dahal, 'Nepal: (Un)Necessary – Doctrine of Necessity' *Telegraph Nepal* (21 September 2011) www.telegraphnepal.com/views/2011-09-21/nepal:-unnecessary-doctrine-of-necessity.html.

[101] *Advocate Vijaya Raj Sakya v. President of Nepal, Mr Ram Baran Yadav, Office of the President, Sital Niwash, Kathamandu & Ors* and in *Advocate Kamlesh Dwivedi v. President of Nepal, Mr Ram Baran Yadav, Office of the President, Sital Niwash, Kathmandu & Ors* (*Supreme Court of Nepal*) [2011] Supreme Court of Nepal Writ No. 066-WS-0050.

[102] *Advocate Bal Krishna Neupane v. The Office of the President, Maharajgunj, Kathmandu & Ors* and *Bharatmani Jangam v. The Office of the President, Maharajgunj, Kathmandu & Ors* (*Supreme Court of Nepal*) [2011] Supreme Court of Nepal Special Writ No. 066-WS-0056.

[103] *Bharatmani Jungam Case* (Writ No. 068-WS-0014) (25 November 2011).

shared intention of improving the practice of interpreting, reviewing, writing or amending constitutions'.[104]

Of course, it is not a characteristic unique to interim constitutions that they sometimes require courts to make political decisions about the application of the constitution that tend to rely on extra-textual justification. However, what is unusual is that courts in interim settings have a tendency to be engaged with the existence and drafting or adoption of the constitution itself or its successor. It is not yet apparent whether the interim-era invisible constitution, including its emphasis on necessity and the dialogic relationship of the Court and the legislature, will endure under the new constitution.

In Albania, the Constitutional Court was created not at the beginning of the interim era, but following April 1992 amendments to the constitution; it represented the first time in Albania's history that it had had a constitutional court.[105] The Court issued some important decisions that displayed its independence and indicated a willingness to take an 'interventionist approach' on some matters.[106] However, at times the Court's independence was less assured; in 1995 it approved legislation which changed the procedure for constitutional amendment which clearly went against the terms of the Constitution. As Ordolli has argued, the Court's approach in the case was not convincing and it ended up with an interpretation far from the reality of the Albanian constitution.[107]

6.4. CONCLUDING OBSERVATIONS

In this chapter, I have explored the ways in which interim constitutions can generate unwritten or invisible, but nonetheless significant, constitutional norms. I want to make three concluding observations about the significance of this link between interim constitutions and the development of the invisible constitution. The first relates to the relationship between amendment of interim constitutions and the development of the invisible constitution. The second concerns the implications of my analysis about the enduring effects of interim constitutions for constitution-drafters. The third is an idea about what a popular invisible constitution might involve.

---

[104] Anne Meuwese and Marnix Snel, '"Constitutional Dialogue": An Overview' (2013) 9 *Utretcht Law Review* 123, 126.
[105] Stiliano Ordolli, *Histoire constitutionelle de l'Albanie: des origines à nos jours* (Geneva: Schulthess, 2008), 347.
[106] John Paul Jones, 'The Tribunal in Tirana (the New Constitutional Courts: Albania)' (1993) 2 *Eastern European Constitutional Review* 52.
[107] Ordolli, Supra note 105, 372–3.

Intuitively, it might seem that interim constitutions would have low levels of amendment. As short-lived documents whose expiry is planned, the demand for constitutional change in an interim-era might be expected to be low.[108] Further, it might be supposed that a high level of amendment and the development of an invisible or expansive constitution would have an inverse relationship, with one obviating the need for the other. Neither of these intuitions is borne out on an analysis of the literature. Interim constitutions often experience high rates of amendment: the fluidity and in some cases volatility of political and constitutional circumstances in states adopting interim texts can be such that the rate of social change or the mismatch between the constitution and the polity can emerge quickly.[109] Moreover, as Ginsburg and Melton have shown with ordinary constitutions, the 'presence of judicial review actually increases the amendment rate'.[110]

There are several reasons why amendments might be adopted, even during a short-lived interim constitutional period. In some cases, a high rate of constitutional amendment, as in South Africa, can be a sign of a democratic and effective drafting process and a climate in which political actors hew closely to constitutional norms. In other cases, high rates of constitutional amendment can be a sign of dysfunction, as seen in the twelve amendments introduced in Nepal. In Albania there was a tendency for ordinary politics to bleed into constitutional debates; in one instance the near-collapse of the country's economy due to a massive pyramid scheme necessitated a constitutional amendment.[111] The Sudanese constitution has, on paper, a relatively high bar for amendment of the interim constitution: a three-quarters majority of 'each Chamber of the National Legislature sitting separately and only after introduction of the draft amendment at least two months prior to deliberations'.[112] However, in practice the three-quarters majority required by s224(1) has operated as a mere formality, given the 90 per cent majority of the party of the President of Sudan, Al-Bashir. As such, several significant amendments have been introduced.

It does not appear that a high rate of amendment discourages the development of an expansive invisible constitution or that it eliminates the evolution of an active constitutional court. In fact in some cases, as seen in the example

---

[108] Tom Ginsburg and James Melton, 'Does the Constitutional Amendment Rule Matter at All? Amendment Cultures and the Challenges of Measuring Amendment Difficulty' (2014) *Coase-Sandor Institute for Law & Economics Working Paper No. 682*, 3 http://chicagounbound.uchicago.edu/cgi/viewcontent.cgi?article=2348&context=law_and_economics.
[109] See discussion of critical junctures in Capoccia and Kelemen, Supra note 41, 341.
[110] Ginsburg and Melton, Supra note 108, 21.
[111] See generally Christopher Jarvis, 'The Rise and Fall of Albania's Pyramid Schemes' (2000) 37 *Finance and Development* www.imf.org/external/pubs/ft/fandd/2000/03/jarvis.htm.
[112] *Interim National Constitution of the Republic of the Sudan*, note 19, Article 224(1).

of Hungary, the very frequency of constitutional amendment can encourage judges to develop a stable and enduring invisible constitution that sits above daily politics. As such, drafters of interim texts will need to consider the possible interconnection between amendment procedures and judicial review and consider which amendment thresholds might best allow for what Arato calls 'constitutional learning' or what Jackson more cautiously hopes for in 'constitutions as a form of continuous conversation'.[113]

Secondly, the tendency for interim constitutions to create permanent effects, including through the generation of enduring invisible constitutions, highlights the importance of the how interim constitutions are drafted. Interim constitutions are typically drafted or agreed to by unelected bodies that represent key parties or bodies that are not fully representative. As such, temporary constitutions are premised on a kind of two-stage legitimacy whereby the first stage of constitutional drafting (the temporary text) is made legitimate by a rejection of the past regime and the promise of a more democratically-negotiated permanent text. However, if the interim text ends up being determinative of significant features of the permanent constitution – both textual and non-textual – then drafters of interim constitutions must be mindful that these texts are not mere placeholders. This knowledge may feed into new norms about the level of public and expert involvement in interim constitutional negotiation and transparency and accountability. It may also lessen the degree to which interim constitutions may claim to 'relax the dead hand' of the past by freeing themselves from a founding moment.[114]

Finally, I want to note that this chapter has focused on the way in which an invisible constitution develops in judicial and legislative spheres. However, I think that what is visible and invisible as part of the constitutional bargain will also be affected by the popular understanding of the constitution. A popular understanding of the constitution will include not only (and perhaps not all of) the written text of the constitution, views about the bargain struck at the interim stage, the degree of departure from the previous regime and perceptions about the desirability of constitutionally relevant practices such as transitional justice mechanisms. This popular understanding of the constitution at the interim stage will influence the kinds of interests represented in public consultations about a final constitution and in the types of claims brought before constitutional courts in the interim and post-interim era. Thus it is possible that the people contribute directly to the formulation of the constitution, in both its visible and invisible formulations.

---

[113] Jackson, Supra note 2, 1287; Andrew Arato, *Constitution Making Under Occupation: The Politics of Imposed Revolution in Iraq* (New York, NY: Columbia University Press, 2009).
[114] Varol, Supra note 44, 448.

PART II

THE VIEW FROM ASIA PACIFIC AND THE MIDDLE EAST

7

Behind the Text of the Basic Law

Some Constitutional Fundamentals

Johannes M. M. Chan[*]

Every constitution is shaped by its unique history and the social and political circumstances of the country in which it operates. Our understanding and interpretation of the constitution cannot be divorced from the social, political and historical contexts of the jurisdiction in which the constitution is to operate. At the same time, constitutions, by their very nature, can only contain general principles. While they prescribe a general framework for assessing the constitutionality of executive acts and in some jurisdictions, statutory provisions, a literal reading of the constitutional text in most cases does not provide an obvious answer to many constitutional issues before the courts. By interpreting the constitution, the courts give life to the constitution. Yet interpretation is rarely a neutral process. It always involves judicial choices among a number of plausible solutions. In making these choices and giving meaning to the general text of a constitution, the courts are from time to time guided by various fundamental values in our constitutional system. Such fundamental values may not be readily visible from the text of the constitution. They are extra-textual, and hence 'invisible', and are shaped by the social, political and historical contexts of the society in which the constitution operates. Professor Lawrence Tribe, in his inspiring work, coined the term 'The Invisible Constitution'.[1] While this term is capable of different interpretations, it does convey a central message that a constitution could not be understood without taking into account these extra-textual dimensions. This chapter tries to identify the content and contours of this layer of invisible constitution in the context of Hong Kong. The approach of this chapter is sociological: it focuses on how judicial choices are made in giving effect to a written constitution, and argues that these choices are guided by some fundamental values, which

---

[*] I am grateful to my colleague Ms Cora Chan for her insightful comments on an earlier draft of this article. Any mistake remains, of course, my sole responsibility.
[1] Lawrence Tribe, *The Invisible Constitution* (Oxford: Oxford University Press, 2008).

I would call 'Constitutional Fundamentals'. These principles exist behind the text; they are interstitial, vague and far from being coherent or structured, and may sometimes even be in conflict with one another. Nonetheless, they exist, guide and influence the development of the constitution, and constitute a deeper layer of constitutional principles. It is not the purpose of this chapter to argue whether these principles are desirable or not, but simply to contend that they exist and are discernible.

Section 7.1 of this chapter sets out the social, political and historical context of the Basic Law. A unique feature of the Basic Law of Hong Kong is that it has to operate in a common law system within a larger socialist/civil law system – the so-called 'One Country, Two Systems' model. It is an asymmetrical model in terms of both economic and political powers. The conflict between the two systems is most intense when it comes to the interpretation of the Basic Law, which serves simultaneously as the constitution of Hong Kong and a domestic statute in Mainland China. Section 7.2 of this chapter outlines this systemic conflict, and argues that the approach adopted by the Court of Final Appeal was guided by the principle of preserving the integrity of the common law system. This principle operated almost in a paradoxical manner in the *Congo* case, when the court was faced with the stark choice of insisting on the common law principles and facing an overrule by the Standing Committee of the National People's Congress, or twisting the common law principles in return for establishing some constitutional convention. Section 7.3 turns to another type of conflict of preserving the past and meeting the future. Given that the promise of One Country, Two Systems is to last for fifty years only, with the position beyond fifty years completely open, preserving the previous system is a rational way to dictate the future. At the same time, the court has to guard against fossilising the system. In the *Kong Yunming* case, the court had to go so far as to twist the meaning of legality in order to preserve the previous social welfare system, and then immediately turned it around by adopting the level of benefits at the point of change of sovereignty as the baseline for measuring progress or retrogression in social welfare rights. Section 7.4 examines briefly the principle of separation of powers, particularly in relation to challenges against the internal operation of the Legislature. Section 7.5 continues the exploration of the theme of separation of powers in the context of proportionality, and shows how the principle of separation of powers leads to an oscillating approach by the court, notably in dealing with social and economic rights. The last part tries to bring together some of the invisible principles.

7.1. THE SOCIAL, POLITICAL AND HISTORICAL CONTEXTS OF THE BASIC LAW

Hong Kong was partially ceded and partially leased to Britain in the nineteenth century under three different treaties. The common law system was transplanted to Hong Kong that was then governed by a relatively benign colonial regime. Traditionally it was a place of refuge for those who wanted to avoid civil unrest in Mainland China. The population soared soon after the Second World War, and it remains today that about half of the population are migrants or refugees from the Mainland. By the 1980s, Hong Kong developed into one of the major financial centres in the world, with a GDP comparable to many developed countries and enjoying a high degree of freedom and liberty. In contrast, China at that time had just emerged from the ten-year-long Cultural Revolution, during which there were widespread persecutions and massive destruction of anything representing the establishment or considered to be non-conforming with the prevailing political ideology. All universities were closed down during the Cultural Revolution. By the end of the Cultural Revolution in 1976, the country was almost on the brink of bankruptcy and at a stage of lawlessness. Since 1978, the country has embarked on a massive rebuilding process with very noticeable success. In 1984, the Sino-British Joint Declaration was concluded under which China would resume sovereignty over Hong Kong under the principle of 'One Country, Two Systems'. Hong Kong would retain 'a high degree of autonomy', and would preserve its own legal, social and economic systems. Mainland law and policies would not apply to Hong Kong, and fundamental rights would be guaranteed. These promises were given effect by the Basic Law, which serves as the constitution of Hong Kong. The Basic Law was promulgated by the National People's Congress of the People's Republic of China ('PRC') in April 1990. On 1 July 1997, Hong Kong became a Special Administrative Region of the PRC ('HKSAR').

It is not surprising that many people in Hong Kong did not feel confident about the future master, especially when half of the population were once refugees fleeing the Mainland and Communist rule. Many provisions in the Basic Law were hence drafted with the Mainland system in mind, such as the right to freedom of choice of occupation,[2] the freedom to engage in

---

[2] Article 33, Basic Law.

academic, literary and artistic creation,[3] a right to judicial remedies,[4] and the right to freely raise a family.[5] There are two special features in the constitution of Hong Kong. While there is no expiry date for the Basic Law, the Joint Declaration expressly stated that it is to last for fifty years, expiring on 30 June 2047. Secondly, the concept of 'One Country, Two Systems' is novel. While there are many precedents of a country with different legal systems, a federal system being one example, Hong Kong is unique in the extent of differences between the two systems. On one side of the border is a common law system embedded in individual liberalism and separation of powers, with the power of interpretation of the law vested exclusively in an independent judiciary. Across the border is a system founded on one party leadership and socialist ideology that expressly rejects separation of powers, and regards the interpretation of law as a political process to achieve a socialist goal, under which the power of interpretation of law is vested in the Standing Committee of the National People's Congress, a predominantly political organ. The two systems are brought under a sovereign under an asymmetrical constitutional model with political and economic powers all vested in favour of the sovereign power. For the common law system, the judiciary, with its power to interpret the Basic Law, has to shoulder the historical challenge of making this constitution work. It has to preserve the previous system to provide the certainty in order to prepare for the uncertainty in the not too distant future. Thus, there are two constant themes in the interpretation of the Basic Law, namely the preservation of the integrity of the common law system, including the enjoyment of liberty and freedom under the common law system and the maintenance and continuity with the previous system.

7.1.1. The Constitutional Context of the Basic Law

Chapter 3 of the Basic Law provides for the protection of the fundamental rights and freedoms of Hong Kong inhabitants. Article 39 of the Basic Law provides that the provisions of the International Covenant on Civil and Political Rights ('ICCPR') and the International Covenant on Economic, Social and Cultural Rights ('ICESCR') shall remain in force and shall be implemented through the laws of the HKSAR. The ICCPR, but not the ICESCR, was incorporated into the domestic law of the HKSAR by the Hong Kong Bill of Rights Ordinance, which reproduced the substantive rights provisions of the

---

[3] Article 34. Intellectuals were severely suppressed and widely persecuted for their writings during the Cultural Revolution.
[4] Article 35.
[5] Article 37. The one-child policy in the PRC was lifted only in 2015.

ICCPR.[6] The PRC has ratified the ICESCR, but not the ICCPR. Article 39 further provides that any restriction of the rights and freedoms enjoyed by Hong Kong residents shall be prescribed by law and shall not contravene the ICCPR and the ICESCR as applied to Hong Kong.

Soon after the Basic Law came into effect, the Hong Kong Court of Final Appeal, in a series of cases, laid down the general approach to the interpretation of the Basic Law. The courts must be vigilant in the protection of fundamental rights and should adopt a generous and purposive interpretation so as to give full measures to individual rights. A literal, technical, narrow or rigid approach should be avoided.[7] Any restriction on a fundamental right must be narrowly interpreted and rigorously examined. Such restriction, in order to pass muster with the constitutional requirements, must be prescribed by law and satisfy the tests of rationality and proportionality. The burden of justification of any restriction rests on the Government.[8]

The Court of Final Appeal noted that a purposive approach to interpretation is necessary 'because a constitution states general principles and expresses purposes without condescending to particularity and definition of terms'.[9] Hence, 'gaps and ambiguities are bound to arise and, in resolving them, the courts are bound to give effect to the principles and purposes declared in, and to be ascertained from, the constitution and relevant extrinsic materials'.[10] Not only must the courts consider the purpose of the instrument, but it must also interpret the language of its text in the light of the context, 'context being of particular importance in the interpretation of a constitutional instrument'.[11] In this regard, it is interesting to note the observation of Sir Anthony Mason, a non-permanent judge of the Court of Final Appeal, made in an extra-judicial lecture, that 'the lack of a fully democratic universal franchise and the relationship created by the Basic Law between a strong executive government and a weak legislature might suggest that the community and the media may

---

[6] The substantive rights provisions of the ICCPR, with the exception of the right of a child to a nationality and a replacement of 'every citizen' by 'every permanent resident' regarding the right to vote and to stand for election, were reproduced in Part II of the Bill of Rights Ordinance. Part II is known as the Bill of Rights. Reservations to the ICCPR that were entered into by the United Kingdom upon ratification of the ICCPR were reproduced in Part III of the Bill of Rights Ordinance.
[7] *Ng Ka Ling v. Director of Immigration* (1999) 2 HKCFAR 4, para 30.
[8] *Ng Ka Ling v. Director of Immigration* (1999) 2 HKCFAR 4, paras 28–30; *Leung Kwok Hung v. HKSAR* (2005) 8 HKCFAR 229, para 116; *Yeung May Wan v. HKSAR* (2005) 8 HKCFAR 137, paras 1–3.
[9] *Ng Ka Ling v. Director of Immigration* (1999) 2 HKCFAR 4, para 28, per Li CJ.
[10] Ibid.
[11] Ibid. For extrinsic materials, Li CJ specifically referred to the Joint Declaration.

place greater expectations in the curial protection of individual rights and due process than is the case in other jurisdictions'.[12]

In construing the Basic Law, the Hong Kong courts have been receptive to a wide range of international and comparative materials.[13] This is partly due to the international origin of the Hong Kong Bill of Rights, which is a replica of the ICCPR, and partly to the practice of having an overseas judge in every substantive hearing before the Court of Final Appeal, which includes a panel of distinguished overseas judges. Thus, apart from case law from both overseas domestic jurisdictions and international tribunals such as the European Court of Human Rights, the Human Rights Committee, the Committee Against Torture, the Inter-American Court of Human Rights and the International Court of Justice, the courts have also freely referred to soft law such as General Comments and Concluding Observations of international treaty bodies, Reports of the Hong Kong Government to various international treaty bodies, the Siracusa Principles, the United States Department of State's Country Reports on Human Rights Practice, as well as Brandeis-type briefs on comparative legislation in the context of flag desecration law,[14] or evidence of comparative medical research on sexual puberty in a claim for equality and privacy in relation to homosexual conduct or the Joint Declaration in resolving a discrepancy in meaning between the English version and the Chinese version of the Basic Law.[15] In *Leung Kwok Hung* v. *HKSAR*, the Court of Final Appeal relied partly on the Government's acceptance of a positive obligation in its period report to the Human Rights Committee pursuant to the ICCPR in upholding a positive obligation to assist the demonstrators to enjoy their right of peaceful assembly and demonstration.[16]

---

[12] Sir Anthony Mason, 'The Role of the Common Law in Hong Kong', in Jessica Young and Rebecca Lee (eds.), *The Common Law Lecture Series 2005* (Hong Kong: Faculty of Law, The University of Hong Kong, 2006), 20. Sir Anthony specifically referred to *Town Planning Board* v. *Society for the Protection of the Harbour Ltd* (2004) 7 HKCFAR 1 as an example of the public looking to the court as an arena for ventilation of grievances and redress when such issues would normally have been addressed and resolved in the political process in other jurisdictions.

[13] See J. Chan, 'Hong Kong's Bill of Rights: Its Reception of and Contribution to International and Comparative Jurisprudence' (1988) 47 *International & Comparative Law Quarterly* 306; J. Chan, 'Basic Law and Constitutional Review: The First Decade'(2007) 37 *Hong Kong Law Journal* 407; J. Chan and C. L. Lim, 'Interpreting Constitutional Rights and Permissible Restrictions', in J. Chan and C. L. Lim (eds.), *Law of the Hong Kong Constitution*, 2nd edn. (Hong Kong: Sweet & Maxwell, 2015), Ch 17.

[14] *HKSAR* v. *Ng Kung Siu* (1999) 2 HKCFAR 442.

[15] *Leung TC William Roy* v. *Secretary for Justice* [2006] 4 HKLRD 211.

[16] (2005) 8 HKCFAR 229, para 22. See also *Ubamaka* v. *Secretary for Security* [2011] 1 HKLRD 359, para 359 (CA); *Kong Yunming* v. *Director of Social Welfare* (2013) 16 HKCFAR 950, paras 177–8.

7.2. PRESERVING THE INTEGRITY OF THE COMMON LAW SYSTEM

Whenever constitutional powers are divided between two different jurisdictions, a classic problem is where and how to draw the dividing line. As an autonomous region, Hong Kong enjoys a high degree of autonomy except in the areas of foreign affairs and defence, and matters concerning the relations of the Central Authorities and the HKSAR. This general principle itself is subject to expressed modifications in the Basic Law. Thus, Hong Kong enjoys, upon authorisation, a considerable degree of autonomy in participating in international events, maintaining and developing with foreign states and regions and international organisations, and even concluding international and regional treaties in specific fields – no doubt a reflection of the expansive international networks of Hong Kong as an international financial centre.[17] At the same time, Hong Kong courts have no jurisdiction over acts of state and are bound by executive certificate on questions of facts concerning acts of state whenever such questions arise in the adjudication of cases.[18] However, apart from such general principles, it is for the courts and the Central Authorities to work out on a case-by-case basis how the demarcation of jurisdictions is to be drawn. Not surprisingly, disagreement and conflicts could arise, and the Basic Law itself provides little guidance on how to address these disputes.

A unique feature of the Basic Law is that the power of final interpretation of the Basic Law is vested, not in the Court of Final Appeal, but in the Standing Committee of the National People's Congress ('NPCSC'). This stems from the fact that the HKSAR is not an independent entity but an autonomous region of the PRC. Under Article 158, in adjudicating a case, the Court of Final Appeal has a duty to refer, before rendering final judgment, a question of interpretation of the Basic Law to the NPCSC if the provision in question falls within the area of defence, foreign affairs and the relationship between the Central Authorities and the HKSAR, and when the interpretation will decisively affect the judgments on the cases. As the Court of Final Appeal explained, this Article embodies two tests: the classification test, which means the provision in question has to be an excluded provision; and the necessity test, which means that the interpretation of the provision in question is necessary for the final disposal of the case before the court.

---

[17] Article 151. The specific fields include economic, trade, financial and monetary, shipping, communications, tourism, cultural and sports fields.
[18] Article 19. Examples of acts of state include defence and foreign affairs.

7.2.1. Delineating the Powers: The Predominant Provision Test

In *Ng Ka Ling* v. *Director of Immigration*, the issue was whether the requirement for a certificate of entitlement, which could not be granted without an exit approval from the Mainland Security Bureau, for claiming a right of abode in Hong Kong was constitutional when there was no such requirement in the definition of the right of abode in Article 24 of the Basic Law. The Government relied on Article 22, which provides that any person from the Mainland coming to Hong Kong shall obtain the approval of the Central Government, to justify the certificate of entitlement system. Before the Court of Final Appeal, on the question of referral pursuant to Article 158, the court held that it was to decide whether the classification test and the necessity test were satisfied. For the purpose of argument, it was accepted that Article 22 was an excluded provision and that Article 22 was arguably relevant to the interpretation of Article 24. The Government argued that in such a case the court was obliged to refer the question of interpretation to the NPCSC. The court disagreed, holding that the proper test was, as a matter of substance, the predominant provision to be interpreted. This, it found, was Article 24, which concerned only domestic affairs. Article 22, which concerns central–local relationships, was relevant only in the background. Li CJ held:

> In our view, the test in considering whether the classification condition is satisfied is ... As a matter of substance, what predominantly is the provision that has to be interpreted in the adjudication of the case? If the answer is an excluded provision, the Court is obliged to refer. If the answer is a provision which is not an excluded provision, then no reference has to be made, although an excluded provision is arguably relevant to the construction of the non-excluded provision even to the extent of qualifying it.

As the classification test was not satisfied, the Court held that there was no need to further consider the necessity test.

Where does this predominant provision test come from? It is by no means obvious from a plain reading of the text of the Basic Law. Professor Albert Chen forcefully criticised the approach of the court for being illogical.[19] He argued that: (1) the court should first consider which provisions are necessary to be interpreted; (2) once the provisions have been identified, whether those

---

[19] Albert Chen, 'The Court of Final Appeal's Ruling in the "Illegal Migrant" Children Case: A Critical Commentary on the Application of Article 158 of the Basic Law', in Johannes Chan, H. L. Fu and Yash Ghai (eds.), *Hong Kong's Constitutional Debate: Conflict over Interpretation* (Hong Kong: Hong Kong University Press, 2000), 73–141.

provisions are excluded provisions. There was no basis for the application of a predominant provision test in applying the classification test.

While it is agreed that the court should first identify the provisions that are necessary to be interpreted before determining whether the relevant provisions are excluded provisions, this does not avoid the need to apply some kind of predominant provision test, albeit in the context of the necessity test. Indeed, Professor Chen himself admitted that in deciding which provisions need to be interpreted, the necessity test is only satisfied by those provisions which would be conclusive or substantially determinative of the outcome of the case before the court. It is unnecessary for the CFA to refer a question to the NPCSC for interpretation if the provisions that have to be interpreted are only marginally relevant. This is obviously desirable for protecting the integrity of the legal system in Hong Kong, for it is not difficult to imagine that a number of provisions in the Basic Law could be invoked in any Basic Law litigation. If the Court of Final Appeal has to make a reference whenever an excluded provision is invoked and is arguably relevant to the final decision of the case, this would be a substantial derogation from the autonomy of the HKSAR. Professor Chen argued that this would not be the case, as the NPCSC was only asked to interpret the meaning of the excluded provision, and it was for the court to adjudicate on other provisions and to apply the interpretation to the case. This explanation is formal rather than practical, for if the excluded provision is crucial to the disposition of the case; once an interpretation is made there is little room left for the Court to decide. In the *Ng Ka Ling* case, once the NPCSC decided that 'people from other parts of China' in Article 22 of the Basic Law included 'Mainland residents who have acquired the status of HK Permanent Residents by virtue of Article 24 upon the commencement of the Basic Law and who would like to come to Hong Kong to take up their right of abode', it follows that the applicants in the case would need an exit approval and therefore a scheme which requires an exit approval would be constitutional.[20]

Therefore, whenever a few provisions of the Basic Law are invoked in a case before the Court of Final Appeal, the Court would have to decide which provisions are 'necessary' to be interpreted in the sense that their interpretation would be determinative of the outcome of the case. This is not always a straightforward exercise. As the Court pointed out, one provision may qualify another provision by way of addition, subtraction or modification, or it may lend colour to the meaning or provide a pointer to the interpretation of another provision. Save in the most straightforward cases, the reference

---

[20] See Albert Chen, ibid., 133. The same is true in the *Congo* case, note 21.

to the NPCSC may not be just the meaning of the excluded provision, for the interpretation has to be made in context, the context being its relations with the other provisions which are not excluded provisions. Hence, a referral most likely means that the NPCSC would effectively determine the outcome of the case, and may even affect other applicable legal principles.[21] As a result, the threshold for referral has to be high so that the necessity test is satisfied only when the interpretation of the provisions are determinative of the outcome of the case. If a few provisions are involved, the court will have to decide which provisions the interpretation of which would be determinative and which provisions the interpretation of which would only be relevant but not determinative. The power to make this decision, if the Hong Kong legal system is to retain its autonomy and to avoid any abuse of the referral procedure, must rest with the Hong Kong courts. The rule of law depends on that. Whether it is called a predominant provision test or a conclusive effect test, the mischief to be avoided is the same, namely to safeguard the integrity of the common law system in Hong Kong. It must also be borne in mind that the interpretation by the NPCSC is essentially a political process without any transparency. Its interpretation is not constrained by legal consideration or the rule of evidence. It is only right for a court at the highest level to act cautiously in giving up its jurisdiction in the process of its adjudication to a political body to effectively determine the outcome of the case. What underlies the reasoning of the court is a higher principle that the constitutional jurisdiction of the courts must be vigilantly safeguarded in order to maintain the integrity of the legal system.

Although the Court of Final Appeal in *Ng Ka Ling* held that it was not necessary to refer any question to the NPCSC for interpretation, the HKSAR Government sought such an interpretation on the basis that the judgment of the Court caused considerable difficulties for Hong Kong, as a large number of Mainland born children would as a result acquire a right of abode in Hong Kong. On 26 June 1999, the NPCSC issued an interpretation that effectively reversed the judgment of the Court.[22]

---

[21] For instance, in *Democratic Republic of the Congo v. FG Hemisphere Associates LLC (No 1)* (2011) 14 HKCFAR 95, the effect of the NPCSC interpretation is that the common law rule on relative immunity is found to be inconsistent with the Basic Law and hence does not form part of the law of the HKSAR.

[22] For a detailed discussion, see Johannes Chan and C. L. Lim, *Law of the Hong Kong Constitution*, paras 2.080–2.093; Chan et al., Supra note 19.

7.2.2. Interpreting the Interpretation: Reasserting the Primacy of the Common Law

The NPCSC interpretation has cast considerable doubt over the independence of the judiciary and the integrity of the Hong Kong legal system. The interpretation is primarily a political decision made without any transparency. There were concerns whether the judiciary could remain independent if its final judgments could be reversed by a political organ across the border, and how independence of the judiciary could reconcile with the NPCSC interpretation, which is constitutional within the Mainland legal system. This question was addressed in *Chong Fung Yuen* v. *Director of Immigration*.[23] The issue in that case was whether a child born in Hong Kong to parents, neither of whom was a Hong Kong Permanent Resident, would acquire a right of abode in Hong Kong. In no uncertain terms the Court of Final Appeal dispelled any concern that a judge would have to look over his shoulder to take into account possible responses from the NPCSC in discharging his judicial duty. It held that the courts in Hong Kong are bound to apply the common law and not the principles in the Mainland system, in interpreting the Basic Law. Under the common law, the courts' role is 'to construe the legislative intent of the Basic Law as expressed in the language. Their task is not to ascertain the intent of the lawmaker on its own. Their duty is to ascertain what was meant by the language used and to give effect to the legislative intent as expressed in the language'.[24] The language was not looked at in isolation, but in light of its context or purpose and the courts must avoid a literal, technical, narrow or rigid approach. At the same time, the courts could not give the language a meaning which it could not bear. In interpreting the Basic Law, while the courts may resort to extrinsic materials such as the Joint Declaration and the Explanations on the draft Basic Law before its enactment, that throw light on the context or purpose of the Basic Law, the courts have to be cautious and should adopt a particularly prudent approach in considering post-enactment materials.[25] This point is of particular significance as the NPCSC in its interpretation reversing *Ng Ka Ling* stated that the intent of the Basic Law could be found in a report of the Preparatory Committee, which was set up six years after the enactment of the Basic Law for the purpose of preparing for the establishment of the HKSAR. The Court in *Chong Fung Yuen* held that this report could not affect the interpretation of a provision when the meaning of its language is clear,

---

[23] (2001) 4 HKCFAR 211.
[24] Ibid., 223.
[25] Ibid., 224–5.

alongside an expression of doubts of the relevance and the appropriateness of considering such extrinsic pre-enactment materials in any event.

With regard to the NPCSC interpretation, the Court respected the power of the NPCSC to interpret the Basic Law under Article 67(4) of the PRC Constitution and Article 158 of the Basic Law, but held that this power operated in a different system and was legislative, not judicial, in nature. Once an interpretation has been made, it is binding on the Hong Kong courts and forms part of the system in the HKSAR. Yet before an interpretation has been made, the courts need only refer to the common law in interpreting the Basic Law. Even after an interpretation has been made, the courts will still have to ascertain the scope of the interpretation. Accordingly, the Court found that some remarks on the nature of Article 24 in the previous NPCSC interpretation were confined to the context of that interpretation and were not binding on the Court in interpreting a different subsection of the same provision in a different context. Having held that the provision before the Court was not an excluded provision, the Court rejected the Director's application for making a judicial reference to the NPCSC.[26]

Chong Fung Yuen is important, not only in restoring public confidence in the independence of the judiciary after the first NPCSC interpretation, but also in the Court's innovative approach of characterizing the NPCSC interpretation, which operates in a different system, as legislative in nature and therefore providing a theoretical justification for the Hong Kong judiciary to legitimately exclude any consideration of possible responses from the legislative organ of a different legal system in interpreting the Basic law. It is clear that protecting the integrity of the common law system is a crucial constitutional principle, if not the *raison d'être*, of the judgment. The point was made even more explicit in the subsequent case of *Vallejos* v. *Commission of Registration*, where the Court of Final Appeal refused to make a judicial reference for the NPCSC on the ground that the necessity test for referral was not satisfied.[27] The Court emphasised that the question for interpretation had to be arguable. An argument that is plainly and obviously bad would not be arguable. The Chief Justice pointed out that 'the arguability factor is implicit in Art. 158(3) to ensure integrity in the operation of a reference. Otherwise, there will be a risk of potential abuse; all sorts of fanciful arguments could then be made just to seek a reference to the Standing Committee'.[28] The Court has to be cautious in making any judicial reference, not only because

---

[26] Ibid., 229.
[27] (2013) 16 HKCFAR 45 paras 103–12.
[28] Ibid., para 104.

it is charged with the responsibility of making final adjudication of cases on its own, but also because there is the 'long established rule that a common law court cannot abdicate any part of its judicial function to any other body'.[29]

7.2.3. Common Law or Foreign Affairs?

The same invisible principle can be discerned in the *Congo* case, although this is a more difficult case to fit into the pattern.[30] In that case, the plaintiff sought to enforce an arbitral award against the Government of Congo Republic in Hong Kong against certain payment that was due by a PRC state-owned enterprise to the Congo Government under a separate mining agreement. The Congo Government resisted the proceeding by raising sovereign immunity in Hong Kong courts. The common law position is that sovereignty immunity is not applicable if the foreign government is engaged in a transaction of a commercial nature ('the restrictive immunity principle'), whereas the foreign policy of China is to accord a foreign state an absolute immunity in her domestic courts. Does the issue involve an application of the common law principle, or does it involve 'an act of state such as foreign affairs' within the meaning of Articles 13 and 19 of the Basic Law so that it falls outside the jurisdiction of the Hong Kong courts? The Court of Appeal held that state immunity was a matter of common law. The Court of Final Appeal, by a three to two majority, reversed this decision. The majority held that in a unitary state, the practice or the doctrine of state immunity applied uniformly across the state, and that the executive and the court had to speak with one voice on the policy of state immunity. Under the Basic Law, the responsibility for foreign affairs was a matter exclusively for the Central Government. The doctrine of state immunity was concerned with relations between states and hence fell within the scope of foreign affairs, over which the Hong Kong courts had no jurisdiction. Accordingly, the Court of Final Appeal decided, for the first time, to refer to the NPCSC a number of questions for its interpretation. Further, the common law on state immunity was overridden by the Basic Law to the extent of inconsistency with the PRC foreign policy.

The minority disagreed, holding that the issue before the court was a matter of common law and should be decided by the Hong Kong court. They drew a distinction between recognition of a foreign state, which was a matter for the executive on which one voice was desirable if not essential, and the extent of

---

[29] Ibid., para 106.
[30] Democratic *Republic of the Congo* v. *FG Hemisphere Associates LLC* (No 1) (2011) 14 HKC-FAR 95.

immunity available in courts, which was a matter of law to be determined by the judiciary. Therefore, whether the immunity was absolute or restrictive, it was a matter of law for the courts. The determination of this question did not involve any exercise of jurisdiction over acts of state, defence or foreign affairs; nor did it involve the interpretation of any provision of the Basic Law.

In considering the arguments, the Court of Final Appeal was heavily influenced by three letters that were placed by the Office of the Commissioner of the Ministry of Foreign Affairs ('OCMFA') before the courts at various stages. The first letter, which was placed before the Court of First Instance, addressed solely the position of the PRC on state immunity. The second letter, which was placed before the Court of Appeal, explained the unchanged position of the PRC despite ratification of the UN Convention on Restrictive Immunity, which had not come into effect. The Court of Appeal held that there was no evidence to show that a restrictive immunity doctrine would jeopardise or prejudice any state interest. So, a third letter was placed before the Court of Final Appeal which identified the prejudice to the sovereignty of the Chinese state had the doctrine of restrictive immunity been adopted in Hong Kong. Unlike the two previous letters, the third letter was drafted in strong language and tone.[31] This prompted Bokhary PJ to extract a concession from the Secretary for Justice that the letter was to draw the court's attention to the policy of the PRC and not to dictate a result.[32] The tone of this letter was clear, that were the court to adopt the doctrine of restrictive immunity, such a decision would likely be reversed by an interpretation of the NPCSC.[33]

The precise status of these three letters was unclear. Under Article 19 of the Basic Law, it is possible for the Chief Executive to certify certain questions of fact concerning acts of state whenever such questions arise in the adjudication of cases. Such certification shall be binding on the courts and be treated as conclusive proof of the facts stated therein. No such certification has been issued in this case. Indeed, the Court itself held that it was unnecessary to do so, as these letters would constitute such certification. This is

---

[31] The letter was reproduced in para 211 of the Judgment.
[32] See para 91 of the Judgment. See also para 294 where the majority expressed the same view.
[33] See Eric Cheung, 'Undermining Our Judicial Independence and Autonomy' (2011) 41 Hong Kong Law Journal 411. Benny Tai argued that as a result, the Court made a calculated decision to make a reference in order to minimise the damage that could have been done to judicial independence by a subsequent adverse interpretation from the NPCSC, given that the context of this case was not political and the issue of foreign affairs was obviously arguable: see Benny Tai, 'The Constitutional Game of Art. 158(3) of the Basic Law' (2011) 41 Hong Kong Law Journal 377. This is an interesting observation but it does not explain why the court could not just go through the common law route without seeking an interpretation and deciding that the common law of restrictive immunity has to be modified.

hardly satisfactory. The fact of state, as it is known, is a procedure to introduce statements of fact which shall be treated as conclusive proof by the court. The purpose is to ensure a proper way of introducing conclusive evidence into the court and a certain formality is required. If a letter from the OCMFA can constitute such conclusive proof, does it suggest in future any letter from any government department of the Central Authority could constitute such conclusive proof? It may be a formality in this case, as it is hardly thinkable that the Chief Executive will not provide a certificate to this effect if requested. Yet the formality is there to avoid any undue pressure to be exerted on the court directly by any department of the Central Government.

7.2.4. What Choices Did the Court Have?

Thus, in light of the clear position of the Central Government, the Court was faced with only limited options. First, it could decide to refer the question of interpretation to the NCPSC, as it chose to do, and the outcome was certain that there would be absolute immunity and the common law of restrictive immunity would be reversed. Second, it could decide to go along with the minority to decide the case on the common law principle of restrictive immunity and not to refer the question to the NPCSC. Its decision would then most likely be reversed by a subsequent NPCSC interpretation. This would be the exact replication of the *Ng Ka Ling* situation and might have a detrimental effect on the Hong Kong legal system. There would also be uncertainty on how far the scope of the NPCSC interpretation would be in such circumstances, especially when the NPCSC interpretation could not affect judgment previously rendered and then the Congo Government would come within the jurisdiction of the Hong Kong court despite the NPCSC interpretation. Third, the Court could avoid the issue of sovereign immunity by holding that whatever be the position on sovereign immunity, the Congo Government had waived its immunity by defending these proceedings.[34] While this is a perfectly defensible position and may be a less controversial route, it may not be an attractive solution as the Central Government is keen not to exercise any jurisdiction over the Congo Government. The consequence of this option would still likely be a reversal of the Court's decision by a subsequent NPCSC interpretation.

---

[34] The dominant position in international law is that mere agreement to arbitration does not mean that there is also waiver to the enforcement of the arbitral award. This position is hardly defensive as a matter of fairness.

There was apparently a fourth option. The majority of the Court of Final Appeal accepted that restrictive immunity represented the common law before the changeover.[35] Under Article 8 and 160, the common law is preserved save to the extent that it is inconsistent with the Basic Law, and may be subject to such modifications, adaptations, limitations or exceptions as are necessary so as to bring them into conformity with the status of Hong Kong after the change of sovereignty.[36] Instead of deciding that the doctrine of state immunity is an act of state and therefore falls outside the jurisdiction of the Hong Kong courts, the majority could have decided, as did the minority, that the extent of state immunity is a matter of common law, which has to be modified to reflect the status of Hong Kong as part of a unified state that adopts the policy of absolute immunity. In this way, the court could have reached a position that the common law principle in Hong Kong after 1997 was no longer restrictive immunity but absolute immunity, and therefore it would be unnecessary to refer any question of interpretation to the NPCSC.[37] On this basis, it would decline jurisdiction over the Congo Government and this option would serve both the interest of China and the interest of protecting the integrity of the common law system.

Instead, the majority chose to refer to the NPCSC a question of interpretation of Articles 13 and 19 of the Basic Law. Arguably Article 13, which provides that the Central Government shall be responsible for foreign affairs, is never an issue. There is no dispute about this fact. The question is, notwithstanding this, whether the doctrine of state immunity is nonetheless a matter of common law that could be decided by the Hong Kong courts. Article 19, which provides that the court has no jurisdiction over acts of state such as foreign

[35] Para 221 of the Judgment.
[36] Decision of the NPCSC on the Treatment of the Laws Previously in Force in Hong Kong in accordance with Article 160 of the Basic Law, referred to at para 313 of the Judgment.
[37] See Yap Po Jen, 'Why Absolute Immunity Should Apply But a Reference was Unnecessary?' (2011) 41 *Hong Kong Law Journal* 391. Yap argued that the one voice policy cases could be distinguished because the executive in Britain had not spoken with another voice, whereas the Secretary for Justice in Hong Kong has spoken with a different voice. It is true that the executive in Britain had not expressed a different view and therefore left the matter of determining the extent of immunity to the court, it does not follow that if the executive has spoken the one voice policy has to be adopted. To make this argument one would have to accept that the determination of state policy on immunity is a matter outside the jurisdiction of the court, an argument which Yap has expressed doubt about. As Cheung pointed out, China has entered into over 100 bilateral agreements that have adopted the position of restrictive immunity and it would be absurd to suggest that there was one voice: see Eric Cheung, Supra note 33. The court accepted that it has to take into account the state policy in determining the content of the common law principle of state immunity. Thus, it is open to the court to take into account the absolute immunity principle of the PRC and modify the common law in Hong Kong accordingly.

affairs, comes closer, and the effect of the NPCSC interpretation is that the court would have to forgo jurisdiction in future whenever state immunity is raised.[38] This is so even when state immunity is raised by a state that has subscribed to the principle of restrictive immunity. The position would have been the same if the Court decided that the common law was now one of absolute immunity. This retrograde position seems like an awkward option for the court to adopt. It would be even more awkward when the UN Convention on Restrictive Immunity, which China has ratified, comes into effect. Would the common law have to be changed again? Thus, instead of surrendering itself to such a dire position, the majority may consider that this position is best assigned to the One Country component, therefore leaving the Two Systems component out of it. This is an ironic position to take. Admittedly the Court has to balance between respecting the PRC sovereignty and limiting the harm to the common law system. In choosing to make a judicial referral, the courts may protect the purity of the common law, but may also have inadvertently given up jurisdiction in relation to what constitutes foreign affairs in future. It is not, for the purpose of this chapter, to say that judicial referral is a desirable approach, indeed much is to be said to the contrary as expressed in the powerful minority judgments, but rather to explain that the majority of the Court may probably consider it to be the least detrimental position to adopt in the circumstances and hence the decision could still be explained, perhaps equally ironically, by the higher principle of keeping the integrity of the common law system!

7.2.5. *Procedural Restraints: Establishing a Constitutional Convention?*

In deciding to make a reference to the NPCSC, the Court of Final Appeal laid down certain parameters. First, it declined to decide the question of referral as a preliminary issue. Instead, it insisted on hearing full arguments on the merits of the case on the grounds that whether certain provisions are necessary and determinative of the outcome of the case could only be fully appreciated when the court was appraised of the merits of the case. Second, the court, after hearing the parties, formulated the questions that it required the NPCSC to interpret. This will define the scope of the interpretation. Although such questions are technically not binding on the NPCSC, the NPCSC did give its interpretation within the framework of these questions. Third, the court itself also rendered a provisional judgment on the issue. It is provisional as it is subject to the interpretation of the NPCSC. The provisional judgment was

---

[38] See P. Y. Lo, 'The Gateway Opens Wide' (2011) 41 *Hong Kong Law Journal* 385.

placed before the NPCSC so that the NPCSC has the benefit of the views of the highest court before it renders its interpretation. This is important in another aspect. The parties to the litigation do not have any right to appear before the NPCSC, yet its interpretation is determinative of the outcome of the case. By allowing the parties to make full submissions on the merits and by giving a provisional judgment, the Court has at least afforded the parties a full and fair hearing, even though its decision is not final. Given that there is no right of audience before the NPCSC, this procedure affords the best the Hong Kong legal system could provide to ensure a fair hearing.

None of these procedures are set out in the Basic Law. The purpose of drawing up these procedures is obviously an attempt to minimise the arbitrariness of the NPCSC interpretation and in turn, to protect the integrity of the legal system in Hong Kong. The invisible constitutional principle is at work again.

7.3. CONTINUITY OF THE PREVIOUS SYSTEM VERSUS A LIVING TREE PRINCIPLE

A constitution should serve its community, and the community changes with time. Thus, the constitution should be able to evolve to respond to social changes. It should be a living tree that is capable of growth and development, and should not be stunted by historical relics. As Justice Bertha Wilson nicely put it, 'a constitution is always unfinished and is always evolving ... [It is like a] chain novel where generations of judges produce their respective chapters. Each judge is constrained to a degree by what has gone on before, but at the same time is obliged to make the novel the best that it can be'.[39]

At the same time, the Basic Law expressly provides that the previous capitalist system and way of life shall remain unchanged for fifty years.[40] The preservation of the previous social, economic and legal system was of great importance in maintaining the confidence of the people in Hong Kong in the future at a time of great uncertainty when the Joint Declaration was signed in 1984, and continues to be of importance as Hong Kong is moving towards the end of the guaranteed period of fifty years, which will expire in 2047.

---

[39] B. Wilson, 'The Making of a Constitution: Approaches to Judicial Interpretation' (1988) *Public Law* 370–372. The famous chain novel analogy comes from Professor Ronald Dworkin, *Law's Empire* (Cambridge, MA: Belknap Press, 1986).

[40] Article 5. This article does not mean that the system has to be changed after fifty years. The position in 2047, when the guaranteed period of fifty years expires, is unclear at this stage. For other provisions that refer to the preservation of the previous system, see for example, 103 (public servants), 136 (education system), 142 (professional qualifications), 144 (subvention for non-governmental organisations), and 145 (social welfare system).

This theme of continuity with the previous system, which does not always sit well with the living tree characteristics of the Basic Law, has come up in a number of cases, and has on some occasions produced awkward consequences.

In *Association of Expatriate Civil Servants of Hong Kong v. Chief Executive of the HKSAR*, the applicants argued that the procedures for the appointment and dismissal of public servants must be established either by legislation or with legislative approval, as Article 48(7) of the Basic Law requires the Chief Executive to appoint or remove holders of public office 'in accordance with legal procedure', whereas the Public Service (Administrative) Order 1997 and the Public Service (Disciplinary) Regulation were executive orders only.[41] The Government relied on Article 103 of the Basic Law, which provides that 'Hong Kong's previous system of recruitment [and] ... discipline ... for the public services ... shall be maintained'. Keith J held that since the previous procedures for the recruitment and dismissal of holders of public office were established by the Crown under the Hong Kong Letters Patent and the Colonial Regulations in the exercise of its prerogative, and by the Governor in the exercise of powers expressly conferred upon him by the Colonial Regulations, the maintenance of the previous system did not require the current system to have the approval of the Legislature. Insofar as the phrase 'in accordance with legal procedure' in Article 48(7) was concerned, this phrase has to be construed together with Article 103 and simply means a procedure established lawfully rather than a procedure to be established by law. Since the procedures laid down by the Chief Executive in the Order and the Regulation maintained Hong Kong's previous system of recruitment and discipline of the public service and were lawfully established, they satisfied the requirement of 'in accordance with legal procedure'. Although this phrase appears a few times in the Basic Law, Keith J held that 'the meaning of a particular provision, whether in an ordinance or in a constitutional instrument such as the Basic Law, depends very much on its context', and the learned judge did not discern a clear pattern as to the rationale behind the use of one phrase and not another in the Basic Law.

Keith J's decision was distinguished by Hartmann J (as he then was) in *Leung Kwok Hung v. Chief Executive of the HKSAR*.[42] In that case, the issue was whether an executive order setting out the procedure for applications for the approval of interceptions of telecommunications complied with the requirement of 'in accordance with legal procedure' in Article 30 of the Basic

---

[41] [1998] 1 HKLRD 615.
[42] HCAL 107/2005, upheld on appeal: CACV 73 and 87/2006. In the further appeal to the Court of Final Appeal, the issue of the legality of the executive order was no longer pursued: (2006) 9 HKCFAR 441 (*sub nom Koo Sze Yiu v. Chief Executive of the HKSAR*).

Law. Hartmann J emphasised that the context in which this phrase was to be interpreted was very different from that in Article 48(7), as Article 30 was concerned with the protection of a fundamental right of privacy. Such context required a different interpretation. Hartmann J held:

> 149. In my view, it is a formalistic outcome to say that the fundamental right contained in art. 30, which the article requires shall be protected by law, may nevertheless be restricted by a body of purely administrative procedures which are not law and which bind only public servants who, in the event of abuse, are subject only to internal disciplinary proceedings. That, in my view, would derogate substantially from the practical and effective value of the right guaranteed by the article. That, I am satisfied – giving the article a generous interpretation in order to protect the full measure of the value of the right it guarantees – cannot have been the intention of those who drafted the Basic Law.
>
> I am satisfied, therefore, that the use of the phrase 'in accordance with legal procedures' in art. 30 means procedures which are laid down by law in the sense that they form part of substantive law, invariably in order to comply with the requirements of legal certainty, within legislation, primary and/or secondary.

The distinction is not satisfactory. It is difficult to see why invasion of privacy has to be provided by law whereas disciplinary action that could have resulted in the removal of a public servant from employment and a substantial loss of pension benefit could be prescribed by administrative procedures. Loss of livelihood would have been the concern of a far higher number of ordinary people than occasional covert surveillance carried out by law enforcement agents. A plausible explanation is that the disciplinary system is a continuation of the previous system, and it is such an overriding principle that the court would be hesitant to upset the system by demanding legislative intervention.

7.3.1. How Far Could It Go: Twisting the Meaning of Legality?

This argument was reinforced in *Kong Yunming v. Director of Social Welfare*.[43] At issue was whether a substantial change of the residence requirement from one year to seven years for Comprehensive Social Welfare Assistance (CSSA) was a violation of the Applicant's pre-existing right to social welfare under Article 36 of the Basic Law. The CSSA scheme is a non-contributory, means-tested social security scheme that is aimed at providing a safety net for people who are unable to meet their basic needs. Like all forms of social security in

---

[43] (2013) 16 HKCFAR 950.

Hong Kong, the CSSA scheme has all along been a non-statutory scheme and is administered by the Social Welfare Department. The Department has issued guidelines which set out the criteria, the procedure for application and even a system of administrative appeal against refusal to provide CSSA. It is not in dispute that these guidelines are administrative in nature and are generally accessible. One of the issues is whether a restriction on the right to social welfare that was imposed administratively satisfied the requirement of Article 36, which provides that 'Hong Kong residents shall have the right to social welfare in accordance with law'.

Both the Court of Appeal and the Court of Final Appeal were concerned about the implications of a requirement of restrictions by law on the social welfare system. At the Court of Appeal, Stock VP noted that Article 36 did not set out any type of social welfare or any level of benefits that a person might enjoy. Nor did it provide for any restriction of the right or the type of restriction that could be imposed. The learned judge then argued that any social welfare must carry with it eligibility conditions. These eligibility conditions should not be regarded as restrictions, and accordingly, the question of restrictions in accordance with law did not arise.[44] Alternatively, the Court relied on Article 145, which provides that '[o]n the basis of the previous social welfare system, the Government of the HKSAR shall, on its own, formulate policies on the development and improvement of this system in the light of the economic conditions and social needs'. It was held that Article 145 itself provided the legal basis; that 'the qualifying conditions may justifiably be described as prescribed by law in that they are authorised by article 145 itself, are accessible, establish rules of general application and do not permit arbitrary or random decision-making'.[45] On the first ground, the distinction between eligibility condition and restriction is a semantic distinction without any difference in substance. In any event, the United Nations Human Rights Committee has commented that 'any qualifying conditions for benefits must be reasonable, proportionate and transparent. The withdrawal, reduction or suspension of benefits should be circumscribed, based on grounds that are reasonable, subject to due process, and provided for in national law'.[46] Thus, the restriction will still have to satisfy the proportionality test whether it is described as a restriction or an eligibility condition. On the second ground, if Article 145 provides the legal basis, the requirement of 'in accordance with law' is tautological and practically meaningless.

[44] CACC 185/2009 (CA, 17 February 2012), paras 53, 73–4.
[45] Ibid., para 74.
[46] General Comment No 19, para 24.

Surprisingly, this reasoning was endorsed by the Court of Final Appeal, which resorted to the 'previous system'. Ribeiro PJ held:[47]

> Article 145 recognizes and endorses the validity of 'the previous social welfare system' which consisted of a non-statutory system of administrative rules and policies. Accordingly, reading Art. 36 together with Art. 145, the intention of the Basic Law must be taken to be that such administrative system – consisting of rules that are accessible, systematically applied and subject to a process of administrative appeal – is to be treated as a system providing 'social welfare in accordance with law' within the meaning of Art. 36.

This reasoning is hardly convincing. Article 145 provides a framework to enable the Government to formulate social welfare policies in accordance with the changing economic conditions. It is at least not clear that Article 145 also endorses an administrative scheme, which would have made a mockery of the requirement of 'in accordance with law' in Article 36. Though the Court of Final Appeal did not agree with the Court of Appeal that Article 36 did not provide any substance other than a right not to be discriminated in the enjoyment of social welfare rights, the Court of Final Appeal did share the concern that the social welfare system had to cater for a wide range of clients with a wide range of different circumstances and therefore it was better served by a flexible, transparent and predictable administrative system rather than by having each benefit spelt out through a legislative process.[48] Yet the desirability for flexibility in administering a social welfare system is not unique to Hong Kong, and many other jurisdictions have found no impediment to introducing a statute on social welfare.[49] The facts that the administrative rules are accessible, systematically applied and include an administrative appeal system to reduce arbitrariness in the decision-making process do not by themselves turn an administrative scheme into law. The requirement of 'in accordance with law' is not formalistic. It serves an important democratic value that any restriction of a fundamental right has to be properly debated and scrutinised by the people's representatives in the Legislature.[50] To regard an administrative scheme as 'law' will defeat the important function of legislative scrutiny

---

[47] (2013) 16 HKCFAR 950, para 25, though the Court of Final Appeal did not accept the first reason on a distinction between eligibility condition and restriction. For a commentary, see Simon Young, 'Does It Matter If Restrictions on the Right to Social Welfare in Hong Kong are Prescribed by Law or Policy?' (2014) 44 *Hong Kong Law Journal* 25.

[48] Para 27.

[49] For example, see the *UK Social Security Act* and the *Australian Social Security Act*.

[50] See 'The word "law" in Article 30 of the American Convention on Human Rights', Advisory Opinion, OC-6/08, Inter-American Court of Human Rights, Series A, No 6 (9 May 1986), paras 21–2.

and is inconsistent with the approach of the court in adopting a wide margin of appreciation. In justifying a wide margin of appreciation, the Court relied heavily on legislative scrutiny because social and economic policies were better judged by the legislature than by the court.[51] Yet by accepting an administrative scheme as 'law', the court leaves no room for legislative scrutiny! It appears that the rather loose requirement on legislative sanction could only be explained partly by the judicial perception of the nature of social and economic rights, an issue that we will come back later, and partly by the eagerness to uphold an invisible principle of continuation of the previous system. The Court was reluctant to upset the previous administrative social welfare scheme that had been in place for many years by imposing a requirement of legal framework.

7.3.2. An Innovative Approach: Crystallising the Previous System

Another significant implication of the continuity principle in this case is the determination of the scope of the right to social welfare. The Court of Appeal has great difficulty in defining the scope of the right under Article 36, which eventually led to its rejection of any substantive right under Article 36, save for a right not to be discriminated in the enjoyment of the right to social welfare. The Court of Final Appeal accepted that the right that received constitutional protection under Article 36 would be the rights as defined by the rules of eligibility on the date of establishment of the HKSAR, namely 1 July 1997.[52] In order to determine progression or retrogression under Article 145, there has to be a baseline for assessment. The obvious, and perhaps the only sensible, baseline would be the rights as they existed at the time when the HKSAR came into being. What the applicant was entitled to on that date included the then eligibility condition, namely the one-year residence requirement: nothing more, nothing less. Thus, in one stroke, the Court constitutionalised the social welfare rights (and conditions) as existed on 1 July 1997, and any further restriction from that level of social welfare benefits has to be justified.[53]

---

[51] See, for example, the judgment of Cheung CJHC at the Court of First Instance, para 56. See also the judgment of the Court of Final Appeal in Fok Chun-wa v. Hospital Authority (2012) 15 HKCFAR 409, para 63–4, where the Court held, in the context of justifying the concept of a wide margin of appreciation, that 'where matters of state or community policy are concerned, these are matters predominantly for the Executive or the Legislature'.

[52] See paras 34–5. See also Catholic Diocese of Hong Kong v. Secretary for Justice (2011) 14 HKCFAR 754, para 45 for a similar holding that the previous education system refers to the system in place just before 1 July 1997.

[53] Bokhary PJ, in his separate judgment, held that if any restriction is to be justified by economic downturn, it has to be so dire as to bring about a situation not contemplated by the constitution,

In contrast, the courts are well aware of the sensitivity of fossilising the previous system, and in this regard they have drawn a distinction based on whether a fundamental right was engaged. In *Catholic Diocese of Hong Kong v. Secretary for Education*, the issue was whether the introduction of a school-based management scheme by the Government, which has the effect of diluting the control of the church in the management board of government-aided schools run by the Catholic Church, was in violation of the right of the religious organisation to continue to run its schools 'in accordance with the previous practice', contrary to Article 141 of the Basic Law.[54] The Applicant argued that the 'previous practice' embodied an exclusive control over the appointment of the school management committee, the supervisor and the principal of its schools. The argument failed, firstly on factual grounds that the previous system did allow the Director of Education to require binding constitution and appoint managers, and secondly that the new system did leave religious organisations free to nominate a majority of the persons serving on the management committees of the aided schools that it sponsored. It also failed on the ground that the 'previous practice' could not prevent the Government from making changes. Article 141 was to preserve the continuity of the previous system, but it did not prevent changes to individual elements of the system.[55] On the other hand, this phrase did protect religious organisations to be able to run their schools in accordance with the previous practice insofar as it involved the exercise of their right to religious belief and religious activities, such as morning prayers or religious instruction, but constitutional protection was not engaged in relation to policies that had no religious content. Thus, the concept of previous practice is extended to cover religious rights and freedom in the educational context, and yet it allows the education system to be further developed in light of changing social conditions.

The theme of continuity has also been invoked in rejecting an argument to outlaw some administrative tribunals such as the Market Misconduct Tribunal or the Inland Revenue Board on the ground that they had usurped powers which were reserved for the judiciary.[56] Administrative tribunals have played an important and valuable role in Hong Kong. Bearing in mind the theme of continuity in the Basic Law, it was held that there have to be very compelling

---

or otherwise Article 145 would be of little practical use: see para 160. See also Albert Chen, '"A Stroke of Genius"' in Kong Yunming' (2014) 44 *Hong Kong Law Journal* 7.

[54] (2011) 14 HKCFAR 754.
[55] Paras 61–2. See also *Secretary for Justice v. Lau Kwok Fai* (2005) 8 HKCFAR 304, para 66.
[56] *Koon Wing Yee v. Insider Dealing Tribunal* [2013] 1 HKLRD 76, para 59; (2008) 11 HKCFAR 170 (CFA); *Luk Ka Cheung v. Market Misconduct Tribunal* (2009) 1 HKC 1, para 35; *Lee Yee Shing Jacky v. Inland Revenue Board* [2011] 6 HKC 307, para 98.

and sound reasons before it could be concluded that the vesting of judicial power in the judiciary under Article 80 of the Basic Law would have the effect of outlawing these tribunals and rendering their statutory jurisdiction unconstitutional for having ousted the jurisdiction of the judiciary or usurped the judicial functions of the courts.

On the other hand, the same theme has also been invoked in justifying restrictions of constitutional rights. It was invoked in justifying legislative action to reduce the pay of civil servants, as the threat of legislative intervention in employment contract with the Government was a feature in the pre-1997 regime.[57] Likewise, corporate voting in the functional constituency system, under which corporations are entitled to vote in functional constituencies to return a member in their constituency to the Legislative Council, was justified on the ground that this system, albeit some distance away from full democracy, represented a feature in the previous political system and has to be considered in its historical context. Accordingly, the Court of Appeal held that the right to vote in Article 26 of Basic Law did not preclude corporate voting.[58] It is not the purpose of this chapter to argue whether the theme of continuity should only be used to advance constitutional entitlements, but rather it is to show that this invisible principle does play a part in constitutional interpretation.

7.4. SEPARATION OF POWERS

One of the perennial debates in Hong Kong is the nature of the governance system. The Mainland authorities keep describing Hong Kong as an 'executive-led system', meaning that both the Legislature and the Judiciary are to support and not to challenge the Executive Government, and accordingly leaves no room for checks and balances against excesses by the Executive Government. This phrase of 'executive-led government' appears nowhere in the Basic Law, but it is contended that the former colonial system under which the Governor enjoyed practically unchecked powers is to be preserved in the HKSAR. This is partly because the former system is regarded as highly efficient, and partly because it is much easier for the Mainland authorities to maintain control on the development of Hong Kong through an appointed Chief Executive. On the other hand, preservation of the colonial system is incompatible with a number of features in the Basic Law. While the Chief Executive is vested

---

[57] *Secretary for Justice v. Lau Kwok Fai* (2005) 8 HKCFAR 304.
[58] *Chan Yu Nam v. Secretary for Constitutional and Mainland Affairs*, CACV 2 and 3/2010 (7 December 2010).

with extensive powers under the Basic Law, he is also subject to extensive checks and balances in the exercise of his powers that were hitherto not in existence in the previous colonial regime. For instance, while the Chief Executive may refuse to give assent to any bill if he considers that the bill is not compatible with the overall interests of Hong Kong and may return the bill to the Legislative Council for reconsideration, his option is limited if the Legislature returns the bill on reconsideration by no less than a two-thirds majority. He has either to give his assent or to dissolve the Legislature, a power that he could exercise only once during his term. If he decides to dissolve the Legislative Council and if the new Legislative Council passes the bill again by a two-thirds majority, the Chief Executive has to resign if he still refuses to assent to the bill. Besides, the Legislative Council is vested with the power to impeach the Chief Executive for a serious breach of law or a dereliction of duty, which power does not exist in the previous system. This has led many observers to conclude that the system under the Basic Law is one of checks and balances, whether it is executive-led or not. This debate is particularly intense in the development of representative government in Hong Kong.[59]

The courts have on a number of occasions expressed their view on the nature of the governance system, and have unambiguously come down in favour of a system of separation of powers.[60] There are a number of implications of this view. It reinforces the principle of legality so that the executive Government is subject to law and, *a fortiori*, judicial review of executive action. It also means that the power of interpretation of law is vested in the judiciary. This includes the Basic Law, which provides that no laws in the HKSAR shall contravene the Basic Law. Accordingly, in the first case on the Basic Law, the Court of Final Appeal held that the power to determine whether any executive act or legislative provision contravenes the Basic Law and to strike down any incompatible legislative provision is vested in the courts.[61] Thus, in one brush the Court of Final Appeal assumed the power of constitutional review and the power to strike down legislative acts that are inconsistent with the Basic Law, when nowhere in the Basic Law expressly confers this power on the judiciary – a power which has been controversial in other jurisdictions. Second, it influences the development of the doctrine of margin of appreciation in that there

---

[59] For a summary of the debates, see Benny Tai, 'The Chief Executive' in J. Chan and C. L. Lim (eds.), *Law of the Hong Kong Constitution*, 2nd edn (Hong Kong: Sweet & Maxwell, 2015), paras 7.013–7.021.
[60] *Leung Kwok Hung v. President of Legislative Council of the HKSAR*, HCAL 87/2006; *Raza v. Chief Executive of the HKSAR* [2008] 3 HKLRD 561; *Society for the Protection of the Harbour v. Chief Executive in Council (No 2)* [2004] 2 HKLRD 902.
[61] *Ng Ka Ling v. Director of Immigration* (1999) 2 HKCFAR 4.

are distinct constitutional roles and areas of competence for each of the three branches of Government so that the courts should afford deference to the other two branches of Government in exercising their powers of constitutional scrutiny. We will come back to this point in the next section.

Third, the courts would be reluctant to interfere with the internal operation of the Legislative Council. There were a number of occasions where the exercise of powers of the Legislative Council was challenged, not only by members of the public, but also by members of the Legislative Council. In *Chim Pui Chung* v. *President of Legislative Council*, a legislator who was convicted and sentenced to three years' imprisonment challenged the order of the President of the Legislative Council to put on the agenda a motion to disqualify him under Article 79(6) of the Basic Law on the ground that 'conviction' and 'sentence' under Article 79(6) referred to a final order of conviction and sentence after the appeal has been exhausted.[62] The application was refused without entering into the question of jurisdiction. In *Leung Kwok Hung* v. *Clerk to the Legislative Council*, the applicant, who was newly elected to the Legislative Council, applied for a declaration that he was free to devise his own form of oath of office so long as the essence of the original oath was retained.[63] His application for leave was refused on the ground that the legislation did not permit a departure from the statutory language of the oath without again entering into the question of jurisdiction. In another case of *Leung Kwok Hung* v. *President of the Legislative Council*, the applicant challenged the ruling of the President of the Legislative Council to disallow him to move an amendment on the basis that it has the object or effect of disposing of or charging part of the revenue.[64] He invited the court to grant a declaration that the relevant Rule of the Legislative Council contravened Article 73(1) of the Basic Law. The application failed on the ground that the remedy was not reasonably arguable. It was noteworthy that the court was not invited to intervene in any internal procedure of the Legislative Council or to pronounce on the legality of the decision of the President. Hartmann J sounded the caution that while the court has jurisdiction to intervene, this jurisdiction, having regard to the doctrine of separation of powers and the sovereignty of the Legislative Council under the Basic Law, should only be exercised in a restrictive manner.[65]

In *Cheng Kar Shun* v. *Li Fung Ying*, the applicant, who was a major real estate developer, challenged the power of a committee of the Legislative

---

[62] [1998] 2 HKLRD 552.
[63] HCAL 112/2004.
[64] [2007] 1 HKLRD 387.
[65] Ibid., 397, para 31.

Council to summons witness in an investigation under Article 73(10) of the Basic Law.[66] It was argued that this power could only be exercised by the Legislative Council and not by one of its committees. For the first time, leave to apply for judicial review of the practice of the Legislative Council was granted. It is significant that the court was invited to intervene in an ongoing proceeding of the Legislative Council. The application was ultimately dismissed on ground of statutory interpretation. The question of jurisdiction was not argued.

Finally, in a further case of *Leung Kwok Hung v. President of Legislative Council*, also known as the filibustering case, the Court of Final Appeal set out clearly the relationship between the courts and the Legislative Council.[67] In that case, the issue was the legality of the ruling of the President of Legislative Council to cut short and close a debate. Having regard to the doctrine of separation of powers, the court held that whether the President has the power to terminate a debate was a matter for the court, but whether the power was properly exercised would be a matter for the Legislative Council. In general, the court shall not intervene in the internal procedure of the Legislative Council. It is for the Legislative Council to decide how it would like to make and apply its own rules to deal with the problem of filibustering, and the courts, in a system of separation of powers, should respect the sovereignty of the Legislative Council in this regard.

The doctrine of separation of powers is not set out in the text of the Basic Law. It was even politically controversial whether this principle was embodied in the Basic Law. Nonetheless, it is clearly an invisible constitutional principle in operation that has guided or influenced the courts in all these cases.

7.5. FROM PROPORTIONALITY TO MANIFESTLY WITHOUT REASONABLE FOUNDATION: PREVALENCE OF CIVIL AND POLITICAL RIGHTS OVER SOCIAL AND ECONOMIC RIGHTS

The doctrine of separation of powers is also seen to be in operation in the context of social and economic rights. Chapter 3 of the Basic Law is titled 'Fundamental Rights and Duties of the Residents', in which it sets out a list of fundamental rights. Among them include both civil and political rights, as well as social and economic rights, culminating in the important Article 39 which provides that no restriction of rights and freedoms shall contravene the ICCPR and the ICESCR as applied to Hong Kong and implemented through

---

[66] [2011] 2 HKLRD 555.
[67] (2014) 17 HKCFAR 689.

the laws of HKSAR. This chapter is not exhaustive of all fundamental rights, as the right to fair trial and the right to jury trial is provided in the chapter dealing with the 'Judiciary', whereas the right to property is protected in the chapter on 'Economy'. While there is nothing in the Basic Law to suggest that there is a hierarchy among different types of rights, the courts have, through a series of decisions on proportionality, reached a stage where not all rights are of equal status.

7.5.1. A Rigorous Proportionality Test

The starting point is that in a civil society, the courts will vigilantly protect fundamental rights and freedoms and vigorously scrutinise any restriction on them. Any restriction will have to satisfy the legality and the proportionality tests. The proportionality test embraces the twin facets that the restriction bears a rational relationship to and does not go beyond what is necessary to achieve the objectives to be pursued. In developing the proportionality test, the courts soon adopt and modify the concept of a margin of appreciation to domestic law. In its original conception, this notion legitimises an international tribunal to defer to the States in determining whether restrictive measures are necessary on the ground that domestic institutions are in a much better and more informed position to evaluate particular local needs and conditions. Formulated in this way, the concept has no place in domestic law, as it is not open to a local judge to claim unfamiliarity with local needs and conditions. However, the concept was soon modified to justify a degree of deference to the Executive Government or Legislature in recognition of their expertise, information advantage or constitutional roles. Thus, in *Lau Cheong v. HKSAR*, the Court of Final Appeal held that whether mandatory life imprisonment replacing a mandatory death sentence was a necessary and proportionate response to murder was a highly charged political decision which the court should defer to the Legislature.[68] While the doctrine of deference is justified on the dual grounds of expertise/competence and constitutional roles, the court is less prepared to defer to the executive or the Legislature if the ground of deference is based on a mere lack of expertise. Thus, in *Kwok Kay Kwong v. Medical Council of Hong Kong*, it was argued that the Courts should defer to the judgment and expertise of the Medical Council who were in a better position to determine what kind of restriction on professional advertising by doctors would be necessary.[69] Yet the Court of Final Appeal was prepared

---

[68] (2002) 5 HKCFAR 415 447.
[69] [2008] 3 HKLRD 524.

to subject the justifications to a searching scrutiny and eventually overrode the judgment of the Medical Council primarily because the decision involved free speech.

7.5.2. An Alternative Test of 'Manifestly without Reasonable Foundations'

In contrast, the Court readily extended the concept to social and economic rights by adopting a new standard of manifestly without reasonable foundations. It readily accepted that allocation of resources in the context of socio-economic policies was a matter for the executive government so that a less vigorous scrutiny would be justified. Thus, in *Fok Chun-wa* v. *Hospital Authority*, the Court held that in the context of allocation of limited public funds, the Government should be left to decide whether to have any social welfare scheme, and if so, its extent and who should benefit thereunder.[70] It was not for the court to find an alternative solution and the courts would intervene only if the impugned measure had clearly transgressed beyond the range of alternatives. In that case, the issue was whether a differential and higher fee for obstetric services for non-Hong Kong residents could be justified. The differential fee regime was introduced to discourage Mainland pregnant mothers from giving birth in Hong Kong, as such incidents, due to their sheer number, have caused considerable anxieties and strains in obstetric services and hospital resources for Hong Kong pregnant mothers. The Court of Final Appeal found that a distinction based on residence status was entirely within the spectrum of reasonableness and that the measure was not discriminatory, taking into account, among other things, the need to ensure the sustainability of providing subsidised health services and the entitlement to subsidised health services not being a fundamental right.

The idea that social and economic rights are not fundamental rights has been expressed in some earlier cases. In *Chan Mei Yee* v. *Director of Immigration*, Hartmann J held that social and economic rights were promotional and aspirational in nature and hence the ICESCR did not create any legally enforceable obligations.[71] This has attracted a rebuke from the Committee on Economic, Social and Cultural Rights in its concluding observation on the Initial Periodic Report on the HKSAR. The Committee, in unusually strong language, 'regrets' such views, which were 'based on a mistaken understanding of the legal obligations arising from the Covenant' and urged

---

[70] (2012) 15 HKCFAR 409, paras 62–81.
[71] HCAL 77/1999, 13 July 2000. See also *Chan To Foon* v. *Director of Immigration* [2001] 3 HKLRD 109, 131–4, and *Mok Chi Hung* v. *Director of Immigration* [2001] 2 HKLRD 125, where a similar sentiment has been expressed.

the Government not to repeat similar views in judicial proceedings.[72] In reply, the Government stated that 'we note the Committee's observation that the Covenant is not merely "promotional" or "aspirational" in nature and accept that it creates binding obligations at the international level'.[73]

While the Government's reply was ambiguous as to its stance on social and economic rights at the domestic level, it did refrain from arguing that social and economic rights are aspirational or promotional in nature in subsequent legal proceedings. Instead, it urged, and to a large extent successfully, the courts to afford a wide margin of appreciation to the Government whenever social and economic rights were engaged. The courts responded by developing the concept of manifestly without reasonable foundation, and in so doing, drew a distinction between cases involving socio-economic policies and cases involving fundamental rights or core values. Thus, in *Kong Yunming* v. *Director of Social Welfare*, the Court of Final Appeal laid down a three-tier test:[74]

> In some cases involving fundamental rights such as freedom of expression or freedom of peaceful assembly, or rights bearing on criminal liability such as the presumption of innocence, the Court has regarded the restriction as disproportionate unless it goes no further than necessary to achieve the legitimate objective in question. This is sometimes called the 'minimal impairment' test.
>
> Similarly, in discrimination cases, where the differentiating inroad is based on certain personal characteristics sometimes referred to as 'inherently suspected grounds' such as race, colour, sex or sexual orientation, the Court will subject the impugned measure to 'intense scrutiny', requiring weighty evidence that it goes no further than necessary to achieve the legitimate objective in question.
>
> However, it would not usually be within the province of the courts to adjudicate on the merits or demerits of government socio-economic policies. Where the disputed measure involves implementation of the Government's socio-economic policy choices regarding the allocation of limited public funds without impinging upon fundamental rights, or involving possible discrimination on inherently suspect grounds, the Court has held that it has a duty to intervene only where the impugned measure is 'manifestly without reasonable justification'.

---

[72] UN Doc E/C.12/1/Add 58, paras 16, 27 (11 May 2011).
[73] 2nd Periodic Report of the HKSAR Government, paras 2.11–2.12, available at www.cmab.gov .hk/en/issues/culturalrights_report.htm.
[74] (2013) 16 HKCFAR 950, para 40.

In short, a less vigorous scrutiny will be adopted in assessing the proportionality of any measures restricting social and economic rights because 'the Art. 36 right to social welfare is not a fundamental right but a right which intrinsically involves the Government setting rules determining eligibility and benefit levels'.[75] In so doing, the courts equated social and economic rights with socio-economic policies and reinforced the second-class nature of social and economic rights. This approach is largely influenced by the courts' perception of separation of powers, namely that allocation of resources in socio-economic policies falls within the domain of executive prerogatives.

Notwithstanding its rhetoric on social and economic rights, the Court of Final Appeal in *Kong Yunming* did, to the surprise of many observers, adopt a rather vigorous scrutiny of the restriction on the right to social welfare and reversed unanimously the decisions of the lower courts. In that case, the issue was whether an extension of the eligibility residence requirement from one year to seven years for comprehensive social welfare assistance was a violation of the right to social welfare under Article 36 of the Basic Law. The Government relied on the familiar argument that the extension was necessary to ensure the sustainability of the social welfare system. The Court, however, subjected this argument to vigorous examination of evidence. It found that the restriction was inconsistent with the family reunion policy and the population policy, that the extension was illogical as young children were exempted but not their parents, resulting in children without parental care or young children having to share their welfare assistance with their parents. It also found that the seven-year residence requirement was in fact targeted at the new arrivals from the Mainland, and the Government failed to substantiate the claim of sustainability when only 12–15 per cent of the expense was attributable to the new arrivals. The Court examined closely the Government's budget, the breakdown of the expenditure on CSSA as revealed in the Legislative Council paper, and various statistics and reports provided by the Government and concluded that there was no rational connection between the justification of sustainability of the welfare system and the seven-year residence requirement, and that the seven-year residence requirement was a restriction on the Applicant's right to social welfare that was manifestly without reasonable foundation.

The approach of the court was exemplary of a vigorous scrutiny of restriction on a fundamental right. It casts doubt on any real difference between the minimal impairment test and the manifestly without reasonable foundation test, which at face value, is reminiscent of the more conservative Wednesbury

---

[75] Ibid.

unreasonableness test in the common law.[76] To that extent it is a welcome development. On the other hand, it would be too early to conclude that this case marks the dawn of a new era for social and economic rights and that the court is prepared to acknowledge social and economic rights as a fundamental right on par with civil and political rights. The Court itself was cautious in pointing out that the right to social welfare was not a fundamental right, that it was dealing with a scheme to provide 'safety net needs', and that its decision may not apply to other forms of social welfare.[77] Its approach may well be conditioned by the special facts in that case.[78]

7.5.3. An Inferior Status of Social and Economic Rights Again?

Indeed, shortly after, the Court seems to have resorted once again to the inferior nature of social and economic rights. In the more recent case of *GA v. Director of Immigration*, the issue was whether the applicants, who were screened-in torture claimants and mandated refugees, were entitled to work when they have been in Hong Kong for 10–13 years and when there was no reasonable prospect of their resettlement in a foreign country.[79] The Court of Final Appeal held that they could not rely on either the ICCPR or the Bill of Rights because of an effective reservation on immigration decisions. Insofar as the right to work in Article 6 of the ICESCR is concerned, the Government accepted that while there was no general domestic law that has given effect to the ICESCR, Article 6 has been implemented in domestic law through various provisions in the Basic Law and provisions in over fifty ordinances. Notwithstanding this concession, the Court held that there was no general, unrestricted right to work. The most that can be said is that 'there is some allowance made for persons like the Applicants to be permitted to

---

[76] Ip criticised that the manifestly without reasonable foundations test as conservative and flawed: see Eric Ip, 'Manifest Unreasonableness: The Doctrinal Future of Constitutional Review of Welfare Policy in Hong Kong' (2014) 44 *Hong Kong Law Journal* 55. While this criticism is valid at face value, the way the test was applied, at least in the case of *Kong Yunming*, is far from conservative. Indeed, others criticised the court for being too invasive: Po Jen Yap and Thomas Wong, 'Public Welfare and the Judicial Over-Enforcement of Socio-economic Rights in Hong Kong' (2014) 44 *Hong Kong Law Journal* 41.

[77] Paras 23 and 138. See also para 40.

[78] In the course of argument, the Court was apparently concerned that the case dealt with a scheme to provide safety-net basic needs. There were also extensive documentations and evidence on the One-Way Permit System and the Population Policies, and the absence of consideration of any other length of residence requirement such that the seven-year residence requirement was obviously targeted at new arrivals from the Mainland.

[79] (2014) 17 HKCFAR 27.

work, but this is far from the general, unrestricted right which is said to exist'.[80] This is a regrettably narrow view of the right to work. In the first place, the right to work may be regarded as a right to freely enter into a contract of employment, which is well recognised in the common law. Second, a right to work does not mean an absolute right to work. It is subject to restrictions that are necessary and proportionate. Framed in this way, the issue would then be whether the restrictions imposed by the Director of Immigration not to allow the applicants to work were proportionate. This would allow the court to examine the substance of the issue and balance the competing considerations. Unfortunately, by rejecting that there is a right to work, the court found it even unnecessary to consider whether the Director of Immigration should exercise his discretion in a manner consistent with treaty obligations under the ICESCR on the basis that the ICESCR was not incorporated into domestic law – reminiscent of the fact that the ICESCR is aspirational and promotional in nature!

The upshot of this line of cases reveals an increasingly restrictive stance towards the rights of aliens. It has first been held that illegal immigrants from the Mainland had no legitimate expectation to a right to fair hearing and that the Director of Immigration had no duty to consider humanitarian grounds.[81] It was then held that there was no discrimination to subject an alien mother from the Mainland to a differential and higher fee for public health services.[82] In another case it upheld the constitutionality of a provision in the Immigration Ordinance that denied foreign domestic helpers ordinary residence in Hong Kong, no matter how long they have stayed in Hong Kong.[83] Then it was held that there was no right to work for mandated refugees or screened-in torture claimants even when they had stayed in Hong Kong for over twelve years with no reasonable prospect of resettlement in another country.[84]

7.5.4. Swinging the Pendulum even Further?

Do these cases foreshadow a reversal of the liberal trend towards treatment of fundamental rights? The original conception of separation of powers that the Government is to abide by law has gradually given way to another conception of separation of powers that the courts should defer to the Legislature or

---

[80] Ibid., para 60.
[81] *Ho Ming Sai v. Director of Immigration* [1994] 1 HKLR 21; *Hau Ho Tak v. Director of Immigration* [1994] 2 HKLRD 202.
[82] *Fok Chun-wa v. Hospital Authority* (2012) 15 HKCFAR 628.
[83] *Vallejos v. Commissioner of Registration* (2013) 16 HKCFAR 45.
[84] *GA v. Director of Immigration* (2014) 17 HKCFAR 27.

the Executive Government when it involves the constitutional competence of another branch of government. This is witnessed by the adoption of the manifestly without reasonable foundation test even in civil and political rights. In *Kwok Cheuk Kin v. Secretary for Constitutional and Mainland Affairs*, the Court of Appeal reinterpreted the three-tier test adopted in *Kong Yunming*.[85] In that case, the issue was whether a prohibition against a legislator who has resigned from the Legislature from taking part in the by-election for the vacant seat that was created by his resignation was a proportionate restriction on the right to vote. The restriction was a response to the attempt of some Legislators who tried to seek popular mandate and force an effective referendum on a controversial issue by resignation and then taking part in the by-election on a single-issue platform. While the right to stand for election is no doubt a civil and political right, the Court of Appeal held that:

> Properly read, in *Kong Yunming*, Ribeiro PJ applied the proportionality test and he was only referring to the difference in the intensity and standard of review in the application of the third limb of that test (proportionate restriction).[86]

By reinterpreting the test in *Kong Yunming*, the Court of Appeal held that there was only one proportionality test and there was no separate minimal impairment test, thereby eschewing the difference between civil and political rights and social and economic rights. It maintained the test of manifestly without reasonable foundations for social and economic rights, but then decided to adopt the same test, or at least a wide margin of appreciation in favour of the Government, for the right to stand for election on the ground that the issue was political in nature. The application for judicial review failed.[87]

The reluctance of the courts to intervene in the allocation of public resources has long been recognised in the common law and could be traced back to the doctrine of separation of powers. This attitude manifested itself in the treatment of social and economic rights in the Basic Law, when the Basic Law itself has not drawn any such distinction. It has led the courts to develop a different notion of proportionality test, namely a test of manifestly without reasonable foundations, and the test was then extended even to the right to stand for election on the ground that the issue was political. The doctrine of separation of powers is not explicit, but it is certainly in operation.

---

[85] [2015] 5 HKLRD 881.
[86] Para 28.
[87] The Court of Appeal has refused to grant leave to appeal to the Court of Final Appeal. The applicant is currently applying for leave to appeal from the Court of Final Appeal.

7.6. CONCLUSION

Hong Kong is not an independent state. Under the One Country, Two Systems model, it has to operate within a country that has adopted a fundamentally different legal, social and political system. It is a precarious model that rests heavily on the goodwill of the PRC. At the time of the Joint Declaration, Hong Kong was already a modern metropolis with great economic success, and was responsible for almost 90 per cent of foreign incomes of the PRC. Thirty years later, China has emerged as the second largest economic power in the world, with Hong Kong responsible for only less than 3 per cent of its GDP. Yet economic progress in the Mainland is not matched by its development of the rule of law, which still flourishes in Hong Kong. Over the years, Hong Kong has been subject to increasing social, economic and political influences from the Mainland. The rule of law, which embodies the independence of the judiciary, is probably the only aspect that distinguishes the two systems now. Thus, it is not surprising that the courts are trying very hard to preserve the integrity of the common law system and in particular, the objective and perceived independence of the judiciary, but at the same time, carefully restrain the exercise of their power.

In preserving the integrity of the common law system, the courts also try to preserve the previous systems, be it the health system, the education system, regulations of civil service or the social welfare system. The promise of One Country, Two Systems is to last for at least fifty years. This promise could only be realised if the essence of the previous system is preserved. At the same time, the courts have to ensure that this would not fossilise the previous systems and allow them to evolve with changing social and economic conditions.

A challenging issue for the courts is the changing relationship of the three branches of government. The rule of law mandates the subjection of Government acts to the principle of legality. At the same time, the power of constitutional review, which the Court of Final Appeal managed to claim, requires the court to respect the sovereignty of the two other branches of government. In this sense, the doctrine of separation of powers goes hand in hand with the power of constitutional review. The influences of the doctrine of separation of powers under this new regime of constitutional review could be seen, not only in delineating the relations between the judiciary and the Legislature in judicial review of the functioning of the Legislative Council, but also in the deference to the Government and the Legislature in reviewing restrictions of social and economic rights.

None of these principles can be found explicitly in the text of the Basic Law. Yet it is also clear that they have been in operation and influencing judicial decisions. Whether they are just distinct constitutional principles or fixed stars that punctuate the night sky that could form a pattern of constitutional constellations remains to be seen.[88] It is probably too early to find an invisible constitutional pattern behind the text in a constitution of barely twenty-five years old. Yet it is clear that there are at least some fundamental principles that lie behind the text. Preservation of the existing system is promised up to the year 2047. The system thereafter remains an open question at this stage, that will probably have to be decided at the latest in around the year 2030.[89] In exploring the future in the not too distant future, there is a practical, if not also imperative, dimension for Hong Kong to identify any invisible constitutional fundamentals. This chapter provides a modest attempt to do so.

---

[88] Tribe, Supra note 1, 72.
[89] The negotiation on the future of Hong Kong was carried out in 1982, some seventeen years before the changeover. This length of period is necessary for proper consultation and for the banking sector to operate on matters regarding finance and mortgages, which were a crucial factor that prompted the negotiation in the late 1970s and the 1980s.

8

The Constitutional Orders of 'One Country, Two Systems'

A Comparative Study of the Visible and Invisible Bases of Constitutional Review and Proportionality Analysis in the Chinese Special Administrative Regions of Hong Kong and Macau

Albert H. Y. Chen and P. Y. Lo[*]

8.1. INTRODUCTION

The last two decades of the twentieth century was not only an era of constitution-making in the People's Republic of China ('PRC'), but also one of the making of 'mini-constitutions' at the sub-national level in China. The PRC's new Constitution of 1982 made it possible for 'Special Administrative Regions' ('SARs') to be established within China that practised economic and social systems different from those applicable in other parts of the PRC. This provision was designed to provide the constitutional foundation for the practice of 'One Country, Two Systems' with regard to Hong Kong and Macau, and possibly also Taiwan, upon their reunification with the Chinese mainland. In 1990 and 1993, the Basic Law of the Hong Kong SAR (HKSAR) and the Basic Law of the Macau SAR (MSAR) were respectively enacted by the Chinese National People's Congress. These two 'mini-constitutions' came into full force in 1997 and 1999, when the British handover of Hong Kong to China and the Portuguese handover of Macau to China took place respectively.

---

[*] Earlier versions of this chapter were presented at the Roundtable of the International Association of Constitutional Law, held at Melbourne University Law School on 2–3 May 2016, and at the Conference on 'Governance, Democratization and Constitutional Reform: Definition of Political Structure of the HKSAR and its Reform' organized by the Centre for Chinese and Comparative Law, City University of Hong Kong Law School on 23–24 June 2016. The authors thank the editors of this book and Cheng Jie, Paula Ling and Yang Xiaonan for their comments on and assistance in the completion of this chapter.

The texts of the two Basic Laws are very similar, and many of their provisions are almost identical. Despite such similarity in the texts of the two Basic Laws, 'the judicial construction of the Basic Law' has resulted in different constitutional orders in Hong Kong and Macau.[1] A comparative study of the constitutional jurisprudence of the Hong Kong and Macau SARs can thus provide an interesting case study of the interaction between the 'visible' and 'invisible' constitutions of each of the two jurisdictions as regards constitutional review and interpretation.

In this chapter, we explore the 'visible' and 'invisible' constitutional bases of the founding and development of constitutional judicial review in the Hong Kong and Macau SARs. We compare the similarities and differences in their textual and extra-textual constitutions, particularly in the contexts of the origins of the power of constitutional judicial review and the use of proportionality analysis in the exercise of such power of review. We conclude that the differences in their constitutional jurisprudence are to a significant extent explicable in terms of the different legal traditions of the two former colonies, their judicial experience accumulated before their handover to the PRC and also partly in terms of the institutional features of their legal systems, different degrees of affinity with foreign constitutional jurisprudence, the political culture of the community and the values of and choices made by the legal and judicial elites of the two SARs.

This chapter will consist of the following sections, apart from this Introduction (Section 8.1). Section 8.2 will introduce the historical and political contexts of the enactment of the two Basic Laws. It will also identify the similarities and differences between the two Basic Laws. Sections 8.3 and 8.4 will review the development of constitutional judicial review and the use of proportionality analysis in Hong Kong and Macau respectively. Finally, Section 8.5 will provide a comparative analysis, and seek to understand and explain the differences in the relevant constitutional jurisprudence.

---

[1] This is the title of P. Y. Lo (Pui Yin Lo)'s book, *The Judicial Construction of Hong Kong's Basic Law: Courts, Politics, and Society after 1997* (Hong Kong: Hong Kong University Press, 2014). As to the courses of construction embarked by the courts of the HKSAR and the courts of the MSAR, see Sections 8.3 and 8.4. As to earlier comparisons of their legal systems and their approaches to constitutional review in the English language, see Ignazio Castellucci, 'Legal Hybridity in Hong Kong and Macau' (2011) 57 *McGill Law Journal* 665; Eric Ip, 'The Evolution of Constitutional Adjudication in the Chinese Special Administrative Regions: Theory and Evidence' (2013) 61 *American Journal of Comparative Law* 799.

8.2. THE HISTORICAL AND POLITICAL CONTEXTS OF THE ENACTMENT OF THE BASIC LAWS OF THE HONG KONG AND MACAU SARS

8.2.1. *The Case of Hong Kong*

The British Empire acquired the colony of Hong Kong from China in three stages: the cession of Hong Kong Island by the Qing Emperor then ruling China to Britain in 1842 after the 'Opium War'; the cession of Kowloon Peninsula (across the harbour from and to the north of Hong Kong Island) by the Qing Imperial Court to Britain in 1860 after the Anglo-French forces invaded Peking; and the ninety-nine-year lease by the Qing Imperial Court to Britain of the 'New Territories' (north of Kowloon) in the midst of the foreign powers' 'scramble for concessions in China' in 1898.[2]

As the British 'lease' over Hong Kong's New Territories would expire in 1997, British Prime Minister Margaret Thatcher visited Beijing in 1982 and initiated negotiations with the PRC Government on Hong Kong's future. The result was the Sino–British Joint Declaration signed at the end of 1984.[3] The Joint Declaration provided for Hong Kong's return to China in 1997.[4] The PRC undertook to allow Hong Kong to practise a high degree of autonomy as a SAR of the PRC after 1997. There would be 'Hong Kong people ruling Hong Kong' instead of the PRC government sending its Communist Party cadres to rule Hong Kong. Hong Kong would be permitted to retain its existing economic, social and legal systems (including capitalism, private ownership of property, the English common law and existing provisions for the protection of human rights and civil liberties) in accordance with Deng Xiaoping's concept of 'One Country, Two Systems': Hong Kong would become an integral part of the 'One Country' of China, but the Chinese mainland and Hong Kong would practise different 'systems' – 'socialism' and 'capitalism' respectively.[5]

---

[2] See generally Peter Wesley-Smith, *Constitutional and Administrative Law* (Hong Kong: China & Hong Kong Law Studies, 2nd edn 1994) 23–30.

[3] See generally Yash Ghai, *Hong Kong's New Constitutional Order* (Hong Kong: Hong Kong UP, 2nd edn 1999), ch. 2.

[4] How Hong Kong was 'agreed' by Britain and the PRC to be returned in 1997 was not only a political struggle between the negotiating parties, but also a legal challenge both in public international law and the domestic constitutional law of the two respective states, bearing in mind that Britain, as described above, acquired parts of Hong Kong by cession through treaty and the remainder (the 'New Territories') by lease through treaty with a term of 99 years as from 1898. The PRC considered those treaties to be 'unequal treaties' and refused to recognise their validity; it preferred to describe the return of Hong Kong to the Motherland as 'resumption of exercise of sovereignty'. The legal consequences of these positions and their implications and consequences for contemporary Hong Kong deserve a separate study.

[5] Section 1 of Annex I to the Joint Declaration provides that 'after the establishment of the Hong Kong Special Administrative Region the socialist system and socialist policies shall not be

The Joint Declaration contains detailed provisions on the systems and policies the PRC declared for practice in the HKSAR to be established on 1 July 1997. The Joint Declaration is a treaty that is binding on the Chinese and British governments in international law, but the PRC would need to translate its provisions into domestic law so as to provide a legal basis for the operation of the HKSAR. The PRC undertook in the Joint Declaration that it would enact such a law.[6] The drafting of such a domestic law began in 1985 and was completed in 1990, when the National People's Congress (NPC) of the PRC enacted the Basic Law of the HKSAR of the PRC. This Basic Law would serve as a 'mini-constitution' for Hong Kong after 1997. It provides for the constitutional relationship between the HKSAR government and the central government in Beijing; it defines the structure, mode of formation and powers of the HKSAR government; it guarantees the rights and liberties of Hong Kong people; it sets out the social and economic policies and systems to be practised in the HKSAR; and it also makes provisions for the continuation of treaties previously applicable to Hong Kong in respect of the HKSAR, as well as for the HKSAR government to conduct certain external affairs under the authorisation of the central government.

8.2.2. The Case of Macau

The successful conclusion of the Sino–British Joint Declaration in 1984 paved the way for the settlement of the question of Macau's future by diplomatic negotiation between the Chinese and Portuguese governments. The geographical size of Macau was less than 30 square kilometres, much smaller than the 1,100 square kilometres of Hong Kong. The Portuguese settlement in Macau had begun three centuries earlier than the British colonisation of Hong Kong. The former took place in the mid-sixteenth century, when China was under the rule of the Ming dynasty, the last of the dynasties of the Han Chinese.[7] After Hong Kong became a British colony in 1842, Portugal sought to turn Macau formally into a Portuguese colony. In 1845, Portugal declared Macau to be a free port and appointed a Governor of Macau. In 1887, Portugal and the Qing Imperial Court entered into the Treaty of Peking, providing expressly for Portuguese governance of Macau. Although this treaty

---

practised in the Hong Kong Special Administrative Region', and 'Hong Kong's previous capitalist system and life-style shall remain unchanged for 50 years'.

[6] See the Joint Declaration, Article 3(12).

[7] The Qing Imperial Court was of Manchu origin from the geographical north-east of the current territory of the PRC. It imposed its rule on China by overthrowing the Ming dynasty and subjugating the Han Chinese to its hegemony.

was abrogated by agreement between the Portuguese government and the Nationalist government of the Republic of China in 1928, Portuguese administration of Macau continued.[8]

After the 1974 Revolution in Portugal, the new government offered to return Macau to China as part of its policy of dismantling colonial rule of territories beyond the seas, but the offer was declined. In 1979, Portugal and the PRC established diplomatic relations. In October 1984, China's paramount leader Deng Xiaoping declared that the resolution of the question of Macau's future would follow the example of Hong Kong. In 1986, the Portuguese and Chinese governments commenced negotiations, leading to the conclusion in 1987 of the Sino–Portuguese Joint Declaration on the Question of Macau (SPJD).

The SPJD was similar to the Sino–British Joint Declaration on the Question of Hong Kong (SBJD) in both structure and content. The former consists of a main text and two annexes, while the latter consists of a main text and three annexes. The main texts of the SPJD and SBJD consist of seven paragraphs and eight paragraphs respectively. Each paragraph in the SPJD has a counterpart in the SBJD, except that the subject matter of the first paragraph of the SPJD corresponds to that covered by the first two paragraphs of the SBJD. Whereas the SBJD provided for the reversion of Hong Kong to China in 1997, the SPJD provided for the reversion of Macau in 1999. The longest paragraph in the main text of the SPJD is paragraph 2, which is divided into twelve sub-paragraphs and sets out the basic policies of the PRC regarding Macau. This corresponds to paragraph 3 of the main text of the SBJD, which is similarly divided into twelve sub-paragraphs, setting out the basic policies of the PRC regarding Hong Kong. Most of the sub-paragraphs of paragraph 2 of the SPJD have counterparts in paragraph 3 of the SBJD.[9]

The lengthy Annex I to each of the two Joint Declarations elaborates the basic policies of the PRC regarding the HKSAR and MSAR respectively. Both Annexes are divided into fourteen sections dealing with various topics. Most of the sections in Annex I to the SBJD and their content have counterparts in Annex I to the SPJD.[10]

As in the case of the SBJD, the SPJD provides that the PRC's basic policies towards the future SAR as set out in the main text of the Joint Declaration and as elaborated in Annex I thereto will be stipulated in a Basic Law to be enacted by the NPC of the PRC, and 'will remain unchanged for 50 years'. Following

---

[8] In 1928, the Sino–Portuguese Treaty of Friendship and Trade was concluded.
[9] Paragraphs 2(5) and 2(11) of the SPJD do not have counterparts in paragraph 3 of the SBJD.
[10] Sections 8 (shipping) and 9 (civil aviation) of Annex I to the SBJD do not have counterparts in Annex I to the SPJD. The subject matter of section 14 (land leases) of Annex I to the SPJD is covered by Annex III (land leases) to the SBJD.

the enactment of the Basic Law of the HKSAR in 1990, the Basic Law of the MSAR was enacted in 1993. We now turn to examine these Basic Laws.

8.2.3. The Basic Laws

There is a close relationship between the Basic Law of each of the two SARs and the corresponding Joint Declaration, which expressly provides that the basic policies set out in the Joint Declaration, shall be stipulated in the Basic Law. A close examination of the text of each of the Basic Laws would reveal that many provisions therein are derived from or even reproduced from the relevant provisions in paragraph 3 of the main text of, and Annex I to, the SBJD (in the case of the Hong Kong Basic Law (HKBL)) or paragraph 2 of the main text of, and Annex I to, the SPJD (in the case of the Macau Basic Law (MBL)). However, there also exist matters not covered by the Joint Declaration but dealt with in the Basic Law. For example, the SBJD does not prescribe the details of how the Chief Executive of the SAR is to be chosen, or how its legislature is to be elected. Detailed provisions in this regard are supplied by the Basic Law.

Both Basic Laws declare the relevant territory to be an inalienable part of China, establish the SAR with a high degree of autonomy and enjoying executive, legislative and independent judicial power (including that of final adjudication), designate the SAR to be a local administrative region of China coming directly under the Central People's Government, provide that the executive and legislative branches of the SAR shall be composed of permanent residents of the HKSAR, require the SAR to protect the fundamental rights and freedoms of its residents and other persons in the SAR and guarantee that the socialist system and policies shall not be practised in the SAR, with the previous capitalist system and way of life to remain unchanged for fifty years.[11]

We now proceed to examine the relevant provisions of the Basic Laws on the relationship between the Basic Law and other laws and on judicial power, with a view to exploring the constitutional basis, if any, for constitutional judicial review in the Hong Kong and Macau SARs. The relevant provisions of HKBL and their counterparts in the MBL are first identified.

> HKBL art. 8: Laws previously in force in Hong Kong shall be maintained, except for any that contravene the Basic Law, and subject to amendment by the legislature. Counterpart in MBL: art. 8.

---

[11] See the Hong Kong Basic Law, arts. 1, 2, 3, 4, 5, 12; and the Macau Basic Law, arts. 1, 2, 3, 4, 5, 12.

HKBL art. 11(2): No law enacted by the legislature shall contravene the Basic Law. Counterpart in MBL: art. 11(2).

HKBL art. 17(3): National People's Congress Standing Committee (NPCSC) may invalidate a law enacted by the Hong Kong legislature on the ground that it is 'not in conformity with the provisions of this Law regarding affairs within the responsibility of the Central Authorities or regarding the relationship between the Central Authorities and the Region'. Counterpart in MBL: art. 17(3).

HKBL art. 19(2): HKSAR courts 'have jurisdiction over all cases in the Region, except that the restrictions on their jurisdiction imposed by the legal system and principles previously in force in Hong Kong shall be maintained'. Counterpart in MBL: art. 19(2).

HKBL art. 39: (1) The provisions of the International Covenant on Civil and Political Rights [ICCPR], the International Covenant on Economic, Social and Cultural Rights, and international labour conventions as applied to Hong Kong shall remain in force and shall be implemented through the laws of the [HKSAR]. (2) The rights and freedoms enjoyed by Hong Kong residents shall not be restricted unless as prescribed by law. Such restrictions shall not contravene the provisions of the preceding paragraph of this Article. Counterpart in MBL: art. 40.

HKBL art. 158: The NPCSC has the power to interpret the Basic Law. The courts of the HKSAR may interpret the Basic Law 'in adjudicating cases', except that if there is a 'need to interpret the provisions of this Law concerning affairs which are the responsibility of the Central People's Government, or concerning the relationship between the Central Authorities and the Region', the Court of Final Appeal (CFA) should seek an interpretation of the relevant provision by the NPCSC before making final judgment. Counterpart in MBL: art. 143.

HKBL art. 160(1): Upon the establishment of the [HKSAR], the laws previously in force in Hong Kong shall be adopted as laws of the Region except for those which the [NPCSC] declares to be in contravention of this Law. If any laws are later discovered to be in contravention of this Law, they shall be amended or cease to have force in accordance with the procedure as prescribed by this Law. Counterpart in MBL: art. 145(1).

It should be noted that the relevant provisions in the HKBL and MBL as mentioned above are almost identical. Thus in both the Hong Kong and Macau SARs, the Basic Law is a superior law relative to other laws in the SAR. The NPCSC has the power to invalidate Hong Kong or Macau laws that contravene the Basic Law in accordance with art. 17(3) of both the HKBL and

MBL (which applies to legislation enacted by the legislature of the relevant SAR), art. 160(1) of the HKBL and art. 145(1) of the MBL (which applied at the transition in respect of the 'laws previously in force'). There is no express provision on the power of the courts of the HKSAR or MSAR to invalidate or determine as invalid any Hong Kong or Macau law that the court considers to be inconsistent with the Basic Law, but the courts of the two SARs are empowered to interpret the Basic Law, subject to the requirement to seek an interpretation from the NPCSC in the circumstances defined in art. 158 of the HKBL and art. 143 of the MBL. Furthermore, art. 19(2) of both the HKBL and MBL defines the scope of the jurisdiction of the courts of the two SARs by reference to their existing jurisdiction before the establishment of the SAR.

8.3. CONSTITUTIONAL JUDICIAL REVIEW AND PROPORTIONALITY ANALYSIS IN HONG KONG

8.3.1. Constitutional Review in Colonial Hong Kong

At the time of the enactment of the HKBL in 1990, there was little case law and jurisprudence in colonial Hong Kong on constitutional judicial review of legislation, though judicial review of administrative action and of delegated legislation in accordance with principles of English administrative law (such as the ultra vires doctrine and the *Wednesbury* unreasonableness standard of 'rationality' review) was well established in the colony.

Hong Kong's colonial constitution[12] was contained in the Letters Patent issued by the British Crown,[13] which established the executive, legislative and judicial branches of the colonial government. Unlike Acts of Parliament which could not be reviewed by British courts because of the doctrine of Parliamentary supremacy, the colonial legislature in Hong Kong, i.e., the Governor acting with the advice and consent of the Legislative Council, only enjoyed limited legislative powers. For example, insofar as its powers were derived from the Letters Patent, it could not act ultra vires the Letters Patent.[14] Furthermore, the Colonial Laws Validity Act enacted by the British

---

[12] The discussion here draws on Albert H. Y. Chen, 'The Interpretation of the Basic Law – Common Law and Mainland Chinese Perspectives' (2000) 30 *Hong Kong Law Journal* 380, 417–20.

[13] See generally Norman Miners, *The Government and Politics of Hong Kong* (Hong Kong: Oxford University Press, 5th edn 1995), ch. 5; Peter Wesley-Smith, *Constitutional and Administrative Law in Hong Kong* (Hong Kong: Longman Asia, 1995), ch. 2.

[14] See *R v. Ibrahim* (1913) 8 HKLR 1 (FC); *Ho Po Sang v. Director of Public Works* [1959] 1 HKLR 632 (FC). Cf *R v. Burah* (1878) 3 App. Cas. 889 (PC), at 904–5; *Powell v. Apollo Candle Co* (1886) 10 App Cas 282 (PC); *Hodge v. R* (1883) 9 App Cas 117 (PC).

Parliament in 1865, which was applicable to Hong Kong as it was applicable to other parts of the British Empire – provided that colonial laws that were repugnant to applicable Acts of Parliament would be null and void.[15] The courts of Hong Kong, including the Judicial Committee of the Privy Council in London which served as the final appellate court of the Hong Kong judicial system, had the power to review whether any statutory provision enacted by the Hong Kong legislature was ultra vires the colonial constitution or otherwise invalid under the Colonial Laws Validity Act 1865 or any other law that limited the legislature's competence.

In practice, however, the courts of colonial Hong Kong had few opportunities to exercise this power of constitutional judicial review of legislation.[16] This was because the Letters Patent were only a crude and rudimentary written constitution for the colony. It did not contain any guarantee of civil liberties and human rights. It did not contain elaborate provisions on the powers of and relationship between the executive, legislative and judicial branches of the colonial government. Nor did it set up any system of division of power as between the colonial government and the metropolitan government.

In the light of this historical background, what happened in 1991 can be regarded as the first constitutional revolution in Hong Kong – the second being, of course, the reversion to Chinese rule and the HKBL coming into force in 1997 (which involved a shift in the Grundnorm).[17] In 1991, in an attempt to restore confidence in Hong Kong's future which had been deeply shaken by the Tiananmen incident of 4 June 1989,[18] the Hong Kong Government introduced and the local legislature passed the Hong Kong Bill

---

[15] See *Rediffusion (HK) Ltd* v. *AG* [1970] AC 1136 (PC). The HKSAR courts even recognised repugnancy under the Colonial Laws Validity Act 1865 in 2003; see *A Solicitor* v. *Law Society of Hong Kong* (2003) 6 HKCFAR 570.

[16] See generally Wesley-Smith, Supra note 13, ch. 7; Ghai, Supra note 3, 305–6. There were, however, a few cases in which the Hong Kong courts were called upon to interpret the provisions of the Letters Patent: see Peter Wesley-Smith, 'Constitutional Interpretation', in Peter Wesley-Smith (ed.), *Hong Kong's Transition* (Hong Kong: Faculty of Law, University of Hong Kong, 1993) 51, 69–70. The leading case in this regard is *Rediffusion (Hong Kong)* v. *Attorney-General of Hong Kong* [1970] AC 1136. See also Peter Wesley-Smith, 'Legal Limitations upon the Legislative Competence of the Hong Kong Legislature' (1981) 11 *Hong Kong Law Journal* 3.

[17] See generally Albert H. Y. Chen, 'The Provisional Legislative Council of the SAR' (1997) 27 *Hong Kong Law Journal* 1, 9–10; Albert H. Y. Chen, 'Continuity and Change in the Legal System' in L. C. H. Chow and Y. K. Fan (eds.), *The Other Hong Kong Report 1998* (Hong Kong: Chinese University Press, 1999) 29, 30.

[18] See generally Albert H.Y. Chen, 'The Suppression of China's Democracy Movement and Hong Kong's Future' (1989) 19 *Hong Kong Law Journal* 283; Albert H. Y. Chen, 'The Basic Law, the Bill of Rights and the British Citizenship Scheme' (1990) 20 *Hong Kong Law Journal* 145.

of Rights Ordinance,[19] which incorporated into the domestic law of Hong Kong the provisions of the ICCPR which had already been applied by the United Kingdom to Hong Kong on the level of international law since 1976. The Ordinance expressly repealed all pre-existing legislation that was inconsistent with it.[20] At the same time, the Letters Patent were amended to give the ICCPR supremacy over future ordinances enacted by the colonial legislature.[21] As the Court of Appeal explained in 1994:[22]

> The Letters Patent entrench the Bill of Rights by prohibiting any legislative inroad into the International Covenant on Civil and Political Rights as applied to Hong Kong. The Bill is the embodiment of the covenant as applied here. Any legislative inroad into the Bill is therefore unconstitutional, and will be struck down by the courts as the guardians of the constitution.

The Bill of Rights and the corresponding amendment to the Letters Patent inaugurated the era in Hong Kong's legal history of judicial review of legislation on the basis of constitutional guarantees of human rights. The case law developed by Hong Kong courts in this new era has been well documented.[23] It demonstrates that Hong Kong courts had already acquired considerable experience in judicial review of the constitutionality of legislation when the HKBL came into force in July 1997. They had introduced into Hong Kong constitutional law basic principles of such judicial review, such as the principle of proportionality and the need for government to justify a restriction of a guaranteed human right.

One of the earliest and most celebrated cases decided under the Hong Kong Bill of Rights in the 1990s was *R v. Sin Yau-ming*, decided by the Hong

---

[19] Chapter 383, Laws of Hong Kong. See generally Raymond Wacks (ed.), *Hong Kong's Bill of Rights* (Hong Kong: Faculty of Law, University of Hong Kong, 1990); Johannes Chan and Yash Ghai (eds.), *The Hong Kong Bill of Rights: A Comparative Approach* (Singapore: Butterworths Asia, 1993); Raymond Wacks (ed.), *Human Rights in Hong Kong* (Hong Kong: Oxford University Press, 1992).
[20] Section 3 of the Ordinance.
[21] The amendment related to article VII of the Letters Patent. See Chan and Ghai, Supra note 19, 539–40.
[22] *R v. Chan Chak Fan* [1994] 3 HKC 145 (CA), 153.
[23] Yash Ghai, 'Sentinels of Liberty or Sheep in Woolf's Clothing? Judicial Politics and the Hong Kong Bill of Rights' (1997) 60 *Modern Law Review* 459; Johannes M. M. Chan, 'Hong Kong's Bill of Rights: Its Reception of and Contribution to International and Comparative Jurisprudence' (1998) 47 *International and Comparative Law Quarterly* 306; Andrew Byrnes, 'And Some Have Bills of Rights Thrust upon Them: The Experience of Hong Kong's Bill of Rights', in Philip Alston (ed.), *Promoting Human Rights Through Bills of Rights: Comparative Perspectives* (Oxford: Oxford University Press, 2000), ch. 9.

Kong Court of Appeal in 1991.[24] The case concerned the constitutional validity of a presumption for the purpose of the law of evidence contained in the Dangerous Drugs Ordinance. The presumption was that if the accused was found in possession of 0.5 grams of dangerous drugs, it would be presumed that he possessed it for the purpose of trafficking unless he could prove otherwise. The Court of Appeal applied the three-stage proportionality test developed by the Canadian Supreme Court in R v. Oakes,[25] which included elements of justification and deference as respect, yet with a bias towards human rights protection, and struck down the presumption as contrary to the presumption of innocence in the Hong Kong Bill of Rights.[26]

8.3.2. Constitutional Judicial Review in the HKSAR

Upon the establishment of the HKSAR in 1997, the colonial constitution embodied in the Letters Patent lost its force. As mentioned above, art. 8 of the HKBL provides for the continued validity of the laws previously in force in Hong Kong, except for any law that contravenes the HKBL and subject to any amendment by the SAR legislature. Under art. 160 of the HKBL, the NPCSC may declare which of Hong Kong's pre-existing laws contravene the HKBL and cannot therefore survive the 1997 transition. Such a declaration was made by the NPCSC on 23 February 1997 in its Decision on the Treatment of the Laws Previously in Force in Hong Kong.[27] The Decision declared the non-adoption, inter alia, of three interpretative provisions in the Hong Kong Bill of Rights Ordinance, apparently on the ground that they purported to give the Ordinance a superior status overriding other Hong Kong laws, which was said to be inconsistent with the principle that only the HKBL is superior to other Hong Kong laws.[28]

---

[24] [1992] 1 HKCLR 127.
[25] [1986] 1 SCR 103. The case is a leading case on the Canadian Charter of Rights and Freedoms incorporated into Canada's constitution in 1982.
[26] However, a less rigorous proportionality analysis was used by the Judicial Committee of the Privy Council in *Attorney General v. Lee Kwong-kut* (1993) 3 HKPLR 72, a case on appeal from Hong Kong. See Lo, Supra note 1, 281–3. The Privy Council and the United Kingdom Supreme Court have since then made an about turn: see *de Freitas v. Permanent Secretary of Ministry of Agriculture, Fisheries, Land and Housing* [1999] 1 AC 69 (PC); and *Gaughran v. Chief Constable of the Police Service of Northern Ireland* [2015] 2 WLR 1303 (UKSC).
[27] For an English translation of this Decision, see (1997) 27 *Hong Kong Law Journal* 419.
[28] The interpretative provisions concerned were sections 2(3), 3 and 4 of the Ordinance. For the effect of the non-adoption of these provisions, see Peter Wesley-Smith, 'Maintenance of the Bill of Rights' (1997) 27 *Hong Kong Law Journal* 15; Johannes Chan, 'The Status of the Bill of Rights in the Hong Kong Special Administrative Region' (1998) 28 *Hong Kong Law Journal* 152.

The operative force of the Hong Kong Bill of Rights and the Hong Kong courts' power of judicial review of legislation on human rights grounds and related principles of proportionality have, however, survived the non-adoption of these provisions in the Hong Kong Bill of Rights Ordinance. This is clear from the case law of the post-1997 era, particularly the CFA's decisions in *Ng Kung Siu* (on the freedom of expression)[29] and *Leung Kwok Hung* (on the freedom of assembly and procession).[30] The Hong Kong courts' post-1997 approach to human rights protection, which has not been challenged by litigants or their lawyers in any case and thus represents the consensus of the legal community in Hong Kong, is that the courts may review whether any legislative or executive action violates the human rights guaranteed by chapter III of the HKBL or by the ICCPR (the applicable provisions of which have, as mentioned above, been reproduced in the Hong Kong Bill of Rights) which is given effect by article 39 of the HKBL. The courts have interpreted article 39 to mean that the relevant provisions of the ICCPR as incorporated into the Hong Kong Bill of Rights have the same constitutional force as the HKBL itself, thus overriding laws that are inconsistent with these provisions.

Another part of Hong Kong's pre-existing laws that continue as part of the laws of the HKSAR is the administrative law based on English common law, including the standard of substantive review of administrative action known as '*Wednesbury* unreasonableness', which limits judicial intervention to cases where the impugned administrative action is 'so unreasonable that no reasonable authority could ever have come to it'.[31] Although the *Wednesbury* standard of review still prevails in English and Hong Kong administrative law, it is noteworthy that 'proportionality' has been mooted as a possible future development of this branch of the law.[32]

---

[29] (1999) 2 HKCFAR 442. The court judgments in the cases discussed in this chapter are all available at the website of the Hong Kong Judiciary, http://legalref.judiciary.gov.hk.

[30] (2005) 8 HKCFAR 229.

[31] Per Lord Greene MR in *Associated Provincial Picture Houses Ltd* v. *Wednesbury Corporation* [1948] 1 KB 223 (EWCA), 230. The *Wednesbury* test has been subject to judicial reformulation and calibration over the course of time; see *Council of Civil Service Unions* v. *Minister for the Civil Service* [1985] AC 374 (HL), 410–11 (per Lord Diplock); *R* v. *Secretary of State for the Home Department; ex p Bugdaycay* [1987] AC 514 (HL), 531 (per Lord Bridge of Harwich); *R* v. *Ministry of Defence ex p Smith* [1996] QB 517 (EWCA), 554 (per Sir Thomas Bingham MR); *R* v. *Chief Constable of Sussex; ex p International Trade's Ferry Ltd* [1999] 2 AC 418 (HL), 452E (per Lord Cooke of Thorndon); *R (Mahmood)* v. *Secretary of State for the Home Department* [2001] 1 WLR 840 (EWCA), [16]–[19] (per Laws LJ); *Kennedy* v. *Charity Commission* [2015] 1 AC 455 (UKSC), [54]–[55] (per Lord Mance). For recent Hong Kong cases discussing and applying the *Wednesbury* test, see *Pagtama* v. *Director of Immigration* (HCAL 13, 45, 56/2014, 12 January 2016) (CFI); and *BI* v. *Director of Immigration* [2016] 2 HKLRD 520 (CA).

[32] Per Lord Diplock in *Council of Civil Service Unions* v. *Minister for the Civil Service*. This possible development has come closer; see *Pham* v. *Secretary of State for the Home Department*

The net effect of the coming into force of the HKBL in July 1997 and the HKSAR courts' interpretation of its judicial review power under the HKBL and of article 39 is that the grounds on which legislative and executive actions may be challenged by way of judicial review have been broadened compared to the post-1997 era. After 1991 but before 1997, it was possible to launch such a challenge on the basis of the provisions of the Hong Kong Bill of Rights, which are identical to those provisions of the ICCPR that are applicable to Hong Kong. After 1997, a challenge may still be launched on this basis, but in addition a challenge may also be based on other provisions of the HKBL, particularly those which confer rights that are not expressly or adequately provided for in the ICCPR, such as the right of abode or the right to travel.[33] In the following text, we will review several leading cases on constitutional judicial review and on the application of proportionality analysis.

The first case on constitutional judicial review in the HKSAR was the decision of the Court of Appeal on 29 July 1997 – less than one month after the HKSAR was established on 1 July 1997 – in *HKSAR v. Ma Wai Kwan*.[34] This case was famous, largely because of what the court said about its lack of competence to review acts of the national legislative organs in Beijing. For our present purposes, the case is significant because it also concerned the power of Hong Kong courts to review acts of the Hong Kong legislature. In this case, the Court of Appeal agreed with the Solicitor General who represented the HKSAR government, that since Hong Kong courts had before 1997 enjoyed the power to review the constitutionality of local legislation, and art. 19 of the HKBL enabled them to retain their former jurisdiction, the courts of the HKSAR have the 'power to determine the constitutionality of SAR-made laws vis-à-vis the Basic Law'.[35] The proposition that Hong Kong courts have this power has never been challenged by any party in subsequent cases. Thus *Ma Wai Kwan* paved the way for subsequent decisions by the Hong Kong courts exercising the power of judicial review of SAR laws alleged to be inconsistent

---

[2015] 1 WLR 1591 (UKSC). See generally, Mark Elliott and Hanna Wilberg, 'Modern Extensions of Substantive Review: A Survey of Themes in Taggart's Work and in the Wider Literature' in Hanna Wilberg and Mark Elliott (eds.), *The Scope and Intensity of Substantive Review: Traversing Taggart's Rainbow* (Oxford: Hart Publishing, 2015) 19–40; and Jeffrey Jowell, 'Proportionality and Unreasonableness: Neither Merger Nor Takeover', in ibid., 41–59.

[33] As well as on the basis that the impugned legislation in question had been repealed by the Hong Kong Bill of Rights Ordinance Section 3 in 1991, the non-adoption of that provision by the NPCSC under the Decision of 23 February 1997 notwithstanding; see *HKSAR v. Lam Kwong Wai* (2006) 9 HKCFAR 574, [59] (per Sir Anthony Mason NPJ).

[34] [1997] HKLRD 761, [1997] HKC 315.

[35] [1997] 2 HKC 315 at 351.

with the HKBL. The *Ma Wai Kwan* case may thus be regarded as the *Marbury v. Madison* of the constitutional history of the HKSAR.[36]

The judicial power to strike down statutory provisions determined by the HKSAR court to be unconstitutional was exercised for the first time in the landmark decision in January 1999 of the CFA in the case of *Ng Ka Ling v. Director of Immigration*.[37] The CFA was established in 1997 to replace the Judicial Committee of the Privy Council as the final appellate court in Hong Kong. It enjoys the power of final adjudication, so that cases litigated in Hong Kong cannot be appealed to Beijing. Although the interpretation adopted by the CFA of art. 22(4) of the HKBL (on the migration to Hong Kong of mainland residents) in *Ng Ka Ling* has subsequently been superseded by an interpretation of the HKBL issued by the NPCSC in June 1999, the *Ng* case is still authoritative on the constitutional review power of Hong Kong courts with regard to local legislation:[38]

> The Region is vested with independent judicial power, including that of final adjudication. Article 19(1) [Basic Law]. The courts of the Region at all levels shall be the judiciary of the Region exercising the judicial power of the Region. Article 80.
>
> In exercising their judicial power conferred by the Basic Law, the courts of the Region have a duty to enforce and interpret that Law. They undoubtedly have the jurisdiction to examine whether legislation enacted by the legislature of the Region or acts of the executive authorities of the Region are consistent with the Basic Law and, if found to be inconsistent, to hold them to be invalid. The exercise of this jurisdiction is a matter of obligation, not of discretion so that if inconsistency is established, the courts are bound to hold that a law or executive act is invalid at least to the extent of the inconsistency. Although this has not been questioned, it is right that we should take this opportunity of stating it unequivocally. In exercising this jurisdiction, the courts perform their constitutional role under the Basic Law of acting as a constitutional check on the executive and legislative branches of government to ensure that they act in accordance with the Basic Law.[39]

The subsequent CFA decisions in *HKSAR v. Ng Kung Siu*[40] and *Leung Kwok Hung v. HKSAR*[41] provide illustrations of constitutional judicial review of

---

[36] 5 U.S. (1 Cranch) 137 (1803).
[37] (1999) 2 HKCFAR 4.
[38] See generally Johannes Chan et al. (eds.), *Hong Kong's Constitutional Debate: Conflict over Interpretation* (Hong Kong: Hong Kong University Press, 2000).
[39] Paragraphs 60–1 of the judgment.
[40] Note 29.
[41] Note 30.

Hong Kong laws restricting human rights on the basis of proportionality analysis. The two cases concerned freedom of expression and freedom of assembly respectively. Whereas the impugned flag desecration law was upheld as a proportionate restriction on freedom of expression for the protection of *ordre public* in *Ng Kung Siu*, one provision in the existing Public Order Ordinance was struck down in *Leung Kwok Hung*. In the latter case, the CFA reiterated the proportionality test for the constitutional review of laws restricting constitutional rights (other than absolute rights such as the right not to be tortured), which involves a three-stage analysis: (1) Is the statutory restriction of the relevant right for the purpose of achieving a legitimate aim? (2) Is the restriction 'rationally connected with one or more of the legitimate purposes'? (3) Is the restriction 'no more than is necessary to accomplish the legitimate purpose in question' (or is the restriction so designed as to involve minimum impairment of the relevant right)? In the 2016 case of *Hysan Development*, the CFA, following English and European jurisprudence, added a fourth step (proportionality *stricto sensu*) to the test, which is to consider whether a 'reasonable balance' has been struck between the interests of the individual or group concerned and the 'societal benefits' flowing from the restriction on the relevant constitutional right of the individual or group, 'asking in particular whether pursuit of the societal interest results in an unacceptably harsh burden on the individual'.[42]

The proportionality test has been applied by the Hong Kong courts not only to human rights guaranteed by the ICCPR and the Hong Kong Bill of Rights, but also to other rights guaranteed by the HKBL, such as the right to travel,[43] and even to adjudicate on the constitutionality of a restriction on appeals from a lower court to the CFA.[44] In the context of the right to equality and non-discrimination, proportionality analysis has been undertaken under the 'justification test', which is structurally similar to the proportionality test. In considering a constitutional challenge on the basis of equality and non-discrimination on the ground of sexual orientation, the CFA decided in *Secretary for Justice v. Yau Yuk Lung*[45] that where persons in 'comparable situations' are subject to differential treatment by law, the Government must justify such differential treatment by showing that (1) the differential treatment pursues 'a legitimate aim', in the sense that there is 'a genuine need for such difference';

---

[42] *Hysan Development v. Town Planning Board* (2016) 19 HKCFAR 372, particularly paras. 73, 76, 78, 135.
[43] See e.g., *Gurung Kesh Bahadur v. Director of Immigration* [2002] 2 HKLRD 775; *Director of Immigration v. Lau Fong* [2004] 2 HKLRD 204.
[44] *A Solicitor v. Law Society of Hong Kong* (2003) 6 HKCFAR 570.
[45] (2007) 10 HKCFAR 335.

(2) 'the difference in treatment' is 'rationally connected to the legitimate aim'; and (3) 'the difference in treatment' is 'no more than is necessary to accomplish the legitimate aim'.

In cases concerning socio-economic policies such as the right to social welfare and the provision of social services, the court has developed a less rigorous version of the proportionality or justification test by modifying the third limb of the test ('no more than necessary to accomplish the legitimate aim', which may be called the standard of 'necessity') to become a standard of 'reasonableness' (or 'manifestly without reasonable foundation'). The modified test was first enunciated by the CFA in *Fok Chun Wa* v. *Hospital Authority*, a case concerning differential charges for obstetric services in public hospitals based on whether the woman giving birth was resident in Hong Kong.[46] The CFA noted that this case concerned a matter of 'socio-economic policies'[47] and 'allocation of public funds' under conditions of 'limited financial resources'.[48] Furthermore, the differential treatment that was challenged in this case was based on residence, rather than 'core values relating to personal characteristics'[49] and involving 'the respect and dignity that society accords to a human being', such as 'race, colour, gender, sexual orientation, religion, politics, or social origin'.[50] In this domain, the court considered it appropriate that a greater 'margin of appreciation'[51] or degree of 'deference'[52] be accorded to the government. Hence in applying the third limb of the 'justification test', the court would only strike down the differential treatment if it is 'manifestly beyond the spectrum of reasonableness' or 'manifestly without reasonable foundation'.[53] Applying this test, the court upheld the differential hospital fees in this case. Subsequently, this modified version of the proportionality test was also applied by the CFA in *Kong Yunming* v. *Director of Social Welfare*, but with the outcome of the impugned restriction (also based on residence) of the right to social welfare being struck down in that case.[54] In *Kwok Cheuk Kin* v. *Secretary for Constitutional and Mainland and Affairs*, the application of the proportionality test was relaxed by the Court of Final Appeal on the ground

---

[46] (2012) 13 HKCFAR 409.
[47] Paragraphs 61, 65 of the judgment.
[48] Ibid., para. 70.
[49] Ibid., para. 78.
[50] Ibid., para. 77.
[51] Ibid., para. 61.
[52] Ibid., para. 62.
[53] Ibid., para. 76.
[54] (2013) 16 HKCFAR 950.

that the constitutional issues raised by the impugned legislation on Legislative Council by-elections involved political or policy considerations.[55]

8.4. CONSTITUTIONAL JUDICIAL REVIEW AND PROPORTIONALITY ANALYSIS IN MACAU

8.4.1. *The Judicial Transition of Macau*

The judicial system of Macau had remained relatively less developed in the course of history. Before 1990, there were established in Macau only courts of first instance jurisdiction belonging to the judicial district of Lisbon, with the result that appeals from first instance decisions had to be heard and determined in the intermediate and supreme courts of Portugal. Judges were then solely of Portuguese in origin appointed to positions in the Macanese courts from the Portuguese judicial establishment. In 1990, the Estatuto Organico de Macau (or the Organic Statute of Macau) was amended to make specific provision for an autonomous judiciary for Macau of independent courts subject only to law, even though this had already been guaranteed in the Portuguese constitution.[56] Later in 1991 and 1992, legislative changes separated the judiciary of Macau from that of Portugal and established a court of second instance, which functioned as the apex court in Macau, save and except in relation to constitutional and certain administrative matters, until the end of Portuguese administration in 1999. The signing of the SPJD and the enactment of the MBL required rapid localisation both of the laws and the judiciary in Macau, but it was only in 1996 that the first Macanese judge of Chinese origin was appointed.[57]

---

[55] (2017) 20 HKCFAR 353.
[56] See the Estatuto Organico de Macau, arts. 51–3 (as amended by Lei No 13-A/90); and Paulo Cardinal, 'Macau: Transformation of an Historic Autonomy', in Yash Ghai and Sophia Woodman (eds.), *Practising Self-Government: A Comparative Study of Autonomous Regions* (Cambridge: Cambridge University Press, 2013) 386–7 (referring to art. 292(5) of the Portuguese Constitution).
[57] See Wei Dan, 'Macao's Legal System Under Globalization and Regional Integration: Between Tradition and Evolution' (2014) 9(2) *Frontiers of Law in China* 233, 234–5, 244–9; Jorge Godinho and Paulo Cardinal, 'Macau's Court of Final Appeal' in Simon Young and Yash Ghai, *Hong Kong's Court of Final Appeal: The Development of the Law in China's Hong Kong* (Cambridge: Cambridge University Press, 2014) 610–11; Huang Henghui, *A Brief History of Macau Law* (Aomen falü jianshi 澳門法律簡史) (Hong Kong: Joint Publishing (Hong Kong) Ltd, 2015) 75–92 (in Chinese). For greater detail, see Alberto Martins and Vitalino Canas, *The Amendments to the Estatuto Organico de Macau* (accessible at: http://library.gov.mo/macreturn/DATA/A12-355/index.htm) (last accessed 5 April 2016).

Another important change made to the Estatuto Organico de Macau in 1990 concerned the laws that the Macanese courts may apply in the adjudication of cases. Article 41 of the Estatuto Organico de Macau declared, among others, that the Macanese courts may not, in respect of matters placed before them for adjudication, apply norms ('normas') that are inconsistent with the Portuguese constitution, the Estatuto Organico de Macau or principles established by them. Nevertheless, as Alberto Martins and Vitalino Canas had pointed out, the jurisdiction of abstract review of laws belonged to the Portuguese constitutional court.[58]

The MBL required the establishment of a court of final instance exercising the power of final adjudication of the judicial power of the MSAR in art. 84. The Macau Court of Final Appeal (Tribunal de Ultima Instancia or TUI) is a court consisting of three members and exercises its jurisdiction usually by way of hearing appeals from the lower courts.[59] The TUI is also vested with the judicial function of ensuring the uniformity of judicial decisions in Macau,[60] the original jurisdiction of conducting criminal proceedings against principal officials accused of crimes committed in respect of the performance of their duties,[61] and the appellate jurisdiction in respect of restrictions on the right of assembly and protest imposed by the police authority of Macau.

---

[58] See Martins and Canas, Supra note 57. See also Jorge Bacelar Gouveia, *Constitutional Law in Portugal* (Alphen aan den Rijn: Wolters Kluwer, 2nd edn, 2015) 129–30.

[59] The TUI that was established upon the establishment of the MSAR consisted of a bench of three judges. The President, Sam Hou-fai, was born in Mainland China and aged thirty-eight at the time of his appointment in December 1999. He had, prior to his appointment to the TUI, worked in the Macau judicial system for four years and as a judge since 1997. Of the other two judges, Justice Virato Manuel Pinheiro de Lima had more than twenty years of judicial experience, the last seven years of which were spent in Macau as a judge. The third judge, Justice Chu Kin, was the first Chinese Macanese judge (mentioned above), having been appointed as a judge in 1996. Justice Chu Kin was declared in 2011 to be incapable of holding office due to critical injuries suffered in a traffic accident in Mainland China and was therefore subject to compulsory retirement. His vacancy was filled by Judge Song Man-lei, formerly the first female prosecutor of Chinese origin in Macau when she was appointed to that position in September 1996.

[60] This may include resolving differences between two TUI judgments; see Godinho and Cardinal, Supra note 57, 613.

[61] Ibid., 627–30 (discussing the case of *Ao Man Long*, a principal official in charge of land policy who, among other things, solicited bribes from property developers). See also 'MDT interview/Paulo Cardinal, Legal Expert: The Denial of the Right of Appeal is Inadequate and Embarrassing', *Macau Daily Times*, 8 March 2016 (accessible at: http://macaudailytimes.com.mo/mdt-interview-paulo-cardinal-legal-expert-denial-right-appeal-inadequate-embarrassing.html) (discussing the case of *Ho Chio Meng*, a former Prosecutor-General who had been accused of corruptly awarding the Prosecutor's Office's contracts to associates) (last accessed on 28 May 2018).

For our present purposes, two aspects of the TUI's activities are examined by reading the Chinese version of its judgments.[62] The first concerns its power to review legislation on the basis of consistency with the MBL. The second involves its application of the principle of proportionality.

8.4.2. *Judicial Review of Legislation and Legal Norms Having Legislative Effect*

Unlike the Hong Kong Court of Final Appeal, the TUI had not been initially active in developing a 'constitutional jurisdiction'. Rather, in 2000, as Paulo Cardinal had described, it dealt 'a deadly blow' to the availability of the traditional continental mechanisms of constitutional review, namely the *amparo* and constitutionality appeal.[63] Jiang Chaoyang considered that the absence of jurisdiction to entertain challenges to the validity of legislation or administrative regulations on the ground of contravention with the MBL was well justified under art. 19(2) of the MBL as well as the previous organic law of the Macau judiciary.[64] On the other hand, the TUI explained in *Case No 9/2006* (25 October 2006) that the Code of Administrative Procedure (Código do Procedimento Administrativo) of the MSAR was at first enacted with an expectation that later there would be conferred upon the TUI an appellate jurisdiction to examine the validity of legal enactments on the ground of inconsistency with the MBL, but this expected jurisdiction of the TUI was not subsequently provided for, with the result that art. 44 of the Law on the Organisation of the Judiciary (Lei de Bases da Organização Judiciária) of the

---

[62] Judgments of the TUI are prepared by one of the judges of the three-person bench hearing the case; this designated author judge or 'relator' can choose to write the judgment in Chinese or Portuguese, one of the two official languages of the MSAR. Judgments of the TUI are accessible in their Chinese version at: www.court.gov.mo/c/cdefault.htm.

[63] See Godinho and Cardinal, Supra note 57, 621, referring to TUI Case No 1/2000 (16 February 2000) and TUI Case No 2/2000 (23 February 2000) in respect of *amparo* and TUI Case No 8/2000 (29 March 2000) and TUI Case No 4/2000 (2 February 2000) in respect of constitutionality appeal.

[64] Jiang Chaoyang, 'The judicial application of the Macau Basic Law' 23(2) *Journal of National Prosecutors College* (*Guojia jianchaguan xueyuan xuebao* 國家檢察官學院學報) (March 2015) 62–70 (in Chinese). See also Zhao Qinglin, 'Research on the Constitutional Review System of the Macau SAR', in Ieong Wan-chong, Huang Laiji and Li Zhijiang (eds.), *Research on Special Administrative Region Systems and the National Basic Political System* (*Tebie xingzhengqu zhidu yu woguo jiben zhengzhizhidu yanjiu* 特別行政區制度與我國基本政治制度研究) (Beijing: China Democracy Press, 2012) 401–3 (in Chinese). Article 19(2) of MBL states: 'The courts of the [MSAR] shall have jurisdiction over all cases in the Region, except that the restrictions on their jurisdiction imposed by the legal system and principles previously in force in Macau shall be maintained.'

MSAR on the nature and jurisdiction of TUI has not included a specific route of litigation for review of the validity of legal enactments.[65]

However, as constitutional issues came to be raised before the Macanese courts, the absence of specific constitutional review mechanisms had not precluded the TUI from raising and examining issues of consistency of laws with the MBL as being incidental to the adjudication of disputes that came before it by ordinary routes of litigation.[66] The TUI did that in *Burmeister & Wain Scandinavian Contractor A/S v. Secretary for Security*, Case No 28/2006 (18 July 2007).[67] The TUI, having referred to the work of Xiao Weiyun (a mainland law professor and former drafter of the MBL who later was the founding dean of one of the law schools of the MSAR), came to the view that even though the MSAR was not a state and the MBL was not in form a constitution, the MBL contained certain formal characteristics related to the political constitution of states. Although the MBL has no provision specifically conferring upon the courts the power to deal with 'those legal norms contravening the Basic Law that are of inferior rank and present in laws, administrative regulations or other normative documents', the TUI considered that the MSAR courts did have such a power on the basis of a joined interpretation of several provisions of the MBL, namely arts. 11(2), 19(2) and 143.[68] 'The Basic Law does not establish any mechanism, especially political mechanism to resolve the question of possible conflicts in judicial proceedings between the Basic Law and legal norms in other laws having effect. Therefore, the conclusion that it must be for the courts to hear these questions in the specific cases committed before them must necessarily be drawn'.[69]

Having considered further the writings of Xiao and another Mainland Chinese jurist Wang Zhenmin,[70] the TUI concluded that as the MSAR courts

---

[65] TUI Case No 9/2006 (25 October 2006) 8.
[66] Ibid., where the TUI specifically indicated that the parties to litigation may seek judicial review of legal enactments of lower rank on the ground of contravention with the MBL, but that this must proceed through ordinary procedures of litigation.
[67] The judgment is published in the *Gazette of the Macao Special Administrative Region*, Issue No 37 (12 September 2007) 7871–929. See also TUI Case No 9/2006 (25 October 2006).
[68] TUI Case No 28/2006 (18 July 2007) 28 (對那些位階較低的、載於法律、行政法規或其他規範性文件中的違反《基本法》的法律規範作出審理的可能). In a footnote to the passage, the Macau Court of Final Appeal referred to the fact that in the United States there was no constitutional provision expressly conferring upon the courts the power of constitutional review.
[69] Ibid., 29 (《基本法》沒有設立任何機制，尤其是政治性的機制去解決在司法訴訟中出現的、《基本法》與載於其他生效法規中的法律規範的可能衝突的問題，因此不得不得出由法院在交付其審理的具體個案中，審理這些問題的結論。).
[70] Wang Zhenmin, then the dean of the School of Law of Tsinghua University, added the point that the courts of the special administrative region are responsible for supervising the implementation of the Basic Law. It follows from this and the conferring of the power to interpret

may interpret the MBL in the course of adjudicating cases, they surely may reach a conclusion that a law or administrative regulation is in contravention of the MBL and in such a situation, they must, without prejudice to art. 143 of the MBL (which makes provision for the power of interpretation on their own of the provisions of the MBL within the limits of the autonomy of the Region), enforce the provision in art. 11 of the MBL, and not apply the legislation/regulation that contravenes a provision of the MBL or a principle of such a provision.[71] The TUI further referred to the work of the Portuguese jurist Gomes Canotilho on constitutional theory, which explained that where the laws applicable to the same case are in conflict, the judge should choose the law of the higher rank (equivalent to constitutional law) and at the same time refuse and not apply the law of the lower rank. The TUI lastly considered that such a power must be exercised as part of the court's function, 'as in all legal orders where the judge may resort to the constitution, this is also the approach in the majority of legal systems'.[72] Applying the above principles, and after referring to the legal systems of pre-1999 Macau, Portugal and the PRC on the enactment and effect of administrative regulations, the TUI then determined the question of interpretation of the MBL concerning the power of the Chief Executive of the MSAR to adopt administrative regulations, and remitted the remainder of the case to the Macau Court of Appeal (Tribunal de Segunda Instancia or TSI).[73]

However, the TSI that heard the remitted case expressed on 13 December 2007 strong disagreement, 'in the spirit of exploring the law',[74] with how the

---

the Basic Law on the courts that the courts shall exercise constitutional review in the special administrative region; see Wang, Zhenmin, *China's Systems of Constitutional Review* (*Zhongguo weixian shencha zhidu* 中國違憲審查制度) (Beijing: China University of Political Science and Law Press, 2004) 356, 357 (in Chinese).

[71] See TUI Case No 28/2006 (18 July 2007) 31 (如果法院在審理案件中可以解釋《基本法》，肯定可以得出某些法律規定或行政法規違反《基本法》的結論，在此情況下，必須執行《基本法》第 11 條中的規定 : 因此，不能適用那些違反《基本法》規定或其中規定的原則的那些法規，但該法第 143 條規定除外。). Jiang Chaoyang, in his survey of the judicial application of the MBL, accepted that the MSAR courts are entitled to directly apply the provisions of the MBL in the adjudication of cases as a ground for the adjudication, or to apply them to resolve a conflict of legal norms, by virtue of art. 11 thereof. Indeed Jiang acknowledged the practical need for such a form of 'incidental judicial review', but warned of the risk of this form of review usurping the constitutional functions of the executive and the legislature; see Jiang, Supra note 64.

[72] See TUI Case No 28/2006 (18 July 2007) 31 (一如在法官可以求諸於憲法的所有法律秩序中那樣，這也是現在在大部分法律制度中的做法。).

[73] The TUI considered the legal system under both the historical constitutions and the current constitution of Portugal and the PRC.

[74] The TSI believed that this was not out of order, for the judgment of the Macao Court of Final Appeal's effect was confined to its decision and not inclusive of the legal reasons for the

TUI had interpreted the relevant provisions of the MBL, suggesting that the TUI's opinion had undermined the mechanism in art. 17 of the MBL for reporting laws of the MSAR to the NPCSC for the record and altered substantially the manner of distribution and check and balance in the enactment of legal norms as between the Legislative Council of the MSAR and the Chief Executive of the MSAR.[75]

In spite of the judicial controversy recounted above, the TUI continued to expound in *Case No 8/2007* (30 April 2008) the constitutional principle of legal normative ranking (*falü guifan weijie yuanze*法律規範位階原則): where a court of the MSAR considers in the course of adjudication that the norm previously applied in the case was in contravention of a norm of superior rank, the court should apply the norm of superior rank or some other lawful norm and must not apply the unlawful norm of inferior rank.[76] The TUI then indicated that it follows that the court may on its own initiative or as requested examine, at the time of application of a law, the validity of that law, particularly on whether it is in contravention of a law of superior rank. But the TUI emphasised that a finding that a norm is in contravention of a law of superior rank is only part of the reasoning of the judgment, a step in the legal logical deduction in the course of reaching the judgment in the end, and not the substance of the determination of the adjudication; the courts may not on the basis of the finding give judgment of general binding effect that a particular norm is in contravention. The relevant finding only has effect in the corresponding case and does not have effect in respect of other cases or other courts. The norm that is considered to be in contravention is not rendered invalid for this

---

decision (裁判書的既判力祇限於裁決本身而非亦包含裁決的法律理由); see TSI Case No 223/2005 (13 December 2007).
[75] Ibid., 64–5. The TUI thereafter upheld in several rulings the effect of administrative regulations the TSI had sought to impugn. In response to the controversy, the Legislative Council of the MSAR enacted Law No 13/2009 (Regime juridico de enquadramento das fontes normativas internas), entitled 'The Legal System for the Enactment of Internal Norms', prescribing the hierarchy of internal norms of laws (lei) enacted by the Legislative Council, independent administrative regulations (regulamento administrativo independente) of the Chief Executive, and supplementary administrative regulations (regulamento administrativo complementar) of the Chief Executive. For an overview of this saga, see Chang, Xu, 'The Right of Formulating the Administrative Regulations of the Macau SAR and Its Solution from the Perspective of Jurisprudence Study' (2010) 6 *Academic Journal of One Country Two Systems* ('*Yiguo liangzhi'yanjiu* '一國兩制'研究) 44–67 (in Chinese).
[76] See TUI Case No 8/2007 (30 April 2008) 8–9 (如果法院在審判時認為，案件原應適用的規範違反了比它位階高的規範時，法院應適用位階高的，或其他合法的規範，而不能適用位階較低、屬違法的規範。).

reason.[77] Rather, if a MSAR court considers a norm to be in contravention of a norm of superior rank and for this reason does not apply it, that court may apply the law/regulation that regulates the matter previously, a law/regulation that is applicable in a supplementary manner or a norm of superior hierarchy directly, in order to reach judgment on the substantive question of the case.[78] The TUI cited in support of its exposition texts of Portuguese jurists on constitutional and administrative law.[79]

The TUI did examine the validity of a legal norm in *Case No 5/2010* where it held, after consulting a text by two Portuguese jurists on the principle of equality, that a norm was in breach of the MBL's constitutional guarantee of equality and that by reason of that breach, the norm, which applied two mutually contradictory systems to the same class of civil servants, was inapplicable, with the consequence that the administrative act under appeal was set aside. And, when the TUI did so, it underlined that it was doing a form of 'passive' determination, which means that the court acts only after excluding all other legal solutions on the basis that they could not be regarded as reasonable, since the court's control of the legality of legal norms on the standard of the provisions of the MBL does not go as far as acting like or substituting for the legislature to produce what it considers to be reasonable, just or ideal for the case at hand.[80] Later, in *Case No 25/2011*, the TUI applied the MBL, particularly the guarantee of the right to demonstrate in art. 27, to hold that where the ordinary law had imposed a restriction on the minimum number of persons that could exercise this right, such a law would be inconsistent with the MBL and not applicable and that priority should be given to an interpretation of that ordinary law that could achieve consistency with the MBL.[81]

---

[77] Ibid., 9 (即法院不能以此判斷而作出某規範違法的具普遍約束力的判決，有關判斷只在本身案件中有效，對其他案件，以至其他法院均不產生任何效力，被認為違法的規範也不會因此而失效。)

[78] Ibid., 9–10. See also TUI Case No 21/2007 (14 May 2008).

[79] See, for example Jorge Miranda, *Manual de Direcito Constitutcional* 2nd edn vol. 6 (Coimbra: Coimbra Editora 2005); and Jose Manuel Santos Botelho, *Contentcioso Administrativo* 4th edn (Coimbra: Almedina 2002).

[80] See TUI Case No 5/2010 (12 May 2010) 34 (在對法律規範之合法性的監控範疇，以《基本法》規定為標準，重要的是要考慮，不是由相關機構本身對法律解決辦法作出'正面'的判斷；或者說這樣判斷，監控機構猶如立法者(及'替代'它)那樣，從分析評估狀況開始，然後以它自己的想法作為法律解決辦法的合理性標準去確定具體個案中的解決辦法為'合理的'、'公正的'或'理想的'。合憲性監控機構不能走得那麼遠：他們應做的僅僅是一種'消極性'判斷，即排除那些從各點上看都不能列為合乎情理的法律解決辦法。).

[81] See TUI Case No 2/2011 (12 January 2011) 5–6 (where the TUI referred to a 2007 annotation of the Portuguese Constitution by the jurists Gomes Canotilho and Vital Moreira on the nature of the rights of assembly and demonstration).

The TUI finally encountered the first right of abode case in 2014, which concerned the application by an Irish national for permanent resident status on the ground that he had ordinarily resided in Macau for a continuous period of seven years immediately before the making of the application and had taken Macau as his place of permanent residence. The TUI affirmed the TSI's judgment in favour of the applicant on the meaning of the requirement in art. 24(5) of the MBL of 'having taken Macau as his place of permanent residence' (as it was implemented in MSAR legislation), after consulting both Mainland Chinese and Macanese texts, as well as the text of the Portuguese jurist Joao de Castro Mendes on the concept of 'domicile'. It held that the Bureau of Identity Establishment's rejection of the applicant's application was contrary not only to the relevant MSAR legislation, but also to the said provision of the MSAR.[82] In the same year, the TUI dealt with a case of a Chinese national claiming to be a permanent resident of the MSAR under art. 24(2) of the MSAR, namely, a Chinese national who has ordinarily resided in Macau continuously for seven years before the establishment of the MSAR. The court referred to the law previously in force before the establishment of the MSAR to determine whether the claimant had ordinarily resided in Macau continuously for seven years by that time.[83]

This series of cases and the legal reasoning in them would have been of little surprise to Vitalino Canas, who wrote in early 2007 that while the Macanese courts before the 1999 handover may conduct judicial review of constitutionality, be it on their own after 1990 or by way of an appeal to the Constitutional Court (Tribunal Constitucional) of Portugal at Lisbon, 'in the context of the Basic Law, there can be no judicial review of the constitutionality by a Constitutional Court. But we may consider whether the MSAR ordinary courts can, under the BLM, Article 143 and 11, second paragraph, refuse the application of rules in conflict with the same BLM'.[84] It also appears to the present authors that anyone who has read art. 41 of the Estatuto Organico de Macau would also find the TUI's exposition of the above constitutional principles unsurprising.[85] Yet, such judicial examinations have had effect only

---

[82] See TUI Case No 21/2014 (7 January 2015).
[83] See TUI Case No 115/2014 (28 January 2015). The TUI relied on the principle in art. 11 of the Macau Civil Code (Código Civil) on the temporal application of laws.
[84] See Canas, Vitalino, 'The General Regime of Fundamental Rights in the Basic Law and the International Instruments' in Jorge Oliveira and Paulo Cardinal (eds.), *One Country, Two Systems, Three Legal Orders – Perspectives of Evolution* (Berlin: Springer Verlag, 2009) 674.
[85] For an empirical survey of the TUI's cases applying the provisions of the MBL, see Xiaonan Yang, 'The Application of the Basic Law of Macao SAR in the Macao Courts: A Comparison with the Hong Kong Courts' (2015) 7 *Hong Kong and Macao Journal* (*Gang'ao yanjiu* 港澳研究), issue 2, 49–58 (in Chinese). Yang's study of the TUI judgments produced these observations:

in respect of the individual concrete case, and the TUI has eschewed any suggestion that these examinations and rulings coming out of them have a general effect binding on all the lower courts and other governmental authorities of the MSAR.[86] For a TUI judgment to have binding effect on the lower courts, it has to be one that seeks to provide a uniform judicial opinion against conflicting decisions of the TUI or decisions between different courts in the MSAR judiciary.[87]

8.4.3. Principle of Proportionality

The MSAR courts apply the principle of proportionality (*shidu yuanze* 適度原則/principio da proporcionalidade) mostly in the adjudication of cases, particularly administrative law cases, but also some cases involving constitutional rights. A survey of about thirty judgments of the TUI determining appeals against judicial decisions in respect of an action against an administrative decision indicates that the MSAR courts recognise the principle of proportionality as a fundamental principle in administrative law that an administrative decision-maker may not contravene in making decisions in the exercise of his discretion. This principle, as it was stated in art. 5 of the Code of Administrative Procedure of the MSAR, requires that where an administrative decision conflicts with the interests of an individual that is protected by law, the impairment by the administrative decision of the relevant interest must be reasonable and proportionate (*shidang ji shidu* 適當及適度/adequados e proporcionais) in respect of the purpose to be achieved. Its core meaning prohibits arbitrariness and requires a reasonable relationship between the means and the purpose. This core meaning gives rise to the three dimensions of the principle, namely reasonableness, necessity and balance/proportionality stricto sensu (adequação, necessidade e equilíbrio). Thus, in order to achieve a relevant purpose, the means taken must be reasonable in respect of that purpose, only the means that least impairs the legal interest amongst all applicable means should be chosen and the standard for evaluation must be public

---

(1) The number of cases was limited; (2) the types of cases were more focused, such as concerning the ownership rights of land, the principle of equality, the right of procession and demonstration, and the right to retirement benefits; (3) there was a stronger tendency of repetition in the contents of the judgments; (4) there were few representative cases, and the Hong Kong experience in the application of the HKBL had not served as an example or reference to the MSAR courts.

[86] Further examination may be needed of the reason and effect of the publication of the TUI's judgment in the *Burmeister* case in the government gazette, especially as to whether this act had clothed the case with binding effect as a governmental measure.

[87] See Yang, Supra note 85.

interest balancing with the yardstick of reasonableness amongst conflicting interests.

Upon application, however, the question for determination by the MSAR court appears to be whether the principle of proportionality has been manifestly violated (*mingxian weibei* 明顯違背/manifestamente violado) in the administrative decision-making, so that the court would intervene to set aside the administrative act in question.[88] This judicial approach of intervention only in respect of a manifest violation or a decision that intolerably contravenes the principle follows to some extent the French judicial approach,[89] as well as, curiously, the English *Wednesbury* unreasonableness approach.[90] Further, when the TUI adjudicates a case on administrative appeal, the threshold for intervention is governed by the Code of Administrative Litigation, so that where the impugned decision was reached by exercising discretion, it could only be properly challenged on the basis that there was a manifest error in the exercise of the power or that the discretion was exercised utterly unreasonably.[91]

The TUI's jurisdiction to hear and determine appeals from decisions refusing or restricting assemblies or demonstrations is provided by legislation. Access to this appellate jurisdiction of the TUI is direct and without conditions, so as to enable the expeditious determination by a court of full jurisdiction in respect of an administrative decision affecting the rights of assembly and demonstration, both of which are guaranteed under art. 27 of the MBL, with the aim of restoring the exercise of such rights as swiftly as possible.[92] In about seventeen judgments spanning the last decade in this type of appeals, the TUI had examined restrictions to meetings or demonstrations in terms of whether the particular restriction was 'prescribed by law' within the meaning

---

[88] See TUI Case No 6/2000 (27 April 2000).

[89] This reference turns out to be unhelpful, as the French Council of State had only explained the nature and structure of the proportionality test (the triple test of suitability, necessity and proportionality) it applied as late as in 2011 and the French administrative law literature had not been able to identify and discuss the applicable degree of control or intensity of the proportionality test, though there has been discussion of 'limited control' where the judge acts only in respect of 'obvious' or 'manifest' errors; see Yoan Sanchez, 'Proportionality in French Administrative Law' in Sofia Ranchordas and Boudewijn de Waard (eds.), *The Judge and the Proportionate Use of Discretion* (London: Routledge, 2016) 45–52, 61–71. Cf. Federico Fabbrini, '"Reasonableness" as a Test for Judicial Review of Legislation in the French Constitutional Council' (2009) 1 *Journal of Comparative Law* 39.

[90] See TUI Case No 26/2003 (15 October 2003), quoting the jurist David Duarte, who indeed referred to the *Wednesbury* case in his 1996 work on the topic. This judicial opinion has been followed continuously thereafter; see TUI Case No 62/2015 (4 December 2015).

[91] See TUI Case No 1/2006 (21 June 2006).

[92] See TUI Case No 16/2010 (29 April 2010) 4–5.

of art. 40(2) of the MBL (including whether there was a ground based on conferred power to impose the restriction (不能根據法律沒有訂定的權利作出決定)), whether a restriction was an 'intolerable restriction to a fundamental right' (對一項基本權利造成不可承受的限制), and ensuring that restrictions to art. 27 should be as small as possible and properly explained.[93] The TUI had even commented that the law should resolve the problems arising out of conflicting rights by prescribing basic principles consistent and proportionate with the aims to be achieved that should be complied with when the same place is used for different demonstrations.[94] However, the TUI had maintained that it would act consistently with the general principle of administrative litigation when it exercises this appellate jurisdiction, so that it would not interfere with the administrative decision-maker's exercise of his discretionary power in respect of whether such power was properly exercised, and would only declare the relevant administrative act unlawful and invalidate it where the exercise of such power amounted to a manifest error or absolute unreasonableness (在行使該權限時出現明顯錯誤或絕對不合理的情況時).[95]

As we have mentioned above, the TUI had applied in *Case No 5/2010* the principle of equality enshrined in the MBL to review a legal or legislative norm concerning the deduction of seniority due to sick leave for teachers and held that the impugned legal norm was inconsistent with the MBL's protection of the principle of equality in art. 25. The TUI, having stated the principle in terms of relevant difference or distinction between two situations, asserted that if the situations were basically the same, but there was unequal treatment, then the principle had been violated from the perspective of prohibition of 'arbitrariness' (proibição do arbítrio/*jinzhi duduan* 禁止獨斷).[96] In this connection, the TUI indicated that this perspective or theory of prohibition of arbitrariness specifies and determines the limits of judicial review, so that this substantively passive standard of review condemns only those unequal situations that are manifest and intolerable; such a situation, the TUI so considered, would only occur where the differential treatment prescribed by the legislator is 'lacking in justification, objectivity and reasonableness'

---

[93] See TUI Case No 16/2010 (29 April 2010), TUI Case No 21/2010 (4 May 2010), TUI Case No 2/2011 (12 January 2011), TUI Case No 95/2014 (30 July 2014), TUI Case No 15/2016 (11 March 2016).
[94] See TUI Case No 16/2010 (29 April 2010) 10.
[95] See TUI Case No 75/2010 (17 December 2010) 6.
[96] The TUI reiterated this principle in a series of cases concerning the appointment and conditions of service of nurses; see TUI Case No 9/2012 (9 May 2012), TUI Case No 19/2012 (9 May 2012), TUI Case No 27/2012 (16 May 2012) and TUI Case No 33/2012 (4 July 2012).

(não fundamentadas, não objectivas, não razoáveis/*meiyou yiju, bu keguan, he bu heli* 沒有依據、不客觀和不合理).[97]

The above discussion suggests that while the MSAR courts maintain their adherence to the principle of proportionality as a tool of review of administrative decisions and legal norms in the European continental tradition, they likewise have followed the tradition of exercising judicial review and declaring an administrative act invalid or a legal norm not applicable only in manifestly unjustified cases, applying a methodology that looks into the matter more intuitively than by way of a structured and progressive examination of normative and operational issues, which is the form of proportionality test that has characterised recent human rights jurisprudence in the HKSAR and the common law world.

8.5. A COMPARATIVE ANALYSIS

8.5.1. *Some Theoretical Considerations*

The Basic Laws of the Hong Kong and Macau SARs both provide that SAR laws may not contravene the Basic Law, but neither of them contains any express provision authorising the courts to review whether a legislative provision of the SAR is inconsistent with the Basic Law and specifying the legal consequences of such inconsistency. In this regard, the written basis – or lack thereof – of constitutional judicial review in the Hong Kong and Macau SARs is as inadequate as that under the Constitution of the United States. As Professor Andrei Marmor has pointed out, even if one accepts the supremacy of the constitution and that there must be some institution having the power to determine in concrete cases whether a conflict between the constitution and ordinary legislation exists or not, 'it simply does not follow that this institution must be the supreme court, or any other institution in particular'.[98] He elaborates as follows:

> First, that [constitutional judicial review] is not a necessary feature of a constitutional regime ... [It] is certainly conceivable to have a legal system with a written constitution without entrusting the power of its authoritative

---

[97] See TUI Case No 5/2010 (12 May 2010) 31–8. See also the subsequent case of TUI Case No 33/2012 (4 July 2012) (which was also a civil service conditions of service case).
[98] Andrei Marmor, *Interpretation and Legal Theory* rev. 2nd edn (Oxford: Hart Publishing 2005) 149. Jutta Limbach agreed, indicating that: 'The power of judicial review is a chief legal instrument in the system of checks and balances. Nevertheless, it is not a universal or necessary element of a democratic constitution': see Limbach, Jutta, 'The Concept of the Supremacy of the Constitution' (2001) 64 *Modern Law Review* 1, 5.

interpretation in the hands of the judiciary, or, in fact, in the hands of anybody in particular. Therefore, secondly, it is also widely acknowledged that the desirability of judicial review is mostly a question of institutional choice: given the fact that we do have a constitution, which is the most suitable institution that should be assigned the role of interpreting it and applying it to particular cases? Finally, it is widely acknowledged that the courts' power of judicial review is not easily reconcilable with general principles of democracy. Even those who support the legitimacy of judicial review, acknowledge the existence of at least a tension between our commitment to democratic decision procedures and the court's power to overrule decisions made by a democratically elected legislature.[99]

Marmor acknowledges the difficulty of *lawyers* in particular in understanding why judicial review of legislation requires justification separate from the supremacy of constitutions:

> For them the reasoning of *Marbury v. Madison* is almost tautological. *We just cannot have it in any other way.* If we have a written constitution which is the supreme law of the land, then surely it follows that the courts must determine what the law is and make sure that it is applied to particular cases. The power of the courts to impose their interpretation of the constitution on the legislature simply follows, so the argument goes, from the fact that the constitution is legally supreme to ordinary legislation. But of course this is a *non sequitur*' (emphasis supplied).[100]

Marmor further points out that even if courts are assigned the power to determine questions of constitutionality, it does not follow that they should have the legal power to invalidate a legislative act which is unconstitutional. The appropriate remedy could be much less drastic, such as a declaratory judgment, or there could be no remedy at all.[101] Marmor emphasised: 'Ultimately, the desirability of judicial review is a matter of institutional choice, and a great many factors which figure in such a complex consideration are empirical in nature'.[102]

---

[99] Marmor, Supra note 98, 149.
[100] Ibid., 149–50.
[101] Ibid., 150.
[102] Ibid., 154. Marmor addressed two other arguments. As to the claim that the interpretation of the constitution, a legal document, is a matter for the courts, the repository of legal expertise, Marmor indicated that this claim rests on the problematic assumption that legal reasoning informs constitutional decision-making solely, as '[most] constitutional decisions are based on

Earlier, examining the United States Constitution, Judge Learned Hand observed in his Oliver Wendell Holmes Lecture that nothing in the powers granted to the courts in the Constitution included the authority to pass upon the validity of the decisions of another 'department' of government as to the scope of that 'department's' powers. The understanding rather was that the three 'departments' of the Executive, the Legislative and the Judicial were separate and co-equal, without any mutual dependence. To subject the validity of a particular decision of one of them to review and reversal by another, in the words of Judge Hand, 'makes supreme the "Department" that has the last word'.[103] Judge Hand also highlighted that the defence of judicial review of legislation by Alexander Hamilton in the Federalist No. 78 was not based upon anything in the constitutional text but rather on the ordinary function of courts to construe statutes:

> The interpretation of the laws is the proper and peculiar province of the courts. A constitution is, in fact, and must be regarded by the judges, as a fundamental law. It therefore belongs to them to ascertain its meaning as well as the meaning of any particular act proceeding from the legislative body ... Nor does this conclusion by any means suppose a superiority of the judicial to the legislative power. It only supposes that the power of the people is superior to both; and that where the will of the legislature declared in its statutes stands in opposition to that of the people declared by the Constitution, the judges ought to be governed by the latter rather than the former.

According to Judge Hand, judicial review of legislation was supportable only after examination of the deficiencies and undesirability of the alternatives. The power was not 'a logical deduction from the structure of the Constitution but only a practical condition upon its successful operation'. Since the Supreme Court's 'authority to keep the states, Congress, and the President within their

---

moral and political considerations'; see ibid., 150. As to the claim that entrusting courts with judicial review secures the rights and principles entrenched in the constitution for the citizens, Marmor called it the argument from consensus, 'a very tenuous agreement which breaks down as soon as a conflict comes to the surface' about rights; see ibid., 151–3.

[103] Learned Hand, *The Bill of Rights* (Cambridge, MA: Harvard University Press, 1958) 4–5. Judge Hand also considered the so-called supremacy clause of Article VI of the United States Constitution to be not supportive of the proposition of the supremacy of the judiciary. Rather it accorded 'with the view that, when it was intended to grant courts the power to declare a statute invalid because it was in conflict with the Constitution, some express grant was thought necessary'.

prescribed powers' was no more than a matter of 'established practice', Judge Hand counselled discretion:

> [judicial review] need not be exercised whenever a court sees, or thinks that it sees, an invasion of the Constitution. It is always a preliminary question how importunately the occasion demands an answer. It may be better to leave the issue to be worked out without authoritative solution; or perhaps the only solution available is one that the court has no adequate means to enforce.[104]

8.5.2. *Constitutional Judicial Review in the Hong Kong and Macau SARs*

The development of constitutional judicial review in the Hong Kong and Macau SARs as discussed previously in this chapter well illustrates the above-mentioned points made by Marmor and Hand. On the basis of Basic Laws that do not expressly authorise constitutional judicial review, the courts of both the HKSAR and MSAR have made the 'institutional choice' of assuming the power to determine questions of constitutionality. As shown previously in this chapter, the approaches of the HKSAR and MSAR courts in the adjudication of cases on the interpretation of the Basic Law share certain similarities. The courts of both SARs seek to enforce the supremacy or superiority of the Basic Law in the adjudication of cases, as part of their exercise of judicial power, even though no provision of the Basic Law of each SAR confers specifically upon the courts the power to investigate, examine or review legal norms for consistency with the Basic Law. The courts of both SARs have sought to justify such enforcement by reference to what other jurisdictions with a written constitution have been doing, referring explicitly in the case of the TUI and implicitly in the case of the HKCFA to the *Marbury* v. *Madison* model of judicial review.[105]

Yet the approach of the TUI to the exercise of examining legal norms to check whether they are consistent with the MBL differs significantly from the exercise by the HKSAR courts of their constitutional jurisdiction, which has been asserted and practised since *Ng Ka Ling*, in that while a finding by a MSAR court of inconsistency operates modestly and momentarily as part of the reasoning of the court towards judgment adjudicating and disposing

---

[104] Ibid., 14–15.
[105] The matter might be more problematic for the TUI since there is no equivalent in the MBL of art. 84 of the HKBL, expressly permitting reference to precedents of other common law jurisdictions.

The Constitutional Orders of 'One Country, Two Systems' 261

of the particular case before the court, a finding by a HKSAR court of inconsistency entails, as a matter of judicial duty as a constitutional check of the other branches of government, a declaration of inconsistency, invalidating the legislative provision or executive act in question for all purposes ('null and void') – it purports to have effect *erga omnes* – and with provisions detailing 'excisions' or other modifications,[106] and time limit for correction.[107]

Professor Yash Ghai observes that if the Macanese approach were to be applied in Hong Kong, then as long as the doctrine of precedent remains part of the legal system, the refusal of the CFA to apply a particular legislative provision would constitute a precedent, and the effect would not be substantially different from declaring it invalid.[108] In contrast, the Macanese approach appears to be what Wang Shuwen and his team of authors counselled,[109] and in keeping with the syllogism theory underlying the continental legal tradition that judges 'apply' the statutes, which express the general will, to solve the particular case.[110] This might find expression in the judicial independence provision in art. 89 of the MBL, which provides that judges of the MSAR shall exercise judicial power according to law, instead of according to any order or instruction, except in the situation as prescribed in art. 19(3) concerning the Chief Executive's certificate binding on questions of fact concerning acts of state. This provision apparently had a counterpart in the previous legal order in art. 53(1) of the Estatuto Organico de Macau.

The divergence in judicial approach between the two jurisdictions can perhaps be explained with reference to the different legal traditions that already existed in the two jurisdictions at the time of the establishment of the SAR.

---

[106] Dong Likun, Zhang Shutian, and other mainland legal scholars often took exception of the elaborate terms of the declarations and relief in *Ng Ka Ling* v. *Director of Immigration* (1999) 2 HKCFAR 4, 45–8; see Dong Likun and Zhang Shutian, 'Power to Review Legislation of the Hong Kong Special Administrative Region Inconsistent with the Basic Law' (2010) 32(3) *Chinese Journal of Law* (*Faxue yanjiu* 法學研究) 3–25 (in Chinese).

[107] See *Koo Sze Yiu* v. *Chief Executive of the HKSAR* (2006) 9 HKCFAR 441.

[108] See Ghai, Supra note 14, 210. Cf. Ip, Supra note 1, 813, suggesting that the TUI's philosophy of constitutional adjudication was '[in] stark contrast' to that of the CFA.

[109] Wang Shuwen (ed.), *Introduction to the Basic Law of the Hong Kong Special Administrative Region*, 2nd edn (Beijing: Law Press China and Joint Publishing (HK) Co Ltd 2009) 536–7 (where the courts of the HKSAR were advised to examine legislative provisions on consistency with the Basic Law and in the case they find any such provisions in contravention of the Basic Law, they should not adjudicate cases in accordance with such provisions but should do so in accordance with other valid legislative provisions).

[110] See Michel Troper, 'Constitutional Law', in George Bermann and Etienne Picard (eds.), *Introduction to French Law* (Alphen aan den Rijn: Kluwer Law International, 2008) 7–9. A near parallel might be drawn with the PRC's socialist state, as the PRC Constitution provides in Article 2 for all power in the PRC to belong to the people, who may exercise state power through the NPC, the highest organ of state power vested with, inter alia, legislative power.

Constitutional judicial review leading to legislative provisions being held invalid and null and void already existed in Hong Kong's common law-based legal system during the colonial era, and rapidly developed after the enactment of the Hong Kong Bill of Rights Ordinance 1991 and the corresponding amendment to the Letters Patent as the written constitution of colonial Hong Kong. After the HKSAR was established, the courts simply carried on the work of constitutional judicial review, now using the provisions of the Basic Law instead of those of the Letters Patent and the ICCPR as the yardstick for review. The legal consequences of a legislative provision being judicially determined to be unconstitutional, i.e., the provision being held to be invalid and null and void, have remained the same as before the 1997 handover, though the HKSAR courts have refined the techniques of and remedies in constitutional adjudication.

By contrast, before the 1999 handover in Macau, there had not existed in this Portuguese colony a well-developed or mature system of constitutional judicial review. The jurisdiction of formally reviewing and invalidating unconstitutional laws vested in the Constitutional Court of Portugal but not in any court in Macau. Nevertheless, the Organic Statute of Macau (1990) expressly provided that Macanese courts may not apply legal norms that were inconsistent with the Portuguese Constitution or the Organic Statute of Macau.[111] The jurisdiction of the MSAR courts after the 1999 handover to determine whether a legal norm is inconsistent with the MBL therefore finds a parallel in the pre-1999 legal system. As MSAR courts accumulated more experience in constitutional adjudication, they have developed jurisprudence on the limited legal consequences of a legal norm being determined to be unconstitutional. It is understandable and by no means surprising that this jurisprudence is distinctive and different from its counterpart in the HKSAR, given the influence of the continental European legal tradition in Macau[112] and the absence under the MBL of a continental-style constitutional court with full power to invalidate unconstitutional laws.[113]

---

[111] Cf. Eric Ip's analysis of the pre-1999 Macau legal system with access to the modern 'mixed' system of constitutional adjudication in Portugal: Ip, Supra note 1, 825–6.

[112] Castelucci considers that the MSAR's civil law based legal system, which does not recognise the binding force of precedents, 'is associated with a high level of observance of the literal provisions of the statutory law, with a conservative attitude and a low level of judicial activism. This rigid attitude seems to be shared by courts in at least some of the former socialist jurisdictions of Eastern Europe …': Castellucci, Supra note 1, 697–8.

[113] Eric Ip has suggested that 'the differing political transaction cost structures faced by the Hong Kong and Macau SAR governments', as well as those faced by the NPCSC, have fostered the more vibrant 'constitutional jurisdiction' of the CFA in the HKSAR and the 'TUI's well known deference to the Macau government', applying a model of strategic judicial behaviour; see Ip,

8.5.3. Proportionality Analysis in the Hong Kong and Macau SARs

It is noteworthy that the principle of proportionality has, following the continental European tradition, been established in the administrative law of Macau. By contrast, the traditional common law approach to judicial review of administrative action in Hong Kong has been based on the triple grounds of illegality, procedural impropriety and irrationality (*Wednesbury* unreasonableness). With the development of constitutional protection of human rights, it has now become possible to apply principles of proportionality to judicial review of administrative actions that restrict human rights.[114] As discussed above in this chapter, the Hong Kong courts have, since the 1990s, practised constitutional judicial review of legislative restrictions on constitutionally guaranteed rights by applying principles of proportionality, and have developed a considerable body of jurisprudence in this regard. By contrast, there is relatively little case law in the MSAR on the application of proportionality analysis in the review of legislative, as distinguished from administrative, acts. This can be explained by the fact that there have been in the MSAR relatively fewer cases of constitutional judicial review of legislation as compared with Hong Kong.[115]

Supra note 1, 816, 818–20. In this chapter, we have focused on the legal and institutional reasons for the development of the judicial power to review legislative enactments in the HKSAR and the MSAR, though we acknowledge the relevance of the myriad of factors discussed in Ip's article, including in each case of Hong Kong and Macau the SAR's economy, the SAR's international connections and significance, the identity of the SAR's population with 'Chinese' identity, the organisation and orientation of the SAR's civil society, the likelihood of opposition politics and social movements in the SAR extending the arena of struggles to the courts, and the organisation and outspokenness of the SAR's legal profession. See also, in this regard, Sir Anthony Mason, 'The Rule of Law in the Shadow of the Giant: the Hong Kong Experience' (2011) 33 *Sydney Law Review* 623. We also note that Ip has not tested his hypotheses quantitatively, stating that '[it] will be difficult to obtain empirical evidence that judges anticipate the responses of the regime if the latter has never retaliated': Ip, Supra note 1, 824. Although Ip has (at 826–7) touched upon the TUI's repeated reversal of the 'assertive' TSI's judgment in the series of cases on administrative regulations beginning with the *Burmeister* case, and suggested that TUI did so 'in order to survive in the face of an implied and credible political threat or retaliation', we are unable to confirm Ip's proposition in this regard in light of the comprehensive judgment of the TUI surveying and analysing the relevant constitutional sources (including citing cases of the Portuguese Constitutional Court) and the complexity of the controversy in question, which was best settled by the enactment of a law (lei) by the MSAR's legislature.

[114] See *Leung Kwok Hung*, Supra note 32.
[115] Relevant factors affecting the number of cases in the MSAR include the size of the economy and society, both in terms of the economic and social interactions and the legal service sector, and features of the MSAR judiciary, including the size of the establishment, the delays in rendering court rulings, the erratic holding of hearings in contentious cases and general efficiency; see Wei Dan, Supra note 57, at 248.

As discussed previously in this chapter, the HKSAR courts have engaged in a step-by-step analysis in reviewing whether a statutory restriction on a constitutionally protected right satisfies the proportionality test (or the similar 'justification test' in cases on equality and non-discrimination). It has also been pointed out previously that the HKSAR courts have adopted a less rigorous version of the proportionality test in certain types of cases, such as cases concerning socio-economic policies, social welfare and social services. By contrast, although notions of necessity, proportionality, reasonableness, arbitrariness and justification exist in the Macanese jurisprudence, it seems that the 'proportionality test' (insofar as it can be said to exist) in Macau has not been as precisely formulated as in Hong Kong. Moreover, the practice of the Macanese courts in applying the proportionality test is apparently such that they will only intervene where the impugned action is manifestly unjustified or involves an intolerable restriction of a protected right. This seems to suggest that the test applied in Macau is close to the 'less rigorous version' of the proportionality test in Hong Kong, or close to the common law standard of '*Wednesbury* unreasonableness'.

As mentioned previously in this chapter, even before the 1997 handover, the Hong Kong courts had already imported the proportionality analysis under the Canadian Charter of Rights and Freedoms into the Hong Kong jurisprudence on the Hong Kong Bill of Rights 1991. With the enactment of the United Kingdom Human Rights Act in 1998, the rapidly developing jurisprudence in Britain on human rights and proportionality also became available to the HKSAR courts. Led by the Hong Kong CFA, which almost invariably includes a distinguished visiting judge from Britain, Australia or New Zealand on its bench when it hears a case, the Hong Kong judiciary seeks to establish its international reputation by ensuring that its jurisprudence is consistent with the general trend in the common law world.[116] Comparatively speaking, the MSAR courts, which operate in the Chinese and Portuguese languages, are less internationally oriented.[117]

Secondly, there have so far been very few cases in which the Macanese courts had the opportunity to apply proportionality analysis, even incidentally, in judicial review of legislation or norms having legislative effect, as

---

[116] Many judges of the superior courts of the HKSAR were educated at some stage in the United Kingdom, be it at the undergraduate or postgraduate level, and some also were called to the English Bar and had undertaken pupillage with English barristers.

[117] This can be noted from the Mainland Chinese and Portuguese sources cited in the TUI's judgments discussed above.

distinguished from judicial review of administrative actions. There were relatively more cases of administrative appeals in Macau, in which the courts' role was constrained by procedural rules and considerations of separation of powers.

Furthermore, the political culture of the community, and the values of and choices made by the legal and judicial elite in Macau are apparently more conservative,[118] as compared to the more liberal political culture and more liberal values of and choices made by the legal and judicial elite in Hong Kong.[119] This is partly reflected in the TUI's 'open embrace' of the PRC's constitutional system and its citations of the texts of Mainland Chinese jurists on the MBL in the *Burmeister* case and other cases concerning the interpretation of the MBL.[120] Some or all of these factors can

---

[118] It is noted that a significant number of the present members of the Macanese judiciary are persons born, raised and educated in Mainland China up to the undergraduate level before they were inducted to the Portuguese language and laws necessary for them to man the judicial system of Macau in preparation for the transition. They happen to include the two Chinese judges on the current bench of the TUI. Castellucci, who had taught in Macau and conversed with members of the local legal community, confirmed that the MSAR's legal community 'is transforming from being characterised by a strong Portuguese legal presence towards a more Chinese-influenced body of judges, lawyers and government officials': Castellucci, Supra note 1, 703.

[119] Ip (Supra note 1) argues that the more conservative orientation of the Macanese courts and the more liberal orientation of Hong Kong courts are results of strategic choices made by the judiciary in the two jurisdictions in response to their different political environments. According to Ip's analysis, the likelihood (as anticipated by the judiciary) of 'retaliation' against or 'punishment' of the judiciary by the regime is lower in Hong Kong and higher in Macau, due to the lack of internal cohesion within the regime and significant 'popular resistance' against it in Hong Kong, as contrasted with a more united regime and 'minimal' popular resistance against it in Macau (thus the 'political transaction costs' of the regime's action to 'discipline' the judiciary would be higher in Hong Kong and lower in Macau); hence the Hong Kong judiciary could choose to be more liberal and activist, while the Macanese judiciary chose to be more conservative and restrained. In our view, such strategic choice is probably one of the relevant factors that can explain the differences in the constitutional jurisprudence of the Hong Kong and Macau SARs, but we doubt that this is the primary and overriding factor.

[120] Castellucci has observed the 'increasing seeping' of the PRC's socialist ideas of governance, including that of using the law to make and further state policy, into 'the political-institutional framework and culture of the SARs'; see Castellucci, Supra note 1, 676. He considers Macau's resistance to such 'infiltration' to be 'lower', as the MSAR's civil law-based legal system, which does not recognise the binding force of precedents, is 'more flexible' in accommodating changes associated with the 'new political environment after the handover to China': ibid., 697–8. A confirmatory comparison is made between the MSAR's legal system with those of European socialist countries, to the effect that such systems are 'more apt, in its language and technicalities, to introduce and enforce more communitarian ideas': ibid., 699. Castellucci has presciently observed at 694–5: '[The] purpose of the basic laws is not just that of isolating the SARs' legal systems, as discernable from their black-letter text from a common law normative perspective. Their purpose is also – ... from the functional Chinese rather than the

perhaps explain the relatively more rigorous application of proportionality analysis in constitutional judicial review in the HKSAR than in the MSAR.

8.5.4. Concluding Remarks

This chapter has demonstrated the high degree of similarity in the structure and content of the Hong Kong and Macau Basic Laws, and the similarities and differences between the two jurisdictions in the practice of constitutional judicial review and the use of proportionality analysis in judicial review of legal restrictions on rights. Whereas the texts of the two Basic Laws provide some support for the exercise of judicial power to determine whether a legislative provision or legislative act is inconsistent with the Basic Law, the jurisprudence in the two jurisdictions on the legal consequences of a judicial determination of such inconsistency forms part of the 'invisible' and extra-textual constitution in each of the two jurisdictions. Although some kind of proportionality analysis may be said to be implicit in the ICCPR that is referred to in each of the two Basic Laws, the development and application of proportionality analysis in the Hong Kong and Macau SARs are also largely an outgrowth of the 'invisible' constitution.[121]

This chapter shows that the similar texts in the two Basic Laws have been similarly used by the courts in the Hong Kong and Macau SARs to support the exercise of judicial power to determine questions of constitutionality. At the same time, there exist both similarities and differences in the relevant parts of the 'invisible' constitutions of the two jurisdictions as regards the legal consequences of a judicial determination of inconsistency between a legislative provision and the Basic Law and as regards the application of proportionality analysis. Thus the texts of the Basic Laws under-determine the constitutional jurisprudence; the texts are open-ended enough to allow and sustain the evolution of 'invisible' constitutions, which are to a significant extent determined by the different legal

---

normative point of view – one of providing Mainland authorities with steering capability over these systems. The Mainland authorities gain that capacity by framing them within a cage of quasi-constitutional, but still flexible, provisions they may interpret according to what they think appropriate'.

[121] Under the ICCPR, many of the rights protected thereby may be subject to such restrictions as are prescribed by law and necessary to protect public safety, public order, national security, public health or morals, etc.

traditions of the two former colonies, their judicial experience accumulated before their handover to the PRC, and also partly by the institutional features of their legal systems, different degrees of affinity with foreign constitutional jurisprudence, the political culture of the community, and the values of and choices made by the legal and judicial elites of the two SARs.

9

The Platonic Conception of the Israeli Constitution

Iddo Porat[*]

America is the only country that went from barbarism to decadence without civilization in between.

— Oscar Wilde[1]

When Tom Ginsburg created, together with other scholars, the website *Constitute* collecting the texts of all the constitutions of the world, he did not include the Constitution of Israel.[2] Subsequently he got an angry email from an Israeli law professor saying – "of course Israel has a constitution, please include it!" This, I believe, could not have happened with regard to any other country. Disagreements on the interpretation of constitutions are omnipresent, but disagreement on whether a country has a constitution or not is quite rare. Indeed this is not due to any oversight on behalf of Professor Ginsburg. The same confusion is present among Israelis today – even among Supreme Court judges[3] and common reference tools such as Wikipedia.[4] To show this,

---

[*] Versions of this article were presented at the San Diego Law School Faculty Colloquium, the CLB Law Faculty Colloquium, Bar Ilan University's conference on the Constitution in Trial Courts, and the University of Sau Paulo Constitutional Law and Political Theory Colloquium. I would like to thank the participants of these conferences for helpful suggestions and comments, and especially Larry Alexander, Moshe Cohen-Eliya, Yossi Dahan, Virgilio da Silva, Rosalind Dixon, Matthias Klatt, Conrado Mendes, Steve Smith, Larry Solum, Gila Stopler, and the editors of this book, Rosalind Dixon and Adrienne Stone.

[1] See "Top Ten Quotes of Oscar Wilde; The Daily Universal Register" *The Times*, July 7, 2008, 27. But see the website http://quoteinvestigator.com/ arguing that the quote is mistakenly attributed to Wilde and was coined after his death.

[2] www.constituteproject.org/.

[3] In a famous plurality decision, Justice Heshin argued against the idea that Israel has a constitution: "We would at least have expected there to be no dispute over the actual authority to enact a constitution. The very existence of disputes on this question indicates the tenuousness of the conclusion that the current Knesset possesses constituent authority:" CA 6821/93 *United Mizrahi Bank Ltd* v. *Migdal Cooperative Village* PD 49(4) 221, 349 (1995) (henceforth *"Mizrahi"*). English translation from the *Versa* website: *Versa, Opinions of the Supreme Court of Israel* http://versa.cardozo.yu.edu/.

[4] Unlike the *Constitute* website, Wikipedia entries maintain that Israel has an "uncodified constitution": https://en.wikipedia.org/wiki/Basic_Laws_of_Israel, downloaded April 12, 2016 or "unwritten constitution" https://en.wikipedia.org/wiki/Constitution_of_Israel, downloaded April 12, 2016.

I open the first class of my constitutional law course each year with a simple question – does Israel have a constitution? There is always a long pause and then conflicting answers of yes and no.[5]

The purpose of this chapter is to document and explain how this situation came about and discuss what it means for the relationship between text and constitutionalism. My own answer to the question I pose to my students is the following: Israel went from parliamentarism to constitutionalism without a constitution in-between. Today, therefore, Israel does have a constitutional system, including a strong form of judicial review and the protection of a full set of constitutional rights, but it does not have a constitutional text. This is not entirely accurate, but it is not very far from the truth. Israel has a fragmented and partial draft of a constitution – its thirteen Basic Laws that were drafted intermittently between 1958 and the present.[6] However, despite the fact that, as a text, these thirteen Basic Laws are no more than an incoherent beginning of a constitution, and despite the fact that there was no political will behind their enactment to make them a constitution (at least not yet), they operate in effect as if they were a full-fledged constitution. The institution that is responsible for bridging this gap and in effect created the Israeli Constitution is not a political organ but the Supreme Court of Israel that has done so in a set of decisions spanning from 1995 until today. One may use the following analogy: the Basic Laws of Israel, which were a political creation, were only a potential for a constitution – an embryo constitution – but the processes of gestation and delivery were done entirely outside of the political sphere, by the Supreme Court of Israel.

What this means in terms of the judicial relationship with the text is quite far reaching. This is so, since in order to bridge this gap between embryonic text and an actual functioning constitution, the Supreme Court of Israel needed to do some radical interpretative adjustments to the text of the Basic Laws. It needed, first, to read into these Basic Laws the proposition that they are indeed a constitution, in the sense that they are superior to regular legislation and that the Supreme Court has the authority to strike down laws that conflict

---

[5] A Israeli colleague reading a draft of this paper tried to correct me on this point arguing that while law students do not know that Israel has a constitution when they begin their constitutional law course, by the time they reach its end, they do. This, to my mind, only strengthens my point regarding the uncertainty around the Israeli constitution.

[6] They are Basic Laws: The Knesset (1958), Israel Lands (1960), The President of the State (1964), The Government (1968, reenacted in 2001), The State Economy (1975), The Army (1976), Jerusalem, The Capital of Israel (1980), The Judiciary (1984), The State Comptroller (1988), Freedom of Occupation (1992, reenacted 1994), Human Dignity and Liberty (1992), Referendum (2014), The State Budget for the Years 2017 and 2018 (Special Provisions) (Temporary Provision) (2017). *See* the Knesset website: "Basic Laws" www.knesset.gov.il/description/eng/eng_mimshal_yesod.htm.

them – which it did. Then, it needed to complete the very partial list of written constitutional rights in these Basic Laws into a full list of rights – and this it also did. Finally, it had to set up rules of "maintenance" and of day to day operation of these Basic Laws and make the entire apparatus cohere – since the Basic Laws were never intended to function as a constitution in their current form, and therefore were not adjusted to do that. To an extent, it also did this.

In addition the Court needed to rely on a legal and normative theory that would justify this radical interpretative move. The doctrinal legal theory was provided by the then Chief Justice, Aharon Barak, in his legal decisions and extra-legal scholarly writings. But behind it is also a deeper theory about the relationship between the constitution and its text, which is not made explicit in the reasoning. I call this theory the "Platonic" conception of the constitutional text. According to this conception, which, I posit, lies behind the judicial pronouncements, the constitutional text is only an approximation – an imperfect shadow – of the "ideal" constitution, which is universal, perfect, unchanging, and also, importantly, accessible to judges regardless of the text. Judges should strive to bridge the gap between the written and the ideal constitution, and owe their allegiance primarily to the latter rather than to the former.

This chapter has two main aims: the first is descriptive. I aim to give a condensed, accessible, and readable account of the judicial move in the 1990s that is sometimes referred to as the Israeli Constitutional Revolution, emphasizing what I take to be its main feature – the judicial bridging of the gap between the partial and embryonic constitutional text, and a the ideal of a full and functioning constitution. Section 9.1 will give the historical background to the move, dividing it between two periods, 1948–92, and 1992–95, and Section 9.2 will concentrate on the move itself and on the doctrines developed by the Israeli Supreme Court as part of this move. My second aim is theoretical and conceptual. I aim to contribute in explicating the conceptual and interpretative assumptions implied by this interpretative move of bridging the gap between text and ideal. This will be done in Section 9.3, titled the Platonic Conception of the Constitution. Section 9.4 will describe some implications of the Platonic conception, discuss how its proponents justify it, and address possible objections to my account.

Two preliminary remarks are in order – the first, normative. My own view is that the judicial move from text to ideal was problematic both in terms of its practical effects and in terms of its democratic legitimacy. I similarly believe that the Platonic conception of the constitution, as a recipe for constitutional interpretation, faces serious implementation problems, and, in particular, a serious democratic legitimacy problem. However, my main aim in this article is descriptive and conceptual rather than normative – it is to show that this conception indeed lies behind the Israeli constitutional revolution, and to explicate its main features, and possible manifestation in other countries as well. Therefore, the description and the conceptual analysis should be congenial also to those with a more favorable view of the move and of the Platonic conception.

The second remark is comparative. Neither the idea of extensive and far-reaching interpretative deviations from the constitutional text nor the Platonic conception of the constitution is unique to Israel. As the other chapters in this book attest, comparative constitutionalism provides ample examples of filling-in the text of the constitution with "unwritten" or "invisible" law, sometimes completely altering or contradicting the textual meaning of the document. In addition what I would term the Platonic conception lies behind much of the attitudes toward the text in European – in particular German – constitutional adjudication, although with some important differences from the Israeli case.[7] It can also be traced in the constitutional adjudication of countries that adopted a European-like constitutional framework, such as Canada,[8] and even, by some accounts, of American constitutional law.[9] However, I believe that the Israeli case presents a more radical endeavor. This is so, since, included in the unwritten part of the Israeli constitution is also its own existence. In other words, whereas other judiciaries may be as radical in their constitutional interpretation as the Israeli one, at least they have *a constitution* to interpret. The difference between the "unwritten-ness" of the Israeli constitution and of other constitutions therefore lies in the political act of creating a constitution through judicial interpretation which is unique to Israel.

[7] The main difference is in the formalism that characterizes German constitutional jurisprudence but not Israeli constitutional jurisprudence. See note 47 and accompanying text. I thank Mattias Klatt for this point.

[8] See the references to Canadian legal scholarship in Section 9.3.1. More generally my assumption is that the Platonic conception is one of the features of what has been termed the "global model of human rights": see Kai Moller, *The Global Model of Constitutional Rights* (Oxford: Oxford University Press, 2013) and of what Moshe Cohen-Eliya and I termed the "culture of justification," see Moshe Cohen-Eliya and Iddo Porat *Proportionality and Constitutional Culture* (Cambridge: Cambridge University Press, 2012); Moshe Cohen-Eliya and Iddo Porat, "Proportionality and the culture of justification" (2010) 59 *American Journal of Comparative Law* 463. Showing this, however, lies beyond the scope of this article.

[9] See e.g., Steven Smith, *Law's Quandary* (Cambridge, MA: Harvard University Press, 2004) 168–9 (criticizing American constitutional jurisprudence for disregarding the text, and for substituting it with the judges conception of ideal rights, and referring specifically to the terms "Platonism" as a heuristic). Some aspects of Dworkin's depiction of American constitutional law also lend themselves to the idea of the Platonic Conception of the constitution (see Edward Foley, "Review Essay: Interpretation and Philosophy: Dworkin's Constitution" (1997) 14 *Constitutional Commentary* 151, 152). See also note 54 and the sources cited there.

9.1. HISTORICAL BACKGROUND: THE CONSTITUTIONAL STORY OF ISRAEL

9.1.1. First Period: A Promise not Fulfilled, 1948–1992

The history of Israel's constitutional law is usually divided into two stages: from the establishment of the State of Israel in 1948 until 1992, and from 1992 onwards.

Israel was established in 1948 after a period of thirty years of British colonial rule over Mandatory Palestine. Although in its defining document – the Declaration of Independence – Israel's early leadership vowed to adopt a constitution,[10] this commitment was made without any deliberation or public debate since the United Nations resolution that provided the formal legitimacy for the State of Israel demanded a constitution as a condition for gaining international recognition of the State.[11] However, this promise was not fulfilled. The initial date that was set in the Declaration of Independence for the elections for a constitutional assembly was postponed because of the 1948 War, and before the second date arrived, a decision was made – in law – that the constitutional assembly would also serve as the first parliament of Israel – the Knesset. The task of drafting and adopting a constitution was therefore conferred on the first Knesset of Israel – a decision that turned out to be fatal to the constitution.

At the time the first Knesset was elected, in January 1949, the international community had already recognized the State of Israel even without a formal constitution, so that the need for a constitution was put again to question. The Knesset debated the issue extensively and finally decided, in the *Harari* decision of 1950, not to adopt a constitution – at least not at that point. Instead, the form of government that was adopted by default was a Westminster-like form of parliamentary sovereignty without a formal constitution, a form of government which characterized Israel at least until 1992.

---

[10] Declaration of the Establishment of the State of Israel, 1 *Laws of the State of Israel* [L.S.I.] 3, 4 (1948). The Declaration refers to "the establishment of the elected, regular authorities of the State in accordance with the Constitution, which shall be adopted by the Elected Constituent Assembly not later than the 1st October 1948." See www.mfa.gov.il/MFA/Peace%20Process/Guide%20to%20the%20Peace%20Process/Declaration%20of%20Establishment%20of%20State%20of%20Israel.

[11] UNGA Resolution 181, A/RES/181(II)(A+B) November 29, 1947. Section I.B.10 of the Resolution provides that "[t]he Constituent Assembly of each State [referring to the Jewish and Arab states. I.P.] shall draft a democratic constitution for its State."

The *Harari* decision, however, did not close the door on a constitution. The decision is very short and is cited here in its entirety:

> The first Knesset directs the Constitutional, Legislative and Judicial Committee to prepare a draft Constitution for the State. The Constitution shall be composed of separate chapters so that each chapter will constitute a basic law by itself. Each chapter will be submitted to the Knesset as the Committee completes its work, and all the chapters together shall be the State's constitution.[12]

The decision was devised so as to avoid a constitution at that stage, but allow for its adoption at a later stage if the political will for that existed. It was also devised so as to give an appearance of faithfulness to the commitment in the Declaration of Independence to have a constitution. As a typical compromise decision it intentionally left unsettled several pertinent questions. First, it set no deadline to the completion of the draft constitution (and indeed since no deadline was set, the work has not been completed up to today). Second, it set no special process for the adoption of these Basic Laws that would serve as the draft of the constitution (therefore they are adopted until today in an ordinary process of legislation as any other regular law of the Knesset). Third, it did not mention which institution is to decide that the draft is complete, how the different Basic Laws are to be collected and compiled, and whether there will be a separate process of adoption and ratification of the entire document, and if so, how would it look like (until today there has not been a decision to the effect that the draft work has been completed and there has been no attempt to collect together the different Basic Laws). Finally, and most importantly to the unfolding of the story, it did not mention what would be the status of these Basic Laws during the interim period until they are collected into a constitution – whether they will have the status of regular laws, or a different status.

The political community interpreted the Harari decision as a decision to defer the question of a constitution to a later stage, but did follow the framework it provided and enacted several Basic Laws. The first Basic Law was enacted eight years after the Harari decision, in 1958 – Basic Law: The Knesset. All in all, until 1992, the Knesset enacted nine Basic Laws at a pace of once every few years. They were all enacted in a regular process of legislation,

---

[12] 5 Knesset Protocols 1743 (1950) (Hebrew). The English translation is taken from the Israeli Knesset website, "The Constitution": www.knesset.gov.il/description/eng/eng_mimshal_hoka.htm#4.

and all of them dealt with the basic institutions of government.[13] There were attempts along the way to push forward for a completion of the Basic Laws, and for their adoption as a full constitution including a Basic Law: Bill of Rights, with a complete list of rights, but they did not come to fruition.[14]

In terms of their normative status, the Basic Laws were not given superiority over other laws and were regarded as regular laws. This was the doctrine in Supreme Court adjudication, made explicit in several decisions, including decisions that gave effect to laws conflicting with a Basic Law, according to the principle of *lex posterior*.[15]

One fact blurred this picture, but not substantially. Some of the Basic Laws included entrenched provisions. Thus, section 4 of Basic Law: the Knesset, discussing the type of elections, contains the following provision: "this section shall not be changed save by a majority of the members of the Knesset" (meaning at least sixty-one of the one-hundred and twenty Knesset members). Section 46, referring to this section, maintained that "under this section, 'change' is either explicit or implicit." In one case, in 1969, the Court invalidated a law that implicitly conflicted with section 4 of Basic Law: The Knesset, but was not enacted by a majority of Knesset members. Striking down the law, however, the Court explicitly maintained that it was not doing this on the assumption that Basic Laws are of a constitutional status higher than regular laws, but on the assumption that the Court would give effect to rules set by the Knesset, regarding the procedure of legislation, including rules regarding entrenchment.[16]

---

[13] Basic Laws: The Knesset (1958), Israel Lands (1960), The President of the State (1964), The Government (1968, reenacted in 2001), The State Economy (1975), The Army (1976), Jerusalem, The Capital of Israel (1980), The Judiciary (1984), The State Comptroller (1988). See the Knesset website: "Basic Laws" www.knesset.gov.il/description/eng/eng_mimshal_yesod.htm. The process of legislation of Basic Laws is the same as of any other governmental bill (i.e., a regular majority of the Knesset Members present in all three readings) except for the fact that they are initiated by the Knesset Constitution, Legislation, and Law Committee and bear a different title than regular laws. See Suzie Navot, *The Constitutional Law of Israel* (Kluwer Law International, 2007) 48–9.

[14] For a description of these attempts see CA 6821/93, *United Mizrachi Bank Ltd. v. Migdal Cooperative Settlement*, P.D. 49(4) 221, [24]–[29] (1995) (Justice Barak).

[15] See H C J *Kaniel v. Minister of Justice*, PD 27(1) 794 (1973); HCJ 60/77 *Ressler v. Chairman of Elections Committee*, PD 31(2) 556 (1977). In both these decisions the Court ruled clearly that the title Basic Law was only semantic, and that Basic Laws have no superiority over regular laws. See also Amnon Riechman "Judicial constitution-making in a divided society – the Israeli case" in Robert Kagan, Diana Kapiszewsk and Gordon Silverstein (eds.) *Consequential Courts: New Judicial Roles in Global Perspective* (Cambridge: Cambridge University Press, 2013) 257.

[16] See HCJ *Bergman v. Minister of Finance*, 23(1) PD 693. For an English translation see (1969) 4 *Israel Law Review* 559.

To conclude, in the first stage of Israeli constitutional law, from its formation in 1948 until 1992, Israel was categorized as a system without a formal constitution. It had, however, nine Basic Laws that were enacted with the idea that they might become part of a constitution one day. None of these Basic Laws protected human rights. One should add, though, that the Court did develop an impressive set of civil rights, including the rights to freedom of speech, equality, freedom of consciousness, freedom of religion and from religion, freedom of occupation, liberty from arrest, due process of law, and the right to fair trial. These rights were made judicially, without a textual basis, and applied only to the executive, through administrative law. They could not be used to defy a formal manifestation of legislative will (i.e., no judicial review over primary legislation).[17]

9.1.2. Second Period: The Two Basic Laws, 1992–1995

All of this changed in two steps – the enactment of two new Basic Laws in 1992, and their interpretation by the Court in a seminal decision in 1995 and in subsequent decisions that complemented it. To tell the story in a nutshell – in 1992 the Knesset enacted two Basic Laws that were a step in the direction of a constitution, and the Supreme Court seized the moment and decided to complete the job. I will leave the description of the Court's reasoning to Section 9.2.

In 1992 two new Basic Laws were adopted by the Knesset – Basic Law: Freedom of Occupation (protecting the freedom of occupation),[18] and Basic Law: Human Dignity and Liberty (protecting the rights to life, bodily integrity, dignity, property, liberty, exit and entry into the country, and privacy).[19] These two Basic Laws therefore included, for the first time, a partial list of civil rights protections. They also included a "limitation clause" based on a similar provision in the Canadian Charter of Rights and Freedoms: "There shall be no violation of rights under this Basic Law except by a law befitting the values of the State of Israel, enacted for a proper purpose, and to an extent no greater than is required, or by regulation enacted by virtue of express authorization in such law."[20] Since the limitation clause set exclusive conditions for when a law can violate a right, it implicitly maintained that a law that did not meet those conditions would be invalid, and hence, that these two Basic Laws were supe-

---

[17] See Navot, Supra note 133, 199; David Kretzmer, "Fifty years of Supreme Court Jurisprudence in Human Rights" (1999) 5 *Haifa Law Review* 297, 298–300 (in Hebrew).
[18] Basic Law: Freedom of Occupation, s 2–3.
[19] Basic Law: Human Dignity and Liberty, s 2–7.
[20] Basic Law: Human Dignity and Liberty, s 8; Basic Law: Freedom of Occupation, s 4.

rior over regular laws. The superiority of these Basic Laws, however, was not written explicitly in the text of either of them, nor did either of them expressly authorize any court to invalidate laws conflicting with them.

The political decision to enact these two Basic Laws was a result of a compromise between the political parties that traditionally objected to a constitutional bill of rights, and those that attempted to enact it.[21] As mentioned above, there were several attempts to complete the enactment of the Basic Laws including a Basic Law: Bill of Rights. The reason why this did not work out was the consistent objection of several political parties. Neither of the two big parties – the Left, Labor party, and the Right, Likud party – was very enthusiastic about the constitution project, and both had their own reservations about it. But they could probably have tolerated the idea, which was promoted primarily by a small minority of left wing and right wing liberal enthusiasts, had it not been for the adamant and consistent objection of the religious parties, whose support they both needed in order to form a coalition government.

Since the debate in the first Knesset and until today the religious parties have been objecting to a constitution for two main reasons: first, they believed that Israel, as the homeland of the Jewish people, should only have one document that is referred to as its constitution – the Torah. Second, and probably more importantly, they were afraid that a judicially enforced bill of rights would infringe on the special privileges that the Jewish religion and the Jewish religious institutions managed to gain through the political process, and through the historic deal between the religious and secular parties, known as the *Status Quo*.[22] What allowed a compromise with the religious parties in 1992 was, amongst other reasons, a tactical shift on the part of the constitution enthusiasts with regard to the bill of rights.[23] Instead of insisting on a complete bill of rights, the left-wing promoters of the constitution, joined by several right wing and religious right liberals, decided to start and enact first those rights for which they could get the religious parties on board. This was the reason for the particular list of rights that was finally included in the two Basic Laws. None of the rights that were considered problematic by the religious parties, such as the rights to equality, freedom of religion and conscience, and

---

[21] Ruth Gavison, "Constitutions and Political Reconstruction? Israel's Quest for a Constitution" (2003) 18 *International Sociology* 53, 63–4.
[22] Ibid., at 58.
[23] See Gideon Sapir, "Constitutional Revolutions: Israel as a Case Study" (2009) 5 *International Journal of Law in Context* 355, 357.

free speech were included.[24] Only those rights that were not considered as a threat by the religious parties were included: freedom of occupation, property, dignity, life, liberty, liberty from arrest, right of movement, and privacy.

As to the limitation clause, it is questionable whether the religious parties were fully aware of the implications of what they were agreeing to. They may have been aware of the possibility that the Court would strike down laws conflicting with these two Basic Laws, because of the limitation clause, but were not too concerned about this, so long as the rights that were included in them did not affect their interests.[25] What is absolutely certain is that no one in the political arena thought that these two Basic Laws amounted to any substantial change in the political system of Israel. Nobody thought they would have any effect on the status of the previous nine Basic Laws, and nobody thought that they amounted to anything close to a full constitution. Indeed, public and political interest around these Basic Laws was quite limited. The first Basic Law was adopted with a vote of twenty-one for and one against, and the second with the vote of thirty-two for and thirteen against – this out of one-hundred and twenty Knesset Members. The newspapers the next day reported on the enactment of the two Basic Laws on their inner pages (some did not report at all, as did the television), and the event did not make any news headlines.[26]

9.2. THE *MIZRAHI* CASE: BRIDGING THE GAP BETWEEN TEXTUAL REALITY AND IDEAL – 1995 AND ONWARDS

While the two Basic Laws of 1992 were not understood as a major change by most, the one institution that thought otherwise was the Israeli Supreme Court, and in particular Justice Aharon Barak, who was soon to become the President of the Israeli Supreme Court. Justice Barak viewed these two Basic Laws as an opportunity, maybe a one-time opportunity, to revamp the potential

---

[24] The religious parties were afraid that a judicially enforced right to equality would conflict with the inferior status of women in rabbinical courts that have exclusive authority over marriage and divorce of Jews under Israeli law. They also feared that a right to equality would conflict with the preference given to Orthodox Jewish organizations over Conservative and Reform Jewish organizations. They were also concerned that it would endanger the privileges of Yeshiva Students such as exemption from army service, or special state stipends. For the same reasons they adamantly objected to a right to freedom of conscience and of religion that could be invoked by Jewish Reform and Conservatives, and by those who wished not to be subject to laws motivated by religious reasons. One other concern they had was that a judicially enforced right to freedom of expression would allow for too much defamation of God and of religious symbols in the public sphere, and would not allow restrictions to speech based on religious feelings. See generally Gavison, Supra note 21.

[25] See Gavison, Supra note 21, 64.

[26] See Sapir, Supra note 23, 10.

constitution of the Basic Laws into a full and operative constitution. In order to do that he had to bridge the gap between text and ideal. This section will describe this move.

Soon after the enactment of the two Basic Laws of 1992, Justice Barak wrote a law review article maintaining that the two new Basic Laws amounted to a "constitutional revolution."[27] In it he already laid down all the principles of the interpretative framework that would later be adopted by the Supreme Court.

It took three more years until most of this framework was adopted. This occurred in the 1995 *Mizrahi* case and a few more judicial decisions that completed it.[28]

9.2.1. The Opening Paragraphs of Mizrahi: Reality and Ideal

The *Mizrahi* case involved an appeal by the Mizrahi Bank and other Israeli banks, in which they wished to invalidate a law which absolved debtors from their debts to the banks, because it conflicted with the right to property protected by the Basic Law: Human Dignity and Liberty. It was the first case in which the Court took upon itself the task of determining the status of the new two Basic Laws of 1992 with regard to conflicting legislation. President Barak's opinion in *Mizrahi* opens with the following two paragraphs, setting the stage for the framework of his interpretation:

> In March 1992, the Knesset enacted Basic Law: Freedom of Occupation and Basic Law: Human Dignity and Liberty. The enactment of these two Basic Laws effected a substantive change in the status of human rights under Israeli law. Such rights became constitutionally protected and were accorded supra-legislative constitutional status. They cannot be changed by "regular" legislation. A regular law cannot infringe a protected human right unless the constitutional requirements set forth in the Basic Law have been met. The failure of a regular law to meet those requirements renders it unconstitutional. Such a law is constitutionally flawed and the Court may declare it void.
>
> Israel is a constitutional democracy. We have now joined the community of democratic countries (among them the United States, Canada, Germany, Italy and South Africa) with constitutional bills of rights. We have become part of the human rights revolution that characterizes the second half of the twentieth century.[29]

---

[27] Aharon Barak, "The Constitutional Revolution: Protected Fundamental Rights" (1992) 1 *Haifa Law Review* 9 (Hebrew).
[28] *Mizrahi*, Supra note 3.
[29] Ibid., at 164.

Note the intermingling of ideal and of fact – of the picture President Barak wishes to see, and the one he encounters in reality – and the heroic attempt to bridge the gap between the two. The second paragraph represents the ideal – "the community of democratic countries (among them the United States, Canada, Germany, Italy and South Africa) with constitutional bills of rights." The ideal is a Western democracy with a full-fledged constitution and a complete bill of rights. This "has become the norm." The first paragraphs starts with reality – "[i]n March 1992, the Knesset enacted Basic Law: Freedom of Occupation and Basic Law: Human Dignity and Liberty." It must be obvious to Barak, as it is to anyone reading these two Basic Laws and knowing the history behind them, that they do not amount to this ideal picture. As mentioned before, they do not include a complete bill of rights, but only a very partial list of rights, and they leave uncertain their superiority and the authority of the court to strike down laws conflicting with them. They are obviously not a complete constitution. The bridging between ideal and reality comes in the words of Barak himself, as if creating reality by stipulation: "Israel is a constitutional democracy. We have now joined the community of democratic countries ... with constitutional bills of rights" – two stipulations of fact, without any holding in the legal reality that existed prior to them. Their mere utterance, however, helped them become reality.

Barak uses very ambiguous terms in these paragraphs in order to mask the facts that do not fit the ideal: "The enactment of these two Basic Laws effected a substantive change in the *status of human rights* under Israeli law. *Such rights* became constitutionally protected and were accorded supra-legislative constitutional status." What do the words "such rights" refer to? One might assume that they refer only to the rights that were included in the two Basic Laws. But the previous sentence refers to a change in "the status of *human rights* in Israeli law" which seems to imply that *all* human rights were affected by the change and given special status. This ambiguity is repeated when Barak refers to the fact that Israel has now "joined the community of democratic countries ... with constitutional *bills of rights*." And has "become part of the human rights revolution." If the change is the result of these two Basic Laws, with the very partial list of rights in them, how is it that Israel has now joined the democracies with full bills of rights? The ambiguity alludes to the sought after ideal – a constitutional protection of all rights.

Another important ambiguity can be found in the following sentence: "A regular law cannot infringe a protected human right unless the constitutional requirements set forth *in the Basic Law* have been met." The words do not refer specifically to the two Basic Laws of 1992, but to the requirements set forth in "the Basic Law" leaving it ambiguous whether the new status of superiority is now accorded not only to the two new Basic Laws but to all Basic Laws – again alluding to the ideal Barak wishes to become a reality.

A close reading of these two opening paragraphs of Barak's opinion in the *Mizrahi* case provides us with a fairly good picture of the interpretative project that he is embarking on and also of the interpretative theory he employs, which I will call the "Platonic" conception of the constitutional text. His goal is to bridge the gap between the limited reality of the fragmented and partial Basic Laws, and the ideal of a full constitution with a full bill of rights, thus also bridging the gap between Israel the rest of the Western world.

9.2.2. The Doctrinal Implementation of the Ideal and Conflicts with the Text

Completing the ideal picture envisioned in these opening paragraphs would require at least four radical interpretative moves, one of which has a limited basis in the text of the Basic Laws, and the rest with no basis at all, or even standing in contradiction to the text. The first interpretative move is to make clear the superiority of the two Basic Laws of 1992 over regular legislation and the authority of the Court to strike down laws conflicting with them. This move has some basis in the text since, as mentioned earlier,[30] one may conclude from the limitation clause included in these two Basic Laws that they are superior to regular legislation, and that the Court has judicial review with regards to them. However, the text of the two Basic Laws does not say anything explicit about the superiority of these two Basic Laws nor about judicial review, and a more cautious Court could have interpreted them differently.

The second move is to declare all Basic Laws, not only the last two ones from 1992, as superior to regular legislation and as having constitutional status. This move has no basis in the text, and stands in contrast to all prior cases that dealt with this question. The two 1992 Basic Laws do not mention the nine older Basic Laws at all, and the nine older Basic Laws do not include any indication as to their superiority in their text either, except for those few provisions that are procedurally entrenched. In addition, as mentioned earlier, a long line of cases ruled very clearly that these old Basic Laws have no constitutional status and no superiority over regular laws.[31] However, declaring the older Basic Laws constitutional was crucial for the project of building up a constitution out of the Basic Laws, since it was hard to create a constitution

---

[30] See note 20 and accompanying text.
[31] See note 15 and accompanying text.

out of only two Basic Laws, and since leaving the older Basic Laws out of the constitutional scheme would have created a strong sense of incoherency.

The first two moves were achieved in the *Mizrahi* case and in an additional case, and are both imbedded in the doctrinal and theoretical framework presented by Justice Barak in *Mizrahi*.[32] I will present this doctrine here only briefly, as it is not my main focus in this chapter, and as I view it as having mainly instrumental value, i.e., its value for those who support it stems mainly from the fact that it is the theory most suited for implementing the ideal of a full constitution. According to Barak's opinion in *Mizrahi*, the first Knesset had the authority to write a constitution, as it was elected as the constituent assembly. While it did not use this authority, it bequeathed it to all subsequent Knessets and they used it when they enacted Basic Laws according to the Harari decision. Therefore, every Knesset has two "hats" simultaneously – the regular legislative hat it uses when it enacts regular laws, and the hat of the constituent assembly, when it enacts Basic Laws. This is known as "the theory of the two hats" or as "the theory of the constituent authority." Basic Laws are thus written not by the Knesset, but by the constituent assembly or, to put it more accurately, by the Knesset in its capacity as the constituent assembly.[33] The theory of the two hats achieves at once the constitutionality of the two 1992 Basic Laws and the constitutionality of all older Basic Laws, as well as all future Basic Laws. This is so since constituent assemblies have the authority to write constitutional law, and since Basic Laws are the product of the constituent assembly. Basic Laws therefore have superiority over regular legislation, even before they are collected and compiled into a constitution, and even if there is no textual indication of their superiority (note that the second interpretative move is not wholly consistent with the first one, since now superiority is derived from theory of the two hats, rather than from limitation clauses). The theory of the two hats itself has no direct indication in any text, and stands in contrast to all prior case law that viewed Basic Laws as regular legislation.[34] It is derived in Barak's opinion from the interpretation of the constitutional history of Israel and the application of jurisprudential analysis to it.[35]

---

[32] While the doctrine of the "two hats" was not adopted by a majority of judges in *Mizrahi*, a majority of judges did rule that the two Basic Laws of 1992 are superior to regular legislation and allow for judicial review. The case that further extended this superiority to the older Basic Laws is HCJ 212/03 *Herut National Movement v. Chairman of Central Elections Committee* PD 57(1) 750 (2003).

[33] *Mizrahi*, Supra note 3, [7]–[33] (Chief Justice Barak).

[34] See note 15 and accompanying text.

[35] *Mizrahi*, Supra note 3, [38] (Chief Justice Barak).

The third interpretative move is as crucial as the first two – the Basic Laws must be interpreted to include a full rather than a partial list of rights, as otherwise the ideal of a full constitution is not achieved and the Court is left with only a very partial list of rights that excludes some of the most central rights, such as equality, free speech, and freedom of conscience. The third interpretative move was not achieved in the *Mizrahi* case, but only in later cases in which the right to human dignity in the Basic Law: Human Dignity and Liberty was interpreted to include in its meaning all other rights. The theory was that human dignity is a basic and foundational concept that includes all manifestation of individual autonomy and therefore implies all rights, including those rights that were not specifically mentioned in the Basic Laws.[36] The theory is sometimes referred to as the theory of implied or unenumerated rights, similar to the theory in the United States constitutional law. However, it seems much more radical than its United States counterpart, or similar interpretative moves in other countries, as it is practically limitless – the unenumerated list of rights includes, in principle, all known rights in the liberal constitutional tradition.

The third interpretative move also has no textual basis in the Basic Laws. Indeed, as indicated by an important law review article from 1997,[37] it stands against the logic and structure of the Basic Laws since, had the Knesset wished the right to human dignity to include all rights, it need not have bothered to write down specific rights in addition to it, such as the right to privacy, property, liberty from arrest, and so on, while leaving other rights out of the text. Of course, this interpretation also directly contradicts the intentions of the drafters of the two Basic Laws of 1992, as the rights that were not included in them were intentionally left out as part of the compromise that allowed for the support of the religious parties. Nonetheless, today, as a result of a series of cases since 1995, all those rights that the religious parties wanted to exclude – the right to equality, the right to religious freedom, the right to freedom of conscience, and the right to freedom of speech – are included in the scope of protection of Basic Law: Human Dignity and Liberty.[38] In addition, the following rights were also included in this Basic Law as stemming from the right to

---

[36] HCJ 6427/02 *Movement of Quality of Government in Israel v. the Knesset*, PD 61(1) 619, [30]–[43] (2006) (Chief Justice Barak).

[37] Hillel Sommer, "The Unenumerated Rights: On the Scope of the Constitutional Revolution" (1997) 28 *Mishpatim* 257 (in Hebrew).

[38] See *Movement of Quality of Government in Israel*, note 36.

human dignity – the right to family,[39] the right to social security and minimal living conditions,[40] and the right to education.[41]

The last interpretative move to be discussed here was required for purposes of coherency and "workability" of the entire project. Since only the last two Basic Laws included a limitation clause, all the earlier Basic Laws had no mechanism that allowed for limiting the provisions that they had set, and any law that conflicted with them had to be struck down. This created a practical problem, and also inconsistency between the different Basic Laws. The interpretative solution was striking. In a case from 1999 the Court simply read limitation clauses into all the earlier Basic Laws, which are now known as "judicial limitation clauses."[42] Another interpretative move that I characterize as stemming from coherency is the judicial theory according to which any change in a Basic Law has to be done itself in a Basic Law.[43] This too has no indication in the text of the Basic Laws, but is required since unlike other constitutions the one stemming out of the Basic Laws does not have a mechanism for its amendments, so that the Court had to provide for one.

Despite attempts at coherency and consistency, several inconsistencies and anomalies were left unresolved. Primary amongst them is the fact that today the Knesset can enact a constitutional norm that will have superiority over regular legislation, and even entrench it in any majority it wishes, and the only formal requirement needed for that is to give it the title "Basic Law." Otherwise the legislative process is of a regular vote, with a regular majority of the Knesset members present at the vote, just like any other law. The Knesset can similarly amend any Basic Law that is not entrenched (and most are not) without the need for any super majority, as long as it calls the amending law a Basic Law. There are several more anomalies and inconsistencies that are left unresolved, which for purposes of brevity I will not discuss here. However, whatever the anomalies and inconsistencies, as of today, the Israeli legal and political system seems to have accepted the idea that the Supreme Court has the authority to strike down laws that conflict with Basic Laws, and that these Basic Laws protect an entire bill of rights. What kind of interpretative theory can justify such radical deviation from the text? This will be the subject of the next section.

---

[39] HCJ 466/07 *Gal-On v. Attorney General* (11.1.2002).
[40] HCJ 366/03 *Commitment to Peace and Social Justice Society and others v. Minister of Finance*, 60(3) 464, [1]–[7] (2005) (Chief Justice Barak).
[41] HCJ 2599/00 *Yated, Children with Down Syndrome Parents Society v. Ministry of Education*, PD 56(5) 834 (2002).
[42] EA 92/03 *Mofaz v. Central Elections Committee*, PD 57(3) 793, [1], [15]–[17] (2003).
[43] *Mizrahi*, Supra note 3 (Chief Justice Barak).

9.3. THE PLATONIC CONCEPTION OF THE CONSTITUTIONAL TEXT

9.3.1. *Distinguishing Socio-Political and Conceptual Questions*

As a matter of political fact, the "constitutional revolution" that started with the *Mizrahi* case was an astounding story of success. The gap between textual reality and ideal was indeed bridged, and the judicial framework set in the case is now the undisputed law of the land. This raises fascinating political, social, and institutional questions regarding why this revolution happened in the first place, why it was so successful, and why did the political branches not react to it. I will briefly discuss these questions here, and then go on to address my main question in this chapter which is conceptual and theoretical.

First, one may give answers to the question why the Court embarked on this project that rely on internal legal reasons. Such an account could be, for example, that the advancement of rights protection jurisprudence worldwide, as well as in the jurisprudence of the Israeli Supreme Court, created an internal legal pressure to expand the set of rights protected, as well as the scope of their protection. In particular, the inclusion of only a limited set of rights in the new 1992 Basic Laws created consistency pressures on the Court to include a full set of rights, as happens in other constitutional systems that have only partial lists of rights, such as Australia.[44]

Second, from a more general socio-political perspective, an account given by several Israeli scholars is that the Court was compensating for changes in Israel that eroded the dominance of the liberal left in Israeli politics and society.[45] The constitutional project was a way of arresting some of these changes, or a way of conferring power on the Court that would protect the interests of the liberal left camp that were eroded in the political sphere.[46] Another related account points to the relative weakness and inefficiency of the political system in Israel at the time of the move, which allowed for a judicial power-grab[47] or, under a different description, created a governance vacuum that pulled in the Court.[48]

---

[44] See Rosalind Dickson's contribution to this book.
[45] See Gavison, Supra note 21 (arguing that the Israeli constitutional project was a way of arresting rather than facilitating change).
[46] See e.g., Ran Hirschle, "The Struggle for Hegemony: Explaining the expansion of Judicial Power through the Constitutionalization of Rights in Culturally-divided Polities" (2000) 36 *Stanford Journal of International Law* 73 (arguing that the Supreme Court of Israel served as a stronghold of the Israeli Left after it had lost power in the political sphere). See also Menachem Mautner, *The Decline of Formalism and the Rise of Values in Israeli Law* (Tel Aviv: Maagalai Daat, 1993) (Hebrew).
[47] See Hirschle, Supra note 46.
[48] See Mautner, Supra note 46.

In terms of the political system's response, or lack thereof, one common account is that the political system was caught off-guard, and by the time it fully realized the scope of the change it was confronted with high legitimacy and path dependency costs in terms of unraveling of the change.[49] In this respect such a revolutionary move by the Court could only happen once, as the political branches would not be caught off guard a second time. Courts, generally, under this explanation, have a one-shot attempt at making revolutionary moves. Other accounts stress the advantages of constitutional judicial review for the political actors themselves – in particular, the fact that the Court would now be the final arbiter on some of the "hot button" issues in Israeli society, thus taking on all the blame for unpopular but unavoidable decisions.

9.3.2. *Theoretical and Conceptual Framework – The Platonic Conception*

While these are all very pertinent and important questions, I will concentrate on another question in this chapter: what kind of theory or conceptual framework could be posited to lie behind and justify the constitutional revolution? Or, to put the question more concretely, what kind of assumptions regarding the relationship between the Court and the constitutional text are necessarily implied by this move? This conception, and these assumptions, one should note, are not necessarily those that the Court explicitly proclaimed to rely on, or was even consciously aware of but, in a sense, the Court must be seen to adopt them, as indicated by its own decisions and reasoning.

Also, it should be noted that the theoretical question is not completely separable from the socio-political questions as the choice of the particular conception that I will identify may have been affected by the extent to which it was congenial to the political aims of the judges. But, nonetheless, the question what this conception is, is a different and to some extent independent one than the question of what were the socio-political reasons behind the judicial move that was described above.[50]

9.3.3. *Plato's Idealism and Constitutional Interpretation*

Plato has famously distinguished between Idea (not to be confused with the modern English use of the word "idea") and Matter, between Form and

---

[49] See Ori Aronson, "Why Hasn't the Knesset Abolished Basic Law: Human Dignity and Liberty? On the Status Quo as Countermajoritarian Difficulty" (2006) 37 *Tel Aviv University Law Review* (Hebrew).

[50] One may view this is a kind of *Transcendental Argument* in the Kantian sense asking "if a theory of interpretation for the constitutional revolution were possible, how must it look like?"

Substance, and between *noumenon* and *phenomenon*.[51] In Plato's theory of Ideas the only real things are the Ideas or the pure Forms or *noumena*, but they are transcendent and beyond the reach of human perception. Ideas are a-spatial and a-temporal, they are eternal, unchanging, abstract, and perfect. Matter, Substance and *phenomena* are imperfect, changing, and temporal. They are an imperfect manifestation, example and instance of the pure and perfect "blueprint" which is the Idea or the Form. For example, a triangle drawn by a chalk on a blackboard is imperfect, spatial and temporal – the hand may shake writing it, it has a width and takes space, and it can be erased and thus cease to exist; but the Idea of a triangle, is abstract, a-special, a-temporal, and therefore also perfect and eternal.

According to Plato, only Ideas are true, whereas the world of Matter and of Substance is an illusion. It is an illusion because we perceive it through our imperfect senses, and can never view directly the real things. Ideas and Forms are also an answer to the problem of universals. They give an answer to the question how is it that there are many different things which are all one and the same. All triangles in the world are instances and manifestations of the Idea of the triangle, and all take part of it, imitate it, and try to be close to it, and in virtue of that fact can all be called triangles.[52]

The famous allegory of the cave exemplifies the relationship between Idea and Matter as the relationship between an object and its shadow. Human beings are analogized to prisoners in a cave who can only see on the cave's walls the shadows of the figures that are behind them. The figures are the real things, while the prisoners can only see their shadows and reflection.[53]

To exemplify what I mean by the term Platonic conception of the constitutional text I will begin with a quote from an important Canadian constitutional scholar – Lorraine Weinrib of Toronto Law School – that most succinctly captures this concept.[54] Weinrib, I will argue, shares the same conception that

---

[51] See Silverman, Allan, "Plato's Middle Period Metaphysics and Epistemology," *The Stanford Encyclopedia of Philosophy* (Fall 2014 edn.), Edward N. Zalta (ed.), https://plato.stanford.edu/archives/fall2014/entries/plato-metaphysics/. These are different terms that are used here interchangeably, although for certain purposes the differences between them may matter.

[52] Ibid.

[53] Plato, Republic, VII 514 a, 2 to 517 a, 7.

[54] Others before me have referred to Plato or to Platonism to describe similar phenomenon to the ones I aim to describe here. Steve Smith in his book, *Law's Quandary* (see note 9) lists a few of those, including Richard Posner, who used the term to describe Langdellian conceptualism (Richard A. Posner, "The Decline of Law as an Autonomous Discipline: 1962–1987" 1987 100 *Harvard Law Review* 761, 762); Brian Bix, who used the term to describe Michael Moore's natural law theory (Brian Bix, *Jurisprudence: Theory and Context*, 2nd edn (Durham, NC: Carolina Academic, 1999), 72); and, most closely to my aim here, David Luban, who used the term to describe the Warren Court's attitude toward rights, although in a much more sympathetic

lies behind the Israeli constitutional revolution. In her important article on constitutionalism after the Second World War, "The Post-WWII Paradigm,"[55] Professor Weinrib writes as follows:

> The rights-protecting instruments adopted in the aftermath of the Second World War share a constitutional conception that transcends the history, cultural heritage and social mores of any particular nation state ... The value structure and corresponding institutional framework are taken to comprise "an objective value order."
> Accordingly, the specific rights guaranteed to individuals as legal subjects – the so-called "subjective rights" – crystallize the more objective abstract constitutional principles of equal citizenship and inherent human dignity[56]... The subjective rights stand as instantiations of an objective normative order based on the principles of equal citizenship and respect for inherent human dignity.[57]

According to Weinrib, therefore, there is an "objective value order" – a term that she derives from German constitutional law. This objective value order "transcends the history, cultural heritage and social mores of any particular nation state" and includes specific legal institutions (of which she brings the examples of "judicial review and possible invalidation of legislation"[58]) and also "objective rights." The objective rights are differentiated from the "subjective rights" which are the particular text found in particular constitutions. The relationship between the two clearly gives primacy to the objective rights over the subjective rights. The latter "crystallize" the objective rights, they are "instantiations" of the objective rights, and they are "important but not exhaustive exemplars" of the objective rights.

The analogy to Plato's Idealism should be clear by now. The constitutional text in this analogy is the Matter, Substance, and *phenomena*. This is so, since it is but an imperfect, flawed, and temporal manifestation of the pure Form and Idea which is the "objective right" or "objective value order." It is, in that

---

view than mine toward it (David Luban, "The Warren Court and the Concept of a Right" (1999) 34 *Harvard Civil Rights – Civil Liberties Law Review* 7, 37). Smith himself uses the term to describe a general attitude to law (164–70). I therefore do not take credit for inventing this concept, but I think that my account puts it to the fore more than most other accounts, and applies it to a particular set of recent phenomena all taking place within constitutional law in ways that are different from other accounts.

[55] Lorraine Weinrib, "The Postwar Paradigm and American Exceptionalism" in Sujit Choudhry (ed.) *The Migration of Constitutional Ideas* (Cambridge: Cambridge University Press, 2006), 84.
[56] Ibid., at 90.
[57] Ibid., at 94.
[58] Ibid., at 90.

sense, not the "real" thing. Texts of constitutions are the result of political compromises, and of the works of humans who are influenced by the contingencies of their time and culture, and the pressures of the hour. They may even be the work of ignorant or racist people. Constitutional texts are thus imperfect things, and are prone to be so. They can also be incomplete or filled with caveats. And they are temporal and can be revoked or changed. The only "real" thing is the Idea of a constitution, or the Idea of a constitutional right, as these Ideas, or ideal Forms, are absolved from the imperfections of the text, transcend national borders and historical circumstances and are, in essence, objective and eternal.

The crucial element in this interpretative theory is the role assigned to the constitutional judge. The judge owes her allegiance to the objective, abstract, and pure Idea of the constitution or of the right, and not to the imperfect contingent manifestation of it in the text. Weinrib writes: "the judicial function is to evaluate whether the state's encroachment on the right violates the constitutional principles of equal citizenship and inherent human dignity [the objective right], of which the specific guarantees [subjective right] are important but not exhaustive exemplars."[59] The judge should apply to the case the ideal Form and not the flawed text, or at least he or she should strive to do so, and should get direction and guidance directly from that ideal Form.

Another important feature of Weinrib's quote, especially if put in the context of my suggested analogy to the Israeli case, is that this Form includes not only constitutional rights, but also some institutional aspects such as judicial review and the ability to invalidate laws. All of them comprise the "objective value order" which "transcend the history, cultural heritage and social mores of any particular nation state."

Note finally that the objective value order also has a substantive focal point, or center – it is "equal citizenship and inherent human dignity." For Weinrib, so it seems, these two principles are the essence of constitutionalism, and from them both the constitutional institutions and the different manifestations of constitutional rights are derived. We might view them as a higher order ideal Form. The text is only a manifestation of the ideal Form of rights, and these rights, in their turn, are only manifestations of the ideal Form of the supreme or overarching right, which is "equal citizenship and human dignity." The influence of German Constitutional jurisprudence and theory is evident here as well, as it similarly has an overarching constitutional value – human dignity. As mentioned earlier Germany is also the birthplace of such concepts as

---

[59] Ibid., at 93–4.

"objective value order,"[60] and in German jurisprudence the idea of the text as only an approximation of the true right is explicitly endorsed.[61] This, although there are some important special characteristics of the German version of the Platonic conception that distinguish it, for example, from the Israeli version - in particular the fact that it is accompanied by legal formalism.[62]

9.3.4. The Platonic Conception and the Israeli Constitutional Revolution

All of this fits very well with Barak's project of bridging the gap between the ideal constitution and the imperfect text of the Basic Laws. For Barak and for those Justices that joined his opinion in *Mizrahi* and in subsequent cases, their allegiance is to the Idea of a constitution and not to its imperfect manifestation in Israeli law, and they therefore strive to move Israeli law as close as they can to that Idea. This ideal Form, as in Weinrib's account, includes both the institution of judicial review itself and the content of the protected bill of rights. Since the ideal Form of a constitution includes judicial review, the Court can imply judicial review, even if it is not clear by the text or (as in the case of the old Basic Laws), has no relation to the text.[63] Second, the limited and imperfect list of rights in the Basic Laws is but a shadow of the true Idea or Form of a bill of rights that the Justices should try and achieve through interpretation. The filling in of the missing rights, despite its contradiction to

---

[60] The term was coined in the Luth case of 1958; Lüth, Bundesverfassungsgericht [BVerfG] [Federal Constitutional Court] January 15, 1958, 7 Entscheidungen des Bundesverfassungsgerichts [BverfGE] 198 (F.R.G.).

[61] Jacco Bomhoff, *Balancing and Constitutional Rights: The Origins and Meanings of Postwar Legal Discourse* (Cambridge: Cambridge University Press, 2013), 107. In describing German constitutional jurisprudence, starting from the 1950s, Bomhoff writes that according to jurisprudence "[t]he written Constitution, on the system-of-values view, might be incomplete and the catalogue of rights haphazard, but ... the value order behind the Constitution could still be comprehensive."

[62] German constitutional jurisprudence is characterized by a high level of formalism and systematization, features that are absent and even antithetical to Israeli constitutional adjudication. The German version of the Platonic conception of the constitution therefore holds within it the tension that is often attributed to German law – between highly abstract and idealized jurisprudence, and highly formalized and technical one: see Jacco Bomhoff, "Lüth's 50th Anniversary: Some Comparative Observations on the German Foundations of Judicial Balancing" (2008) 9 *German Law Journal* 121, 124. That different systems may have different versions of the Platonic conception, however, does not mean that they do not share a similar conception. I have suggested elsewhere though that the absence of the text as a limitation on judicial discretion is balanced in Germany by the formalism that characterizes it, but that such balance is absent in the Israeli jurisprudence: see Iddo Porat, "Sixty Years of Balancing: On the Transformation from Instrumental to Substantive Balancing in Israeli Law" (2010) 10 *Law and Business* 347 (Hebrew).

[63] See notes 32–35 and accompanying text.

the structure of the text and to the political compromise behind it, is therefore justified since this political compromise is only behind the human and flawed "subjective rights" and does not affect the validity of the "objective rights" that are derived directly from general principles of personhood and dignity.

The Platonic conception helps explain several key aspects of the relationship to the text in Israeli constitutionalism, as well as in other constitutional systems that share this model. First this conception helps explain how the Court completely ignores the original intent behind the Basic Laws, and why originalism as a constitutional theory has absolutely no place in Israeli constitutionalism. According to a Platonic conception of the text the will of the drafters is irrelevant. The will of the drafters of the text cannot affect the truth of the Idea of the right or of the constitution, of which the text is an imperfect manifestation. Hence, for Barak, the obvious and undisputed will of the drafters of the Basic Law: Human Dignity and Liberty not to include certain rights in the text was inconsequential for its interpretation.[64] Equality, freedom of speech, and freedom of religion "truly" inhere in the right to human dignity, and in the more general Idea of a constitution, whether the drafters of the Basic Law willed this or not.

Second, this account also explains why Barak chose the right to human dignity to carry on its shoulders the weight of the entire bill of rights. This is the same right that serves as the Archimedean point for Weinrib, is the center of German constitutionalism, and can be seen as the true Form of all the different manifestations of the specific rights. Third, the Platonic conception can explain why Barak and others view their doctrines as "interpretation" of the text, although not being constrained by the human will behind it. This point can be made clear if we compare the Platonic conception with the idea of Natural Law.

There is much similarity between the Platonic conception of constitutional law and constitutional rights, and the idea of Natural Law and Natural Rights. There is also of course a historic connection between the two, as the Catholic Natural Law theory is a derivation of Greek Platonic and Aristotelian philosophy. Like the Platonic Ideas, Natural Law is unchanging, pure, and unaffected by human imperfection. Like the Ideas Natural Law is the "real" thing, and holds priority over the human and imperfect Positive Law.[65] However, there seems to be the following difference: unlike the relationship between Form and Substance there is no necessary connection or similarity between Natural

---

[64] See notes 37–41 and accompanying text.
[65] See Natural Law Tradition in Ethics, *Stanford Encyclopedia of Philosophy*, https://plato.stanford.edu/entries/natural-law-ethics/.

Law and Positive Law. Some positive legal systems may be more just and therefore closer to Natural Law, and some not, but the two are conceptually different, and there is no causal or conceptual necessary connection between them. Therefore their relationship is usually portrayed as one of conflict – the Natural Law that lead Antigone to bury her brother, in the Greek play that carries her name, conflicted with Creon's positive law that forbade it.[66] The relationship of Form and Substance and of Idea and Matter is, on the other hand, one of reflection and manifestation. This is the reason why the act of bridging the gap between the imperfect constitutional text and the perfect Idea of the constitution is usually referred to by judges and lawyers as an act of "interpretation" rather than an act of conflict and of "overriding." The true Form is thought to lie somehow in the heart of its imperfect manifestation in the constitutional text, and the judge, interpreting the text, only finds it there and brings it to light.

Fourth, the Platonic conception can also help explain the extensive use of foreign constitutional law in the jurisprudence of the Israeli Supreme Court,[67] as well as in the jurisprudence of other constitutional courts that share this model, such as the German[68] and the Canadian[69] ones. The same attempt at getting at the ideal Form that is embedded somehow in the imperfect text, is shared by constitutional judges all over the world, as different constitutions are all manifestations (flawed and imperfect each in their own way) of this ideal. Since judges all over share the same project they can be aided by the products of each other.

Fifth and finally, the Platonic conception can also explain why judges can annul constitutional provisions even without a "super" constitutional text that lies above the constitution. Judges can invalidate even the constitution itself, if it deviates too much from the Platonic Idea of a constitution. This conclusion may sound extreme, but it is also part of actual Israeli constitutional doctrine.

---

[66] Sophocles, *Antigone* (trans. Robert Fagles) (Penguin Classics 2015). It has been pointed out to me that this perception of the relationship between Natural Law and Positive Law is true from a positivistic perspective, but not necessarily from a Natural Law one. I thank Steve Smith for this point.

[67] See Iddo Porat, "The Use of Foreign Law in Israeli Constitutional Adjudication", in Gideon Sapir, Daphne Barak-Erez and Aharon Barak (eds.), *Israeli Constitutional Law in the Making* (Hart Publishing 2013), 151.

[68] Hannes Unberath, "Comparative Law in the German Courts," in Guy Canivet, Mads Andenæs and Duncan Fairgrieve (eds.), *Comparative Law before the Courts* (British Institute of International and Comparative Law 2004), 307.

[69] Peter McCormick, "The Supreme Court of Canada and American Citations 1945–94: A Statistical Overview" (1997) 8 *Supreme Court Law Review* 527; Peter McCormick, "American Citations and the McLachlin Court: An Empirical Study" (2009) 47 *Osgoode Hall Law Journal* 83.

According to Justice Barak and other Justices, the Supreme Court could invalidate a Basic Law if it conflicted in a strong way with the "basic principles of the system."[70] This doctrine is associated by these judges with the doctrine of "unconstitutional constitutional amendments" known also in other constitutional systems,[71] but it seems more far-reaching, as the unconstitutionality in the Israeli case would not emanate from the constitution itself, but from higher principles – the Idea of a constitution according to my interpretation.

9.4. THE PLATONIC CONCEPTION TAKEN TO THE EXTREME, JUSTIFICATIONS, AND ANSWERS TO OBJECTIONS

9.4.1. Constitutionalism without a Text

Do we need therefore a text at all? Taken to its logical extreme it would appear that according to the Platonic conception text is not required at all. We could have constitutionalism without a constitution. Indeed, text could even be counterproductive to constitutional adjudication, as it might drive judges away from the true Idea of the constitution or of constitutional rights.[72] In one of his most striking opinions, Justice Barak seems to arrive at this same conclusion. This occurs in an opinion from 1989, before the two Basic Laws of 1992 and the constitutional revolution. In the *Laor* case Barak writes the following as an obiter dicta:

> In principle and theoretically, there exists the possibility that a court in a democratic society would declare void a law that violates the basic principles of the system, even if these basic principles are not enshrined in an entrenched constitution or Basic Law. There is nothing axiomatic in the approach that a law is not invalidated because of its content.[73]

A constitutional text, according to Barak, is therefore not required for the understanding of the principles according to which a law can be invalidated (what Barak terms the "basic principles of the society" and could be viewed as a placeholder for what I called the Idea of a constitution), nor for the legitimacy

---

[70] HCJ 4908/10 *Bar-On v. Knesset* (11.1.2011 not published yet).
[71] See generally Yaniv Rosnai, *Unconstitutional Constitutional Amendments* (Oxford University Press 2017).
[72] For a similar claim made by way of critique of American constitutional law, see Foley, Supra note 9, 152: "I shall suggest an account of constitutional interpretation in which the actual language of the Constitution serves as little more than a potential obstacle to judicial decisions reached independently by considerations of pure political philosophy. (By 'pure political philosophy,' I mean the judge's own normative beliefs about what the Constitution ideally ought to say.)"
[73] HCJ 14/86 *Laor v. Films and Plays Censorship Board* 41(1) PD 421 (1989), [30] (Justice Barak).

for invalidating a law. According to Barak, there is "nothing axiomatic" in the view that you need a constitution for a court to strike down a law. Justice Barak could, in principle, have done everything he did when using the Basic Laws even without them.

If there is no purpose for the text at all, according to the Platonic scheme, how is it that Barak nevertheless did not embark on the constitutional revolution project without some anchoring in a constitutional or quasi-constitutional text – i.e., the two 1992 Basic Laws? Even for Barak and for the Platonic view, there seems therefore to be some importance to the constitutional text, though it is purely instrumental. The text is required to provide legitimacy to the Court in the eyes of the public. It is required in order to achieve the cooperation of the political branches with the Court and its rulings. There may be other instrumental reasons, such as coordination, or education, or reducing litigation costs, or litigation volume. But, for the judicial task itself, for its essence and moral justification, the text is completely redundant. As long as a judge can convince the public and the political branches that what he does is legitimate because it emanates from the text, the text has served its purpose.

9.4.2. Democratic Justification and Judicial Review

The Platonic conception of the constitution presents formidable normative challenges to those who adopt it; foremost amongst them is the democratic challenge. Shouldn't the constitution – the highest law of a people – be adopted by the people themselves, rather than by a court? As I mentioned in the introduction, I believe this normative challenge is very serious. The advantage of the account I offer, hopefully, is in exposing the full thrust of this challenge since it exposes much of current constitutionalism in the European tradition for what it is – a project in which The People have no substantial or foundational place. Since the normative account is not my main aim, I only present here the way Justice Barak gives an answer to this challenge. Note how this answer is itself a rare moment of clarity in which there is no attempt to find democratic will behind the constitution. Here is Barak's answer in the *Laor* case, quoted above, when justifying his position that text is not required for judicial review:

> In invalidating a law by the court because of its extreme infringement of basic principles the principle of parliament sovereignty is not harmed, since sovereignty is never indefinite. There is no harm to the principle of separation of power, since this principle is based on checks and balances that restrict each one of the branches. There is no harm to democracy, since

democracy is a delicate balance between majority rule and human rights and basic principles and in this balance the safeguarding of human rights and basic principles cannot be seen, in itself, as undemocratic. It is not harmful to the office of the judiciary since it is the task of the judiciary to safeguard the rule of law, including the rule of law over the legislator.[74]

Democracy is therefore not hurt, according to Barak, since democracy is not only the rule of the majority, but a delicate balance between the rule of the majority and human rights and basic principles. The court does not need a text in order to know what human rights and basic principles are – this is established already if we accept the assumption of the Platonic conception of the constitution – and, according to Barak in this quote, applying these principles on the legislator is not contrary to democracy, although it is not done in the name of the people's will as expressed in a constitution, since the will of the people is not the only thing that matters in a democracy. When the court restricts the will of the people because of principles of human rights "this cannot be seen, in itself, as undemocratic."

The theory of judicial review and of democracy, therefore, is based on a substantive rather than a formal conception of democracy, and is not based on the idea that the will of people stands behind the constitution. Hence, also, the fact that the Basic Laws were not voted on with any substantial majority in the Knesset, nor did they reflect any robust process of public deliberation, is inconsequential for Barak, and does not hamper their legitimacy in his eyes. The Basic Law's legitimacy comes from the fact that they are an imperfect instance of the true Form of a constitution, and even if they were not voted on by any of the Knesset members, to the extent that they partook in this ideal they were valid. What is also clear from Barak's account is that the only institution from which we should not be afraid of subverting the ideas of human rights, basic principle, and the rule of law, and who therefore can impose those ideas on every other organ but need not be supervised or restricted itself – is the court.

9.4.3. Answers to Objections

The Platonic conception is a heuristic device to illuminate some of the main features of the Israeli Court's, as well as other courts, attitude toward the constitutional text. As such this heuristic is not hermetically sealed against inadequacies and cannot present a perfect analogy. In addition, it is not the only

---

[74] Ibid.

heuristic that can be used to describe the phenomenon I wish to describe. In this last section I wish to explain this choice and defend it from possible objections. I will review three main objections.

One objection may stem from the difficulty of accepting the metaphysics of the Platonic account. According to Plato, the Ideas or true Forms really exist. They are not just an interpretative construct, but actual entities in the world. This makes the Platonic philosophy implausible to many. Other accounts which resemble the Platonic account evade this difficulty by not adopting its metaphysics. Such is, for example, Michael Moore's idea of "functional kinds" which he uses to describe the law.[75] My reply is, first, that using the Platonic account as a heuristic does not require adopting it as truth. I argue that the relationship between text and the ideal (or template) constitution resembles the relationship between Matter and Idea. This does not mean that the ideal constitution actually exists as a real entity. Second, as mentioned earlier, the adoption of the Platonic account for the analogy is not a necessary one, and does not exclude other effective analogies. It is, however, advantageous to other possible heuristic accounts (such as Moore's functional kinds), even if those might be less philosophically demanding, because of its simplicity and ability to catch the public imagination. Plato and his idealism are well known cultural constructs, and are therefore effective in making the point if, as I hope, they resemble closely enough the phenomenon I wish to describe.

Other possible objections can address the inadequacies in the analogy, some of which have already been discussed. I will discuss here two. First, one may ask how far does the analogy go – do all constitutional rights have an ideal Form? Does the ideal Form of a constitution include all institutional arrangements that constitutions have, some of which are very technical? The answer to these questions is that this is a matter of degree, and that while there may be borderline cases, some examples fall clearly either on the side of being part of the ideal Form or not. For example, the central human rights, such as equality, political freedom, freedom of conscience are quite clearly (in the eyes of those to whom I assign the Platonic conception, such as Justice Barak) part of the ideal Form of the constitution. Such is also the institution of judicial review itself. However, other rights may be viewed as contingent or culturally based, and therefore not part of the ideal Form, such as, for example, the right to bear arms in the American Constitution.[76] The same may apply to some institutional arrangements, such as the type of judicial review adopted (e.g.,

---

[75] See Michael Moore, "The Semantics of Judging" (1980) 54 *Southern California Law Review* 151; Michael Moore, "Law as a Functional Kind", in Robert George (ed.) *Natural Law Theories* (Oxford: Oxford University Press, 1992). I thank Larry Solum for this point.
[76] The Constitution of the United States, Amendment 2.

with or without an override clause), or the type of doctrine applied (e.g., tiers of scrutiny or proportionality). Some rights or institutional arrangements may be borderline cases. The doctrine of proportionality, for example, is viewed by some as part of the essence of constitutionalism, and as following logically from the idea of human rights, and hence as having left the realm of contingent doctrine and entered into what I would term the ideal Form of a constitution.[77]

Second, one may ask how is it that the ideal Form of a constitution can be perceived by judges. After all, according to the Platonic analogy, the ideal Forms are imperceptible to the human eye, and only their manifestations as matter or object can be perceived. Similarly, how is it that judges can annul constitutional provisions or amendments (using such doctrines as unconstitutional constitutional amendments), if such provisions are analogized to objects and Matter that cannot be erased from reality by an act of human will. As to the first question, judges may indeed acknowledge that they do not have direct access to the ideal constitution, or the ideal Form of human rights – they can only strive to approximate them, and get closer to them, and the different manifestations of constitutional texts worldwide are helping them in this project. Second, the idea of annulling a constitutional provision can be analogized to declaring a classification of an object as wrong. Viewing a provision in a constitution that deprives people of their basic rights, as a constitutional provision, would be like looking at a dog and saying that it is a cat. Some objects are so far from the ideal Form that they cannot be regarded as manifestations of it. While not all parts of the analogy fit exactly, I hope to have shown that it is close enough to be a useful and effective heuristic.

9.5. CONCLUSION

Israeli constitutional adjudication includes a very substantial amount of unwritten constitutional law. Indeed, most of the constitution in Israel can be said to be unwritten. Even the fact that it is a constitution and not a piece of regular legislation is unwritten. I have argued that this fact is the result of continuous attempts by the Supreme Court, and in particular by its most intellectually influential Justice, Justice Aharon Barak, to bridge the gap between the ideal – having a full-fledged constitution with a full bill of rights, and reality – only a partial and fragmented text which is the beginning of a constitution.

---

[77] See Robert Alexy, *A Theory of Constitutional Rights* (Oxford: Oxford University Press, 2002), 66 (Julian Rivers trans.) arguing that the doctrine of proportionality "logically follows" from the nature of rights as principles.

I have also argued that behind this project, that turned out to be phenomenally successful, lies a theory of constitutional interpretation which I called a Platonic conception of the constitutional text.

Is Israel only an extreme case of the Platonic conception of the text, or should it be regarded as qualitatively different than, let us say, German constitutionalism which also shares some of the premises of the Platonic conception, or even the American constitution, of which great parts are unwritten? The answer is not clear. However, sometimes differences of degree become differences in kind. Courts have been known to engage in very loose methods of constitutional interpretations, but they at least were interpreting a *constitution*. In the case of Israel, the judicial act can only be described as an act of pure statesmanship on behalf of the Court – since it amounted to constitution building and creation, and not only interpretation.

10

The Indonesian Constitutional Court

Implying Rights from the 'Rule of Law'

Simon Butt

Indonesia's Constitutional Court was established in August 2003. It has nine judges, with three each appointed by the three arms of government – the national parliament, the Supreme Court and the president. Most of its judges have been law professors, former politicians and judges from other Indonesian courts, including the Supreme Court itself. Though it is not the first Indonesian judicial institution to have some form of judicial review power, the Court is the first to have exercised constitutional review. However, this power is limited. In particular, the Court can only determine whether legislation enacted by Indonesia's national parliament complies with the Constitution. It lacks jurisdiction to review executive regulations or government action for constitutionality.

This chapter considers the handful of cases in which the Court has sought to 'imply' constitutional rights. In these cases, the Court has identified, and then applied, rights that it considers essential to the 'rule of law', as understood in Indonesia. Problematically, the Court has attempted to explain neither its approach to implying rights, nor precisely what the rule of law entails.

While implying rights raises the ire of legislatures and legal commentators in other countries, it has almost entirely escaped attention in Indonesia. Indeed, when the national legislature attempted to curb the Court's powers in 2011, in response to perceived judicial activism, it ignored these implied rights cases. Instead, the legislature sought to prohibit the Court exceeding its jurisdiction in other ways. Nevertheless, after an enthusiastic start during its earlier years, the Court's rights implication appears to have slowed, if not ceased, in more recent years. The Court's implied rights jurisprudence may well have already reached its zenith.

This chapter provides an account of the rise, and the apparent fall, of rights implication in Indonesia's Constitutional Court. I begin by introducing the Court and its jurisdiction, before discussing the Court's implied rights cases and the vagaries of the Indonesian version of the 'rule of law' – the concept upon which the Court has relied to imply rights, at least in the cases thus far. I then seek to explain why the Court began – and then stopped – implying rights.

10.1. INTRODUCING THE CONSTITUTIONAL COURT

Indonesia is a large archipelagic state, comprising over 17,000 islands, stretched across over 5,000 kilometres from east to west. Its population of over 250 million is culturally and religiously diverse and, though it has a rising middle class, the gap between rich and poor is becoming more marked. A former Dutch colony, it follows the civil law tradition and continues to apply large bodies of Dutch law dating back many decades. (In particular, its Civil Code, first applied in Indonesia in 1848, and Criminal Code, applied from 1918, remain largely intact, despite piecemeal attempts at legislative reform in some fields, such as marriage, land law, corruption and terrorism.) Though not an Islamic state, Indonesia has more Muslims than any other nation and has religious courts to decide particular types of disputes between Muslims. Customary law, or *adat*, is widely practised, particularly outside urban centres.

For most of its independent history, Indonesia has been an authoritarian state. Indonesia's first Constitution – introduced on 18 August 1945, the day following the declaration of independence – was threadbare and ambiguous, referring to the need for an independent judicial system and an elected legislature, but leaving much scope for the exercise of strong presidential power. This was justified as necessary to bring Indonesia's disparate population together, in part to fight against the Dutch when they returned to reclaim Indonesia after World War II. After this so-called revolution against the Dutch concluded in 1949, Indonesia's rulers experimented with a liberal democratic system – complete with independent courts, constitutional rights, democratic elections and a strong legislature. A constituent assembly was established to decide whether Indonesia should maintain that system or choose another. Two of the systems the assembly considered were an Islamic state and authoritarianism. However, instability, both within the national parliament and in Indonesia's outer regions, led the then President Soekarno to reinstate the 1945 Constitution by decree in July 1959 – before the Assembly could decide on the basis of the state. From then, until the fall of Indonesia's second President, Soeharto, in May 1998, Indonesia was authoritarian, backed by a very strong military that played a central role in politics.

Within a few years of Soeharto's fall, Indonesia had already made significant progress along the path to becoming a functioning democracy. One early reform was amending the Constitution to give more power to the national legislature, elected in free and fair elections, and to entrench a catalogue of internationally protected human rights. Judicial reform was also prioritised. By the late 1990s, Indonesia's courts had become decrepit – in terms of physical infrastructure and budgets, judicial competence, administrative capacity, susceptibility to bribery and dependence on government. They were widely considered unable to reliably resolve disputes between citizens, much less between citizens and the state. During the Soeharto years in particular, the government had used its administrative control over the courts – including when to pay or promote judges, if at all – to elicit favourable decisions. One of the first judiciary-related reforms, then, sought to improve judicial independence by giving administrative control of all lower court judges to the Supreme Court itself.

Another important post-Soeharto judiciary-related reform was the establishment, in 2003, of the Constitutional Court – the focus of this chapter. This Court, institutionally separate from the Supreme Court, has various constitutionally delineated powers. These include constitutional review – that is, assessing whether statutes enacted by Indonesia's parliament comply with the Constitution; resolving disputes over election results; deciding jurisdictional contests between state institutions established under the Constitution; hearing government – brought motions for the disbandment of political parties; and considering parliamentary allegations of misconduct by the president or vice president, as part of impeachment processes.

The Court has, mostly, exercised these powers professionally – that is, independently, industriously, consistently, transparently and with a concern to justify its decisions by reference to the law. This sets it apart from most of Indonesia's other courts, which, as mentioned, have traditionally been considered corrupt, incompetent and dependent on government. The Constitutional Court has not shirked 'difficult' cases, including those involving significant governmental interests or controversial issues such as human rights, religion and ethnicity. It has invalidated dozens of statutory provisions and has even invalidated entire statutes. For these reasons, the Court is often described as a model for judicial reform in Indonesia.

However, the Court has not been beyond reproach. Some of its staff and judges have been accused – and convicted – of corruption. Most notable was the conviction of Justice Akil Mochtar for taking bribes to fix the outcome of regional head electoral disputes. Mochtar was Chief Justice of the Court when he was arrested. Further, the Court's decision-making has been criticised, most often for the outcomes produced. It is also criticised for issuing inconsistent decisions, for economic conservatism, for failing to uphold important constitutional rights and for guarding its own institutional interests, even against legitimate legislative intervention directed at ensuring that the Court does not overstep its constitutional mandate. Yet despite these perceived inadequacies, the Court's decisions have been largely respected. This is particularly significant, because many of its cases involve the interests of the government, or government institutions, whether national, provincial, city or county. For many decades, government institutions have not had the exercise of their powers subjected to judicial scrutiny.

The Court has also been criticised for using inadequate or questionable legal reasoning to support some of its decisions. Critics have focused on the Court's insufficient disclosure, in its decisions, of the legal reasoning or interpretative methods it employs. These criticisms, however, have largely fallen on deaf ears, even within Indonesian legal and political communities. While lawyers and politicians often criticise the Court for the decisions it reaches, they rarely criticise the processes or principles the Court uses to arrive at those decisions. This is surprising. Some politicians are particularly forthright in their condemnation of the Court for invalidating legislation enacted by a democratically elected parliament, but they have let this 'opportunity' to criticise the Court pass by. Also, Indonesia's legal community is particularly vibrant, and usually keeps a close eye on the Court and the way it operates. Given the need for lawyers to present arguments before the Court, one might expect that they would be interested in discovering how the Court chooses between those arguments. One explanation, explored later in this chapter, is that Indonesian politicians and lawyers alike understand neither what rights implication is nor what its consequences are.

I now turn to briefly outline the Court's implied rights jurisprudence. As we will see, the primary constitutional basis upon which the Court has implied rights is Article 1(3) of the Constitution, which declares that Indonesia is a *Negara Hukum* – a country that observes 'the rule of law'. What comprises the *Negara Hukum* has never been entirely clear and remains hotly contested in Indonesia today. Nevertheless, after initially providing little guidance on what the concept means in modern Indonesia, the Court has, more recently, begun providing clues about its key components.

10.2. IMPLIED RIGHTS CASES

The Court began referring to the *Negara Hukum* concept and emphasised its importance in its earliest decisions. In *Bali Bombing* (2003), for example, the majority stated that

> the essence of the Constitutional Court's existence ... to guard the Constitution and to uphold the principle of the supremacy of the law in the Indonesian state system after the *Reformasi* era ... is nothing other than an effort to strengthen the realisation of the ideas of the *Negara Hukum*.[1]

---

[1] Constitutional Court Decision 013/PUU-I/2003, 46.

In subsequent cases the Court uncovered various rights that emanate from the *Negara Hukum*. These rights appear to include the right to legal aid, to due process, to a fair trial and to be presumed innocent until proven guilty. I now turn to outline key cases in which the Court has 'discovered' these rights.

10.2.1. *The Right to Legal Aid and Access to Justice*

In the *Advocates Law* case (2004), the Court was asked to review the constitutionality of provisions of the 2003 Advocates Law that prohibited those who were not formally qualified as advocates or lawyers from providing any form of legal services or advice.[2] Those who did so faced criminal penalties of up to five years' imprisonment and significant fines. This prohibition put in jeopardy the operation of many hundreds of legal aid clinics – most of which are housed in universities – run by students and staff who were not formally qualified as advocates. These clinics provided the primary, if not sole, means by which Indonesia's poor accessed legal services. For the Court, depriving these citizens, and others, of legal assistance violated the *Negara Hukum* concept:

> [T]he right to legal assistance, as a part of human rights, must be considered a constitutional right of citizens, even though the Constitution does not explicitly regulate or mention it. The state must, therefore, guarantee the fulfilment [of this right].[3]

In this context, the prohibition caused injustice for those who needed legal services but could not afford to pay for them, and for those who lived in an area where there was a clinic but no practising advocates. For the Court, this further restricted or closed off the

> community's access to justice. Yet access to justice is an inseparable part of another feature of the *Negara Hukum* – that the law must be transparent and accessible to all, as is recognised in developments in modern thinking on *Negara Hukum*. If, for financial reasons, a citizen does not have this access, then it is the obligation of the state [to provide it], and it is truly also the obligation of advocates to facilitate [that access] not to close it.[4]

---

[2] Constitutional Court Decision 006/PUU-II/2004.
[3] Ibid., 29.
[4] Ibid., 32.

10.2.2. Right to a Fair Trial?

In several cases, the Court has declared that the right to a fair trial is also required by the *Negara Hukum*.[5] In the *Bali Bombing* case (2003), for example, the Court reviewed a law purporting to allow a new terrorism law to be applied retrospectively to aid the investigation, prosecution and conviction of those involved in the Bali bombings in Kuta in 2002. In its decision, the majority explained that the right to a fair trial was an essential element of the *Negara Hukum*. The Court stated that procedural justice requires

> the presumption of innocence; equality of opportunity for the parties; announcement of the decision open to the public; *ne bis in idem* [the double jeopardy rule]; the application of less serious laws for pending cases and the prohibition against retrospectivity ... Law No 16 of 2003 ... clearly breaches one requirement ... that is, it applies the retrospectivity principle.[6]

In the *Advocates Law* case, mentioned above, the Court also appeared to associate the right to a fair trial with access to justice:

> Article 31 is ... excessive and ... impedes ... the community's access to justice, which in turn, can prevent the fulfilment of the right to a fair trial, particularly for those who are indigent. Article 31 is, therefore, contradictory to the ideal of the *Negara Hukum*, which is clearly formulated in Article 1(3) of the Constitution.

The Court then drew a parallel with the requirements of the 'rule of law':

> As a comparison, access to justice in the context of fulfilling the right to a fair trial attaches to the ideal of the rule of law and, therefore, is considered a constitutional right. This constitutes the *communis opinio* [community of opinion], as is shown in the English court case of R v. *Lord Chancellor ex p Witham* (1998), in which it was stated ' ... **the right to a fair trial, which of necessity imports the right of access to the court, is as near to an absolute right as any which I can envisage ... It has been described as a constitutional right, though the cases do not explain what that means**'.[7]

---

[5] In addition to the cases discussed in this section, see Constitutional Court Decision 69/PUU-II/2004, 137, para 3.10.1.

[6] Constitutional Court Decision 013/PUU-I/2003, 38. In the *Soares* case (2004), Justice Roestandi's dissent listed the same minimum standards for a fair trial, albeit in a different order. He confirmed the importance of fair trials, describing them as 'a mainstay of the rule of law' (2004: 62–3).

[7] Constitutional Court Decision 006/PUU-II/2004, 33 (emphasis in original).

10.2.3. Due Process

The Court has also referred to due process being a component of the *Negara Hukum*.[8] Although hardly stated with clarity, the 'due process right' appears to flow from the presumption of innocence. (The Court's jurisprudence on the presumption of innocence is discussed later in this chapter. As mentioned previously, the Court appears to view the presumption as one of the five elements of a fair trial, which is an aspect of the *Negara Hukum*.) Apparently, the Court considers that a defendant not given an opportunity to defend himself or herself is presumed guilty.

The Court first considered this argument in the *Broadcasting Law* case (2003).[9] In it, the applicants had objected to a provision that required broadcasters to 'correct' broadcasts or news about which a complaint was made, regardless of whether the complaint had any foundation.[10] The Court upheld the objection, deciding that a piece of news or broadcast is not proven to be untrue or mistaken merely because a complaint is made about it.[11] The Court declared that no correction would be necessary if the broadcaster simply published the objection:

> Under the principle *'cover both sides'*, if there is an objection or complaint against a piece of news or a broadcast, then broadcasting the objection or protest itself is sufficient to fulfil the principle of *'cover both sides'*, unless there is other strong supporting evidence which accords with the principle of *'due process of law'*.[12]

The Court stated that:

> it would be extraordinary if a correction was made in response to an objection or complaint, indicating that the objection or protest was correct, but in court it was proven that the objection or protest was incorrect.[13]

The Court concluded that to find otherwise would breach the *Negara Hukum*:

> [T]he obligation to make a correction based on an objection or complaint sets aside the presumption of innocence ... because it suggests that if a complaint

---

[8] In addition to the cases discussed in this section, see the *Praperadilan case* (Constitutional Court Decision 21/PUU-XII/2014), 96–7, 100.
[9] Constitutional Court Decision 005/PUU-I/2003.
[10] The law stated that 'broadcasters must make a correction if the contents of news or a broadcast are discovered to contain an oversight or mistake, or if a protest is made against the contents of news or a broadcast'.
[11] Constitutional Court Decision 005/PUU-I/2003, 83.
[12] Ibid., 83–4 (emphasis in original).
[13] Ibid., 84.

or objection is made, the broadcast or piece of news is definitely wrong and that a correction must be made, and it is insufficient only to broadcast the objection or protest. The infringement of the presumption of innocence means a breach of the '*due process of law*' and, therefore, is contrary to Article 1(3) of the Constitution, which states that Indonesia is a *Negara Hukum*.[14]

The Constitutional Court made similar comments in the *PKI* case (2003).[15] This case concerned Article 60(g) of Law 12 of 2003 on General Elections, which sought to prohibit from standing for election to the national or regional legislature candidates who had been members of any of a number of prohibited organisations including the Indonesian Communist Party (*Partai Komunis Indonesia*, PKI), or who had been directly or indirectly involved in the 1965 coup. This case was brought by about thirty people, some of whom had been imprisoned for direct or indirect involvement in the coup of 30 September 1965 and had been labelled communist.

This case was primarily won on the argument that Article 60(g) was discriminatory. The Court held that, because Article 60(g) purported to prohibit a group of citizens from nominating themselves for these parliaments, it clearly 'had a nuance of political punishment for the group'.[16] However, the Court added:

> [A]s a rule of law state, prohibitions which directly relate to the rights and freedoms of citizens must be based on a binding court decision.[17]

The majority appeared to emphasise that citizens cannot be punished without due process:

> Criminal responsibility can only be sought against the perpetrator, an accomplice, and/or an accessory. To place criminal responsibility upon a person who was not directly involved conflicts with the law, justice, legal certainty and rule of law principles.[18]

The Court's strongest and clearest use of the due process ground comes from its decision in the *Book Banning* case (2010).[19] In it, a large coalition of Non-Governmental Organizations (NGOs) supporting authors and journalists challenged laws under which the Attorney General could ban books

---

[14] Ibid.
[15] Constitutional Court Decision 011-017/PUU-I/2003.
[16] Ibid., 36.
[17] Ibid.
[18] Ibid.
[19] Constitutional Court Decision 6-13-20/PUU-VIII/2010.

and then confiscate them.[20] While the Court held that these laws violated freedom of expression and the right to not have property arbitrarily seized, it appeared to be most concerned about the laws giving unfettered power to the Attorney General to ban and seize books without judicial oversight.[21] The Court declared:

> In a *Negara Hukum* like Indonesia, due process – that is, law enforcement through a judicial system – is imperative. If an act is to be characterised as illegal, it must be [declared as such] by judicial decision. Banning the distribution of items, such as printed materials, because they may breach public order cannot be simply left to a government agency without a judicial decision. The Attorney General's power to prohibit the distribution of written materials ... without judicial process is one of the things an authoritarian state [would do], not a *Negara Hukum* like Indonesia.[22]

10.2.4. Presumption of Innocence

The Court held, in the *Bibit and Chandra* case (2009),[23] that citizens are entitled to the presumption of innocence.[24] The applicants were two embattled Commissioners of the Anti-corruption Commission (*Komisi Pemberantasan Korupsi* or KPK), Chandra Muhammad Hamzah and Bibit Samad Rianto. They had been suspended from office while being investigated for misusing their authority as Commissioners by issuing and revoking travel bans. However, it was widely believed that they had been 'set-up' by senior police they were investigating for corruption.[25] They feared that, once brought to

---

[20] Specifically, Articles 1 and 6 of Law 4/PNPS/1963 on Securing Printed Materials that Impede Public Order; and Article 30(3)(c) of Law 16 of 2004 on the Public Prosecution.
[21] Indeed, the majority even declared that book seizure would not necessarily breach these rights and freedoms, if obtaining judicial permission was a prerequisite to seizure.
[22] Constitutional Court Decision 6-13-20/PUU-VIII/2010, para 3.15.
[23] Constitutional Court Decision 133/PUU-VII/2009.
[24] Though the Court had, in earlier cases, already made important statements about the presumption. For example, the Court declared, in Constitutional Court Decision 24/PUU-II/2005, 36, that

> [t]he presumption of innocence is a principle [under which] a suspect or defendant is considered not guilty until there is a final and binding decision of a court. **This** right is not only guaranteed by the 1945 Constitution, as the constitution of a *negara hukum*, but has universally been accepted as a part of civil and political rights that must be respected, protected and guaranteed (emphasis added).

[25] These claims were proved true when the Constitutional Court, during its first hearing of the case, allowed KPK-recorded taped conversations between suspects the KPK was investigating and senior prosecutors and police to be played in open court. These conversations revealed a plot to frame Bibit and Chandra: Simon Butt, *Corruption and Law in Indonesia* (London: Routledge, 2012).

trial, they would be dismissed under Article 32(1)(c) of Law No 30 of 2002 on the Anti-corruption Commission, which states:

> Anti-corruption Commission leaders are to leave their position or be removed from their positions if they become a defendant (*terdakwa*) in a criminal case.

One of their arguments was that the Constitution gave citizens the right to be presumed innocent until proven guilty, despite the Constitution not expressly stating this presumption. Article 32(1)(c) breached that right, they said.

The Court affirmed that due process of law is a fundamental constitutional guarantee. It requires that all legal processes are fair: people must be informed of legal processes against them and must have the right to be heard before their rights, freedoms or property are taken away.[26] In particular, the Court argued, due process of law and the presumption of innocence are primary principles of Indonesia's democratic *Negara Hukum*. It agreed that Article 32(1)(c) contravened the presumption of innocence because it imposed a sanction without trial. As the applicants had argued, they could be dismissed before being found guilty of an offence – indeed, even if they were never found guilty of an offence.

10.3. CRITICISMS

In these cases, the Court has provided scant reasoning to support its decisions. Most significantly, the Court has not explained the 'version' of the rule of law it has adopted or applied in these cases. This is highly problematic because, as we will see, the 'rule of law' (or *Negara Hukum* in the Indonesian context) is a concept that has been misused as a legitimising tool for decades to sustain authoritarianism.

This failure to adequately explain has not been recognised as a significant shortcoming by Indonesian lawyers and politicians who, as mentioned, have focused their critiques on the particular outcomes of these cases. This is partly because Indonesian judicial decisions have not traditionally provided detailed reasoning. Indonesia's legal system follows the civil law tradition. Under that tradition, many courts produce short decisions, leaving much of the reasoning and contextualisation of decisions to other actors, such as legal academics, and there is generally no formal system of precedent.[27]

---

[26] Constitutional Court Decision 6-13-20/PUU-VIII/2010, para 3.18.
[27] Mitchell Lasser, 'Anticipating Three Models of Judicial Control, Debate and Legitimacy: The European Court of Justice, the Cour de Cassation and the United States Supreme Court', Jean Mooet Working Paper 1/03.

However, the unique status that Constitutional Court decisions have in the Indonesian system – legally, politically and historically – increases the transparency and accountability threshold the Court must reach, beyond those of Indonesia's other courts. The Court's roles – as adjudicator of the Constitution and its meaning, by which the Court can displace the decisions of a democratically elected legislature and as arbiter of important matters of state – encumber it with a significant 'explanatory burden'.[28] Other Indonesian courts can point out that their decisions do not formally create law, and argue that accountability and transparency mechanisms are, therefore, less critical for them because their decisions affect only the parties. By contrast, the Court has no such 'defence' at its disposal and, indeed, the Court's identification and application of unexpressed constitutional rights appears to further increase its 'burden'.

Another reason why the Court must explain its reasoning in more detail is the widespread presence of judicial impropriety. Most Indonesian courts are notorious for corruption.[29] The more detailed and convincing the reasoning, the less likely are suspicions that 'something else' is behind the Court's decision-making. While the Constitutional Court is almost certainly much cleaner than most other Indonesian courts, opportunities for graft abound, as the Akil Mochtar conviction demonstrates.

10.3.1. *The* Negara Hukum *as a Self-Explanatory Concept*

In the cases discussed above, the Court appears to have treated the *Negara Hukum* concept, and its necessary implications, as uncontentious and self-explanatory. However, nothing could be further from the truth in Indonesia. The *Negara Hukum* is one of Indonesia's most contentious legal concepts. The Constitution does not define it, and no other law explains the concept in significant detail. Indonesian jurists have long debated what it entails in both theory and practise, without reaching consensus. Hosen neatly summarises some of the differing scholarly views:

> The debate over *Negara Hukum* in Indonesian legal history is reflected in the writings of (to name but a few): Sunaryati Haryono, who interpreted *Negara Hukum* in light of the rule of law; Oemar Seno Adji, who opined that

---

[28] Mitchel de S.-O.-L'E. Lasser, *Judicial Deliberations: A Comparative Analysis of Judicial Transparency and Legitimacy* (Oxford: Oxford University Press, 2009), 303.
[29] Simon Butt and Tim Lindsey, 'Judicial Mafia: The Courts and State Illegality in Indonesia', in Edward Aspinall and Gary van Klinken (eds.), *The State and Illegality in Indonesia* (Leiden: KITLV Press, 2010).

Negara Hukum had its own Indonesian characteristics based on the family principle; Padmo Wahyono, who related the concept *Negara Hukum* with the political philosophy of organic statism (integralism or *integralistik*); Ismail Suny, who adhered to the literal meaning of *Negara Hukum* as *rechsstaat*; and Hartono Marjono, who took the view that elements of *Negara Hukum* are supremacy of law, equality before the law and due process of law.[30]

Here, we see the concept of *Negara Hukum* equated with all 'versions' of the rule of law, both 'thick' and 'thin'.[31] On one extreme are views that *Negara Hukum* encompasses the Western concept of the 'rule of law', including its democracy and human rights components. On the other is a much more limited version of rule by law, with no guarantees against authoritarianism. For example, the 'family principle' and 'organic statism' both provide scope for a very strong state, with limited democracy and human rights. As described by Indonesian jurists, the organic state is one in which the state and its people are an inseparable whole, in which there is no need to guarantee rights against the state or provide institutions citizens can use to challenge the state. Because the state was 'integrated', the state can never be at odds with the individuals comprising it.[32] As one prominent Indonesian jurist, Professor Soepomo, put it during constitutional debates in the lead-up to Indonesian independence:

> There will be no need for any guarantee of *Grund- und Freiheitsrechte* [basic rights] of individuals against the state, for the individuals are nothing else than organic parts of the state, having specific positions and duties to realise the grandeur of the state.[33]

The 'family principle' was similar:

> The duties which father asks his wife and children to carry out are happily accepted, and there is no grumbling. What father says is right, because father is wise![34]

The need for a clear and well-reasoned description of what the *Negara Hukum* entails in post-Soeharto Indonesia is highly desirable, particularly given that

---

[30] Nadirsyah Hosen, *Human Rights, Politics and Corruption in Indonesia: A Critical Reflection on the Post-Soeharto Era* (Doredrecht: Republic of Letters, 2010), 45–6 (footnotes omitted).
[31] Tim Lindsey, 'Indonesia: Devaluing Asian Values, Rewriting Rule of Law', in Randall Peerenboom (ed.), *Asian Discourses of Rule of Law* (London: RoutledgeCurzon, 2004) 479.
[32] Butt and Lindsey, 'Judicial Mafia: The Courts and State Illegality in Indonesia'.
[33] Muhammad Yamin, *Naskah-Persiapan Undang–Undang Dasar 1945* (Djakarta: Jajasan Prapantja, 1959–60) 114.
[34] Herbert Feith and Lance Castles (eds.), *Indonesian Political Thinking, 1945–1965* (Ithaca: Cornell University Press, 1970) 185.

the concept was used, or rather misused, almost exclusively as a political tool during the Soekarno and Soeharto presidencies. Because no law or judicial decision explained the *Negara Hukum* – and legal scholars were divided or muted by the military – the regimes could interpret it to suit their own purposes.[35] For example, Soekarno's Old Order (*Orde Lama*) used the *Negara Hukum* concept as a nation-building ideology, which gained strong popular support because many Indonesians were optimistic for change after the long revolution against the Dutch.[36] Yet Soekarno introduced policies and laws that were contrary to the 'rule of law'. For example, in 1964, he issued a decree that purported to dissolve the separation of powers doctrine and allow the government to directly interfere in judicial decision-making.

By contrast, Soeharto (1965–98) used the concept of *Negara Hukum* as a legitimising tool – both to present himself as the legitimate successor to Soekarno and to set his regime apart from Soeharto's. According to Soeharto's government, Soekarno had failed to uphold the *Negara Hukum*, which caused dire economic and social consequences.[37] The New Order promised to 'consistently and purely' implement the 1945 Constitution, including the *Negara Hukum*, outlining the concept as follows:

1. legality, in the sense of law in all its forms;
2. a judiciary which is independent, impartial and free from the influence of any other power in force; and
3. recognition and protection of fundamental rights, embodying equality in politics, law, and in the social, economic, cultural and educational spheres.[38]

Ironically, though using the *Negara Hukum* to legitimise itself during its early years, the New Order in practice became the very antithesis of the rule of law, at least as understood in many Western countries. Contrary to *Negara Hukum* ideals, the regime became highly repressive of its citizens and set-up mechanisms to ensure that the government and military enjoyed virtual

---

[35] T. Lubis, *In Search of Human Rights: Legal–Political Dilemmas of Indonesia's New Order, 1966–1990* (Jakarta: PT Gramedia Pustaka Utama in cooperation with SPES Foundation, 1993), 88.
[36] D. S. Lev, 'Judicial Authority and the Struggle for an Indonesian Rechtsstaat' (1978) 13 *Law and Society Review* 44.
[37] See the Preamble (point 2) of MPR Decree No. XX/1966, which claims that divergence from the 1945 Constitution partially caused the 1965 coup attempt.
[38] As contained in the MPR's first Five Year Development Plan (*Rencana Pembangunan Lima Tahun, Repelita*) of 1969–70. Sudargo Gautama and Robert N. Hornick, *An Introduction to Indonesian Law: Unity in Diversity* (Bandung: Penerbit Alumni, 1983), 191.

impunity for illegal actions, including human rights violations and massive corruption. The regime's co-option of the judiciary meant that the courts could never hold the government to account for breaching the law or human rights, let alone add any 'flesh' to this three-pronged definition.

After Soeharto's fall, reformists called for greater 'rule of law' as part of broader democratic and governance reforms and sincere attempts were made to improve judicial independence, to ensure the government was subject to law, and to provide legal protection for human rights. The *Negara Hukum* concept itself was also constitutionally 'elevated'. Before the post-Soeharto constitutional amendments, the Constitution's Elucidation mentioned that Indonesia was a 'rechtsstaat', not a 'machtsstaat'; but in 2001, the statement that Indonesia was a *Negara Hukum* was inserted into Article 1(3) of the Constitution's text. At the same time, other foundational principles were inserted. These included that Indonesia is a Unitary Republic (Article 1(1)) and that sovereignty lies in the hands of the people (Article 1(2)).

10.3.1.1. The Court and the Rule of Law: Majority Perspectives

Unfortunately, while the Court has repeatedly emphasised the importance of the *Negara Hukum*, the Court has not comprehensively explained what Indonesia's version of the rule of law is and what it entitles citizens to, beyond its bald uncovering of rights in the cases mentioned above. Nevertheless, majority decisions have provided clues about the elements of the *Negara Hukum* in cases where the Court has not implied rights but has applied specific constitutional rights. However, the Court's statements have been mostly brief and piecemeal.

The Court has, for example, appeared to include within the rule of law the concept of 'government by law', holding that:

> a principle of the *Negara Hukum* is that the state and citizens must submit to the law in performing their respective functions and tasks. Whenever a violation of the law occurs, the law must be upheld through a legal mechanism that has been stipulated democratically (due process of law).[39]

In other cases, the Court has indicated that the *Negara Hukum* also embodies equality before the law[40] and an understanding that every person has human

---

[39] Constitutional Court Decision 69/PUU-X, 137, para 3.10.1.
[40] Constitutional Court Decision 21/PUU-XII/2014, 101; Constitutional Court Decision 73/PUU-IX/2011, para 3.23.

rights that the state must respect.[41] Another principle included within the *Negara Hukum* is that:

> judicial decisions must be considered to be correct (*res judicata pro veritate habetur*) until there is a decision of a higher court overturning that decision ... [and] there is a right for justice seekers to appeal a judicial decision.[42]

These additional implied *Negara Hukum* entitlements do not, however, appear to stand alone. Rather, they seem dependent upon, or at least linked with, rights expressly provided in the Constitution. As the Court said in the *Muhlis Matu* case (2007), due process elements of the *Negara Hukum* are 'related to' other constitutional rights, including Article 28D(1), which expressly provides rights to legal recognition, protection and certainty, and to equality before the law.[43] Likewise, Article 28I(5) of the Constitution states that human rights are to be 'upheld and protected', in accordance with the principle of the democratic *Negara Hukum*, and thus the 'implementation of human rights' is to be 'guaranteed, regulated and contained' in law.

The Court has also emphasised that the *Negara Hukum* requires judicial independence, declaring:

> One principle of a democratic state and the *Negara Hukum* is independent judicial power ... without independent judicial power there can be no democratic state and *Negara Hukum*.[44]

Again, judicial independence is guaranteed elsewhere in the Constitution.[45]

A majority of the Court has also revealed, in its decision in the *Blasphemy Law* case (2009), that the rule of law has a religious element.[46] This case was a review of Indonesia's Blasphemy Law, under which the government can restrict the practises of religions or beliefs that identify as one of the religions adhered to in Indonesia but which deviate from the orthodox teachings of that religion. If the government-imposed restrictions are ignored, then the government can move to ban those practices. If that ban is itself ignored, then adherents face criminal penalties, including imprisonment.

---

[41] Constitutional Court Decision 21/PUU-XII/2014, 96–7; Constitutional Court Decision 109/PUU-XI/2014, p. 27; Constitutional Court Decision 18/PUU-XII/2014, 119; Constitutional Court Decision 13/PUU-XIII/2015, 122.
[42] Constitutional Court Decision 69/PUU-X, 137, para 3.10.1.
[43] Constitutional Court Decision 14–17/PUU-V/2007, 128.
[44] Constitutional Court Decision 43/PUU-XIII/2015, 114.
[45] See Article 24(1).
[46] Constitutional Court Decision 140/PUU-VII/2009.

Near the end of its decision, the Court made these observations:

> The meaning we give to the Indonesia *Negara Hukum* does not need to be the same as the ... *rechtsstaat* or *the rule of law*. The *Negara Hukum* principle must be viewed through the lens of the Constitution, that is, a *Negara Hukum* that positions 'Almighty God' as the primary principle, and in which religious values underlie the life of the nation and the state. It is not a state that separates religion and state and does not follow purely individualistic or communal principles. The Indonesian Constitution does not allow campaigns pushing for freedom to have no religion, to promote 'anti-religion' or to offend or discredit religious teachings or texts which are the source of religious beliefs, or which sully the name of God. This is one thing that sets Indonesia's *Negara Hukum* apart from the Western rule of law. In the administration of government and the judiciary, and in lawmaking, religiosity and religious teaching and values are yardsticks to determine whether the statute is good or bad – even for determining whether law is constitutional or unconstitutional. In line with this thinking, the restrictions on human rights [can be] on the basis of 'religious values', as mentioned in art. 28J(2) of the Constitution. This is different from art. 18 of the ICCPR, which does not include religious values as a ground for limiting individual freedoms.[47]

Unfortunately, the Court's statement seems to raise more questions than answers about Indonesia's version of the *Negara Hukum*. The primacy of 'Almighty God' is undoubtedly a reference to Indonesia's five-principle national ideology, *Pancasila*, which is contained in the Preamble to the Constitution. Its first principle is 'Belief in Almighty God', making Indonesia a religious state. However, the Preamble does not specify the religion or religions to which it refers. This has created countless problems throughout Indonesia's independent history, with some – perhaps most – Indonesians seeing it as an ideology of tolerance for all religions, and others – probably a relatively small percentage of the population – seeing it as providing constitutional validity for conservative interpretations of Islam. (As mentioned, Islam is Indonesia's majority religion, though it is commonly said that most Indonesians are moderate Muslims.) Given the differences between the tenets of the religions formally recognised and practised in Indonesia – Islam, Catholicism, Protestantism, Hinduism, Buddhism and Confucianism – the Court's statements about religion and the *Negara Hukum* are not instructive. Which religion's values can or should be a 'yardstick' for constitutional validity? Most commentators have concluded that the Court was referring to the conservative version of Islam expounded by Indonesia's Council of Islamic

---

[47] Ibid., 275.

Scholars (Majelis Ulama Indonesia or MUI). This result is unsatisfactory, particularly given that many views of the MUI appear to sit uncomfortably alongside other constitutional rights, such as freedom of religious belief, freedom of expression and the like.

10.3.1.2. The Court and the Rule of Law: Minority Perspectives

Some of the clearer expositions of the *Negara Hukum* concept have come from the dissents of individual judges. For example, in his dissent in the *KPK* case (2004), Justice Siahaan set out a formulation of *Negara Hukum*: recognition and protection of human rights; the principle of legality, meaning that all state bodies and institutions and citizens must base their actions on legal rules; and an independent and impartial judiciary. In the same case, Siahaan explained further that the *Negara Hukum*'s principle of legality requires lawmakers to obey the hierarchy of laws when lawmaking – that is, lower-level laws must be based on higher-level laws, with the Constitution at the apex. He noted that every lower-level law that is inconsistent or conflicts with a higher-level law breaches the principle of legality.[48] In this case, Justice Soedarsono also confirmed that '[t]he purpose of the *Negara Hukum* ... is to protect human rights'.[49]

Perhaps the most substantial discussion of the concept has been provided by Justice Hidayat. In a recent dissent, he stated the following:

> The Indonesian *Negara Hukum is* based on *Pancasila* and the 1945 Constitution and choses a prismatic or integrative concept between the two concepts of *rechtstaats* and the *rule of law*, which integrates the principle of 'legal certainty' from the *rechtstaats* and the principle of 'justice' from the rule of law. Therefore, Indonesia does not choose which one is better and superior, but combines these two principles into one ... including the positive elements of the two principles in monitoring the exercise of government power and law enforcement, with the aim of achieving utility and order in the community, in accordance with the aim of the law, as declared by Gustav Radbruch – that is, justice, certainty and utility.[50]

Justice Hidayat continued:

> As a *Negara Hukum*, the state constitution is placed in the highest position in the hierarchy of laws. In the context of the hierarchy, the legal order is

---

[48] Constitutional Court Decision 006/PUU-I/2003, 111.
[49] Ibid., 125.
[50] Constitutional Court Decision 43/PUU-XIII/2015, 220.

described as a pyramid with the constitution as the highest law, and the laws below it being an elaboration of the constitution ... the creation of lower norms is determined by other higher norms the creation of which are determined by higher laws, with the chain ending with the highest fundamental norm – the constitution.[51]

10.3.2. Implying Rights

The Court has ignored debate on the wider issue of the propriety of implying rights. In many countries, the implication of constitutional rights has been controversial. Some theorists argue that it undermines the legitimacy of judicial review, which is only democratically justifiable if judges strictly interpret the Constitution, rather than add to or reduce it according to their personal preferences. After all, most judges are not elected and judicial review allows them to overrule laws made by a democratically elected legislature.[52] Most countries, however, consider judicial review legitimate when permitted by the Constitution – the 'highest law' or the ultimate source of legal legitimacy, assumed to express the will of the people.[53] Yet arguably when the Court implies rights that are not expressly stated in the Constitution, it breaches the very Constitution that empowers it.

The Court has also not addressed compelling arguments against implying rights. If the Constitution intended to provide rights, then why did it not clearly express them, instead of leaving them open to supposition? After all, the Constitution was only recently amended. Why did the People's Consultative Assembly (*Majelis Permusyawaratan Rakyat*, MPR) not insert specific provisions on *Negara Hukum* rights if it wanted the Court to enforce them? And if the rights flowing from the *Negara Hukum* are so fundamental that they need not be expressed, then why is the right to protection from retrospective prosecution – one of the five pillars of a fair trial, which itself formed part of the rule of law as identified by the Court expressly included in the Constitution?

---

[51] Ibid., 221.
[52] Ilya Somin, 'Political Ignorance and the Countermajoritarian Difficulty: A New Perspective on the Central Obsession of Constitutional Theory' (2004) 89 *Iowa Law Review* 1287; Lisa Hilbink, 'Beyond Manicheanism: Assessing the New Constitutionalism' (2006) 65 *Maryland Law Review* 15.
[53] Alec Stone Sweet, *Governing with Judges: Constitutional Politics in Europe* (Oxford: Oxford University Press, 2000), 135.

10.3.3. Practical Consequences of 'Discovering' Rights

In these decisions, the Court has proclaimed the existence of these rights almost in the abstract, considering no practical implications of their coming into being. For example, the Court has not explained the consequences of a breach of process-related rights. If a trial is procedurally unfair or due process is ignored, will the final judicial decision be invalid? Will trials in which these rights are ignored be automatically open to appeal because an error of law has been made?

The Court's decision about legal aid in the *Advocates Law* case is particularly simplistic and lacking in foresight. It is unclear whether the Court intended that the right to legal aid was a broad right to legal aid for any Indonesian citizen for any case, regardless of financial means, or only for those without sufficient means to afford an advocate. This lack of elaboration leaves unanswered fundamental questions about the right's practical operation. If the right applies only to those unable to afford a lawyer, then how 'poor' must one be to qualify for legal aid? Does the right apply in all cases – criminal, civil and administrative? Does the right apply to support vexatious litigants or unrealistic claims? Further, the Court did not specify who was to fund and administer the provision of legal aid apparently required by its decision.

10.4. EXPLANATIONS AND CONCLUSIONS

Despite having a significant basis upon which to complain, the government has not responded to any of the democratic or constitutional objections to implying rights mentioned above. Indeed, in 2011, when Indonesia's national parliament changed the Constitutional Court's governing law – directed at reining in the Court, which appeared to have been expanding its powers and usurping the legislative function – the Court's implied rights jurisprudence was ignored. The amendments focused on other ways in which the parliament thought the Court was pushing the boundaries of its jurisdiction, such as by issuing orders to government, invalidating laws or provisions that applicants had not requested and, most importantly, issuing declarations of conditional constitutionality or unconstitutionality.[54] That implied rights escaped unscathed appears to indicate that the state did not see their 'discovery' and 'application' as a threat to legislative power.

There are several possible explanations for this, four of which I now turn to discuss. One is that, as mentioned, the constitutional rights the Court appears

---

[54] Simon Butt and Tim Lindsey, *The Indonesian Constitution: A Contextual Analysis* (Oxford: Hart Publishing, 2012).

to have implied were already provided as express statutory rights. On this reading, these implied rights added no substantive legal entitlements to those citizens already enjoyed, about which there is no controversy. The presumption of innocence is, for example, found in several Indonesian statutes, including Indonesia's basic judiciary laws,[55] and the 1999 Human Rights Law.[56] The Code of Criminal Procedure and the Human Rights Law also provide other rights and guarantees commonly associated with a fair trial and due process.

However, this explanation underplays the significance of what the Court has done in these implied rights cases. It ignores that the Court appears to have elevated to constitutional status rights that had previously only been provided by statute. This is an important development, because it brings these rights within the jurisdiction of the Court to enforce. (As mentioned, the Court's judicial review power is limited to ensuring the constitutionality of statutes. It has no power to apply or enforce statutes. Only the Supreme Court and the courts below it in Indonesia's judicial hierarchy have power to do this.) Various judges of the Constitutional Court have indicated that it often takes on the responsibility to provide 'justice' when other state institutions, including other courts, have failed to do so.[57] This analysis – of the Court as 'the backstop of justice' – seems to encompass a critique of other courts in Indonesia for failing to ensure that the state and its officers do not trample on important process-related rights of citizens.

A second explanation emphasises that sometimes the rights the Court has implied from the *Negara Hukum* concept have, as mentioned, been reflected in or encompassed by other express constitutional rights. In most cases in which the Court appears to have favoured this approach, the Court could probably have reached the same decision simply by applying only the express constitutional rights provisions, without recourse to the *Negara Hukum* concept.

Perhaps the strongest example of this approach is found in Constitutional Court Decision 16/PUU-VIII/2010 – a case in which the Court was asked to review legislative provisions that prohibited a person from asking the Supreme Court to reopen a case more than once. This process, called *peninjauan kembali*, allows the Supreme Court to review an earlier court decision – even one of its own appeals – in the interests of justice because of new evidence or obvious judicial error.

---

[55] See, for example, Article 8 of Law 4 of 2004 on Judicial Power.
[56] See, for example, Article 18(1).
[57] Rita Triana Budiarti, *Kontroversi Mahfud M.D.* (Jakarta: Konstitusi Press, 2012).

One objection to the impugned statute was that allowing only one application for reopening closed off the possibility of a future application being made, even if new exculpatory evidence emerged that would likely have led to a different result. The applicant argued that this breached the *Negara Hukum* concept and several express constitutional rights.[58] The Court turned down the application, holding that the limitation promoted legal certainty and, because it applied to all, was not discriminatory.[59] Nevertheless, the Court made this statement about the *Negara Hukum*:

> [T]he *Negara Hukum* is a state which adheres to principles including supremacy of law, equality of law and due process of law which are constitutionally guaranteed. The *Negara Hukum* principle is a general principle adhered to in the administration of the state of Indonesia and in its implementation must be connected with other provisions in the Constitution. Therefore, whether the provisions put forward for review by the applicants breached Article 1(3) will be considered interrelated with the other constitutional provisions put forward by the Applicant.[60]

On this view, an important use of the *Negara Hukum* by the Court appears to be as a legitimising tool – that is, to provide further legal strength to its application of other constitutional rights – perhaps ultimately to give its decisions more weight. It is not clear why the Court feels the need to do this, given that its decisions are usually respected by the government and private citizens alike. As mentioned, the main reaction to the Court's decisions from lawyers, the government and the public, is almost exclusively concerned with the outcome, rather than the decision itself and the reasoning it employed.

A third possible explanation for the lack of reaction to the Court's implying rights in 2011 is that the high water mark of the Court's implied rights jurisprudence had already been reached by that time. According to this view, the government has nothing to fear from the Court implying rights because the Court now rarely does it. The practice of implying rights first emerged during the reign of Indonesia's first Constitutional Court Chief Justice, Professor Jimly Asshiddiqie, a well-respected constitutional law scholar.[61] Just as the Indonesian Constitutional Court was designed using the South

---

[58] Namely, Articles 27(1), 28D(1), 28H(2) and 28I(2).
[59] Constitutional Court Decision 16/PUU-VIII/2010, 67.
[60] Ibid., 66.
[61] For an excellent discussion on the importance of the personalities of the Court's chief justices to the Court's successes, see Stefanus Hendrianto, 'The Puzzle of Judicial Communication in Indonesia: The Media, the Court, and the Chief Justice' in Richard Davis and David Taras (eds.), *Justice and Journalists: The Global Perspective* (Cambridge: Cambridge University Press, 2017).

Korean Constitutional Court as a model, so too did the Indonesian judges, in their decision-making, draw on some of the 'activist' tendencies of the South Korean Court, including the implication of rights. In this context, the Court's earlier implied rights cases, discussed above, are consistent with Asshiddiqie's widely reported desire for the Court to establish as large a body of constitutional jurisprudence as possible, in the shortest possible time. (Unfortunately, though, the Court paid little heed to establishing an overarching structure or philosophy of interpretation to guide it in this endeavour.) The Court's activism, including rights implication, was continued by Asshiddiqie's successor, Professor Mahfud. However, it appears that the adventurousness of Asshiddiqie and Mahfud has not been sustained by their successors, under whom no new implied rights have been discovered.

Finally, it is possible that the rights the Court has 'implied' are largely unenforceable and, therefore, usually require the state to take no action. While the Court can invalidate statutes in which such rights are ignored, most of the rights that the Court has declared flow from the *Negara Hukum* are breached in the daily practice of law, such as during investigations or trials, or in judicial decisions, rather than in legislation. As mentioned, the Constitutional Court's review jurisdiction limits it to assessing whether statutes enacted by the national parliament comply with the Constitution. The Constitutional Court's implied rights decisions can, therefore, often be ignored by all but the national legislature, because the Court lacks jurisdiction to review the constitutionality of government action and the judicial processes of other courts.

11

Is the Invisible Constitution Really Invisible?

Some Reflections in the Context of Korean Constitutional Adjudication

Jongcheol Kim

11.1. QUESTIONS: DOES AN INVISIBLE CONSTITUTION MATTER? FOR WHAT?

11.1.1. *Tribe's Version of an Invisible Constitution*

In his seminal work, *The Invisible Constitution*, Professor Laurence H. Tribe of Harvard Law School argued that without "the invisible, non-textual foundations and facets of a Constitution," the constitution itself, even its explicit text alone is not able to work properly: "So the visible constitution necessarily floats in a vast and deep – and, crucially, invisible – ocean of ideas, propositions, recovered memories, and imagined experiences that the Constitution as a whole puts us in a position to glimpse."[1] To him, it is "the invisible Constitution" that is "at the center of the Constitution's meaning and of its inestimable value."[2] Having said that, the task of understanding and abiding by the "invisible" constitution is imposed on not only the judges whose functional task is to interpret the constitution, but also on all the people who are abiding by the Constitution.[3]

For him, there are two levels of invisibility: trivial and genuine invisibility. While "trivially invisible" parts refer to what can be easily made visible by simple construction of the text, as they are to be regarded as implied by the text alone, "genuinely invisible" ones are those "*no* reasonable reader could claim to extract or infer from the text alone."[4] He then suggests some examples of the

---

This research was supported by the Ministry of Education and the National Research Foundation of Korea (NRF-2015S1A3A2046920).
[1] L. Tribe, *The Invisible Constitution* (Oxford: Oxford University Press, 2008) 9.
[2] Ibid., 22.
[3] Ibid., 31.
[4] Ibid., 28.

genuinely invisible principles that a "vast majority of educated citizens" would agree with in the context of the American constitutionalism: "government of the people, by the people, for the people," "government of laws, not men," "rule of law," and so on.[5]

Quite naturally, he also argued that this invisible part of the constitution can be organized or evolved through historical and cultural processes of formation[6] identified in at least "six distinct but overlapping modes of construction:" geometric, geodesic, global, geological, gravitational, and gyroscopic.[7]

Professor Tribe attempted to justify his quest for the invisible constitution by saying that "My hope is to nudge the nation's constitutional conversation away from debates over what the Constitution *says* and whether various constitutional claims are properly rooted in its written text and toward debates over what the Constitution *does*. Put otherwise, I hope to shift the discussion from whether various constitutional claims are properly rooted within the Constitution's written text to whether claims made in its name rightly describe the content, both written and unwritten, of our fundamental law."[8]

11.1.2. *A Point of Comparison: Dicey's Distinction of Two Elements of the Constitution*

In following Professor Tribe's quest for the invisible constitution, I happened to recall a dualist conception of the constitution made by a renowned Victorian jurist, Albert Venn Dicey, who has been regarded as a founding authority of British constitutionalism. He defines constitutional law or the constitution as "all rules which directly or indirectly affect the distribution or the exercise of the sovereign power in the state."[9] These rules include "all rules which define the members of the sovereign power, all rules which regulate the relation of such members to each other, or which determine the mode in which the sovereign power, or the members thereof, exercise their authority."[10] He intentionally used the word "rules" instead of "laws" to "call attention to the fact that the rules which make up constitutional law, as the term is used in England, include two sets of principles or maxims of a totally distinct character."[11]

---

[5] Ibid., 28.
[6] From this observation, it may be assumed that the boundary of the invisible constitution varies according to the history and culture of each country it governs.
[7] Ibid., 155 ff (Tribe).
[8] Ibid., 22.
[9] A. V. Dicey, *Introduction to the Study of the Law of the Constitution* (Indianapolis: Liberty Fund Inc., 1982) cxl.
[10] Ibid., cxl.
[11] Ibid., cxl.

According to Dicey, constitutional law to use a broader term, or the constitution consists of two sets of rules: "constitutional law in the proper sense of that term" or "the law of the constitution" and the "conventions of the constitution" or "constitutional morality."[12] While the latter is a set of rules consisting of "conventions, understandings, habits, or practices which, though they may regulate the conduct of the several members of the sovereign power, of the Ministry, or of other officials, are *not in reality laws at all* since they are not enforced by the Courts"(*italics* are added); the former is a set of rules which are "in the strictest sense 'laws,' since they are rules which (whether written or unwritten, whether enacted by statute or derived from the mass of custom, tradition, or judge-made maxims known as the Common Law) are enforced by the Courts."[13]

In using this conception of the constitution or constitutional law in a broader sense, according to Dicey, two things should be noted. First, although the word "convention" suggests a notion of insignificance or unreality, some constitutional conventions or practices are as important as any laws. Second, this distinction differs essentially from the distinction between "written law" and "unwritten law," as laws of the constitution such as the Bill of Rights, the Act of Settlement, and Habeas Corpus Acts, are "written law," while other most important laws of the constitution, such as the responsibility of the Ministers,[14] are "unwritten" laws.[15] Interestingly, the main reason for Dicey's lengthy explanation on this dual form of the constitution is to clarify the main duty or calling of the constitutional lawyer, that is, to find the subject of constitutional law in the study of the law of the constitution, instead of the conventions of the constitution the subject of which is not "one of law but of politics."[16]

This is, in a sense, in the same vein as Tribe attempted to use in dealing with the theme of invisibility of the constitution, though their specific objectives are different; both tried to discern what should be focused on in dealing with the constitution. Truly, both Tribe and Dicey point out that the

---

[12] Ibid., cxl–v.
[13] Ibid., cxl–i.
[14] According to Dicey, this responsibility of the Ministers is derived from "the combined action of several legal principles, namely, first, the maxim that the King can do no wrong; secondly, the refusal of the Courts to recognize any act as done by the Crown, which is not done in a particular form, a form in general involving the affixing of a particular seal by a Minister, or the countersignature or something equivalent to the countersignature of a Minister; thirdly, the principle that the Minister who affixes a particular seal, or countersigns his signature, is responsible for the act which he, so to speak, endorses." See *Ibid.* cxlii.
[15] The form of rules, written or unwritten, is totally up to the choice of the sovereign in each country.
[16] Ibid., cxlv–cxlvi (A. V. Dicey).

traditional conception of the constitution needs to see a genuine face of the constitution by recognizing its newly formulated aspects, and they have commonalities in stressing the limited role of the written text. However, the results of distinctions are very different. While Dicey appears to stress the importance of positivity of the constitution, Tribe stresses that of the invisible parts of the constitution. In terms of the usefulness of the dichotomy both tried to discern, I would give a better grade to Dicey than to Tribe. Dicey was arguably successful in propagandizing what constitutional lawyers do or how positivist approaches should be focused at the center of constitutional law, while Tribe appears to fail to achieve anything new in constitutional discourse.[17] His expositions can be seen as an artificial reformulation of the self-evident nature of the constitution that gives rise to so many fundamental questions: is such an invisible constitution really invisible, or can only what we can see in the form of the written text of a constitution be said to be visible? Is "what the constitution says" different from "what it does?," and finally "does it matter at all whether the form of the constitution is visible or invisible?"

11.2. ARGUMENT ONE: THE NATURE OF THE CONSTITUTION AS THE SUPREME LAW OF THE LAND AND ITS IMPLICATIONS

The straightforward answer to those questions raised above should be in the negative. The reason why constitutional writers have delved into what the constitution *says* is mainly to verify what the constitution *does* so that they can provide not only governmental powers, but also a general public abiding by the rule of the government with the guidance of practices and actions. So Tribe's distinction between constitutional saying and doing is a misleading one ignoring the identical interconnection between the two. Put otherwise, what the constitution says is the other side of the same coin, that is, what the constitution does. Then, what we have to ask is why the constitution matters.

My answer to this founding question is that it is because the constitution is the supreme law of the land. Once the sovereign decided the basic form and values of government, and if it is a constitutional democracy with or without a written constitution, the first principle is that the constitution is the supreme norm to which everything shall be subordinate. Is this maxim invisible in the Constitution of the USA? No. Article IV Clause two of the Constitution of the United States provides that the Constitution, federal

---

[17] His conclusion in this regard is arguable, partly because the subject of constitutional lawyers should not be confined to the ambit of a judicial process-oriented ideal. They need to play a role in making the conventions of the constitution or political morality compatible with the constitutional principles, hopefully in collaboration with political scientists.

laws made pursuant to it, and treaties made under its authority, constitute the supreme law of the land. Independent of its federalist implications, this clause can be regarded as the cornerstone of the American form of government. Also, the premise of the Supremacy clause is the principle that American people or the Founding Fathers adopt constitutionalism as their basic principle of constitutional arrangements. What naturally follows from this premise are a couple of what Tribe called "genuinely invisible" principles or "bedrock" principles, such as "government by law, not men," and the rule of law.

Then, if there were no Supremacy clause, what would happen to the constitutional conversations about the American constitution? As Tribe himself properly described in several parts of his book on the invisible constitution, there would be no other option to take mostly the same construction as if there were a supremacy clause; governments, state or federal, cannot help but be limited by the Constitution because the structure and meaning of the constitutional texts as a whole do not allow any construction contrary to what the Supremacy clause has produced. Therefore, what matters is not whether the constitution is visible or invisible, but only the ideal of constitutionalism. The basic ideal of constitutionalism or government according to the constitution, with or without a written constitution, is envisaged to found the very base of most of what Tribe terms the invisible constitution.

This argument may be justified further by a study of comparative constitutional law on the list of genuinely invisible principles of the American constitution. If most constitutional democracies have those basic principles in either their constitutional texts or common laws, i.e., in what Dicey called the law of the constitution, they need to be called "universal principles" of contemporary constitutional democracies rather than "invisible principles" in a specific constitutional democracy like the United States, because the invisible form itself cannot be said to carry any significant meaning, but the very ideal of constitutional democracy can.

Let me take the Korean case as an example. The first principle of "Government of the People, by the People, for the People" is explicitly provided in Article 1 of the Korean Constitution stating that "The Republic of Korea shall be a democratic republic" (Paragraph 1), and "The sovereignty of the Republic of Korea shall reside in the people and all state authority shall emanate from the people" (Paragraph 2). "Government of law, not men" and "the rule of law" suggested as "genuine invisible constitutions" in Tribe's understanding of the American Constitution can be found in Article 37 Paragraph 2 of the Korean Constitution providing that "The freedoms and rights of citizens may be restricted by Act only when necessary for national security, the maintenance of law and order or for public welfare. Even when such restriction is imposed, no essential aspect of the freedom or right shall be violated." Tribe's invisible principle assuming judicial review is also constitutionalized in the Korean Constitution by Article 111 Paragraph 1 and Article 107 Paragraph 2, allowing the Constitutional Court and the Supreme Court respectively to review the constitutionality of statutory legislation and subordinate legislation. The constitutional command prohibiting torture is enshrined (together with the prohibition of self-incrimination clause) in Article 12 Paragraph 2, while the constitutional norms protecting privacy are guaranteed by several constitutional provisions like Article 17 (private life and secrecy) and Article 18 (communication privacy).[18]

It is very clear that the Korean Constitution has a very magnificent list of "visible" principles or rights. However, can we Koreans dare to say that the Korean constitutionalism is far further developed than the American constitutionalism because the latter lacks a visible list of principles and rights of the people? On the contrary as far as, for example, the autonomy of individuals in their personal life is concerned, it can be said that the American constitutionalism has maybe accomplished the ideal of constitutional democracy far further than the Korean constitutionalism, because the latter does still fail to protect, for example, the autonomy in same-sex marriage, while the former is quite successful in this field.[19]

From the comparison of the American invisible constitution as Tribe envisaged and the Korean visible constitution as I have argued, we now get to the concluding point that what matters in constitutional practice or discourse is not the appearance but the ideal or spirit of the constitution and, furthermore, that what the constitution does or says is far less important than how to put the ideal into practice. Actually, Tribe's invisible bedrock principles should be considered as "visible," as they are well ordered by the constitution as a whole under the umbrella of constitutionalism. So my argument is that the dichotomy of a visible and invisible constitution is of no use in finding and understanding universal principles immanent in the constitution.

Then, the next question would be whether it is useless in constitutional thinking and practice at all. I assume that the effective function of an invisible constitution could be found in solving the question of constitutional silence

---

[18] Along with these specific provisions related to intimate private life, the autonomy of individuals that can be equated with the constitutional right to privacy developed by the Supreme Court of the United States is to be protected by the human dignity and the pursuit of happiness clause of Article 10 of the Korean Constitution as the KCC interpreted. See Jongcheol Kim, "'Constitutional Law' in the Korea Legislation Research Institute" (ed.), in *Introduction to Korean Law* (Berlin: Springer, 2013) 66–7.

[19] *Obergefell v. Hodges*, 576 U.S. – (2015).

or abeyance. If there are no explicit provisions on the matters of constitutional implication and thus there is room for critical constitutional construction, what may be called an invisible constitution may turn up to resolve the deadlock. For example, the Korean Constitution remains silent on the term of the President of the Korean Constitutional Court (KCC), while it has a provision for the term of constitutional justices (Article 112 Paragraph 1 gives them a term of six years with the possibility of reappointment), as well as a process of appointment; (Article 111 Paragraph 4 states that "The president of the Constitutional Court shall be appointed by the President from among the Justices with the consent of the National Assembly"), which is too vague to avoid political conflict. If a new president of the KCC is to be appointed from among the incumbent justices, there would be at least two options to determine their term as the president. The first option is to make them serve for the remaining term as a constitutional justice. The second is to provide a new six-year term assuming they are newly appointed as a constitutional justice on a different legal basis. Until an explicit law concerning this constitutional omission is made, the key to resolve this problem may lie in the hands of the appointers designated by the constitution, i.e., the President and the National Assembly and/or the justice in that situation. The fifth president of the KCC, Park Han-Chul, was appointed as the president in 2013 during his term as a justice since his appointment to that position in 2011. His case was the first in the history of the KCC, as his predecessors had been appointed at the same time as their appointment as a justice. As he retired on January 31, 2017 when his term as a justice came to the end, we may now say a new constitutional convention is evolving. It means that the space for invisible constitution can be mostly found in what Dicey called the "conventions of the constitution" rather than the law of the constitution.

11.3. ARGUMENT TWO: THE IMPORTANCE OF CONSTITUTIONAL DIALOGUE AND THE POLITICAL CHARACTER OF CONSTITUTIONAL ADJUDICATION

Having said that the ideal of constitutional democracy rather than its appearance matters in constitutional discourse, what comes next would be the questions of how the constitution ought to evolve on the one hand and, on the other, how it actually does.

Both questions are separate but interrelated, because they can interact with each other. In answering these questions, it is important to see who is entitled to take part in this constitutional discourse. Under the ideal of constitutional democracy, not only the representative authorities of the state, but also the people who are the sovereign authority should be regarded as constitutional actors. The role of the people as constitutional actors is not direct but indirect, in the sense that in terms of "legal" principle they cannot change the decisions of their representatives. However, their involvement in constitutional discourse is very important in that in terms of "constitutional" principles their will should be sovereign in finalizing constitutional conflicts. The decisions, even the judicial decisions in specific cases, cannot be final in a broader sense since they should be politically reviewed by the sovereign people. Of course, this does not mean that the people may overturn specific decisions of their representatives. It means that the will of the people will affect the fate of those decisions by influencing changes in the law, including constitutional interpretation in the end. Furthermore, even the will of the people is not omnipresent. The common ground for desirable constitutional discourse would be that all the actors should be supposed to accept the normative boundary within which the discourse or dialogue among them takes place.[20]

Put differently, a constitutional discourse is by nature a political process, in the sense that as far as they are within the constitutional boundary they are entitled to decide freely what to do. But "political" is not meant to be equated with "partisan." Constitutional adjudication is one of the important areas where political decision-making takes place. It is important in constitutional discourse not only because it is a designated place for that purpose by the constitution itself in most contemporary constitutional democracies, but also because its own function is involved directly with the determination of what the constitution does or says or how to draw a line between what is constitutional and unconstitutional, regardless of whether they are based upon either a visible or invisible constitution. However, whatever important roles the judges or the adjudicating bodies may assume, they should be open to the political review of other constitutional actors, including the sovereign people. Therefore, they should be very cautious not to override the constitutional boundary that commands self-limitation on the part of all the constitutional actors, as well as checks and balances among competing actors. The guidance of self-limitation is the ideal of constitutional democracy: whether or not their decisions are compatible with the explicit texts, histories, and objectives of the constitution. More concretely, in constitutional adjudication, they should make sure that their decisions contribute to the protection of human rights and the democratic basic order, or otherwise it may devalue constitutionalism

---

[20] In this regard, we may be helped from the insightful ideas of Habermas. See Jürgen Habermas, *Between Facts and Norms: Contributions to a Discourse Theory of Law and Democracy* trans. William Rehg (Cambridge, MA: MIT Press, 1996).

just by endorsing political decisions of other actors. Furthermore, in adjudicating constitutional cases they should not be hindered by their partisan hindsight, but should do their best to keep logical consistency and persuasiveness in their reasoning.[21]

11.4. SOME REFLECTIONS ON INVISIBLE OR VISIBLE CONSTITUTIONS IN KOREAN CONSTITUTIONAL CASES

Now we seem to be ready to examine some constitutional adjudication cases delivered by the KCC from the angle of the "invisible" constitution in Tribe's terminology (or "visible" but "unwritten" constitution based on the ideal of constitutional democracy). I am going to review three cases which have had a vital influence on the political structure: the Capital relocation case; the presidential impeachment case; and the election reapportionment case. The first two cases heard in 2004 can be seen as a watershed in the Korean history of constitutional review. They were in reality the result of political strife between the then President Roh Moo Hyun and the opposition parties. The first case was the KCC's invalidation of the Construction of the New Administrative Capital Act that was a top priority in the political agenda of the Roh Government. The second case was the KCC's ruling turning down the National Assembly's impeachment against President Roh who had been alleged to intervene illegally in the parliamentary election in 2004.

The last case is the most recent case in a series of the same kind, though the rule made by the KCC has been changed step by step. This case forced the National Assembly to change the election alignment which affects the distribution of political power among territorial regions.

By playing a crucial role in these three constitutional crises, the KCC was eager to represent its ambitious intention to become the final constructor of the Constitution and a constitutional coordinator controlling political conflicts. The task before us is to ask if it, fulfilling the virtue of self-limitation, complied with the required constitutional command not to override the constitutional boundary, although in principle I am sympathetic to such a conception of the KCC. My hypothesis is that the first case yielded a wrong decision, defying their constitutional obligation to respect the constitutionally ordained legislative power, while the remaining two cases contributed to the

---

[21] See Jongcheol Kim and Jonghyun Park, "Causes and Conditions for Sustainable Judicialization of Politics in Korea" in Björn Dressel (ed.), *The Judicialization of Politics in Asia* (Oxford: Routledge, 2012) ch. 3.

enhancement of Korean constitutionalism by not automatically deferring to the policy choices made by the legislature.

11.4.1. Sagas of "Customary Constitution" in the Relocation of the Capital City Case

In the sixteenth presidential election in 2002, a controversial issue dividing major presidential contenders was the plan to construct an administrative capital in which the office and residence of the President (the Blue House) and major governmental ministries would be relocated from Seoul to Choongcheong Province in order to enhance decentralization. Roh Moo Hyun, who endorsed the plan as one of his top pledges, finally won the election and initiated the plan to be put into practice by proposing a Special Bill on the Construction of the New Administrative Capital. The Bill was passed and promulgated in the wake of fierce political controversies in early 2004. A number of citizens who were unsatisfied with the plan, including the then Mayor of Seoul Lee Myong Bak (the seventeenth president succeeding Roh), organized an anti-relocation-of-the capital movement. Some of the dissenters brought their complaints before the KCC, alleging that the Special Act was unconstitutional because it violated their constitutional right to vote on a referendum allegedly required by the Constitution and other constitutional rights, including the right to property, the right to become civil servants, and so on.

The KCC accepted the complaints in an eight to one majority decision.[22] The main thrusts of the majority opinion were fourfold. First, the relocation of the capital is a core constitutional matter that forms a requisite element of the Constitution. Second, although "Seoul is the capital" is not expressly stated in the written constitution, the fact becomes a customary constitution as a part of the unwritten constitution directly chosen by the people even prior to the enactment of the written constitution of the Republic of Korea. Third, since a customary constitution is also a part of the constitution with the same effect as that of the written constitution, its revision should be carried out only by way of revision of the written constitution. Fourth, Article 130 of the Constitution requires a mandatory referendum for constitutional revision, the Act on the review intended to relocate the capital encroached upon their constitutional right to vote on the referendum.

The basic issue underlying the Relocation of the Capital case can be questioned from two aspects which are internally intertwined with each other and actually constitute two sides of the same coin. The first aspect of the question

---

[22] Constitutional Court Decision 2004Hun-Ma554, October 21, 2004, 16–1(B) KCCR 1.

is a judicial one which can correspond to the position of the KCC's majority opinion: *whether a customary constitution is a proper form of law having enough justification to strike down statutes*. The second one is a constitutional aspect which the KCC veiled, intentionally or unintentionally, but it concerns the constitutional effects in terms of the separation of powers delegated by the sovereign people in constitutional arrangements: *which is better positioned to fill the gap caused by, if any, constitutional abeyance, the National Assembly or the Constitutional Court?* Why are these two aspects intertwined with each other? My assumption is that the reason why the KCC's majority opinion lifted the controversial legal tool of customary constitution from the unknown expanse of constitutional theories is to take over the legislature's role to represent the will of the people in the form of constitutional construction or review. In other words, if the answer to the first judicial aspect of the issue is No, the natural result of the KCC's majority opinion is nothing but the usurpation of the legislative power of the National Assembly on political matters.

Two preliminary questions should be answered in order to get to the correct conclusion of the major issue. First, is it possible to identify a customary constitution in a constitutional democracy with a written constitution? Second, if so, does the customary constitution have the same effect as the written constitution? The answer to the first question may depend upon the structure of the written constitution, the constitutional history regarding the form of the constitution, and the extent of constitutional stipulation. However, the KCC's majority recognized the form of customary constitution as a kind of *a priori* source of constitutional law by assuming that

> notwithstanding the existence of a written constitution, it is impossible to completely provide a written constitution, and, in addition, the Constitution pursues succinctness and implication as the basic law of the nation. Therefore, there is room for recognizing certain matters though not written out in the formal code of the Constitution as unwritten constitution or customary constitutional law. Especially, there may be certain circumstances where no express provision is necessarily included in the text for those matters that are self-evident or presupposed or that are general constitutional principles at the time of the establishment of the written constitution.[23]

A lot of constitutional and legal arguments about each statement of this extract may arise. But since our focus is on the role of the unwritten constitution and

---

[23] Ibid. (English translation by KCC), available at http://english.ccourt.go.kr/cckhome/eng/decisions/majordecisions/majorDetail.do (last accessed on July 20, 2017).

on the consistency of the constitutional reasoning based upon this invisible constitution, it would be enough to mention just two major flaws here. First, the scope of the unwritten constitution explained by the majority is not cautious enough to be persuasive. The majority opinion made a great effort to include "those matters that are self-evident or presupposed or that are general constitutional principles at the time of the establishment of the written constitution," so that it can take advantage of the reliable effect inherent in such universal principles in the course of justification for a customary constitution with no reliable image. As I have argued in challenging Tribe's "genuinely invisible" principles previously, those self-evident principles cannot be regarded as an "unwritten constitution," but as the written constitution itself. They are the very *base* upon which constitutional text is written. They are "invisible" because they are too obvious to deny. Therefore, they should not be abused or misused to justify the constitutional value of a controversial conception of customary constitution that is by nature the *result* of constitutional practice and interpretation.

Second, even if a customary constitution could be regarded as *a priori* source of law, further justifications would be required to give it the same status as the written constitution. The majority moved on to undertake this task as follows:

> [As] the citizens of the Republic of Korea are the holders of the sovereignty of the Republic of Korea and of the highest authority to establish the constitution, the citizens not only participate in the establishment and the revision of the written constitution, but also may directly form as necessary constitutional law matters that are not included in the text of the written constitution, in the form of customs. Then, the customary constitutional law should be deemed as the expression of intent of the constitutional determination of the citizens as the holders of sovereignty, like the written constitution, and should also be deemed to have the same force as that of the written constitution ... The principle of sovereignty or democracy requires the participation of the citizens in the establishment of the positive law, written or customary, in the entirety, and the customary constitutional law established by the people binds the legislator and has the force as constitutional law.[24]

The majority of the KCC reached the conclusion that *a priori* recognition of a customary constitution can be justified by the people's sovereignty that also provides a justification for the customary constitution's status having the same effect as the written constitution.

[24] Ibid.

The majority of the KCC needed further twists to carry out the self-imposed task to strike down the Act at issue completely, because the recognition of a customary constitution itself is not enough to find the violation of an individual's constitutional rights, a legal requirement in the constitutional complaints procedure. For that purpose, further reasoning on two counts are required. First, the question why the fact that Seoul has been the capital should become the norm with which the legislator is supposed to comply must be answered. Second, even if the first question were to be answered properly, there should be another requirement to meet, i.e., a violation of an individual's constitutional rights to make the Act at issue invalidated.

The majority opined on the first question as follows:

> that Seoul is the capital of our nation has been a given normative fact concerning the nation for over six-hundred (600) years since the Chosun period as the meaning of the word Seoul also indicates, therefore it can be estimated as a continuing convention practice traditionally formed in the nation (continuance); such practice has never been interrupted in the continuum as it has existed in actuality for a long period of time without change (maintainability); the fact that Seoul is the capital has a clear meaning to the extent that none among the citizens of our nation would hold a different opinion over it individually (unequivocalness); and, further, such practice is a basic element of the nation in whose effectiveness and enforceability the citizens believe, by obtaining the approval and the wide consensus of the citizens through firm establishment over a long period of time (national consensus). Therefore, that Seoul is the capital is part of the unwritten constitution established in the form of customary constitutional law, as it is a customary constitutional law that has traditionally existed since prior to our written constitution, and is a norm that is self-evident and presupposed in the constitution notwithstanding the absence of an express constitutional provision indicating this.[25]

I am still unsatisfied with the majority's reasoning that the fact that Seoul has been regarded as the capital in Korean history is a "dormancy of its normative nature behind the factual proposition." There is plenty of counter-evidence from various perspectives challenging its assertion that the factual proposition met even the elements of customary constitutional law. However, the crucial argument showing the inconsistency of the majority is the majority's final step to meet the formal requirement of the constitutional complaints, i.e., the recognition of the violation of a citizen's right to vote on a referendum.

---

[25] Constitutional Court Decision 2004Hun-Ma554, October 21, 2004, 16–1(B) KCCR 1(English translation by KCC), available at http://english.ccourt.go.kr/cckhome/eng/decisions/majordecisions/majorDetail.do (last accessed on July 20, 2017).

The majority moved on to the argument that even a customary constitution as an unwritten constitution can be revised only by way of the constitutional revision process of the written constitution. It said that

> [In] the case of our constitutional law, Articles 128 through 130 under Chapter 10 of the Constitution set forth a strict procedure for the constitutional revision that is different from the revision procedure for general statutes, and such constitutional revision procedures designates its object merely as the "constitution." Therefore, as long as customary constitutional law constitutes part of the constitution, it is within the meaning of the constitution that is the object of the constitutional revision procedure referred to here. Then, in order to eliminate the customary constitutional law that the capital of our nation is Seoul, constitutional revision pursuant to the procedure set forth by the Constitution is mandatory.

The logical consequence of this proposition is that even though the people may have the right to choose in which form they constitute the constitution, written or unwritten, as far as revision of the constitution is concerned, there is no right to choose the procedure as they wish but the duty to comply with the revision procedure of the written constitution. Upon a quick glance, the reasoning on this part seems to be very logical. However, if the true nature of the revision procedure in the Constitution is recognized, the majority's hindsight can be unveiled. Constitutional revision clauses require both the concurrent votes of two-thirds or more of the total members of the National Assembly, with the determination confirmed by more than one-half of all votes cast by more than one-half of the voters eligible to vote in elections for members of the National Assembly. Therefore, the natural consequence of the majority opinion is that only one-third of the total number of the National Assembly can block the transfer of the capital. Then, we can finally realize how feeble it is that the constitutional status of the customary constitution can be justified by the "visible" principle of the people's sovereignty. Ironically enough, they held that the people themselves are not entitled to change, if any, a customary constitution and therefore should be subject to the will of minority representatives, instead of a majority, while the formation of a customary constitution can be done only by the will of the people. Is this what the invisible constitution is intended to be or should it play a role in constitutional discourse?

In my opinion, the proper role of the KCC in this case was not to intervene in a typically political issue, considering that there is no explicit provision concerning the capital or its relocation. To be faithful to the ideal of constitutional democracy, the KCC should have held that it might be more desirable for social integration to allow civic participation in the decision-making process for the relocation of the capital city but in principle it is not constitutionally commanded, and since the constitution is silent on the location of the capital city and the process to change it, this issue would be better decided by the regular political process among elected representatives, and under such a constitutional circumstance, the constitutional court is not the right place to discuss the constitutional validity of the decision to construct a New Administrative Capital. For one thing, there was no clear evidence that its intervention contributed to the enhancement of democracy and human rights as the justification for active constitutional review. An invisible or unwritten constitution is of no use in this arena.

11.4.2. *Protection of the Presidency from the Abusive Use of Impeachment in the Presidential Impeachment Case*

In 2004, President Roh Moo Hyun was impeached for, among others, violations of the Election Act, corruption stemming from abuse of power, and the unfaithful performance of presidential duties. When he was impeached, he had just completed less than one year out of five years of his term, while the four-year term of the National Assembly was almost finished so that a new general election was in process. The general public challenged this attempt at impeachment and in the ensuing election, the supporters of impeachment, who were used to obtaining more than two-thirds of the total seats in the National Assembly, faced a humiliating defeat and the pro-president party won the majority of the new National Assembly.

After the general election, the KCC came to a conclusion in an especially speedy process. The KCC found wrongdoings on President Roh's part on three accounts. First, his open support for a political party at a press conference prior to the scheduled general election violated Article 9(1) of the Public Official Election Act requiring public officials' neutrality in elections. Second, his seemingly defiant comments on the warning of the National Election Commission which prohibited him from making political speeches in relation to a general election was in violation of the presidential duty to uphold and protect the Constitution. Third, his proposal of a national referendum on the people's confidence in his presidency was not compatible with Article 72 Paragraph 1 allowing a referendum only on specific policies, and thus breached his duty to uphold and protect the Constitution.[26]

Despite these findings, however, the KCC refused to dismiss him from the presidency on the ground that these wrongdoings were not grave enough to

---

[26] Constitutional Court Decision 2004Hun-Na1, May 14, 2004, 16–1 KCCR 601, 609.

deprive him of the presidency.[27] In reaching this conclusion, the KCC relied upon a "balancing test" or the principle of proportionality in the sense that constitutional punishment should be proportionally correspondent to the responsibility of the person charged with wrongdoings:

> Article 53(1) of the Constitutional Court Act provides that, "when there is a valid ground for the petition for impeachment adjudication, the Constitutional Court shall issue a decision removing the respondent from office." The above provision may be interpreted literally to mean that the Constitutional Court shall automatically make a decision of removal from office in all cases where there is any valid ground for impeachment as set forth in Article 65(1) of the Constitution. However, if every and any minor violation of law committed in the course of performing official duties were to mandate removal from office, this would offend the request that punishment under the Constitution proportionally correspond to the obligation owed by the respondent, that is, the principle of proportionality. Therefore, the "valid ground for the petition for impeachment adjudication" provided in Article 53(1) of the Constitutional Court Act does not mean any and all incidences of violation of law, but the incidence of a "grave" violation of law sufficient to justify removal of a public official from office.

The KCC also held that "the question of whether there was a 'grave violation of law' or whether the 'removal is justifiable' cannot be conceived by itself. Therefore, the existence of a valid ground for ... the removal from office, should be determined by balancing the 'degree of the negative impact on or the harm to the constitutional order caused by the violation of law' and the 'effect to be caused by the removal of the respondent from office'."

Here we can see that the KCC formulated an "invisible" discretion of striking balances between competing interests and values in impeachment. It is interesting to see that the KCC tried to rely on Article 53 Paragraph 1 of the Constitutional Court Act to as the statutory base for a balancing test in the impeachment procedure. As the KCC acknowledged, this provision can be literally construed as the recognition of the power of final say in the hands of the KCC. However, the existence of the power to declare impeachment of a public official is one thing, and how to wield this power is a totally different matter. That is, the KCC did not justify sufficiently their choice of a balancing test in the impeachment process. It means that the KCC just assumed the discretion of striking balances between competing interests and values

---

[27] The protection of the President from outside interference is reinforced by the provision of Article 84 vesting him with the privilege exempted from criminal charges except for insurrection or treason during his term.

from the fact that it is entitled to have a final say on impeachment. This is exactly the same way in which it derived the principle of proportionality from an overarching basic principle of the rule of law (or *Rechtsstaat*)[28] or Article 37 Paragraph 2 envisaged putting limitations on governmental activities.[29] In Korea, there has been so far no serious examination of whether the principle of proportionality is part of an invisible constitution because, as I believe, not only the ideal of constitutional democracy pertaining to the rule of law in general, but also the natural construction of all the relevant provisions including Article 37 Paragraph 2 as a whole cannot help but support such understanding. From the viewpoint of comparative constitutional law, the fact that, regardless of a visible or invisible basis, most constitutional democracies have developed a similar principle in whatever title which would strengthen this seemingly unanimous understanding in Korea. The remaining issue is how and to what extent this principle can be applied to a variety of constitutional cases.

As far as the impeachment is concerned, the judicial discretion of a balancing test can also be justified by the very ideal of constitutional democracy or a democratic republic under which the Korean constitutional arrangement as a whole is made up. The KCC as the constitutionally designated institution of impeachment justice may elaborate the legal requirements. In this context, the use of a balancing test is a part of elaboration or articulation of legal reasoning. The outcome of impeachment is of constitutional importance, so that the judicial body entrusted with the power of impeachment should consider the constitutional causes and consequences of impeachment. For example, the importance of the presidency as the unique representative of the sovereign people would not accept an easy and extra-political dismissal without the sovereign people's consent:

> On the other hand, a decision to remove the President from office would deprive the "democratic legitimacy" delegated to the President by the national constituents through an election during the term of the office and may cause political chaos arising from the disruption of the opinions among

---

[28] The principle of the rule of law may be discerned from that of *Rechtsstaat*, at least in terms of its diverse ideological origins and different paths of development. However, the KCC has used these two ideas as similar principles in their constitutional meanings by often citing them together in the same context (e.g., "The system of impeachment against the President intends to realize the rule of law or the principle of *Rechtsstaat* that every citizen is governed by law and even a man of national power does not stand above the law [emphasis added]." Constitutional Court Decision 2004Hun-Na1, May 14, 2004, 16–1 KCCR 632).

[29] For the principle of proportionality as a standard of constitutional review in the context of constitutional adjudication in Korea, see generally Jongcheol Kim, "The Structure and Basic Principles of Constitutional Adjudication in the Republic of Korea" in K. Cho (ed.), *Litigation in Korea* (London: Edward Elgar Publishing, 2010) 130.

the people, that is, the disruption and the antagonism between those who support the President and those who do not, let alone a national loss and an interruption in state affairs from the discontinuity of the performance of presidential duties. Therefore, in light of the gravity of the effect to be caused by the removal of the President, the ground to justify a decision of removal should also possess corresponding gravity.

Although it is very difficult to provide in general terms which should constitute a "grave violation of law sufficient to justify the removal of the President from office," a decision to remove the President from office shall be justified in such limited circumstances as where the maintenance of the presidential office can no longer be permitted from the standpoint of the protection of the Constitution, or where the President has lost the qualifications to administrate state affairs by betraying the trust of the people.

To sum up, the KCC persuasively derived an "invisible" limitation on impeachment of the president from the "visible" text which states the requirements of impeachment by way of applying the universal constitutional principle of the rule of law into the impeachment procedure. I believe that this approach of the KCC took the right stance in a way of applying the "invisible" constitutional principle in Tribe's terminology (or "visible" in my understanding) to the proper place, and thus successfully struck the balance among constitutional powers by preventing the legislature from exercising impeachment power abusively.

11.4.3. Materialization of the Principle of Equality in Election in the Election Reapportionment Cases

In Korea, Article 67 Paragraph 1(*in re* presidential election) and Article 41 Paragraph 1(*in re* election of the National Assembly) of the Constitution declare four principles of election: universality, equality, directness, and secrecy of ballot in election. The KCC have used these principles to review the constitutionality of election laws. Here, we will discuss the principle of equality as a host of an "invisible" constitutional principle.

The KCC's basic understanding of equality in election is that the parliamentary electoral system should guarantee not only equal votes for each voter,[30] but an equal value for each vote.[31] The key element in this regard

---

[30] For a judgment of the KCC invalidating an electoral scheme on the ground of the "one person, one vote" rule, see Constitutional Court Decision 2000Hun-Ma91, July 19, 2001, 13–2 KCCR 77.

[31] For a judgment of the KCC invalidating an electoral scheme on the ground of the "one vote, one value" rule, see Constitutional Court Decision 95Hun-Ma224, December 27, 1995, 7–2 KCCR 760.

is to formulate the constitutionally justifiable population disparity among all election districts.

In 2001, the KCC held that the population disparity should meet a limit of 50 percent deviation (in which case the maximum permissible ratio between the most populous district and the least would be 3:1), though in principle, a limit of 33⅓ percent deviation would need to be achieved in the future.[32] This temporary permissible range was tightened compared to the KCC's previous decision requiring a limit of 60 percent deviation (the maximum permissible ratio would be 4:1).

However, in 2014, the KCC moved to further tighten the permissible range as it anticipated in 2001, that is, it declared that a limit of 33⅓ percent deviation must be accomplished until 2015.[33]

In addition, since its first decision on this matter in 1995,[34] the KCC held that the average population of all the constituencies, rather than the actual population of each constituency, should be used in deciding whether they can be said to abide by the equality principle in election alignment.[35]

In fact, the issue of election reapportionment has been considered so important that once it has been regarded as out of the jurisdiction of judicial review on the ground that it might fall into the category of a "political question." As we all know, this story can be found only in past history,[36] and in most constitutional democracies election reapportionment is required to abide by the constitutional guidelines including the principle of equality, otherwise the electoral system can be found to be invalid.[37]

---

[32] Constitutional Court Decision 2000Hun-Ma92•240(consolidated), October 25, 2001, 13-2 KCCR 502.

[33] Constitutional Court Decision 2012Hun-Ma92, October 30, 2014, 26-2(A) KCCR 668. On March 3, 2016, the National Assembly revised electoral district apportionment according to the judgment of the KCC.

[34] Constitutional Court Decision 95Hun-Ma224, December 27, 1995, 7-2 KCCR 760.

[35] However, as far as local election constituencies are concerned, the KCC applied a different permissible range of population. In 2007, the KCC ruled that considering the peculiarity of social circumstances, for example, unbalanced urbanization, a limit of 60 percent deviation is acceptable. See Constitutional Court Decision 2005Hun-Ma985, March 29, 2007, 19-1 KCCR 287.

[36] It was the Supreme Court of the United States that broke the old standard of "political question" in election arrangements and opened the way for judicial review on electoral laws. See Baker v. Carr, 369 U.S. 186(1962).

[37] The "one person, one vote" standard that was first set up at both Baker v. Carr, 369 U.S. 186(1962) and Reynolds v. Sims, 377 U.S. 533(1964) was recently reconfirmed in Evenwel v. Abbott, 578 U.S. – (2016) in which the Supreme Court of the United States rejected a challenge to the "one person, one vote" rule and allowed the use of total population in drawing legislative districts.

Then, we can ask if these principles and their derivatives which emerged in the course of constitutional evolution are to be respected just because they are expressed in the written constitution, or because they are essential to constitutional democracy. If the answer is in the former, the appearance of visibility becomes very important, while if it is in the latter, the ideal rather than the appearance matters. I believe that the provisions declaring the principles of election in the Korean Constitution are basically the confirmation of universal principles derived from the ideal of constitutional democracy or a democratic republic as Article 1 of the Korean Constitution declares.[38] And the step-by-step elaboration made by the KCC, e.g., the gradually tightened election disparity, is nothing but an emanation of universal principles which have been developed to meet the growing demands of the sovereign people. I cannot imagine that without equal and universal suffrage a civilized country may declare itself a democratic republic. Under this constitutionalist or democratic understanding, I do not think that it really matters whether we have visible or invisible constitutions covering election principles.

Let me finish this section by giving a short assessment of the KCC's performance in these election reapportionment cases. In principle, the KCC finally played its constitutionally designated function of implementing visible or invisible constitutional principles very well. Thanks to the efforts of the KCC to enhance constitutional democracy, the notoriously undemocratic election system in Korea had a momentum to be reformed, at least at the lowest level.[39] It is hoped that similar efforts on the part of the KCC should be

---

[38] It is interesting to see that the Korean Constitution has a specific provision of equality in election, while the Supreme Court of the United States articulated rules of electoral equality from the general provision of equal protection in the Fourteenth Amendment.

[39] The Korean electoral system is basically a majoritarian system, because only one-sixth of the overall representatives (currently 47 out of 300) are elected by a party list system. This majoritarian system has been generally accused of producing an "unfair," distorted representation on the ground that it tends to give grossly exaggerated representation to the two major parties by simply focusing on who tops the poll and ignoring the size of the majority. The huge number of "wasted votes" of ordinary citizens in every constituency in reality results in the disenfranchisement of many millions of voters within the country. The major victim of these wasted votes is the smaller party whose vote obtained, across the local constituencies, cannot be transferred into the seats in the National Assembly. In addition, the Public Officials Election Act provides too many regulations on campaigns to be called a free election system. Very harsh regulation on political parties is also responsible for a democratic deficit in the political system as a whole in Korea. For a general account of political reform in Korea, see Jongcheol Kim and Jimoon Lee, "The Necessity and Conditions of a Political Reform for the Republican Co-prosperity: Beyond Inconsistent Proposals for Constitutional Revision of the Presidential System" [available only in Korean] (2014) 20–1 *World Constitutional Law Review* 63–92, 77–86.

made for other remaining electoral reforms by reviewing more strictly election related laws.[40]

11.4.4. Political Reactions and Implications in Relation to the Role of the KCC

For the sake of foreign readers who do not have enough background of Korean society, I would like to add some background explanations, especially in regard to the first two cases concluded in the same year, 2004.

Although these cases provided a good opportunity for the KCC to represent its ambition to be a constitutional coordinator, it is true that their political outcomes polarized Korean society and thereby the raison d'être of the KCC became vulnerable to popular opinion. In the impeachment case which, as a matter of fact, was the first impeachment trial against the president in Korean modern history since its formal establishment as a new Republic in 1948, the KCC attempted to get into the middle ground of the political spectrum by trying to make both supporters and opponents on the issue of impeachment of President Roh satisfied. Its conclusion in refusing to remove him from office might have relieved his supporters while it tried to amuse the other side, recognizing President Roh's constitutional and legal violations on three counts and stating some warnings to the President. However, the KCC's seemingly ambivalent ruling, on the one hand, drew fierce criticism from "the Old Forces" who have had vested interests for more than sixty years in Korean Society, in the sense that a group of social forces have had a very vital influence on the allocation of political, social, cultural, and economic resources, and on opinion formation in Korean society. On the other hand, it was respected as the bastion of democracy by "the New Forces" who have driven political and social reforms challenging the Old Forces' continuous ruling of Korean society.

The political reaction about the KCC's ruling in the relocation of the capital city case was exactly the reverse of the impeachment case. The KCC's ruling that the Construction of the New Administrative Capital Act 2004 encroached upon the people's constitutional right of referendum by relocating the capital without the direct consent of the people was welcomed by the Old Forces which have strong economic and social assets in the present capital, Seoul. However, the New Forces, believing that the relocation of the

---

[40] The National Assembly is endowed with comprehensive legislative power, especially in relation to the electoral system, by Article 41 of the Constitution, especially those parties with vested interests in the current system that have been criticized for their ignorance of or reluctance to support electoral reform.

capital is a key tool in a decentralization project crucial to dismantle the social base of the Old Forces and distribute social recourse centralized in Seoul area across the nation, attacked the KCC as a destructor of the Constitution mainly because the KCC's decision made it almost impossible to move the capital by using a very controversial conception of customary constitution.

This roller coaster public reaction toward the KCC in 2004 has not changed very much and remains even today. This situation has ambivalent anticipations. On the one hand, constitutional dialogue is becoming institutionalized gradually in Korean society, whereas in the past the overwhelming political influence put inroads to a constructive dialogue. On the other, it can show the uncertain status of the KCC in the constitutional arrangements, so that if constitutional amendment movements can get enough support from the people and political elite, it could suddenly be abolished and its powers transferred to the Supreme Court.[41] Which outcome is realized will depend upon the sovereign people's evaluation on how the KCC performs its designated role as a constitutional bastion of democracy and human rights. The third case study on the electoral reapportionment case may be a good example of the desirable role of the KCC, because its activist approach in these cases has been admired as enhancing democracy and political equality in Korea. If the KCC continues to perform this self-imposed function properly, its role as a constitutional coordinator in constitutional dialogue will be well established in Korean constitutional arrangements.

11.5. CONCLUDING REMARKS

In the process of implementing constitutional functions, it is inevitable that the constitutional actors, including public authorities, refer to some constitutional propositions established by its own precedents, or by guidance from

[41] During the revision period of this chapter, Korea experienced a dynamic political change. In the wake of a series of "candlelight protests" joined by more than 16 million people since late October 2016, President Park Geun Hye was finally impeached by the judgment of the KCC on March 10. On May 9, a new presidential election took place and the newly elected President Moon Jae In and the National Assembly agreed to amend the constitution until mid-June 2018. During this dramatic political change, the KCC has gained strong support from the general public and it is highly likely that the KCC will remain as an independent constitutional institution in the amended constitutional arrangements. And it is worthwhile to mention that the first presidential impeachment was accomplished through the harmonized combination of "unofficial" or "deinstitutionalized" will-formation of candlelight citizens and "official" or "institutionalized" constitutional processes of impeachment on the parts of the National Assembly and the KCC. This experience that may be called a "candlelight revolution," may contribute to the upgrading of the mechanism of constitutional dialogue among constitutional actors in Korean society.

judicial bodies. The references can be often derived from explicit texts in the constitution, while some can be from unwritten parts of the constitution. This difference of references may have some substantive meanings, but it should not be exaggerated. What, in reality, should guide constitutional discourse is not the appearance of the constitution, but the ideal overarching the constitution as a whole. From some case studies in the context of Korean constitutional adjudication, this argument has been proved true. What is important is that all the constitutional actors participating in constitutional dialogue designed or envisaged by the ideal of constitutional democracy are to abide by the limitation the constitution imposes, regardless of the appearance of those references, visible or invisible. At the same time, it is also noteworthy to recognize that they perform its constitutionally designated functions providently, consistently, and persuasively within such limitations. Constitutional adjudicators are not an exception to this proposition, but should be leading actors to provide a role model for other actors.

12

Constitutional Implications in Australia

Explaining the Structure – Rights Dualism

Rosalind Dixon and Gabrielle Appleby

Constitutional implications play a significant part in many important aspects of Australian constitutional law. For instance, under the *Boilermakers*' principle, the High Court has recognised an implication protecting the separation of federal judicial power from non-judicial power; under the *Kable* principle this has been extended to protect the institutional integrity of state courts. The Court has recognised implied principles protecting states as bodies politic under the *Melbourne Corporation* doctrine, and the Commonwealth and its powers under the *Cigamatic* doctrine. The Court has recognised implied guarantees of freedom of political communication and universal access to the franchise. Most recently, in the protection of the federal system and responsible government, the Court has articulated an extra-textual constitutional limitation on the Commonwealth's executive power to spend and contract in the absence of explicit statutory authorisation.

Implications are thus critical to the shape of doctrines that protect fundamental constitutional structures in Australia – the separation of powers, federalism, political democracy and responsible government – and are thus critical to day-to-day government practice in a range of important policy areas. Yet, outside of these protections for the structural features of the Constitution, in the context of non-politically associated individual rights, Australian constitutional culture remains deeply suspicious of most forms of implication. Our conception of individual rights in this context is, of course, itself contestable: on one view, a constitutional 'right' exists wherever the Court upholds an individual's constitutional claim.[1] The view we take, however, is that at least in this context the concept of a constitutional right is best understood as referring to

---

[1] See e.g., W. N. Hohfeld, 'Fundamental Legal Conceptions: As Applies in Judicial Reasoning' (1917) 26 *Yale Law Journal* 710. See also discussion in Frederick Schauer, 'The Generality of Rights' (2000) 6 *Legal Theory* 323, 328.

a somewhat narrower class of legal claim, where the *explicit basis* of the claim lies in shared commitments in a democracy to individual freedom and equality or human dignity and not simply a more instrumental or structural set of constitutional commitments.[2]

This chapter considers this important dimension to Australia's 'Invisible Constitution', and in particular, the possible explanations for this structure–rights 'dualism' in extra-textual Australian constitutional practice.[3] One potential explanation, we suggest, is *legal*–cultural in origin, and lies in the combined influence of early decisions of the High Court of Australia, most particularly the *Engineers' Case*, and the choices of the drafters of the Constitution regarding the protection of individual rights. Ever since 1920 and the Court's landmark decision in *Engineers*, the Court has insisted that constitutional implications must be securely grounded in the 'text and structure' of the Constitution. However, the Australian framers were variously suspicious of and unperturbed about constitutional rights protection, and thus the text and structure of the Constitution provide limited express support for the protection of individual rights.[4]

A second possible explanation is *political*–cultural in nature, and is drawn from the longstanding resistance among legal and political elites in Australia to forms of judicial review that involve open-ended, proportionality-style judgments about the justice or merits of various legislative policies. From the outset, views of this kind have been an obstacle to the adoption of rights-based judicial review in Australia.[5] In recent decades, there have also been a series of opportunities for the Australian Parliament, and voters, to amend Australia's constitutional framework to introduce greater individual rights protection – for instance, by adding express constitutional rights guarantees, or broad statutory rights guarantees. These attempts to create capital and small 'c' constitutional change, however, have consistently failed in the domain of individual rights, in large part due to resistance from political and legal elites.

---

[2] See e.g., Schauer, Supra note 1 (distinguishing between rights in a truly *ex post* and particularistic sense and a more general *ex ante*-sense). Compare also Ronald Dworkin, *Taking Rights Seriously* (Massachusetts: Harvard University Press, 1977) (articulating a conception of rights is grounded in mutual respect and concern, or respect for equal human dignity). Compared to Dworkin, of course, we take a far less definitive view of the relative weight to be afforded to rights-based claims, compared to other competing interests.

[3] In this sense we adopt the conceptual definition of the invisible constitution, referred to by Dixon and Stone in Chapter 1, and a relatively broad view of extra-textual constitutional practice or influence, which does not seek directly to parse what might be considered as internal versus external to legitimate processes of constitutional construction. Contrast Goldsworthy, and Solum in Chapters 3 and 4 of this book.

[4] Rosalind Dixon, 'An Australian (Partial) Bill of Rights' (2016) 14 *International Journal of Constitutional Law* 80.

[5] See e.g., Sir Isaac Isaacs as discussed in ibid.

The two explanations are interrelated: the political resistance to change in this area is itself informed by the reasoning and methodology favoured by the Australian High Court since the *Engineers' Case*, which emphasises the need for judicial judgments to be strongly grounded in constitutional text and structure, rather than more open-ended inquiries.

The potential broader lessons from the Australian experience, therefore, are that the trajectory of constitutional implications in a particular constitutional jurisdiction can be shaped both by the express language and structure of a particular constitution *and* more contingent local legal- and political-cultural factors. The scope of implied constitutional rights protection in Australia might look quite different, we suggest, if *either* the general language and structure of the Constitution were more supportive of individual rights, the High Court were more open to 'looser' forms of construction or the background political culture were more supportive of rights-based judicial review. It is the combination of these factors that seems to explain the continuation of what, in global terms, is a striking bifurcation between structural and rights-based judicial review in Australia, or the willingness of the High Court consistently to draw and enforce a broad range of structural constitutional implications, while largely rejecting most rights-based implications, beyond those core political rights associated with representative democracy. Even there, the Court has taken explicit care to frame the implications as limitations on government power as opposed to rights.[6]

The remainder of the chapter is divided into three sections. Section 12.1 sets out the key modern structural constitutional implications identified and enforced by the High Court, and explains their centrality to current Australian constitutional practice. Section 12.2 discusses the ongoing resistance by the Court to other more squarely rights-based implications. Section 12.3 speculates on the potential explanations for this structure–rights dualism, or tale of resistance, in relation to the acceptance of implications in Australia. Section 12.4 offers a brief conclusion as to the lessons of this experience for broader comparative constitutional understandings.

12.1. THE CENTRALITY OF IMPLICATIONS AS AN INVISIBLE DIMENSION OF AUSTRALIAN CONSTITUTIONAL LAW AND PRACTICE

Today, the High Court's jurisprudence on the existence and development of implied limits is an important – indeed increasingly central – part of Australian constitutional law, and has a growing impact on how government is practiced. This is true for the separation of federal judicial and non-judicial power,

---

[6] See e.g., *Lange v. Australian Broadcasting Corporation* (1997) 189 CLR 520, 560.

constitutional federalism in relation to the protection of the states and the Commonwealth, implied guarantees of freedom of political communication and universal access to the franchise to protect the operation of representative democracy. Most recently, the Court has also found a non-textual limitation on the Commonwealth's executive power to preserve and promote federalism and responsible government.

This heavy reliance on implications has added an important 'invisible' dimension to Australian constitutional law and practice. On some level, it could be said that constitutional implications are indistinct from the constitutional document, the visible constitution. This might even be thought to be particularly persuasive in the Australian context, where the Court has insisted that implications are grounded in the interpretation of the text and structure of the Constitution and may thus be viewed as emanations of that text. Indeed, in many contexts in Australian constitutional law, successive courts have attempted to ground previously broadly drawn implied limitations more closely in the text and individual words of the Constitution. However, constitutional implications differ in their nature from more direct judicial interpretation. What generally distinguishes constitutional implications from direct judicial interpretation is that the Court's drawing of an implication comes not from an attempt to interpret the words of a provision in its application to a particular dispute, but rather to draw on inferences from text and structure of the Constitution to find a principle and rules that will resolve the dispute, which could not be resolved by the direct application and interpretation of the constitutional text alone. As Cheryl Saunders and Adrienne Stone have explained:

> The form of these arguments is to reason from specific provisions ... to a more general principle ... to a more specific set of rules.[7]

Further, implications are generally drawn from the combined force of text and structure, and the interplay between specific provisions and the structural framework of the constitutional document, rather than the application and interpretation of individual provisions.

12.1.1. The Separation of Judicial Power

One of the most important implications under the Australian Constitution concerns the separation of judicial and non-judicial power at the Commonwealth

---

[7] Cheryl Saunders and Adrienne Stone, 'Constitutional Reasoning in the High Court of Australia' in Andras Jakab, Arthur Dyevre and Giulio Itzcovich (eds.), *Comparative Constitutional Reasoning* (Cambridge: Cambridge University Press, 2017).

level, or the so-called '*Boilermakers*' principle'. The implication is drawn from the structural division of powers between the three branches of government in Chapters I, II and III of the Constitution, coupled with the extensive treatment of judicial power in Chapter III itself.[8]

The two limbs of the *Boilermakers*' principle prohibit the vesting of federal judicial power in a body other than a Chapter III court, and the vesting of any power other than federal judicial power (and powers incidental to the exercise of it) in federal Chapter III courts, with their constitutional protections of tenure and remuneration.[9] The principle requires the Court to grapple with the definition of 'judicial power'. In *TCL Air Conditioner (ZhongShan) Co. Ltd v. Judges of the Federal Court of Australia*, French CJ and Gageler J identified three aspects of federal judicial power: the nature of the function conferred; the process by which the function is exercised; and the necessity for the function to be compatible with the essential characteristics of the court as an impartial and independent institution.[10] In *Nicholas v. The Queen*, Gaudron J explained the centrality of the protection of fair judicial process to the *Boilermakers*' principle, including notions of equality before the law and procedural fairness.[11]

The *Boilermakers*' principle has had a major role in shaping legislative policy in a wide variety of areas in Australia, from tribunal and court design, to antiterrorism and anti-organised crime, to immigration policy. In the 1995 decision of *Brandy v. Human Rights and Equal Opportunities Commission*, the High Court struck down an attempt by the Commonwealth government to introduce greater efficiencies into its tribunal system.[12] The government had introduced amendments that allowed the Human Rights and Equal Opportunities Commission's determinations to be registered with the Federal Court, thus giving them the effect of court orders. *Brandy* threw doubt on the constitutional validity of several federal tribunals and eventually led to the introduction of the Federal Magistrates Court, now the Federal Circuit Court.

In the 2007 case of *Thomas v. Mowbray*, the *Boilermakers*' principle was the basis of a challenge to a provision conferring on the Federal Magistrates Court the power to issue interim control orders against individuals for the purpose of preventing a terrorist act, and which included a statutory requirement that

---

[8] *R v. Kirby; Ex parte Boilermakers' Society of Australia* (1956) 95 CLR 254, 275–8.
[9] Constitution s 72.
[10] (2013) 251 CLR 533, 553 [27].
[11] (1998) 193 CLR 173, 208–9.
[12] *Brandy v. Human Rights and Equal Opportunity Commission* (1995) 183 CLR 245. See further discussion of this case and the consequences in Gabrielle Appleby, 'Imperfection and Inconvenience: Boilermakers' and the Separation of Judicial Power in Australia' (2012) 30(2) *University of Queensland Law Journal* 265.

the orders be issued *ex parte*.[13] The Court dismissed the challenge to the particular regime, which has led to the spread and adaptation of the control order regime in the states to target members of organised crime gangs.

The *Boilermakers'* principle has also been at the heart of constitutional disputes over the legality of executive detention, particularly immigration detention. In *Chu Kheng Lim v. Minister for Immigration, Local Government and Ethnic Affairs*, Brennan, Deane and Dawson JJ accepted that 'the involuntary detention of a citizen in custody by the state is penal or punitive in character and, under our system of government, exists only as an incident of the exclusively judicial function of adjudging and punishing criminal guilt'.[14] However, the Court accepted that executive detention for non-punitive purposes, such as the processing and deportation of immigrants pursuant to the aliens' power, would not fall foul of this norm. Justice Gummow explained in *Kruger v. Commonwealth* that non-judicial detention would infringe Chapter III of the Constitution where it was in substance punitive, to be determined by reference to whether the detention is 'reasonably capable of being seen as necessary for a legitimate non-punitive purpose'.[15] However, in *Kruger*, the Court dismissed a challenge to the *Aboriginals Ordinance 1918* (NT), which authorised the involuntary removal and detention of Indigenous children from their families, on the basis that – however misguided – the policy was implemented for non-punitive, welfare and protection purposes.

The Court has also subsequently rejected a number of challenges to immigration detention, accepting as constitutionally permissible the potentially indefinite detention of stateless individuals,[16] the detention of children,[17] and irrelevancy of the conditions to the constitutionality of detention.[18] Thus, while the *Boilermakers'* principle may appear to have great possibility for rights protection in this area, it has proven weak in doing so in practice.

The Court, over time, has also recognised a related implication protecting the institutional integrity and independence of state courts: the *Kable* principle.[19] The *Kable* principle emerged in the case of *Kable v. DPP (NSW)* as a

---

[13] *Thomas v. Mowbray* (2007) 233 CLR 307.
[14] (1992) 176 CLR 1, 27.
[15] (1997) 190 CLR 1, 161. While the relevance proportionality of detention to the non-punitive purpose was doubted, it has more recently been affirmed in *Plaintiff S4-2014 v. Minister for Immigration and Border Protection* (2014) 253 219, 231 [26], 232 [29] (French CJ, Hayne, Crennan, Kiefel and Keane JJ).
[16] *Al-Kateb v. Godwin* (2004) 219 CLR 562.
[17] *Re Woolley; Ex parte Applicants M276/2000* (2004) 225 CLR 1.
[18] *Behrooz v. Secretary of the Department of Immigration and Multicultural and Indigenous Affairs* (2004) 219 CLR 486.
[19] *Street v. Queensland Bar Association* (1989) 168 CLR 461, 521 (Deane J).

limitation on state legislative power in response to the extraordinary *Community Protection Act 1994* (NSW). The Act empowered the Supreme Court of New South Wales to issue a preventative detention order against Mr Kable, and no other person. Justices Toohey, Gaudron, McHugh and Gummow rejected the argument that fundamental common law rights would restrict the breadth of plenary state legislative power. However, they accepted that there was an implied limitation on state power that protected the existence and structural integrity of state courts in Chapter III of the Constitution. This was based on the integrated nature of the Australian judicial system, in which appeals are available from state Supreme Courts to the High Court under section 73(ii) and the provision in sections 71 and 77(iii) that state courts may be vested with federal judicial power.[20] The *Kable* principle restricts state legislative power in two ways: state Parliaments cannot abolish their Supreme Court, so as to frustrate the integrated judicial system, and they cannot interfere with their courts so as to create 'two grades or qualities of justice, depending on whether judicial power is exercised by State courts or federal courts created by the Parliament'.[21] This second restriction was framed in terms of 'incompatibility' with the role of the state courts in the federal system as institutions capable of being vested with, and exercising, federal judicial power.

The establishment of the *Kable* principle gave rise to a number of challenges testing the scope of this new implied limit, including challenges to the preventative detention of serious sexual offenders,[22] the appointment of acting judicial officers,[23] and the remuneration arrangements of Magistrates.[24] The Court's creation of the limitation undoubtedly resulted in more cautious state legislative drafting in relation to their courts.[25] The High Court, however, would not be drawn to extend the principle outside the extraordinary facts of *Kable* itself until the 2009 case of *International Finance Trust Co v. New South Wales Crime Commission*,[26] in which the Court struck down part of the New South Wales *Criminal Assets Recovery Act 1990* (NSW) that relied on *ex parte* hearings. Up until this point, while the Court sometimes used the principle

---

[20] *Kable v. Director of Public Prosecutions* (NSW) (1996) 189 CLR 51, 102 (Gaudron J).
[21] Ibid., 103.
[22] *Fardon v. Attorney-General (Qld)* (2004) 223 CLR 575.
[23] *Forge v. Australian Securities and Investments Commission* (2006) 228 CLR 45.
[24] *North Australian Aboriginal Legal Service Inc v. Bradley* (2004) 218 CLR 146.
[25] *South Australia v. Totani* (2010) 242 CLR 1, 95 [245] (Heydon J).
[26] (2009) 240 CLR 319. In this time the Queensland Court of Appeal did strike down a criminal confiscation statute using the principle: *Re Criminal Proceeds Confiscation Act 2002 (Qld)* [2003] QCA 249.

to construe state statutory schemes so as to mitigate their worst excesses, it was reluctant to deploy the principle to strike down legislation.[27]

Since *International Finance Trust Co*, the High Court has upheld a number of *Kable* challenges, which have in turn shaped important aspects of state law and order policy. Many of these challenges have arisen in the context of the states' anti-organised crime policies, which the states have had to revise substantially following the decisions. In *South Australia v. Totani*, the Court struck down part of South Australia's anti-organised crime control order regime that required the Magistrates Court to issue a control order against a member of a criminal organisation if that organisation had been declared such by the Attorney-General. In *Wainohu*, the Court struck down the New South Wales control order regime because of its inclusion of a provision that relieved judges of the duty to provide reasons for decisions to declare organisations criminal. In the subsequent decision of *Condon v. Pompano*, the Court upheld the validity of the Queensland control order regime, which has now largely been replicated in many states.[28]

Since *Kable*, the Court's formulation of the limits of the principle has evolved, and the protections afforded to the institutional integrity of state courts are now framed by reference to maintaining the defining characteristics of 'courts', as referred to in the Constitution.[29] This represents a move to more closely ground the implied limits of the *Kable* principle in the text of the Constitution. Framed in this way, in *Kirk*, the Court struck down state legislation that removed the supervisory jurisdiction of the New South Wales Supreme Court, effectively extending the express constitutional protections of access to the courts in section 75(v) of the Constitution for review of the actions of Commonwealth officers to the state sphere.[30] This has had fundamental implications for the use of privative clauses at the state level.

The *Boilermakers'* and *Kable* principles are both implied structural limitations on Commonwealth and state legislative power to interfere with the courts, judicial process and, at the federal level, the bestowal of judicial power on non-judicial bodies. While they may have had some beneficial effects for individual rights – such as in relation to due process accorded to individuals in judicial proceedings and protection from arbitrary executive detention – they have explicitly and repeatedly been framed as *structural* guarantees, with any rights-benefits being incidental and narrow.

---

[27] Such as in *Gypsy Jokers Motorcycle Club Incorporated Inc v. Commissioner of Police* (WA) (2008) 234 CLR 532; *K-Generation Pty Ltd v. Liquor Licensing Court* (2009) 237 CLR 501.
[28] *Assistant Commissioner Michael James Condon v. Pompano Pty Ltd* (2013) 252 CLR 38.
[29] *Forge v. ASIC* (2006) 228 CLR 45, 76 (Gummow, Hayne and Crennan JJ).
[30] *Kirk v. Industrial Court of New South Wales* (2010) 239 CLR 531.

12.1.2. Federalism

In the domain of federalism, two implied doctrines operate, albeit in different ways and to different degrees, to protect the structural integrity of the state and Commonwealth governments: the *Melbourne Corporation* and *Cigamatic* doctrines.

The High Court relies on the *Melbourne Corporation* doctrine to protect the role of the states under the Constitution. This doctrine holds that the Commonwealth may not interfere with the states as independent constitutional entities within the Australian federal system.

The current iteration of the principle was first identified in 1947, in *Melbourne Corporation v. Commonwealth*, as the basis of a decision by the Court striking down attempts by the Commonwealth Parliament to compel state governments (and their instrumentalities) to bank with the Commonwealth Bank of Australia.[31] The Court reasoned that, while giving broad power to the Commonwealth Parliament to make various laws under section 51 of the Constitution, the Constitution also contemplated both 'a central government and a number of state governments separately organised', or 'the continued existence [of states] as independent entities'.[32] This, a majority of the Court found, further implied a limitation on Commonwealth power preventing the Commonwealth from passing laws 'preventing a state from continuing to exist and function' as an independent entity, or 'restricting or controlling' a state in the exercise of its constitutional functions. Justice Dixon in particular also emphasised the connection between this limitation and the notion that the Commonwealth does not have power to pass laws imposing 'special burdens' or 'disabilities' compared to other actors.

In subsequent cases, the Court has repeatedly affirmed the status of the *Melbourne Corporation* doctrine as an independent (implied) limitation on Commonwealth power, not simply a limitation on the kinds of laws that may reasonably be characterised as within the scope of the Commonwealth's express power under section 51.[33] For the last thirty-five years at least, the only debate as to the scope of the doctrine has been as to the relationship between the first and second aspects of the Court's reasoning in *Melbourne Corporation* – i.e., the concern with the continued existence of states of independent entities and the principle of non-discrimination identified by Dixon J. In the Court's

---

[31] (1947) 74 CLR 31.
[32] Ibid., 82 (Dixon J).
[33] See *Fairfax v. Federal Commissioner of Taxation* (1965) 114 CLR 1; *Victoria v. Commonwealth* (1971) 122 CLR 353 ('*Payroll Tax Case*') (Menzies, Walsh Gibbs JJ) (Barwick CJ, McTiernan J dissenting); *Commonwealth v. Tasmania* (1983) 158 CLR 1.

more recent jurisprudence, *Austin*[34] and *Clarke*,[35] it has held that the doctrine is best articulated as a single, unified principle, with discrimination only one of several indicators of whether the limitation is in fact engaged.

In its various formulations, the Court has applied the doctrine across a wide variety of important policy areas limiting the Commonwealth's capacity to affect state governments. These have included industrial relations, tax and superannuation, education and environmental policy.[36] Most notably, the Court has held that the principle protects the states' autonomy in determining the terms and conditions of higher-level employees,[37] and the numbers and identity (although not minimum conditions) of all other employees.[38] In *Austin* and *Clarke*, the Court also held that the principle prevents the Commonwealth from levying certain kinds of superannuation tax on state judicial and legislative officers, which might have the capacity to impair the ability of states to recruit and retain suitably qualified individuals.

The High Court has implied a markedly broader protection for the Commonwealth and its constitutional powers, known as the *Cigamatic* doctrine. This doctrine was first recognised by Dixon J in his dissent in the 1947 decision *In re Foreman & Sons Pty Ltd; Uther v. Federal Commissioner of Taxation* (*Uther's Case*).[39] *Uther's Case* concerned a challenge to state legislation that removed the Commonwealth's priority for debts. While a majority of the Court dismissed the challenge, Dixon J upheld it, explaining that '[i]n a dual political system you do not expect to find either government legislating for the other'. But, he explained, the Constitution, through section 109, had given 'supremacy' to the Commonwealth,[40] and the state Parliaments, with their powers drawn from those of the colonial Parliaments, had no power to regulate the legal relations of the Commonwealth with its subjects.[41]

This position was then adopted by a majority of the Court in the 1962 case of *Commonwealth v. Cigamatic Pty Ltd (in liq)*,[42] where Dixon, now Chief Justice, explained the principle as one that 'must go deep in the nature and operation

---

[34] *Austin v. Commonwealth* (2003) 215 CLR 185.
[35] *Clarke v. Commissioner of Taxation* (2009) 240 CLR 272.
[36] See e.g., *Queensland Electricity Commission v. Commonwealth* (1985) 159 CLR 192; *Re Australian Education Union; Ex parte Victoria* (1995) 184 CLR 188; *Victoria v. Commonwealth (Payroll Tax Case)* (1971) 122 CLR 353; *Austin v. Commonwealth* (2003) 215 CLR 185; *Clarke v. Commissioner of Taxation* (2009) 240 CLR 272; *Commonwealth v. Tasmania* (1983) 158 CLR 1 ('Tasmanian Dam Case').
[37] *Re Australian Education Union; Ex parte Victoria* (1995) 184 CLR 188.
[38] Ibid.
[39] (1947) 74 CLR 508.
[40] Ibid., 529.
[41] Ibid., 531.
[42] (1962) 108 CLR 372.

of the federal system'.[43] Since then, in the 1997 *Henderson's* Case decision, the Court has affirmed the principle, while also somewhat reformulating it, as an implied immunity that protects the capacities of the Commonwealth, but subjects them to state regulation in their exercise.[44] That case involved a challenge to the application of the *Residential Tenancies Act 1987* (NSW) to the Commonwealth's statutory authority, the Defence Housing Authority. A majority of the Court affirmed the doctrine, but reformulated it so as to turn on a distinction between an implied immunity that protected the capacities of the Commonwealth, but subjected them to state regulation in their exercise. The usefulness of such a distinction was criticised heavily by McHugh J, and Kirby J argued that the only coherent formulation of the implication was as a reciprocal version of the doctrine in *Melbourne Corporation*.

Tracing their providence back to Dixon J, one of Australia's most celebrated legalistic jurists, the *Melbourne Corporation* and *Cigamatic* doctrines are now well-established and accepted implications of Australian federal constitutional law. They are fundamentally structural protections of government institutions and, at least for the Commonwealth, constitutional powers. In their formulation and application, they have had little rights-salience.

12.1.3. *Representative and Responsible Government*

In the last three decades, the High Court has developed important implications protecting the operation of political democracy in Australia or, in the Westminster-derived language of the Court, the institutions of 'representative and responsible government'. The first implication that was drawn by the Court in this context was the implied freedom of political communication. The principle was initially identified by the Court in *ACTV v. Commonwealth* and *Nationwide News v. Wills* in 1992. In these earlier cases, however, there was substantive disagreement between the judges as to the basis for the implication and the strength of its relationship to the text of the Constitution. It was finally refined in the 1997 decision of *Lange v. ABC*, where a unanimous Court held that 'freedom of communication on matters of government and politics is an indispensable incident of [the] system of representative government which the Constitution creates', via provisions such as sections 7, 24, 64 and 128.[45]

---

[43] Ibid., 377.
[44] Re Residential Tenancies Tribunal of NSW v. Henderson; Ex parte Defence Housing Authority (Henderson's Case) (1997) 190 CLR 410.
[45] *Lange v. Australian Broadcasting Corporation* (1997) 189 CLR 520, 557. The Court in this context also cited s 128, on the Amendment of the Constitution, and ss 1, 8, 13, 15 and 30: see at 557.

The Court thus emphasised the importance of grounding the implied principle and rules in the constitutional text, rather than extraneous constitutional principles such as 'democracy' or even 'representative government'.

The Court in Lange held that, in ascertaining whether this freedom of communication was infringed by Commonwealth or state law, it was necessary to ask two questions: whether a law 'effectively burden[s] freedom of communication about government or political matters either in its terms operation or effect' and if so, whether it is 'reasonably appropriate and adapted to serve a legitimate end the fulfilment of which is compatible with the maintenance of the constitutionally prescribed system of representative and responsible government on the procedure prescribed by section 128 for submitting a proposed amendment of the Constitution to the informed decision of the people'.[46]

Since then, the Court has restated and refined this test,[47] most recently in 2015 by suggesting that the notion of a law being 'reasonably appropriated and adapted' to its end can best be understood as a requirement of reasonable proportionality – i.e., as requiring the law be suitable and narrowly tailored to a legitimate end, and achieve an adequate balance between that end and the implied freedom.[48]

The Court has been quite consistent in adopting a broad approach to the first stage of the inquiry invited by Lange. The Court has held that the implied freedom is broad enough to protect a protest against duck shooting within a legally restricted zone;[49] virulent criticism of the conduct of individual police officers;[50] political campaign donations;[51] statements to the media by a person on parole;[52] religious leafleting in a public shopping mall;[53] and 'offensive' communication via the post of the families of deceased Australian military officers, criticising their conduct and that of the Australian government in military activities overseas.[54] While the Court has often gone on to uphold the legislative restriction of communication of this kind as reasonably appropriate and adapted or proportionate to serving a legitimate government end, it has

---

[46] Ibid., 567.
[47] Coleman v. Power (2004) 220 CLR 1, 51 (McHugh J); Brown v. Tasmania [2017] HCA 43, [104] (Kiefel CJ, Bell and Keane JJ); [156] (Gageler J).
[48] See McCloy v. New South Wales (2015) 89 ALJR 857, 862ff (French CJ, Kiefel, Bell and Keane JJ).
[49] Levy v. Victoria (1997) 189 CLR 579.
[50] Coleman v. Power (2004) 220 CLR 1.
[51] Union NSW v. New South Wales (2013) 252 CLR 530; McCloy v. New South Wales (2015) 89 ALJR 857.
[52] Wotton v. Queensland (2012) 246 CLR 1.
[53] A-G (SA) v. Corporation of City of Adelaide (2013) 295 ALR 197.
[54] Monis v. The Queen (2013) 295 ALR 259.

also done so only after debate and deliberation over the reasonableness or justifiability of limitations of this kind.

The Court in recent years has also extended and expanded this understanding of the requirements of representative government in sections 7 and 24 of the Constitution to imply protections around access to the franchise. In *Roach v. Electoral Commissioner*, in the context of federal legislation disqualifying all prisoners from voting in federal elections, a majority of the Court held that legislation of this kind amounted to an arbitrary or disproportionate limitation on a principle of universal access to the franchise protected by the Constitution.[55] Chief Justice Gleeson held that changed historical circumstances over the course of the twentieth century were such that the language of 'directly chosen by the people' in sections 7 and 24 of the Constitution had 'come to be a constitutional protection of the right to vote', on the basis of universal adult suffrage.[56] Justices Gummow, Kirby and Crennan, in a joint judgment, likewise held that 'voting in elections for the parliament lies at the very heart of the system of government which the Constitution provides', and that the Constitution thus supported at least some 'minimum bedrock' of voting rights, where what was 'at stake [was] legislative disqualification of some citizens from exercise of the franchise'.[57]

In the implied freedom of political communication and franchise cases, the relevant implied limitations have thus operated both to promote a robust form of judicial review of the constitutionality of Commonwealth and state legislation and, in some cases, the protection of the political rights of individuals involved. However, even in this context, with the notable exception of Gleeson CJ's statement in *Roach*, the Court has repeatedly stressed that the relevant implications are to be seen as *limitations* on power, rather than as the source of individual rights;[58] thus, as we saw with the structural protections implied from Chapter III, rights protection through implication in Australia remains indirect, and closely tied to the structural features of the Constitution.

12.1.4. Federalism, Responsible Government and Executive Power

In one of the most recent extra-textual judicial developments, in the 2012 decision of *Williams v. Commonwealth (No. 1)*,[59] the High Court relied on textual

---

[55] (2007) 233 CLR 162.
[56] Ibid., 174, [7].
[57] Ibid., 198, [81]–[82].
[58] In the recent decision of *Gaynor*, the Full Federal Court emphasised the importance of this distinction: *Chief of Defence Force v. Gaynor* [2017] FCAFC 41.
[59] *Williams v. Commonwealth (No. 1)* (2012) 248 CLR 156.

and structural implications, and more specifically, the combined effect of the federal structure of the Commonwealth Parliament and the role of the Senate, and the doctrines of responsible government, to identify extra-textual limits on the exercise of federal executive power to spend and contract.

Williams (No. 1) involved a constitutional challenge to the federal funding of chaplaincy services in schools. This funding was provided pursuant to an appropriation only, with no other statutory basis. Responding to the increase in the government achieving, in effect, regulation through federal funding and the distorting effects on the federal balance of powers, a majority of the Court held that, with only some exceptions, Commonwealth spending must be accompanied by authorisation in both the form of an appropriation *and* an explicit statutory provision. This, the judges explained, was a necessary implication from the structure and limits of the Australian Senate, which has only limited powers over appropriation legislation under section 53. Thus, to give full effect to the doctrine that the government is responsible to both houses of Parliament, it must seek statutory approval above and beyond appropriations legislation for much of its spending (with some exceptions, for example in relation to the ordinary services of government). This places the federal executive in Australia in a markedly different constitutional position from that in the United Kingdom, where the executive's power to spend and contract is unfettered, subject only to the requirement that it be authorised under an appropriation.

This limitation on executive power had an immediate effect on the legislative structuring of federal spending programs, with wide-ranging remedial legislation rushed through to support more than 400 federal spending programs. The High Court has indicated that much of this remedial legislation is likely to be invalid; the Court in *Williams (No. 2)*[60] struck down that part of the scheme which purported to provide statutory authorisation for the national school chaplaincy program on the basis that it lacked a connection to a federal head of power.

In drawing the extra-textual limitation in *Williams (No. 1)*, the majority of the Court emphasised that the constitutional structure established in Australia is a result of the unique combination of our constitutional history. The limitation is overwhelmingly structural in nature, with the protections it offers having little, if any, effect on individuals.

---

[60] *Williams v. Commonwealth (No. 2)* (2014) 252 CLR 416.

12.2. RESISTANCE TO CERTAIN CONSTITUTIONAL IMPLICATIONS BY THE COURT

Despite this central role played by implications in Australian constitutional law and discourse around the structures of the separation of powers, federalism and representative and responsible government, there remains strong resistance in Australia to broader implications involving the protection of individual *rights*. Even in the context of principles of political democracy, since *Lange* the High Court has consistently emphasised that it does not see such a principle as creating a freestanding or true individual right.[61] Beyond any core political rights to freedom of political expression and participation, the Court has also consistently rejected claims brought before it in the form of implied constitutional rights.

In the context of associational rights, such as the right to freedom of movement and association, the Court has held that these rights are protected insofar as they involve association or movement for the purposes of facilitating the democratic process, particularly freedom of access to the institutions of government, including the seat of government.[62] Several justices in *Kruger* held that this was implicit in the constitutionally prescribed system of responsible and representative government, or in the logic underpinning the implied freedom of political communication.[63] But beyond that, in the case of *Tajjour*, the Court has found that the Constitution does not support the making of any independent implication protecting a wider-ranging right to freedom of association.[64]

Similarly, for rights such as the right to equality or non-discrimination, the Court has expressly held that the text and structure of the Constitution do *not* support the making of any implications of this kind. In *Leeth*, where the issue was one of the discriminatory application of federal sentencing laws across different states, a majority of the Court held that this was a form of discrimination

---

[61] Of course, in a Hohfeldian sense this does create some form of individual right to freedom of political expression, but there is debate as to the extent of this individual right or privilege: see e.g., Adrienne Stone, 'Rights, Personal Rights and Freedoms: The Nature of the Freedom of Political Communication' (2001) 25 *Melbourne University Law Review* 374. See also notes 1–2.
[62] See e.g., *Kruger v. Commonwealth* (1997) 190 CLR 1, 115–16 (Gaudron J), 142 (McHugh J), 157 (Gummow J).
[63] See especially Gaudron J.
[64] *Tajjour v. New South Wales* (2014) 254 CLR 508. See also *Kruger v. Commonwealth* (1997) 190 CLR 1, 157 (Gummow J).

explicitly contemplated by the federal structure of the Constitution. And in *Kruger*, where the issue was one of discrimination against Aboriginal and Torres Strait Islander Peoples as part of a policy of forced removal of children from their families, the Court held that the text of the Constitution did not support the implication of any general principle of substantive equality. 'Whatever may be said of the policy which underlay the impugned provisions', Brennan CJ held, it was 'impossible to derive a restriction of substantive equality to control the legislative power conferred by section 122': there is 'nothing in the text and structure of the Constitution' to support such a limitation.[65] Justice Dawson likewise stressed that 'a doctrine of equality in the operation of laws made under the Constitution [does not] appear from the Constitution' itself, and that, in his view, it was impermissible for the Court 'to read into the fact of agreement any implications which do not appear from the document upon which agreement was reached'.[66] Justice Gaudron held that there was 'no room for any implication of a constitutional right to equality beyond that deriving from Chapter III',[67] and Gummow J that 'in the absence of an anchor in the constitutional text it was [too] a large step to extract from the whole corpus of the common law a "general doctrine of legal equality" and treat it as constitutionally entrenched'.[68]

Even in the context of 'hybrid' rights cases, that is, cases which involve potential limits on federal power in the name of individual rather than state rights, such as sections 51(xxvi) and 51(xxxi), the Court has been reluctant to identify any form of implied limitation on Commonwealth legislative power.[69] In *Kartinyeri*, the Court was asked to consider the scope of the Commonwealth's power, under section 51(xxvi), to make laws with respect to 'the people of any race for whom it is deemed necessary to make special laws'. The Court was urged to construe the power as limited to a power to pass laws for the 'benefit' of the Aboriginal race. Arguments to this effect were made both on the basis of evolving community standards on international human rights law, and the amendment to the Constitution in 1967, which aimed to expand the rights of Indigenous Australians by including them within the scope of the power, or deleting previous language in section 51(xxvi) providing that 'race' for this purpose was any race 'other than the aboriginal race in any State'. Several members of the Court found it unnecessary to address this question, but of

---

[65] (1997) 190 CLR 1, 44–5.
[66] Ibid., 67.
[67] Ibid., 113.
[68] Ibid., 154.
[69] See e.g., discussion in Erin Delaney, 'Justifying Power: Federalism, Immigration, and "Foreign Affairs"' (2013) 8 *Duke Journal of Constitutional Law and Policy* 153.

those justices who did consider the issue, a majority found that there was simply insufficient basis in the *text* of the Constitution for inferring such a limited view of the power.[70] This was despite a very clear shift in other constitutional jurisdictions and internationally toward recognition of a principle of racial non-discrimination.[71] It is also arguably one reason why debate continues in Australia over the need *further* to amend the Constitution to provide constitutional recognition to Aboriginal and Torres Strait Islander Peoples.[72]

12.3. EXPLAINING THE RESISTANCE

What explains this opposition by Australia's High Court to the drawing of rights-based constitutional implications, when in a structural context so many aspects of the Australian constitutional order depend on constitutional implications?

12.3.1. A Legal–Cultural Explanation: Text, Structure and Australia's Partial Bill of Rights

One possible explanation is legal–cultural: it rests on the limited express support in the language and structure of the Australian Constitution for the protection of individual rights *together with* the influence of the *Engineers' Case*, an early decision of the High Court emphasising the centrality of 'text and structure' in Australian constitutional interpretation.

12.3.1.1. Limited Express Textual Recognition of Rights

Compared to many modern democratic constitutions, the text of the Australian Constitution provides limited support for the High Court to play a robust role in the protection of individual rights. It is sometimes suggested that Australia is now the only constitutional democracy in the world without a written Bill of Rights.

---

[70] See Gummow and Hayne JJ in *Kartinyeri v. Commonwealth (Hindmarsh Island Bridge Case)* (1998) 19 CLR 336. Contrast Kirby J.

[71] See e.g., discussion in ibid. (Kirby J, dissenting). See also Expert Panel on Constitutional Recognition of Indigenous Australians, *Recognising Aboriginal and Torres Strait Islander Peoples in the Constitution* (2012) ch. 2; Australian Human Rights Commission, *Can International Comparison of the Racial Discrimination Act 1975* (2008); M. Cherif Bassiouni, 'Human Rights in the Context of Criminal Justice: Identifying International Procedural Protections and Equivalent Protections in National Constitutions' (1993) 3 *Duke Journal of Comparative and International Law* 235, 258–9.

[72] Expert Panel on Constitutional Recognition of Indigenous Australians, note 71, chs 4, 6; Referendum Council, *Final Report* (2017).

But as one of us has suggested elsewhere, this statement is also somewhat misleading: Australia does in fact have at least four express constitutional rights guarantees that, together, could readily be considered a narrow or 'partial' bill of rights. The text of the Constitution explicitly guarantees a right to trial by jury in certain Commonwealth trials (section 80), a right to freedom of religion (section 116), freedom of movement across state lines (section 117) and protection of the right to property against acquisitions by the Commonwealth, other than on just terms (section 51(xxxi)).[73]

What is striking about these provisions, however, is their extreme narrowness in both comparative and democratic terms. Where international human rights law, and most modern democratic constitutions, protect a range of due process rights or rights on the part of criminal defendants, section 80 of the Australian Constitution guarantees a trial by jury for *Commonwealth* indictable offences, where the Commonwealth Parliament itself defines an offence as triable on indictment.[74] Further, the Court has historically divided over the purpose of the guarantee in section 80, whether it is an individual right – 'a protection of the citizen' against the power of the government[75] – or whether it is an institutional guarantee, of predominantly 'public concern', protecting the standards, integrity and impartiality of the administration of criminal justice.[76]

Where international and comparative law gives strong protection to religious liberty, against any form of unreasonable limitation, section 116 of the Australian Constitution simply prohibits the *Commonwealth* Parliament from passing laws with the *purpose* of imposing undue burdens on religious liberty. And where international and comparative human rights instruments protect broad rights to individual liberty, dignity and equality, the Commonwealth Constitution protects only rights to property and free movement across state lines. The narrowness of the Australian Constitution, in this context, is also far from supported by contemporary democratic understandings of rights.[77]

---

[73] See further discussion in George Williams and David Hume, *Human Rights under the Australian Constitution*, 2nd edn (Oxford: Oxford University Press, 2013); Dixon, Supra note 4.

[74] *Ex parte Lowenstein* (1938) 59 CLR 556, 571 (Latham CJ); *Kingswell v. The Queen* (1985) 159 CLR 264; *Cheng v. The Queen* (2000) 203 CLR 248.

[75] See e.g., *Ex parte Lowenstein* (1938) 59 CLR 556, 580 (Dixon and Evatt JJ).

[76] See e.g., *Brown v. The Queen* (1986) 160 CLR 171, 208–9 (Dawson J). The views are not mutually exclusive: Deane J has taken a view of the position that incorporates both objectives: *Kingswell v. The Queen* (1985) 159 CLR 264, 300 (Deane J); *Brown v. The Queen* (1986) 160 CLR 171, 201 (Deane J). Most recently, in *Alqudsi v. The Queen* [2016] HCA 24, the Court endorsed this institutional understanding of the guarantee.

[77] Dixon, Supra note 4, 86–7, citing Brian Galligan, 'Australia Rejection of a Bill-of-Rights' (1990) 28 *Journal of Commonwealth and Comparative Politics* 344; 'Majority Support the Introduction of a Law to Protect Human Rights in Australia' *Amnesty International*, 12 March 2009 www.amnesty

For the High Court, this has meant a number of things. The first is that the text and structure of the Constitution, as a whole, provide limited support for the Court assuming an active role in protecting individual rights or inserting rights protections in areas where the framers were clear they did not wish to grant such protections, such as due process and equal protection rights.[78]

Second, in any given case where the Court is asked to recognise an implied constitutional right, it also means that the Court will face a 'slippery slope' based argument: if it chooses to recognise a right as implicitly protected by the Constitution, it will likely be asked to recognise a large number of other, rights-based implications in the future, which themselves are not strongly grounded in the text and structure of the Constitution. The Court, in such a case, can attempt to identify some reason why the relevant right is particularly tied to the text of the Constitution or is specially deserving of judicial protection from the perspective of other constitutional values or commitments – for example, by connecting it to broader commitments to political democracy or a system of 'representative and responsible government'.[79] But if such an 'allocational' account is unavailable, it will be faced with the clear difficulty that, by deciding to recognise one right, it may end up committing the Court, in the future, to a quite radical departure from existing interpretive principles.[80] This is exactly the kind of 'slippery slope' argument that can persuade a court *not* to endorse a particular principle in the first place.[81]

Members of the High Court have, at times, arguably been quite explicit in identifying this kind of logic as a reason for rejecting various implied rights principles as implicit in the concept of representative democracy recognised by the Constitution. In *Theophanous*, for instance, McHugh J directly challenged the basis of the Court's earlier decision in *ACTV*, identifying an implied right to freedom of political communication, on slippery slope type grounds. If the principle in *ACTV* were grounded in the free-standing notion of representative democracy, McHugh J suggested, it would be difficult to confine the logical consequences of this to the protection of political communication. Instead, the notion of 'representative democracy' could be understood to support a broad range of implications connected to the notions of political

---

.org.au/news/comments/20560/; National Human Rights Consultation Committee, *National Human Rights Consultation Report* (2009); Expert Panel on Constitutional Recognition of Indigenous Australians, note 71.

[78] See further explanation of the lack of concern by the Australian regarding the inclusion of constitutional human rights protections in Williams and Hume, Supra note 73, 60–73.
[79] See e.g., discussion in Dixon, Supra note 4.
[80] On allocational accounts, see e.g., ibid., 91–2.
[81] Compare Eugene Volokh, 'The Mechanisms of the Slippery Slope' (2003) 116 *Harvard Law Review* 1026 on slippery slope arguments generally.

equality, or 'equality or rights and privileges' among citizens.[82] This was also one reason McHugh J favoured a narrower view of the scope and basis of the implied freedom, as more directly connected to the type of 'representative and responsible government' that was given effect to in sections 7, 24, 64 and 128 – a position that logically supports various *political* rights and liberties, but not broader implications protective of individual equality or liberty.[83]

12.3.1.2. *Engineers*' and the Dominance of 'Text and Structure'

These text-based limits in Australia are also reinforced in significance by the longstanding emphasis in legal culture in Australia on the importance of arguments from constitutional 'text and structure'.

This emphasis on text and structure, in Australian legal culture, is often traced to the 1920 decision of the High Court in the *Engineers' Case*:[84] The Court, in the *Engineers' Case*, issued a landmark decision overruling earlier implied doctrines of the Court known as the immunity of instrumentalities and reserved state powers, and in doing so, began a path of asserting the primacy of constitutional text as the basis for constitutional interpretation in Australia.

It was clearly open to the Court in *Engineers*' to justify its decision in more purposive, 'living' constitutional terms: when the Constitution was first adopted, the dominant view of the Constitution was that it was a compact between states, designed to create only limited power on the part of the Commonwealth Parliament to pursue certain common economic and defence interests. Over time, as economic and political conditions changed – i.e., the idea of Australian nationhood was consolidated by war, economic and commercial integration, the unifying force of federal law, the decline of dependence upon British naval and military power and a recognition and acceptance of common external interests and obligations among the states – there was also clearly increased support for a broader definition of Commonwealth power and a weaker notion of state immunity.[85] The Court, however, did not express its decision in these terms.[86] Instead, it framed its decision in terms of a *methodological* critique of earlier cases, as taking too broad and flexible an approach to constitutional interpretation generally and

---

[82] *Theophanous v. Herald & Weekly Times Ltd* (1994) 182 CLR 104, 199–200.
[83] Ibid., 198–201.
[84] See e.g., George Williams, '*Engineers* is Dead, Long Live the Engineers!' (1995) 17 *Sydney Law Review* 62.
[85] *Victoria v. Commonwealth* (1971) 122 CLR 353, 395 (Windeyer J) ('*Payroll Tax Case*').
[86] Cf ibid.

particularly to the drawing of constitutional implications.[87] The majority was particularly critical of the variable, subjective, inconsistent and uncertain nature of the earlier implications as drawn by different judges, noting, for example, that implications drawn from the principle of 'necessity' were 'referable to no more definite standard than the personal opinion of the Judge who declares it'.[88] The Court suggested that the only 'safe course' in interpreting the Constitution was 'to read its language' like any ordinary statute – that is, according to its ordinary and natural meaning, and not by reference to any general theory of *constitutional* interpretation, which depended on individual judges' 'hopes and expectations respecting vague external conditions', or 'implications formed on a vague individual conception of the spirit of the [Constitution as a political] compact'.[89]

The legal orthodoxy in Australia since *Engineers'* has generally been to accept the correctness of the Court's reasoning in these terms, rather than to insist on reinterpreting it in more historically specific terms. This, in turn, has perpetuated a strong emphasis on legalistic approaches to constitutional interpretation, which are firmly grounded in the 'text and structure' of the Constitution, and a wariness of broad forms of constitutional implication, which are more directly founded on value-based, and thus more subjective, constitutional arguments.

In the 1980s and early 1990s during Sir Anthony Mason's tenure as Chief Justice, the High Court sought – to some degree – to challenge this orthodoxy, by encouraging a more transparent, policy-oriented approach to constitutional reasoning.[90] In cases such as *ACTV*, the Court also relied on a more of substantive form of constitutional reasoning to support the development of the implied freedom of political communication to protect political democracy. The Court, however, did not create anything like a complete shift in prevailing legal-cultural understandings or orthodoxies. As Theunis Roux notes, while the Court was operating against the backdrop of important legal changes, such as the *Australia Acts 1986* and an increasingly globalising legal community, there were no *major* external legal or political changes during this period sufficient to *fundamentally* reshape prior legal orthodoxies.[91]

---

[87] (1920) 28 CLR 129, 148 (Knox CJ, Isaacs, Rich and Starke JJ).
[88] Ibid., 142 (Knox CJ, Isaacs, Rich and Starke JJ).
[89] Ibid., 145, 19 (Knox CJ, Isaacs, Rich and Starke JJ).
[90] Leslie Zines, 'Sir Anthony Mason' (2000) 28 *Federal Law Review* 171.
[91] Theunis Roux, 'Re-interpreting "the Mason Court Revolution": An Historical Institutionalist Account of Judge-Driven Constitutional Transformation in Australia' (2015) 43 *Federal Law Review* 1.

A historically specific factor during this period of potentially fundamental change that militated against any seismic shift in Australia's legal-cultural orthodoxy was, at least for several members of the Court, the relatively recent attempts by Justice Lionel Murphy to expand the scope of implied rights under the Constitution. The freshness of Murphy J's legacy at this crucial juncture made it more difficult, both psychologically and politically, for the Court to adopt such an approach. Murphy, a justice of the Court between 1975 and 1986, was a former Labor Attorney-General and an important actor in Prime Minister Gough Whitlam's reform agenda. During his political tenure he had sought to introduce a statutory bill of rights. When he was appointed to the Court he quickly asserted a broad range of implied constitutional right protections, very similar to those contained in his proposed statutory bills of rights.[92] In doing so, he made little attempt to ground those assertions in processes of orthodox legal reasoning, thus attracting the ire of traditional Australian constitutional commentators, practitioners and judges.[93] Over time, Murphy J also became mired in significant personal controversy.[94] The combination of Murphy J's political background, unorthodox legal reasoning and personal controversy also arguably contributed to other justices of the Court distancing themselves, both at the time and in later years, from an approach that in any way resembled that of Murphy J.[95]

In *Miller v. TCN Channel Nine Pty Ltd*, for example, Mason J explicitly rejected Murphy J's suggestion that the Constitution contains an implied common law-style bill of rights, suggesting he could not 'find any basis for implying a new section 92A into the Constitution'.[96] And in later cases, such as *ACTV*, where the Mason Court itself identified the implied freedom of political communication, the majority was quite careful to delimit the scope of such an implication, suggesting that structural implications of this kind

---

[92] *R v. Director-General of Social Welfare, Ex Parte Henry* (1975) 133 CLR 369, 388; *General Practitioners Society v. Commonwealth* (1980) 145 CLR 532; *Ansett Transport Industries (Operations) Pty Ltd v. Wardley* (1980) 142 CLR 237, 267; *Ansett Transport Industries (Operations) Pty Ltd v. Commonwealth* (1977) 139 CLR 54, 88; *Miller v. TCN Channel Nine Pty Ltd* (1986) 161 CLR 556, 582–3. See further Paul Bickovskii, 'No Deliberate Innovators: Mr Justice Murphy and the Australian Constitution' (1977) 8 *Federal Law Review* 460.

[93] George Winterton, 'Extra-Constitutional Notions in Australian Constitutional Law' (1986) 16 *Federal Law Review* 223; Lisbeth Campbell, 'Lionel Murphy and the Jurisprudence of the High Court Ten Years on' (1996) 15 *University of Tasmania Law Review* 22, 26; Bickovskii, Supra note 92, 460.

[94] See discussion in Jenny Hocking, *Lionel Murphy: A Political Biography* (Cambridge: Cambridge University Press, 1997).

[95] Cf Campbell, Supra note 93, 45 (on the rejection of the Murphy approach by Deane, Mason and others on the Mason Court.).

[96] (1986) 161 CLR 556, 579.

could be made only where they were 'logically or practically *necessary* for the preservation of the integrity' of the structure from which they were derived.[97]

In recent years, in affirming and applying various structural constitutional implications such as those recognised in *Kable* and *ACTV*, the Court has gone out of its way to emphasise the degree to which these implications are grounded in express provisions of the constitutional *text*. In the unanimous judgment in *Lange*, which restated the basis and nature of the implied freedom, the Court, now under the leadership of Sir Gerard Brennan, was careful to link it to concepts of representative and responsible government found in the text and structure of the Constitution, rather than more general (Murphy-style) notions of representative democracy. Indeed, in *Lange*, many of the original members of the Court in *ACTV* joined the decision of the Court restating the *ACTV* principle, and emphasising the basis of the implied freedom in particular in the words of sections 7 and 24 of the Constitution, which provide for members of Parliament to be 'directly chosen' by the people. This move, George Williams and David Hume have postulated, can be explained as a response of the Court to the 'activist' criticism that was levelled at it following its earlier decisions, a shift in the composition and therefore interpretative orientation of the Court, a desire to create more certainty for the freedom and 'to confer legitimacy on the exercise of the Court's professed power to strike down legislation on the basis of an implication discerned 90 years after federation'.[98]

Kable cases decided in the last decade have also reframed the doctrine by reference to the essential characteristics of a 'court', a term used in various provisions of Chapter III of the Constitution. In *Forge v. Australian Securities and Investments Commission*, Gummow, Hayne and Crennan JJ explained the *Kable* principle by reference to the requirement in Chapter III that the States retain 'a body fitting the description of "the Supreme Court of a State"', and that State 'courts' maintain 'the defining characteristics of a "court"'.[99] The Court has explained that it is from these textual hooks that limiting concepts such as 'institutional integrity' and 'incompatibility' arise.

The majority's continued distancing of its rights-implication jurisprudence from the approach of Murphy J also arguably continued, or was at least replicated, in its response to later attempts by Justice Michael Kirby to develop more expansive implied rights jurisprudence. Justice Kirby's approach to constitutional interpretation was very different from that of Murphy J. He spent

---

[97] *Australian Capital Television Pty Ltd v. Commonwealth* (1992) 177 CLR 106, 135 (emphasis added).
[98] Williams and Hume, Supra note 73, 173.
[99] (2006) 228 CLR 45, 76.

many pages justifying his judicial conclusions, and he developed a consistent jurisprudential approach across cases. But like Murphy J, Kirby J also ultimately adopted an unorthodox approach to constitutional interpretation: Kirby J argued that international law should not only play an important role in shaping the development of the common law and interpretation of statutes in Australia, but also in the interpretation of the Constitution, particularly in relation to those provisions and limitations that protect rights. For Kirby J, such a role included interpreting the scope of implied constitutional limits – such as the need for an independent and impartial tribunal under the *Kable* principle – consistently with international human rights standards[100] and the resolution of ambiguities in constitutional text by reference to international law.[101]

The most direct – and blistering – criticism of Kirby J's approach came from McHugh J in *Al-Kateb v. Godwin*. McHugh J, a strong proponent of the strict – and by that time uncontroversially orthodox – approach to drawing implications grounded in the text and structure of the Constitution, explained that there was a danger such that the approach advocated by Kirby J could result in judicial amendment of the Constitution, subverting the purpose of the referendum requirements of s 128.[102] 'As a matter of constitutional doctrine', McHugh J declared, 'it must be regarded as heretical'.[103] He then took aim at the position that judges should refer to foreign authority in approaching constitutional interpretation. This, he said, would result in judges being given 'a "loose-leaf" copy of the Constitution'.[104] A constitutional Bill of Rights, he argued, must be achieved through section 128 or not at all. Justice Heydon tallied up the score in *Roach*, noting that Kirby J's approach to using international law in constitutional interpretation has been 'denied by 21 of the Justices of this Court who have considered the matter, and affirmed by only one'.[105] The rejection of Kirby J's approach in this context also had potential connections to, or at least parallels with, the role played by Murphy J in an earlier era. Justice Kirby was unusual among members of the Court in publicly celebrating Murphy J's legacy as a jurist,[106] and because of this, his embrace of international human rights law may itself have suffered from an indirect association

---

[100] See e.g., *Forge v. Australian Securities and Investments Commission* (2006) 228 CLR 45.
[101] See e.g., *Newcrest Mining (WA) Ltd v. Commonwealth* (1997) 190 CLR 513, 657–8; *Kartinyeri v. Commonwealth* (1998) 195 CLR 337, 418 (Kirby J).
[102] *Al-Kateb v. Godwin* (2004) 219 CLR 562, 591–4.
[103] Ibid., 593.
[104] Ibid., 595.
[105] *Roach v. Australian Electoral Commissioner* (2007) 233 CLR 162, 225.
[106] See e.g., www.google.com.au/webhp?sourceid=chrome-instant&ion=1&espv=2&ie=UTF-8#q=justice+kirby+justice+murphy.

to Murphy J.[107] Like Murphy J, by the end of his time on the Court Kirby J was also something of an outsider to the inner workings of the Court and thus not in a position to command broad support for his preferred approach to constitutional interpretation.[108]

12.3.2. A Political–Cultural Explanation: The Shadow of Parliamentary Supremacy and Process-based Theory

Another important explanation for the Court's reluctance to draw particular types of rights implications relates to more distinctly political understandings and attitudes in Australia.[109]

12.3.2.1. Suspicion of Judicial Review of Political Judgments

There is, after all, clear scope for the Australian Parliament to *amend* the scope of both the visible and invisible constitution in this context, to give more express constitutional protection to individual rights. There has been a range of proposals to amend the Constitution, to add further rights protections, over the last few decades, as well as proposals to adopt a range of quasi-constitutional or statutory rights protections.[110] However, almost all of these proposals have failed either at the proposal or referendum stage. Australians

---

[107] For examples of those making connection, albeit in a positive way, see e.g., Scott Guy and Kristy Richardson, 'Justice Murphy and Kirby: Reviving Social Democracy and the Constitution' (2010) 22(1) *Bond Law Review* 26.

[108] See A. J. Brown, *Michael Kirby: Paradoxes and Principles* (Annandale, NSW: Federation Press, 2011).

[109] Legal cultural and political understandings, of course, inevitably transect. Compare Roux, Supra note 91. In some cases, leading members of the judiciary and legal profession have also been at the forefront of public arguments in favour of political over legal constitutionalism in this context. See e.g., *Momcilovic* v. *The Queen* (2011) 245 CLR 1, 177–8 [444]. But contrast James Spigelman, 'The Common Law Bill of Rights' (2008) 3 *Statutory Interpretation and Human Rights: McPherson Lecture Series*; *Al-Kateb* v. *Godwin* (2004) 219 CLR 562 (McHugh J).

[110] One of the interesting questions about statutory rights protection of this kind in Australia is whether, if it had succeeded more generally, it would in fact have been understood as constitutional or quasi-constitutional in status, or rather relegated to a more purely 'statutory' status, in ways that would have made it a candidate for being described as part of the 'invisible constitution' in a more sociological sense. For debate about this question of the relationship between statutory and common law norms, and the definition of the Constitution in a sociological sense, in Australia, see e.g., Rosalind Dixon and Jason Spinak, 'Common law liability of clubs for injury to intoxicated persons: *Cole* v. *South Tweed Heads Rugby League Football Club Ltd*' (2004) 27 *University of New South Wales Law Journal* 816; Rosalind Dixon and George Williams, 'Introduction' in Rosalind Dixon and George Williams (eds.), *The High Court, the Constitution, and Australian Politics* (Cambridge: Cambridge University Press, 2015).

are variously suspicious of judicial review of human rights protections and complacent about the sufficiency of current protections.[111]

In a capital "C" constitutional context, the most recent constitutional amendment attempt – in 1988 – to expand rights protection met with a notable lack of support. When recommendations were made by the Constitutional Commission to amend the Constitution to insert a number of additional rights-based guarantees, the Parliament chose to put only a narrow portion of those proposals to the electorate at a national referendum – i.e., proposals to broaden the existing guarantees of freedom of religion, trial by jury and acquisition of property on just terms.[112] At the relevant referendum, the proposals also gained only 30.79 per cent of the national vote. Earlier, more successful referendums – such as the 1967 referendum that removed two provisions that discriminated against Indigenous Australians and the 1977 referendum, providing a mandatory retirement age for federal judges and giving people in the Territory the right to vote in referendums held under section 128 of the Constitution have also not been explicitly rights-oriented or conferred broad discretion on the judicial branch to determine their scope.[113]

In a quasi-constitutional or statutory context, there has been successful reform in the last two decades in Australia at a *state and territory level*. In 2004, the Australian Capital Territory enacted the *Human Rights Act*, giving courts broad power to reinterpret legislation so as to render it rights compatible, and to make non-binding declarations of 'inconsistent interpretation' modelled on the remedies available under section 4 of the United Kingdom *Human Rights Act*. In 2006, Victoria enacted a similar form of statutory charter in the form of the Victorian *Charter of Rights and Responsibilities*. While both models empower the judiciary to consider the severity of rights breaches and weigh them against other public objectives in the context of statutory interpretation, they fall far short of giving the judiciary ultimate power in determining such questions.

At a federal level, however, there has been far more limited change, driven at least in part by reluctance to involve the judiciary in rights analysis. Several attempts were made in the 1970s and 1980s to introduce a statutory bill of rights at a Commonwealth level, but these proposals consistently failed to gain the necessary degree of political support.[114] And in 2011, despite calls by a special

---

[111] Hilary Charlesworth, 'The Australian Reluctance about Rights' (1993) 31 *Osgoode Hall Law Journal* 195, 196.
[112] *Constitution Alteration (Rights and Freedoms)* 1988 (Cth).
[113] On the nature of the amendments, and the interpretive questions raised, see e.g., Rosalind Dixon, 'Amending Constitutional Identity' (2012) 33 *Cardozo Law Review* 1847. See also Beryl Bainbridge etc., history cited in Amending Identity.
[114] See e.g., Williams and Hume, Supra note 73, 207–8; Constitutional Commission, *Final Report of the Constitutional Commission* (1988) ss 9.148–9.151; Expert Panel on Constitutional Recognition of Indigenous Australians, note 71, 169.

committee headed by leading lawyer Father Frank Brennan, tasked with investigating the question of enacting a UK-style national human rights charter, the Commonwealth Parliament adopted a far more modest form of legislative change. Vocal opponents to the introduction of a national human rights charter – who were often political and legal elites – pointed to a shift in power from the political branch to the judicial branch in the jurisdictions of Canada, New Zealand and the United Kingdom, despite the 'ultimate' authority resting with the politicians. They therefore argued that even a statutory bill of rights would result in a fundamental shift in constitutional and political power from the elected legislature to the 'unelected judges'.[115] Parliament's muted response to the Brennan Report was to enact the *Human Rights (Parliamentary Scrutiny) Act 2011*, which requires a parliamentary committee to test the compatibility of legislation against a range of international human rights norms, but explicitly attempts to avoid any form of judicial enforcement of relevant rights.[116]

More recently, the political suspicion of judicial review of parliamentary judgment in the rights arena also manifested in opposition to a proposal by a government-commissioned Expert Panel to introduce a racial anti-discrimination clause into the Constitution as part of the wider recognition of the history, culture and rights of Indigenous peoples. Opposition to the proposed section 116A – which would have banned racial discrimination – relied on similar arguments to those raised against a statutory bill of rights. This opposition has significantly shaped the course of the debate on constitutional recognition, including the development of a new proposal to insert a *political* limitation rather than a *legal* limitation to protect the interests of First Nations. The proposal takes the rough form of a constitutionalised Indigenous representative body that must be consulted by Parliament in legislating on matters affecting Indigenous peoples.[117] The turn in this debate towards a legislative, *political* protection of rights, and away from conferring any power on the judiciary for making unreviewable judgments that might require the

---

[115] See e.g., Bob Carr, 'Bill of Rights is the Wrong Call' *The Australian*, 9 May 2009, www.theaustralian.com.au/news/inquirer/bill-of-rights-is-the-wrong-call/story-e6frg6z6-1225710664130; James Allen, 'Let's Draw a Line through a Bill of Rights', *Sydney Morning Herald*, 26 September 2005 www.smh.com.au/news/opinion/lets-draw-a-line-through-a-bill-of-rights/2005/09/25/1127586742586.html, and Philip Ruddock, 'Bills of Rights Do Not Protect Freedoms' *Sydney Morning Herald*, 31 August 2007, www.smh.com.au/news/opinion/bills-of-rights-do-not-protect-freedoms/2007/08/30/1188067275092.html.

[116] See Rosalind Dixon, 'A New (Inter)National Human Rights Experiment for Australia' (2012) 23 *Public Law Review* 75; George Williams and Lisa Burton, 'Australia's Exclusionary Parliamentary Model of Rights Protection' (2013) 34 *Statute Law Review* 58.

[117] See further on this political proposal, referred to as a 'Voice to Parliament', the *Uluru Statement from the Heart*; and the Referendum Council, *Final Report* (2017).

balancing of rights and other constitutional values is consistent with Australia's dominant political-legal community's greater comfort with legislative judgment in such areas.

This, we suggest, is also ultimately explained by the longstanding resistance in Australian *political* culture – particularly elite political culture – toward almost any forms of rights-based judicial review – whether based on express or implied (or extra-textual) constitutional sources.

The wider Australian public has not always been suspicious of judicial review of this kind. In a public poll conducted in 1991, 59 per cent of respondents supported the courts having the ultimate authority to determine rights and freedoms, in comparison to 41 per cent who thought that role should fall to Parliament.[118] This survey was undertaken prior to the Mason Court's controversial decisions in *Mabo*, *ACTV* and *Nationwide News* (all decided in 1992).[119] While there has been no equivalent survey undertaken subsequently, in 2009 the Brennan Committee conducted a large public consultation regarding the implementation of a statutory national human rights charter. The Committee received written submissions and conducted sixty-six community roundtables. The Committee summarised these consultations to the effect that there was clear 'majority support' for a *statutory* human rights instrument, though also substantial opposition to any constitutional and statutory rights instruments that would cause a transfer of power to 'unelected judges'.[120]

Australian political and legal elites have tended to be consistently wary of broad-based judicial scrutiny in the domain of individual rights – or open-ended forms of judicial scrutiny of legislative policy choices. Foundationally, this suspicion can be traced back to the inherently contradictory nature of the two constitutional traditions that most heavily influenced Australian constitutionalism: the British principle of parliamentary supremacy, and the principle inherent in the adoption of a written, US-style constitution that sets out the minimum rules that all actors within the legal system must comply with, enforced by an independent judicial branch. In the context of individual rights (that is, outside of federalism and separation of powers), British traditions have also largely predominated. While, as we identify previously, it is not correct to say that the Australian Constitution contains no bill of rights, it is

---

[118] Brian Galligan et al., *Rights in Australia 1991–1992: National Household Sample* (Canberra, ACT: Australian Data Archive, Australian National University, 1992).
[119] Paul Kildea and George Williams, 'The Mason Court' in Rosalind Dixon and George Williams, *The High Court, The Constitution and Australian Politics* (Cambridge: Cambridge University Press, 2015) 244, 257.
[120] Commonwealth of Australia, *National Human Rights Consultation Report*' (September 2009) ('Brennan Report') 16.

notable, however, that the rights it protects are extremely narrow or 'partial' compared to background rights commitments in Australian society. Indeed, the Australian framers were either expressly antagonistic to the inclusion of too many individual rights guarantees in the Constitution, concerned, as they were, about maintaining the colonies' racially discriminatory policies and promoting the White Australia Policy, or unperturbed about the need for such guarantees, being inclined to trust the democratic institutions of government to provide the necessary protections.[121] Hilary Charlesworth has explained the framers lack of concern with constitutional rights protection by reference to a 'confidence in a philosophy of utilitarianism'.[122]

In interpreting various express rights, the High Court has also adopted an extremely narrow approach which largely eliminates any role in second-guessing legislative choices regarding, for example, the appropriate relationship between the government and the church under section 116 or when an individual ought to be accorded the right to trial by jury under section 80.

Despite the adoption of a written constitution, Australian legal and political elites have thus tended to maintain strong resistance to forms of judicial review that depend on open-ended, proportionality-style judgments about the justice or merits of legislative policies. This reflects a historically grounded, cultural assumption of the wisdom of legislative judgment in achieving just, fair and equitable government and the protection of individual liberty.[123]

Where the Court has confronted issues involving proportionality-style judgments, it has also often encountered resistance. This is particularly true for areas touching on individual rights, or broad-ranging social and political questions. In the context of section 92 of the Constitution, the constitutional guarantee of freedom of interstate trade and commerce, for instance, the Court has adopted a proportionality-style test largely without controversy. Thus in *Betfair v. Western Australia,* in 2008, the Court indicated that the preferred test for determining whether a burden on interstate trade and commerce would breach the guarantee should be one of 'reasonable necessity' for achieving a non-protectionist regulatory purpose or whether it was *not disproportionate* to such a purpose.[124] The same is also true for attempts by the

---

[121] See Dixon, Supra note 4; Sir Anthony Mason, 'The Role of a Constitutional Court in a Federation: A Comparison of the Australian and the United States Experience' (1986) 16 *Federal Law Review* 1, 4.

[122] Charlesworth, Supra note 111, 197.

[123] Jeffrey Goldsworthy, 'The Constitutional Protection of Rights in Australia' in Greg Craven (ed.) *Australian Federation Towards the Second Century* (Melbourne: Melbourne University Press 1992) 151, 152–4.

[124] (2008) 234 CLR 418.

Court to articulate limits on the scope of the Commonwealth's purposive and incidental legislative powers: in *Burton* v. *Honan*, a case involving the scope of the Commonwealth's power to seize goods as part of a customs regime, Dixon CJ again held that the scope of the incidental power was to be understood in terms of a test of 'reasonable necessity' and the proportionality judgment this implies has occasioned little comment or resistance.[125]

But in the domain of individual rights or areas involving broader social and political choices, there has been far more resistance to such an approach. In the context of the implied freedom of political communication, for example, for a long period the Court explicitly argued that the proportionality-style analysis that it engaged in in this context was quite *different* from the four stage-test employed in foreign and international rights-jurisprudence – i.e., a test of the *legitimacy* of the government's purpose, the *suitability* of the law to achieving the stated objective, the *necessity* of the law to achieving that objective and to which the law was *adequate in the balance* of benefits versus costs it imposed or proportionate in the true or strict sense.[126] Indeed, there was an explicit rejection by the Court of the idea that its test involved the kind of subjective judicial 'balancing' of competing rights and interests of the kind implicit in the fourth stage of any proportionality analysis. In *Coleman* v. *Power*, for instance, McHugh J responded to Adrienne Stone's argument that the Court's insistence that the implication was drawn from the text and structure of the Constitution disguised a value-laden form of review of legislative action by *denying* the role of judicial value judgment in the test.[127]

Only in 2015, in *McCloy* v. *New South Wales*, did a majority of the Court endorse the three-stage proportionality test that is now seen in various forms in Europe and in the Supreme Court of Canada, and for the first time explain that the Court would often be engaged in a value judgment, a necessarily somewhat subjective weighing of the objective and the rights incursion. Even in this admission, the Court was also wary of claiming too broad a discretion to review legislative policy. The majority explained the test 'does not entitle the courts to substitute their own assessment for that of the legislative

---

[125] (1952) 86 CLR 169.
[126] Moshen Cohen-Eliya and Iddo Porat, *Proportionality and Constitutional Culture* (Cambridge: Cambridge University Press 2013); Alec Stone Sweet and Jud Mathews, 'Proportionality Balancing and Global Constitutionalism' (2008) 47 *Columbia Journal of Transnational Law* 72; Matthias Klatt and Moritz Meister, *The Constitutional Structure of Proportionality* (Oxford: Oxford University Press 2012); Vicki Jackson, 'Constitutional Law in an Age of Proportionality' (2015) 124 *Yale Law Journal* 3094.
[127] Adrienne Stone, 'The Limits of Constitutional Text and Structure: Standards of Review and the Freedom of Political Communication' (1999) 23 *Melbourne University Law Review* 668, 704.

decision-maker'.[128] They explained it remained the role of the legislature 'to determine which policies and social benefits ought to be pursued'.[129] They reinforced the importance of the boundaries between the branches of government. In that same case, Gageler J also noted reservations about the majority's approach, including that the final 'adequate in its balance' criterion failed to provide an appropriate degree of guidance for the exercise of the judicial discretion; he argued that such a generalised and abstract principle would not be able to promote consistency or predictability in judicial decisions.

12.3.2.2. Process-based Theory

Another potential-related explanation for this unwillingness to support rights-based judicial review by the High Court could be a belief, in Australia, in a form of John Hart Ely-style 'process-based' theory of judicial review – according to which the key function of the Court is to police the boundaries of the political process and ensure that the channels for political change remain open, rather than to adjudicate on the substantive merits of the laws and policies produced by that process.[130] Representation-reinforcing theories of this kind have been extremely influential in many constitutional democracies outside the United States,[131] and have been openly defended by some of the current members of Australia's High Court.[132] They also clearly have some resonance with the emphasis by the Court, in cases such as *Lange*, on its role in protecting principles of 'representative and responsible government' – and not commitments to substantive democracy, more generally.[133]

One difficulty with this account, however, is that it is not one that is explicitly endorsed by the broader political culture in Australia or by key political elites who oppose the expansion of rights-based judicial review.[134] It is also an account that suggests that the High Court should have been willing to

---

[128] (2015) 89 ALJR 857, [89].
[129] Ibid. [90].
[130] John Hart Ely, *Democracy and Distrust: A Theory of Judicial Review* (Cambridge, MA: Harvard University Press 1980). We are indebted to Iddo Porat for pushing us on this point.
[131] See e.g., discussion of New Zealand in Rosalind Dixon, 'Partial Bills of Rights' (2015) 63 *American Journal of Comparative Law* 101.
[132] Stephen Gageler, 'Beyond the Text: A Vision of the Structure and Function of the Constitution' [2009] *NSW Bar Association News* 14.
[133] See *Lange v. Australian Broadcasting Corporation* (1997) 189 CLR 520; *Theophanous v. Herald & Weekly Times Ltd* (1994) 182 CLR 104 (McHugh J).
[134] See e.g., Julian Leeser and Ryan Haddrick (eds.), *Don't Leave Us with the Bill: The Case Against an Australian Bill of Rights* (Barton, ACT: Menzies Research Centre 2009); Bob Carr, Supra note 115; Bernice Carrick, 'Freedom on the Wallaby: A Comparison of Arguments in the Australian Bill of Rights Debate' (2010) 1 *Western Australian Jurist* 68.

recognise at least some form of implied right to equality or implied protection for 'discrete and insular minorities' in the political process.[135] The Court, however, in cases such as *Leeth* and *Kruger* has consistently rejected the suggestion that it should play a role in protecting minorities in this way, or recognise any form of general implied principle of non-discrimination under the Constitution.

While the political and judicial resistance to rights-based review may be weaker for core political rights than other more substantive rights it is still an important source of pressure pushing against the recognition of almost all forms of rights-based judicial review in Australia – of both an express and an implied kind.

12.4. CONCLUSION

Constitutional implications play a central role in the jurisprudence and the day-to-day working of Australia's constitutional order. They inform the scope and operation of the constitutional structures: the separation of powers, federalism, and responsible government and key aspects of the Australian democratic system including freedom of political communication and universal access to the franchise. Yet Australian constitutional culture remains suspicious of the idea of constitutional implications in the domain of individual rights.

In this chapter, we explored two broad, interrelated reasons for this division. First, we suggest, it can be traced to Australia's early embrace of legalistic constitutional interpretative methodology and wariness of drawing implications from outside the constitutional text and structure of the Constitution, combined with the narrow recognition given to individual rights in the text and structure of the Australian Constitution, which make any form of rights-based implication under the Constitution susceptible to significant *legal-methodological* objections. Second, we suggest that it can be traced to Australia's longstanding embrace of political over legal forms of constitutionalism in respect of the protection of individual rights or resistance to both express and implied forms of rights-based judicial review.

What does this tell us more generally about the drawing, scope and operation of 'the invisible constitution' in the form of constitutional implications from a comparative perspective? It suggests that, in each country, the acceptance and scope of implications will be shaped by a number of factors,

---

[135] Ely, Supra note 130, on footnote 4 in *United States v. Carolene Products Co*, 304 U.S. 144 (1938).

including formal features of the written or visible constitution, such as its language and structure and more informal aspects of local constitutional culture, including a constitution's history and relationship to contemporary legal and political understandings. Ultimately these factors intersect and interact in complex ways, and cannot be analysed independently. But they are important factors to consider if we are to try to understand the invisible constitution in comparative perspective.

In Australia, we suggest, the current dualism in the High Court's role in protecting constitutional structure versus individual rights is sustained by a combination of a legal interpretive orthodoxy that emphasises the importance of 'text and structure' in the interpretation of the Constitution, prior textual and structural choices by the drafters of the Australian Constitution, which give limited express support to individual rights and political-cultural obstacles to achieving change to this position via either formal or informal means.[136] If any one of these three dimensions explaining Australian constitutional practice were to change, we believe, it might be enough to create a more robust rights-based invisible constitution in Australia. But without such a change, it seems likely that the trajectory of 'the invisible constitution' in the form of constitutional implications in Australia will remain firmly bifurcated.

---

[136] Compare Roux, Supra note 91.

13

Malaysia's Invisible Constitution

Yvonne Tew

13.1. INTRODUCTION

Religion has become the great fault line of the Malaysian constitutional order. Contemporary Malaysian politics and adjudication are divided by competing views over the constitutional identity of the modern Malaysian state as secular or Islamic. At the heart of this debate is Article 3(1) of the Federal Constitution of Malaysia, which declares 'Islam is the religion of the Federation; but other religions may be practised in peace and harmony'. Over the last two decades, the clause constitutionalising Islam as the state religion has increasingly been pitted as being in tension with the right of religious freedom guaranteed under Article 11(1).[1] This chapter considers the invisible constitution in connection with the Malaysian Constitution's religion clauses. It explores the conceptual aspect of the unwritten, extra-textual influences surrounding the interpretation of the religion clauses, and also examines the deeper foundations of the constitutional framework underlying the visible text of Article 3(1).

Malaysia's religion clauses provide a focal point for examining the invisible constitution in two main ways. The first aspect of invisibility is connected to the expansion of Islam's position in the constitutional order by political and judicial actors through means outside textual constitutional change. Although the text of Article 3(1) has remained unchanged since the nation's founding, Islam's role in the Malaysian Constitution has been expanded through unwritten, extra-textual means in contemporary constitutional discourse. The invisible elevation of Islam's supremacy in recent decades has taken place through expansive judicial interpretations of Article 3(1) by prioritising Islam's place over other constitutional norms. This approach, in effect, amounts to a claim that Article 3(1) gives rise to an implication of Islam's primacy in Malaysia's constitutional order. The invisible Islamisation of judicial discourse

---

[1] Fed. Const. (Malay.), Article 11(1) ('[e]very person has the right to profess and practice his religion ...').

has also taken place through judges referring to sources beyond the Constitution, like Islamic texts and principles, in judicial reasoning when deciding cases in the civil courts.

A second, contrasting approach to Malaysia's invisible Constitution is to have recourse to the Constitution's original framework. Invisibility in this sense refers to the architecture of the Constitution – the overarching constitutional structure and commitments underlying the surface of its visible text. Malaysia's Constitution came into force at the birth of a newly independent state, setting in place a framework for constitutional governance at the nation's founding. Those who defend the Constitution's secular nature argue that constitutional history and the original understanding of the constitutional bargain at the time it was framed are crucial sources establishing the secular basis underlying the text of Article 3(1). Understood properly, these unwritten constitutional fundamentals supply the framework for interpreting the written document. On this account of Malaysia's invisible Constitution, the secular basis on which the Constitution was founded as well as its structural principles and fundamental rights guarantees are integral to Malaysia's constitutional core.

Section 13.2 of this chapter begins by setting the background for discussing the Malaysian Constitution's religion clauses. It describes the constitution-making process behind the constitutional provisions on religion and the growing Islamisation phenomenon in the contemporary Malaysian state. Section 13.3 examines the role of the courts and the constitutional adjudication relating to religion in Malaysia. Section 13.4 discusses the religion clauses and their connection to the invisible constitution in Malaysia. It explores the expansion of Islam's place in the constitutional order through extra-textual means, as well as the use of constitutional history to uncover the Constitution's unwritten secular basis. Section 13.5 offers some concluding reflections on the observations gained from the Malaysian example for broader comparative understandings.

13.2. CONSTITUTIONALISING RELIGION

13.2.1. *Constitution-making and the Islamic Establishment Clause*

The Constitution of Malaya was conceived in the post-colonial climate of a nation on the cusp of independence.[2] The Independence Constitution

---

[2] See generally Rais Yatim, 'The Road to Merdeka,' in Andrew Harding and J. P. Lee (eds.) *Constitutional Landmarks in Malaysia: The First 50 Years 1957–2007* (Kuala Lumpur: LexisNexis, 2007), 1.

came into force when the Federation of Malaya ceased to be a British colony and became an independent state on 31 August 1957, following negotiations between the newly elected local political leaders and the departing British colonial powers. It would later become the basis for the Federal Constitution of Malaysia, when Singapore and the North Borneo states of Sabah and Sarawak joined Malaya in 1963 to become a new Federation: Malaysia.[3]

Five legal experts from the United Kingdom and the Commonwealth were appointed to form a constitutional commission chaired by Britain's Lord Reid, a Lord of Appeal in Ordinary, to draft the constitution for the newly independent state.[4] This was the result of a deliberate decision by the local Alliance political party led by Tunku Abdul Rahman;[5] the Malayan leaders gave the Reid Constitutional Commission specific terms of reference that the local representatives had already negotiated and agreed on.[6] The Commission's task was essentially to translate into legal terms that which had already been politically settled.[7]

The Constitution that was drafted established a federal system of government with a legislative, executive and judicial branch,[8] and a constitutional monarch – the *Yang di-Pertuan Agong* – as the head of the Federation.[9] Malaysia's constitutional structure is based on a parliamentary system modelled after Westminster, and contains an explicit bill of rights.[10] The power of judicial review over the constitutionality of legislation and executive action is implicitly assumed as a natural corollary of the Constitution's supremacy clause.[11]

---

[3] Singapore would leave the Federation two years later to form its own separate, independent state. Sabah and Sarawak remain within the Malaysian Federation, which currently consists of thirteen states and the three federal territories of Kuala Lumpur, Labuan and Putrajaya.

[4] See Joseph M. Fernando, *The Making of the Malayan Constitution* (Kuala Lumpur: MBRAS, 2002), 95.

[5] See Joseph M. Fernando, *Federal Constitutions: A Comparative Study of Malaysia and the United States* (Kuala Lumpur: University of Malaya Press, 2007), 12–13 (explaining that 'the choice of an independent body made up of legal experts from the Commonwealth was a conscious choice of the ruling Alliance party and was intended to avoid local prejudices in the framing of the Constitution').

[6] Federation of Malaya Constitutional Commission, *Report of the Federation of Malaya Constitutional Commission* (1957) [3], [hereinafter 'Reid Report'].

[7] Andrew Harding, *The Constitution of Malaysia: A Contextual Analysis* (Oxford: Hart Publishing, 2012), 32.

[8] Fed. Const. (Malay.), pt. IV, arts. 39–65; pt. IX, arts. 121–31.

[9] Ibid., pt. IV, arts. 32–7.

[10] Ibid., pt. II, arts. 5–13.

[11] Ibid., pt. I, Article 4(1) ('[t]his Constitution is the supreme law of the Federation and any law ... which is inconsistent with this Constitution shall, to the extent of the inconsistency, be void'.).

The Independence – or *Merdeka* – Constitution was fashioned at the birth of a new nation attempting to accommodate the competing demands of a pluralistic society made up of a Malay ethnic majority group and non-Malay – primarily Chinese and Indian – ethnic minorities.[12] It was a document founded on the basis of the constitutional bargain established at independence. As the result of inter-ethnic negotiations and compromise, a clause declaring that 'Islam is the religion of the Federation; but other religions may be practised in peace and harmony' was eventually included as Article 3(1) of the Constitution.[13] Understanding the text of Article 3(1) requires locating it in its historical and political context.

The Reid Constitutional Commission, the drafters of the Independence Constitution, initially rejected the suggestion that a provision declaring Islam as the religion of the Federation be included in the draft Constitution.[14] The Malay rulers of the various Malayan states, concerned that a clause establishing an official religion would encroach on their traditional positions as the head of Islam in their respective states, supported the Reid Commission's decision not to include an Islamic establishment clause.[15]

The main push for a declaration of Islam as the religion of the Federation came from the Alliance, a coalition of three political parties – the United Malays National Organization (UMNO), the Malayan Chinese Association (MCA) and the Malayan Indian Congress (MIC) – which would later become the *Barisan Nasional* ruling coalition after the country's independence.[16] UMNO, the Malay constituent of the Alliance, sought the inclusion of the Islamic establishment clause as part of a larger package of demands in which religion was connected to Malay special privileges and quotas, language and citizenship, not because it had a particular vision of imposing Islamic law on the Federation.[17] The Reid Commission rejected the Alliance's initial proposal; its Report also emphasised that there was 'universal agreement' that 'if

---

[12] *Merdeka* is the Malay word for independence.
[13] Fed. Const. (Malay.), pt. I, Article 3(1). See generally Joseph M. Fernando, 'The Position of Islam in the Constitution of Malaysia' (2006) 37 *Journal of Southeast Asian Studies* 249.
[14] See Reid Report, note 6. For a comprehensive examination of the historical sources surrounding the drafting of the position of Islam in the Constitution of Malaysia, see Fernando, note 7. See Harding, note 7; Kristen Stilt, 'Contextualizing Constitutional Islam: The Malayan Experience' (2015) 13 *International Journal of Constitutional Law* 407.
[15] Harding, Supra note 7, 39.
[16] The Alliance Party was the precursor to the National Front (*Barisan Nasional*), the ruling political coalition in Malaysia. *Barisan Nasional* is made up of three parties, each representing one of the three major ethnic communities.
[17] Stilt, Supra note 14, 410, 430.

any such a provision were inserted it must be made clear that it would not in any way affect the civil rights of non-Muslims'.[18]

Significantly, there was no suggestion that the new nation would not be a secular state, even from the proponents of a clause declaring Islam as the religion of the Federation. The Alliance Party's own memorandum stated: 'The religion of Malaysia shall be Islam. The observance of this principle shall not impose any disability on non-Muslim nationals professing and practicing their own religions, and shall not imply that the State is not a secular State'.[19]

Only one member of the Constitutional Commission supported the inclusion of a declaration establishing Islam as the state religion: Justice Abdul Hamid from Pakistan. Yet he, too, thought that such a provision would be 'innocuous', writing in the Reid Report that such a clause would not 'impose any disability on non-Muslim citizens' nor 'prevent the State from being a secular State'.[20]

Negotiations between the Alliance Party and the Working Party in charge of reviewing the draft Constitution proceeded on the understanding that a provision declaring Islam as the official religion would not undermine the secular basis of the new nation. The Alliance coalition maintained that such a provision would serve a symbolic purpose, rather than have any practical effect.[21] Tunku Abdul Rahman, the leader of the Alliance Party and later Malaysia's first Prime Minister, declared unequivocally that 'the whole Constitution was framed on the basis that the Federation would be a secular state'.[22]

On the basis of these explicit assurances that the insertion of the declaration would be symbolic and would not comprise their rights as non-Muslims, the non-Malay political parties accepted the insertion of the declaration on Islam.[23] Numerous historical sources document this common understanding among all the parties involved in the nation's founding. The Colonial Office in London finally accepted the insertion of the Islamic constitutional clause, noting in its memorandum that the Alliance delegation had 'stressed that they had no intention of creating a Muslim theocracy and that Malaya would be a secular State'.[24]

---

[18] Reid Report, Supra note 14, [169].
[19] Alliance Memorandum to the Reid Constitutional Commission, 27 September 1956, 19.
[20] Reid Report, Supra note 14, [11].
[21] Joseph M. Fernando, Supra note 13, 258.
[22] Ibid., 258 (citing Minutes of the 19th Meeting of the Working Party, 17 April 1957, CO 941/87).
[23] Ibid., 258.
[24] Ibid., 260 (citing Memorandum by Jackson, Colonial Office, 23 May 1957, CO 1030/494 [20]).

Back in Malaya, the Alliance government tabled a White Paper on the new draft Constitution in Parliament, which explained:

> There has been included in the proposed Federation Constitution a declaration that Islam is the religion of the Federation. This will in no way affect the present position of the Federation as a secular state, and every person will have the right to profess and practice his own religion and the right to propagate his religion.[25]

Soon after, the British Parliament passed the Federation of Malaya Independence Bill, creating a sovereign state and crystallising the newly drafted Constitution into force.

Article 3(1) of the new Federal Constitution states: 'Islam is the religion of the Federation; but other religions may be practised in peace and harmony in any part of the Federation'. The intentions of those involved in the constitution-making process affirm that the provision was not meant to affect the secular basis of the state.

The text of Article 3 reflects this basic understanding. The Article 3(1) clause establishing Islam as the religion of the Federation provides in the same provision that 'other religions may be practised in peace and harmony'. Additionally, Article 3(4) specifies that: 'Nothing in this Article derogates from any other provision of this Constitution'. And, under the Constitution's bill of rights, Article 11(1) guarantees that 'every person has the right to profess and practice' his or her religion.[26]

13.2.2. *The Politicisation of Islam*

Growing Islamist political and social discourse in Malaysia over the past three decades, however, has challenged the established understanding of the Article 3 clause declaring Islam as the state religion. The politicisation of Islam has increasingly been at the forefront of the battleground between the UMNO, which is part of the *Barisan Nasional* coalition, and the opposition Islamic party, the Pan-Malaysian Islamic Party (PAS). PAS's political platform has been to project itself as the authentic Islamic party as compared to the ruling party. In response to PAS, UMNO expanded its own campaign of Islamisation. This set the stage for an Islamisation race between PAS and

---

[25] *White Paper on the Federation of Malaya Constitutional Proposals 1957* (Kuala Lumpur: Government Printer, 1957), 18; *Legislative Council Paper No. 42 of 1957*.
[26] Article 11(1).

UMNO beginning in the 1980s and intensifying in the 1990s to secure the support of the Malay–Muslim electorate.

Against this backdrop of political competition between UMNO and PAS, on 29 September 2001, then Prime Minister Mahathir Mohamad made the unprecedented declaration that 'Malaysia is an Islamic state'.[27] In 2007, Deputy Prime Minister Najib Tun Razak – now the current Prime Minister – endorsed Mahathir's pronouncement with his assertion that: 'Islam is our official religion and we are an Islamic state'.[28]

The Islamisation phenomenon has pushed the position of Islam in the Malaysian constitutional system into the spotlight of public discourse. At the centre of this debate is the Article 3(1) declaration that 'Islam is the religion of the Federation; but other religions may be practised in peace and harmony in any part of the Federation'. Those who support Islam's supremacy argue that the establishment of Islam in Article 3(1) provides the justification for an expanded role for Islam in the public sphere.[29] Secularists, on the other hand, argue that the clause was intended by the framers to establish Islam as the official religion for ceremonial purposes and that the foundations of the Malaysian constitutional order are generally secular in nature.[30]

---

[27] See 'Malaysia Recognised as Islamic Nation' *New Straits Times* (11 August 2001) 4. See also ibid., clxxv.

[28] 'Malaysia Not Secular State, says Najib,' *Bernama* (17 July 2007) www.bernama.com/bernama/v3/news_lite.php?id=273699. See also Clarence Thomas, 'Islamic State Label Sparks Controversy in Malaysia,' *Reuters* (25 July 2007). For recent affirmations of the *Barisan Nasional* government's position, see 'BN Government Committed to Make Malaysia an Islamic State,' *Malay Mail Online* (14 October 2017), www.themalaymailonline.com/malaysia/article/bn-government-committed-in-making-malaysia-an-islamic-state.

[29] See e.g., Abdul Aziz Bari, 'Islam in the Federal Constitution: A Commentary on the Decision of Meor Atiqulrahman' (2000) 2 Malayan Law Journal cxxix, cxxxv (arguing that 'history and the essential character of the country' are the 'most important' reasons supporting Islam's supremacy); Mohamed Ismail Shariff, 'The Legislative Jurisdiction of the Federal Parliament in Matters Involving Islamic Law' (2005) 3 Malayan Law Journal cv, cx ('[t]here is nothing in Article 3 that restricts the natural meaning of the term "Islam". And there is no reason to circumscribe its meaning to rituals and ceremonies only ... It is suggested that what the framers of the Constitution have in fact done is to resurrect the lost or hidden power relating to Islamic law, that which was taken away by the British, and entrenched it in Article 3'.).

[30] See e.g., Ahmad F. Yousif, *Religious Freedom, Minorities and Islam* (Selangor: IIUM Press, 1998), 171 ('[f]irst and foremost, it should be stated that Malaysia is not an Islamic state'); Ismail Mohamad Abu Hassan, *Introduction to Malaysian Legal History* (Selangor: Ilmiah Publishers, 2004), 147 (supporting the view that Islam is meant to be recognised formally in rituals and government ceremonies of the Federation, and not as the basis for the law of Malaysia); Benjamin Dawson and Steven Thiru, 'The Lina Joy Case and the Future of Religious Freedom in Malaysia' (2007) *Lawasia Journal* 151; Tommy Thomas, 'The Social Contract: Malaysia's Constitutional Covenant' (2008) 1 Malayan Law Journal cxxxii. See also Andrew Harding, 'The Keris, the Crescent and the Blind Goddess: The State, Islam and the Constitution in Malaysia'

This push for an Islamic state, involving a prioritised role for Islam in the constitutional order, is further complicated by the broader social and political context in Malaysia. Religious and racial identity are perceived as inextricably intertwined in Malaysian society. The Federal Constitution's definition of 'a person who professes the religion of Islam' as one of the elements of being Malay adds a religious dimension to ethnic nationalism.[31] Viewed in this context, claims for Islamic supremacy are perceived as connected to a religious nationalism that seeks to protect the special position of the Malays. The connection of the Islamic establishment clause to Malay special privileges engenders increased polarisation in a country divided along ethnic lines. The politicisation of Islam's supremacy fuels tensions between the Malay community and the non-Malay ethnic minorities, who increasingly perceive themselves as being treated as second-class citizens.[32]

13.3. ADJUDICATING RELIGION IN MALAYSIA

Initially, the Supreme Court affirmed the secular nature of the Malaysian Constitution in two apex court decisions.[33] In the 1988 decision of *Che Omar bin Che Soh* v. *Public Prosecutor*, the Supreme Court declared that the Malaysian Constitution was founded on a secular basis.[34] Lord President Mohamad Salleh Abas, writing for the Supreme Court, concluded that the history of British colonialism and the drafting history of the Constitution showed that Islam's role was confined only to 'rituals and ceremonies'.[35] The appellants in this case faced the mandatory death penalty for drug trafficking and firearm offenses. They argued that the death penalty was unconstitutional because crimes involving drugs and firearms were not offences requiring the death penalty under Islamic law. Since Islam is constitutionally declared as the religion of the Federation, the appellants' counsel argued, Islamic precepts

---

(2002) 6 *Singapore Journal of International and Comparative Law* 154; Li-ann Thio, 'Apostasy and Religious Freedom: Constitutional Issues Arising from the Lina Joy Litigation' (2006) 2 Malayan Law Journal i; Jaclyn Ling-Chen Neo, 'Malay Nationalism, Islamic Supremacy and the Constitutional Bargain in the Multi-ethnic Composition of Malaysia' (2006) 13 *International Journal on Minority and Group Rights* 95, 104.

[31] Fed. Const. (Malay.), Article 160.
[32] Take, for example, Member of Parliament Badruddin bin Amiruldin's declaration in a House of Representatives debate in 2005: 'Malaysia is an Islamic state! You don't like it you get out of Malaysia!' (translated from Malay). Hansard (11 July 2005) 34, video clip available at www.youtube.com/watch?v=pkqyhBDU5HM.
[33] The Supreme Court (now the Federal Court) is Malaysia's highest appellate court.
[34] *Che Omar bin Che Soh* v. *Public Prosecutor* [1988] 2 Malayan Law Journal 55.
[35] Ibid., 56–7.

should be regarded as the source of all legal principles; on this basis, the death penalty could not be imposed for offences that were not in line with Islamic law.

The Malaysian Supreme Court unanimously rejected the idea that laws passed by Parliament contrary to Islamic principles could be struck down, dismissing the notion that laws 'must be imbued with Islamic and religious principles' as 'contrary to the constitutional and legal history of the Federation'.[36] Indeed, the Court noted that the opposite is true: the Constitution 'purposely preserves the continuity of secular law prior to the Constitution ...'.[37] The Lord President of the Supreme Court emphasised that 'the law in this country is still what it is today, secular law, where morality not accepted by the law is not enjoying the status of law'.[38]

Two years later, the Supreme Court reaffirmed the secular basis of the Constitution in its *Susie Teoh* decision.[39] In this case, the Court relied on the Constitution's secular founding principles and the framers' intent to uphold a statute allowing a parent or guardian to decide the upbringing, education, and religion of a minor.[40] Historical documents written by the constitutional framers at the time they drafted the Constitution stated that the recognition of Islam as the state religion 'would not in any way affect the civil rights of non-Muslims'.[41] Since 'under normal circumstances' a non-Muslim parent had the right to decide various issues affecting a minor's life, the Supreme Court upheld the civil family law statute that gave a parent the right to determine a minor's religious upbringing.[42] The new Lord President, Abdul Hamid, emphasised that the Malaysian Constitution 'was not the product of an overnight thought', but represented a negotiated constitutional settlement among local representatives.[43]

In these two early decisions, the Supreme Court affirmed the secular basis of the Malaysian Constitution, viewing Islam's position under Article 3(1) as serving a chiefly ceremonial role in the constitutional order.

This dynamic would soon change. Recent judicial decision-making in religion cases has moved away from the Supreme Court's affirmation of the Constitution's secular basis toward prioritising Islam's supremacy in Malaysia's constitutional order. I begin by exploring several examples that demonstrate

---

[36] Ibid., 57.
[37] Ibid., 56.
[38] Ibid., 57.
[39] *Teoh Eng Huat v. Kadhi Pasir Mas (Susie Teoh)* [1990] 2 Malayan Law Journal 300.
[40] Ibid.
[41] Ibid., 301–2 (citing the Reid Report, Supra note 6, [169]).
[42] Ibid., 302.
[43] Ibid., 279.

the major areas in which the civil courts have expanded Islam's constitutional scope and the authority of the religious courts.

Apostasy is one major area of controversy. Cases involving Muslims who wish to convert out of Islam bring into sharp tension the Article 3(1) declaration of Islam as the religion of the state and the Article 11(1) right of religious freedom. Civil courts have refused to exercise jurisdiction over such cases, even when they clearly engage the constitutional right to religious freedom, deferring these matters to the religious Sharia courts instead. One prominent example is the case of *Lina Joy v. Majlis Agama Islam*.[44] Lina Joy, a Malay woman born and raised by a Malay-Muslim family, converted to Catholicism in her adulthood. She wanted to marry her Christian fiancé but could not do so under civil law unless she too was officially recognised as not being Muslim.[45] She applied to the National Registration Department to have her name and religion changed on her national identity card. Her application to remove 'Islam' as the religion on her identity card was rejected. The Department refused to change her religious status without a certificate of apostasy from the Sharia court declaring that she had converted out of Islam.

Obtaining a declaration of apostasy from the Sharia courts for a Malay-Muslim is a practical impossibility. Apostasy is regarded as an offence in several Malaysian states, punishable in some states by fines, imprisonment, or whipping.[46] In other states, Sharia courts can order apostates to be detained at Islamic faith centres for mandatory rehabilitation.[47]

---

[44] *Lina Joy v. Majlis Agama Islam Wilayah Persekutuan* (2007) 3 All Malay. Rep. 585 (F.C.).

[45] The Law Reform (Marriage and Divorce) Act 1976 governs marriages between non-Muslim couples only. Muslims must contract their marriage under the Islamic Family Law (Federal Territories) Act 1984, which prohibits marriage with non-Muslims. *Laws of Malaysia* vol. 14 163–4 (2006). See also Brief of Amicus Curiae on Behalf of the All Women's Action Society, Sisters in Islam, Women's Aid Organisation, Women's Centre for Change and Women's Development Collective for Lina Joy [3.2]; Julia E. Barry, 'Apostasy, Marriage, and Jurisdiction in Lina Joy: Where was CEDAW,' Note (2008) 41 *New York University Journal of International Law and Politics*: 407.

[46] See e.g., Administration of the Religion of Islam and the Malay Custom of Pahang Enactment of 1982 (amended 1989), § 185 ('[a]ny Muslim who states that he has ceased to be a Muslim, whether orally, in writing or in any other manner whatsoever, commits an offence, and on conviction shall be liable to a fine not exceeding five thousand ringgit or to imprisonment for a term not exceeding three years or to both and to whipping of not more than six strokes'.) See Jaclyn Ling-Chen Neo, 'Competing Imperatives: Conflicts and Convergences in State and Islam in Pluralist Malaysia' (2015) *Oxford Journal of Law and Religion* 1, 16–17; Mohammad Azam Mohamed Adil, 'Law of Apostasy and Freedom of Religion in Malaysia' (2007) 2 *Asian Journal of Comparative Law* 29.

[47] One case illustrating this is that of Revathi, an Indian Malaysian woman who converted to Hinduism. When she applied to the Malacca Sharia Court regarding her renunciation of Islam, the Sharia Court ordered that she be detained for 100 days at an Islamic rehabilitation centre. See Claudia Theophilus, 'Malaysian Family Split by Faith,' *AlJazeera* (7 May 2007) www.aljazeera.com/news/asia-pacific/2007/05/20085251339076o277.html.

Lina Joy brought a challenge before the civil courts arguing that her constitutionally guaranteed right to religious liberty under Article 11(1) had been infringed. The High Court held that the constitutional right to profess and practice one's religion did not extend to Muslims who wished to leave Islam without the approval of the Sharia courts.[48] According to the high court judge, the Article 3(1) declaration of Islam as the religion of the Federation 'has a far wider and meaningful purpose than a mere fixation of the official religion'.[49] As the High Court judge declared, the upshot of this approach is that: 'A Malay ... remains in Islamic faith until his or her dying days'.[50]

In 2007, the Federal Court, in a two-to-one decision, dismissed Lina Joy's appeal.[51] The majority held that 'freedom of religion under Article 11 of the Federal Constitution requires [the individual] to comply with the practices or law of the Islamic religion in particular with regard to converting out of the religion'.[52] In effect, the majority's decision prevents a Muslim from exiting the Islamic religion without obtaining the approval of the Sharia court. In a robust dissent, Justice Richard Malanjum emphasised that the civil courts had a duty to uphold the individual's right to religious freedom and the supremacy of the constitution.

A second area in which the civil courts have abdicated their jurisdictional responsibility involves family law disputes between a non-Muslim parent and a parent who converts to Islam.[53] These cases involve a parent (typically the father) who converts himself and the children to Islam, and then applies to the Sharia courts for divorce and custody of the children. This leaves the non-Muslim parent unable to contest the custody or conversion of the children because she has no recourse to the Sharia court.

---

[48] *Lina Joy v. Majlis Agama Islam Wilayah & Anor* [2004] 2 Malayan Law Journal 119 (H.C.), 144.

[49] Ibid., 129 [19]. The High Court's decision was affirmed by a majority in the Court of Appeal: *Lina Joy v. Majlis Agama Islam Wilayah Persekutuan* (2005) 5 All Malay. Rep. 663, 690 [27]–91 [29], 690 (C.A.).

[50] Ibid., 143 [58]. See Fed. Const. (Malay.), Article 160(2) ('"Malay" means a person who professes the religion of Islam, habitually speaks the Malay language, conforms to Malay customs ... ').

[51] *Lina Joy v. Majlis Agama Islam Wilayah Persekutuan* (2007) 4 Malayan Law Journal. 585 (F.C.).

[52] Ibid., [14].

[53] See e.g., *Viran a/l/ Nagapan v. Deepa a/p Subramaniam*, Civil Appeal No 02(f)-4-01-2015 (2016) (F.C.); *Shamala Sathiyaseelan v. Jeyaganesh Mogarajah* [2004] Current L. J. 516 (H.C.) [hereinafter '*Shamala*']; *Subashini Rajasingam v. Saravanan Thangothoray* [2008] 2 Malayan Law Journal 147 (F.C.) [hereinafter '*Subashini*']; *Indira Gandhi a/p Mutho v. Pengarah Jabatan Agama Islam Perak* [2013] 5 Malayan Law Journal 552 (H.C.).

Consider, for example, the case of *Indira Gandhi*.[54] At stake in this case was whether a parent could unilaterally convert a child to Islam without the knowledge or consent of the other parent. Indira Gandhi's ex-husband had converted from being Hindu to Muslim. Without her knowledge, he then converted all their three children to Islam and obtained custody over the children from the Sharia court – a religious court which Indira Gandhi could not access as a non-Muslim. Indira Gandhi brought her case to the civil courts, arguing against the children's conversion to Islam without her knowledge and requesting custody. The Court of Appeal majority ruled against Indira Gandhi, holding that the Sharia courts had exclusive jurisdiction to determine the validity of any conversion to Islam.[55] In 2018, the Federal Court set aside the Court of Appeal's decision. In a landmark judgment the apex court affirmed that the civil courts had jurisdiction over matters relating to Islamic law when constitutional issues are involved.[56]

These apostasy and child conversion cases highlight how the prioritisation of Islam over religious liberty claims is often framed as a jurisdictional matter between the secular courts and the religious courts. The Federal Court's decision in *Indira Gandhi* is welcome for its robust affirmation of the civil courts' jurisdiction over child conversion disputes; however, the Court has not been as willing to exercise judicial review over matters of apostasy, continuing to defer such cases to the Sharia courts.[57]

Another example illustrating the growing prioritisation of Islam's constitutional position is the litigation over the ban on non-Muslim publications using the word 'Allah'. In 2014, Malaysia's Court of Appeal upheld a government order prohibiting a Catholic publication from using the term 'Allah' to refer to God.[58] The Court of Appeal overturned the High Court's decision that the government's ban of the use of the word 'Allah' by non-Muslims violated the Catholic Church's right to religious freedom.[59] In a unanimous decision,

---

[54] *Pathmanathan a/l Krishnan* v. *Indira Gandhi a/p Mutho* [2016] Current Law Journal 911 (C.A.).

[55] Ibid., [33]. The Federal Court has allowed Indira Gandhi leave to appeal on this matter. Qishin Tariq, 'Federal Court: Indira Gandhi Can Question Validity of Children's Unilateral Conversion,' *The Star Online* (19 May 2016) www.thestar.com.my/news/nation/2016/05/19/federal-court-allows-indira-gandhi-to-question-validity-of-childrens-unilateral-conversion/.

[56] Indira Gandhi a/p Mutho v. Pengarah Jabatan Agama Islam Perak & Ors. [2018] 1 Malayan Law Journal 545 (F.C.).

[57] See Sulok Tawie, 'Federal Court Defers to Shariah Courts in Sarawak Apostasy Cases,' *Malay Mail Online* (27 February 2018) www.themalaymailonline.com/malaysia/article/federal-court-defers-to-shariah-courts-in-sarawak-apostasy-cases#iKsoGVrDM1fR1qdE.97.

[58] See Jaclyn L. Neo, 'What's in a Name? Malaysia's "Allah" Controversy and the Judicial Intertwining of Islam with Ethnic Identity' (2014) 12 *International Journal of Constitutional Law* 751.

[59] *Titular Roman Catholic Archbishop of Kuala Lumpur* v. *Menteri Dalam Negeri & Anor* [2010] 2 Malayan Law Journal 78 (H.C.).

the intermediate appellate court held that there was no infringement of any constitutional rights because the use of the word 'Allah' is not an integral part of the faith and practice of Christianity.[60]

In a striking endorsement of the view that Article 3(1) established Islam's supremacy,[61] the Court of Appeal ruled that the reference to 'other religions may be practised in peace and harmony' in Article 3(1) meant that the freedom of religion guaranteed by Article 11(1) of the Federal Constitution must be read in line with 'the doctrine that the welfare of an individual or group must yield to that of the community'.[62] The Federal Court dismissed the Catholic Church's application for leave to appeal, holding that the Court of Appeal had applied the correct test.[63]

13.4. RELIGION AND THE INVISIBLE CONSTITUTION

Malaysia's religion clauses provide a case study for exploring the unwritten constitution in two main ways. The first is through the unwritten expansion of the place of Islam in the Malaysian Constitution. Although the text of Article 3(1) has remained the same, Islam's position in the constitutional order has been vastly expanded through the use of informal, extra-textual means in judicial discourse. In contrast, others defend the nature of the Constitution through the use of constitutional history and originalist arguments to protect the Constitution's unwritten secular basis.

13.4.1. *(Invisible) Elevation of Islam's Constitutional Position*

Judicial discourse over Malaysia's religion clauses has gradually expanded Islam's supremacy in the constitutional order. The Islamic prioritisation by the courts has far-reaching effects on the nature of Malaysia's Constitution and on the protection of constitutional rights like religious liberty and equality.

---

[60] *Menteri Dalam Negeri & Ors v. Titular Roman Catholic Archbishop of Kuala Lumpur* [2013] Malayan Law Journal 468 (Court of Appeal) [hereinafter '*Allah Case*' (C.A.)].
[61] Fed. Const. (Malay.), Article 3(1) ('Islam is the religion of the Federation; but other religions may be practised in peace and harmony in any part of the Federation').
[62] *Allah Case* (C.A.), note 60, 495 [48].
[63] *Titular Roman Catholic Archbishop of Kuala Lumpur v. Menteri Dalam Negeri & Ors* 4 (2014) Malayan Law Journal 765. See 'Top Malaysian Court Dismisses "Allah" Case', *AlJazeera* (23 June 2014) www.aljazeera.com/news/asia-pacific/2014/06/top-malaysian-court-dismisses-allah-case-20146232448487953.html; Ida Lim and Shaun Tan, 'Last Nail in Catholic Church's "Allah" Case as Federal Court again Says No', Malay Mail Online (21 January 2015) www.themalaymailonline.com/malaysia/article/last-nail-in-catholic-churchs-allah-case-as-federal-court-again-says-no.

Yet this constitutional change has not taken place though formal amendment but through informal constitutional change.

This invisible elevation of Islam's position in the constitutional system, I argue, has largely taken place through less visible means in the judicial discourse. The primary means has been through expansive interpretation of the Article 3(1) Islamic declaration clause which has led to judicial prioritisation of Islam's position vis-à-vis other constitutional norms. Proponents of this view are, in essence, claiming that Article 3(1) gives rise to a constitutional implication of Islam's primacy in the Malaysian constitutional order. Another means has been through the civil courts' use of non-constitutional sources – such as Islamic texts and principles – in judicial reasoning.

Perhaps the most marked approach toward Islam's expansion in the Malaysian courts' jurisprudence has been to endorse Islam's position under Article 3(1) as a lens through which the rest of the Constitution must be interpreted. This prioritisation of Islam's status is often used in turn to justify a restrictive interpretation of constitutional rights like religious freedom. In *Lina Joy* v. *Majlis Agama Islam*,[64] for example, the High Court declared that, '[f]reedom of religion under art 11(1) must be read with art 3(1) which places Islam in a special position as the main and dominant religion' of the Federation.[65] The trial judge rejected the precedent in *Che Omar* that Islam had a merely ceremonial role, asserting that Article 3(1) had 'a far wider and meaningful purpose than a mere fixation of the official religion'.[66] Lina Joy had interpreted the religious freedom right under Article 11 in a 'limited and isolated manner' without due regard to other constitutional provisions relating to Islam.[67] According to the judge, there was a 'clear nexus' between Article 3(1) and 11(1), which necessarily restricts the scope of religious freedom. In sum, on the court's account, Article 3(1) provides an interpretive lens through which to read the right to religious liberty.[68]

The Federal Court's majority reasoning in *Lina Joy* that 'one cannot renounce or embrace a religion at one's own whims and fancies' likewise reveals a conception of apostasy from an Islamic perspective, rather than generally accepted common law principles.[69] The Chief Justice, writing for the majority, reasoned: 'If a person professes and practices Islam, it would definitely mean that he must comply with the Islamic law which has prescribed

---

[64] *Lina Joy* v. *Majlis Agama Islam Wilayah & Anor* [2004] 2 Malayan Law Journal 119 (H.C.).
[65] Ibid., 144 [60].
[66] Ibid., 127 [19].
[67] Ibid.
[68] Ibid., 128 [21].
[69] *Lina Joy* [2007] 3 All. Malay. Rep. 693, 715 [14].

the way to embrace Islam and convert out of Islam'.[70] The overall tenor of the Federal Court's majority judgment prioritises Islam's supremacy in the Constitution at the expense of the constitutionally guaranteed right of religious liberty.

Judicial endorsement of Islam's primacy in the constitutional order is also evident in the High Court's decision in *Meor Atiqulrahman bin Ishak* v. *Fatimah bte Sihi*.[71] Schools in Malaysia prohibit Muslim students from wearing religious headgear – like the *serban* – according to the education policy on school uniforms. The High Court judge found the school ban on wearing the *serban* unconstitutional and explicitly asserted that Article 3(1) established Islam's supremacy in the constitutional system:

> [The Article 3 declaration that] 'Islam is the religion of the Federation, but other religions can be practiced in peace and harmony' means that Islam is the dominant religion among the other religions which are professed in this country like Christianity, Buddhism, Hinduism and others. Islam is not of the same status as other religions; it does not sit shoulder to shoulder or stand at the same height. Islam sits at the top, it walks first ... If this were not the case, Islam would not be the religion of the Federation but just one of the several religions practiced in the country and every person would be equally free to practice any religion he or she professes, no one better than the other.[72]

Civil courts have used this expansive reading of the Article 3(1) Islamic constitutional clause to justify adopting a restrictive interpretation of the Article 11(1) religious freedom guarantee.[73] In *Daud Mamat* v. *Majlis Agama Islam*,[74] for example, the High Court held that to find that Article 11(1) protected the right to profess and practice the religion of one's *choice* 'would stretch the scope of Article 11(1) to ridiculous heights, and rebel against the canon of construction'.[75]

Another means by which growing Islamisation has crept into judicial reasoning has been through the use of extra-constitutional sources, such as

---

[70] *Lina Joy* [2007] 3 All Malay. Rep. 693 720 [17.2].
[71] *Meor Atiqulrahman bin Ishak* v. *Fatimah bte Sihi* [2000] 5 Malayan Law Journal 375.
[72] Ibid., 375, 377 (translated from Malay).
[73] Fed. Const. (Malay.), Article 3(1) ('Islam is the religion of the Federation ... '); Fed. Const. (Malay.), Article 11(1) ('Every person has the right to profess and practice his religion and, subject to Clause (4), to propagate it.').
[74] *Daud Mamat* v. *Majlis Agama Islam* [2001] Current Law Journal 161.
[75] Ibid., 172.

Islamic texts and principles.[76] Judges in the secular *civil* courts – not the religious Sharia courts – have explicitly referred to Qur'anic verses and Islamic principles in several decisions. Consider, for example, the High Court's judgment in *Shamala*, where the judge cited a verse from the Qur'an regarding polygamy while interpreting a civil statutory provision providing the spouse of a convert to Islam with a ground to elect for divorce.[77]

> [T]he defendant husband, now a Muslim though [he] cannot file a petition for divorce against his plaintiff Hindu wife, can take another wife – a Muslim wife because the defendant husband being a Muslim is now practising a polygamous marriage ... The word used in the Section is 'may', i.e., to maintain the status of the civil marriage (Hindu marriage) if the unconverted wife wishes to remain the wife of her converted husband although the converted husband can take another wife if he can do justice as the Holy Quran *Al-Nisa* (IV) Ayat 3 states and which reads, 'if ye fear that ye shall not Be able to deal justly With the orphans, Marry women of your choice, Two, Three, or Four; But if ye fear that ye shall not Be able to deal justly (with them), Then only one or two (a captive)'.[78]

Likewise, in *Subashini*, the Court of Appeal judge, Justice Suriyadi, upheld the Sharia Court's jurisdiction reasoning that the Islamic judge's position would 'squarely fall' under 'Quranic revelations' to follow the sacred law.[79]

What is striking is the explicit use of religious texts as extra-constitutional sources by *civil* court judges who are meant to apply the general, secular law of the land. The use of Islamic sources and religious rhetoric in civil court opinions is deeply concerning. While Islamic sources may properly be regarded as within the domain of the Sharia courts, civil courts deal with general legislation and common law, which are not meant to have any religious basis.

Religion cases are fraught because of their connection in the socio-political context with racial–religious nationalism, where Islam's position is seen as

---

[76] See Amanda Whiting, 'Desecularising Malaysian Law?' in Sarah Biddulph and Penelope Nicholson (eds.), *Examining Practice, Interrogating Theory: Comparative Legal Studies in Asia* (Leiden: Martinus Nijhoff, 2008), 229, 249–52.
[77] *Shamala* [2004] Malayan Law Journal 241.
[78] Ibid., [13].
[79] *Subashini* [2008] 2 Malayan Law Journal 147, [61] ('[h]is position would squarely fall under these Quranic revelations: And We have set you on a road of Our Commandment (a Syariah, or a Sacred Law of Our Commandment, Syaria'tin min al-amr); so follow it, and follow not the whims of those who know not (45:18).').

intertwined with the protection of the Malay community's special position. Cases involving religious conversion out of Islam, in particular, bring these tensions to the fore; they are further complicated by the perceived inextricability between religious and racial identity. Such perceptions are exacerbated by the reasoning used by the civil court judges in highly contentious religion cases. In *Lina Joy*, for example, the Court of Appeal's majority, consisting of two Malay-Muslim judges, declared: 'Renunciation of Islam is generally regarded by the Muslim community as a very grave matter'.[80]

13.4.2. *Constitutional History and the Original Secular Framework*

Secularists have sought to defend the Malaysian Constitution's secular basis against the expansion of Islam's constitutional position through the use of constitutional history. Interpreting the written Constitution's religion clauses, they argue, requires recourse to the original constitutional framework behind the text. The Article 3(1) declaration of Islam as the religion of the Federation must be viewed with an understanding of the historical context of the Constitution's founding and the original meaning of the text. On this view, the Constitution's original founding and fundamental core, understood properly, provides the proper framework for interpreting the written text.

Originalist arguments have typically focused on the intent of the framers to affirm the Constitution's secular foundations. The Supreme Court in *Che Omar bin Che Soh* v. *Public Prosecutor* declared the secular nature of the Constitution by relying on the framers' original intent.[81] The Lord President of the Supreme Court made clear the Court's focus of inquiry: 'The question here is this: Was this the meaning intended by the framers of the Constitution?'[82] Using a historical lens, the Lord President concluded that the history of British colonialism and the drafting history of the Constitution showed that Islam's role was confined only to 'rituals and ceremonies'.[83]

Likewise, in *Susie Teoh*, the Supreme Court again employed an interpretive approach based on the framers' intent to affirm the secular foundations of the Constitution:[84]

> Although normally ... we base our interpretative function on the printed letters of the legislation alone, in the instant case, we took the liberty ... to

---

[80] *Lina Joy* [2005] 5 All Malay. Rep. 663, 690 [29].
[81] *Che Omar bin Che Soh* v. *Public Prosecutor* [1988] 2 Malayan Law Journal 55.
[82] Ibid., 56.
[83] Ibid., 56–7.
[84] *Teoh Eng Huat* v. *Kadhi Pasir Mas* (*Susie Teoh*) [1990] 2 Malayan Law Journal 300.

ascertain for ourselves what purpose the founding fathers of our Constitution had in mind when our constitutional laws were drafted.[85]

To fuel the movement toward greater Islamisation, however, some of its proponents have mobilised historicist rhetoric to promote judicial elevation of Islam's constitutional position. In *Meor Atiqulrahman*,[86] for example, to support its vastly expansive interpretation of Islam's position under Article 3(1), the High Court judge focused heavily on constructing a historical account of the constitutional bargain to argue that the constitutional framers had intended to secure Islam's dominant position as the result of a social contract between the Muslims and non-Muslims.[87] And in *Lina Joy*, the same High Court judge insisted that an interpretation of religious freedom that would allow Muslims to freely convert out of Islam 'would result in absurdities not intended by the framers' of the Constitution.[88] '[T]o give effect to the intention of the framers of our [C]onstitution', the judge claimed, religious freedom must be qualified by other constitutional provisions relating to Islam.[89] The historicist accounts of the High Court in these decisions have been heavily criticised by scholars as 'revisionist' and 'erroneous'.[90] But what is striking is the courts' insistence on using history and original intent in support of their expansive interpretation of the Islamic clause despite established Supreme Court precedent in *Che Omar* confining Islam's scope in Article 3 to a ceremonial role.

Judges who viewed this expansion of Islam's position with alarm fought back on originalist turf. In a robust dissent against the Federal Court's majority opinion in *Lina Joy*, Justice Richard Malanjum asserted that the civil courts had a duty to uphold an individual's right to religious freedom guaranteed in the Constitution.[91] Significantly, Justice Malanjum viewed his interpretation as faithful to the original intent of the constitutional framers: 'Sworn to uphold the Federal Constitution, it is my task to ensure that it is upheld at all times by giving effects to what I think the founding fathers of this great nation had in mind when they framed this sacred document'.[92] He emphasised that Islam's

---

[85] Ibid., 301.
[86] *Meor Atiqulrahman bin Ishak v. Fatimah bte Sihi* [2000] 5 Malayan Law Journal 375 (High Court, Seremban). The High Court occupies the lowest tier in Malaysia's appellate court structure, which comprises of the High Court, the Court of Appeal and the Federal Court.
[87] Ibid., 385; see also ibid., 384.
[88] Ibid., 129 [18].
[89] Ibid., 129 [19].
[90] See Li-ann Thio and Jaclyn Ling-Chien Neo, 'Religious Dress in Schools: The Serban Controversy in Malaysia' (2006) 55 *International and Comparative Law Quarterly* 671, 681–3.
[91] *Lina Joy*, 4 Malayan Law Journal (2007) 585, at 631 [85].
[92] Ibid., 619 [23].

special position in Article 3(1) 'was never intended to override any right, privilege or power explicitly conferred by the Constitution'.[93]

Recourse to constitutional history as an extra-textual constitutional source in Malaysia has reached beyond issues of religion and the state. Judges advocating a purposive and rights-expansive approach to interpreting the Malaysian Constitution's bill of rights have also used the language of originalism to support their constitutional adjudication approach. Liberals promoting a robust rights-oriented approach to constitutional interpretation systematically refer to the original commitments of the framers.[94] Those who support this living constitutionalist approach do so on originalist grounds, exhorting the courts 'to adopt a liberal approach in order to implement the true intention of the framers of the Federal Constitution'.[95] On this account, the framers themselves contemplated the necessity of constitutional construction by future generations. As Justice Gopal Sri Ram declared, 'the terms in which these provisions of the Constitution are expressed necessarily co-opts future generations of judges to the enterprise of giving life to the abstract statements of fundamental rights'.[96]

Proponents of this form of framework originalism support empowering judges to protect individual rights from legislative infringement by *expanding* the scope of enforceable constitutional rights.[97] Judges who endorse this approach have been willing to find implied fundamental rights and to expand a number of constitutional rights – such as the right to life,[98] equality,[99] and the

---

[93] Ibid., 623 [53]–24 [53].
[94] Sivarasa Rasiah v. Badan Peguam Malaysia & Anor [2010] 2 Malayan Law Journal 333, 339 (observing that 'the provisions of the Constitution, in particular the fundamental liberties guaranteed ... must be generously interpreted'.).
[95] *Tan Tek Seng v. Suruhanjaya Perkhidmatan Pendidikan* [1996] 1 Malayan Law Journal 261, 288. See also *Sukma Darmawan Sasmitaat Madja v. Ketua Pengarah Penjara Malaysia* [1999] 1 Malayan Law Journal 266, 271 ('[T]he Federal Constitution, unlike any ordinary statute, does not merely declare law ... It also confers upon individuals certain fundamental and inalienable human rights, such as equality before the law. Its language must accordingly receive *a broad and liberal construction in order to advance the intention of its framers*'.) (emphasis added).
[96] *Lee Kwan Woh v. Pub. Prosecutor* [2009] 5 Malayan Law Journal 301, 312 (quoting *Boyce v. The Queen*, [2004] UKPC 32).
[97] See Jack M. Balkin, *Living Originalism* (Cambridge, MA: Harvard University Press, 2011), 23 (arguing that framework originalism holds that 'interpreters must be faithful to the original meaning of the constitutional text and to the principles that underlie them').
[98] Courts have found that the right to life in the Constitution of Malaysia protects the right to access to court (*Sivarasa Rasiah v. Badan Peguam Malaysia & Anor* [2010] 2 Malayan Law Journal 333); employment (*Tan Tek Seng v. Suruhanjaya Perkhidmatan Pendidikan*, [1996] 1 Malayan Law Journal 261); livelihood under native customary land rights (*Nor Anak Nyawai* [2005] 3 Current Law Journal 555); and the right to fair trial (*Lee Kwan Woh v. Public Prosecutor* [2009] 5 Malayan Law Journal 316).
[99] *Sivarasa Rasiah*, 2 Malayan Law Journal 333.

freedom of expression and association[100] – by applying a purposive interpretive approach in line with the founding principles of the Constitution.

Originalist arguments have not been confined to the courts. Scholars and commentators regularly invoke originalist appeals in debates over Malaysia's secular or Islamic identity.[101] Secularists vigorously defend the original commitments of the Malaysian Constitution as secular, arguing that historical evidence of the founding demonstrates that the framers had intended the nation to be a secular state.[102] As scholar Thio Li-ann notes, '[o]riginalists underscore the secular nature of the Constitution, which Article 4(1) declares supreme' while '"revisionists" ... defy precedent and constitutional history in contending that Article 3 has broader practical significance'.[103]

Outside the academy, reference to the framers and constitutional founding occur frequently and forcefully in political and social discourse and are part of the national conversation on a variety of issues.[104] What seems clear is that constitutional history is an unwritten constitutional feature that has popular salience in Malaysia: it is the subject of legal and academic debates and occupies a significant space in public discourse.

13.5. REFLECTIONS ON MALAYSIA'S INVISIBLE CONSTITUTION

The story of Malaysia's religion clauses and the invisible features of the Constitution give rise to several broader observations. In this section, I end with three concluding reflections on the observations gained from the Malaysian example for wider comparative constitutional understandings.

First, the constitutional jurisprudence surrounding Malaysia's religion clauses adds to accounts regarding the use of constitutional history and

---

[100] *Muhammad Hilman bin Idham v. Kerajaan Malaysia* [2011] 6 Malayan Law Journal 507.
[101] For proponents of Islam's supremacy in the Malaysian constitutional order, see e.g., Bari, Supra note 29; Shariff, Supra note 29; Faiza Thamby Chik, 'Malay and Islam in the Malaysian Constitution' (2009) 1 Malayan Law Journal cxxix, cxlii.
[102] See e.g., Fernando, Supra note 4; Tommy Thomas, 'Is Malaysia an Islamic State?' (2006) 4 Malayan Law Journal xv; Dawson and Thiru, Supra note 30, 160; Li-ann, Supra note 30, i, xi–xii.
[103] Thio Li-ann, 'Jurisdictional Imbroglio: Civil and Religious Courts, Turf Wars and Article 121(1A) of the Federal Constitution,' in Andrew Harding and H. P. Lee (eds.) *Constitutional Landmarks in Malaysia: The First 50 Years 1957–2007* (Kuala Lumpur: LexisNexis, 2007), 197.
[104] See e.g., 'DAP Firmly against the Idea of Islamic State' *New Straits Times* (Malay.) (12 July 2001) 8 (Opposition figure Karpal Singh called the issue of setting up an Islamic state 'an affront to the solemn will of the framers of the Constitution, who, undoubtedly, had as their objective Islam as the religion of the country in the context of a secular state'); see also Malik Munip, 'Is Malaysia an Islamic or Secular State?' *New Straits Times* (Malay.) (16 November 2012) www.nst.com.my/opinion/columnist/is-malaysia-an-islamic-or-secular-state-1.171584; Art Harun, 'Secular or Non-secular: What History Tells Us' *Malaysian Insider* (8 November 2012); David Tih, 'Uphold Founding Fathers' Legacy' *New Straits Times* (Malay.) (31 August 2010) 40.

originalist arguments.[105] In the United States, the originalist movement arose out of frustration with the perceived rights-expansive judicial activism of the Warren and Burger Courts.[106] As a result, originalism in America has been closely associated with a conservative political movement and the promotion of judicial restraint.[107] The inverse phenomenon is apparent in Malaysia: originalism is frequently the domain of political liberals seeking to increase the courts' oversight of the legislative process or judicial expansion of individual rights.[108] Originalist arguments in Malaysia tend to be employed in service of a more rights-expansive constitutional adjudication approach than the status quo, and are not associated with judicial constraint. Constitutional history is used to support the protection – in many cases, the expansion – of constitutional rights. Secularists in Malaysia routinely reach back to the founding premises of the Constitution to argue for more robust protection of religious freedom and other individual rights. The constitutional history and founding premises in Malaysia facilitate a form of originalism that envisages a Constitution based on a more robust vision of fundamental rights protection that can be applied in a manner that accommodates legitimate constitutional change.

Originalist discourse in Malaysia is characterised by a focus on constitutional history and the intent of the framers, rather than text.[109] Original intent dominates the Malaysian courts' originalist jurisprudence.[110] Originalist arguments in the Malaysian context have not centred on the textual public meaning of the Constitution at the time of drafting; rather, interpretation of the Constitution is strongly influenced by the constitutional history surrounding

---

[105] I explore this argument in greater length in Yvonne Tew, 'Originalism at Home and Abroad' (2014) 52 *Columbia Journal of Transnational Law* 780, 801–18, 832–49.
[106] See Keith E. Whittington, 'The New Originalism' (2004) 2 *Georgetown Journal of Law and Public Policy* 599, 601 (noting that 'originalism was a reactive theory motivated by substantive disagreement with the recent and then-current actions of the Warren and Burger Courts'); Thomas B. Colby, 'The Sacrifice of the New Originalism' (2011) 99 *Georgetown Law Journal* 713, 716 (explaining that originalism 'arose as a by-product of the conservative frustration with the broad, rights-expansive decisions of the Warren and Burger Courts').
[107] See Colby, Supra note 106, 714 (observing that 'originalism was born of a desire to constrain judges.').
[108] See Yvonne Tew, 'Comparative Originalism in Constitutional Interpretation in Asia,' (2017) *Singapore Academy Law Journal* 719, 726–9.
[109] Tew, Supra note 105, 817, 845–9.
[110] See *Che Omar Bin Che Soh v. Pub. Prosecutor* [1988] 2 Malayan Law Journal 55, 56; *Teoh Eng Huat v. Kadhi Pasir Mas (Susie Teoh)* [1990] 2 Malayan Law Journal 300, 301; *Meor Atiqulrahman bin Ishak v. Fatimah bte Sihi* [2000] 5 Malayan Law Journal 375, 384F; *Lina Joy v. Majlis Agama Islam Wilayah & Anor* [2004] 2 Malayan Law Journal 119 (H.C.), 129 [18]; *Lina Joy v. Majlis Agama Islam Wilayah Persekutuan* [2007] 3 All Malay. Rep. 585 (F.C.), 3; *Lee Kwan Woh v. Pub. Prosecutor* [2009] 5 Malayan Law Journal 301, 311.

its drafting.[111] Secularists and Islamists do not battle over distinctions between the framers' intent and the original meaning of the text, but over whether constitutional history supports their particular originalist interpretation. The overriding theme that emerges from originalist practice in Malaysia is that it is focused on historical understandings and the intent of those involved in the framing of the Constitution.

The Malaysian experience suggests that the form of originalist methodology that takes hold in certain nations is profoundly influenced by the orientation of its constitutional culture toward the authority of the past. In countries where the founders or framers have popular resonance in the nation's constitutional narrative, originalist arguments thrive because of their historicist appeal.[112] The comparative perspective sheds light on how the approaches a nation takes towards the written and unwritten aspects of its Constitution – and the salience of originalist arguments to its constitutional interpretation – is deeply connected to a country's particular constitutional culture and history.

The second observation concerns the relationship between the unwritten constitution and constitutional change.[113] Part of the appeal of originalist arguments in the Malaysian context is also connected to the *formal* features of its Constitution, such as its constitutional amendment procedure. The United States Constitution is highly difficult to amend, which lends weight

---

[111] Historical evidence is viewed favourably as an extrinsic interpretive aid to determine the actual intentions of individual framers. For example, in *Zambry bin Abd Kadir v. Mohammad Nizar bin Jamaluddin* [2009] 5 Malayan Law Journal 464 (C.A.), the Court of Appeal relied on an academic article published in the *Cambridge Law Journal* written by Professor Ivor Jennings – one of the framers of the Malaysian Constitution – as extrinsic evidence in deciding how to interpret constitutional provisions about the head of state's right to dismiss a chief minister. Justice Zainun Ali exhorted the Court 'have regard to extraneous matters such as [the Jennings'] article … in order to distill the original and true intent behind constitutional provisions'. Ibid., 534.

[112] In the United States, originalism – whether focused on intent or meaning – has also been characterised by constitutional historicism. The original intent of the framers dominated the first wave of American originalist jurisprudence and the United States' 'constitutional practice continues to privilege intentionalism'. Jamal Greene, 'The Case for Original Intent' (2012) 80 *George Washington Law Review* 1683, 1686. Although academic originalist theory has shifted away from original intent toward original public meaning, historicist original understanding continues to matter in practice and popular discourse because of the central role the framers play in America's constitutional culture and national identity. See ibid., 1696–7. As Jack Balkin observes, '[d]espite the dominance of original public meaning originalism in academic theory, lawyers … continue to treat particular members of the founding generation differently than a dictionary or concordance'. Jack M. Balkin, 'The New Originalism and the Uses of History' (2013) 82 *Fordham Law Review* 641, 653.

[113] Yvonne Tew, *Stealth Theocracy*, 58 *Virginia Journal of International Law* (forthcoming 2018).

to the concern that interpreting the Constitution according to its original understandings binds contemporary society to the dead hand of the past.[114] By contrast, the Federal Constitution of Malaysia is easily amendable in practice. The most common amendment rule is a requirement for at least a two-thirds legislative majority in Parliament;[115] the dominance of the ruling coalition has meant that the government can, and often has, revised the Constitution at will.[116]

In Malaysia, the threat to democratic legitimacy does not stem from the people's perceived inability to change a rigid inherited Constitution; instead, it lies in the monopoly possessed by the dominant ruling party over amending the Constitution. Until recently, the *Barisan Nasional* coalition has been in power since the nation's independence and has controlled more than two-thirds of the majority in Parliament for much of Malaysia's history.[117] Executive ability and willingness to use the amendment process have given rise to many constitutional amendments that undermine institutional safeguards.[118] In a dominant party system with circumstances like these, the Constitution risks being altered out of line with the framer's vision and the original framework

---

[114] See e.g., Henry Paul Monaghan, 'Doing Originalism' (2004) 104 *Columbia Law Review* 32, 35 (describing the United States Constitution as 'practically unamendable').

[115] The general rule is that a constitutional amendment of the Constitution of Malaysia must be supported by a two-thirds majority of the total membership of each House of Parliament Fed. Const. (Malay.), Article 159(3), Const. of the Rep. of Sing., Article 5(2). There are some exceptions to this rule. In Malaysia, some constitutional provisions can be amended by ordinary law without the requirement for a two-thirds parliamentary majority, such as amendments to restrict freedom of movement and freedom of speech, assembly and association; and to legislate against subversion and pass emergency laws so as to override constitutional provisions. Fed. Const. (Malay.), Article 9(2)–(3), Article 10(2)–(3), Article 149(1), Article 150(5). A number of constitutional provisions, such as those affecting the privileges and positions of the Rulers, cannot be amended without the consent of the Conference of the Rulers. Ibid., Article 158(5).

[116] More than fifty constitutional amendment Acts and 700 individual textual amendments have been passed in Malaysia since its independence in 1957. Cindy Tham, 'Major Changes to the Constitution,' *Sun* (17 July 2007) www.malaysianbar.org.my/echoes_of_the_past/major_changes_to_the_constitution.html.

[117] Until its stunning upset in Malaysia's historic 2018 national elections, the *Barisan Nasional* coalition has been the dominant ruling party in power since Malaysia's independence. It has also controlled more than a two-thirds majority in Parliament for much of Malaysia's history, until it lost its super majority in the 2008 general elections.

[118] Following executive frustration with several judicial decisions in the 1980s, for example, the Malaysian Parliament amended the Federal Constitution to remove the reference to the judicial power being 'vested' in the courts; the altered Article 121(1) provision now states that the courts 'shall have such jurisdiction and powers as may be conferred by or under federal law'. Fed. Const. (Malay.), Article 121(1). For further detail, see Yvonne Tew, 'On the Uneven Journey to Constitutional Redemption: The Malaysian Judiciary and Constitutional Politics' (2016) *Washington International Law Journal* 673, 678–1.

established at the nation's independence. For secularists, recourse to the original Constitution provides a safeguard for the Malaysian Constitution's basic structure and minimum core.

My third point involves the link between the unwritten constitution and constitutional identity. Secularists and Islamists in Malaysia battle so deeply over the unwritten features of the constitutional provisions on religion because of its profound relationship to conceptions of the nation's identity. Argumentation over the invisible core underlying the Constitution's text provides a way for a society to articulate and cement constitutional narratives about itself.[119] The use of originalist arguments in Malaysia is not primarily about interpretive method; rather, historicist arguments of this kind are best understood as an argument about constitutional *ethos*.[120] Originalism has popular appeal in a nation conditioned by particular cultural and political influences to identify with its constitutional history. As Jamal Greene has observed of the United States, originalism is an argument 'driven by a narrative about the American ethos'.[121] In Malaysia, too, originalist arguments have salience because of the historical and political traditions associated with the nation's independence and constitutional founding. In contexts like these, 'the deeper power of originalist argument sounds in the romance of national identity'.[122]

Malaysia's invisible Constitution is not confined to the courts; it has a distinctly popular dimension. Constitutional arguments over the nation's constitutional identity as secular or Islamic have public salience. Debate over the interpretation of the Article 3(1) Islamic declaration clause extends well beyond the judicial sphere; and originalist arguments have rhetorical potency in the political and popular discourse.[123] Judges, lawyers, scholars, politicians, journalists and civil society activists mobilise constitutional arguments in debates over Islam's position because of the public appeal of such arguments.

---

[119] See Carolyn Evans, 'Constitutional Narratives: Constitutional Adjudication on the Religion Clauses in Australia and Malaysia' (2009) 23 *Emory International Law Review* 437, 438 ('[C]onstitutional narrative in this context is a culturally and legally created story about the role, purpose, history, and relevance of the constitution in a particular society'.).

[120] Tew, Supra note 105, 834–6.

[121] See Jamal Greene, 'On the Origins of Originalism' (2009) 88 *Texas Law Review* 1, 84 (arguing that originalist argument is a species of ethical argument, i.e., an argument 'driven by a narrative about the American ethos'.)

[122] Richard Primus, 'The Functions of Ethical Originalism' (2010) 88 *Texas Law Review* 79, 80.

[123] Turkey provides another comparative example for originalism abroad. Ozan Varol observes that in Turkey originalism is 'not confined to the judicial sphere' and that '[e]ven the Turkish politicians' criticisms of the judiciary feature heated debates over originalism'. Ozan O. Varol, 'The Origins and Limits of Originalism: A Comparative Study' (2011) 44 *Vanderbilt Journal of Transnational Law* 1239, 1274.

Like in the United States, where the Constitution – and originalism – occupies a prominent place in its political and popular culture,[124] Malaysia's Constitution has public salience and its constitutional founding is frequently invoked in popular discourse.[125] The popular perception of the Malaysian Constitution goes beyond its text; it is influenced by unwritten features like the historical and political traditions associated with the nation's founding and perceptions of the social contract struck at the constitutional framing. In constitutional cultures like Malaysia, where the nation's founding is central to its constitutional narrative, the invisible Constitution may feature prominently – both in the judicial and popular sphere – because of its role in linking constitutional history and national identity.

13.6. CONCLUSION

The history of the contest between secular and Islamic constitutional ideas over the Article 3(1) Islamic declaration clause illustrates the profound extent to which invisible means can impact a nation's constitutional identity. At the same time, the Malaysian story provides an insight into how such invisible influences may be more open to gradual renegotiation and change – and by more diffuse actors and processes – than formal mechanisms of constitutional change, like the amendment process controlled by the dominant ruling party.

Malaysia's religion clauses illustrate how the deepest struggles over a nation's constitution often go beyond the visible constitutional text. The battle over the soul of the Malaysian Constitution continues in contemporary Malaysia. Secularists and Islamists collide over their competing visions of Malaysia's invisible Constitution, which they attempt to construct through using non-textual means to elevate Islam's supremacy or by inviting a return to the Constitution's original secular basis. The invisible aspects of the Constitution are crucial to understanding the continuing struggle over the meaning of the words contained in the written Constitution and its constitutional commitments.

---

[124] See Jamal Greene, 'Selling Originalism' (2009) 97 *Georgetown Law Journal* 657, 672–96.
[125] See e.g., Malik Imtiaz, 'Latifah Mat Zin: Reaffirming the Supremacy of the Constitution,' *Disquiet Blog* (29 July 2007) malikimtiaz.blogspot.com/2007/07/latifah-mat-zin-reaffirming-supremacy.html; David Tih, Supra note 104, 40; Malik Munip, Supra note 104; Art Harun, Supra note 104.

14

The 'Invisible Constitution' seen Realistically

Visualising China's Unitary System

Han Zhai

14.1. LOCATING THE SCENE

To engage the real world, comparative constitutional scholarship needs to endeavour to cover politics while maintaining the boundary between constitutional normativity and political realities. The notion of the 'invisible constitution' presents an opportunity for deeper and more contextually sensitive investigations into constitutional implications in different constitutional regimes. In an authoritarian party-state without any judicial review or formal constitutional interpretation, what picture can the concept of the 'invisible constitution' draw from China's incomplete 1982 Constitution? Beyond identifying the 'invisible constitution' as an interpretative approach, we hold that it has the potential to become a theoretical framework for studying the constitution and its function through a realistic perspective. When the functions of a constitution might not be entirely predicted by a written constitution, then between the ideal of a normative constitution and the reality of its implementation, there is usually a departure that might be more significant in the case of a reforming constitution. From this gap, constitutional scholarship has offered theoretical frameworks such as constitutional conventions, informal constitutional changes and now the likely development of the 'invisible constitution'. In this chapter, the 'invisible constitution' refers to the unforeseen changes that occur during the implementation of a written constitution and the implicit logic behind the fundamental arrangements offered by the 1982 Constitution of China in a historical-social context.

The 'invisible constitution' gained its specific influence over Chinese constitutional scholarship through the translation of Tribe's work in 2010. Inspirations about the 'invisible constitution' can be found in articles and debates on the material constitution during the reform period. This research trend is underpinned by the pursuit of a proper theory to explain the uniqueness both in and beyond the written text of the 1982 Constitution. However, in post-1978 China, the 'invisible constitution' implies possible intellectual access to study the 1982 Constitution in the realistic context of constitutional changes.

The incomplete nature of the 1982 Constitution necessitates a theoretical framework such as the 'invisible constitution'. With a minimalist unitary system, the text of China's 1982 Constitution keeps silent on almost every crucial issue that a constitution should articulate during the reform period, and this constitutional silence invites us to see the de facto picture. As China's 'reforming' constitution, the 1982 Constitution aims to move beyond the country's totalitarianism past and relaunch the modern state-building of China.[1] It offers the rebalancing of the entire power structure of the Chinese state, establishing a symbolic state president, a central military commission and an operative national legislative body by empowering its Standing Committee with more special committees. In practice, effective local laboratories subsequently developed formal national policy and could even cause textual constitutional changes.[2] The 1982 Constitution provides a unitary system that allows the initiative and enthusiasm of local authorities under the unified leadership of the central authorities.[3] This model provides enough constitutional leeway for the ongoing trial-and-error practise and future developments during the reform period.[4] During the reform era, the 1982 Constitution reflected policy changes rather than setting the parameters of the reform itself. Amendments to the 1982 Constitution mainly incorporated and legitimated changes in the direction and operation of economic reform.[5] The changes in the Constitution that were unforeseen or developed later were invisible indeed.

The invisible part of China's 1982 Constitution not only refers to what is textually unwritten, which can be easily identified in the implementation of the

---

[1] Li Qiang, 'State Capacity, Democratic Principles, and Constitutional Order: Modern State-Building in Post-totalitarian Society' in Xiaoming Huang (ed.), *The Institutional Dynamics of China's Great Transformation* (New York: Routledge, 2012) 157.
[2] The 1982 Constitution has been amended four times in 1988, 1993, 1999 and 2004, involving thirty-two particular articles, amounting to nearly a quarter of the Constitution. Over 75 per cent of amendments resulted from the evolving economic practice, featuring in the constitutional recognition of private economy and protection of private property subsequently.
[3] Article 3(4), the 1982 Constitution (rev. 2004).
[4] Best illustrated by the revolutionary reform of rural land use which was substantially against the socialist ideology and the economic practices in the Special Economic Zone since the 1979. See Sebastian Heilmann, 'From Local Experiments to National Policy: The Origins of China's Distinctive Policy Process' (2008) 59 *The China Journal* 1, 1. For an institutional analysis, see Zhou Xueguang, 'The Institutional Logic of Collusion among Local Governments in China' (2009) 36 *Modern China*, 1.
[5] Robert Benewick, 'Towards a Developmental Theory of Constitutionalism: The Chinese Case' (1998) 33 *Government and Opposition* 441, 443.

Constitution, but also includes the implicit logic of its unitary system, which requires systematic deduction from the basic structure provided in both the text of the 1982 Constitution and its organic laws. The reality that any Chinese constitution must address is China's regional diversity in various aspects throughout the country's wide territory. To unify both geographic and political peripheries in the pursuit of national prosperity, the 1982 Constitution provides a unitary system that accommodates three types of decentralisation: the unsettled decentralisation in fiscal powers during the reform period, regional national autonomy (RNA) and the Special Administrative Regions (SARs).[6] Previous academic inquiries have focused on the contrast between the authoritarian appearances of the Chinese regime, which theoretically provides central control over subnational units, with the conspicuous gaps in policy implementation over many arenas.[7] These decentralised arrangements are usually discussed separately and form a large body of existing literature.[8] This chapter will therefore explain how subnational units are designed for central governance if we match them with the 1982 Constitution and its organic laws concerning decentralisation arrangements, rather than following the paradigm of Chinese federalism. In a more implicit sense, the invisible part of the 1982 Constitution is how sub-state decentralisation arrangements are designed to fit in the unitary system.

To provide a (relatively) full picture of the implementation and implicit logic of the unitary system, with proper methodological reflections, the following discussion will start with a brief review of the intellectual link between

---

[6] The central-local relationship remains one of the core issues since the founding of the People's Republic of China. See Linda Chelan Li, 'Central-Local Relations in the People's Republic of China: Trends, Progress and Impact for Policy Implementation' (2010) 30 *Public Administration and Development* 177.

[7] Linda Chelan Li, 'Central Relations' in Chris Ogden (ed.), *Handbook of China's Governance and Domestic Politics* (London: Routledge, 2013) 143.

[8] To name a few, on the RNA, see Pitman B. Potter, 'Governance of China's Periphery: Balancing Local Autonomy and National Unity' 19 (2005) *Columbia Journal Asian Law* 293; Maria Lundberg and Yong Zhou, 'Regional National Autonomy under Challenge: Law, Practice and Recommendations' (2009) 16 *International Journal on Minority and Group Rights* 269. On the autonomous issues of Hong Kong SAR, see Albert H. Y. Chen, 'Further Aspects of the Autonomy of Hong Kong under the PRC Constitution' (1984) 14 *Hong Kong Law Journal* 341; Albert H. Y. Chen, 'Some Reflections on Hong Kong's Autonomy' (1994) 24 *Hong Kong Law Journal* 173; Albert H. Y. Chen, 'The Law and Politics of Constitutional Reform and Democratization in Hong Kong' *University of Hong Kong Faculty of Law Research Paper No. 2014/035*; Yash P. Ghai, *Hong Kong's New Constitutional Order: The Resumption of Chinese Sovereignty and the Basic Law* (Hong Kong: Hong Kong University Press, 1999). There is little typical research so far concerning the fiscal decentralisation during the reform with constitutional analysis. For an overall picture of the 1980s and 1990s, see Donald J. S. Brean (ed.) *Taxation in Modern China* (New York, London: Routledge, 1998).

Tribe's *Invisible Constitution* and the debates over China's unwritten constitution. It will continue with an existing study on China with some methodological notes for discussion in the following parts. In particular, existing critiques on Tribe's work have echoed in the debates on China's *unwritten* constitution, which implies the dangerous potential to confuse constitutional issues with political reality when applying the invisible or unwritten constitution in China, although they are conceptually equal to each other. Then, with a methodological modification on applying the 'invisible constitution' into China's 1982 Constitution, we will start from the articulated political structure and analyse all three types of sub-state decentralisations with regard to both their fundamental framework and any crucial changes during the reform. The discussion concludes with a visualisation of the picture of China's unitary system with specific features in each of the three decentralisations, which might be a new opportunity for further research.

14.2. FROM TRIBE'S INVISIBLE CONSTITUTION TO THE UNWRITTEN CONSTITUTIONAL DEBATES

14.2.1. Reviewing Tribe's 'Invisible Constitution'

Tribe's book fails to provide a clear definition of the 'invisible constitution', but it does try to build the interpretative methods for the constitution itself. The constitutional interpretation of specific articles should be guided by constitutional principles structured by different influences and priorities. Tribe claims there are two sets of constitutional principles: the meta-principles and the fundamental constitutional principles; the former will determine how to read the rest of the text.[9] In Tribe's work, this type of constitutional interpretation connects constitutional provisions, forming the 'resulting triangle' from the 'geometric structure' of the constitution. In general, interpretative methodology with non-textual foundations might be an issue in discovering the 'invisible constitution'. The legitimacy of the 'invisible constitution' is 'enhanced by its apparent malleability'; a concept that actually allows non-judicial and even non-governmental actors to present their own views regarding constitutional meaning.[10] The 'invisible' constitution even implies criticism, as it might draw careless interpretation from scholars, especially considering that the 'invisible

---

[9] Laurence H. Tribe et al. 'The Invisible Constitution and the Rule of Law' (2009) 62 *Bulletin of the American Academy of Arts and Sciences* 59, 61.

[10] Kermit Roosevelt III, Book Review: 'The Indivisible Constitution' (2008) 25 *Constitutional Commentary* 321, 340.

constitution' is 'more malleable and less permanent' than the visible one.[11] The unreliability of this idea is also questioned. If the answer cannot be found in the text, history, structure or precedents which are solid enough for inference, how can constitutional scholars draw the line between 'the unthinkable and the unconstitutional'?[12] This issue is echoed in Chinese constitutional research, where the 'invisible' is conceptually equal to the 'unwritten'.

Indeed, the transparent part of Tribe's work is considered to be proof of a robust *unwritten* constitutional law.[13] Tribe's methods for interpreting the 'invisible constitution' might cause 'constitutional confusion' because they do address the 'inevitable starting place', which necessitates an effective analysis of the unwritten constitution. The question of how to explain the 'invisible' part of the constitution is addressed by detecting the unwritten part of the written constitution if the written constitution is an ideal, aspirational and symbolic charter of the state as well as the political reality that translates constitutional aspirations into action.[14] This conceptual reduction is crucial if the distinction between 'visible' and 'invisible' is to make any analytical sense, as focusing on the 'invisible constitution' might 'by the same token' invalidate such a distinction.[15]

The Invisible Constitution was translated into Chinese in 2010. In the special foreword to Chinese readers, Tribe suggests that the core idea concerning the 'invisible constitution' is applicable to any modern written constitution by denying the constitutional exceptionalism of America.[16] He insists that the whole meaning of a written constitution cannot be captured by merely reading its text. Essentially, the constitution consists of a set of ideas that are located in their own historical context. Furthermore, these ideas are underpinned by more fundamental principles.[17] The written constitution remains an incomplete expression of these historical ideas and principles; the supposed invisible part of it cannot be understood through its textual expressions, but still contains its fundamental sense. Tribe's specific introduction to Chinese readers displays the flexibility of the 'invisible constitution' from a scholarly interpretative

---

[11] Eric J. Segall, 'Lost in Space: Laurence Tribe's Invisible Constitution' (2009) 103 *Northwestern University Law Review Colloquy* 434, 434.
[12] Ibid., 437.
[13] Ibid., 440.
[14] Martin Loughlin, 'Constitutional Imagination' (2015) 78 *Modern Law Review* 1, 20.
[15] Segall, Supra note 11, 339.
[16] Laurence H. Tribe, *The Invisible Constitution* (Chinese version), Tian Lei trans. (Beijing: Law Press, 2011) X [【美】劳伦斯·却伯 ：《看不见的宪法》，田雷译，北京 ：法律出版社，第 3 页].
[17] Ibid., 4.

methodology for a broader research approach, underpinned by the idea that the substantive rules really matter.[18] In other words, the determinative factor that bonds textualism in constitutional interpretation is the substance of the constitution.[19]

14.2.2. Trends in Researching the 'Invisible Constitution' in China

By equating the 'invisible' aspects of the 1982 Constitution with the unwritten constitution, Chinese constitutional scholarship followed the Chinese translation of Tribe's *The Invisible Constitution* in 2010. In the meantime, there have been two research currents in China's constitutional law research: one that debates the content and implications of the 'unwritten constitution' beyond the text of the 1982 Constitution, and one that offers preliminary theories about the ongoing constitutional practice along the central-local relationship. Sharing the context of the emergence of Chinese political constitutional scholarship, both of these research threads can contribute essential methodological reflections for our analysis into China's reforming constitution.

The debate concerning the unwritten constitution has been triggered by Jiang Shigong's research into the unwritten constitution in China as part of an effort to justify the constitutional legitimacy of the Communist Party of China (CPC).[20] While reviewing similar discussions among American constitutional scholars, Jiang noticed Tribe's work on the 'invisible constitution' and became intellectually interested in the departure of the written constitution from its practice. Jiang believes that there have been aspects of an 'invisible' constitution underpinning the political operation of the PRC for over six decades. Through a realistic perspective and with a remarkable break from mere textual analysis, Jiang has analysed four different aspects of China's unwritten constitution: the party's constitution, constitutional conventions, constitutional doctrines and constitutional statutes.[21] Then, in a 2010 paper, Jiang summarised the four resources of China's unwritten constitution as: (1) the party's constitution as the substantive constitution in China; (2) the 'trinity' system of rule combining the party, the National People's Congress (NPC) and Chinese people together to realise the leadership of the party; (3) local initiatives under

---

[18] Roosevelt III, Supra note 10.
[19] Cass R. Sunstein, *The Impartial Constitution* (Cambridge, MA: Harvard University Press, 1993) 123.
[20] This study has been published in both Chinese (2009) and in English with a modified version in correspondence to the 'historical-empirical' approach advocated by Professor Philip C. C. Huang (2010).
[21] See Jiang Shigong, 'Written and Unwritten Constitutions' (2010) 36 *Modern China* 12.

democratic centralism, which is constitutionally articulated as the unitary system; and (4) the Basic Laws of Special Administration Regions, consisting of 'One Country, Two Systems' as an essential part of the fundamental framework together with the 1982 Constitution.

With a significant break from constitutional normativism, Jiang provides a comprehensive and persuasive account concerning the realistic picture of China's constitutional-political practice in its dual constitutional system.[22] Jiang's methodological approach reflects a sociological concern that fundamental principles, including institutions, rules and conventions significantly influence patterns of political behaviour in governing China.[23] Jiang's research also addresses the self-consciousness of Chinese constitutionalism, which has been appreciated, presented and has tried to defend the legitimacy of constitutionalism, Chinese style.[24]

To Jiang, the 'unwritten constitution' is equated with the rules of real politics outside the text of China's Constitution.[25] Since the Chinese version of Jiang's argument was published in 2009, domestic constitutional scholars have been criticising Jiang's inexact adoption of the 'unwritten constitution' and his suggestion that the party's constitution is the material constitution in China. Zhou Yongkun argues the 'unwritten constitution' should address human rights protections as the fundamental value of modern constitutionalism.[26] With a contextual and historical study on the notion of the 'unwritten constitution' in British tradition, Zhai Zhiyong convincingly argues that the 'unwritten constitution' is an improper label from an outdated taxonomy and can contribute little to the substantive discussion.[27] Other critics have argued that only the written constitution can determinatively underpin a country's constitutional framework, although other factors can also influence the operation of state powers and the protection of civil rights.[28] In Jiang's theoretical

---

[22] For a recent study echoing China's dual constitutional system with further empirical construction, see Shucheng Wang, 'Emergence of a Dual Constitution in Transitional China' (2015) 45 *Hong Kong Law Journal* 819.

[23] Kevin J. O'Brien, 'How Authoritarian Rule Works' (2010) 36 *Modern China* 79, 82.

[24] Larry Catá Backer, 'Towards a Robust Theory of the Chinese Constitutional State: Between Formalism and Legitimacy in Jiang Shigong's Constitutionalism' (2014) 40 *Modern China* 168, 173.

[25] Heike Holbig, 'China's Unwritten Constitution: Ideological Implication of a "Non-ideological" Approach' (2014) 132 *The German Journal of Contemporary China* 53, 55.

[26] Zhou Yongkun, 'Some Issues in Studying the Unwritten Constitution' (2009) 3 *Law Science* 26, 29. [周永坤: "不成文宪法的几个问题"1, 《法学》2011年第3期, 第29页。]

[27] See Zhai Zhiyong, 'The Conceptual Change of the Unwritten Constitution: On Misusing the Unwritten Constitution in China' (2013) 7 *Tsinghua Law Journal* 86. [翟志勇: "英国不成文宪法的观念流变 – – 兼论不成文宪法概念在我国的误用", 《清华法学》2013 年第 3 期 (总第7卷), 第86–97页。]

[28] Ibid., 97.

effort defending China's constitutional uniqueness as a party-state, Tu Zhenyu notes Jiang's overenthusiasm in adopting concepts (such as the notion of the 'invisible' or 'unwritten' constitution) that lack reflection on both the Chinese political status quo and Western discourses. More dangerously, this strongly labelled 'conception-borrowing' could be disrespectful to real Chinese efforts that are part of the country's move towards constitutionalism.[29] Arguably, Jiang failed in his nationalist intention in exactly the same way.

The criticism of Jiang's work by his Chinese colleagues is not targeted at the notion of the unwritten constitution. Rather, the aspect with which most constitutional scholars disagree is Jiang's conclusion that the 'party's constitution' – the unwritten political practices of governance in China – is the material constitution of China. Jiang's critics argue that the notion of the 'unwritten constitution' is open enough to allow any political factors to be considered constitutional. These factors could include identifying the party as a constitutional subject for further study, rather than admitting the party is beyond the constitution, especially concerning the relationship between the constitution and modern political parties.

As it was the thirtieth anniversary of the 1982 Constitution, the year 2012 witnessed another rising research current concerning what is 'unwritten' in the 1982 Constitution, mainly exemplified by Tian Lei's research on pragmatic local practices during the reform period.

Conscious of 'rediscovering the 1982 Constitution in China', Tian employs a new framework to present preliminary theories about the implementation of the 1982 Constitution. Starting from the country's internal 'differential pattern' as the reality of regional diversity in various aspects of governing, there cannot be a formal pattern set for economic policy implemented locally.[30] From the modern semi-feudal and semi-colonial society that inherited the basic territorial structure of the Qing Empire to the military triumph of the CPC, China's historical experience is a testament to the importance of 'differential pattern' in understanding the fundamental situation of China. The practice of the reform, which included nationwide projects such as the South–North Water Diversion Project and the West–East Gas Pipeline Project to close regional disparities in resources and economy, also confirmed the differential pattern

---

[29] Tu Zhenyu, 'Reflecting the Debate on the Unwritten Constitution' (2015) 6 *Political Science and Law* 65, 70. [屠振宇："中国不成文宪法的争论与反思"，《政治与法律》2015年第6期，第70页。]

[30] Tian Lei, '"Differential Patterns", Anti-patterning and the "Incompletely Theorised Agreements": Outlining China's Constitutional Narrative' (2012) 24 *Peking University Law Journal* 927, 927. [田雷："'差序格局'、反定型化与未完全理论化合意：中国宪政模式的一种叙述纲要"，《中外法学》2012年第五期（总第24期），第927页。]

as the determinant factors in governance.[31] Referring to Sunstein's critique on Rawls, Tian adopts 'incompletely theorised agreements' to explain Deng Xiaoping's political pragmatism and its implementation throughout the whole design and ongoing practice of the reform.[32]

In the landscape of Chinese constitutional research during the latest decade, Jiang and Tian's work together represents the growing influence of political constitutional scholarship, which is said to have emerged in 2008 following the publication of a paper concerning the nature of the 1982 Constitution.[33] Going against the grain to see the establishment of judicial review as China's near future, Chen Duanhong brings the CPC, as a constitutional subject, under the framework of popular sovereignty and constituent power. By abstracting the 'five fundamental rules' from the 1982 Constitution, Chen argues that the Constitution cannot be practised through judicial review because its normative characteristics are too fragile.[34] Thus, in the political context of the party-state lacking a judicial review system, the function of regulating public factors is now vested in the internal discipline regulators of the party, administrative supervision of lower level government offices is conducted by higher level offices and the people's congress supervises other state organs, together with subsequent legal sanctions.[35] Further, most of the controversial cases concerning fundamental rights are involved with institutional changes and could even involve the evolution of legal principles based on the transforming social values during the reform. Therefore, it is actually improper for the courts to decide those fundamental political issues, and they are unable to do so.[36] Thus, Chen argues that it is more appropriate to view the 1982 Constitution as a political charter in which lies the possibility of Chinese political constitutionalism.[37]

---

[31] Ibid., 935.
[32] Ibid., 945.
[33] For the starting point of the emerging domestic political constitutionalists and their research, see Gao Quanxi, 'The Rise of Political Constitutional Study and Its Evolution' (2012) 1 *Shanghai Jiao Tong University Law Review* 22, 22 [高全喜："政治宪法学的兴起与嬗变",《交大法学》2013 年第1期, 第 22 页。] In fact, the political constitutional study has been developing by consistent debate between the political constitutionalist and the leading scholars who side with the normative constitutionalism.
[34] Chen Duanhong, 'The Constitution as the Fundamental Law and the Higher Law' (2008) 20 *Peking University Law Journal* 485, 504. [陈端洪："论宪法作为国家的根本法与高级法",《中外法学》2008 年第 4 期（第 20 卷）, 第 504 页。]
[35] Ibid., 502.
[36] Ibid., 502.
[37] Ibid., 511.

14.2.3. *Methodological Reflections: The Written Constitutional Matters*

In studying China's developmental constitutionalism, constitutional scholars can be easily influenced by the political status quo of the ruling party, resulting in some perspectives reflecting the constitutional realism of China's dual constitutional context within a party-state system. As these differences in approach indicate and justify, there is no universally employed methodological approach to determine what forms part of a country's unwritten or 'invisible constitution'. However, the text of the written constitution should clearly be the source restricting the usage and scope of the 'unwritten' constitution. Otherwise, the unlimited use or further construction of the concept of the unwritten or 'invisible constitution' would endanger the unwritten constitution itself as lacking normative justification. This unlimited use would raise a question similar to one raised by those who have reviewed Tribe's work, namely, *who* is to say what the unwritten constitution contains.[38]

Political constitutional study should safeguard the text of the Constitution as the premise for further inquiry into its invisible parts, especially with respect to the essential reforming features and the fundamental framework that the 1982 Constitution has provided for governance. These reform features are not only in place to accomplish practical goals during the reform, but also to ensure the rigid arrangement needed to govern such a wide territory. For example, both Jiang's and Tian's works see the evolving picture of the central-local relationship under the written arrangements of the 1982 Constitution despite of the party and state. Inspired by the methodological review above, taking the unitary system in the 1982 Constitution of China as a case study, this chapter will move to a substantive discussion of the unitary influence on the three types of decentralisation arrangements.

14.3. CASE STUDY: DECENTRALISATION ARRANGEMENTS UNDER THE UNITARY SYSTEM

14.3.1. *Fiscal Decentralisation*

The 1982 Constitution provides total constitutional silence regarding the central-local fiscal arrangements that are entirely textually unwritten. Under the unitary system, fiscal decentralisation from the central government to the provincial governments and lower is deemed to be the key to China's

---

[38] Daniel Lazare, 'No Exit: Laurence Tribe and "The Invisible Constitution"' www.thenation.com/article/no-exit-laurence-tribe-and-invisible-constitution/.

achievement in economic reform in terms of remedying defective institutions.[39] According to an early political-economic study in 1995, fiscal decentralisation resulted in Chinese-style federalism and further enhanced the country's regionalisation.[40] However, China remains a centralised political economy.[41] As a result of this democratic centralism, political control from the centre of the ruling party through its *nomenklatura* ensures both the formality of the central-local relationship and central control over provincial practices during China's continuing economic reform.[42] More importantly, legislative power over taxes was taken into the hands of the central authorities in 1977, before the fiscal contract system started, and it is supposed to stay there through the increasingly formalised legal system; this also indicates the irreversible nature of centralisation as a result of the evolution of China's legal system, which was initially established by clarifying central-local relations formally.

The fiscal federalism model for China calls for a specific context. From the 1980s until 1993, the financial system operating in China was the fiscal contract system. By establishing separate contracts with the central government, provincial governments could retain local revenues, directing only a small portion – consisting of customs, direct taxes and taxes paid by state-owned enterprises in different localities – to the central government. Fiscal contracts between the central government and a particular province were negotiated every five years.[43] In practice, local governments exceeded their limited authority and provided tax reductions that substantively altered the national fiscal policy established by the central government. Informal practices such as this had a negative impact on central revenues in two important indicators. First, the central ratio to the total revenue declined significantly, dropping from 40.5 per cent in 1984 to 28 per cent in 1993. Second, the central revenue share of GDP declined dramatically from 25.5 per cent in 1980 to 12.3 per cent in 1993. However, China's GDP grew at an average annual rate of 9.9 per

---

[39] See Wang Shaoguang, 'Defective Institutions and Their Consequences: Lessons from China, 1980–1993' (2002) 35 *Communist and Post-Communist Studies* 133.
[40] Gabriella Montinola, Yinyi Qian and Barry R. Weingast, 'Federalism, Chinese Style: The Political Basis for Economic Success in China' (1995) *World Politics* 55, 80.
[41] Louis Chih-hung Liu, 'The Typology of Fiscal Decentralisation System: A Cluster Analysis Approach' (2011) 31 *Public Administration and Development* 363, 371.
[42] See Susan L. Shirk, *The Political Logic of Economic Reform in China* (Berkeley: University of California Press 1993); Yumin Sheng, 'Central-Provincial Relations at the CCP Central Committees: Institutions, Measurement and Empirical Trends' (2005) 182 *The China Quarterly* 338.
[43] Jun Ma, 'Modelling Central-Local Fiscal Relations in China' (1995) 6 *China Economic Review* 105, 105.

cent from 1980 to 1993.[44] In other words, the first decade of economic reform resulted in conflicts between a weakened central government and energetic economic development at the local level, especially in the eastern regions. This imbalance placed pressure on the central government to adopt a 'tax separation system' in 1994 in order to strengthen China's state capacity for its transition.[45]

During the 1980s, the unitary system seemed to be evolving into a form of de facto federalism, but normative evidence regarding the power of legislating tax law assists in maintaining the vertical unitary nature of intergovernmental fiscal relations. Institutional centralisation of tax power started with the decision of the Finance Ministry on the Tax Management System in 1977 (the 1977 Decision), which seeded the basic structure of the central-provincial fiscal relationship for the reform. This decision was released one year ahead of the official beginning of the reform and two years earlier than the establishment of the first four Special Economic Zones that are the only exceptions to the centralised legislative tax power for special authorisation from the NPC. According to the decision, the central government was exclusively in charge of any changes to the revenue policy, the adoption and implementation of the tax law, the imposition and cessation of specific taxes, and the addition or reduction of tax items and rates. The decision also authorised very limited financial powers exercisable by the provincial governments in different situations; these powers required the approval of the finance ministry. Moreover, these authorised powers (with particular emphasis) *in general* shall not be reauthorised to any government lower than the provincial level. For provincial governments, re-delegating authorised fiscal power was not totally forbidden; reach from the central government into local fiscal affairs existed only in the central-provincial relationship, which is still an institutional feature within China's unitary system, with further development in administration.[46]

What was really decentralised by the 1977 decision was administrative power over taxes. This was part of the preparation for the coming fiscal decentralisation during the 1980s. When the 1977 decision was implemented, the

---

[44] Anping Chen and Nicolaas Groenewold, 'The National and Regional Effects of Fiscal Decentralisation in China' (2013) 51 *The Annals of Regional Science* 731, 732.

[45] See Wang Shaoguang and Hu An'gang, *The Chinese Economy in Crisis: State Capacity and Tax Reform* (New York: M. E. Sharpe, 2001). For a highly influential research urging separation of the tax system in the 1990s, see Wang Shaoguang and Hu Angang, *Report on the State of the Nation: Strengthening the Leading Role of the Central Government during the Transition to the Market Economy* (New Haven: Yale University Press, 1993).

[46] The latest evolution is the direct provincial governance over the counties, bypassing the municipalities in between since 2005.

tax collection and management system was relatively decentralised. Local tax departments were subordinate to both the local governments and the tax offices from the central government, indicating that local governments could influence local tax collection and management according to their own interests. Before adopting the fiscal contract system, there were nationwide restructurings of the tax management system in 1978 and 1982, but the administrative decentralisation of tax collection and taxation was preserved until the tax-separating reform started in 1994.[47] However, lacking the complete legal system of the Chinese state and the legal consciousness of its officials, the violation of the exclusive authority of the Finance Ministry not only occurred in local governments, but also occurred in other departments of the central government.[48]

The power of tax legislation has not been returned to lower governments since the central authorities took it back – until now. Following this trend, the 1994 tax-separation reform echoed and enhanced the centralisation spirit of the tax power, which had been expected early in 1977 when national taxes were separated from local ones; in particular, there have been national tax offices established locally for independent collection of national taxes. After 1994, under the framework of the tax-separating system, bargains between the central government and the local authorities have centred on the interpretation of tax laws rather than the former implementation of direct alternatives without authorisation in 1980.[49]

Even more important, but usually neglected by both legal scholars and political scientists, is that the lawmaking law was drafted in 1993 when the tax-separating reform was underway. During its long drafting process, the formality and centralisation of legislative power had been emphasised by the relevant officials repeatedly.[50] When implemented in 2000, this law provided a more orderly and formal legal system, with particular arrangements

---

[47] Xu Jian, 'Centralising the Allocation of Financial Power: Process and Influences' (2012) *Peking University Law Journal* 800, 802. [徐键："分税制下的财权集中配置：过程及其影响"，《中外法学》2012年第4期，第802页。]

[48] In 1982, there were nine regulatory documents made by other departments of the State Council during September 1981 to February 1982 ultra vires relating to tax affairs, out of thirteen selected randomly by the financial ministry. See Cui Wei, 'The Origin of the Highly Centralised tax Legislative Power' (2012) *Peking University Law Journal* 762, 776. [崔威："税收立法高度集权模式的起源"，《中外法学》2012年第4期，第776页。]

[49] Xu Jian, Supra note 47, 811.

[50] Qiao Xiaoyang, 'Legislating the Law-making Law, Promoting the Rule of Law: A Speech in the Workshop of Drafting the Law-making Law' (1997) 3 *Administrative Law Review* 1, 2, 3. [乔晓阳："制定立法法，促进依法治国——在《立法法》起草工作研讨会上的讲话（1997年4月9日）"，《行政法学研究》1997年第3期，第2、3页。] Qiao was then the deputy director of the legislative affairs commission of the NPC Standing Committee.

concerning the national legal hierarchy. This system has been further consolidated by its recent amendment in 2015, which places further limitations on delegated legislation with a stronger tone of the tax legality.[51] Centralisation of tax legislation power essentially established the constitutional bottom line of the unitary system.

The system of separating tax revenues has been evolving along a clear chronology entwined with two core issues: its implementation below the provincial level, and the distribution of administrative functions and responsibilities in line with the central-provincial fiscal relationship. In 1996, the Finance Ministry released an official notice of its intention to improve the administration of the system separating tax revenue below the provincial level.[52] In 2002, the State Council approved and transmitted a similar suggestion to the Finance Ministry, which indicated the chaotic administration of fiscal affairs below the provincial level.[53] Direct provincial administration at the county level was established in 2009 and has enhanced provincial power in fiscal administration and aims to implement the separation of tax reform at levels lower than every province.[54]

The 1994 tax-separating reform was not complete; it left an uncoordinated system of administrative and expenditure responsibilities at the local level. Following the State Council's decision in 1993, the Budget Law confirmed the system separating tax revenues in 1994.[55] In the following year, the State Council released regulations implementing the Budget Law. These regulations, which separated tax attribution between the central and local governments, theoretically complied with vertical administrative distribution.[56] However, since the objective of separating the tax revenues was to strengthen the fiscal capacity of the central government, the central government has been slow to promote tax and revenue reform that distributes expenditure responsibilities in proportion to the fiscal capacity of governments at each lower level.

---

[51] Article 8(6), the Law-making Law of the PRC (2000, rev. 2015).

[52] The Finance Ministry of the PRC, 'Notice on improving the separating tax revenues administration system below the provincial level' [《关于完善省以下分税制财税管理体制有关问题的通知》] (1996) www.reformdata.org/content/19951226/7992.html.

[53] 'Opinions on improving the separating tax revenues administration system below the provincial level' [《关于完善省以下财政管理体制有关问题的意见》] (2009) www.moa.gov.cn/zwllm/zcfg/flfg/200601/t20060123_541180.htm.

[54] 'Opinions of the Ministry of Finance on boosting the reform of public finance of counties directly governed by provinces' [《财政部关于推进省直接管理县财政改革的意见》] (2009) www.mof.gov.cn/pub/czzz/zhongguocaizhengzazhishe_daohanglanmu/zhongguocaizhengzazhishe_zhengcefagui/200909/t20090914_207256.html.

[55] Article 15, Budget Law of the PRC (1995, rev. 2014).

[56] Article 6, Regulation for the Implementation of the Budget Law of the PRC (1995).

The absence of a constitutional principle of expenditure responsibility division between the central government and the local ones has been criticised as an inconsistent drawback delaying the separating tax reform.[57] The tax revenue system is intended to be based on the vertical distribution of public administration with proper expenditure responsibilities, but this crucial principle of modern fiscal systems has remained largely unimplemented in China's case for over three decades. The system separating tax revenues eventually evolved into a system that contains a centralised fiscal system and a growing local expenditure burden. In 2016, the State Council released guidelines on promoting reform relating to the division of financial powers and expenditure responsibilities between the central and local governments.[58] These reforms aim to clarify the expenditure responsibilities of governments at different levels and improve government efficiency in providing public services.

14.3.2. Regional National Autonomy with Ethnic Features

Unlike the clear distribution of power between the state and federal governments and the residual powers left to the states in some federal constitutions, RNA under China's constitutional framework lacks a list of reserved autonomous powers. Beyond regional autonomy is the authority at the upper levels of government, including the central authorities.

The real power structure of the autonomous regions under the unitary system is the premise of discussing what type of power the autonomous areas essentially enjoy. Article 4(3) of the 1982 Constitution provides the establishment of the RNA, 'Regional autonomy is practised in areas where people of minority nationalities live in compact communities; in these areas, organs of self-government are established for the exercise of the right of autonomy. All the national autonomous areas are inalienable parts of the People's Republic of China'. This expression offers some basic characteristics of the RNA, such as its ethnic features, organs of self-government and the supremacy of national unity. While this Article does not provide sufficient information about the operation of regional autonomy, the picture becomes clearer when we refer to Article 30, which concerns the 'administrative division' of power.

---

[57] Zhou Feizhou, 'A Decade of Tax-Sharing: The System and Its Evolution' (2006) 6 *Social Sciences in China* 100, 102. [周飞舟："分税制十年：制度及其影响",《中国社会科学》2006年第06期, 第 102 页。]

[58] 'The State Council's Guideline on Promoting the Reform of Dividing Financial Powers and Expenditure Responsibilities between Central and Local Governments' [2016] 26 *Bulletin of the State Council of the People's Republic of China* 16–22. ["国务院关于推进中央与地方财政事权和支出责任划分改革的指导意见",《国务院公报》2016年第26号, 第 16–22 页。]

Article 30 of the 1982 Constitution provides the fundamental structure of the unitary system and its 'administrative division', which is established based on the province-city/county-town structure as a three-tiered division. Notably, the RNA areas in this chapter are institutionally 'integrated' into the unitary system. There are also three levels of authorities in the RNA system exercising both autonomous powers and ordinary powers of the non-autonomous authorities. Autonomous regions, autonomous prefectures and autonomous counties are parallel to provinces, cities and counties in general.

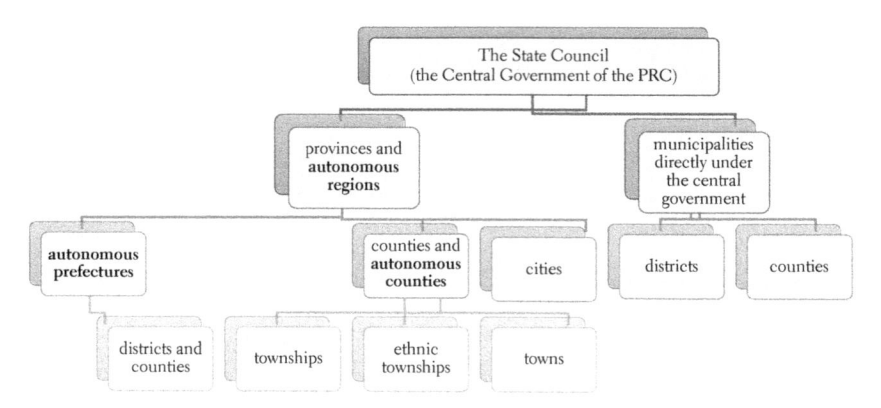

```
                    The State Council
            (the Central Government of the PRC)
                          |
        ┌─────────────────┴──────────────────┐
        |                                    |
   provinces and                      municipalities
   autonomous                         directly under
   regions                            the central
                                      government
        |                                    |
   ┌────┴─────┬──────────┐          ┌────────┴────────┐
   |          |          |          |                 |
autonomous  counties and  cities  districts        counties
prefectures autonomous
            counties
   |          |                ethnic
districts   townships         townships    towns
and
counties
```

The RNA is interlaced with the unitary system throughout the three levels of national administration. In other words, within one autonomous region, smaller autonomous areas such as autonomous prefectures and autonomous counties can exist. For example, Xin Jiang Uygur Autonomous Region (AR) also accommodates six autonomous prefectures and six autonomous counties where communities of Kazakh, Mongolian, Hui people and Kyrgyz live.[59] This interlaced system also implies that even for the same ethnic people, autonomy could be exercised in different areas. Outside the Tibet AR, Tibetans also enjoy ten autonomous prefectures and two autonomous counties across four provinces.[60] Moreover, some autonomous areas have two or three ethnic minorities as 'multi-ethnic' counties, such as the Enshi Tujia/Miao Autonomous Prefecture in Hubei Province or the Weining Autonomous County for the Yi, Hui and Miao people in Guizhou Province. However, for

---

[59] The State Ethnic Affairs Commission of People's Republic of China, 'Basic Information about the 155 Autonomous Regions' (2005) www.seac.gov.cn/gjmw/zwgk/2005-02-28/1177034000717203.htm.

[60] Barry Sautman, 'Scaling Back Minority Rights? The Debates about China's Ethnic Policies' (2010) 46 *Stanford Journal of International Law* 51, 59.

a specific ethnic group that lives in an autonomous area, the closest higher authority will either be an autonomous one due to the presence of another group of ethnic people, or it will be non-autonomous. This institution is very different from the understanding of autonomy based on specific groups of ethnic minority people. On the contrary, these groups fall under different governments in the areas where they live.

The *interlaced* system provides contours for the RNA, and the system will be clarified by investigating who enjoys autonomous power in autonomous regions, what autonomous power includes and how autonomous powers are exercised. Article 4 of the Law of Regional National Autonomy (LRNA), together with Article 30 of the 1982 Constitution as its constitutional foundation, is supposed to be the key to understanding the constitutional nature of the RNA. In accordance with the interlaced system provided in Article 30 of the 1982 Constitution, Article 4 of the LRNA articulates that the 'state organs of self-government' in national autonomous areas exercise the power of regional autonomy together with powers enjoyed by the regular local governments.[61] In addition, Article 4(3) and Article 115 of the 1982 Constitution provide the 'organs of self-government' that are the means of exercising autonomous power. According to the LRNA, the 'organs of self-government' in autonomous regions include regional people's congresses and governments.[62] This means that the autonomous powers in ethnic minority areas refer to both legislative and administrative powers. Judicial power is excluded from ethnic minority regional autonomy. The lack of an independent judicial system indicates the fundamental differences in China's RNA practice compared to more commonly practised local discretion.[63]

In practice, autonomous power under RNA is exercised in the ordinary operation of those areas' governments and congresses. In an ideal situation, when exercising autonomous power on specific issues, the people's congress and the government in one autonomous area would work as the 'organs of self-government'. In other issues, the non-autonomous government might also address the legislative body and the administration of an autonomous county, prefecture or region, which function in the same way as the non-autonomous

---

[61] Article 4, the Law of the People's Republic of China on Regional National Autonomy (1984, rev. 2001).
[62] Article 15, the Law of the People's Republic of China on Regional National Autonomy (1984, rev. 2001).
[63] Erik Friberg, '"Master of Their Homelands": Revisiting the Regional Ethnic Autonomy System in China in Light of Local Institutional Developments' in M. Weller and Stefan Wolff (eds.), *Autonomy, Self-governance, and Conflict Resolution: Innovative Approaches to Institutional Design in Divided Societies* (London, New York: Routledge, 2005) 220.

bodies. In this light, the next question concerns which 'specific issues' fall under autonomous powers, which directly concern the scope and limitation of autonomy that the autonomous organs in one autonomous area enjoys.

The scope of autonomy in ethnic areas pertains to 'internal affairs', which mainly covers the protection of the unique culture and traditions of a specific minority group. This general principle is implicit in both the 1982 Constitution and the LRNA, where the principle is only textually referred to in the preamble. However, it could still be interpreted from the existing provisions of the 1982 Constitution, which contains six basic issues that fall in the autonomous scope:

- *With the approval of the standing committee of the people's congress from a higher level*, to legislate autonomous regulations and specific regulations; the regulations of the autonomous prefectures and the autonomous counties should also be reported to the Standing Committee of the NPC to be recorded (Article 116);
- *With the approval of the State Council*, to organise local public security forces (Article 120);
- *In accordance with autonomy regulations*, to employ the spoken and the written language or languages in common use in the locality (Article 121);
- *Under the guidance of state plans*, to develop the economy in the respective areas (Article 118);
- To *independently* administer their own finances in the autonomous areas (Article 117);
- To *independently* govern educational, scientific, cultural, public health and physical culture affairs (Article 119).[64]

The internal scope of autonomous areas under RNA rests in the five issues listed above. They also highlight the key terms for autonomous areas with various types of state control.[65] More importantly, the limitation varies with respect to different regional issues, and the formal independent exercise of autonomous power exists merely in their own finance and cultural development. According to the LRNA, the latter power includes ethnic culture, regional education and the use of ethnic languages, regional scientific development and the heritage of ethnic traditional medicine.[66] However, autonomous

---

[64] Articles 116–21, the 1982 Constitution (rev. 2004).
[65] In fact, Chapter 3 of the Law of the People's Republic of China on Regional National Autonomy (1984, rev. 2001) unfolds and enriches these fundamental issues articulated in the Constitution with details.
[66] Articles 36–45 the Law of the People's Republic of China on Regional National Autonomy (1984, rev. 2001).

legislative power, which represents the core characteristic of a RNA institution, is burdened by supervision from the central authorities.[67]

Although the 1982 Constitution permits autonomous areas to modify higher laws and policies by legislating their own specific regulations, legislative bodies at the provincial and municipal levels are required to submit their local legislation to the Standing Committee of the NPC for approval.[68] By comparison, the general regulations and the implementation of non-autonomous local legislation do not require the approval of the NPC. It seems that under the current constitutional arrangement, the more autonomy an area enjoys, the more central control will be designed to regulate the exercise of that autonomy in order to ensure it will not endanger the central authorities.

Aside from the central supervision of autonomous legislatures, approval from the central authority is also required in cases of alternative implementation or delayed practice of national policies, the organisation of local public security forces, changes to regional boundaries and the establishment of the foreign trade ports.[69] These 'approval' procedures highlight the continuing central control over national autonomous regions and the limits of national regional autonomy.

The reform has brought new issues to public governance on ethnic affairs beyond the rigid constitutional structure, and these new issues require more engagement of the central government in balancing regional development. During the first two decades of the reform, national economic developments prioritised the eastern part of China, as the fiscal decentralisation analysis in the former section shows. As a consequence, the western part of China has lagged behind. The minority-majority income inequality in rural China rapidly widened between 1988 and 1995.[70] Policies from the central authority to counteract the national minority-majority income gap in rural China are needed.[71] Since 2000, the Western Development Project has been under development with the aim of addressing the regional disparity through more balance in regional economic development.[72] Together with this project, the

---

[67] Article 116 the 1982 Constitution (rev. 2004).
[68] Article 100 the 1982 Constitution (rev. 2004).
[69] Article 116 the 1982 Constitution (rev. 2004); Articles 19, 20, 24, 31 the Law of the People's Republic of China on Regional National Autonomy (1984, rev. 2001).
[70] With data from nineteen provinces. Björn Gustafsson and Li Shi, 'The Ethnic Minority-Majority Income Gap in Rural China during Transition' (2003) 51 *Economic Development and Cultural Change* 805, 819.
[71] Ibid., 820.
[72] For an overview on policy changes in the Mao era and the Reform see: Susan K. McCarthy, 'The State, Minorities, and Dilemmas of Development in Contemporary China' (2002) 26 *Fletcher Forum of World Affairs* 107.

State Council has established the fiscal transfer system in ethnic regions, covering all five autonomous regions, three provinces treated like those regions, including Qing Hai, Yunnan and Guizhou and all regional autonomous prefectures outside the five autonomous regions.[73] During 2000–15, the revenues transferred to the ethnic areas mentioned above reached 395.5 billion RMBs in total, with 58.2 billion RMBs solely in 2015.[74] In some specific cases, such as the Tibet AR, subsidies from the central government in all terms took over 95 per cent of regional expenditures from 1952 to 2013. At the same time, the way in which money from the central government has been spent remains another issue worth further investigation beyond the legal context.[75]

The regional disparities have also resulted in a massive immigration of ethnic minorities to the cities. This has strengthened urban ethnicity identity, especially through labour market development.[76] To address the growing mobile ethnic populations in cities, the State Council implemented the Regulation of Urban Ethnic Affairs for governments in 1993. The Regulation is in effect in both cities under the direct governance of the State Council and municipalities lower than the provincial level, with a focus on social welfare and specific preferential policies of mobile ethnic workers.[77] After practices that lasted more than ten years, the State Council sought public opinions for the amendment of the Regulation in 2016.[78] Online submissions indicated a strong public will for greater integration between different ethnic groups, including Han Chinese, through an 'embedded social structure'.[79] This corresponds to the rise of ethnic awareness among both Han Chinese and ethnic minorities. With China deepening its process of urbanisation, cities are becoming increasingly important sites for the negotiation, contestation and remaking of ethnic identity.[80]

---

[73] This scope was expanded to all ethnic counties in 2006.
[74] The Financial Ministry of the PRC: 'Further increase of the central avenues transfer to historical revolutionary base areas, ethnic areas, borderlands and poverty areas' [中华人民共和国财政部："中央财政2015年进一步加大转移支付力度支持革命老区、民族地区、边疆地区、贫困地区发展"] www.gov.cn/xinwen/2015-12/07/content_5020833.htm.
[75] For a policy evaluation from the sociological perspective on Tibetan market participation under central investment, see Wang Shiyong, 'Policy Impact on Tibetan Market Participation' (2009) 10 *Asian Ethnicity* 1.
[76] See Wu Jiaping, 'The Rise of Ethnicity under China's Market Reforms' (2014) 38 *International Journal of Urban and Regional Research* 967.
[77] 'Regulations on the urban ethnic affairs' (1993).
[78] Before 28 July 2016, the draft was available on the public opinions soliciting system of the China Government Legal Information Website which is supported by the Legislative Affairs Office of the State Council.
[79] Ibid.
[80] Jiaping, Supra note 76, 981.

14.3.3. *The Hong Kong SAR under 'One Country, Two Systems'*

When considering regional autonomy under the unitary system, Hong Kong is a more significant case, both in terms of the limitation on autonomy in the SAR and the resulting tension with the central authorities for complex reasons. Still under the principle of 'One Country, Two Systems' (OCTS) that is not written in the 1982 Constitution, Macau has experienced a more peaceful transition than Hong Kong and has experienced little friction with the central authorities.[81] In fact, before reunification, Macau and Hong Kong had already taken different perspectives in terms of their attitudes towards integration with China.[82]

For Hong Kong, the post-1997 constitutional framework inherited some similar structural elements to its past. The Basic Law of Hong Kong SAR sets out Hong Kong's high degree of autonomy in some details through a specific set of constitutional arrangements in nine of its chapters and three of its annexes.[83] The Hong Kong SAR enjoys autonomous powers in administration, legislation and an independent judiciary with its own final adjudication.[84] In Hong Kong's pre-1997 colonial political system, the Governor – who represented the British monarch – took full control of Hong Kong's internal affairs, and the United Kingdom authorities de jure controlled its external links. The constitutional design in both the Joint Declaration between China and the United Kingdom (1984) and the Basic Law of the Hong Kong SAR (1990) have considered and echoed this historic institutional feature. The Basic Law of the Hong Kong SAR adopts the general political system and is 'executive-led'. The Chief Executive represents the core of the constitutional structure in the Hong Kong SAR and is accountable to the Hong Kong SAR in addition to the central government.[85] Although foreign affairs and regional defence in the Hong Kong SAR rest with the obligations of the central government in Articles 13 and 14 of the Basic Law of the Hong Kong SAR, it is also clearly provided that the military force of the People's Liberation Army garrisoned in Hong Kong shall not interfere in local affairs.[86] Providing a workable constitutional structure for Hong Kong's politics after 1997, the Basic Law of the

---

[81] Stuat Lau, 'China Hails Macau's Adherence to Basic Law in Subtle Warning against Democracy Movements' *South China Morning Post* (9 December 2014) www.scmp.com/news/hong-kong/article/1659229/macau-held-role-model-obeying-basic-law?page=all.
[82] Ming K. Chan, 'Different Roads to Home: The Retrocession of Hong Kong and Macau to Chinese Sovereignty' (2003) 12 *Journal of Contemporary China* 493, 493.
[83] Kate Olley, 'Introduction to Judicial Review in Hong Kong' (2003) 8 *Judicial Review* 109.
[84] Article 2, Basic Law of the Hong Kong SAR (1990).
[85] Article 43, ibid.
[86] Article 14(3), ibid..

Hong Kong SAR also functions as the constitutional source of judicial review in Hong Kong's courts: 'No law enacted by the legislature of the Hong Kong Special Administrative Region shall contravene this law'.[87]

Treating the Hong Kong SAR as a separate constitutional system 'in territory' obscures the full picture of its autonomy, which is designed to be read together with the unitary system.[88] The limitation is, first and fundamentally, somewhere between a generally high degree of autonomy and the direct governance of the central government. Article 12 of the Basic Law of the Hong Kong SAR reads that Hong Kong is under *the direct governance of the central government* while enjoying its special autonomy. Such a notion of 'under the direct governance' (直辖) is not novel in the unitary system. Municipalities 'under the direct governance' exist in the mainland according to Article 31 of the 1982 Constitution. As *zhi xia shi* (直辖市), they are of national importance and equal to provinces in legal status and practical conditions, including area and population. The history of this type of institution in modern China can be dated back to the 'special municipalities' (特别市) established by the Beiyang Government during the 1920s. Now, there are four in total: Beijing, Tianjin, Shanghai and Chongqing. They are authorised to have more powers than ordinary cities under provinces, this includes, for example, the power to legislate their own municipal laws and administrative regulations. This authorised power is not considered autonomous in China's constitutional law.[89] In the analogical reasoning of the Chinese unitary system, 'under the direct governance' indicates that Hong Kong, as the SAR under the OCTS, still ranks on the same level as provinces, autonomous regions and *zhi xia shi* under the whole unitary system of China.

Early constitutional controversies rose from Hong Kong's independent judicial power and the Standing Committee of the NPC's authority, which resulted in the 'dual track system' in interpreting the Basic Law of the Hong Kong SAR.[90] With the maintenance of the pre-1997 common law system, the

---

[87] Article 11(3), ibid..
[88] Ever since the Joint Declaration signed by Chinese and British governments, the promise of Hong Kong's 'high degree of autonomy' captured the major research concerns towards Hong Kong's fate towards and after 1997. This trend arose even after the Basic Law of Hong Kong SAR was approved by the Seventh National People's Congress of China in 1990, for it takes the same wording from the Joint Declaration.
[89] Article 63 the Legislative Law (2000; rev. 2015).
[90] See Dai Yaoting and Wang Xiaonan, 'The Constitutional Review in Hong Kong' in Tang Dezong and Wang Pengxiang (eds.), *Legal Developments in Two Coasts and Four Areas* vol. 1 (Taipei: Institutum Iurisprudentiae, Academia Sinica, 2007) 143–85. [戴耀廷、杨晓楠："香港的违宪审查制度", 汤德宗、王鹏翔《两岸四地法律发展（上册）》（台北：中央研究院法学研究所，2007），第143-185页。]

Basic Law of the Hong Kong SAR leaves significant scope for judicial independence. The explicit limitation on judicial power is only in Article 19, which excludes state acts from the jurisdiction of Hong Kong courts. Therefore, the Standing Committee of the NPC has the final say on the interpretation of the Basic Law of the Hong Kong SAR.[91] In early controversial cases, the Court of Final Appeal actively probed the scope of its judicial autonomy through judicial review of laws made by the preliminary legislative council, resulting in unavoidable friction during the post-transition period between the Hong Kong SAR and the central government.[92] Independent judicial power is considered to be a challenge to the central governance and a means of safeguarding the spirit of rule of law in Hong Kong.[93]

As time has passed, constitutional disharmonies between Hong Kong and Beijing have turned their focus to the post of Chief Executive for complex economic and social reasons. As the core 'joint' of the relationship between the Hong Kong SAR and the central authorities, the Basic Law of the Hong Kong SAR provides Section 1 of Chapter IV on the Chief Executive, but it only defines the political function of the Chief Executive as 'accountable to the Central People's Government and the Hong Kong Special Administrative Region' in accordance with the provisions of the Law.[94] The Chief Executive's accountability to the central government appears logical and substantially echoes central governance in Article 12 of the Basic Law of the Hong Kong SAR. However, this accountability remains vague in the Basic Law. How does it apply to 'the Hong Kong SAR'? If it refers to the Hong Kong people, then this vagueness left by the drafters of the Basic Law is understandable for further amending towards electoral reform, according to Annex 1, which shall be proposed from the central authorities. Since the Chief Executive should be appointed by the central government, it can also be assumed that even if universal suffrage of the Chief Executive were realised, without a nomination committee substantially controlled by the central authorities and no matter who is elected by what amended procedure, the central authorities have the final say on the appointment; namely, they can deny the appointment, though in practice, this may result in a constitutional crisis.[95]

Compared to the over-cooperative interactions between the legislature body and the Chief Executive in Macao, the political structure of Hong

---

[91] Article 158, Basic Law of the Hong Kong SAR (1990).
[92] Two typical cases are *Ng Ka Ling v. Director of Immigration* [1999] 1 HKLRD 315; *Chong Fung-yuen v. The Director of Immigration* [2001] 2 HKLRD 533.
[93] Benny Y. T. Tai, 'Judicial Autonomy in Hong Kong' (2010) 24 *China Information* 295.
[94] Article 43(2), Basic Law of the Hong Kong SAR (1990).
[95] Article 45, Basic Law of the Hong Kong SAR (1990).

Kong is deemed more 'restrictive' in terms of the Legislative Council and the Chief Executive.[96] However, in regard to the impeachment conducted by the Legislative Council against the Chief Executive, even the motion of impeachment must be passed by a two-thirds majority of all members of the Legislative Council.[97] In fact, the interplay between the Chief Executive and the legislature is a fundamental issue of Hong Kong's political structure. On the one hand, the Chief Executive leading the civil service bureaucracy is accountable to the central government through the central appointment process; on the other hand, the democratic process for locally electing legislators and political parties is becoming increasingly inflexible. The tension between these two formulates the 'halfway house' within Hong Kong's political system, founded by the Basic Law of the Hong Kong SAR.[98] In other words, the Basic Law establishes a government that is 'answerable' to the Legislative Council rather than accountable to it.[99]

In practice, the problematic design of the Chief Executive's accountability could be accurately presented correlatively through the universal suffrage issue. Since Article 45 of the Basic Law of the Hong Kong SAR reads that the candidates for Chief Executive should be nominated by a special committee, the way to achieve universal suffrage based on that article has been a central part of the subsequent Chief Executive's political reform proposals after 1997. These reforms gained the most opposition from Hong Kong residents who want 'one person, one vote' and consider the elective committee to be the mechanism for central control. In 2004 and 2014, the Standing Committee of the NPC made an interpretation on the Basic Law of the Hong Kong SAR and one decision that substantially amended the universal suffrage proposed in the Basic Law of the Hong Kong SAR.[100]

---

[96] See Yin Yi fen, 'The Restrictive and Cooperative Relationship between the Legislature and the Chief Executive in Hong Kong and Macau' (2008) 49 *Macau Studies* 35. [邓奋益：" 港澳地区立法会于行政长官的制约配合关系", 《澳门研究》第49期，第35-39页。]

[97] Article 73(9), Basic Law of the Hong Kong SAR (1990).

[98] Albert H. Y. Chen, 'The Theory, Constitution and Practice of Autonomy: The Case of Hong Kong' in Jorge Oliveira and Paulo Cardinal (eds.), *One Country, Two Systems, Three Legal Orders: Perspectives of Evolution* (Berlin, London: Springer, 2009) 764.

[99] Ian Schott, 'The Government and Statutory Bodies in Hong Kong: Centralisation and Autonomy' (2006) *Public Organization Review* 185, 189.

[100] Secretariat of the Legislative Council, 'A Brief Overview on the Interpretations Made by the Standing Committee of the National People's Congress According to Article 158 of the Basic Law' 3 www.legco.gov.hk/yr11-12/chinese/sec/library/1112in29-c.pdf. The 2014 '8·31' Decision www.2017.gov.hk/filemanager/template/tc/doc/20140831a.pdf.

As the result of accumulating civic dissents towards Beijing, the Occupy Central Movement in fact raised harsh questions for both Hong Kong residents and the central authorities: do the people of Hong Kong have the right to oppose the Basic Law? In 2014, the citizens' discontent turned into the Occupy Central Movement and then developed into the so-called Umbrella Movement, which has received worldwide coverage.[101] In other words, if the people of Hong Kong are deeply disappointed with certain articles in the Basic Law of the Hong Kong SAR, how can they change it? Again, seeking a proper answer to this question will reveal the fundamental limitations of the Hong Kong SAR's autonomy. Article 159 of the Basic Law of the Hong Kong SAR confers the amending power on the NPC. The Hong Kong government has the power to propose amending the Basic Law of the Hong Kong SAR to the NPC in line with the Standing Committee of the NPC and the central government. However, such amendments must be approved by the Hong Kong representatives of the NPC, a two-thirds majority of the legislative council and the Chief Executive. Following this procedure, even if an amending proposal went through the regional procedure in Hong Kong, it may not be passed by the NPC. It is not surprising that the final say still belongs to the central authorities according to the implicit logic of the unitary system.

In the winter of 2016, the Standing Committee of the NPC released a new interpretation of Article 104 in the Basic Law of the Hong Kong SAR in response to the separationist oath-taking of two members of the Legislative Council when assuming office.[102] This interpretation clarifies both the content and procedure of the oath-taking. Once this procedure is violated, the oath-taker will be disqualified forthwith from assuming the specified public office. In addition, it also imposes legal consequences on oath-takers who intentionally read out words incorrectly. Since the oath-taking interpretation was released before judicial decisions on the same issue, the Standing Committee aims to bind the court and control the decision, which might damage judicial authority in the Hong Kong SAR, which is guaranteed to be independent according to the Basic Law of the Hong Kong SAR.[103]

---

[101] For an overview of the 2014 Hong Kong pro-democracy protests, see Jonathan Kaiman 'Hong Kong's Umbrella Revolution: *The Guardian* briefing' *The Guardian* (30 September 2014) www.theguardian.com/world/2014/sep/30/-sp-hong-kong-umbrella-revolution-pro-democracy-protests.

[102] The Standing Committee of National People's Congress, 'Interpretation of Article 104 of Basic Law of Hong Kong SAR' news.xinhuanet.com/english/2016-11/07/c_135811504.htm.

[103] Wilson Yuen, 'The Crisis of Judicial Independence in Hong Kong' (*I·CONnet*, 4 November 2016) www.iconnectblog.com/2016/11/the-crisis-of-judicial-independence-in-hong-kong/.

14.4. CONCLUSION

The 'invisible constitution', as a methodological approach rather than a mere metaphoric term, invites constitutional scholars to investigate constitutional implications, practices and disharmonies more deeply. The special intellectual link between the 'invisible constitution' and Chinese constitutional study is a cause for caution in the methodological design of this study in the sharing context of political constitutional scholarship. In general, what is invisible in a written constitution has its own malleability that might blur the borders between constitutional law scholarship and political studies. However, political constitutional study should safeguard the written constitution as the premise for further inquiry into its invisible content. Even from the perspective of constitutional realism, it is crucial to read the 'invisible constitution' out of a written constitution, rather than to refer to more political factors that might be only relevant to the written constitution.

The incomplete nature of the 1982 reforming Constitution of China drives scholarly efforts to consider the whole picture of its unwritten but de facto evolution in the reform and, more implicitly, the internal logic of the constitutional unitary system. A general conclusion from the whole picture of China's sub-state decentralisation is that the implicit limitation of these decentralisation arrangements exists in the institutional design itself rather than the written articles. In other words, they not only fall constitutionally under the central authorities with their 'visibly' articulated central control; they are also designed to fit within the unitary system, and the central authorities have the final say on the central-local relationship in any case. This is exactly why sub-state decentralisation arrangements are easily considered defective in comparative studies that search for some 'real' autonomy.

Lacking a proper mechanism that can resolve the central-local disputes has different results.

During early fiscal decentralisation in the 1980s, the provincial governments caused collusion against central policies even as they were, hopefully, combined with the centralist norms. At the same time, the autonomous regulations remained absent, for they might lead to vertical separation between the national autonomous regions and the central authorities. A significant institutional feature is that the unitary system is reinforced by the newly amended Lawmaking Law in 2015 after pragmatic practice during last three decades. The new Lawmaking Law regulates local legislation more formally and rigidly, including the local legislation of ethnic autonomous areas. In the case of the Hong Kong SAR, the central government has been displaying some self-restraint according to OCTS by growing its political governance through the Chief Executive.[104] Notably, tightening central control can be blamed for intervening in autonomous affairs even with a legal explanation from the central authorities; however, it is still in accordance with the unitary system.

---

[104] A new constitutional convention after 1997 is the annual work report of the Chief Executive to top central officials. Both Chief Executives in person do this report from two SARs, which started from the report meeting between the first HKSAR Chief Executive Mr Tung Chee-hwa and the former State President Mr Jiang Zemin in Beijing in December 1997. In December 2015, when Mr Li Keqiang, the Premier of the State Council, met Mr Leung Chun-ying, the current Chief Executive of HKSAR, the mass media noticed that during the meeting the reception for Leung was the same as other top provincial officials for the first time.

PART III

THE VIEW FROM EUROPE AND NORTH AMERICA

15

The Evolution of Natural Law in Ireland

Eoin Carolan

15.1. INTRODUCTION

From an Irish perspective, the notion of an 'invisible constitution' most obviously calls to mind the controversy over the influence of natural law philosophy on Ireland's constitutional order. The Constitution of Ireland contains several provisions which can be plausibly construed as having a natural law dimension. Quite what these allusions to an external moral code meant for constitutional practice, however, proved contentious. This partly reflected the Constitution's lack of textual clarity on these questions. It can also be traced, however, to the contestable character and content of this 'natural law' itself. Acknowledged but ambiguous, endorsed but arguably unknowable, natural law provides perhaps the most high-profile experiment in Ireland with an 'invisible' constitutional resource. It serves therefore as the most relevant Irish source of reflection on this theme.

This chapter is divided into a number of sections. Section 15.2 describes the history of natural law references in Irish constitutional jurisprudence. This section sets out the conventional narrative, which is that natural law enjoyed a period of prominence during the period between the mid-1960s and mid-1990s before being decisively and completely rejected by the Supreme Court in its Abortion Information Bill decision in 1995.[1] This heralded the 'death of natural law' within the Irish legal system.[2]

The next section of the chapter challenges that narrative in several respects. It is argued, first of all, that the 'death of the natural law' narrative is based on a series of questionable assumptions about the natural law jurisprudence of the

---

[1] In re *Article 26 and the Regulation of Information (Services outside the State for the Termination of Pregnancies) Bill 1995* [1995] 1 IR 1 ('the Abortion Information Bill' reference).
[2] Adrian F. Twomey, 'The Death of the Natural Law?' (1995) 13 *Irish Law Times* 270.

Irish courts in the 1960s to 1990s. A careful reading of the case law from this period confirms that the Supreme Court's 1995 decision was not necessarily inconsistent with (at least some of) the judicial determinations that preceded it.

Nor, it is suggested, does it necessarily mean the end of natural law in Ireland. The second argument advanced in Section 15.3 is that the Supreme Court continues to draw on natural-law-style reasoning in some of its recent cases. Specifically, the Supreme Court's willingness to have regard to values of dignity, autonomy and justice in certain instances of constitutional adjudication bears comparison, in some respects, with the earlier invocations of natural law. While the terminology and (perhaps) content of these 'invisible' norms may have changed, their interpretative potential as extra-textual sources of constitutional understanding seems broadly similar.

The final section of the chapter considers the implications of this analysis for the book's wider interest in 'invisible' constitutional values. In particular, the fact that the Irish courts continue to make use of quasi-moral or normative concepts that are not clearly enumerated in the text, that are ambiguous in their content and that may carry with them connotations of inalienability is argued to suggest either a reluctance or inability to rely on purely textual readings alone. Section 15.4 considers why this might be the case. What the Irish experience indicates, the chapter tentatively concludes, is that there may be social and systemic benefits to a degree of opacity in the constitutional order.

15.2. NATURAL LAW AND THE CONSTITUTION OF IRELAND

15.2.1. *Natural Law in Ireland's Early Constitutional History*

Natural law's first major appearance in Ireland's constitutional history came under the 1922 Constitution, the opening provisions of which declared that 'all lawful authority comes from God to the people'. This was relied upon by Kennedy CJ (dissenting) in *State (Ryan)* v. *Lennon* to oppose the enactment by the Oireachtas (Parliament) of a draconian constitutional amendment which provided, inter alia, for the establishment of a quasi-military Constitution (Special Powers) Tribunal with powers of criminal conviction and sentencing for certain offences.[3] This included a power to impose the death penalty. Because the 1922 Constitution imposed no substantive limits on the power of the Oireachtas to introduce constitutional amendments within a transitional period (a period which the Oireachtas had extended by use of

---

[3] [1935] 1 IR 170.

the same unfettered amendment power), it was argued (and accepted by the majority) that the amendment was not contrary to the Constitution. Kennedy CJ, however, suggested that the derivation of lawful authority God introduced additional (invisible) requirements for the valid exercise of lawful power.

> Every act, whether legislative, executive or judicial, in order to be lawful under the Constitution, must be capable of being justified under the authority thereby declared to be derived from God. From this it seems clear that, if any legislation of the Oireachtas (including any purported amendment of the Constitution) were to offend against that acknowledged ultimate Source from which the legislative authority has come through the people to the Oireachtas, as, for example, if it were repugnant to the Natural Law, such legislation would be necessarily unconstitutional and invalid, and it would be, therefore, absolutely null and void and inoperative.[4]

Applying that approach to the amendment before the Court, he concluded that it was contrary to the natural law. Furthermore, he suggested that the judiciary's authority could similarly – and directly – be traced back to God in a manner which effectively carved out the judicial power as an independent, distinct and exclusively court-based function.

Coming, as it did, as part of a dissenting judgment, the Chief Justice's assertion of an independent natural law jurisdiction on the part of the courts had little immediate influence. It should not be overlooked, however, that Kennedy CJ's 'celebrated dissent'[5] was – and continues to be[6] – regarded within legal circles as a brave and powerfully expressed effort to resist an unjust attack on fundamental rights.

In 1937, a new Constitution of Ireland was introduced. Article 6 of the Constitution retained a link between governmental authority and God, stating that 'All powers of government, legislative, executive and judicial, derive, under God, from the people'. In addition, however, the 1937 Constitution contained several new provisions with a more avowedly religious dimension.

---

[4] *State (Ryan)* v. *Lennon* [1935] IR 170, 204–5.
[5] Tom Hickey, 'Revisiting *Ryan* v. *Lennon* to Make the Case against Judicial Supremacy' (2015) 53 (1) *Irish Jurist* 125, 130.
[6] For example, the Supreme Court's website lists it first in the thirty or so most important cases in Irish constitutional history. It has also been the subject of numerous academic articles including G. Hogan, 'A Desert Island Case Set in the Silver Sea: The *'State (Ryan)* v. *Lennon*' in E. O'Dell (ed.), *Leading Cases of the Twentieth Century* (Dublin: Sweet & Maxwell, 2000); G. Quinn, 'Dangerous Constitutional Moments: The "Tactic of Legality" in Nazi Germany and the Irish Free State Compared' in John Morison, Kieran McEvoy and Gordon Anthony (eds.), *Judges, Transition and Human Rights* (Oxford: Oxford University Press, 2007); and Hickey, Supra note 5.

Aside from specific acknowledgements that 'the homage of public worship is due to Almighty God'[7] and of the special position of the Catholic Church,[8] the text's description of certain rights pertaining to the family as 'inalienable', 'imprescriptible' and 'antecedent and superior to all positive law' followed Catholic natural law philosophy. Perhaps most notably, the Preamble to the Constitution as one judge later put it, 'reflects a firm conviction that we are a religious people',[9] proclaiming:

> In the Name of the Most Holy Trinity, from Whom is all authority and to Whom, as our final end, all actions both of men and States must be referred,
> We, the people of Éire,
> Humbly acknowledging all our obligations to our Divine Lord, Jesus Christ, Who sustained our fathers through centuries of trial,
> Gratefully remembering their heroic and unremitting struggle to regain the rightful independence of our Nation,
> And seeking to promote the common good, with due observance of Prudence, Justice and Charity, so that the dignity and freedom of the individual may be assured, true social order attained, the unity of our country restored, and concord established with other nations,
> Do hereby adopt, enact, and give to ourselves this Constitution.

These provisions were to prove important in the next phase of natural law jurisprudence within the Irish courts.

15.2.2. *Natural Law and the Unenumerated Rights Doctrine*

This second and more extended engagement with natural law began with the decision of Kenny J in the High Court in *Ryan v. Attorney General*.[10] This judgment has foundational significance for modern constitutional jurisprudence in Ireland because of its inauguration of a doctrine of unenumerated personal rights. Kenny J held that the Constitution conferred protection upon a set of unenumerated (or invisible) rights. This followed, in his view, from the wording of Articles 40.3.1 and 40.3.2 of the Constitution. The former committed the State to defend and vindicate the 'personal rights of the citizen'. The latter explained that the State shall 'in particular' defend and vindicate

---

[7] Article 44.1.
[8] Now deleted by reason of a constitutional amendment.
[9] *Quinn's Supermarket v. Attorney General* [1972] IR 1, per Walsh J.
[10] [1965] IR 294.

'the life, person, good name and property rights of the citizen'. For Kenny J, the reference to 'in particular' confirmed that subsection 2 was a non-exhaustive statement of the personal rights of the citizen and that 'the general guarantee in sub-s. 1 must extend to rights not specified in Article 40'. The courts, accordingly, were charged with 'the difficult and responsible duty of ascertaining and declaring what are the personal rights of the citizen which are guaranteed by the Constitution' – with making visible the values and entitlements protected by a provision that was pregnant with possibilities. This reading of Article 40 as a guarantee of unspecified rights was accepted on appeal by the Supreme Court, and led over time to the recognition by the Irish courts of many textually 'invisible' entitlements such as the right to bodily integrity, the right to privacy, the right to marry, the right to dignity and autonomy, and so on.

However, as the passage cited from Kenny J's decision acknowledges, the idea of a power to identify and declare unenumerated rights gave rise to obvious challenges. This included the immediate question of how such rights ought to be ascertained. In Kenny J's view, the personal rights protected by this general guarantee were those that followed from the 'Christian and democratic' nature of the State. Kenny J did not expand on this criterion in any detail in his decision, while the Supreme Court, in circumspectly confining itself to the observation that 'to attempt to make a list of all the rights which may properly fall within the category of "personal rights" would be difficult and, fortunately, is unnecessary in this present case', did not even go that far.[11] Nonetheless, by construing Article 40.3.1 as a laconic and incomplete acknowledgment of invisible – and arguably Christian – values, *Ryan's* unenumerated rights doctrine became the vehicle for a more explicit consideration of natural law issues in subsequent litigation.

In these later cases, natural law tended to be discussed either as an extra-constitutional source of the values textually protected by the Constitution, or as a justification for the elevated status of the rights described by Articles 41, 42 and 43 as inalienable, imprescriptible or antecedent and superior to all positive law.[12] The former account of natural law is the one that is the more direct focus of the analysis here, but both senses are relevant to important definitional questions about the nature of the relationship between natural law and the Constitution. Was the natural law external to the 1937 Constitution? An invisible extra-textual constitution? An extra-constitutional source of textual meaning? Or something not textually explicit but wholly internal to the interpretation of the constitutional text? As Barrington J's summary of the position

---

[11] [1964] IR 294, 344–5.
[12] *Northants Co. Council v. A.B.F* [1982] ILRM 164.

in *Finn v. Attorney General* demonstrated, the relationship was one which was complicated by the immanent superiority of natural law claims.[13]

> It is arguable that [the fundamental rights protected by the Constitution in Articles 40 to 44] derive not from a man's citizenship but from his nature as a human being. The State does not create these rights, it recognises them and promises to protect them ... Articles 41, 42 and 43 recognise that man has certain rights which are antecedent and superior to positive law. By doing so, the Constitution accepts that these rights derive not from the law but from the nature of man and society, and guarantees to protect them accordingly.

The impression here is of two distinct and free-standing bodies of rights: one visible, the other invisible but accessible by reason. However, the precise interaction between the two remains unclear. The Constitution, at the very least, provides a textual basis for a natural law influence on Irish constitutional reasoning. However, the justification – and perhaps authority – for so doing derived not from the text but from the Constitution's inherent status and value. This is invisibility in a deeply normative sense but it is not immediately clear where, if at all, intra-constitutional meaning ends and extra-constitutional morality begins.

Perhaps the most extended and influential engagement with natural law is that found in the decision of the Supreme Court in *McGee v. Attorney General*.[14] In seeking a more precise understanding of the role of natural law in Irish constitutional adjudication, it is, accordingly, deserving of detailed scrutiny. The proceedings involved a challenge to the statutory prohibition on the import or usage of contraceptives in Ireland. The plaintiff, a married mother, contended that this was a breach of her unenumerated right to marital privacy. This argument was accepted by a 4:1 majority of the Court. In the course of his judgment as part of that majority, Walsh J considered in some detail the nature, content and status of the natural law insofar as it is implicated by the Constitution.

> Both in its preamble and in Article 6, the Constitution acknowledges God as the ultimate source of all authority. The natural or human rights to which I have referred earlier in this judgment are part of what is generally called the natural law. There are many to argue that natural law may be regarded only as an ethical concept and as such is a reaffirmation of the ethical content of law in its ideal of justice. The natural law as a theological concept is the law of God promulgated by reason and is the ultimate governor of all the laws

---

[13] [1983] IR 154.
[14] [1974] IR 284.

of men. In view of the acknowledgment of Christianity in the preamble and in view of the reference to God in Article 6 of the Constitution, it must be accepted that the Constitution intended the natural human rights I have mentioned as being in the latter category rather than simply an acknowledgment of the ethical content of law in its ideal of justice.[15]

This was a fairly clear (if, as we shall see, ambiguous in other respects) acceptance of certain propositions: that the Constitution acknowledged the existence of natural law and natural rights; that the version of natural law and natural rights endorsed by the Constitution had religious and specifically Christian roots; and that, in particular, the natural law recognised by the Constitution was that version which, represented 'the law of God' as 'the ultimate authority'.

Walsh J's confirmation of the religious character of the Constitution's natural law dimensions therefore left open the possibility of an invisible 'shadow' corpus of non-constitutional norms, values which the Constitution acknowledged but which were neither derived from it nor dependent on it for their authoritative status.

15.2.3. *The End of Natural Law: The Abortion Information Bill Reference*

This religious understanding of the natural law is one that can be read to include a supremacist claim to super-constitutional status. The potential for such an anti-constitutional understanding of this 'shadow' constitution emerged fully in 1995 when the Supreme Court was faced with the argument that an amendment to the Constitution which had been endorsed by a majority vote in a referendum should be annulled on the grounds that it violated the natural law.[16] The amendment, introduced in the aftermath of litigation concerning the legality of a teenage rape victim travelling to the United Kingdom for the purposes of obtaining an abortion, confirmed the existence of a right to travel and of access to information.[17] The Bill which was introduced to give effect to this amendment was referred by the President to the Supreme Court under Article 26 of the Constitution, which provides for a test of a Bill's constitutional validity prior to enactment. The Court-appointed counsel to act on behalf of the interests of the unborn[18] argued that '[f]or as long as the

---

[15] [1974] IR 284, 317–18.
[16] In re *Article 26 and the Regulation of Information (Services outside the State for the Termination of Pregnancies) Bill 1995* [1995] 1 IR 1.
[17] *Attorney General v. X* [1992] 1 IR 1.
[18] The right to life of the unborn is expressly recognised in Article 40.3.3 of the Constitution.

present constitution remains in force, nothing in it or in any laws passed by the Oireachtas, or any interpretation thereof by the judiciary can run counter to the natural law'.[19]

This argument had been foreshadowed in a debate in the academic literature about the same abortion controversy.[20] A High Court judge, writing extra-judicially,[21] had argued that the Constitution's recognition of the existence of the natural law logically required an equivalent acknowledgement of its superior and inalienable status:

> It is clear ... that the protection of fundamental rights in the Irish Constitution (and in particular the right to life of the unborn) is firmly grounded on what is called the Natural Law ... It would appear to follow ... that no law could be enacted, no amendment of the Constitution could lawfully be adopted, and no judicial decision could lawfully be given, which conflicted with the Natural Law (which we recognise as being of divine origin).[22]

This view was rejected by the Supreme Court. Echoing some of the academic response to the O'Hanlon thesis, the Court's decision was primarily based on the democratic character of the state, as described in Articles 5 and 6 of the Constitution.[23] It was clearly inconsistent with the Constitution's textual affirmation of popular sovereignty to suggest that a referendum result could be judicially invalidated on the grounds of invisible religious values.

This also required the Court, however, to address the relationship between the constitutional text and a natural law which, as we have seen, previous authorities had described as a superior and antecedent normative code. This it did in relatively cursory terms. Following a brief citation of some of the unenumerated rights case law, the Court concluded:

> From a consideration of all the cases which recognised the existence of a personal right which was not specifically enumerated in the Constitution, it is manifest that the Court in each such case had satisfied itself that such personal right was one which could be reasonably implied from and was guaranteed by the provisions of the Constitution, interpreted in accordance with its ideas of prudence, justice and charity.

---

[19] [1995] 1 IR 1, 8–9.
[20] R. J. O'Hanlon, 'Natural Law and the Constitution' (1993) 11 *Irish Law Times* 8; 'The Judiciary and the Moral Law' (1993) 11 *Irish Law Times* 129. T. Murphy 'Democracy, Natural Law and the Irish Constitution' (1993) 11 *Irish Law Times* 81; D. Clarke, 'The Constitution and Natural Law: A Reply to Mr Justice O'Hanlon' (1993) 11 *Irish Law Times* 177.
[21] O'Hanlon, 'Natural Rights and the Irish Constitution'.
[22] Ibid., 9–10.
[23] Murphy, Supra note 20.

The courts, as they were and are bound to, recognised the Constitution as the fundamental law of the State to which the organs of the State were subject and at no stage recognised the provisions of the natural law as superior to the Constitution.[24]

And so, 'with these brief but unequivocal statements, it seemed that the influence of natural law on Irish constitutional jurisprudence had been stopped in its tracks'.[25] The Court's reasoning has been criticised as illogical,[26] as disingenuous in its treatment of the authorities,[27] or as having outright 'abandoned precedent by using positive law'.[28] Whatever one thinks about the historical accuracy of the Courts' account, the decision marked a clear step away from the religious rhetoric and moral reasoning that characterised the earlier jurisprudence. The accepted view of the Abortion Information Bill reference is thus that it heralded 'the death of natural law' in Ireland. This has also been linked in the literature with an asserted abandonment of the unenumerated rights doctrine.[29]

Perhaps of particular relevance to the broader questions addressed in this book is the view of these developments as a rejection of an illegitimate 'lack of objectivity in recognition of rights' by allowing judges to make decisions by reference to unspecified values. This account holds that the 'none of the techniques used to identify these implied constitutional rights seemed to give any objective guide to what rights were contained within the Constitution', instead involving a 'breadth of ... discretion [which] eclipsed the discretion ordinary afforded in interpreting ambiguous text'.[30] This is a view that appears to take direct issue with both the possibility and appropriateness of invisibility in constitutional adjudication.

As the next section contends, however, this 'death of the natural law' narrative may be misconceived. The proposition that the Irish courts have eschewed the invisible (be that natural law or unenumerated rights) in favour of an

---

[24] [1995] 1 IR 1, 42–3.
[25] A. Kavanagh, 'Natural Law, Christian Values and the Ideal of Justice' (2012) 48 (2) *The Irish Jurist* 71, 91.
[26] G. Whyte, 'Natural Law and the Constitution' (1996) 14 *Irish Law Times* 8.
[27] Twomey, Supra note 2.
[28] Kristen E. Carder, 'Liberalizing Abortion in Ireland: In re Article 26 and the Passage of the Regulation of Information (Services Outside the State for the Termination of Pregnancies) Bill' (1996) 3 *Tulsa Journal of Comparative and International Law* 253, 254.
[29] Oran Doyle, 'Legal Positivism, Natural Law and the Constitution' (2009) 31 *Dublin University Law Journal* 206.
[30] David Kenny, 'Recent Developments in the Right of the Person in Article 40.3: Fleming v Ireland and the Spectre of Unenumerated Rights' (2013) 36 *Dublin University Law Journal*, 322.

objective (and visible) approach to constitutional reasoning is contradicted by subsequent developments, by the original natural law jurisprudence properly construed and, arguably, by the nature of constitutional adjudication itself.

15.3. THE DEATH OF NATURAL LAW: A REPORT GREATLY EXAGGERATED?

In rejecting the claim advanced on behalf of the unborn in the Abortion Information Bill reference, the Supreme Court has commonly been portrayed as having rejected the constitutional status of natural law itself. This may, however, represent an overreaction to the outcome of that reference. As Gerry Whyte has pointed out, the proposition on which the Court was asked to adjudicate in this reference was a stark one which went far beyond its previous jurisprudence.

> [Here t]he Supreme Court was asked to take one variant of natural law theory beyond its previous role as a source of implied rights to its logical, anti-majoritarian extreme so as to empower an unelected, unrepresentative judiciary to set aside decisions of the people made by way of referendum.[31]

Indeed, it may be questioned whether this proposal was, from a legal perspective, the logical corollary of the Constitution's endorsement of natural law. The fact that the natural law was undoubtedly invisible in the sense of being non-explicit did not thereby mean that it was invisible in the non- or extra-constitutional sense of standing outside or above the legal regime. Even O'Hanlon's argument drew a distinction between natural law as a source of constitutional value and natural law as *the* constitutionally authoritative value, although it seems to regard the two as logically intertwined. In seeking to understand the precise implications of the Abortion Information Bill ruling, it is important to carefully consider what the courts' earlier references to natural law may or may not have meant.

15.3.1. *What Was the Natural Law in Ireland?*

A first and critical point of cultural context is the likely relationship between the courts' acknowledgment of natural law and the 'manifesto' or 'identitarian' aspects of the Irish Constitution. As the Preamble demonstrates, the Constitution of 1937 was conceived in explicitly nationalistic terms. Given the complicated but undeniable links between Irish nationalism and the majority

---

[31] Whyte, Supra note 26, 9.

Catholic population, a constitutional invocation of Christian values could also function as an assertion of a specifically Irish identity. For prominent legal figures, natural law seems to have had additional value as a statement of Irish legal and intellectual independence. Given its colonial past, Irish nationalism was often defined by contrast to what was understood as British – and in legal terms, that appears to have been regarded as a Benthamite positivism that famously treated the notion of natural rights as nonsense on stilts. Thus 'natural law was part of Ireland's rebellion against what was perceived to be Britain's positivist tradition'.[32]

This has important implications for any understanding of this 'Irish' conception of natural law. References to natural law, in some instances at least, were as much a statement of opposition to a specific idea of British positivism – one connected (arguably inaccurately) with logically distinct concepts of parliamentary supremacy, strict precedent and Benthamite philosophy – as a comprehensive endorsement of a single version of Thomistic natural law.

The extent to which this consciously anti-Benthamite position shaped judicial attitudes to natural law is well illustrated by Walsh J's extra-judicial writings on the topic:

> The concept of natural law and natural rights for many years was overshadowed by the positivist legal philosophy, of which the arch exponent was Jeremy Bentham. Bentham summed it up by saying 'rights are the fruit of the law and of the law alone. There are no rights without law, no rights contrary to the law, no rights anterior to the law' ... In both South Africa and Nazi Germany, positivism led to a mechanical approach to the judicial function, so that no law could be invoked to invalidate the barbaric acts undertaken in each of those countries. However, the experience of Nazi Germany also proved to be the ultimate absurdity of positivism and led to its downfall.[33]

The easy equation of Benthamite positivism with apartheid South Africa and Nazi Germany is an instructive insight. What this means for reading Irish judicial references to the natural law (especially those of Walsh J) is that they may be motivated at least in part by a desire to reject, and be seen to reject, ideas of unfettered parliamentary supremacy, or of rigid and unthinking obedience to text and precedent. The positions associated by Irish jurists with English positivism were clearly inconsistent with the Constitution's express recognition of fundamental rights and of a judicial review power. Such a binary

---

[32] Kavanagh, Supra note 25, 99.
[33] Brian Walsh, 'The Constitution and Constitutional Rights' in Frank Litton (ed.), *The Constitution of Ireland 1937–1987* (Dublin: Institute of Public Administration, 1987), 92.

characterisation of the choice between natural law and positivism was, of course, problematic in that it encouraged 'the fallacy that rejecting formalist judicial reasoning entails support for a natural law approach'.[34] Nonetheless, natural law explained and justified these textual choices in a manner that spoke to powerful aspects of the Irish identity.

The specifically negative nature of this usage means, however, that it overstates the position to present the constitutional jurisprudence in the thirty years after *Ryan* as an extended engagement with natural law. Judicial references to 'natural law' often signified no more than a repetition of the text of Article 41 or of a vague characterisation of the Constitution of Ireland as acknowledging a natural law. Indeed, as Kavanagh notes, 'it has often been noted that whilst the Irish courts tended to refer to natural law or natural rights in their judgments, this was never matched by a willingness to examine in any detail what the requirements of the "natural law" were or what its source or sources might be'.[35] Certainly, the more complex issues explored elsewhere in this book around the respective roles of the visible text and invisible values were rarely, if ever, considered.

15.3.2. What Was It Not?

In the absence of an authoritative judicial account of natural law within the Irish system, some guidance may be gleaned from an examination of certain indications of what it was not. As Whyte has observed, the deciding authorities had never declared that natural law should take precedence over the result of a referendum to amend the Constitution. Less starkly than that, however, there are also several indications in the case law that natural law was never conceived as a superior or antecedent source of *legal* values. In fact it seems possible, contrary to Twomey's and Carder's claims, to read the natural law jurisprudence in a manner that is consistent with the conclusions drawn by the Supreme Court in the Abortion Information Bill reference.

Take, for example, Walsh J's decision in *McGee*. This is of central importance to this discussion because of Walsh J's general position as an intellectual leader of the Court, because of his position as perhaps the leading advocate of natural law and because of his unusually detailed analysis in *McGee* not only of the natural law dimensions to the Constitution, but also of what that meant

---

[34] Kavanagh, Supra note 25.
[35] Ibid., 94, citing T. Murphy, 'The Cat amongst the Pigeons: Garrett Barden and Irish Natural Law Jurisprudence' in E. Carolan and O. Doyle (eds.), *The Irish Constitution: Governance and Values* (Dublin: Thomson Round Hall, 2008).

for the practice of constitutional adjudication. The following passage has been read by some as an endorsement of the supremacy of the natural law over the Constitution.

> Articles 41, 42 and 43, emphatically reject the theory that there are no rights without laws, no rights contrary to the law and no rights anterior to the law. They indicate that justice is placed above the law and acknowledge that natural rights, or human rights, are not created by law but that the Constitution confirms their existence and gives them protection. The individual has natural and human rights over which the State has no authority; and the family, as the natural primary and fundamental unit group of society, has rights as such which the State cannot control.[36]

Although it contains language that describes certain values as being 'above the law', there are several reasons to suggest that it should not properly be read as supporting – even as a logical extreme – O'Hanlon's later belief in the natural law as a non- or anti-constitutional norm.

First of all, the language in the first sentence about the relationship between rights and the law is a direct paraphrase (and rejection) of Bentham's work. For the reasons already explained, this, it is suggested, should be understood as a renunciation of a specific conception of English legal philosophy rather than as a positive assertion of the supremacy of rights over law.

Second, the supremacist language used in relation to the position of the family is similar to that used in the text of the Constitution itself, so that this also cannot necessarily be characterised as an extra-textual reliance on a 'shadow' natural law, still less as an endorsement of natural law as a distinct and superior form of legal authority.

Finally, and perhaps most importantly, the portion of the passage which quotes neither Bentham nor Articles 41 and 42 outlines a view of natural rights as morally free-standing but dependent for their legal protection on their having been incorporated into the Constitution. Walsh J accepts the core logic of the natural law that it is an enduring and overarching set of values which does not depend on positive law for its existence. He does not, however, extend that logic to the O'Hanlon conclusion about the legal effect of the natural law. The Constitution seems to provide the important and necessary link between the moral or normative notion of a natural law and the capacity of the courts to protect it. This is a very different constitutional role. Here natural law is

---

[36] [1974] IR 284, 310.

invisible in the much more limited sense that its legal status is textually visible but its content is not. On this view, it is an unwritten source of textual meaning.

In fact, even leaving aside the positivist aspect of this argument, Walsh J's account of natural rights as legally contingent on their recognition in the constitutional text seems to logically reject the O'Hanlon thesis that they should be regarded by the courts as superior to all positive law, including the text of the Constitution. If natural law is capable in its own terms of requiring and commanding obedience, natural rights should be self-executing rather than dependent for their protection on an 'inferior' legal authority.

This reading of Walsh J's analysis is further supported by the guidelines outlined later in his decision concerning how courts should approach natural law arguments:

> What exactly natural law is and what precisely it imports is a question which has exercised the minds of theologians for many centuries and on which they are not yet fully agreed ... In a pluralist society such as ours, the Courts cannot as a matter of constitutional law be asked to choose between the differing views, where they exist, of experts on the interpretation by the different religious denominations of either the nature or extent of these natural rights as they are to be found in the natural law. The same considerations apply also to the question of ascertaining the nature and extent of the duties which flow from natural law ... In this country it falls finally upon the judges to interpret the Constitution and in doing so to determine, where necessary, the rights which are superior or antecedent to positive law or which are imprescriptible or inalienable. In the performance of this difficult duty there are certain guidelines laid down in the Constitution for the judge ... The judges must, therefore, as best they can from their training and their experience interpret these rights in accordance with th[e] ideas of prudence, justice and charity [recognised in the Preamble].[37]

Perhaps because of its focus on the practicalities of the litigation process, this passage has sometimes been less cited than other aspects of Walsh J's judgment. It is, however, of critical importance to the question of the precise relationship between natural law and the text of the Constitution because it expressly disavows the proposition that the courts should treat religious teachings as a distinct source of constitutional value. This runs counter to the misconception evident in much of the Irish commentary that any acknowledgement

---

[37] [1974] IR 284, 317–19.

of natural law necessarily commits the courts to enforce a freestanding and non-constitutional set of religious (or even moral) norms.

Desmond Clarke, for example, has criticised the reasoning of Kenny J in *Ryan* for a perceived logical delegation of constitutional decision-making to Christian institutions:

> [T]he State in Ireland is governed by laws that were inspired by Christianity, and their proper interpretation requires the courts to understand them as reflecting specifically Christian values. The wide diversity of Christian beliefs, especially since the Reformation, would require judges to decide authoritatively between alternative theological interpretations of Christianity, or to consult Christian theologians about what Christianity would require in disputes about legal rights in much the same way as De Valera consulted Revd McQuaid when drafting the text. Alternatively, courts could refer disputed theological claims to an authoritative Christian court.[38]

Similarly, Doyle's discussion of the natural law unenumerated rights case law seems in places to overstate the breadth of the discretion as both envisaged and exercised by the post-*Ryan* courts.

> [T]he unenumerated rights doctrine leaves open the possibility that *all* unjust rules can be overturned once they are sought to be applied. The avoidance of an injustice is considered more important than the general need for law to have and maintain a determinate position that can be identified in a way that does not call for moral judgment. Of course, this does not just undermine the certainty of laws only when a particular law is overturned: it leaves open a standing possibility that any law can be overturned. The test for overturning such a law is 'the Natural Law'.[39]

This would be a valid concern if, for example, the Supreme Court had ever endorsed Albert Keating's suggestion that the basic norm of Ireland is that 'one ought to obey the natural law'.[40] Keating's argument, however elides the existence, authority, obligatory character and legal status of natural law in a way that is unnecessary, arguably confused and certainly without obvious support in the Supreme Court's case law.

The O'Hanlon thesis similarly assumes that a natural law dimension logically requires that constitutional adjudication be subordinated to a separate set

---

[38] Desmond M. Clarke, 'Unenumerated Rights in Constitutional Law' (2011) 34 *Dublin University Law Journal* 101, 119–20.
[39] Doyle, Supra note 29.
[40] A. Keating, 'The Basic Norm and Concept of a Constitution' (2012) 30 *Irish Law Times* 137.

of religious doctrines. That was, however, expressly contradicted by Walsh J's view of how religious experts should be treated, by his specific reminder that the exercise of determining these natural rights was undertaken as part of an interpretation of the Constitution and conducted according to the 'guidelines laid down in the Constitution' for the judge and, of course, by the outcome of the *McGee* litigation as contrary to the official teaching of the Catholic Church.

Walsh J's judgment suggests, therefore, that natural law reasoning was influential in his era as a source of constitutional value, but not as a form of constitutional or legal authority. In effect, it was an extant if invisible repository of normative or moral value, with a particular utility in making explicit the content of other similarly less visible aspects of the constitutional order. The Constitution may have acknowledged a natural law dimension to Irish law, but it was also the Constitution that provided the courts with the authority, basis and parameters for referring to it in their rulings. While judges were entitled to have regard to the natural law, they did so as judges – and were therefore subject to the other constitutional and institutional constraints applicable to that position. Until the Abortion Information Bill reference, the courts' natural law jurisprudence never considered the existence or otherwise of an obligation to obey and apply the natural law *as law*.[41] Or, to put it in the terminology of the invisible constitution discussion, the courts had never prior to 1995 had to determine whether natural law was non-explicit or extra-textual; contextually embedded or free-standing; intra-, extra- or non-constitutional. It was therefore arguably open to the Supreme Court to adopt the position that it did without necessarily being understood (as it has been) to eschew the influence of natural law reasoning on constitutional adjudication in its entirety.

15.3.3. *The Survival of the Natural Law?*

This leads into the second main argument of Section 15.3: that the Abortion Information Bill decision did not, in fact, bring about the end of natural law-style reasoning in Irish constitutional adjudication. This argument depends, in part, on a separate question (which there is not space to consider here) as to how to properly define natural law, and to what extent invocations of moral norms in legal interpretation reflect a natural law position. The argument in this section is confined to a much narrower claim that the approach adopted by the Irish courts in the 1965–95 period to the 'invisible' natural law

---

[41] This brings in a related but separate argument about whether it is misleading to describe natural law as law.

is comparable to that applied in some of the courts' more recent case law on fundamental rights. In particular, Irish constitutional adjudication continues in certain instances to be informed by indeterminate norms, the content of which is textually 'invisible' and the conceptual basis for which is quasi-moral. This contradicts not only the 'death of natural law' narrative, but also the associated assertion of a more objective style of constitutional reasoning that makes little, if any, allowance for an 'invisible' constitution.

On this analysis, the major change in natural law-style reasoning in Ireland has been not its abandonment, but rather its symbolic (and primarily rhetorical) evolution from a Christian concept to one expressed in the more secular terminology of dignity, autonomy or justice. This shift may have been most clear in the Abortion Information Bill decision, but it can arguably be traced to an earlier strand of the natural law jurisprudence that favoured a dignitarian conception of Christian values.

This strand is most noticeable in the judgments of Henchy J in *McGee* and in *Norris* v. *Attorney General*.[42] In *McGee*, Henchy J agreed with Walsh J that a prohibition on contraception was inconsistent with the Constitution's fundamental values. His account of the origin of these values placed considerably less emphasis on the divine:

> It is for the Courts to decide in a particular case whether the right relied on comes within the [unenumerated Article 40.3.1] constitutional guarantee. To do so, it must be shown that it is a right that inheres in the citizen in question by virtue of his human personality. The lack of precision in this test is reduced when [Article 40.3.1] is read (as it must be) in the light of the Constitution as a whole and, in particular, in the light of what the Constitution, expressly or by necessary implication, deems to be fundamental to the personal standing of the individual in question in the context of the social order envisaged by the Constitution.[43]

This focus on the 'human personality' of the individual as a foundational constitutional norm was even more pronounced in his dissent in *Norris*. This concerned a challenge to the criminalisation of male homosexual conduct in Ireland. The majority held that there was nothing in a conspicuously Christian text to ground a conclusion that such a ban should be struck down as unconstitutional. By contrast, Henchy J relied on the natural law to contend that an individual was entitled to a measure of dignity and privacy which was violated by this statutory prohibition.

---

[42] [1984] IR 36.
[43] [1974] IR 284, 325.

> Having regard to the purposive Christian ethos of the Constitution, particularly as set out in the preamble ... to the denomination of the State as 'sovereign, independent, democratic' in Article 5, and to the recognition, expressly or by necessary implication, of particular personal rights ... there is necessarily given to the citizen, within the required social, political and moral framework, such a range of personal freedoms or immunities as are necessary to ensure his dignity and freedom as an individual in the type of society envisaged. The essence of those rights is that they inhere in the individual personality of the citizen in his capacity as a vital human component of the social, political and moral order posited by the Constitution.
>
> Amongst those basic personal rights is a complex of rights which vary in nature, purpose and range (each necessarily being a facet of the citizen's core of individuality within the constitutional order) and which may be compendiously referred to as the right of privacy.[44]

His fellow dissenting judge echoed this dignitarian analysis. McCarthy J drew a distinction between a conception of natural law which blindly reflected Christian theology and, on other hand, one informed by 'Christianity itself, the example of Christ and the great doctrine of charity which He preached'. Favouring the latter, he concluded:

> I would uphold the view that the unenumerated rights derive from the human personality ... The dignity and freedom of the individual occupy a prominent place in th[e Constitution's] objectives and are not declared to be subject to any particular exigencies but as forming part of the promotion of the common good.[45]

The rhetoric and reasoning of these judgments is telling in two respects. First of all, it is notable that the dissenting judges still felt it appropriate (or necessary) to connect their dignitarian analysis of the rights of the individual with the self-declared Christian ethos of the constitutional text. This may have something to say to about the political value of connecting constitutional adjudication to prevailing social and moral norms.[46]

Second, and somewhat conversely, while these judgments make a rhetorical genuflection to Christian values, the reasoning is in principle consistent with secular conceptions of natural law and of human rights. Like the earlier natural law authorities, the *Norris* dissents are based on a claim that there are certain rights, the normative or moral value of which can be derived from

---

[44] [1984] IR 36, 71.
[45] [1984] IR 36, 99–100.
[46] This point is considered in a little more detail in Section 15.4.

particular overarching principles. However, while these can (and were) attributed to God, they exist not as arbitrary expressions of God's will but as certain common principles of humanity: prudence, justice, charity, dignity and so on.

Crucially, the Preamble makes specific reference to a number of these principles. This meant that, in terms of constitutional adjudication, the notion of God as the origin of natural law fulfilled an explanatory but strictly superfluous role in the Irish constitutional order. Divine authority was neither the basis nor touchstone of natural law reasoning in the constitutional sphere. Recourse to the natural law as a source of value could occur because of and by means of a constitutional commitment to certain textual if incompletely specified norms – but it is the meaning of the norms themselves rather than their religious origins that are constitutionally critical. Mark Tushnet has suggested that the Rawlsian idea of overlapping consensus may have value here, observing that this is also consistent with the Thomistic claim that 'its conclusions are available to anyone exercising the capacity of human reason, without regarded to his or her religious commitments'.[47] On this view, Clarke's concern about an invisible and theocratic 'shadow' constitution may be based on no more than a fairly conventional instance of constitutional abstraction.

If this is correct, the decision in the Abortion Information Bill reference is less a cynical sidestep and more the evolution of a trend towards 'a more gradual de-emphasis in the case law on the Christian strand of the constitutional jurisprudence'.[48] However, this also means that an abandonment of religious rhetoric does not necessarily signify an equivalent move away from judicial reliance on invisible (or incompletely specified) moral norms. While the summary of the jurisprudence in the Abortion Information Bill reference is notably shorn of Christian rhetoric when compared to its predecessors, its basic claim that the courts engaged in the unenumerated rights jurisprudence regarded themselves as seeking to identify rights 'which could be reasonably implied from and was guaranteed by the provisions of the Constitution, interpreted in accordance with its ideas of prudence, justice and charity' is not inconsistent with decisions such as *McGee* or *Norris*. Prudence, justice and charity may have been described (perhaps even explained) in those decisions as Christian values, but their immediate derivation and constitutional force came from the text of the Preamble.

---

[47] Mark Tushnet, 'National Identity as a Constitutional Issue: The Case of the Preamble to the Irish Constitution of 1937' in Eoin Carolan (ed.), *The Constitution of Ireland: Perspectives and Prospects* (Dublin: Bloomsbury Professional, 2012) 49, 54.
[48] Kavanagh, Supra note 25, 93.

There is also the important consideration that the Irish courts have continued in certain instances to have regard to values such as dignity, autonomy or justice in a manner that assumes (and depends for its justification on the assumption) that they can be attributed to an independent code of morality from which they derive some normative force. That is not to say that dignity or autonomy are treated as freestanding values to which unlimited appeal can be made – any more than natural law was in the past. But there is evidence of the Irish courts using these textually invisible values as a source of constitutional meaning where similar considerations of ambiguity, indeterminacy or moral contestation arise.

In *PP* v. *HSE*, for example, a divisional High Court found that a pregnant women who was brain dead but being kept alive while her body rapidly (and gruesomely) deteriorated had an entitlement to dignity to which the Court could have regard.[49] Furthermore, the Court explained and justified its position by reference to the kind of universal (if non-religious) norm associated with a natural law position.

> [The right to retain dignity in death is] an approach has been the hallmark of civilised societies from the dawn of time. It is a deeply ingrained part of our humanity and may be seen as necessary both for those who have died and also for the sake of those who remain living and who must go on.

Somewhat similar references can be found in the *Roche* v. *Roche* decision, where several Supreme Court judges referred to the necessity to show 'respect' for the dignity and potential humanity of a frozen embryo that the Court had, in its same decision, found not to fall within the scope of the constitutional protection of 'the unborn'.[50]

Most notably, the Supreme Court's 2013 decision in *Fleming* v. *Ireland* provides a reaffirmation of the unenumerated rights doctrine and of its continued relationship with certain natural law-style norms.[51] *Fleming* involved a challenge to the absence of an assisted suicide regime under Irish law. The applicant, who was suffering from motor neuron disease, asserted a right to terminate her life and to have assistance with that if necessary (as it was in her case). Her claim was based on the contention that the rights to life and of the person protected by Article 40.3.1 should be considered in light of the constitutional values of autonomy, self-determination and dignity as including a right to assisted suicide.

[49] [2014] IEHC 622.
[50] [2010] 2 IR 321.
[51] [2013] 2 IR 417.

While her claim was ultimately unsuccessful, the Court appeared in its reasoning to accept that these invisible values can be relevant to constitutional adjudication, and that this relevance follows from the Constitution's overarching commitment to certain normative values or goals.

> Whether therefore values of autonomy, self-determination and dignity, as they find expression in the rights guaranteed by the Constitution, provide constitutional protection for the performance of specific acts depends on a concrete analysis of the impact of any law which is impugned in a particular case on the life of the individual, and a careful consideration of the provisions of the Constitution *and the values it protects in the rights it guarantees.*[52]

This last phrase draws a distinction between the rights specifically guaranteed by the text and a distinct set of values which the Constitution (implicitly?) protects. The Court seems to suggest that the Constitution protects and guarantees both visible rights and invisible values, and that both have a role to play in constitutional adjudication. The meaning of the Constitution can be influenced by a distinct set of values which the express provisions of the Constitution aim to protect. This is a clear endorsement of some kind of invisible constitution: one which appears to be conceptual, normative in character, and – at the very least – with an extra-textual dimension. The parallels with the role performed by the 'natural law' in the earlier case law are obvious, and arguably made explicit, by the courts' direct citation of Henchy J's 'human personality' approach in *McGee*. Notably, the Court accepted the continued relevance of the unenumerated rights jurisprudence, outlining an interpretive methodology which takes account of concerns around certainty, legitimacy and the authority of the written text, but which also nonetheless embraces a natural law-style recourse to non-textual normative principles.

> [T]he test for the identification of an unenumerated right, or the determination of the extent of an enumerated right, is a test necessarily lacking in precision, and there are irreducible areas of choice. It is all the more important therefore that the reasoning be as explicit as possible. The approach that any right inheres in a citizen by virtue of his or her personality and should be fundamental to the personal standing of the individual in the context of the social order envisaged by the Constitution provides a useful structure and focus for analysis.[53]

The Court went on:

---

[52] [2013] 2 IR 417, 444. Emphasis added.
[53] [2013] 2 IR 417, 446.

> Here, while the Constitution does not expressly refer to any right similar to those asserted on behalf of the appellant, it does by Article 40.3.2 commit the State to protect and vindicate the life and person of every citizen. Can it be said that the right to life as so guaranteed, whether on its own or in conjunction with the guarantee of the protection of the person, necessarily implies as a corollary, the right of every citizen to terminate his or her life and to have assistance in so doing? ... [I]t is not possible to discern support for such a theory in the provisions of the Constitution without imposing upon it a philosophy and values not detectable from it ... In the social order contemplated by the Constitution, and the values reflected in it, that would be the antithesis of the right rather than the logical consequence of it.
>
> Thus, insofar as the Constitution, in the rights it guarantees, embodies the values of autonomy and dignity and more importantly the rights in which they find expression, it does not extend to a right of assisted suicide.[54]

Leaving aside the religious rhetoric of the natural law case law, there is much in the Court's reasoning that finds echo in the earlier jurisprudence. Like many of its predecessors did in the 1965–95 period, the Court accepts that the specific rights guaranteed by the Constitution are the expression of a deeper set of values which may have greater moral or normative force. As the courts did in these earlier decisions, the *Fleming* Court also accepts that these values may be relevant to constitutional adjudication as a source of constitutional meaning or value. However, like Walsh J in *McGee*, the Court also reiterates that such an acknowledgement of these values does not justify treating them as a standalone source of moral value. The question is not whether the proposition before the court is one which is capable of being justified by a philosophical (or theological) account of dignity, autonomy or natural law.

This makes this understanding quite different from the Platonic conception of a constitution explored in Iddo Porat's Chapter 9. The Irish natural law approach (and arguably the Thomistic theory of natural law too) foregrounds the fallibility of human and judicial reason in a way that runs counter to the entitlement of judges under the Platonic conception to directly interpret and apply what they regard as an ideal form of rights.

In practice, the differences between these two approaches may be less stark. Both, after all, allow a court to consider textually invisible normative values in determining a question of constitutional law. Both, therefore, allow a degree of relatively unguided normative reflection to inform constitutional adjudication. There are, however, conceptually important differences between an approach that treats a written constitution as an imperfect placeholder for an

---

[54] [2013] 2 IR 417, 446–8.

invisible and directly effective ideal form and one which regards the visible constitution as the imperfect but currently operative instantiation of a particular normative vision. As the Abortion Information Bill reference demonstrates, these differences may also have practical significance in extreme cases involving issues about the role of, and relationship between, visible and invisible norms. Under a Platonic approach, the text is conceptually and inevitably inferior; under the Irish approach, the text is authoritative if incomplete. The invisible values that it promotes may be normative ideals, but they are ultimately subject in the judicial sphere to the limits imposed by the constitutional text and institutional context. They remain, in the final analysis, internal to the constitutional order.

15.4. CONCLUSION

Does the Irish experiment with natural law have potential implications for the concept of an invisible constitution? For the reasons explained above, the Irish courts' invocations of natural law have to be interpreted first and foremost in light of the somewhat idiosyncratic conceptions of positivism and natural law that were at one time prominent in Irish legal thinking. It is also necessary to bear in mind the limited and narrow role which natural law reasoning performed in this early case law. Natural law never functioned as *a law*, let alone as a distinct (if invisible) *constitution*. Indeed, perhaps the first lesson of the Irish experience is of the risks of describing non-textual norms in terms that carry with them the connotations of more formal legal texts.

More generally, the survival in Ireland of a form of constitutional reasoning that looks much like a non-religious version of natural law may speak to the difficulty (or impossibility) of the kind of objective adjudications of constitutional value by reference to which the original natural law jurisprudence was unfavourably compared. The bare assertion that natural law involves an illegitimately broader discretion than other forms of constitutional reasoning seems somewhat flimsy when compared to the *Fleming* Court's reliance on concepts of dignity, autonomy or self-determination. A similar point might be made about other abstract legal standards like natural justice or procedural fairness.

Two points may follow from this. The first is that the Supreme Court's decision in the Abortion Information Bill reference may not represent the renunciation of abstract or subjective reasoning by the Irish courts that some have claimed. Rather, it arguably reflected the anachronistic and socially unacceptable nature of continued references to Christian teachings in a more pluralistic and less religious society. If this is the case, however, it may be more plausible to explain this as a readjustment in the judiciary's description of the normative underpinnings of the constitutional order. This would fit with Tushnet's point about the possibility of an overlapping consensus: the values that are incorporated into and underpin the Constitution remain the same even if the inspiration for their inclusion varies.

This in turn leads to a second point about the relationship between abstract or invisible values and the social and political functions of a constitutional system. I have argued in more detail elsewhere that constitutionalism's political utility derives from the extent to which it helps to foster a unitary sense of social consciousness.[55] That is a necessary element of the system's stability in the face of inevitable pluralism.

One way in which this can be achieved is by the constitution's system declaration and ongoing reinforcement of a sense of common identity and value. This provides one explanation of the rise, fall and residual influence of natural law reasoning in Ireland. Whereas the drawing of a connection between the Constitution and Christian morality would have reinforced the unifying authority of the constitutional text in the 1960s and 1970s, the invocation of Christian morality in more recent times would be likely to have imperilled that same broad social acceptance. This would also account for the shift to the less explicitly religious rhetoric of dignity, autonomy and justice.

This is, of course, no more than a descriptive explanation of the social and political dynamics of the Irish experience. It does, however, raise a related question about the general relationship between abstract moral values and constitutional adjudication. The Irish experience provides anecdotal support for the argument that constitutional adjudication ought to involve some degree of reliance on invisible (or at least textually undeveloped) norms. If it is assumed that legal adjudication requires some degree of reason-giving, that there is a social and political necessity for a constitutional order to be accepted by (at least a portion of) its citizens and that this social and political utility also requires that it must be publicly seen to be so accepted, then there would seem to be a political value (at the very least) in the constitutional system being regarded as a social good. Connecting the Constitution to broad normative principles, the contents of which are not made explicit, provides a means of publicly declaring the system's goodness, while nonetheless preserving a politically necessary space for moral contestation. In this account, invisibility has real political and social utility in maintaining the constitutional system.

---

[55] See the discussion of constitutional stability and public reason in Eoin Carolan, *The New Separation of Powers: A Theory for the Modern State* (Oxford: Oxford University Press, 2009), ch 1.

While the idea that there may be a political or social value in maintaining invisibility on certain issues shares some similarities with Sunstein's work on incompletely theorised agreements, the Irish experience is quite different in that it reverses his preferred focus on outcomes instead of abstractions. While Sunstein acknowledges the possibility of 'incompletely specified agreements' in the constitutional sphere, his work is more interested in (and advocates strongly) a judicial approach that consciously avoids discussion of general principles in favour of low-level principles and particular outcomes.[56] A presumption against high-level reasoning would, in his view, provide a prudential and minimalist means of promoting consensus by obtaining no more agreement than is necessary.

The Irish experience, by contrast, suggests that these abstract high-level principles may have value as a unifying source of social stability. While citizens will disagree on the appropriate outcome in particular cases, there may be scope for a reciprocal consensus on the system's commitment to certain broad normative goals. As the discussion of the Preamble showed, this can be based in part on the constitution's declaration of a normative identity which might be anticipated to be socially or politically attractive. There is also, however, a more actively long-term sense in which the use of abstract constitutional norms, the content of which are invisible, may foster stability. This follows from the participatory and reason-focused nature of constitutional adjudication. Where citizens differ on particular outcomes, high-level constitutional norms can offer a grammar of disagreement that encourages deliberation on these different views. The significance of this is that any disagreement remains internal to the constitutional order. Furthermore, the disagreement is dealt with in a way that promotes reciprocity and reason-giving. This affirms both the autonomy of the individual and legitimacy of the system by providing the loser with a public justification of the outcome. From the point of view of both the particular outcome and the general reputation of the system, there is an obvious incentive for that justification to be expressed in terms that are more likely to enjoy broad social acceptance. General normative principles provide one way that this can be achieved.

This offers support for a hypothesis that textual indeterminacy – the possibility of invisible values – may not necessarily be the problem sometimes suggested in Ireland; in fact, it may be that this incompleteness creates a space for pluralistic contestation within a framework that makes disagreement manageable. This has some parallels with Rawls' concept of public reason without

---

[56] Cass R. Sunstein, 'Incompletely Theorized Agreements' (1995) 108 *Harvard Law Review* 1733, 1739.

necessarily imposing the same kind of substantive constraints on permissible reasons. Rather, the more basic point that – whether for moral,[57] minimialist[58] or Machiavellian[59] considerations – a process that explains its outcomes by reasons that invite a social consensus has the potential to support constitutional stability. The lesson from Ireland might therefore be that recourse to invisible normative values is not only an inevitable response to textual ambiguity, but also a systemically valuable aspect of constitutional adjudication. However, the Irish experience also cautions that this invisibility presents an enduring challenge to the authority and status of the principles involved, so that they may prove more susceptible to political and social pressures than other more visible aspects of the constitutional order.

---

[57] John Rawls, *Political Liberalism* (New York, NY: Columbia University Press, 2010). See also John Rawls, 'The Domain of the Political and Overlapping Consensus (1989) 64 *New York University Law Review* 233.

[58] Sunstein, Supra note 56; Cass R. Sunstein, *Legal Reasoning and Political Conflict* (Oxford: Oxford University Press, 1996).

[59] Maritn Loughlin, 'Constitutional Law: The Third Order of the Political' in Nicholas Bamforth and Peter Leyland (eds.), *Public Law in a Multi-Layered Constitution* (Oxford: Hart Publishing, 2003).

16

"Additive Judgments"

A Way to Make the Invisible Content of the Italian Constitution Visible

Irene Spigno

16.1. INTRODUCTION

The Italian Constitutional Court was introduced by the Constitution of 1948. It was a year in which a constitutional democracy was established in Italy as a form of government in which sovereignty belongs to the people who exercise it within the limits established by a "rigid" written Constitution (Article 1 of the Constitution). The rigidity of the Constitution is entrenched by means of a more complex amendment procedure compared with the ordinary legislative one (Article 138 of the Constitution).

In addition to its rigidity, the 1948 Italian Constitution was conceived by its Constituent Fathers as a "supreme" norm, hierarchically superior to the laws approved by Parliament. The position the Constitution holds within the sources of law is protected by its more complex amendment procedure, as well as by the constitutional justice system which, in fact, envisages a Constitutional Court with the power, *inter alia*, to declare the illegitimacy of laws and legally binding acts produced by the State and the Regional organs.[1]

Since the start of its activity as privileged interpreter of the Constitution in 1956, the Court has displayed a high level of interpretative creativity and activism in its interpretation of the text of the Constitution.[2] This is possible also thanks to the formulation of constitutional norms conceived by the Constituent Fathers as provisions capable of adapting to the changing times. Thus, the Italian Constitution, like many other constitutional texts, has both a visible and an invisible content, and the Constituent Fathers were well aware

---

Inter-American Academy of Human Rights.
[1] For the other competences of the Italian Constitutional Court see Section 16.2.
[2] Tania Groppi, *Le grandi decisioni della Corte cosituzionale italiana* (Naples: Editoriale Scientifica, 2010) XII.

of this aspect of constitutional invisibility within the 1948 text. The invisibility of the Italian Constitution, to be considered as "extra-constitutional understanding," as Rosalind Dixon and Adrienne Stone point out in Chapter 1 in this book, is mainly linked to two elements. On the one hand, it is a widely shared opinion that the Republican Constitution was clearly intended to be a "charter of principles," since it was originally conceived as regulating the functioning of the State's powers. On the other hand, its invisibility derives from the specific structure of the Constituent Assembly, whose composition was a mirror of the post-war political panorama.[3] In that period, Italian society was divided into two main political blocs with hugely differing goals and relationships with the dominant social forces: on one side, there was the Catholic party (*Democrazia Cristiana*) and, on the other side, the left-wing parties (*Partito Comunista* and *Partito Socialista*). They had different and competing claims, and the only way to have them recognized in the Constitution was to accept a constitutional compromise.[4] The Constitution thus acknowledges their claims in the form of – sometimes contrasting – principles to be balanced at the moment of application and/or interpretation.

In this sense, the "formal Constitution" is quite different from the "material Constitution": the former is the constitutional act adopted according to the modalities and forms required by the law.[5] The latter could be characterized as a "fundamental Constitution" that transposes the original meaning of the Constitution itself. Thus, in the words of Costantino Mortati, the "material Constitution" could be understood as a "costitution that could be called a second power running alongside the formal one, derived from it, never fully absorbed into it, but sharing its same nature."[6]

The Court accepted the mandate entrusted to it by the Constituent Fathers with great enthusiasm and sense of responsibility: extending beyond the constitutional text, the Constitutional Court has become one of the actors in its "silent transformation and accommodation" through informal constitutional changes.[7]

---

[3] The Constituent Assembly was elected on June 2, 1946 with the task of writing the new Republican Constitution.

[4] See Piero Calamandrei, *La Costituzione e le leggi per attuarla* (Torino: Einaudi, 1955) 209 ff., according to whom many parts of the Constitution represent the transactive and probably temporary effect of contrasting forces and conceptions.

[5] The Italian Constitution was approved on December 22, 1947 and entered into force on January 1, 1948.

[6] Costantino Mortati, *La Costituzione materiale* (Milano: Giuffré, 1939).

[7] Enzo Cheli, *Il Giudice delle leggi* (Bolonga: Il Mulino, 1996); Tania Groppi, "The Constitutional Court of Italy: Towards a Multilevel System of Constitutional Review?" (2008) 3 *Journal of Comparative Law* 2, 10. See Sergio Bartole, *Interpretazioni e trasformazioni della*

This has been possible in part because a rich variety of judgments have been handed down since the very early years of its activity, thanks to the need recognized by the Constitutional Court itself to consider the impact that its decisions have on the legal system as a whole, and on the other branches of government. Among them, those most affected are the judiciary, through the application of the technique known as *interpretazione conforme* (consistent interpretation), which evolved in accordance with the *diritto vivente* (doctrine of the living law) paradigm, and Parliament.

In particular, in its dialogue with Parliament, the Court has created a specific type of decision. The so-called "additive judgments" (*sentenze additive*), are rulings whereby the Court declares a statute unconstitutional, not because of what it provides for, but rather what it does not provide for. In this way, the Court manages to insert new norms into the legal system that cannot be found in any statutory text and transforms itself – or so it would appear – into a creator of legal rules, thereby playing a role that in the Italian system belongs almost exclusively to Parliament (with some exceptions related to regional competences[8] and to the Government).[9]

In such a context, this chapter aims to analyze the functioning of "additive judgments" in order to see how the Italian Constitutional Court uses this type of judgment to make visible the sense of constitutionality to which legislative power can be blind. A number of criticisms have been leveled against "additive judgments" in legal scholarship, the first being that they contradict the classical Kelsenian idea of constitutional justice whereby constitutional courts must be confined to being "negative legislators." Through "additive judgments," however, the Constitutional Court seems to become a "creator" of legal norms by taking over competences that the Constitution entrusts only to Parliament (and exceptionally the government). Other criticisms, however, focus on the effects such rulings may have, since they are decisions that ought not to be able to produce real legal effects, but merely represent a warning to the legislator.[10]

The following chapter, therefore, aims to provide a brief description of the Italian constitutional model. Later on, I will describe the conditions that the Constitutional Court itself identifies to justify the adoption of additive judgments as the only possible constitutionally compulsory solution, and the

---

Costituzione repubblicana (Bologna: Il Mulino 2004) for whom the "living" Constitution in Italy is very far removed from the "written" Constitution.

[8] Constitution Article 117.
[9] Ibid., 76, 77.
[10] Marcello Gallo, "Il fascino indiscreto delle sentenze additive della Corte Costituzionale" (2011) *Critica del diritto* 119.

different types of additive judgments traceable in the Italian Constitutional Court's case law. Lastly, I propose some concluding considerations on the ability of such rulings not only to satisfy the "need to protect challenged normative acts," but also to allow the Constitutional Court to make some invisible parts of the Constitution visible. It is my opinion that, with all due reserve, additive judgments are nothing more than an additional mechanism that allows the Italian Constitutional Court to work as the Constitution's supreme guardian, not only in relation to the constitutional text, but also to the "material Constitution" that Costantino Mortati had envisaged since 1939.

16.2. THE ITALIAN MODEL OF CONSTITUTIONAL JUSTICE

Breaking with a past dominated by the principle of parliamentary supremacy (with the 1848 Albertine Statute),[11] the Fathers of the Republican Constitution opted for a rigid constitution protected by a system of constitutional guarantees. Together with the provision of a constitutional review system more complex than that envisaged for the ordinary legislative process,[12] they set up a system of judicial review of legislation, strongly inspired by the Kelsenian model: a centralized system where the guarantee of the constitutionality of laws is entrusted to a constitutional court.[13]

The composition of the Italian Constitutional Court reflects the search for a balance between technical needs and legal expertise on the one hand, typical of judicial bodies, and the need to take into account the inevitably political nature of constitutional review on the other. It is made up of fifteen judges chosen from justices (including retired ones) of the ordinary and administrative higher courts, university professors of law, and lawyers with at least twenty years' practice behind them. A third of the members are nominated by the President of the Republic, a third by joint sitting of Parliament, and a third by the ordinary and administrative supreme courts.[14]

Article 134 of the Constitution sets out the jurisdiction of the Constitutional Court. According to Article 134, the Constitutional Court can pass judgment on controversies regarding the constitutional legitimacy of laws and enactments having force of law issued by the State and Regions, conflicts arising from the allocation of powers of the State and those powers allocated to the

---

[11] Giorgio Rebuffa, *Lo Statuto albertino* (Bologna: Il Mulino, 2003).
[12] Constitution Article 138.
[13] Alessandro Pizzorusso, Vincenzo Vigoriti and Giuseppe LeRoy, Certoma "The Constitutional Review of Legislation in Italy" (1983) 56 *Temple Law Quarterly* 503.
[14] Constitution Article 135.

State and the regions, and among the regions themselves. It may also rule on charges brought against the President of the Republic and Ministers according to the provisions of the Constitution.

Article 2 of Constitutional Law no. 1 of 1953 added a further power, namely to adjudicate on the admissibility of requests for referendums to repeal laws (abrogative referendums), which may be proposed by 500,000 voters or five regional councils, pursuant to Article 75 of the Constitution.

The Constitutional Court's powers are limited and minimalist from various points of view, especially if considered from the comparative perspective, in particular with regard to the modalities of access to constitutionality proceedings, the object of the judgment, and to the types of decisions that can be taken, as well as their effects. On the first point, despite the possibility of "direct-abstract control" that can be activated only by Regions against State laws or other regions' laws depleting their own powers, and by the national government against regional laws within sixty days of publication, no direct action can be taken by private citizens, parliamentary groups, or local authorities at sub-regional level.[15] The more typical way to access constitutionality proceedings is "incidental control" brought about by legal proceedings (called an "*a quo* proceeding") against a provision that a judge has applied in order to close a case. "The keys to open the door of constitutional review" are therefore in the hands of ordinary courts, which play an important role in selecting the matters on which the Court will then pronounce.[16]

As for the limits regarding the object of the constitutional proceedings, it should be noted that constitutional review may only cover laws and acts with the force of law, excluding all other kinds of law (such as delegated or administrative legislation that is reviewed only by ordinary and/or administrative courts). These courts, however, cannot strike down statutes, although they can strike down or set aside secondary legislation. In addition, the Court cannot stray from the *thema decidendum*, i.e., the object and the parameter identified in the application (as stated in Article 27 of Law no. 87 of 1953, which states that "when the Constitutional Court receives an application or appeal concerning a question of constitutionality of a law or an act having the force of law, it declares within the limits of the appeal, namely unconstitutional legislative dispositions.").

---

[15] Ibid., 127; Gianluca Gentili, "A Comparison of European Systems of Direct Access to Constitutional Judges: Exploring Advantages for the Italian Constitutional Court" (2012) 4 *Italian Journal of Public Law* 159.

[16] Tania Groppi and Irene Spigno, "Constitutional Reasoning in the Italian Constitutional Court" (2014) *Rivista AIC* 1.

The kinds of decisions the Court can adopt are also limited. From the formal point of view, it can hand down *sentenze* (judgments) and *ordinanze* (orders).[17] The latter is a decision which does not decide the question, playing a merely interlocutory role or rejecting an application on procedural grounds. These are usually justified due to lack of standing or lack of other admissibility requirements.[18] The former are decisions that concern the substantive part of a question. According to the constitutional and legislative provisions pertaining to the Constitutional Court, the range of judgments available is limited: they can either accept or reject constitutional challenges, and these are known respectively as *sentenze di accoglimento* and *sentenze di rigetto*.[19] The effects produced by these two types of decision are defined by law. According to Article 136 of the Constitution, when the Court declares the constitutional illegitimacy of a law or enactment having force of law, the law ceases to have effect the day following the publication of the decision. This decision of the Court must be published, and Parliament and the Regional Councils concerned must be notified, so that wherever deemed necessary, they act in conformity with constitutional procedures. The typical effect of judgments whereby the Italian Constitutional Court declares the constitutional illegitimacy of a statutory provision is simply striking down, which deletes the unconstitutional norm from the legal system (with retroactive [*ex tunc*] and *erga omnes* effects).

Conversely, if the Court rejects an issue because it finds the question regarding constitutionality groundless, this decision only binds the referring court (*a quo* judge) and does not produce *erga omnes* effects. Another judge could challenge the same rule (it produces no retroactive [*ex nunc*] and *inter partes* effects). However, if the latter judge does not present new arguments in favor of unconstitutionality, the "reiterated" question will be declared "manifestly unfounded" in an order (*ordinanza*) deliberated in closed session.

Despite all those limitations imposed by the Constitution and the legislation, and under pressure to solve practical problems for which no help comes from the functions explicitly bestowed upon the Court, since the earliest days, the Constitutional Court has shown great creativity by "producing" different kinds of decisions characterized by a special modulation of the effects on the legal order (but also in its relations with the other branches of government and parliament, and the courts in particular).[20]

---

[17] Law no. 87 of 1953 Article 18.
[18] Groppi and Spigno, Supra note 16.
[19] Constitution Articles 134–7; Law no. 87 of 1953.
[20] The Constitutional Court became operational in 1956.

Establishing a distinction between provisions (*disposizione*, i.e., the linguistic expression by which the will of the legislative power is manifested) and rules (*norma*, i.e., the result of an interpretive process built around the *disposizione*; the interpretative process of a provision can lead to the production of more than one rule from a single provision or a single rule from a plurality of provisions), the Constitutional Court departed from the rigid idea of being only a "negative legislator," preferring to consider itself as having the implicit power to "manipulate" legal texts.[21]

The Court applied this distinction right from its first decision, adjudicating questions relating to the constitutionality of legislative acts enacted before the 1948 Constitution and conflicting with its dispositions.[22] Given the failure of the new Republican legislator in its responsibility to give effect to the constitutional principles by modifying or repealing the existing laws, the Court considered the need to reinterpret legislative texts and derive constitutionally compatible meanings from them. The Court gradually disaggregated the disputed provisions and eliminated only the incompatible interpretations without formally altering the text. But this was not all. The Court not only functioned as a body with the power to interpret provisions and to declare any provisions contrary to the Constitution void, but it also came to define itself as a body able to "manipulate" provisions through different strategies: (1) ablation; (2) replacement; or (3) addition.

(1) In "ablative" decisions, the Court declares the unconstitutionality of a provision "in the part in which" it provides for something for which "it should not provide," thereby deleting a fragment of the text.[23]
(2) In "substitutive" decisions, the provision is declared unconstitutional "in the part in which" it provides for something "instead" of providing for something else: the decision of the Constitutional Court usually has the effect of replacing one fragment with another.[24]
(3) In "additive" decisions, the declaration of unconstitutionality affects the provision not in terms of what it provides for but for what it fails to

---

[21] Distinction introduced by Crisafulli (1956).
[22] Judgment 1 of 1956.
[23] See Judgments 63 of 1966 and 11 of 1979. For a further description of these judgments, see the Report of the Constitutional Court of the Italian Republic, *Legislative omission in constitutional jurisprudence*, in *Les problèmes de l'omission législative dans la jurisprudence constitutionnelle/Problems of legislative omission in constitutional jurisprudence* (XIV Congrès de la Conférence des Cours constitutionnelles européennes, 2008) 551 ff.
[24] See Judgments 15 of 1969 and 409 of 1989. For both, see Report of the Constitutional Court of the Italian Republic, *Legislative Omission in Constitutional Jurisprudence*.

provide for "in the part in which it does not provide that ...:" the Court decision adds a fragment to the provision declared unconstitutional.

These "manipulative" decisions come under the category of judgments the Court uses to declare the unconstitutionality of a disposition, a provision, or a norm with force of law, thus producing the same effects set out in Article 136 of the Constitution. However, they present several theoretical problems related to the fact that the Court, especially with reference to "substitutive sentences" and "additive sentences," is introducing new legal provisions that are the sole province of Parliament in the Italian legal system.

16.3. THE CONSTITUTIONAL COURT'S REACTION TO LEGISLATIVE OMISSION: ADDITIVE JUDGMENTS

The Constitutional Court issued its first additive judgment in 1967. With Judgment 151, the Court recognized the unconstitutionality of Article 376 of the 1889 Italian Code of Criminal Procedure (the Zanardelli Code, in force until 1988) for not providing for the obligation to dispute the facts and the questioning of the defendant in the case of their acquittal with a formula stating anything other than that the fact did not take place or was not committed by the accused. For a similar reason, the Court also declared the unconstitutionality of Articles 395, last paragraph, and 398, last paragraph, of the Code of Criminal Procedure. The contested provision, Article 376 of the Code of Criminal Procedure, stipulated that the defendant may not be acquitted by the granting of judicial pardon or for lack of evidence or under amnesty if they have not been heard or if they have not been informed of the fact by means of a mandate that has remained without effect. It has been argued that, in all other cases of acquittal, questioning or rebuttal of the charge were not necessary. The question of constitutionality was directed precisely against this unwritten part of the norm, implicit in the normative disposition.

The Court emphasized how the legislature itself recognized that, in some cases, an acquittal may affect the dignity of the citizen as much as an indictment, so it ruled that both be preceded by questioning or a contestation of the fact, in order to allow the accused to defend themselves and avoid such a sentence. According to the Court, some cases, such as acquittal for lack of evidence, were already included in these norms at the time of publication of the Code (in 1889). Others were added later with the 1955 reform.[25] However, there was no doubt that among the different possible political or social reasons

---

[25] Law no. 517 of 1955.

behind these changes, the need to guarantee the right to a defense provided by Article 24 of the Constitution (posterior to the Zanardelli code) was the main one.

The Court acknowledges the effort made by the legislator, but states that

> the legislator has stopped halfway. It did not consider that the acquittal decision under certain circumstances may contain or imply a restrictive measure of personal freedom (e.g., acquittal for mental infirmity); in some other hypothesis, not even referred to by Article 376, it may even have defamatory effects, greater than or at least equaling a conviction (e.g., the acquittal for chronic alcohol or narcotic poisoning); all of them, except for judgments issued because the fact did not take place or was not committed by the defendant, attribute something or do not exclude the attribution of something that may not constitute a crime but may nevertheless be unfavorably judged by public opinion or otherwise by the social conscience.

Respect for Article 24 of the Constitution led the Court to declare the disputed disposition unconstitutional.[26]

It has been clear since the very first additive judgment that they effectively fill legislative gaps. A legislative gap can be understood in two ways: as a "non-fulfillment" – in the sense of "inertia" – and as a "not-complete-fulfillment" in the sense of an "incomplete action," which constitutes a deficiency in the part that is incomplete in terms of what the action should have produced.

Additive judgments should only serve to fill cases of "incomplete action." The Court can adopt an additive decision only if there is a legislative product, albeit an incomplete one. In the absence of a law or an act having the force of law, a constitutional proceeding could not even begin. Moreover, the need must arise for the Court to make the disputed provision compatible with the Constitution (and in reality this need drastically reduces the characteristics of originality of additive judgments in comparison to other unconstitutional decisions).

The most original aspect of additive decisions lies in the part of the judgment where the Court explicitly states the new normative fragment deduced from the Constitution. Even if these features do not have any influence on the Court's argumentation, they have a great influence on the *ratio decidendi*. It is the Court itself that dictates the limitations and characteristics additive judgments must have. These characteristics may be described from three different perspectives: equality and *tertium comparationis*, the concept of the compulsory constitutional solution referred to as the doctrine of *rime obbligate*

---

[26] Judgment 151 of 1967.

("necessary choice," literally "prescribed verse"), and substantive limitations to additive judgments in criminal matters.

16.3.1. *Equality and* Tertium Comparationis

The logical-deductive process that leads to the identification of the normative fragment lacking in the provision (and that should be added) must be clear and evident in the Court's argumentation. The added fragment must be the result of a comparative process where the disputed provision is subject to the constitutional process (working here as a *tertium comparationis*). The object of this comparative analysis is to identify common areas and differences able to justify or otherwise the extension of the scope of the provision through an addition to the text. In other words, depending on the outcome of this comparative process, the Constitutional Court evaluates whether the principle of equality (to be considered according to Article 3 of the Constitution, i.e., to treat equal situations equally and different situations differently) is applicable. As a matter of fact, the "constitutional addition" is possible only in cases where this comparison has provided a positive result vis-à-vis the assimilability of the cases. Moreover, the Court must also explain the existing relationship between this provision and the norm that it has been asked to add in explicit terms.

With regard to the principle of equality, the Court states that the rule referred to as *tertium comparationis* must be valid for the role, and making the omission unconstitutional through the additive judgment must be the only possible option.[27] In this sense,

> the principle of equality cannot be invoked when the provision of law from which the *tertium comparationis* has been taken represents a derogation from a general rule. In this case, the function of the constitutional review according to Article 3 of the Constitution can be nothing less than the restoration of the general discipline, unjustifiably derogated from by that particular provision, and not the extension to other cases of the latter, which would worsen rather than eliminate the lack of coherence of the regulatory system.[28]

Based on this idea, Judgment 97 of 1996 declared groundless the question of constitutional legitimacy concerning Article 2, letter (c) of Act no. 469 of 1961 on the National Fire Brigade "in the part in which" it did not provide for the

---

[27] Judgment 2 of 1998.
[28] Judgment 383 of 1992. See also Judgment 295 of 1995 discussed in the Report of the Constitutional Court of the Italian Republic, *Legislative Omission in Constitutional Jurisprudence*.

possibility of the owners of areas used for public performance being able to establish their own fire prevention and extinguishing systems by recourse to private firefighting teams, even within the limitations of, and based on the criteria established by, the competent Ministry of the Interior.[29] According to that law, only the owners of factories, warehouses, and similar enterprises were allowed to set up a private service. According to the *a quo* judge, this amounted to discriminatory treatment of these two categories and, furthermore, the compression of the right to private economic initiative by the owners of public entertainment areas. The Court replied pointing out that the diversity of the rules regarding industrial factories and places of public entertainment, as far as the faculty to make use of a private service rather than the public one is concerned, is justified because it concerns specific and distinct realities and the object of the protection granted by the legislation is totally different. This object is to be identified, on the one hand, in the safety of employees at work, and on the other in the safety of the public during a show or entertainment. The difference between the two situations leads the Court to consider the different treatment justified "even setting aside any consideration that the possibility that the principle of equality would have been usefully evoked in this case considering that the provision assumed as *tertium comparationis* [was] an exception, in derogation from the general rule deducible from the overall regulatory system."[30]

However, in a subsequent judgment, the Court worked on the idea of the "equality" (*omogeneità*) of the cases being compared; "equality" must be evaluated in relation to the *ratio* of the contested norm, verifying in particular whether this *ratio* can be applied to all the cases under comparison with absolutely no distinction. Once this "equality" is found, the difference in legal treatment wholly removes any reasonable justification from the contested provision, and therefore infringes the principle of equality.[31]

---

[29] *Ordinamento dei servizi antincendi e del Corpo nazionale dei vigili del fuoco e stato giuridico e trattamento economico del personale del sottufficiali, vigili scelti e vigili del Corpo nazionale dei vigili del fuoco.*

[30] For a discussion of this case see the Report of the Constitutional Court of the Italian Republic, *Legislative Omission in Constitutional Jurisprudence.*

[31] See Judgment 322 of 1998 in which the Court declares the unconstitutionality of Article 2941 no. 7 of the Italian Civil Code, in the part in which it does not provide that statutory limitations are suspended in connection with relations between a mixed limited-unlimited liability partnership (*società in accomandita semplice*) and its administrators, as long as they are in office, with regard to liability actions against them, as already envisaged for companies with legal personality, because the *ratio* for the suspension of statutory limitations refers to the managerial relationship that binds the company to the administrator; in this sense, it is obviously

16.3.2. The Compulsory Constitutional Solution or the "Rime Obbligate" ("Necessary Choice") Doctrine

The elements that the Court includes in the wording of the disputed provision are the result of the incorporation of an element set out in a constitutional provision (as in Judgment 364 of 1988 on the recognition of the principle of the personality of criminal liability). Otherwise, they may derive from a general legal principle which, if not observed, brings about a violation of Article 3 of the Constitution by omission, as it is contrary to the principle of reasonableness.

The Court can pronounce an additive judgment only if the normative fragment which is added is something indefectible, when it represents a "compulsory constitutional solution." In this sense it is said that the Court rules from "necessary choice" (*rime obbligate*).[32] According to the Court, "an additive decision is allowed ... only when the adjusting solution is not the result of a discretionary evaluation but is necessarily the consequence of the judgment of legitimacy, so that the Court actually proceeds to a logically necessitated extension, often implied in the interpretative potential of the regulatory environment in which the contested provision is inserted." By contrast, "when ... there are a plurality of solutions, resulting from various possible evaluations, the Court's intervention is not an option and the relevant choice belongs to the legislator alone."[33]

In reality, the decisions where the discretion of the legislator represents an insurmountable barrier to the Court are fairly frequent: in addition to criminal law, the Court is also cautious in other politically sensitive constitutional areas.[34] The Court has developed the concept of the "constitutionally compulsory solution" in a number of orders by which it has declared the issue of constitutionality manifestly inadmissible or unfounded. In Order 463 of 2002, the Court ruled that extension to a separated spouse of the measure against their property rights envisaged in divorce cases would entail the Court issuing an addendum to introduce, in the absence of any constitutional obligation, an institution other than the one the current complaints address. This would represent an obvious and unjustified intrusion in the sphere of attribution

---

irrelevant insofar as it is a matter of a company with legal personality or – as in the case before the referring court – of a limited partnership, which has no legal personality.

[32] Vezio Crisafulli, "Questioni in tema di interpretazione della Corte costituzionale nei rapporti con l'interpretazione giudiziaria" (1978) *Giurisprudenza costituzionale* 929.

[33] See Judgment 109 of 1986, discussed in the Report of the Constitutional Court of the Italian Republic, *Legislative Omission in Constitutional Jurisprudence*.

[34] See later.

reserved to the discretion of the legislator, and so the Court declared the question manifestly inadmissible.[35]

These criteria have been applied by the Court with regard to the question of constitutionality regarding the lack of a specific discipline in the Italian system on homosexual unions. In Judgment 138 of 2010, when the Court was called to pronounce on the unconstitutionality of several articles of the 1942 Italian Civil Code that do not allow homosexual couples to marry, the constitutional judge stated that "The question raised by the two referral orders, regarding Article 2 of the Constitution, must be declared inadmissible, because its purpose is to obtain a non-constitutional compulsory additive judgment."[36] It follows, therefore, that, within the scope of Article 2 of the Constitution, it is the responsibility of the Parliament, in the exercise of its full discretion, to identify forms of guarantee and recognize homosexual unions, leaving the Constitutional Court the opportunity to intervene in the protection of specific situations (as was the case of *more uxorio* relationships).[37] In fact, it may be that, in relation to specific situations, there is a need for equal treatment of the married couple and that of the homosexual couple that the Court can guarantee through recourse to the parameter of reasonableness.[38]

The expression *rime obbligate*, rather than the much more frequent "constitutionally compulsory solution," has been used by the Court since the nineties with the purpose of identifying its presence and thereby pronouncing an additive judgment,[39] as well as its absence, consequently denying the possibility of an additive judgment.[40] In Judgment 70 of 1994, which decided the questions of constitutionality raised against the provision which established the mandatory postponement of the execution of a sentence against a person infected with HIV in cases of incompatibility with the state of detention, the Court stated that it belongs to the parliamentary prerogative to decide between the immediate execution of the prison sentence or its temporary suspension, so it does not involve any kind of *rime obbligate* solution.[41]

In Judgment 432 of 2006, the Court dismissed as manifestly inadmissible the question of constitutionality over which it was asked to add a new rule that

---

[35] See also Order 185 of 2007 with reference to administrative process.
[36] *Considerato in diritto* 5.
[37] See Judgments 559 of 1989 and 404 of 1988.
[38] *Considerato in diritto* 8.
[39] As in Judgment 218 of 1995.
[40] Among others, see Judgments 298 of 1993, 70 of 1994, 258 and 308 of 1994, and Order 432 of 2006.
[41] Article 146, first paragraph, no. 3, of the Criminal Code, added to Article 2 of Decree Law no. 139 of 1993, converted with amendments by Law no. 222 of 1993.

would have brought about a change in the administrative law process. With the required addition, the administrative judge would have been given the *ex officio* power to transfer the extraordinary appeal to the courts if an act after the extraordinary appeal to the Head of State were challenged before the administrative court itself. The question of constitutionality was meant to introduce forms of coordination between the two remedies mentioned within the system of administrative justice without taking into account that "the concrete ways of coordination between the two remedies may be multiple and respond to divergent objectives, ... without which none of them can be considered constitutionally mandatory." The decision on the merits of the issue stemmed ultimately from the need to recognize "the existence of normative evaluation characterized by high legislative discretion," and therefore "the issue raised is [resolved] in the request for an adjustment to the present [Constitution] and not to *rime obbligate*."[42]

The Court explicitly acknowledges the presence of *rime obbligate* in order to pronounce an additive sentence in only one case. In Judgment 218 of 1995, on the (supposed) illegitimacy of the system of incompatibility between an allowance (or pension) for disability and unemployment benefit, the Court pointed out that even if it falls within the discretion of the legislator to establish the non-cumulation or incompatibility between different social security or welfare benefits, balancing the needs provided for in Article 38 of the Constitution (welfare support for some categories of citizens in disadvantaged circumstances, such as citizens without work or disabled people), and the need to preserve the balance of public finance (Article 81 of the Constitution), it has to consider and satisfy the principle of equality and reasonableness (Article 3 of the Constitution), since it is not possible to exclude in the abstract the possibility that those people who suffer multiple adverse events may be exposed to a situation of greater need than those who suffer only one adversity. According to the Court, the system provided by the Italian legislation was a system of rigid incompatibility, not tempered by the possibility of choice. For these reasons, it manifested "intrinsic unreasonableness" because it was possible that a person on a disability allowance might have another disability at the same time, and this ought to justify, according to the Court, the concurrence of unemployment benefit and the subsidy (or pension) for disability.[43]

---

[42] See Judgment 432 of 2006 and, for its discussion, Report of the Constitutional Court of the Italian Republic, *Legislative Omission in Constitutional Jurisprudence*.

[43] On this case, see the Report of the Constitutional Court of the Italian Republic, *Legislative Omission in Constitutional Jurisprudence*.

16.3.3. Substantive Limitations to Additive Judgments: Criminal Law

There are some sectors of the legal system where additive judgments are not envisaged: namely those causing expenses to be borne by public bodies and criminal matters.[44]

According to Article 25 of the Constitution, "No one may be punished except by virtue of a law already in force before the offense was committed." Thus, the Constitutional Court may not adopt additive judgments in criminal matters which act *in malam partem*, i.e., extending the scope of criminal law.

A leading case on this subject is Judgment 42 of 1977. In this case, the Court was asked to rule on the constitutionality of a provision on making libel committed through the press a criminal act, which excluded the possibility of punishment for the same conduct if committed by other means.[45] Given the a *quo* judge's request to extend the punitive discipline to cases of defamation committed by other means, the Court clearly stated that it had no way of subtracting specific cases from the ordinary discipline to place them under a special and more restrictive discipline. Since this is a highly political issue, reserved by Article 25 of the Constitution to the legislator alone, there can be no possibility of intervention using additive sentences. This approach has gradually been consolidated and confirmed in the Court's case law.[46]

The principle of strict legality in criminal matters does not operate in an absolute sense, however. The Court may introduce legislation and practices able to bring about reductions in the range of the penal precept (*in bonam partem* intervention). Judgment 108 of 1974 thus declared the unconstitutionality of Article 415 of the Criminal Code, which provided for prison sentences ranging from six months to five years for actions inciting others to breach laws of public order or instigating hatred between social classes. The Court found this law unconstitutional because it conflicted with the exercise of the right to freedom of speech guaranteed by Article 21 of the Constitution, failing to specify that the incitement to hatred between social classes had to be manifest in a form that would lead to disorderly conduct.

On the same lines, with Judgment 71 of 1983, when asked to pronounce an additive decision to exclude the contravention pertaining to advertising tobacco products from decriminalization, the Court declared the inadmissibility of the question pointing out that "such decisions exceed the powers of

---

[44] See Judgment 42 of 1997, *Considerato in diritto* 4.
[45] Article 1 of the Law no. 47 of 1948.
[46] In this sense, see Orders 187 of 2005 and 437 of 2006. For their discussion see Report of the Constitutional Court of the Italian Republic, *Legislative Omission in Constitutional Jurisprudence*.

the constitutional court, which does not remove specific cases from the common rules, adding a new exception to a series absolutely fixed by law; and even more so when it is – as in the case under consideration – a way of creating a new type of crime that will affect the fundamental principle of rule of law in criminal matters."[47] According to the Court, this disposition did not indicate incitement to a specific criminal action or activity against public order or disobedience of the law; it simply punished action intending to bring about a feeling or sensation without requiring the modalities used to necessarily constitute a danger to public order and peace. It did not, however, rule out the possibility that it could affect the mere manifestation and incitement to the persuasion of the truth of a political or philosophical doctrine and ideology. Due to this lack of precision, the provision was declared contrary to Article 21 of the Constitution (on freedom of expression) "in the part in which" it punished anyone who publicly incites hatred between the social classes, insofar as the same article did not specify that this instigation had to take place in a manner that represented a danger to public peace.[48]

This approach was partially specified in Judgment 42 of 1997, in which the Court stated that,

> Even granted that this Court may remove from the criminal law provisions *in bonam partem* with the purpose of restoring the general vigor of derogated rules, and it remains the sole province of the courts to assess the effectiveness of such a pronouncement in the ongoing criminal proceedings, it is certain that it cannot, however, subtract specific cases from the common discipline in criminal matters in order to bring it under a special discipline which is deemed more appropriately safeguarded by the interests involved, and even less when this entails an aggravation of the punishment. Such a choice, which must be defined as eminently political, is in fact reserved to the legislature alone by Article 25 of the Constitution, excluding any possibility of intervention through so-called additive judgments.[49]

---

[47] The Court took the same position in its Judgment 8 of 1987 on the presumed unconstitutionality of the provision establishing that a parent intending to proceed to the belated recognition of his/her son, already recognized by the other parent, needed the consent of the latter, waivered only by a judgment of the Court which takes the place of the lacking parental consent: see the Report of the Constitutional Court of the Italian Republic, *Legislative Omission in Constitutional Jurisprudence*.

[48] An additive action in the criminal field is contained, *inter alia*, in Judgment 139 of 1989, pertaining to Article 266 of the Criminal Code, regarding the crime of inciting members of the armed forces to disobey the law.

[49] *Considerato in diritto* 4.

16.4. THE VARIOUS TYPES OF ADDITIVE JUDGMENTS

According to the classification proposed in the *doctrine*, additive judgments come under the category of "manipulative judgments," together with substitutive judgments.[50] Within the category of additive judgments, it is possible to distinguish between additive performance judgments and additive procedural judgments. Despite the name, additive judgments of principle form an autonomous category. There are also some new types of additive judgments for which it is not yet possible to identify a category.

16.4.1. Additive Judgments

16.4.1.1. Additive Performance Judgments

With additive performance judgments, the Court introduces a "new" provision or, more frequently, extends the economically favorable effects of a law to categories originally excluded in an "unreasonable way" from the benefit.[51] Additionally, there may be additive judgments of performance adopted under the principle of solidarity, as envisaged in Article 38 of the Constitution.[52] The peculiarity of this type of decision lies not so much in the ruling itself as in the reasoning and in the effects it produces, as they create an economic burden on public spending.

According to the third paragraph of Article 81 of the Constitution, which introduces the necessary "financial coverage" clause, "any law involving new or increased expenditure shall provide for the resources to cover such expenditure."[53] Strictly speaking, this provision does not apply to the decisions of the Constitutional Court, being directed only to Parliament and the Government. However, the Court cannot ignore this provision when addressing the necessary balancing between the rights guaranteed by the added benefits, and respect for the principle of proper management of public finances. If the Court considers that the disputed provision is unconstitutional because of the breach of the principle of equality, two different scenarios are possible.

---

[50] See Judgments 15 of 1969 and 409 of 1989.
[51] See Judgment 1 of 1991.
[52] See Judgment 250 of 1994 on the integration of the minimum pension.
[53] Article 81 of the Constitution was modified by Constitutional Law no. 1 of 2012 in response to the 2012 Euro-crisis: see Tania Groppi, Irene Spigno and Nicola Vizioli, "The Constitutional Consequences of the Financial Crisis in Italy" in Xenophon Contiades (ed.), *Constitutions in the Global Financial Crisis: A Comparative Analysis* (New York: Ashgate 2013) 89. The same financial coverage clause was provided in the previous version of the fourth paragraph of Article 81 of the Constitution.

In the first one, if the Court fails to take into account the financial coverage clause, it will "extend" the number of recipients of the benefits including those who, unconstitutionally, were not originally contemplated. According to the second scenario, if the Court takes into account the financial coverage clause, respect for the principle of equality will impose a "limit" on the number of recipients of a given benefit, thus excluding those people who are not in a comparable condition to those considered in the disputed provision. This approach is mainly based on the idea that "available resources are limited, and the Government and Parliament have to introduce changes to spending legislation in the financial maneuver where this is necessary to safeguard the State budget's equilibrium and to pursue the objectives of financial programming"; "[m]oreover, it is undeniable that [t]he legislature, in balancing the exercise of its discretion and taking into account fundamental economic policy requirements, must balance all the legally relevant factors."[54] On the other hand, "the principle of equality does not operate unidirectional and is necessarily directed to extend the scope of a more favorable discipline referred to as *tertium comparationis*, but it may also develop in the sense of removing the unjustified privilege arising from a more favorable discipline than the one indicated for comparison."[55] The Court imposed this approach due to the "evolution of the social conscience" and the "serious crisis of public finances." However, the legislator remains free to act as it sees fit in handling the issue by bringing it under normative discipline.

There have been some decisions in which the Constitutional Court has adopted an additive judgment that has brought about new expenses, albeit indirectly.[56] It is also true that, beyond any need for balancing, the Court may consider, when it is necessary, to declare the unconstitutionality of an act, doing so irrespective of any economic effects on the institutions. Nowadays, the constitutional court tends to take "costing" decisions on matters such as public employment, social security, public assistance (e.g., on minimum wages, social and health care, contributory capacity, or the minimization of pension benefits). In Judgment 455 of 1990, the Court pointed out that when

---

[54] See Judgment 99 of 1995.
[55] See Judgment 421 of 1995.
[56] See Judgments 284 of 1987 (which allows lecturers who have not done a certain number of years' service to take part in the procedures for the inclusion in the list of researchers who have not done that number of years' service), 399 of 1988 (which allows "temporary workers" to benefit from the positions left over on the reserve list of teachers) and 39 of 1989 (which allows lecturers who take part in examinations to be put on the official list of confirmed university researchers who are regulated by Article 24 of the Law no. 62 of 1967): Report of the Constitutional Court of the Italian Republic, *Legislative Omission in Constitutional Jurisprudence*.

fundamental rights imply claiming positive benefits from public facilities, they are subject to precise conditions, especially from the point of view of expenditure.

It has been established in this regard that the right to health is subject to "the determination of the instruments, the timing and the means of implementation" of the relevant protection indicated by the ordinary legislator. The dimension of the right to health implies that, as with any right to positive benefits, the right to obtain medical treatment is guaranteed to every person as a "conditional" constitutional right by the implementation of the ordinary legislature. In balancing the interest protected by that right with the other constitutionally protected interests, the Court takes into account the objective constraints that the legislature encounters in its implementation work in relation to the necessary organizational and financial resources. This principle, which is common to other constitutional rights, certainly does not imply degrading the fundamental protection enshrined in the Constitution to a purely legislative one. Rather, it implies that the constitutionally mandatory protection of a given good (in this case the right to health) will be implemented gradually as a result of reasonable balancing with other interests or assets enjoying the same constitutional protection, and with the real and objective possibility of having the necessary resources for the same implementation.

As additive performance judgments represent a serious burden on public budgets (a particularly acute problem in times of financial crisis), over the last twenty years, the number of these pronouncements has gradually declined. A mechanism the Court has adopted to limit the financial consequences of these judgments is that of the additive judgments of principle.[57]

16.4.1.2. Additive Procedural Judgments

These additive judgments are wholly comparable from the structural point of view with the "classic" additive and additive judgments of principle.[58] The difference lies in the content of the addition, which concerns the procedure for the formation of the disputed law from the point of view of constitutionality, or – more often – other acts enacted according to the dispositions of the said law. In other words, the Court adds normative content to a procedural disposition in order to insert stages or phases in the approval process.

This type of decision, theoretically applicable to any procedure, takes on special importance in relations between the State and the regional organs,

---

[57] See in detail later; see also: Judgments 307 of 1990, 26 of 1999 and 385 of 2005.
[58] See later.

since the recent decisions of the Court have spread a pervasive application of the principle of loyal cooperation (*leale collaborazione*) between local organs, suggesting a departure from "dual regionalism" (originally only an Italian phenomenon) in favor of a greater connection between the different levels of government.

In this context, it should be noted that additive judgments have become particularly significant in recent years as a result of the new division of legislative and administrative powers between the State and the territorial autonomies (brought into being by Constitutional Law no. 3 of 2001 under which Title V of the Constitution was modified). Subject matter and skills interact, often in the absence of any certain, unambiguous criterion for bringing the contested regulation within well-defined constitutional parameters. Given this situation, the use of cooperative modules is essentially a remedy for a regulatory gap and, at the same time, for the failure of the legislator to provide for the intervention of a joint body, whose institutional role would be the resolution of conflicting interests between the State and territorial autonomies.[59]

16.4.2. Additive Judgments of Principle

In some cases, the Court remarks the existence of a gap to fill, but at the same time notes that if it were to fill the gap itself, it would invade the sphere of legislative competence. Due respect for legislative discretion produces the double effect of not precluding the declaration of the existence of unconstitutionality, and stops the Court in its labor of mending the legal system in a coherent way: as has already been pointed out, in the case of more than one possible (and constitutionally allowed) addition, the Court has no power to choose.

If the Court were to opt for a declaration of unconstitutionality *tout court*, the discretion of the legislator would be safeguarded, but many collateral problems would arise, relating, for example, to provisions that offer guarantees to a certain category of persons or situations. In this case, it is clear that declaring an entire provision unconstitutional would not provide a remedy against non-compliance with the Constitution, but would worsen the defect arising from the (further) reduction of the protected situations.

To address situations of this kind, the Court began to adopt the so-called "additive judgments of principle" in the late eighties. These are decisions in

---

[59] See Judgments 219 of 2005, 231 of 2005, 133 of 2006, 213 of 2006, and 165 of 2007. For a discussion, see the Report of the Constitutional Court of the Italian Republic, *Legislative Omission in Constitutional Jurisprudence*.

which the Court, after declaring the unconstitutionality of the provision at issue "in the part in which it does not provide" (as in the "classic" additive judgments), does not indicate the missing normative fragment, but states the general principle in an attempt to fill the gap (on the assumption that the intervention in terms of legislation will follow, with effect *erga omnes*). In the *ratio* of these judgments, the Court sometimes sets a deadline for the legislator to intervene and lays down the principles from which the lawmaker should take inspiration: in this way, the content of a true additive judgment and the content of a delegated decision are combined, reconciling the immediacy of the declaration of unconstitutionality with safeguarding the legislator's discretional sphere.

The Court has used this type of decision in particularly "sensitive" areas, such as the question of the protection of working mothers.[60] Pronouncing on the legitimacy of the rules under which it was expressly prohibited to make women return to work during the three months after childbirth but excluded premature parturition from protection, the Court stated that despite the possibility of different solutions with specific regard to the commencement of the period of leave, moving commencement to the moment the child was to be moved to the family home or rather the presumed date of the physiological end of pregnancy, the choice between the various possible options fell to the legislator. But, given the evident unconstitutionality of the norm, and in the absence of legislative action, it was the Constitutional Court's responsibility to identify the legal principle suited to govern the situation in accordance with constitutional principles. From this perspective, the declaration of unconstitutionality targeted the contested provision "in the part in which it does not provide for the application of the terms of the compulsory abstention from work in the case of premature parturition required to ensure adequate protection of mother and child."[61]

By recourse to the additive judgment of principle, the Court therefore establishes a dialogue, not only with the legislator called to fill legislative lacunae,

---

[60] Examples include compensation for harm suffered by victims of road accidents, in which the Court declared the unconstitutionality of the existing regulation for not providing for the re-evaluation of the monetary value of compensation "in the part in which it does not provide for the adjustment of the value of currency" (Judgment 560 of 1987), ordinary unemployment benefits, stating the unconstitutionality "in the part in which it does not provide for the adjustment of the monetary value mechanism" (Judgment 497 of 1988), the liability of carriers for damages arising from loss or damage to transported goods "in the part in which it does not provide a mechanism for updating the maximum amount of compensation" (Judgment 420 of 1991). See also the Report of the Constitutional Court of the Italian Republic, *Legislative Omission in Constitutional Jurisprudence*.

[61] Judgment 270 of 1999.

but also with judges who are tasked, pending parliamentary intervention, with following up the principle relied on in the decision of unconstitutionality. In fact, the Court has stressed that

> the declaration of constitutional illegitimacy of a legislative omission – such as that recognized in the event of failure to provide a suitable mechanism to ensure its effectiveness through a norm of constitutionally guaranteed right – leaves the legislator with the task of introducing and regulating such a mechanism retroactively by recourse to abstract standards, administered by a principle which the merits judge is authorized to refer to in order to find a remedy to the omission in the process of identifying the rule applicable to a specific case.[62]

16.4.3. New Types of Additive Judgments

After the reform of Title V of Part II of the Constitution, there has been a significant increase in litigation between the State and the Regional Authorities. The difficulty of resolving such disputes has sometimes obliged the Court to develop new types of additive judgments in order to achieve the full realization of the principle of loyal cooperation between the State and the Regions.

The full realization of this principle has, in some cases, made it sufficient to merely add an opinion;[63] in others, however, the Court has held that the unconstitutionality of the contested provision resides in the failure to include an agreement with the State-Regions Conference,[64] or with the individual Region concerned.[65]

A special additive effect occurs when the Constitutional Court, pursuant to Article 117 of the Constitution, declares a conflict with the provisions of the European Convention on Human Rights as interpreted by the Strasbourg Court (in the orientation begun with Judgments 348 and 349 of 2007). In such situations, the Court may find it necessary to introduce, for example, new procedural rules to guarantee the effective protection of a fundamental right, which the European Court of Human Rights has found to be infringed by Italian law.[66]

---

[62] Judgment 295 of 1991.
[63] Among the most recent, Judgment 33 of 2011.
[64] *Ex plurimis*, Judgments 163 of 2012 and 79 of 2011.
[65] Among many others, see Judgment 263 of 2011. See the Report of the Constitutional Court of the Italian Republic, *Legislative Omission in Constitutional Jurisprudence*.
[66] See Judgment 113 of 2011 on the *Dorigo* case.

In some cases, before proceeding to a declaration of unconstitutionality, the Court makes an "admonition" to the legislature, indicating areas of unconstitutionality or normative contradiction, which it is first of all up to the legislator to remove. This can happen for various reasons: it may be a criminal matter and striking it down would cause an expansion of criminal penalties, which are only the province of statutory law (so-called additive sentences in *malam partem*). It may be a case in which the areas of unconstitutionality cannot be eliminated by an additive judgment, because there is no single constitutionally imposed solution; it may be a case involving dispositions whose elimination would result in the transformation of an entire sector of the regulatory system. In other cases, it may involve norms whose elimination would result in a vacuum in some delicate matter for the protection of fundamental rights.

Other hypotheses could be formulated, and others have definitely occurred over the more than fifty years of the Court's activity.

The follow-up to these judgments may vary: the legislator may accept the admonition and consequently amend the contested provision according to the indications of the Court. On the other hand, Parliament may entirely fail to act, and this inertia will force the Court to declare the norm unlawful, based on the prevalence of the need to eliminate the unconstitutional norm on the grounds of systemic impediments, for which the legislator has already been admonished.

16.5. CONCLUSION

From a theoretical point of view, it seems clear that in its use of additive judgments the constitutional judge is no longer a mere "negative legislator," but has become a "creator of legal norms," thus invading a space that the Italian constitutional system reserves to Parliament.[67]

In the overall contexts of the 1948 Italian Constitution, the Constitutional Court is the body that must ensure compliance with, and guarantee, the supremacy of the Constitution, and in doing so it can also make the will of Parliament ineffective: the last word when constitutional values are at stake belongs to the Constitutional Court.[68] In its activities as guarantor of the Constitution, the Court has adopted different types of decisions which, despite leaving the narrow confines indicated in the Constitution and the laws are meant to "clean up" the existing legislation. Some authors have called the

---

[67] Article 70 of the Constitution.
[68] Valerio Onida, *La Costituzione* (Bologna: Il Mulino, 2007).

creative power of the Court "a genuine constitutional revolution"[69] driven by a *horror vacui*,[70] or by the search for a "less intrusive solution,"[71] or as a means of political mediation.[72]

There can be no doubt that the Court's creative power was – and still is– needed to fill both historical and contemporary legislative omissions that, as we have already seen, do not represent the absence of a legislative product (a circumstance that would not even allow the constitutional proceeding to come before the Court, since according to Article 134 of the Constitution, the Court considers only the legitimacy of laws and enactments having the force of law), but rather incomplete legislative activity that leaves regulatory gaps or lacunae to change and/or update the legislation.

In doing so, the Court has been cautious, making explicit that:

> an additive decision is permitted, being *ius receptum*, only when adjusting a solution is not the consequence of a discretionary assessment, but must necessarily follow the judgment of legitimacy, so the Court actually carries out an extension that is a logical necessity and is often implicit in the interpretative potential within the legal order in which the contested provision is inserted. However, faced with a plurality of solutions arising from different possible assessments, it is not lawful for the Court to intervene, and the relevant choice pertains exclusively to Parliament.[73]

Or, in simpler terms, "additive judgments ... are permitted only when the issue is presented in *rime obbligate*, i.e., when the solution is logically necessitated and implicit in the legislative context"[74]; as we have already seen, the expression *rime obbligate* has been used by the Court to underline presence,[75] as well as its absence,[76] and consequently to affirm or deny the possibility of pronouncing an additive decision. Consequently, given a plurality of possible solutions, the Court declares the inadmissibility of the question.

Actually, the theory of *rime obbligate* has been widely criticized: according to some authors, if it is true that the solution proposed by the Constitutional Court is already present in the legal order and it only needs to be developed

---

[69] Gaetano Silvestri, "Le sentenze normative della Corte costituzionale" in AA.VV., *Scritti su la giustizia costituzionale in onore di V. Crisafulli* (Padova: Cedam, 1985) 755 ss.
[70] Franco Modugno, "Ancora sui controversi rapporti tra Corte costituzionale e potere legislativo" (1988) *Giurisprudenza Costituzionale* 16.
[71] Gustavo Zagrebelsky, *La giustizia costituzionale* (Bologna: Il Mulino, 1988).
[72] Silvestri, Supra note 69.
[73] See Judgments 109 of 1986 and 125 of 1988.
[74] See Order 380 of 2006.
[75] Judgments 218 of 1995.
[76] Judgments 298 of 1993, 70 of 1994, 258 and 308 of 1994, Order 432 of 2006.

and translated into law, then why should ordinary judges not reach the same solution through interpretation? From this point of view, the intervention of the Constitutional judge is not considered necessary.[77]

An answer to this is that in the centralized Italian system of constitutional justice, the Constitutional Court alone has the power to derive a somehow "forced" solution with *erga omnes* effects.

Despite criticisms in this regard, I would not say that the Court has its own "political direction." Indeed, I believe that additive judgments are decisions that do not lose their judicial nature, so I wholly subscribe to the position of those who underline that a normative addition introduced by the Court is not a pure creation. It is rather something taken from what already exists within the legal system, in the constitutional system itself: something that was waiting to be developed and translated into an express rule.[78] It is the *rime obbligate* theory that involves the development through additive judgments of "constitutionally obliged case law," that prevents the Constitutional Court from taking any discretionary action.

I consider additive judgments to be an instrument the Constitutional Court can use to reveal the invisible meaning of the Constitution. It has a latent meaning that is invisible to the legislator but is evident in the part of the sentence that declares a law unconstitutional "for what it does not provide."

---

[77] Zagrebelsky, Supra note 71.
[78] A view shared by Crisafulli, "Questioni in tema di interpretazione della Corte Costituzionale nei confronti con l'interpretazione giudiziaria", for example.

17

Germany's German Constitution

Russell A. Miller

17.1. INTRODUCTION

Not long ago I visited the German Federal Constitutional Court (*Bundesverfassungsgericht*) with a group of my American law students. When our tour of the Court reached the luminous, wood-and-glass hearing chamber our guide triumphantly declared: "Welcome to the only common law court in Germany!"

It would have pleased the legendary comparative law scholar H. Patrick Glenn to hear it.[1] In his seminal work *Legal Traditions of the World* he argued that legal systems such as Germany's cannot be categorically classified as emblematic of a single legal tradition.[2] Glenn contended that state legal systems are the sites of encounters between the world's complex, commensurable and interdependent legal traditions.[3] He used words such as "bridging" and "dialogue" and "interchange" to describe this unavoidable dynamic, which he imagined to be something similar to Russian nesting dolls, with lateral-traditions and sub-traditions supporting and complementing a system's leading or primary tradition.[4] The tour guide at the Constitutional Court seemed to

---

[1] Sadly, McGill University Law Professor H. Patrick Glenn passed away in 2014. A memorial essay in the *American Journal of Comparative Law*, a publication produced by the American Society of Comparative Law (over which he presided as President at the time of his death) described him as "one of the most respected comparatists of our time:" David J. Gerber, "In Memoriam, H. Patrick Glenn (1940–2014)" (2015) 63 *American Journal of Comparative Law* 1. See also Daniel Jutras, "Saying Goodbye to Professor H. Patrick Glenn (1940–2014)," *McGill University Faculty of Law News* (October 3, 2014), available at www.mcgill.ca/law/channels/news/saying-goodbye-professor-h-patrick-glenn-1940-2014-239330.

[2] H. Patrick Glenn, *Legal Traditions of the World: Sustainable Diversity in Law*, 5th edn (Oxford: Oxford University Press, 2014), 368 ("[a]ll categories are vague, [...] all efforts at separation are arbitrary and artificial").

[3] Ibid., 43. See also H. Patrick Glenn, "Are Legal Traditions Incommensurable?" (2001) 49 *American Journal of Comparative Law* 133.

[4] Glenn, Supra note 2, 366–7, 373–4.

have all of this in mind, implying that German constitutional law (embodied by the Constitutional Court) represents the subaltern common law tradition asserting itself in the German legal culture, which is predominantly shaped by the continental or civil law tradition.

This is not a novel characterization of Germany's postwar legal culture. Others have remarked on the tension that resulted from the encounter between the new constitutional law and the old civilian legal order.[5] In fact, the story is usually cast in less reconciliatory terms than Glenn would have preferred. Germany's ordinary courts, our tour guide was suggesting, are the carriers of the German legal culture's predominant civil law gene.[6] But the Constitutional Court represents a recessive – albeit thriving – common law genetic adaptation that has gradually conquered and colonized Germany's civilian legal culture.[7] According to this account the Constitutional Court, facing resistance from the ordinary courts and the German legal culture's entrenched civil law orientation, has heroically overcome formalism and positivism in a common law-like pursuit of constitutional justice. In fact, few courts have shaken off the continent's old civilian shackles and taken up the common law judicial role with as much gusto as the German Constitutional

---

[5] See Thomas Dietrich, "Bedeutung der grundrechte im zivilrecht" in Institut für Wirtschaftsrecht der Universität Kassel (ed.) *60 Jahre Grundgesetz – Vortragsreihe* (Kassel: Kassel University Press, 2010), 97, 101. Dietrich refers to a "krachende Konfrontation der Grundrechte mit dem geltende Zivilrecht ..." ("crashing confrontation between constitutional rights and private law").

[6] See René David and John E. C. Brierley, *Major Legal Systems in the World Today*, 3rd edn (London: Stevens & Sons Ltd, 1985), 58–60, 63–72; Mathias Siems, *Comparative Law* (Cambridge: Cambridge University Press, 2014), 76; John Henry Merryman and Rogelio Pérez-Perdomo, *The Civil Law Tradition*, 3rd edn (Stanford, CA: Stanford University Press, 2007), 31; John Henry Merryman, "How Others Do It: The French and German Judiciaries" (1988) 61 *Southern California Law Review* 1871 ("[t]he 'old' individual rights ... have largely been achieved and solidified in the work of ordinary courts quietly applying the traditional sources [principally the civil codes] and methods of private law.")

[7] Merryman, Supra note 6 ("[t]he rise of constitutionalism is thus an additional form of decodification: the civil codes no longer serve the constitutional function, which has moved from the most private of private law sources – the civil code – to the most public of public law sources – the constitution"). See also A. Pearce Higgins, "The Making of the German Civil Code" (1905) 6 *Journal of the Society of Comparative Legislation* 95, 96 ("for the first time in the history of Germany, there came into being a veritable common law, which, sweeping away all anomalies and local customs, was ... to regulate the relations of all the members of the German Empire in the most important details of private law").

Court.[8] The Herculean role the Court now plays in the German polity might even make a native common law jurist blush.[9]

This story of dynamic diversity and pluralism within the German legal system (what Glenn referred to as "multivalence") is an important facet of postwar Germany's determined effort to confront and overcome the National Socialist past,[10] a process the Germans call *Vergangenheitsbewältigung*.[11] In this version of the story the civil law tradition helped to shape the preexisting legal culture, and it serves as the negative frame against which Germany's postwar constitutionalism serves as a rebuke.[12] As a matter of substantive law, the fronts in this *Kulutrkampf* especially involved family law and gender equality, but noteworthy skirmishes have also taken place in contract law, tort law, property law, and criminal law. The triumph of German constitutional law (and its common law orientation), so the myth would have it, required a number of innovative jurisprudential devices that are now closely identified with

---

[8] Donald P. Kommers and Russell A. Miller, "Das Bundesverfassungsgericht: Procedure, Practice and Policy of the German Federal Constitutional Court" (2009) 3 *Journal of Comparative Law* 194, 208 ("[t]he Court's record ... reveals a self-confident tribunal deeply engaged in Germans' lives and politics ... The number and range of cases in which the Federal Constitutional Court has acted to dramatically impact German politics are too great to systematically or comprehensively recount in this brief introduction"). See also B. S. Markesinis, "Conceptualism, Pragmatism and Courage: A Common Lawyer Looks at Some Judgments of the German Federal Court" (1986) 34 *American Journal of Comparative Law* 349, 359 ("[t]he 1900 Civil Code could not have survived without some very daring judicial interventions which, if not hallowed by the term judicial law-making, come as close as any common law judge has come into making new law").

[9] See Ronald Dworkin, *Law's Empire* (Cambridge, MA: Belknap Press, 1986), 239–40. See also Walter Mattli and Anne-Marie Slaughter, "Revisiting the European Court of Justice" (1998) 52 *International Organization* 177, 201 ("[i]n the German case, the commitment to *Verfassungspatriotismus*, or constitutional patriotism, results in the Constitutional Court's unusual willingness to decide cases with important foreign policy implications. According to Juliane Kokott, this willingness flows from the renewed German commitment to the *Rechtstaat* in the wake of the Second World War – no questions are above or beyond the law. The Constitutional Court thus conceives itself as an equal participant with the political branches of the German government in the process of European integration").

[10] Glenn, Supra note 2, 368–72.

[11] See Peter Reichel, *Vergangenheitsbewältigung in Deutschland: Die Auseinandersetzung mit der NS-Diktatur in Politik und Justiz* (Munich: C. H. Beck, 2001); Thomas McCarthy, "Vergangenheitsbewältigung in the USA on the Politics of the Memory of Slavery" (2002) 30 *Political Theory* 623. See also "Word of the Week: Vergangenheitsbewältigung", *Deutsche Welle*, available at www.dw.de/vergangenheitsbew%C3%A4ltigung/a-6614103.

[12] See Gerhard Casper, "Guardians of the Constitution" (1980) 53 *Southern California Law Review* 773, 781 ("[i]t was because of those very discontinuities in German constitutional history ... that the German post-war discussion centered on the failure of the German constitutions ... Above all, attention was turned to the Weimar Constitution, that professionally engineered document, so widely acclaimed in its time, such a dismal failure in operation" [internal quotations omitted]).

German constitutional law. For example, the Constitutional Court pioneered the idea that the constitution's basic rights must be regarded as "objective values" applicable across the entire society – and not merely as a set of subjective and negative limits on the state's interactions with its citizens.[13] Flowing inevitably from this innovation, the Constitutional Court also concluded that the Basic Law's objective values may be applied horizontally – albeit indirectly – across all of German law, even in private legal disputes that do not involve state action.[14] Finally, the Constitutional Court championed the use of proportionality in constitutional interpretation, giving itself the discretion to weigh constitutional harm and consider constitutional priorities on a case-by-case basis.[15] Ultimately, this is the myth of the postwar Basic Law (*Grundgesetz*) overcoming Germany's turbulent constitutional history and indigenous civilian tendency toward formalism and positivism to truly and at last bind the legislature, the executive and the judiciary to (constitutional) law and justice.[16]

The story of the common law's triumph in Germany depends on a number of fundamental premises, which I will survey and – for the most part – confirm in Section 17.2. The first premise is that the civil law tradition is the primary tradition in the German legal culture. The second premise is that constitutional law as practiced by the Constitutional Court bears many of the hallmarks of the common law tradition. The third premise is that there is a tension – perhaps even a hard-fought rivalry – between these different jurisprudential orientations in the postwar German legal order. The final premise is that the German Constitutional Court can claim victory in this struggle because it has succeeded in giving the constitution, with its common law orientation,

---

[13] Lüth Case, 7 BVerfGE 198 (1958). See Donald P. Kommers and Russell A. Miller, *The Constitutional Jurisprudence of the Federal Republic of Germany*, 3rd edn (Durham, NC: Duke University Press, 2012), 59–62; Donald P. Kommers, "German Constitutionalism: A Prolegomenon" (1991) 40 *Emory Law Journal* 837, 855–61.

[14] Lüth Case, 7 BVerfGE 198 (1958). See Kommers and Miller, Supra note 13; Bernhard Schlink, "German Constitutional Culture in Transition" (1993) 14 *Cardozo Law Review* 711, 718 ("[t]he Court found that because fundamental rights had importance not only as subjective rights of citizens against the state, but also as society's most important values, they governed the entire legal order, including civil laws that regulated the relationship of citizens to each other").

[15] See Kommers and Miller, Supra note 13, 67. See also Aharon Barak, *Proportionality: Constitutional Rights and Their Limitations* (Cambridge: Cambridge University Press, 2012); Robert Alexy, *A Theory of Constitutional Rights* (Oxford: Oxford University Press, 2002) (Julian Rivers trans.); Schlink, Supra note 14, 729 ("[w]hile methodologically convincing decisions still occur every now and again, there are many others that simply arise from the Court's feel for what is indicated by social and political life – for what is accepted and 'fits' into the social and political landscape. Decisions thus encompass only the individual cases *sub judice*, and are expressed and handed down as such").

[16] Grundgesetz für die Bundesrepublik Deutschland [Grundgesetz] [GG] [Basic Law] May 23, 1949, BGBl. I., Articles 1(3) and 20(3).

priority (as a legal-cultural matter and not as a doctrinal matter of constitutional supremacy) over the entrenched civil law tradition and especially the revered German Civil Code.[17]

Yet, Glenn understood that the encounters between legal traditions within a legal system are reciprocal affairs. The postwar constitutional regime profoundly introduced elements of the common law tradition into the German legal culture.[18] But the old, predominant civilian legal tradition in Germany has influenced German constitutional law, too. Glenn suggested that the interaction of these legal traditions would "blur the distinction between the two" and that both traditions would become subject to "multivalent, bridging, complexity" involving "rejection, limitation, accommodation or even adoption."[19] It is on this unremarked dynamic – the civil law tradition's influence on Germany's constitutional law – that I want to focus in this chapter. In Section 17.3 I document the civil law tradition's symbiotic influence on German constitutional law. There is evidence of this in the character of the constitutional text, in some constitutional theory, in the lingering priority given to the legislature (as opposed to the judiciary) to develop and refine the constitutional framework, in the civilian character of the Constitutional Court's jurisdiction, and in the Constitutional Court's civilian decisional style.

My analysis is significant for comparative lawyers' work because it suggests that German constitutional law – if it is to be studied and understood at all – must be taken on its own complex, multivalent terms. Of course, the common law/civil law interdependence I describe here is just one such distinctly contextual facet of German constitutional law. There are other influences – ranging from the raging sweep of political history to the contributions made by discrete individuals – that make equally important explanatory and determinative contributions to the tapestry of German constitutional law.[20] As comparative lawyers we ignore this thick web of meaning at the risk of engaging with nothing more than a chimera of German constitutional law. The object

---

[17] "The legislature shall be bound by the constitutional order ..." Grundgesetz für die Bundesrepublik Deutschland [Grundgesetz] [GG] [Basic Law] May 23, 1949, BGBl. I., Article. 20(3) (German Bundestag translation).

[18] Glenn noted the reverse phenomenon in the United States, suggesting that the civil law tradition had come to shape American constitutional law: Glenn, Supra note 2, 265.

[19] Glenn, Supra note 2, 374.

[20] Pierre Legrand calls these elements "traces" and identifies the following as a non-exhaustive list of possibilities: "traces of historical configurations enmeshed with traces of political rationalities intertwined with traces of social logics interwoven with traces of philosophical postulates plaited with traces of linguistic orders darned with traces of economic prescriptions interlaced with traces of epistemic assumptions:" see Pierre Legrand, "Negative Comparative Law" (2015) 10 *Journal of Comparative Law* 405, 419–20.

of comparative lawyers' study cannot be an abstract classification or taxonomic archetype of constitutional law, at least not if we want to be saying anything about something.[21] As this study demonstrates, the Basic Law anchors a highly contingent and contextually determined constitutional regime that features a mix of the common law and civil law traditions – and much, much more. It is Germany's German constitutional law.

17.2. HALF THE STORY: GERMAN CONSTITUTIONAL LAW AS THE TRIUMPH OF THE COMMON LAW TRADITION OVER THE CIVIL LAW TRADITION

There is an almost messianic narrative about postwar German law that suggests that the Basic Law has vanquished the formalistic and positivistic impulses in the German legal culture that are the residue of the civil law tradition's historical predominance in Germany. This myth depends on four premises. The first is that German legal culture is steeped in the civil law tradition's statutory formalism and positivism. The second is that constitutional law, with its focus on judicial interpretation and case-by-case decision-making, resembles the common law. The third is that the German Constitutional Court, as the guardian of the constitution (and thereby, the prophet of the common law tradition in Germany's civilian desert), has had to struggle against the enduring dominance of the civil law in postwar Germany.[22] The fourth is

---

[21] Cf David S. Law, "Constitutional Archetypes" (2016) 95 *Texas Law Review* 153.
[22] Kommers, Supra note 13 ("[m]eeting in 1948–1949, the Parliamentary Council generated the text that functions as the German constitution, known as the Grundgesetz [Basic Law]. In outlining the institutional infrastructure of the new Federal Republic, the Basic Law provided for a Federal Constitutional Court. The debate in the Parliamentary Council over constitutional review boiled down to a dispute over whether the new constitutional institution should be like Weimar's Staatsgerichtshof [State Court] and serve mainly as an organ for resolving conflicts between branches and levels of government [i.e., a court of constitutional review], or whether it should combine such jurisdiction with the general power to review the constitutionality of legislation [i.e., judicial review]? The framers finally agreed to create a constitutional tribunal independent of other public-law courts, but they disagreed over how much of the constitutional jurisdiction listed in the proposed constitution should be conferred on the court as opposed to other high federal courts. The controversy over the scope of the Federal Constitutional Court's jurisdiction centered on the distinction between what some delegates regarded as the "political" role of a constitutional court and what others considered to be the more "objective" law-interpreting role of the regular judiciary. Some delegates preferred two separate courts – one to review the constitutionality of laws [i.e., judicial review], the other to decide essentially political disputes among branches and levels of government [i.e., constitutional review]. Others favored one grand, multipurpose tribunal divided into several panels, each specializing in a particular area of public or constitutional law. This proposal was strenuously opposed by many German judges who were alarmed by any such mixing of law and politics in a single institution. The upshot was a compromise resulting in a separate constitutional tribunal with

that the German Constitutional Court has triumphed in this struggle, ushering in an era of previously unattainable constitutional law and justice – of *Rechtsstaatlichkeit*. Each of these premises has a basis in truth and I will explore them in this section.

Before turning to that endeavor I will first offer brief definitions of the "civil law" and "common law" traditions – two concepts that are fundamental to this study.

17.2.1. The Civil Law and Common Law Traditions Defined

Throughout this chapter I refer to the "civil law" and "common law" to represent two distinct legal traditions from among the many that find expression in the world. These are old labels with considerable explanatory force.[23] They are also quite dangerous. In the worst cases they are asserted as taxa – static and exclusive categories – into which many of the world's legal systems can be dumped in our mania to classify or map global legal phenomena.[24] Drawing almost satirically from the natural sciences, comparative lawyers have sometimes called these categories "legal families,"[25] as if they represent empirically discoverable biological species.[26] Elsewhere, I argue that this kind of taxonomic thinking in comparative law is perilous because it is superficial, and because it allows us to ignore the dynamic and discursive character of sociological phenomena such as the law.[27] These legal families (and other encompassing archetypes) seem to tell us so much about a legal system only because they tell us nothing at all.

I do not use legal traditions as a taxonomic device. I am not interested in trying to definitively classify Germany (or any other legal system) as belonging to an exclusive *legal family*. First, I embrace Glenn's definition of "legal

---

exclusive jurisdiction over all constitutional disputes, including the authority to review the constitutionality of laws' [internal citations omitted]).

[23] See David and Brierley, Supra note 6. See also Jorge L. Esquirol, "René David: At the Head of the Legal Family," in Annelise Riles (ed.) *Rethinking the Masters of Comparative Law* (Oxford: Hart Publishing, 2001), 212.

[24] See Siems, Supra note 6.

[25] See Mariana Pargendler, "The Rise and Decline of Legal Families" (2012) 60 *American Journal of Comparative Law* 1043; H. Patrick Glenn, "Comparative Legal Families and Comparative Legal Traditions", in Mathias Reimann and Reinhard Zimmerman (eds.) *The Oxford Handbook of Comparative Law* (Oxford: Oxford University Press, 2006), 421; Jaakko Husa, "Legal Families", in Jan M. Smits (ed.) *Elgar Encyclopedia of Comparative Law* (Cheltenham: Edward Elgar Publishing Ltd, 2006), 382; Jaako Husa, "Classification of Legal Families Today: Is It Time for a Memorial Hymn?" (2004) 56 *Revue Internationale de Droit Compare* 11.

[26] Pargendler, Supra note 25, 1051.

[27] Russell A. Miller, *Comparative Law's Taxonomy Problem* (April 15, 2016) (unpublished manuscript, on file with the author).

traditions," which represent identifiable epistemic constellations of normative information about ways of doing (and not doing) the law.[28] Glenn explains: "tradition emerges as a loose conglomeration of data, organized around a basic theme or themes ..."[29] That information, he argues, counts as tradition because it is carried forward from the past to the present. I do not know if he would have objected, but I find that Merryman and Pérez-Perdomo have helpfully clarified Glenn's concept of "legal traditions," concluding that they are

> [a] set of deeply rooted, historically conditioned attitudes about the nature of law, about the role of law in the society and the polity, about the proper organization and operation of a legal system, and about the way the law is or should be made, applied, studied, perfected, and taught.[30]

Second, I share Glenn's conviction that many different legal traditions can exist as part of a dynamic discourse within a single legal system. For example, Glenn tells of the churning mix of Hindu legal tradition, Islamic legal tradition, and the British common law tradition in India.[31] Hindu digests "continued to be written through the arrival of the British," Glenn explains. But the "arrival of the British was to supplant both hindu and islamic law as territorial law," leaving these traditions with a "special status, as personal laws of hindu or Islamic people."[32] This colonial "reception" of western law, perhaps better understood as the violent imposition of the colonizer's legal traditions,[33] was repeated along the knife-edge of western expansion in the world.[34] Still, Glenn could conclude that "[t]he effect of English law on Hindu law [in India] was ... not immediate or abrupt, nor did it prejudice the legitimacy and availability of classic Hindu sources. The change was more subtle ..."[35] Used in this way, legal traditions merely provide a means for talking about the multivalent legal attitudes that can be seen to be in conversation within any legal system, such as the interchange between the civil law tradition and the common law tradition in Germany.

---

[28] Glenn, Supra note 2, 12–14.
[29] Ibid., 16.
[30] Merryman and Pérerz-Perdomo, Supra note 6, 2.
[31] Glenn, Supra note 2, 312.
[32] Ibid., 310–11.
[33] See Upendra Baxi, "The Colonialist Heritage", in Pierre Legrand and Roderick Munday (eds.) *Comparative Legal Studies: Traditions and Transitions* (Cambridge: Cambridge University Press, 2003), 46.
[34] See Glenn, Supra note 2, 345.
[35] Ibid., 311.

As a way of thinking about what the law is or should be, the civil law tradition is commonly understood to be the heir to the Roman *ius civile*.[36] This ancient provenance – and the civil law's far-reaching reception around the world – led David and Brierley to refer to it as the "first family of laws."[37] Legal scholars play a prominent role in developing and extending the tradition,[38] even if the ideal source of law within the civil law tradition is now a highly systematic and comprehensive code.[39] It is the legislator's and professor's law, and not the judge's. The latter is thought to play an almost bureaucratic function in the formalistic, positivistic, and deductive application of the code's settled concepts to the facts of any given case.[40] The spirit of the civil law tradition, it is argued, has always been its moral recognition of the individual.[41] It is necessary to point out, however, that this rough sketch of the civil law tradition glosses over what many see as discursive diversity within the so-called civil law family. It is often subdivided between French and German siblings.[42] David and Brierley felt obliged to call it the "Romano-Germanic family."[43] A fundamental difference between these siblings is thought to be the high degree of systematization found in the German codifications that is lacking in the French Civil Code.[44] This is one of the civilian features of German constitutional law that I will illuminate in this chapter. For that reason I have to concede that I am really only talking about the reverse influence of *German* civil law on *German* constitutional law, while at the same time accepting that all of these labels represent dynamic and evolving conditions – depending on

---

[36] See Merryman and Pérerz-Perdomo, Supra note 6, 6.
[37] David and Brierley, Supra note 6, 33. See Merryman and Pérerz-Perdomo, Supra note 6, 3 ("[t]he civil law tradition is older, more widely distributed, and more influential than the common law tradition ... It should be added that many people believe the civil law to be culturally superior to the common law, which seems to them to be relatively crude and unorganized").
[38] See Merryman and Pérerz-Perdomo, Supra note 6, 56.
[39] Ibid., 27.
[40] Ibid., 36 ("[t]he picture of judicial process that emerges is one of fairly routine activity; the judge becomes a kind of expert clerk ... the judge's function is merely to find the right legislative provision, couple it with the fact situation, and bless the solution that is more or less automatically produced from the union").
[41] See Glenn, Supra note 2, 147–51.
[42] "The German Civil Code [*Bürgerliches Gesetzbuch*] appeared at the end, and the French Civil Code at the beginning, of the turbulent century of the Industrial Revolution. The German Code emerged from an intellectual and political background that differed in many ways from the Enlightenment and revolutionary thought that informed the Code Civil. It is thus not surprising that Germany and France have inspired somewhat different sub-traditions in the civil law world": Mary Ann Glendon, Paolo G. Carozza and Colin B. Picker, *Comparative Legal Traditions in a Nutshell*, 3rd edn (Eagan: West, 2008), 38.
[43] David and Brierley, Supra note 6, 33.
[44] Ibid., 71.

what kind of normative information is being carried forward from the past into the contemporary life of the law in Germany.

The civil law's foil is imagined to be the common law tradition.[45] The common law does not share the civil law's Roman roots (or at least not in the same degree).[46] It is the product of the Norman conquerors' efforts to govern occupied – and often hostile – England.[47] This led to some of the common law tradition's most distinctive characteristics, including an empowered judiciary working on a case-by-case basis with local norms and in cooperation with local populations to settle on the most acceptable (or least offensive) substantive rules to resolve disputes as they arise.[48] The galvanizing focus of the tradition was on the process leading to the court's jurisdiction over the case, and not the substantive resolution of the case once the courthouse doors had been pried open.[49] The accretion of these judicial decisions is the case law that has priority in the common law tradition.[50] The common law is altogether less conceptual and less systematic. It is inductively focused on facts, which we are told "are the life of the law."[51] But here, too, I cannot neglect the practice of recognizing distinct Anglo and American currents within the so-called common law family.[52] A key difference between the two, according to David and Brierley, is the Americans' unique and less rigorous application of the rule of precedent or *stare decisis*.[53] "All that can really be said with certainty about the American rule of *stare decisis*," David and Brierley concluded,

> is that, as compared to the corresponding rule in England, it has and important limitation the United States Supreme Court and the supreme courts of the different states are not bound to observe their own decisions and may, therefore, operate a reversal of previously established judicial practice.[54]

It is this kind of unbounded judicial authority, among other factors, that convinces me of the temperamental link between the common law tradition

---

[45] David and Brierley, Supra note 6, 334 ("English legal structure is not the same as that of French law and it poses the greatest difficulty for a continental jurist since it is, in fact, totally different to anything with which he is familiar."); Merryman and Pérerz-Perdomo, Supra note 6, 1–5; Siems, Supra note 6, 43–64.
[46] David and Brierley, Supra note 6, 309–11.
[47] Ibid., 311–18; Glenn, Supra note 2, 237–41.
[48] Glenn, Supra note 2, 237–41.
[49] Ibid., 254–5.
[50] Glenn, Supra note 2, 243; David and Brierley, Supra note 6, 366–7, 376–8.
[51] "The life of the law has not been logic; it has been experience": Oliver Wendell Holmes, *The Common Law* (Boston, MA: Little, Brown & Co, 1881), 1.
[52] David and Brierley, Supra note 6, 397, 407.
[53] Ibid., 434–5.
[54] Ibid.

and constitutionalism. And so I have to concede that I may only be talking about the American-style common law constitutionalism.

Glenn knew that the traditions that interested him were complex and evolving and confoundingly contingent – and that they could only do limited service as fixed concepts.[55] Still, he believed that they maintained "some form of external coherence."[56] It is in the same spirit that I rely on them here, where they do just enough to allow us to look for the surprising interplay of diverse approaches to the law in the context of the German legal system.

17.2.2. The Predominance of the Civil Law Tradition in Germany

In any myth worthy of the name a hero must achieve his enlightenment by passing a test.[57] In fact, the odds were long that the common law tradition – with the priority and privilege it extends to judges at the expense of the legislature – would gain a prominent foothold in Germany. The German legal culture, after all, is definitively civilian.[58] The German Federal Justice Minister once insisted that German law is steeped in the tradition of the system of codified law that has evolved throughout continental Europe and that has proven its worth even in difficult times."[59] German law is presented as an example

---

[55] Glenn, Supra note 2, 366–76.
[56] Ibid., 374. See James R. Fox, "Common Law", in *Dictionary of International and Comparative Law*, 3rd edn (Dobbs Ferry: Oceana Publications, 2003), 62; James R. Fox, "Civil Law", in *Dictionary of International and Comparative Law*, 3rd edn (Dobbs Ferry: Oceana Publications, 2003), 55. See also Holmes, Supra note 51; Merryman and Pérez-Perdomo, Supra note 6; Glenn, Supra note 6, 133, 237 (4th edn 2010). See also Caslav Pejovic, "Civil Law and Common Law: Two Different Paths Leading to the Same Goal" (2001) 32 *Victoria University of Wellington Law Review* 817, 819 ("[o]ne of the basic characteristics of the civil law is that the courts main task is to apply and interpret the law contained in a code, or a statute to case facts. The assumption is that the code regulates all cases that could occur in practice, and when certain cases are not regulated by the code, the courts should apply some of the general principles used to fill the gap ... The most obvious distinction between civil law and common law systems is a that civil law system is a codified system, whereas the common law is not created by means of legislation but is based mainly on case law. The principle is that earlier judicial decisions, usually of the higher courts, made in a similar case, should be followed in the subsequent cases, i.e., that precedents should be respected").
[57] "Our hero, then, has to qualify for the throne in two ways: he must pass a test in some such subject as rain-making or riddle-guessing, and he must win a victory over the reigning king:" Lord FitzRoy Raglan, *The Hero: A Study in Tradition, Myth, and Drama* (Mineola, NY: Dover Publications 1956). See Joseph Campbell, *The Hero with a Thousand Faces*, 3rd edn (Novato, CA: New World Library, 2008).
[58] Axel Filges et al. (eds.), *Law – Made in Germany*, 2nd edn (2012), 7, available at www.lawmadeingermany.de/Law-Made_in_Germany.pdf ("German law belongs to the long-standing family of continental European legal systems in the tradition of Roman law ... This legal family is characterised by its codified system of legal provisions, e.g., in the form of statutes.")
[59] Ibid., 3.

of the continental civil, or codified, legal tradition in most comparative law projects,[60] including the best-known English-language introductions to the German legal system.[61]

The German Civil Code (*Bürgerliches Gesetzbuch* or BGB), and the prominence it enjoys in Germany, is the clearest indication of the far-reaching influence the civil law tradition has had over the German legal culture.[62] The Civil Code has been an intense point of pride for Germans and is a leading export of one of the world's leading exporters.[63] The Civil Code, after all, was a source of political and cultural unity for a long-fragmented people.[64] For

[60] See, e.g., Glendon et al., Supra note 42, 63; David and Brierley, Supra note 6, 49–75; Glenn, Supra note 2, 133–80.
[61] See Reinhard Zimmermann, "Characteristic Aspects of German Legal Culture", in Mathias Reimann and Joachim Zekoll (eds.), *Introduction to German Law* (Leiden: Kluwer Law International, 2005), 1, 9 (" … the civilian tradition … still provides a fair idea of what may be dubbed German legal culture"); Nigel Foster and Satish Sule, *German Legal System and Laws*, 3rd edn (Oxford: Oxford University Press, 2002), 3 ("[t]he German legal system belongs to the central European family of legal systems, broadly classified as civil law countries"); Howard D. Fisher, *The German Legal System and Legal Language* XXVII, 4th edn (London: Routledge-Cavendish 2009) ("[t]he German legal system remains, generally speaking, a system of [positive] norms i.e., traditional German legal thinking revolves, in the vast majority of cases, around the twin immutable 'pillars' of an established system and norms regarded as authoritative."); E. J. Cohn and W. Zdzieblo, *1 Manual of German Law*, 2nd edn (London: British Institute of International and Comparative Law, 1968–71), 1, 3 ("German law is a member of a family of laws, which one might well call the European Continental laws … Notwithstanding many and striking differences between the branches and members of this family, the basic structure … is very similar"); Gerhard Robbers, *An Introduction to German Law*, 4th edn (Baden-Baden: Nomos Publishers, 2006), 15 (" … German law [has] the characteristics of a codified legal system, in other words, one whose rules are laid down in legislation which cover all aspects of the law. This characteristic is not the least of the factors which identify Germany law as Continental European").
[62] Bürgerliches Gesetzbuch [BGB] [Civil Code] August 18, 1896, Reichsgesetzblatt [RGBl.]. See The Editors of Encyclopædia Britannica, German Civil Code, *Encyclopædia Britannica*, available at www.britannica.com/EBchecked/topic/230659/German-Civil-Code ("[t]he concept of law embodied in the code was the gemeines Recht, the common law based on the 6th-century codification of Roman law put in force by the emperor Justinian … Although altered to some extent by feudal law, customary law again came under Roman influence in the 15th century, when Roman law was received into Germany in an effort to systematize customs and legal institutions").
[63] The BGB has strongly influenced civil law codifications around the world, including in China. Indeed, the first English-language translation of the BGB was prepared by the Chinese scholar Chung Hui Wang. See Chung Hui Wang, *The German Civil Code: Translated and Annotated with an Historical Introduction and Appendicies* (London: Stevens and Sons, 1907). Cf Ernest J. Schuster, "A Chinese Commentary on the German Civil Code" (1907) 8 *Journal of the Society of Comparative Legislation* 247. See Russell Miller, "Law Land: Germany as a Legal Super Power", *AICGS Policy Reports* (2015), available at www.aicgs.org/site/wp-content/uploads/2015/12/GAI-17-Germany-Law-Land.pdf.
[64] See Neil MacGregor, *Germany: Memories of a Nation* (London: Allen Lane, 2014). See also Higgins, Supra note 7, 96.

more than a century the Civil Code has been law's foundation in German society. In one English-language introduction to the German legal system the point is made this way: "In Germany, all important legal issues and matters are governed by comprehensive legislation in the form of statutes, codes and regulations. The most important legislation [is] ... the Civil Code."[65] At the time of its enactment and entry into force the Civil Code was described in nearly breathless terms:

- "The greatest among [Germany's] exploits is a Civil Code";[66]
- "[The Civil Code is] a monument of legal learning and ... one of the ripest expressions of the aims and methods of modern civil jurisprudence";[67]
- "[The Civil Code] works an almost unprecedented revolution in the jural life of the German Empire. It may well be questioned whether an upheaval of like extent has ever taken place anywhere";[68]
- "[The Civil Code] is the most carefully considered statement of a nation's laws that the world has ever seen."[69]

More than a century after its promulgation the Civil Code is in force almost exactly in its original form. One commentary summed up the wonder of the Civil Code's endurance in these terms: "The fact that the BGB has lasted so long, providing legal solutions to a variety of social and economic problems arising under imperial, social democratic, totalitarian and liberal social state political regimes, provides a lasting tribute to the wisdom and foresight of its drafters. The BGB has served Germany well."[70] Another contemporary scholar simply called the Civil Code "one of the masterpieces of European legal culture."[71]

What makes the Civil Code – and the German legal culture it both embodies and enraptures – so paradigmatically civilian?

---

[65] *Law – Made in Germany*, Supra note 58, 7, available at www.lawmadeingermany.de/Law-Made_in_Germany.pdf.
[66] Frederic William Maitland, "The Making of the German Civil Code", in H. A. L Fisher (ed.), *The Collected Papers of Frederic William Maitland* (Cambridge: Cambridge University Press, 1911), 474, 476.
[67] Ernst Freund, "The Proposed German Civil Code" (1890) 24 *American Law Review* 237, 254.
[68] Arthur Ameisen, "The new Civil Code of the German Empire" (1899) 33 *American Law Review* 396, 407.
[69] Higgins, Supra note 7, 105 (quoting Otto Friedrich von Gierke, *Political Theories of the Middle Age xvii*, Frederick William Maitland trans. [Archivum Press, 1900]).
[70] Joseph J. Darby, "The Influence of the German Civil Code on Law in the United States" (1999) *Journal of South African Law* 84.
[71] Karl-Heinz Ladeur, "The German Proposal of an 'Anti-discrimination' Law: Anticonstitutional and Anti-common Sense. A Response to Nicola Vennemann" (2002) 3 *German Law Journal*, available at www.germanlawjournal.com/index.php?pageID=11&artID=152.

First – although it is circular to say it – the Civil Code itself is profound evidence of the civil law tradition's grip on the German legal culture. After all, codification is a central feature of the civil law tradition.[72]

Second, as with the other achievements of the civil law tradition, the Civil Code traces its roots to Roman law.[73] Yet, the German process of codification did not involve a direct adoption of the Justinian legacy. Under the influence of von Savigny, the Civil Code instead sought to Germanize the Roman heritage so that it would be reflective of the spirit of the German people, a concept von Savigny called the *Volksgeist*.[74] According to Catherine Valcke, the French civilian orientation (surely the world's "other" great codification) is characterized by a single conceptual framework, namely the revolutionary force of rationality. Only rationality could explain the violent rupture with the historical inertia of tradition and caste that ordered French society prior to the Revolution.[75] "Centuries of history were to be erased," Valcke explained, "and a whole new nation rebuilt out of ideas."[76] As its complex, systematic structure demonstrates, rationality also has a vital place in the German Civil Code. But Valcke's point is that the BGB accommodated the experiences Germans had made with law prior to codification. The fact that von Savigny's historicism ultimately played a fundamental role in the German codification process is evidence of the Civil Code's irrational – culturally contingent – possibilities. It might be better to understand the Civil Code as a rationalization and codification of the historical facts of German law. It was not a clean, rational, and revolutionary break with the jurisprudential past. Still, the Roman legacy's rationality and systematics are strongly present in the Civil Code, perhaps most obviously in the fact that it is arranged in five parts or "books" that roughly reflect the Pandects' division of the Roman law into its relevant fields.[77]

---

[72] See Foster and Sule, Supra note 61, 3 ("[o]ne of its basic features is that a country which has adopted the civil law tradition would usually have as the core of its legal system five codes, normally including civil law in the Roman law definition, criminal law, civil procedure law, criminal procedure law, and commercial law").

[73] Catherine Valcke, "Comparative History and the Internal View of French, German, and English private law" (2006) 19 *Canadian Journal of Law and Jurisprudence* 133 ("[i]t is well-known that German law shares the *ius commune* heritage of French law and indeed resembles it in many ways").

[74] Susan Gaylord Gale, "A Very German Legal Science: Savigny and the Historical School" (1982) *Stanford Journal of International Law* 123, 131.

[75] See Valcke, Supra note 73, 139. See also Sarah Maza, "Luxury, Morality, and Social Change: Why There was No Middle-class Consciousness in Pre-revolutionary France" (1997) 69 *Journal of Modern History* 199 (illustrating the social debate that was raging among thinkers prior to the Revolution).

[76] See Valcke, Supra note 73, 139.

[77] William L. Burdick, *The Principles of Roman Law and Their Relation to Modern Law* (Clark: The Lawbook Exchange, 2007), 7; Foster and Sule, Supra note 61, 3.

Third, the Civil Code unvaryingly embodies the jurisprudential features that are typically attributed to the civil law tradition. It is an expression of the preference for positively enacted legislation, as opposed to judge-made law. But the Civil Code is no ordinary statute. It is highly systematic, it has comprehensive ambitions, and it aspires to a tightly fitted ordering of life's affairs. The Civil Code superseded all prior-existing law. It is viewed as a complete and absolute normative framework. In its completeness, it is thought to provide cherished certainty and predictability. Judges are meant only to apply the Civil Code's clear and systematic framework. To achieve all of this the Civil Code relies extensively on conceptual logic and abstraction in identifying prescribed solutions to human dilemmas.

The Civil Code is conceptual and rational and scientific and deductive. This is a defensible characterization of Germany's thoroughly civilian legal culture, which Pierre Legrand described as "the land of Rechtswissenschaft, of seemingly relentless legal conceptualism and systematization, or apparently incessant categorical thinking, the country where one appreciates being told one is a good dogmatician."[78]

17.2.3. *The Common Law Character of Constitutional Law*

The civil law tradition emphasizes statutory law – for example, taking the form of the German Civil Code – and it relies on notions of formalism and positivism to greatly limit judicial discretion in the interpretation and application of legislation. This is not the way of the common law. More than any other legal tradition, the common law has been viewed as "the civil law's other, the difference of its identity."[79] The common law's champions are judges, and its raw materials are the particular facts of each case. The common law is inductive and it is shaped by the logic of analogy.

Especially in the power it bestows on judges at the expense of legislation, constitutional law can be seen as possessing many of the hallmarks of the common law tradition. Thomas Poole suggested that this claim advances the idea that constitutional law is grounded in fundamental common law principles and is structured around the institution of the common law court.[80] Two arguments support the claim. First, Poole maintained that it is possible to deduce a set of values and political commitments that are central to constitutionalism and are uniquely expressed by the common law tradition. Second, Poole

---

[78] Legrand, Supra note 20.
[79] Pierre Legrand, "Antivonbar" (2006) 1 *Journal of Comparative Law* 13, 23.
[80] Thomas Poole, "Questioning Common Law Constitutionalism" (2005) 25 *Legal Studies* 142.

contended that the core features of constitutional law are most consistently recognized and protected by the common law, particularly in the context of judicial review.[81]

Walter Murphy argued for the nexus of the common law and constitutionalism in his article "Civil Law, Common Law, and Constitutional Democracy."[82] "Wondering" about the viability of the new constitutions being adopted in Eastern Europe in the 1990s, Murphy worried that the new democracies' civil law orientation might prejudice those heady efforts every bit as much as the East-Bloc countries' postwar totalitarian experiences.[83] Had Murphy looked into the roiling constitutional futures of Hungary and Poland? On one hand, he noted that the "most successful" constitutional projects were founded in common law legal systems. On the other hand, Murphy concluded that civil law legal systems had produced repeated, dramatic constitutional failures.[84] But more than just projecting from this rough accounting of constitutional history, Murphy advanced the fundamental argument that the character of the civil law is at odds with constitutionalism, and that the character of the common law is aligned with constitutionalism. He contrasted "the civil law's tense commitment to order" with the common law's embrace of chaos.[85] The civil law, Murphy concluded, "leaves judges no respectable room to maneuver"[86] while the common law instructs judges "to walk around rather than try to fill in the abyss, to hunker down when the great wind blows rather than to attempt to contain it."[87] The common law's inductive, case-by-case approach,

---

[81] Ibid., 162.
[82] Walter F. Murphy, "Civil Law, Common Law, and Constitutional Democracy" (1991) 52 *Louisiana Law Review* 91.
[83] Ibid., 99.
[84] Ibid., 93 ("[t]he preeminent constitution-making feat was pulled off more than two centuries ago in a backward but developing country whose nascent legal systems were offshoots of the Common Law. If we measure success by continuance over time, a pair of Common Law countries, Canada [1867] and Australia [1900], generated the other most 'successful' constitutional democracies ... In stark contrast, Latin American countries – all consumers of the Civil Law – have changed their constitutions with a regularity analogous to that with which modern farmers rotate crops. Moreover, as was also the case in Mejei Japan and the Russian, German, and Austro-Hungarian empires, these 'constitutions' have sometimes made scant pretense of trying to establish regimes that were either democratic or limited. And when constitutional democracy was the objective in other Civil-Law nations, as in Germany and Poland after World War I, the resulting polities were often unstable, providing only one phase in a sequence that quickly cycled back to authoritarian rule").
[85] Ibid., 96.
[86] Ibid., 95.
[87] Ibid., 96.

Murphy concluded, involves a "supple pragmatism over tight logic" that is inherent in the "messiness of constitutional politics."[88]

Murphy is not the only scholar to remark on the correlation between the common law tradition and constitutionalism. Others have noted that the non-textual balancing tests and constitutional standards that have developed in constitutional jurisprudence are more akin to the common law than to the practice of any other legal tradition. David Strauss, for example, argued that "it is the common law approach ... that best explains, and best justifies, American constitutional law today."[89] Henry Monaghan was so persuaded by the linkages that he fashioned a theory of the "constitutional common law" that accounts for the law constitutional courts develop, either through authoritative constitutional interpretation, or as a "substructure of substantive, procedural, and remedial rules drawing their inspiration and authority from" the constitution.[90] It is easy to see why this uncontroversial description of the work of constitutional courts might be seen as closely allied with the common law tradition. In fact, Monaghan's thesis has gained adherents in the generation since he proposed it. More recently, Abigail Moncrieff once again confirmed that "the judicial habit of enforcing broad constitutional norms" was precisely the "feature of modern constitutionalism that Henry Monaghan famously

---

[88] Ibid.
[89] David A. Strauss, "Common Law Constitutional Interpretation" (1996) 63 *University of Chicago Law Review* 877, 879. The notion that American constitutional law is a common law system has occurred to many. See e.g., Frederick Schauer, "Is the Common Law?" (1989) 77 *California Law Review* 455, 470 and note 4; Paul Brest, "The Misconceived Quest for the Original Understanding" (1980) 60 *Boston University Law Review* 204, 228–9, note 90 (cited in note 4) (identifying "adjudication" and the "common law method" with "nonoriginalist strategies of constitutional decision-making"). Harry H. Wellington has endorsed what he describes as a "common-law method of constitutional interpretation." Harry H. Wellington, *Interpreting the Constitution: The Supreme Court and the Process of Adjudication* (New Haven, CT: Yale University Press, 1990), 127. See Harry H. Wellington, "Common Law Rules and Constitutional Double Standards: Some Notes on Adjudication" (1973) 83 *Yale Law Journal* 221, 265–311. See also Ely, *Democracy and Distrust* 63–9, 218, note 112 (cited in note 14) (criticizing Wellington); Bruce Ackerman, *We the People, Volume 1: Foundations* (Cambridge: Harvard University Press, 1993), 17–18 (cited in note 2) (describing a "Burkean sensibility" that is "pronounced amongst practicing lawyers and judges," but that lacks a full theoretical justification). The "Burkean tendency" Ackerman describes – which he says is to some degree reflected in Charles Fried, "The Artificial Reason of the Law or: What Lawyers Know" (1981) 60 *Texas Law Review* 35 and Anthony T. Kronman, "Alexander Bickel's Philosophy of Prudence" (1985) 94 *Yale Law Journal* 1567 – seems substantially more conservative than the common law approach I defend here, which, as I will discuss later, allows for innovation and even sudden change. Compare Ackerman note 2 17–18, with text accompanying notes 40–2.
[90] Henry P. Monaghan, "The Supreme Court Term 1974 – Foreword: Constitutional Common Law" (1975) 89 *Harvard Law Review* 1, 3–4.

identified [as] 'the constitutional common law.'"[91] Advocates of common law constitutionalism have described their approach as the idea "that courts do and should develop the meaning of general or ambiguous constitutional texts by reference to tradition and precedent, rather than original understanding, and the related idea that courts do and should proceed in a Burkean, rather than ambitiously rationalist or innovative fashion."[92] The Burkean common law tradition – and its near cousin constitutionalism – contrast sharply with the civil law tradition. Burke, of course, is celebrated for his practical reason, which built its arguments in response to specific political circumstances and did not aspire to the generality, broad theory, and abstract conceptualism that characterize the civil law.[93] This very common law understanding of constitutional law engages with two distinct claims.[94] First, it accepts that judges possess some form of latent wisdom and that they will "generally do best by deferring to the wisdom embodied in precedent and tradition, rather than trusting" reason.[95] Second, it claims that "legal principles such as fairness and equality reside within the common law, are constitutive of legality, and inform (or should inform) statutory interpretation on judicial review."[96]

There is no doubt, as our tour guide at the Constitutional Court understood so well, that constitutionalism possesses many of the characteristics of

---

[91] Abigail R. Moncrieff, "Validity of the Individual Mandate" (2012) 92 *Boston University Law Review* 1245, 1248.

[92] Adrian Vermeule, "Common Law Constitutionalism and the Limits of Reason" (2006) 107 *Columbia Law Review* 1482, 1482.

[93] See Francis P. Canavan, "Edmund Burke's Conception of the Role of Reason in Politics" (1959) 21 *The Journal of Politics* 60 ("[t]he essential difference between Burke's political thought and the type of thinking of which he accused his opponents, is that he thought in terms of practical reason, and they, as he saw it, did not. That is to say, Burke thought primarily of the end to be achieved and then of the ways of attaining it in the given circumstances. The questions to be answered were: what do we really want? how must we act in order to obtain it?" [citation omitted]).

[94] See Mark D. Walters, "The Common Law Constitution and Legal Cosmopolitanism", in David Dyzenahus (ed.) *The Unity of Public Law* (Oxford: Hart Publishing, 2004), 431; J. Goldsworthy, "Interpreting the Constitution in Its Second Century" (2000) 24 *Melbourne University Law Review* 677. But see Poole, Supra note 80, 142.

[95] See Vermeule, Supra note 92; Thomas Poole, "Back to the Future? Unearthing the Theory of Common Law Constitutionalism" (2003) 23 *Oxford Journal of Legal Studies* 435, 439 ("[t]he essence of the theory of common law constitutionalism is the reconfiguration of public law as a species of constitutional politics centred [sic] on the common law court. The court, acting as primary guardian of a society's fundamental values and rights, assumes, on this account, a pivotal role within the polity").

[96] See e.g., T. R. S. Allan, *Constitutional Justice: A Liberal Theory of the Rule of Law* (Oxford: Oxford University Press, 2001).

the common law tradition and that the processes Monaghan described have emerged as the "pervasive mode of constitutional enforcement."[97]

17.2.4. The Postwar Civil Law/Common Law Clash in the German Legal Culture

If the first two premises have been confirmed, then what have been the consequences of the emergence of a vital and effective constitutional law regime in a German legal culture long-dominated by the civil law tradition? The third premise of this prevalent narrative is that the civil law and the common law traditions have found themselves in conflict with one another, vying for the soul of the German jurist.

In fact, that tension is on spectacular display in Karlsruhe, Germany. On the northern edge of this charming little city the "new" Constitutional Court serves as the "protector of the *Grundgesetz*" from its sleek, modern, Bauhaus-influenced building. But the Constitutional Court has had to carve out a place for itself alongside the revered Federal Court of Justice (*Bundesgerichtshof*). From its baroque residence in a leafy neighborhood in the southwest corner of Karlsruhe, the Federal Court of Justice – a most civilian institution – presides as the last-instance jurisdiction over Germany's four great codifications, including the Civil Code. The Federal Court of Justice, in particular, is seen as a bastion of civilian formalism and positivism in Germany. Its judgments

---

[97] Moncrieff, Supra note 91, 1248. Others have identified and discussed this trend. See Dan T. Coenen, "A Constitution of Collaboration: Protecting Fundamental Values With Second-Look Rules of Interbranch Dialogue" (2001) 42 *William and Mary Law Review* 1575, 1582; Dan T. Coenen, "The Rehnquist Court, Structural Due Process, and Semisubstantive Constitutional Review",' (2002) 75 *Southern California Law Review* 1281, 1282–3; William N. Eskridge, Jr. and Philip P. Frickey, "Quasi-constitutional Law: Clear Statement Rules as Constitutional Lawmaking" (1992) 45 *Vanderbilt Law Review* 593, 596–7; Richard H. Fallon, Jr., "The Supreme Court 1996 Term – Forward: Implementing the Constitution" (1997) 111 *Harvard Law Review* 54, 57; Roderick M. Hills, Jr., "Federalism as Westphalian Liberalism" (2006) 75 *Fordham Law Review* 769, 769–70 (arguing that federalism is a good way to deal with deep and intense disagreements over individual liberty); Roderick M. Hills, Jr., "The Individual Right to Federalism in the Rehnquist Court" (2006) 74 *George Washington Law Review* 888, 888–9 (making the case for state elaboration of substantive rights, at least as a way of evolving national consensus prior to federal judicial enforcement); Hans A. Linde, "Due Process of Lawmaking" (1976) 55 *Nebraska Law Review* 197, 199; John F. Manning, "Clear Statement Rules and the Constitution" (2010) 110 *Columbia Law Review* 399, 399; Monaghan, Supra note 90, 2–4; Matthew C. Stephenson, "The Prices of Public Action: Constitutional Doctrine and the Judicial Manipulation of Legislative Enactment Costs" (2008) 118 *Yale Law Journal* 2; Laurence A. Tribe, "Structural Due Process" (1975) 10 *Harvard Civil Rights-Civil Liberties Law Review* 269; Ernest A. Young, "Constitutional Avoidance, Resistance Norms and the Preservation Of Judicial Review" (2000) 78 *Texas Law Review* 1549, 1550–1.

have been described as formulaic, abstract, "highly conceptual, even metaphysical," and containing "detailed consideration of the views of contemporary (and past) academic writers."[98] That is classic civilian justice.

Knut Wolfgang Nörr characterized this clash of cultures as a struggle between codification and the constitution.[99] There was good reason to believe that codification would persist as the *Leitbild* of German law even after the Basic Law entered into force.[100] After all, Nörr explained, "the civil code had survived the Nazi regime, at least in its outward shape."[101] The question was whether German law "would find its identity" by returning to codification's formalism and positivism? Or would Germany turn to the new Basic Law and constitutionalism?[102]

The horizontal effect principle (*Drittwirkung*), fashioned early-on by the Federal Constitutional Court, is significant evidence of the struggle in the German legal culture between the constitutional common law and the civil law tradition. Horizontal effect refers to the application of the constitution's basic rights protections in the "horizontal" relationships between equally-positioned individuals. That, however, is the realm of the Civil Code. Horizontal effect is the Basic Law's response to the prominence of the German Civil Code, which was thought to comprehensively regulate these private relations. Nörr explained how horizontal effect sought to resolve the conflict between the civil law and constitutional law:

> Of course, the question came up from which source [post-war] norms should be taken. One usually turned to the values of the Codification, of the codes themselves to extract from them the standards for the development of law. In this respect a crucial change occurred [after the promulgation of the Basic Law]. Certain constitutional jurists founded the doctrine of the [Civil Code's] general clauses being the link between the Codification and the Basic Rights of the Constitution [so-called *"Drittwirkung der Grundrechte"*]. The doctrine maintains that also the relationship between individuals ought to be measured to a certain extent by the standards of the Basic Rights. Whereas according to the traditional view the Basic Rights serve to protect the citizen against the power of the state, now they shall protect one citizen against the other. The Constitutional Court in 1958 adopted this theory [in the *Lüth Case*,

---

[98] Basil S. Markesinis and Hannes Unberath, *The German Law of Torts – A Comparative Treatise*, 4th edn (Oxford: Hart Publishing, 2002), 8–14.
[99] Knut Wolfgang Nörr, "From Codification to Constitution: On the Changes of Paradigm in German Legal History of the Twentieth Century" (1992) 60 *Tijdschrift voor Rechtsgeschiedneis* 145.
[100] Ibid.
[101] Ibid.
[102] Ibid.

BVerfGE 7, 198]. In this way, the Constitution – through the general clauses of the Codification – found its way into the Codification itself, and right into its zones of growth.

17.2.5. The Myth of German Constitutional Law's Triumph Over Civilian Formalism and Positivism

According to the myth, the result of this clash has been constitutional law's victory over the civil law tradition. But constitutional law's triumph in Germany is just another way of saying that the common law tradition now plays a prominent role in the German legal culture where it is in dialogue with the still-predominant formalism and positivism of the civil law tradition.

In many ways, this victory is Gustav Radbruch's story. The twentieth-century German legal philosopher's life and work have come to embody the prevailing myth.[103] The University of Heidelberg law professor is widely seen has having championed legal positivism alongside Kelsen and others before he was dismissed from the university by the Nazis because of his social-democratic politics.[104] According to the accepted version of events,[105] the horror of witnessing the immoral uses to which the Nazis could put Germany's strictly formalist and positivist jurisprudence turned Radbruch against the civilian tradition, a conversion he is supposed to have consecrated in his famous postwar essay "Statutory Lawlessness and Supra-Statutory Law" (*Gesetzliches Unrecht und übergesetzliches Recht*).[106] In the essay Radbruch seethed with disdain for the Nazis' reliance on legal positivism as a defense in their postwar criminal trials.[107] The Nazis' claim that "a law is a law," Radbruch agonized, "expressed the positivistic legal thinking that, almost unchallenged, held sway over German jurists for many decades."[108] The essay is still celebrated for Radbruch's resounding rejection of the positivist tradition. But it was a struggle

---

[103] See e.g., Thomas Mertens, "Nazism, Legal Positivism and Radbruch's Thesis on Statutory Injustice" (2003) 14 *Law and Critique* 277; Thomas Mertens, "But was it law?" (2006) 7 *German Law Journal* 191; Stanley L. Paulson, "Lon L. Fuller, Gustav Radbruch, and the 'Positivist' Theses" (1994) 13 *Law and Philosophy* 313; Stanley L. Paulson, "Statutory Positivism" (2007) 1 *Legisprudence* 1.

[104] See Arthur Kaufmann, *Gustav Radbruch* (Munich: Piper, 1987); Günter Spendel, *Jurist in einer Zeitenwende: Gustav Radbruch zum 100. Geburtstag* (Heidelberg: Müller, 1979).

[105] See Stanley L. Paulson, "Radbruch on Unjust Laws: Competing Earlier and Later Views?" (1995) 15 *Oxford Journal of Legal Studies* 489.

[106] Gustav Radbruch, "Statutory Lawlessness and Supra-statutory Law" (2006) 26 *Oxford Journal of Legal Studies* 1 (Bonnie Litschewski Paulson and Stanley L. Paulson trans.).

[107] Ibid., 7.

[108] Ibid., 1.

that he said was "being taken up everywhere."[109] Radbruch proposed a formula that would free judges from the fetters of banal statutory interpretation and blind application of the codes so that they might pursue supra-statutory justice. If that sounds nothing like the civil law tradition, with its technocratic judges unquestioningly applying the legislature's statutes,[110] then it just might be Radbruch's call for the ascendance of the common law.[111]

Or it might be the triumph of constitutional law. In fact, the Constitutional Court rather self-consciously imagines itself to be Radbruch's heir. The Court's justices are the rarefied German jurists who are at last truly free of the formalist and positivist bonds of unjust statutes. We know this because, from its earliest decisions, the Constitutional Court acknowledged its authority to refuse to enforce unjust laws. This exceptional circumstance, the Court explained, would exist if the "norm in question so evidently contradicts the principle of justice that prevails in all formal law, such that the judge who would be applying or accepting the legal consequences of the norm would in fact be enforcing injustice rather than justice."[112] This is just Radbruch's formula, which provided that "the positive law, secured by legislation and power, takes precedence even when its content is unjust and fails to benefit the people, unless the conflict between statute and justice reaches such an intolerable degree that the statute, as 'flawed law,' must yield to justice."[113] And in case there was any doubt, the Constitutional Court explicitly invoked Radbruch's formula when it denied East German leaders and border guards the benefit of a formalistic and positivistic application of the Basic Law's prohibition on the *ex post facto* application of criminal law.[114] After reunification the complainants had been convicted of murder for the shooting deaths of East Germans attempting to flee across the border to West Germany. Of course, the mortal

---

[109] Ibid., 6.
[110] See e.g., Hermann Kantorowicz, "The Battle for Legal Science" (2011) 12 *German Law Journal* 2005 (Cory Merrill trans.) ("[t]he reigning ideal image of the jurist is as follows: a higher civil servant with academic training sits in his cell armed only with a thinking machine, certainly one of the finest kinds. His cell is furnished with nothing more than a green table on which the State Code lies before him. Present him with any kind of situation, real or imaginary, and with the help of pure logical operations and a secret technique understood only by him, dutifully he is able to deduce the decision with absolute precision from the legal code that is predetermined by the legislature").
[111] See e.g., Vivian Grosswald Curran, "Romantic Common Law, Enlightened Civil Law: Legal Uniformity and the Homogenization of the European Union" (2001) 7 *Columbia Journal of European Law* 63.
[112] Civil Servant Case, 3 BVerfGE 58, 119 (1953) (Russell Miller trans.).
[113] Radbruch, Supra note 106, 7.
[114] Grundgesetz für die Bundesrepublik Deutschland [Grundgesetz] [GG] [Basic Law] May 23, 1949, BGBl. I., Article 103(2).

defense of East Germany's "anti-fascist barrier" was legal under – was mandated by – East German law.[115] The defendants could be convicted by courts in a newly unified Germany that were applying old West German criminal law only if the civilian formalism "a law is a law" were to be rejected. That is what the ordinary courts did.[116] And that is how the Constitutional Court upheld the convictions in the *Wall Shooting Case*.[117] The Constitutional Court explained that the lesson of the Radbruch formula is that the "fundamental principle of legal certainty," which is the promise of civilian formalism and positivism, "can be given less weight than material justice if the law would otherwise lead to an intolerable violation of justice."[118] The Constitutional Court's *Wall Shooting Case* decision was regarded as a profound victory for justice over civilian legal formalism and positivism. At the same time it was a victory for the justices – and the common law tradition that gives them priority.

The myth has no less force with respect to more commonplace jurisprudence that does not involve the constitutional reckoning with Germany's totalitarian pasts. The mere exercise of unexceptional judicial review is a species of the same common law judicial power, and it is a significant departure from the formalist and positivist tradition in the German legal culture.[119] The German Constitutional Court has assumed this new role with great enthusiasm and confidence. It is no exaggeration when the German Federal Constitutional Court is characterized as the "most powerful constitutional court in the world."[120] Elsewhere, I have remarked that the "Court's

---

[115] See Kif Augustine Adams, "What is just?: The Rule of Law and Natural Law in the Trials of Former East German Border Guards" (1993) 29 *Stanford Journal of International Law* 271, 289–93; Peter E. Quint, "Judging the Past: the Prosecution of East German Border Guards and the GDR Chain of Command" (1999) 61 *The Review of Politics* 303; Peter E. Quint, "The Border Guard Trials and the East German Past-Seven Arguments" (2000) 48 *American Journal of Comparative Law* 541; A. James McAdams, *Judging the Past in Unified Germany* (Cambridge: Cambridge University Press, 2001), 23.

[116] Kif Augustine Adams, Supra note 115, 297 ("Judge Seidel held that shooting to kill was authorized under East German law. Nonetheless, he concluded, the order infringed a higher moral law. Although the defendants were 'at the end of a long chain of responsibility,' they violated 'a basic human right' by shooting at someone whose only crime was trying to emigrate.' Judge Seidel applied natural law when he argued that 'not everything that is legal is right: There is a central area of justice, which no law can encroach upon. The legal maxim, 'whoever flees will be shot to death' deserves no obedience." Consequently, "[a]t the end of the 20th century, no one has the right to ignore his conscience when it comes to killing people on behalf of the power structure'").

[117] Wall Shootings Case, 95 BVerfGE 96 (1996) (Russell Miller trans.).

[118] Ibid., 134–5.

[119] Kommers and Miller, Supra note 13, 5 ("[t[he doctrine of judicial review ... was alien to the theory of judicial power in Germany. A judge's only duty under the traditional German doctrine of separation of powers was to enforce the law as written").

[120] Kommers and Miller, Supra note 8, 210 (quoting Uwe Wesle, *Der Gang nach Karlsruhe* [2004] 7).

decision-making record might suggest a tribunal embarked on a path of relentless activism."[121] Others have simply taken to calling reunified, postwar Germany the "Karlsruhe Republic."[122] A former Federal Justice Minister concluded that "in Germany, all power issues have become constitutional issues," to be resolved by the Court.[123] And true to the myth, the Court is not seen as meddlesome or over-reaching. To the contrary, the Court consistently is the most respected social institution in the country.[124] In fact, the Court is widely credited with having established democracy, the rule of law, rights protections, and general prosperity for what seemed to be an ungovernable and treacherously unruly German nation. As one comparative law scholar put it: "[T]he stability and prosperity ... Germany enjoyed over the last half of the 20th Century bespeaks the integrity and efficacy of the *Bundesverfassungsgericht*."[125]

And some now believe that constitutional law (with its common law character) has supplanted the civil law tradition as Germany's dominant jurisprudential frame. Donald Kommers' concluded that much of the Basic Law's regime derives from "the gloss the Federal Constitutional Court has put on the text of the Basic Law," implying a nature and style of judicial decision-making that is much more closely attuned to the common law's vision of judging, and that is far removed from the judicial restraint typical of the civil law tradition.[126] In a commemoration written on the two-hundredth anniversary of the United States Supreme Court's seminal decision *Marbury v. Madison*, former Federal Constitutional Court Justice Wolfgang Hoffmann-Riem underscored the importance of constitutional law's counter-civilian influence in postwar German legal culture.[127] With the supremacy of the postwar Basic Law, as interpreted and enforced by the Federal Constitutional Court's justices, Hoffmann-Riem concluded that this paradigm shift finally and decisively had overtaken Germany. Hoffmann-Riem confirmed the prominent role played by the Federal Constitutional Court when he concluded that "the jurisdiction of this court is particularly wide-ranging," and considerably greater than

[121] Kommers and Miller, Supra note 13, 35.
[122] Gerhard Casper, "The 'Karlsruhe Republic" – Keynote Address at the State Ceremony Celebrating the 50th Anniversary of the Federal Constitutional Court" (2001) 2 *German Law Journal* www.germanlawjournal.com/index.php?pageID=11&artID=111.
[123] Brigitte Zypries, "The Basic Law at 60 – Politics and the Federal Constitutional Court" (2010) 11 *German Law Journal* 87 (citing Heinrich Wefing, "Der bonner reflex", *Die Zeit* [April 30, 2009] 19).
[124] See Peter E. Quint, "Leading a Constitutional Court: Perspectives from the Federal Republic of Germany" (2006) 154 *University of Pennsylvania Law Review*, 1853, 1870; Kommers and Miller, Supra note 13, 39.
[125] See Kommers, Supra note 13; Kommers and Miller, Supra note 8.
[126] Kommers and Miller, Supra note 13, 57.
[127] *Marbury v. Madison*, 5 U.S. 137 (1803).

the review jurisdiction of the US Supreme Court.[128] The Federal Constitutional Court, Hoffmann-Riem said, "has been proactive," and has "continually expanded its identity."[129] This has placed it, unbending, in conflict with the high federal courts.

Nörr concluded that, with the dawning of Germany's postwar (common law) constitutional order, "the Basic Law became the point of reference for the [West German] legal system and in this function superseded the Codification: for good, it seems."[130] In his estimation, and in the estimation of our tour guide at the Constitutional Court, this has been a definitive and irreversible paradigm shift.

17.3. GERMANY'S CIVILIAN CONSTITUTION

The encounter between the civil law tradition and the common law tradition in the German legal system has not been a one-way street. It is not just Germany's old civilian approach to the law that has been touched by the common law tradition. The civil law tradition has also had an influence on German constitutional law. The gravitational pull of the civil law tradition in Germany is simply too strong for it to have been otherwise.

The evidence of the persistent civilian orientation of German law – even German constitutional law – can be seen, *inter alia*, in the code-like text of the Basic Law; in some theories about constitutional law in Germany; in the jurisdiction of the Constitutional Court; and in the Constitutional Court's judicial style.

17.3.1. *The Basic Law as Code*

In many places the text of the Basic Law has the characteristics of a civilian code. Some provisions are famously short and open-textured, such as the terse promise in Article 1 that "human dignity shall be inviolable."[131] These provisions naturally demand a rambling, unfettered interpretive role from the Constitutional Court. And in those places, German constitutional law lurches decisively in the direction of the common law tradition with its confidence in

---

[128] Wolfgang Hoffmann-Riem, "Two Hundred Years of *Marbury v. Madison*: The Struggle for Judicial Review of Constitutional Questions in the United States and Europe" (2004) 5 *German Law Journal* 685, 697.
[129] Ibid.
[130] Nörr, Supra note 99.
[131] Grundgesetz für die Bundesrepublik Deutschland [Grundgesetz] [GG] [Basic Law] May 23, 1949, BGBl. I., Article 1(1).

the judiciary. But many other provisions in the Basic Law are long, detailed and systematic – exceeding even the depth and scope of many paragraphs of the Civil Code. These provisions, in their precision, seem designed to prescribe a very specific constitutional result rather than map the stars of constitutional values. These code-like constitutional provisions necessarily limit the Constitutional Court's interpretive room to maneuver. The so-called "Financial Constitution," among the Basic Law's other structural provisions, is especially exemplary of the Basic Law's civilian orientation. Article 106, as just one example, covers the "apportionment of tax revenue" in ten subparagraphs and more than 1,000 words.[132] This is not a framework of broad principles to be interpreted – in the style of the common law – by the Constitutional Court. It is a detailed and definitive arrangement for revenue distribution, involving all sources, and attributable across all levels of government in Germany. The federation, the Basic Law tell us, is entitled to revenues generated by the "the road freight tax."[133] The states are entitled to the revenues generated by the "motor-vehicle tax."[134] The Basic Law's specific accounting of all tax revenues proceeds in the same detail in the rest of Article 106 and across a number of other provisions. This feels more like legislation than constitutional law.

Several basic rights provisions also contain nearly definitive detail. Article 7, for example, addresses the "school system" in six subparagraphs and more than 250 words.[135] Article 12a, speaking to "compulsory military service," involves six subparagraphs and 500 words.[136] Article 13, which provides constitutional protection for the "inviolability of the home," consists in seven subparagraphs and more than 400 words. It is a detailed text that very clearly aspires to a systematic and comprehensive solution to the issues involved. Article 13 is patently deductive in its content and structure. It begins with the broad principle that the home is sacrosanct. It then descends through a series of evermore precise exceptions and their accompanying procedural requirements.

American constitutional law may offer similar protection for the sanctity of the home.[137] But it does not build from a similarly concrete textual

---

[132] Grundgesetz für die Bundesrepublik Deutschland [Grundgesetz] [GG] [Basic Law] May 23, 1949, BGBl. I., Article 106.
[133] Grundgesetz für die Bundesrepublik Deutschland [Grundgesetz] [GG] [Basic Law] May 23, 1949, BGBl. I., Article 106(1)[3].
[134] Grundgesetz für die Bundesrepublik Deutschland [Grundgesetz] [GG] [Basic Law] May 23, 1949, BGBl. I., Article 106(2)[3].
[135] Grundgesetz für die Bundesrepublik Deutschland [Grundgesetz] [GG] [Basic Law] May 23, 1949, BGBl. I., Article 7.
[136] Grundgesetz für die Bundesrepublik Deutschland [Grundgesetz] [GG] [Basic Law] May 23, 1949, BGBl. I., Article 12a.
[137] U.S. Const. amends. III and IV.

commitment.[138] The extensive regime of exceptions to that protection have been mapped through generations of the Supreme Court's decisions, which mold the constitution's meaning at its joints and in its ambiguities.[139] It would not have dawned on the drafters of the American Fourth Amendment, steeped as they were in the common law's judicial suppleness, that they might have aspired to anything like the rigid and comprehensive constitutional codification found in Article 13 of the Basic Law.[140]

17.3.2. Constitutional Theory and Constitutional Codification

Theorists in Germany have embraced this codified understanding of the constitution. Peter Unruh has explained that some constitutional theory in Germany, under the influence of the civil law tradition, has sought to treat the Basic Law as part of the civil law tradition.[141] This theoretical approach accepts that constitutions are not a classical example of codification. But it insists that there is no reason why constitutions must be treated as antithetical to civilian codification. In particular, Unruh noted, the Basic Law creates a closed constitutional system that is similar to the comprehensive and complete order framed by the Civil Code.[142] On one hand, the Basic Law requires that all constitutional change be achieved by constitutional amendment. On the other hand, the Basic Law prohibits some constitutional changes.[143]

---

[138] See e.g., Morgan Cloud, "The Fourth Amendment during the Lochner Era: Privacy, Property, and Liberty in Constitutional Theory" (1996) 48 *Stanford Law Review* 555, 555–6 ("Fourth Amendment theory is in tatters at the end of the twentieth century. The disarray in the Supreme Court's recent case law has been explored in numerous scholarly articles and judicial dissents. Two of the most common complaints are that these opinions lack any unifying theory and fail to preserve the rights embodied in the Amendment" [internal citations omitted]).

[139] Helen J. Knowles, "From a Value to a Right: The Supreme Court's Oh-so Conscious Move from 'Privacy' to 'Liberty'" (2007) 33 *Ohio Northern University Law Review* 595.

[140] See Stanley N. Katz, "Looking Backward: The Early History of American Law [review]" (1966) 33 *University of Chicago Law Review* 867, 872 ("[i]f one examines the actual substance of colonial law, however, it seems difficult not to conclude that early American law was a quite sophisticated combination of English and indigenous ideas which evolved in response to the changed conditions of life in the New World. To notice that the common law was not transported in toto to Massachusetts does not demonstrate that English law had no influence there. It was out of the familiar English local law that the Puritans framed their own system").

[141] Peter Unruh, *Der Verfassungsbegriff des Grundgesetzes* (Tübingen: Mohr Siebeck, 2002).

[142] Ibid.

[143] Grundgesetz für die Bundesrepublik Deutschland [Grundgesetz] [GG] [Basic Law] May 23, 1949, BGBl. I., Article 79(3) ("[a]mendments to this Basic Law affecting the division of the Federation into Länder, their participation on principle in the legislative process, or the principles laid down in Articles 1 and 20 shall be inadmissible").

The result of this arrangement is the suggestion that there is no constitutional law beyond the text of the Basic Law.

A constitution can claim to be a comprehensive and systematic regime addressing the state's organization, as well as the relation between the citizen and the state.[144] A constitution can be civilian. In fact, the Basic Law's extensive coverage of the state's financial competences in Articles 104a–115 (requiring more than 2,000 words in total) suggests that the German constitution seeks to comprehensively define and demarcate all state power, in the same way that a code aspires to definitively occupy the field it governs. This is a possible reading of the whole Basic Law, which objectively defines the individual and citizen,[145] frames the boundaries for and roles of the states and the federation,[146] provides for the legislative power,[147] establishes the executive power,[148] and institutes the judicial power.[149] Very little relating to state power, and its relationship with individuals, is left unaddressed.

Similar to other codes, the Basic Law seeks to establish a reasonable, consistent, and permanent legal order. Historically, constitutionalism originates from the same era of Enlightenment rationality as the classical codification in France, when Napoleon sought to give the legal system – and society with it – a rational basis in the code.[150]

The Basic Law is a code in all of these respects and, consequently, it is often treated as a codification in German jurisprudence. This also involves the

---

[144] Ruth Gavison, "What Belongs in a Constitution?" (2002) 13 *Constitutional Political Economy* 89, 89–90 ("[t]here are three standard candidates for inclusion in a constitution: basic governmental structures and the relations between the main powers and functions of government; basic values and commitments; and human rights. Some constitutions describe language and flags and other symbols. These may either be seen as an additional group, or be seen as a part of the main commitments of the state. In addition, a constitution usually specifies the mechanisms for its own amendment and enforcement, and proposed constitutions often contain provisions about the mechanisms of their adoption ... The main purpose and functions of constitutions are at least three. First, to both authorize, and to create limits on, the powers of political authorities. Second, to enhance the legitimacy and the stability of the political order. Third, to institutionalize a distinction between 'regular politics' and 'the rules of the game' and other constraints [such as human rights] within which ordinary politics must be played").
[145] Grundgesetz für die Bundesrepublik Deutschland [Grundgesetz] [GG] [Basic Law] May 23, 1949, BGBl. I., Article 116.
[146] Grundgesetz für die Bundesrepublik Deutschland [Grundgesetz] [GG] [Basic Law] May 23, 1949, BGBl. I., Articles 20–37.
[147] Grundgesetz für die Bundesrepublik Deutschland [Grundgesetz] [GG] [Basic Law] May 23, 1949, BGBl. I., Articles 70–82.
[148] Grundgesetz für die Bundesrepublik Deutschland [Grundgesetz] [GG] [Basic Law] May 23, 1949, BGBl. I., Articles 54–69.
[149] Grundgesetz für die Bundesrepublik Deutschland [Grundgesetz] [GG] [Basic Law] May 23, 1949, BGBl. I., Articles 92–104.
[150] Merryman and Pérez-Perdomo, Supra note 6, 27–31.

approach scholars take toward constitutional law. Similar to the way the other codes are studied German constitutional law scholars write commentaries on the Basic Law.[151] These commentaries pursue a systematic exegesis of each article in the constitution. This tradition, a distinct part of the civil law culture, has no equivalent in America's common law-oriented constitutional scholarship and practice.[152] Of course, casebooks are almost unknown in Germany.[153]

Werner Heun explained that, in technical terms, constitutional law in Germany has been treated as if it were codified civil law.[154] Constitutional law, Heun noted, is assessed in almost complete accordance with the conditions of the dogmatic science that dominates the practice and study of the codes. This can be seen in several ways. First, "the Constitution is regarded as a predetermined normative decision, which is beyond criticism within the system."[155] Second, constitutional analysis aims for the "systematization of all written and unwritten rules, their interpretation and development."[156] Third, "the interpretation of the Basic Law essentially follows the commonly accepted classical rules and methods that were established already by Friedrich Carl von Savigny in the early nineteenth century."[157] This interpretive canon, similar to civilian statutory interpretation, gives priority to text, system, structure, and teleology. "Original intent," Heun noted, "plays only a minor role."[158] Finally, Heun explained that the "Constitutional Court, affirmed by the overwhelming majority of scholars, has always stressed the 'objective meaning' of a provision."[159] This, of course, is the abstract and conceptual approach taken to interpreting comprehensive codes.[160]

17.3.3. The Basic Law's Deference to Statutory Law

The Basic Law's civilian orientation is also evident in its preference for legislative resolution of its interpretive ambiguities. Especially with respect to the protection of basic rights, where the constitutional text might never have

---

[151] Kommers and Miller, Supra note 13, 73.
[152] See e.g., Merryman and Pérez-Perdomo, Supra note 6, 61.
[153] See Basil Markesinis, "Judicial Style and Judicial Reasoning in England and Germany" (2000) 59 *Cambridge Law Journal* 294, 298.
[154] Werner Heun, *The Constitution of Germany: A Contextual Analysis* (Oxford: Hart Publishing, 2010), 5.
[155] Ibid., 6.
[156] Ibid.
[157] Ibid.
[158] Ibid.
[159] Ibid.
[160] Markesinis, Supra note 153, 296–9.

achieved code-like detail and precision, the Basic Law often assigns the task of rounding-out the meaning of the enumerated rights to the legislature. The common law solution to these uncertainties is to entrust the matter to the courts. The approach adopted by the Basic Law, however, denies the Constitutional Court the fullest possible authority over the Basic Law's meaning. The civil law's confidence in legislation – and its distrust for the judiciary – is unmistakable in this arrangement.[161]

The Constitutional Court is not troubled by its subordination. "The Court has ... stated on numerous occasions that it will not substitute its judgment of sound or wise public policy for that of the legislature."[162] Thus, the Court exercises significant restraint when reviewing legislation enacted pursuant to the legislature's authority to define and limit constitutional law, despite the fact that the legislation directly touches upon the enjoyment of a basic right. One example of this framework can be found in Article 5, which provides for "Freedom of expression, arts, and sciences."[163] The freedom of expression, information, and press that is unequivocally asserted by the article's first subparagraph is framed by the second subparagraph, which gives the legislature the central role in defining the scope of the right: "These rights shall find their limits in the provisions of general laws, in provisions for the protection of young persons, and in the right to personal honour."[164] The Court's role when reviewing these constitutionally ordained legislative limits on the freedom of expression is largely to assess them for their proportionality.[165] That, however, is not that same thing as judging the substance of the parliament's decisions about the scope of and limits on the freedom of expression. In terms that simply radiate with the residual ethos of the civil law tradition, Hans Jarass explained that, "for the exercise of basic rights, fundamental questions must be settled by the parliament."[166]

---

[161] See e.g., Grundgesetz für die Bundesrepublik Deutschland [Grundgesetz] [GG] [Basic Law] May 23, 1949, BGBl. I., Articles 2(2), 4(3), 5(2), 8(2), 10(2), 11(2), 14(1). But see Grundgesetz für die Bundesrepublik Deutschland [Grundgesetz] [GG] [Basic Law] May 23, 1949, BGBl. I., Article 19(2).

[162] Kommers and Miller, Supra note 13, 34–5.

[163] Grundgesetz für die Bundesrepublik Deutschland [Grundgesetz] [GG] [Basic Law] May 23, 1949, BGBl. I., Article 5.

[164] Grundgesetz für die Bundesrepublik Deutschland [Grundgesetz] [GG] [Basic Law] May 23, 1949, BGBl. I., Article 5(2).

[165] Hans Jarass, "Art. 5", in Hans Jarass and Bodo Pieroth (eds.) *Grundgesetz für die Bundesrepublik Deutschland – Kommentar*, 10th edn (Munich: C. H. Beck, 2009), margin note 57.

[166] Ibid., margin note 55.

17.3.4. The Nature of the Constitutional Court's Jurisdiction

The civilian orientation of German constitutional law is also apparent in the Constitutional Court's jurisdiction. First, the fact that the Court does not have discretion to select the cases it will review suggests that its decisions – although profoundly influential – do not formally establish precedent.[167] Precedential authority, however, is a central feature of the common law's embrace of judicial lawmaking.[168] Second, the Court's abstract review jurisdiction anticipates constitutional judgments that will be taken wholly on the basis of the abstract legal principles involved and without reference to the specific facts of a discrete and actual controversy.[169] This is the civil law's deductive approach to law, and not the common law's inductive, case-specific orientation.

17.3.5. The Constitutional Court's Civilian Decisional Style

The Constitutional Court's decisional style also suggests the strong influence the civil law tradition maintains over German constitutional law. Maybe this should not be surprising. After all, the Federal Constitutional Court Act (*Bundesverfassungsgerichtsgesetz*) provides that eight of the Court's justices must have served as judges at the federal high courts, such as the Federal Court of Justice.[170] These federal high courts sit as the last instance of review in disputes arising out of distinct code regimes, including the Civil Code. Judges reach these prestigious ranks of the judiciary by having demonstrated mastery over the civilian application and interpretation of codified law.

The Constitutional Court's decisions unwaveringly hew to a formulaic structure that seems to yearn for the systematic and orderly nature of the civil law, even in the midst of the chaos and liberty judges confront in the constitutional common law. Every one of the Constitutional Court's judgments

---

[167] Kommers, Supra note 13, 845 ("the Federal Constitutional Court is not formally bound to the rule of stare decisis. In the culture of Germany's code law world ... judicial decisions do not enjoy the status of law as in the common law world").

[168] See e.g., Harlan F. Stone, "The Common Law in the United States" (1936) 50 *Harvard Law Review* 4, 5 ("[d]istinguishing characteristics are [the common law's] development of law by a system of judicial precedent, its use of the jury to decide issues of fact, and its all-pervading doctrine of the supremacy of law ...").

[169] Grundgesetz für die Bundesrepublik Deutschland [Grundgesetz] [GG] [Basic Law] May 23, 1949, BGBl. I., Article 93(1)[2]. See Christian Hillgruber and Christoph Goos, *Verfassungsprozessrecht*, 4th edn (Heidelberg: C. F. Müller, 2015), 207–37.

[170] Grundgesetz für die Bundesrepublik Deutschland [Grundgesetz] [GG] [Basic Law] May 23, 1949, BGBl. I., Article 94(1). See Kommers and Miller, Supra note 16, 22–4; Rudolf Streinz, "The Role of the German Federal Constitutional Court: Law and Politics" (2014) 31 *Ritsumeikan Law Review* 95, 102.

follows the same pattern. In Section A, the Court provides an objective presentation of the relevant law, facts, procedural background, and the arguments of complainants. In Section B, the Court provides an objective presentation of the respondents' arguments and the presentations made at a hearing (if one was held), including the contributions to the proceeding from experts in the relevant facts and law. In Section C, the Court announces and justifies its decisions regarding admissibility and the merits of the case. Anyone familiar with the rambling and unsystematic judicial style of the US Supreme Court's judgments is immediately struck by the systematic and rational structure of the Constitutional Court's decisions.

Other practices confirm the Constitutional Court's civilian understanding of constitutional law because they reinforce the law's abstract or conceptual nature.

First, the Court almost always reaches its decisions by unanimous judgments.[171] This helps to avoid the impression that constitutional decision-making is a matter of the justices' personal or political preferences. Constitutional law is presented as a coherent and objective normative framework. It does not appear, as is often the case in the judgments of the US Supreme Court, as a pluralistic and disputed enterprise that lurches toward results only through sometimes fragile majorities of the justices. The Constitutional Court justices have had a right to publish dissenting opinions since the early 1970s but, in keeping with the civil law's principled conceptualism, they rarely do so.[172]

Second, the Court has developed highly systematized approaches to its practice in the areas of constitutional interpretation that otherwise would have demanded the greatest discretion and flexibility. In this way, the Court has sought to limit and restrain its role in ways that resonate with the civil law tradition's suspicion for judicial power.

The Court invariably approaches the review of alleged basic rights violations by resorting to a formula prominently promoted by the scholars Bodo Pieroth and Bernhard Schlink (now joined by Thorsten Kingreen and Ralf Poscher).[173] Adjudicating the constitution's basic rights might have involved a nearly unbounded jurisprudential practice, especially when one considers the broad textual framing rights such as dignity, personality, and equality must be

---

[171] See Kommers and Miller, Supra note 13, 28–9.
[172] Ibid. See Bundesverfassungsgericht, Jahresstatistik 2014 – Entscheidungen mit oder ohne Sondervotum in der amtlichen Sammlung (BVerfGE) – Bände 30–134 (1971–2014), available at www.bundesverfassungsgericht.de/DE/Verfahren/Jahresstatistiken/2014/gb2014/A-I-7.html (154 dissents in 43 years).
[173] Bodo Pieroth et al., *Grundrechte – Staatsrecht II* (Heidelberg: C. F. Müller, 2014).

given. But the Court has yoked itself to a three-part formula that gives its work in this context the feeling of objectivity and scientific inquiry. In the first step, the Court begins by defining the scope of the asserted constitutional protection. This, for example, requires the Court to answer the question "to whom or what does the basic right apply?" In the second step the Court assesses whether there has been a direct or indirect encroachment upon the protectable scope of the basic right. In the third step the Court determines whether an encroachment on the basic right has been justified. This, in turn, requires the Court to follow one of two systematic paths, one for rights that can be limited by statute,[174] and another for rights that are absolute.[175] Each of these tracks involves a distinct, systematized assessment.

The central component of step three (the determination whether an encroachment is justified) is the application of the proportionality principle for which the Court is well-known.[176] The proportionality principle might be characterized as an open-ended balancing test that gives the justices unchecked and dangerously subjective discretion to assign "weight" to competing interests and to reach conclusions on the basis of an unsystematic balancing exercise.[177] There is some truth in this critique. But the criticism should grapple with the Constitutional Court's highly methodical approach to proportionality analysis. In fact, in the system developed by the Court, the proportionality principle involves balancing or weighing only as the last of four steps in the analysis.[178] Before determining whether measures that encroach upon basic rights are proportional to the benefits they are intended to produce, the Court first examines whether the measures are legitimate, suitable, and necessary.

---

[174] Kommers, Supra note 13, 857 ("[a] close look at the Basic Law discloses an interesting hierarchy of rights. Some are cast in unqualified language").

[175] Ibid. ("[a]ll other rights are conditional, and they fall into three categories. First are those rights which can only be limited by the terms of the Basic Law itself ... The second category of conditional rights are those whose contours are to be defined by law ... Finally, certain rights may be restricted by the 'general laws'. The reference here is to the general provisions of the civil and criminal code").

[176] See e.g., Dieter Grimm, "Proportionality in Canadian and German Constitutional Jurisprudence" (2007) 57 *University of Toronto Law Journal* 383.

[177] See Vicki C. Jackson, "Ambivalent Resistance and Comparative Constitutionalism: Opening Up the Conversation on 'Proportionality', Rights, and Federalism" (1999) 1 *Journal of Constitutional Law* 583, 603–4 (quoting William Stuntz as asserting "[t]here is no nonarbitrary way to arrive at the proper legal rules, no way to get to sensible bottom lines by something that looks and feels like legal analysis. Whether proportionality review is lodged in appellate or trial courts, the only way to do it is to do it, to decide that this sentence is too great but not that one. There is no metric for determining right answers, no set of analytical tools that defines what a given sentence ought to be").

[178] Robert Alexy, "Constitutional Rights, Balancing, and Rationality" (2003) 16 *Ratio Juris* 131, 135.

The Court faithfully resolves each of these threshold standards before taking up the less-bounded challenge of balancing or weighing interests.[179]

17.4. CONCLUSION

My American law students were relieved to hear the tour guide's claim that the German Constitutional Court was the country's common law tribunal. Implied in the claim was the idea that the entire German legal culture was now keyed to the common law. After all, whatever else the American students might have understood about their visit to the Court in Karlsruhe, they knew that the Constitutional Court is Germany's most powerful and important judicial organ. The common law – the tour guide wanted them to believe – now radiates across all German law. This put the young American jurists on stable and familiar ground. It was a different country and a different legal tradition, the sentiment ran, but at least when it comes to constitutional law we speak the same (common law) language. It must have been the familiarity that the tour guide sought to engender with her remark that emboldened that group of too-often reluctant students to join the discussion about the Court with real interest and vigor. The questions they raised quickly exposed the problems with the tour guide's claim about the Constitutional Court's common law orientation. "Who is the best known justice," one of the students asked. The tour guide explained that the Court's President often has a significant public profile. But she noted that the Constitutional Court's justices, mostly working anonymously and unanimously, do not enjoy anything like the celebrity of the US Supreme Court justices. "What was her favorite dissenting opinion," another student asked. The justices of the Constitutional Court are rarely divided in their votes, the tour guide explained. And when they are, it is even rarer for the dissenters to write a separate opinion. "What is the Court's process for deciding which cases it will consider," a third student asked. The tour guide explained that the Constitutional Court doesn't select the cases on its docket, but must decide all admissible cases. Another student asked, "What are the standards the Court follows if it wants to abandon its own precedent?" The tour guide explained that the Constitutional Court does not follow the common law doctrine of *stare decisis*. The magic of the earlier moment, stirred when the tour guide declared the Court to be Germany's only common law

[179] Grimm, Supra note 176, 387 ("[o]nly a legitimate purpose can justify a limitation of a fundamental right ... [T]he German Court asks whether the law is suitable to reach its end[,] whether the law is necessary to reach its end or whether a less intrusive means exists that will likewise reach the end, and [t]he third step ... is a cost-benefit analysis, which requires a balancing between the fundamental rights interests and the good in whose interest the right is limited").

court, was waning. Maybe it was the bank of clouds that had crept in front of the sun and muted the glow of the Constitutional Court's hearing chamber. But one of my students put it more bluntly. "Well," she said, "this doesn't sound like any common law court I'm familiar with."

German constitutional law is civilian in character and style. Constitutional law has not only been the vehicle for the common law's triumph over civilian formalism and positivism as the prevailing myth would suggest. German constitutional law has also been colored by the still-predominant civil law tradition. This is nothing more than the symbiotic interchange between legal traditions that Glenn envisioned. The distinct and continuously evolving mix of these traditions – as well as of history, and politics, and culture – leaves us undeniably with Germany's uniquely German constitutional law. It suggests that any credible study of German constitutional law must account for the German constitutional regime's civilian orientation, and a potentially infinite array of other "traces."[180] More broadly, my thesis serves as a warning for comparative lawyers who might be tempted to neglect a particular constitutional culture's unique socio-legal frame in pursuit of comparisons that rely on generalized or universal notions of constitutionalism. It is all marvelously more complex than that.

---

[180] See Legrand, Supra note 20.

18

Unwritten Constitutional Principles in Canada

Genuine or Strategic?

David Schneiderman

Appearances can be deceiving, no more so than in the constitutions of states. Tribe maintains that the United States Constitution, "*at every moment* depends on extratextual sources of meaning."[1] One cannot understand what is going on in the United States Constitution, in other words, without having recourse to nontrivial understandings beyond the text.[2] Tribe's "invisible constitution" refers not merely to what judges say the constitution means, and something less than the "complex superstructure" operating around the constitution, but what is going on "within it."[3] Such goings on are informed by "constitutional principles that go beyond anything that reasonably could be said to flow simply from what the Constitution expressly says."[4]

Likewise, Canada's Constitution easily misleads readers.[5] The Constitution Act, 1867, treated by many as Canada's first Constitution (though it is not), purports to confer absolute authority on the monarch, with the legislative and executive branches granted a subsidiary role.[6] Because British parliamentary traditions are incorporated as a matter of conventional constitutional law, Canada's monarch is, in actuality, subordinate while the executive controls prerogatives formerly falling within monarchical discretion (e.g., the powers

---

[1] Lawrence H. Tribe, *The Invisible Constitution* (Oxford: Oxford University Press, 2008) 6 (emphasis in original).
[2] Amar writes that the written and unwritten are intertwined in Akhil Reed Amar, *America's Unwritten Constitution: The Precedents and Principles We Live By* (New York: Basic Books, 2012) 20.
[3] Tribe, Supra note 1, 10.
[4] Ibid., 28.
[5] See Rosalind Dixon and Adrienne Stone, "The Invisible Constitution in Comparative Perspective" Chapter 1 in this book.
[6] It more appropriately should be counted as the fifth. See Peter Russell, *Constitutional Odyssey: Can Canadians Become a Sovereign People?* 3rd edn (Toronto: University of Toronto Press, 2003) 12.

to make war and peace).[7] This is presaged by the Constitution's suggestive preamble that declares the Constitution of 1867 to be one "similar in Principle to that in the United Kingdom."

Much of the Canadian Constitution evinces elements of both specificity and generality, calling for numerous enhancements through the application of judicial methods together with intergovernmental practice.[8] Judges in Canada have been granted license to adapt the constitution, within "natural limits," to modern times.[9] The Supreme Court of Canada has enthusiastically embraced this judicial practice of "filling in the gaps" of Canada's constitutional order in the 1990s with reference to constitutional principles. The preamble, the Supreme Court declared, serves as the "grand entrance hall to the castle of the Constitution."[10] Swept onto its threshold was the unwritten constitutional principle of "judicial independence." The Court was there answering a question concerning the independence of provincial court judges who did not have constitutional security equivalent to that available to federally appointed justices.[11] The Court construed the preamble as "inviting" the use of "organizing principles to fill" in "gaps in the express terms of the constitutional scheme."[12] Judicial independence could be inferred, in this way, as an "unwritten norm, recognized and affirmed by the preamble."[13] As a consequence, provincial court judges were entitled to a semblance of institutional and financial security. The opinion helped to kick-start Canada's contemporary preoccupation with unwritten principles. The Court's ruling in *Reference re Secession of Quebec* represents its apotheosis. The Court articulated a new "constitutional duty to negotiate," drawing on what the Court described as four "constitutional principles" underlying the constitutional text (without mention of the Constitution's preamble or convention).[14] These decisions

---

[7] See Andrew Heard, *Canadian Constitutional Conventions: The Marriage of Law and Politics* 2nd edn (Oxford: Oxford University Press 2014).

[8] For example, it declares, in its third schedule, that "Lighthouses and Piers, and Sable Island" fall within federal jurisdiction. The text also confers authority on the federal government to make laws in relation to various omnibus classes including a general one concerning "peace, order and good government."

[9] This refers to the "living-tree" metaphor. It took some fifty years after its initial articulation, in *Edwards v. AG Canada* [1930] AC 124, for this interpretive rule to truly gain ground in Canada. See Vicki C. Jackson, "Constitutions as 'Living Trees'? Comparative Constitutional Law and Interpretive Metaphors" (2006) 75 *Fordham Law Review* 921, 947.

[10] *Reference re Remuneration of Judges of the Provincial Court* (P.E.I.) [1997] 3 S.C.R. 3 para. 109.

[11] They are not mentioned in s. 96 of the Constitution Act, 1867, which provides a semblance of such security. See W. R. Lederman, "The Independence of the Judiciary" (Part II) (1956) 34 *Canadian Bar Review* 1139.

[12] *Reference re Remuneration of Judges of the Provincial Court* (note 10), para. 95.

[13] Ibid., para. 109.

[14] *Reference re Secession of Quebec* [1998] 2 SCR 217.

signaled a novel enlargement and significant departure from, the stock of readily available legal techniques.[15]

Informed by literature on judicial politics, I argue that the Court invoked unwritten constitutional principles for "strategic" reasons. Though it often is hard to separate out strategic judicial choices from legal ones, the Court in the Secession Reference drew upon salient features of Canada's constitutional order, but without recourse to typical legal methods in order to reveal a novel constitutional duty to negotiate. This had the distinct advantage of getting the court out of a difficult predicament. What the Secession Reference together with later decisions signals is that when the Court embraces unwritten principles it is likely engaging in some version of strategic behavior. This leads me to a second hypothesis: that the Court's invocation of unwritten constitutional principles in the Secession Reference was not intended to determine constitutional outcomes going forward. It was not meant, in other words, to harden into doctrinal precedent. In short, the justices were being legally disingenuous.

Such an interpretation helps to explain the most recent test case of unwrittenness in *Quebec* v. *Canada*,[16] concerning the destruction of Canada's firearms registry by the federal Conservative government. The Government of Quebec sought to preserve those records for the purposes of law enforcement within the Province. Quebec argued that the unwritten constitutional principle of cooperative federalism required that the federal government hand over to its provincial counterpart registry records constructed using Quebec data. The Supreme Court rejected this argument by a five to four vote (all three Quebec justices dissenting). I hypothesize that a reluctance to innovate in *Quebec* v. *Canada*, in the direction of adopting an unwritten constitutional principle of federal loyalty, underscores the degree to which the Supreme Court of Canada acted strategically in the past. As the Court was divided in *Quebec* v. *Canada*, and as its personnel changes over time, one cannot say that the justices are *not at all* interested in unwritten constitutional principles, only that most are less interested than originally thought.

The discussion also provides an opportunity to consider the appeal of comparative constitutional law to the Supreme Court of Canada. This is because the government of Quebec sought to import into Canadian constitutional doctrine via unwritten principles, though not explicit about this, the continental idea of "federal loyalty." This would have required that the federal

---

[15] But see David J. Mullan, "Underlying Constitutional Principles: The Legacy of Justice Rand" (2010–11) 34 *Manitoba LJ* 73, who describes "judicial support" in the period in which an implied bill of rights was read into the division of powers of the Constitution Act, 1867 as "equivocal at best and the seeming ambit of the doctrine's operation limited" 76.
[16] *Quebec (Attorney General)* v. *Canada (Attorney General)* [2015] 1 SCR 693.

government act in ways consistent with the constitutional sinews that connect the two orders of government.[17] As others have observed, the Canadian justices are not that interested in foreign constitutional law. This is despite the long-standing tradition of drawing upon English constitutional law (the law of the mother country), together with the occasional citation of American constitutional law (the law of the parent company). There is, apart from these exceptions, a tendency to be mostly disinterested in constitutional developments elsewhere.

I begin in Section 18.1, with a brief discussion of the judicial politics literature and strategic decision-making. In Section 18.2, I turn to the Secession Reference and, in Section 18.3, address a selection of the subsequent case law, including *Quebec* v. *Canada*.[18] Section 18.4 turns to arguments made by scholars from within Quebec who sought to adapt comparative constitutional developments to Canadian circumstances. This provides an occasion to reflect on the state of the constitutional law of federalism and comparative constitutional influences.

18.1. STRATEGIC

If we understand judges as being constrained principally by text, precedent, and history, together with practices of judicial propriety – the traditional legal tools with which judges reason legally – it can be said that high court decision-making operates under few other constraints.[19] In vexatious constitutional disputes, where there will be no single obvious answer, there is even more room for judicial maneuvering.[20] The political science literature on judicial behavior turns out to be helpful insofar as it offers up a number of models, beyond traditional legal methods, with which to understand high court decision-making. In the interests of brevity, two are taken up for discussion here. The "attitudinal model" suggests that judicial preferences,

---

[17] *Concordat Case* (1957) 6 BVerfGV 309 in Donald P Kommers, *The Constitutional Jurisprudence of the Federal Republic of Germany*, 2nd edn (Durham: Duke University Press 1997) 80–2.

[18] I have elected not to discuss in this chapter the full complement of lower court and Supreme Court of Canada decisions that invoke unwritten principles. For a broader discussion, see Jean Leclair, "Canada's Unfathomable Unwritten Constitutional Principles" (2002) 27 *Queen's Law Journal* 389.

[19] Richard A Posner, *How Judges Think* (Cambridge, MA: Harvard University Press, 2008) 12.

[20] Michael McCann, "How the Supreme Court Matters in American Politics: New Institutionalist Perspectives" in Howard Gillman and Cornell Clayton (eds.), *The Supreme Court in American Politics: New Institutionalist Interpretations* (Lawrence, KS: University of Kansas Press, 1999) 65–6.

particularly as reflected in the ideology of the appointing authority, explain judicial outcomes. Judicial voting behavior in the United States, it is said, is best explained by sincere judicial policy preferences and these will get channeled in the opinions of individual justices.[21] A "strategic" model, by contrast, understands judges as rational actors who pursue strategies in order to attain their preferred outcomes, but these are constrained by their institutional interdependence.[22] While fidelity to law matters, the response that judges elicit from the institutional environment within which they operate better explains outcomes.[23] We should understand strategic decision-making as constrained by law's imagined possibilities, but departing from traditional methods of judicial decision-making.

Though these two models originated simultaneously as a way of understanding the US Supreme Court output,[24] they have been conscripted as techniques with which to study foreign court behavior,[25] including the Supreme Court of Canada. The attitudinal model, however, has not been a helpful explanatory device of Canadian developments. In contrast to the United States, Alarie and Green find that there is "not at all a strong relationship between the party of the prime minister who appointed the judges and their subsequent voting preferences."[26] Not only is there a weak connection between purported policy preference and voting outcomes, Canadian Supreme Court justices are likely to agree more often in divisive cases than their United States counterparts and, when they do disagree, voting patterns

---

[21] Jeffrey A Segal and Harold J Spaeth, *The Supreme Court and the Attitudinal Model* (Cambridge: Cambridge University Press, 1993) 32–3.

[22] Lee Epstein and Jack Knight, *The Choices Justices Make* (Washington, D.C.:Congressional Quarterly Press, 1998) 12; Lee Epstein and Jack Knight, "Toward a Strategic Revolution in Judicial Politics: A Look Back, a Look Ahead" (2000) *Political Research Quarterly* 625, 626.

[23] Walter F. Murphy, *Elements of Judicial Strategy* (Chicago, IL: University of Chicago Press, 1964) 199. There is a third institutionalist approach that looks to the constraining influence of institutional norms and path dependence to explain judicial behavior. Here legal norms play a role in addition to institutional settings in which judges operate. See e.g., Rogers M. Smith, "Historical Institutionalism and the Study of Law" in Gregory A. Caldeira, R. Daniel Keleman and Keith E. Whittington (eds.), *The Oxford Handbook of Law and Politics* (Oxford: Oxford University Press, 2008) and Nancy Maveety, "The Study of Judicial Behavior and the Discipline of Political Science" in Nancy Maveety (ed.), *The Pioneers of Judicial Behavior* (Ann Arbor, MI: University of Michigan Press, 2002) 28–9. This account is not taken up here.

[24] Maveety, *The Pioneers of Judicial Behavior*, 25.

[25] Pablo T. Spiller and Rafael Gely, "Strategic Judicial Decision-Making" in Gregory A. Caldeira, R. Daniel Keleman and Keith E. Whittington (eds.), *The Oxford Handbook of Law and Politics* (Oxford: Oxford University Press, 2008) 38–9.

[26] Benjamin Alarie and Andrew Green, "Policy Preference Change and Appointments to the Supreme Court of Canada" (2009) 47 *Osgoode Hall LJ* 1, 28.

are harder to predict than in the United States.[27] Songer et al. maintain, nevertheless, that ideology and attitude play a role, particularly in criminal appeals.[28]

Even if the strategic model has prompted only a handful of scholarly studies, it may have more explanatory force.[29] That is, the Court will issue reasons in some cases that are better explained with reference to the institutional environment in which the Court operates in particular, its relationship to the political branches, both national and sub-national. Former Prime Minister Pierre Trudeau, for instance, explained the Supreme Court's historic decision in the Patriation Reference in strategic terms.[30] The Court ruled that Trudeau's federal government could not unilaterally bring the Constitution home from Britain without offending a constitutional convention, that of securing "substantial" provincial consent beforehand. The majority's ruling, Trudeau complained, long after he left office, left "little doubt that the majority judges had set their minds to delivering a judgment that would force the federal and the provincial governments to seek a compromise."[31] Knopff et al. claim that in a series of high profile but "jurisprudentially suspect" decisions, including the Patriation and Secession References, strategic decision-making is the only plausible explanation for their results.[32] Sauvageau et al. suggest that the Supreme Court's opinion in R. v. *Marshall* (No. 2)[33] can only be explained as a means of mollifying the indignation that was directed at the Court as a consequence of its ruling in *Marshall* (No. 1), which seemingly expanded the scope of Indigenous rights across Atlantic Canada.[34] Johnson's study of Supreme Court decision-making in the period prior to 1949, at which

---

[27] Benjamin Alarie and Andrew Green, "Should They All Just Get Along? Judicial Ideology, Collegiality and Appointments to the Supreme Court of Canada" (2008) 58 *University of New Brunswick LJ* 73, 74.

[28] Donald R. Songer, Susan W. Johnston, C. L. Ostberg and Matthew W. Wetstein, *Law, Ideology, and Collegiality: Judicial Behaviour in the Supreme Court of Canada* (Montreal and Kingston: McGill-Queen's University Press, 2012) 152.

[29] See discussion in Emmett Macfarlane, *Governing from the Bench: The Supreme Court of Canada and the Judicial Role* (Vancouver: UBC Press, 2013) 30.

[30] *Reference re Resolution to Amend the Constitution of Canada* [1981] 1 SCR 753.

[31] Pierre Elliott Trudeau, "Convocation Speech at the Opening of the Bora Laskin Law Library" (1991) 41 *University of Toronto LJ* 295, 302.

[32] Rainer Knopff, Dennis Baker and Sylvia LeRoy, "Courting Controversy: Strategic Judicial Decision Making" in James B. Kelly and Christopher P. Manfredi (eds.), *Contested Constitutionalism: Reflections on the Canadian Charter of Rights and Freedoms* (Vancouver: UBC Press, 2009) 67, referring to *Reference re Resolution to Amend the Constitution of Canada* (note 30) and *Reference re Secession of Quebec* (note 14).

[33] *R v. Marshall* [1999] 3 SCR 456.

[34] *R v. Marshall* [1999] 3 S.C.R. 533. See discussion in Florian Sauvageau, David Schneiderman and David Taras, *The Last Word: Media Coverage of the Supreme Court of Canada* (Vancouver: UBC Press 2006) 165; Vuk Radmilovic, "A Strategic Approach to Judicial Legitimacy: Supreme Court of Canada and the Marshall Case" (2010) 15 *Review of Constitutional Studies* 77.

point appeals to the Judicial Committee of the Privy Council were abolished, and after proclamation of the Charter of Rights and Freedoms reveals that both the threat of reversal, in the first case, and constitutional amendment, in the second case, "legally constrained" Supreme Court justices.[35]

This selected evidence points to the likelihood that strategic decision-making has, at the very least, an episodic presence in Canadian judicial decision-making. It is likely, then, to be one among several factors that drive judicial outcomes.[36] Indeed, it is probably correct to say that judicial choices typically exhibit elements of the legal, strategic and even attitudinal, and that it is often hard to isolate any one of these elements.[37] We should be hesitant, then, to characterize strategic decision-making as something other than "law."[38] Though some commentators view the Court's performance in the Secession Reference as not constitutional law "in any conventional sense" or amounting to "extralegal amendment,"[39] all that we need acknowledge here is that it represents a significant deviation from standard, and usually-to-be-expected, judicial technique. Strategic decision-making informed by unwritten constitutional principles, in other words, represents a novel departure from the typical Canadian constitutional forms of argumentation.[40] In which case, a strategic model of judicial behavior may aid in understanding judicial outcomes, particularly in those high profile disputes that have political salience.[41] It also might help to explain when the Court will have recourse to unwritten constitutional principles.

---

[35] Susan W. Johnson, "The Supreme Court and Strategic Decision Making: Examining Justices' Voting Patterns During Periods of Institutional Change" (2012) 42 *American Review of Canadian Studies* 236.

[36] Emmett Macfarlane, Supra note 29, 185.

[37] Mark A. Garber, "Legal, Strategic or Legal Strategy: Deciding to Decide During the Civil War and Reconstruction" in Ronald Kahn and Ken I Kersch (eds.), *The Supreme Court and American Political Development* (Lawrence, KS: University of Kansas Press, 2006) 33, 48, 60.

[38] For one who does not, see Phillip Bobbitt, *Constitutional Fate: Theory of the Constitution* (Oxford: Oxford University Press, 1982) 61.

[39] Jamie Cameron, "The Written Word and the Constitution's Vital Unstated Assumptions" in Pierre Thibault, Benoit Pelletier and Louis Perret (eds.), *Essays in Honour of Gerald A. Beaudoin: The Challenges of Constitutionalism* (Montreal: Les Éditions Yvon Blais Inc, 2002) 89, 108 and Sujit Choudhry, "Ackerman's Higher Lawmaking in Comparative Constitutional Perspective: Constitutional Moments as Constitutional Failures?" (2008) 6 *Int J Const Law* 193, 214.

[40] Choudhry, "Ackerman's Higher Lawmaking in Comparative Constitutional Perspective", 218.

[41] Though not exclusively in high profile disputes. A strategic account might explain any number of judicial outcomes. Moreover, any number of objectives (and not just judicial policy preferences) can be served by strategic decision-making. See discussion in Epstein and Knight, "Walter F. Murphy: The Interactive Nature of Judicial Decision Making" in Nancy Maveety (ed.), *The Pioneers of Judicial Behavior* (Ann Arbor, MI: The University of Michigan Press, 2002) 197, 200–1. In this paper, I argue that reliance upon unwritten principles can be understood as a signal that the Court is acting strategically.

18.2. EMBRACE

It is by now commonplace to explain the Court's opinion in the Secession Reference with reference to legitimacy concerns.[42] It is less common, however, to link the identification of unwritten constitutional principles to the judicial strategy that was in play.[43] These, typically, are treated as less controversial and play a subsidiary role in the legitimacy narrative, as compared to the constitutional duty to negotiate and the Court's withdrawal from any supervisory role in furtherance of that duty.[44] I argue that the unwritten constitutional principles revealed in the Secession Reference were a response to legitimacy concerns then facing the Court and which no longer are present. Judges and scholars from Quebec mistook these signals as genuinely novel legal developments rather than strategic responses intended to get the Court out of a jam. Though operating within a legal frame, the Court sought out a method to resolve legal problems that looked suspiciously situational. Rather than the age, rigidity, or prolixity of the constitution as factors driving the Supreme Court down this path, I argue that legitimacy concerns, which periodically

---

[42] Sujit Choudhry and Robert Howse, "Constitutional Theory and the Quebec Secession Reference" (2000) 13 *Canadian J of Law and Jurisprudence* 143; Vuk Radmilovic, "Strategic Legitimacy Cultivation at the Supreme Court of Canada: Quebec Secession Reference and Beyond" (2010) 43 *Canadian J of Political Science* 843; David Schneiderman, "Introduction" in David Schneiderman (ed.), *The Quebec Decision: Perspectives on the Supreme Court Ruling on Secession* (Toronto: Lorimer, 1999); Robert Young, "A Most Politic Judgment" in David Schneiderman (ed.), *The Quebec Decision: Perspectives on the Supreme Court Ruling on Secession* (Toronto: Lorimer, 1999).

[43] A recently discovered exception is Jean Leclair "Constitutional Principles in the Secession Reference" in Nathalie Des Rosiers, Patrick Macklem and Peter Oliver (eds.), *The Oxford Handbook on the Canadian Constitution* 1010 (Oxford: Oxford University Press, 2017). Choudhry and Howse, "Constitutional Theory and the Quebec Secession Reference" (note 42) purport to be providing an account of the Secession Reference that is internal to law, but their explanation draws upon the motifs of context and legitimacy, the kinds of considerations that drive strategic accounts external to law. On internal and external influences, see Ronald Kahn and Ken I Kersch, "Introduction" in Ronald Kahn and Ken I. Kersch (eds.), *The Supreme Court and American Political Development* (Lawrence, KS: University of Kansas Press, 2006) 1, 17–18.

[44] Radmilovic, for instance, provides a strategic account of the Secession Reference but describes the Court as having "moderated" its activism in "Strategic Legitimacy Cultivation at the Supreme Court of Canada" (note 42) 858. Gaudreault-Desbiens argues that meta-principles fell within "constitutional parameters already known or suspected" in Jean-François Gaudreault-Desbiens, "Quebec Secession Reference and the Judicial Arbitration of Conflicting Narratives about Law, Democracy, and Identity" (1999) 23 *Vermont L Rev* 793, 828. I argue, by contrast, that the Court exaggerated the degree to which the Constitution is unwritten so as to provide cover for its innovative constitutional strategy of devising a new constitutional duty to negotiate.

dog high court decision-making in Canada as it does elsewhere in the world, was the principal factor pushing the Court in this direction.[45]

The Secession Reference was, by most every indicator, a legally momentous occasion. After the near loss for federalist forces in the 1995 Quebec referendum on sovereignty (49.2 percent voted yes to secession, 50.58 percent voted no), the federal Liberal government identified a two-pronged strategy by way of a response, one political and the other legal.[46] The first was to encourage the provinces to think about reform of the federation.[47] The second was to refer constitutional questions to the Supreme Court of Canada regarding the unilateral secession of Quebec from the federation.[48]

Three short questions were referred to the Court: is unilateral secession lawful under the Canadian Constitution; is it condoned under international law; and should there be a conflict between national and international law, which legal order takes precedence? The questions were drafted in such a way as to prompt self-evident responses. Prima facie, a unilateral declaration of independence (UDI) is not authorized by the amending formulae in Part V of the 1982 Constitution. Whatever international law might have to say on the matter, in Canada's dualist system international law would not have supremacy over national constitutional law. So the questions were expected to elicit predictable answers from the court. So much so that international law professor Alain Pellet described himself as "shocked" by the questions asked. They were so biased he declared in the course of a television interview, that if they had been submitted to the International Court of Justice, there would be talk about manipulation of jurisdiction.[49]

This is one of the reasons why the government of Quebec refused to recognize the jurisdiction of the court over such matters. Questions concerning the terms upon which Quebec could secede were matters that Quebecers, alone, had authority to decide. These were not questions susceptible to legal answers. Quebec political leadership, moreover, did not expect to gain much sympathy from Canada's federally appointed apex court. In the advertising campaign conducted contemporaneous with the hearings, the governing Parti Quebecois invoked the image of the leaning Tower of Pisa to infer that,

---

[45] See Dixon and Stone, Chapter 1 in this book.
[46] The referendum was styled by the governing Parti Quebecois as being a vote on "partnership."
[47] Resulting in the Calgary Declaration of 1997, which outlined seven principles for discussion among nine provinces and the federal government (not including Quebec). See "Calgary Declaration" (September 14, 1997) www.exec.gov.nl.ca/currentevents/unity/unity1.htm accessed February 27, 2017 and David Schneiderman, "Introduction", Supra note 42, 5.
[48] The background to the Reference can be found in David Schneiderman, "Introduction," Supra note 42.
[49] Sauvageau et al., Supra note 34, 103.

when the Supreme Court decides constitutional questions, it leans in a decidedly federalist direction. This was a sweeping attitudinal narrative that had been pushed by Quebec political and legal elites since the 1960s: that justices appointed by the federal government (under s. 96) could not be expected to rule against the interests of the appointing authority.[50] The Supreme Court was compelled, by reason of Quebec's absence, to appoint Quebec City lawyer André Jolicoeur as amicus in order to make arguments that the Quebec government would have made had it been present. The predictability of the outcome also helps to explain the desultory nature of the proceedings. No members of the court asked any questions of legal counsel during oral argument, giving rise to depictions of the justices as "nine clams."[51] The legitimacy of the Court, in other words, hung in the balance. The justices would seemingly do whatever it took to maintain and, if need be, restore the Court's reputation.

If most court watchers were certain about the outcome, the reasons issued by the court were unexpected. In regard to the first critical question, the Court declared that UDI would be unconstitutional because it ignored the Constitution's amending formula. It said nothing further about what level of consensus would be required.[52] In so doing, the Court, significantly, would not rule out constitutional breakup by the withdrawal of a constituent unit of the federation. The Court opined that international law would not condone a UDI by Quebec and, on the question of conflict international law could not trump national constitutional law. It is in the course of answering the first question that the court articulated a new constitutional duty to negotiate. "If a clear majority answering a clear question" decided to pursue secession, other provinces and the federal government had a constitutional duty "to acknowledge and respect" that decision by entering into good faith negotiations.

The Court began, early in its reasons, to identify unwritten constitutional principles out of which the constitutional duty to negotiate could be derived.[53] These unwritten principles underlying the Constitution – federalism, democracy, constitutionalism and the rule of law, and protection of minorities – were

---

[50] Andrée Lajoie, Pierrette Mulazzi and Michele Gamache, "Political Ideas in Quebec and the Evolution of Canadian Constitutional Law' in Ivan Bernier and Andrée Lajoie (eds.), *The Supreme Court of Canada as an Instrument of Political Change*, Royal Commission on the Economic Union and the Development Prospects for Canada vol. 47 (Toronto: University of Toronto), 60.

[51] Sauvageau et al., Supra note 34, 108.

[52] *Reference re Secession of Quebec* (note 14), paras 76, 84.

[53] The duty was derived, specifically, from two unwritten constitutional principles: democracy and the rule of law. All four of the constitutional principles, however, would be expected to guide negotiations between the two principal "majorities."

not "explicit," the Court wrote, but represented the "vital unstated assumptions upon which the text is based."[54] The "principles dictate major elements of the architecture of the Constitution itself and are as such its lifeblood."[55] This was "not an invitation to dispense with the written text of the Constitution," the Court added. Nevertheless, underlying constitutional principles "may give rise to substantive legal obligations."[56] This looked like an invitation to question, under the umbrella of broad constitutional principles, all variety of government action.

It is curious that the Court would describe these features as unwritten. Each is given expression in constitutional text. Federalism is, of course, a key element: a division of powers between federal and provincial levels is expressly provided for in sections 91 and 92 of the Constitution Act, 1867. Democracy, admittedly, was not expressly provided for in 1867, though "having a Constitution similar in principle to that of the United Kingdom" probably ensured this by convention, in addition to the practice of having an executive responsible to the elected chamber. It is now expressly provided for, however, in the "democratic rights" sections of the Constitution Act, 1982 (ss. 3–5). Constitutionalism and the rule of law, both old ideas, are present in contemporary constitutional text. Supremacy of the Constitution is provided for in section 52 of the 1982 Constitution, where it is described as "supreme law," while Canada is described as having been "founded upon ... the rule of law" in the 1982 preamble. There are multiple textual references to the protection of minorities in 1867 and 1982, among them, aspects of provincial autonomy, guarantees of denominational education rights and, later, official minority language education, together with equality rights and religious freedom. Reference to unwritten constitutional principles seemed overwrought, therefore, in light of the available constitutional text. These unwritten principles were not invisible to the Court's audience. They could reasonably be derived from the text and from practice, but this not what the Court purported to be doing.

I surmise that the Court was acting strategically. It was providing cover for yet another unwritten feature of Canada's constitutional order that it had newly discovered for the purposes of resolving this particularly fraught constitutional dispute, namely, the constitutional duty to negotiate. By elucidating a number of powerful constitutional principles, apparently not derived from, but familiar to, the constitutional text, the Court would not be seen to be overreaching if, in addition, it found another unwritten principle that would

---

[54] *Reference re Secession of Quebec* (note 14), para. 49.
[55] Ibid., para. 51
[56] Ibid., para. 54.

guide the behavior of the political branches in the event of a "clear majority" voting to pursue secession. A more orthodox legal analysis would have focused on Part V of the Constitution. A UDI on the part of one of the constituent units of the federation would, as the Court declared in passing, run afoul of Part V's amending formulae. But there was no specificity to the discussion. The Court exhibited little interest in these, more conventional, legal details.[57] Instead, it chose to emphasize unwritten elements, like a constitutional duty to negotiate. Though the federalist side had asked for a more conventional legal analysis, this was not what the Court embraced. Instead, it chose an outcome that ensured maintenance of the Court's legitimacy within Quebec. It was, in short, an adroit performance.

The ruling was greeted with applause by both sides. Federalists and sovereignists could both claim victory. Each side would battle things out in the media circus that followed release of the opinion, each side seeking interpretive control over the ambiguities in the Court's ruling.[58] Members of the Court could quietly resume their role as neutral arbiters in federalism disputes, deflating the long-standing Quebec narrative of the Court as partisan in such conflicts. The Court's reputation was greatly enhanced. Indeed, the Court recognized that the outer reaches of its legitimacy had been reached when it declared the four unwritten constitutional principles would guide future negotiations. The Court would not enforce or supervise those negotiations, nor would it play any role in determining whether either party had discharged its constitutional duty. It could safely return to the task of shuffling papers.

18.3. ABANDONMENT

Unwritten constitutional law was now trending in Canadian scholarship. The intensity with which scholars and lawyers took up unwritten principles was startling. Warren Newman, for instance, described the Court's opinion as "a ringing declaration on the importance of constitutionalism and the rule of law in Canada, and a powerful affirmation by the Supreme Court of the legal and normative value that must be accorded to these principles by governments and citizens alike."[59] The Court's objective, observed Mark Walters, was to "articulate basic legal assumptions that inhere in the human condition itself and that

---

[57] Donna Greschner, "*Goodbye to the Amending Formulas?*" in David Schneiderman (ed.), *The Quebec Decision: Perspectives on the Supreme Court Ruling on Secession* (Toronto: Lorimer, 1999), 153.
[58] Sauvageau et al., Supra note 34, 121–5.
[59] Warren J Newman, "The Principles of the Rule of Law and Parliamentary Sovereignty in Constitutional Theory and Litigation" (2005) 16 *National J of Constitutional L* 175, 183.

therefore possess normative force independent of legislative enactment."[60] Fervor dampened significantly six years later, when the Court signaled that it was not very interested in such arguments. In *British Columbia v. Imperial Tobacco Canada Ltd.*, the Court was dismissive of arguments made by tobacco manufacturers premised on unwritten principles.[61] Tobacco manufacturers argued that British Columbia's Tobacco Damages and Health Care Costs Recovery Act, SBC 2000, c. 30, which authorized novel civil action to recover healthcare expenditures incurred by the provincial government treating patients suffering from the health effects of consuming tobacco products, violated the constitutional principles of judicial independence and the rule of law. Justice Major, writing for a unanimous Court, found that no principles of judicial independence were violated and that the broad version of the rule of law that was invoked "would render many of our written constitutional rights redundant."[62] Justice Major wrote:

> The rule of law is not an invitation to trivialize or supplant the Constitution's written terms. Nor is it a tool by which to avoid legislative initiatives of which one is not in favor. On the contrary, it requires that courts give effect to the Constitution's text, and apply, by whatever its terms, legislation that conforms to that text.[63]

What the Imperial Tobacco case signaled is a Court disinterested in arguments based upon unwritten constitutional principles. It underscored the hunch that the Court, in the Secession Reference, did not mean what it said when it described underlying principles as having "powerful normative force."[64]

It would be wrong, however, to leave readers with the impression that the Court gave up entirely on unwritten constitutional principles. Unwrittenness played a modest role in *Reference re Senate Reform*, which considered the constitutionality of a federal plan to hold provincial elections for appointment to the Canadian Senate.[65] The Canadian Senate is divided into four regions, and senators are appointed to sit as representatives from each of the ten provinces. As appointments are entirely under the control of the Prime Minister, the Senate has served mostly as a house of patronage rather than an

---

[60] Mark Walters, "The Common Law Constitution in Canada: Return of Lex Non Scripta as Fundamental Law" (2001) 51 *University of Toronto LJ* 91, 93.
[61] [2005] 2 SCR 473.
[62] *British Columbia v. Imperial Tobacco Canada Ltd.* ibid., para. 65.
[63] Ibid., para. 67.
[64] *Reference re Secession of Quebec* (note 14) para. 54.
[65] [2014] 1 SCR 704.

institution representative of the provinces.[66] The Conservative government promised to initiate a process that would transform Canada's upper house into an elected body but without amending the Constitution. This was a problem, as the "method of selecting Senators" was contemplated by the amending formula, requiring substantial provincial consent (s. 42[1]).[67] A federal scheme was introduced that would authorize, in consultation with willing provinces, the holding of elections from which persons could then be appointed to sit in the Senate (in addition to limiting their tenure from eight- to nine-year terms). Federal lawyers argued that this did not amount to an amendment requiring provincial consent, a position with which only two intervening provinces agreed. All others insisted that such a change could not be initiated without their participation.

The Supreme Court of Canada agreed that provincial consent was required (it should be acknowledged, which the Court did not, that the federal scheme could not have succeeded without provincial cooperation). The Court was not content merely to rest its opinion on the text of the amending formula – which would have sufficed – and, instead, invoked the "basic structure" and "fundamental nature" of the Constitution. Changes to the Senate's "fundamental nature" that would "fundamentally alter the architecture of the Constitution required provincial consent." The Court was not willing to accept the argument that consultative elections preserved discretion in whom the Prime Minister appoints. The argument, they wrote, "privilege[d] form over substance."[68] "While the provisions regarding appointment of senators remain textually untouched," the Court continued, "the Senate's fundamental nature and role as a complementary legislative body of sober second thought would be significantly altered."[69] The Court thereby informed its interpretation of text with reference to structure. Here is how the Court described its method: "The assumptions that underlie the text and the manner in which the constitutional provisions are intended to interact with one another must inform our interpretation, understanding, and application of the text."[70]

It is hard to explain the ruling's repeated non-textual references to "basic structure" and "fundamental nature" in light of the amending formula command

---

[66] David Schneiderman, *Red, White and Kind of Blue? The Conservatives and the Americanization of Canadian Constitutional Culture* (Toronto: University of Toronto Press, 2015) 191–5.
[67] The general amending formula is required for amendments concerning "the method of selecting Senators," requiring, at a minimum, the consent of seven out of ten provinces representing more than 50 percent of the Canadian population.
[68] *Reference re Senate Reform* [2014] 1 SCR 704 para. 52.
[69] *Reference re Senate Reform*, ibid., para. 60.
[70] Ibid., para. 26.

that amendment to the "method of selecting Senators" required the consent of provincial governments. It could be that the Court wished to signal continuity with its earlier, pre-amending formula, decision responding to another unilateral federal proposal to abolish and then erect a reformed (but still appointed) Senate. The federal proposal, the Court ruled in 1979, would destroy the fundamental features and "essential characteristics" of the Canadian Senate.[71] The justices may have been desirous of drawing upon the logic of the Court's earlier ruling. Yet, this seemed an unnecessary strategy in light of the amending formula in Part V.[72] Perhaps the justices were fortifying their reasons because they were fearful of federal government blowback?

This is precisely what happened a week after release of the Senate Reference, at which time the Prime Minister and the Chief Justice of the Supreme Court publicly drew swords. In an unprecedented assault on judicial independence, the government alleged that the Chief Justice acted "inappropriately" by contacting the Prime Minister's Office about a legal dispute likely to come before the Court. The attack appeared precipitated by the anger directed toward the Court by the governing federal Conservative Party for ruling against them in the Senate Reference, released a week earlier.[73] The allegation turned out to be without substance, and the Prime Minister quickly retreated.[74] However frigid the relationship was between the executive and the judicial branches, there was little or no threat at this time to the Court's legitimacy owing to these false allegations. The reference to unwritten constitutional principles turns out not to have succeeded in forestalling this kind of response.

The intuition that the Court did not fully mean what it said in the Secession Reference was fortified by the decision in *Quebec* v. *Canada*.[75] The constitutional dispute concerned the destruction of federal firearms registry data that had been collected with the effort and cooperation of provincial governments. The registry was a 1995 initiative of the Chretien Liberal government responding to the 1989 massacre of fourteen female engineering students at the École

---

[71] *Re Authority of Parliament in Relation to the Upper House* [1980] 1 SCR 54, 78. See discussion in Schneiderman, Supra note 66, 195–8.

[72] A similar unnecessary reliance upon the unwritten constitution appears to have been embraced in *Trial Lawyers Association of British Columbia* v. *British Columbia (Attorney General)* [2014] 3 S.C.R. 31 where the Supreme Court of Canada invoked the "rule of law" (without referring to it as an unwritten principle) as supplemental to a reading of the judicature section of the Constitution Act, 1867, s. 96. The majority, as a consequence, were able to "resolve the fundamental issue of principle in this appeal" with reference to the text of the constitution (para. 38). The majority's appeal to the rule of law, however, signals that something more was going on.

[73] See discussion in Schneiderman, Supra note 66, 234–5.

[74] Sean Fine, 'High Court Drama' *The Globe and Mail* (May 24, 2014) A1.

[75] *Quebec (Attorney General)* v. *Canada (Attorney General)* (note 16).

Polytechnique at the Université de Montréal by a gunman who professed to hate women. Destruction of the registry, like Senate reform, was an election promise of the federal Conservative Party intended to appease a gun toting rural, mostly western, electorate. Having secured a parliamentary majority in 2011, Prime Minister Harper's government proceeded to roll back the scheme. In 2012, Parliament enacted the Ending the Long Gun Registry Act, which terminated the registry and mandated the destruction of all records associated with the 1995 initiative. The Quebec government sought to block destruction of the data so that it could maintain its own long gun registry in the province. The Harper government, committed to destroying all registry data, was not willing to cooperate.

The political context of the dispute could not be more different than that in the Secession Reference. The Parti Québécois (the political party having the independence of Quebec as its principal goal) was the party in power in the period leading up, and subsequent, to the Secession Reference. Political debates and media reports were centered on the Court and the question of UDI. The future of the federation, in the event of another referendum on independence, was weighing on the justices' minds. The stakes were nowhere near as high in *Quebec* v. *Canada*. The Quebec Liberal Party, an avowedly federalist one, had been in power for nine consecutive years (2003–12) and had returned to power in April 2014, six months before the oral hearing. Any threat that unsatisfied autonomy claims would fuel claims for independence, and another sovereignty referendum, simply was not credible.[76] While there certainly was attention being paid in Quebec to the destruction of firearms registry data – it was sufficiently concerning to warrant launching a constitutional challenge – it did not attract the kind of heated debate between Quebec and the rest of Canada as occurred in 1998. The Court could be expected to go about doing its business in the usual way.

There was some foundation, however, for Quebec to proceed with the reference, and some expectation that they could succeed. In addition to the principle of federalism articulated in the Secession Reference, the Supreme Court had envisaged itself as playing the role of facilitator of cooperative federalism or, as Wright labels it, "intergovernmental dialogue." The Court's record in

---

[76] See Valérie-Anne Mahéo and Éric Bélanger, "*Is the Parti Québécois Bound to Disappear? A Study of the Generational Dynamics of Electoral Behaviour in Contemporary Quebec*" (September 2016) http://csdc-cecd.ca/wp-content/uploads/2016/09/MaheoBelanger_PQ_Generations_2016_September21-2.pdf accessed September 23, 2016, who predict that, as a consequence of generational change and disinterest, sovereignty will cease to be on Quebec's agenda by 2034.

this regard has been confined to rewarding parties who have cooperated by deferring to their "mutually acceptable allocations of jurisdiction."[77]

In the Quebec Superior Court, the trial judge held that the federal law violated the principle of cooperative federalism and was beyond the capacity of the federal government to enact (and so ultra vires).[78] The Quebec Court of Appeal unanimously reversed, holding that the principle of cooperative federalism could not be used to abrogate the federal division of powers.[79] The lower court judge erred, the appeal court declared, by applying the principle of cooperative federalism "not as a mere interpretive tool but as the legal basis" for a declaration of constitutional invalidity. The Supreme Court of Canada agreed: "Quebec's position has no foundation in our constitutional law and is contrary to the governing authorities from this Court."[80] Cooperative federalism is a label that can be used to describe a number of doctrinal rules. It also has its limits, namely, when it runs up against the written constitution.[81] "The principle of cooperative federalism ... cannot be seen as imposing limits on the otherwise valid exercise of legislative competence," five justices declared.[82] The majority stomped all over Quebec's argument when it wrote that neither the:

> Court's jurisprudence nor the text of the Constitution Act, 1867 supports using that principle to limit the scope of legislative authority in order to impose a positive obligation to facilitate cooperation where the constitutional division of powers authorizes unilateral action. To hold otherwise would undermine parliamentary sovereignty and create legal uncertainty whenever one order of government adopted legislation having some impact on the policy objectives of another.[83]

---

[77] Wade K. Wright, "Courts as Facilitators of Intergovernmental Dialogue: Cooperative Federalism and Judicial Review" (2016) 72(2d) *Supreme Court L Rev* 365, 430. But see the Securities Act Reference, discussed below.

[78] *Quebec (Attorney General)* v. *Canada (Attorney General)* [2012] QCCS 4202; [2012] R.J.Q. 1895.

[79] *Quebec (Attorney General)* v. *Canada (Attorney General)* [2013] QCCA 1138; [2013] R.J.Q. 1023, para. 52.

[80] *Quebec (Attorney General)* v. *Canada (Attorney General)* (note 16) para. 16.

[81] Ibid., para. 18.

[82] Ibid., para. 19. The majority echoes objections to relying upon unwritten principles voiced by Justice Rothstein in his dissent in *Trial Lawyers Association of British Columbia* (note 72) para. 98. Yet, as mentioned, the majority in the *Trial Lawyers Association* case appears to have resolved the constitutional question, principally, with reference to Constitution Act, 1867, s. 96.

[83] Ibid., para. 20. To similar effect, see *Rogers Communications Inc.* v. *Châteauguay (City)* [2016] 1 S.C.R. 467 at para. 39 (per JJ. Wagner and Côté).

In a jointly written opinion, the three Quebec-based judges, together with Justice Abella, strongly disagreed. Describing the circumstances as "novel," the dissenting justices characterized cooperative federalism as the "dominant tide," in which case, "our courts must protect such schemes both when they are implemented and when they are dismantled."[84] In order to dismantle the federal registry, which had been erected with the cooperation and partnership of the provinces, it "must be carried out in a manner that is compatible with the principle of federalism that underlies our Constitution."[85] The scheme "cannot be dismantled unilaterally by one of the parties without taking the impact of such a decision on its partner's heads of power into account."[86] Though unacknowledged, this looks precisely like the German idea of federal loyalty. The justices' silence about this fact is consistent with the Court's general unwillingness to refer to constitutional developments abroad.[87]

The dissenting justices also turned to more traditional constitutional methods. They distinguished between the provisions of the law that terminated the collection and those that mandated the destruction of data.[88] The former was entirely within federal authority; the latter had as its principal object the termination of a partnership that had required the "administrative, financial, and legislative participation of Quebec."[89] Not only was this ultra vires the federal government, it was not sufficiently integrated into an intra vires scheme to survive constitutional scrutiny (applying the "ancillary" doctrine).

In contrast to the ruling in the Secession Reference, the majority of the Supreme Court in *Quebec v. Canada* reverted to more orthodox legal methods, associated with a traditional "dualist" (or "watertight compartments") style of federalism, with a reliance on text above all else.[90] Unlike the former case, where the Court constructed a novel constitutional apparatus of unwritten constitutional principles upon which could be derived an unwritten

---

[84] Ibid., para. 152.
[85] Ibid., para. 153.
[86] Ibid., para. 154.
[87] Though they do mingle and exchange ideas with other apex court justices. See Tonda MacCharles, "Canada's Supreme Court Justices Travel to Exchange Ideas, Discuss Legal Issues With International Judges" *The Toronto Star* (February 18, 2017).
[88] Paul Daly, "Dismantling Regulatory Structures: Canada's Long-Gun Registry as Case Study" (2015) 33 *National J of Constitutional L* 169, 189. Daly's argument relies less on unwritten constitutional principles than on constitutional doctrine informed by those principles (181).
[89] *Quebec (Attorney General) v. Canada (Attorney General)* (note 16) para. 172.
[90] This is how the ruling is described in Jean-François Gaudreault-Desbiens and Johanne Poirier "From Dualism to Cooperative Federalism and Back? Evolving and Competing Conceptions of Canadian Federalism" in Nathalie Des Rosiers, Patrick Macklem and Peter Oliver (eds.), *The Oxford Handbook on the Canadian Constitution* 410–11 (Oxford: Oxford University Press 2017).

constitutional duty to negotiate, in the latter, the majority chose to exert little energy in this regard. The justices disposed of the appeal in a short, forty-four paragraph opinion by relying on a robust federal criminal law power. It is the justices in the minority who had the work cut out for them, working up an unwritten federalism principle, earlier identified in the Secession Reference, in order to restrain broad federal authority over the criminal law. Such a course of action could have been open to the majority, but the circumstances of the case likely did not force the justices' hands as did those in the Secession Reference.

That the Court split principally along civil versus common law lines is evidence of a divide that is not easily explained by invoking standard Anglophone accounts of judicial reasoning. Rather, the rupture may best be explained with reference to the differing modes of thinking utilized in the common law and civil law traditions. In the civilian tradition, text can be understood as an elaboration of a shared normativity that is the substratum underlying constitutional instruments. If Gaudreault-Desbiens is correct to claim that this helps to explain the outcome in the Secession Reference, it may also help to explain the gulf between the common law and civilian justices in *Quebec* v. *Canada*.[91]

It is no great surprise that the Court, in *Quebec* v. *Canada*, made no reference to foreign law or scholarship. Close readers of Supreme Court of Canada jurisprudence will have observed that the justices are not that interested in foreign constitutional law. Apart from occasional references to United Kingdom and United States developments, the Court has exhibited a disinterestedness in constitutional developments elsewhere. According to McCormick's 2009 study, citations from other countries, though present, have "always occurred at a very modest level," ranging from 1 percent of total judicial citations pre-Charter of Rights to just fewer than 2 percent post-Charter.[92] This reluctance in foreign citations can be explained, in part, by Canadian anxieties about having a political (and constitutional) identity separate from, and distinctive of, the neighboring geopolitical hegemon to the South. Yet, there are good reasons to think that developments beyond the United States would be of interest to Canadian justices, particularly as the Supreme Court of Canada

---

[91] Jean-François Gaudreault-Desbiens, "*Underlying Principles and the Migration of Reasoning Templates: A Trans-Systemic Reading of the Quebec Secession Reference*" in Sujit Choudhry (ed.), *The Migration of Constitutional Ideas* (Cambridge: Cambridge University Press, 2006) 178, 204; also Jean-François Gaudreault-Desbiens, "Le juge comme agent de migration de canevas de raisonnement entre le droit civil et la common law: Quelques observations à partir d'évolutions récentes du droit constitutionnel canadien" in Ghislain Otis (ed.), *Le juge et le dialogue des cultures juridiques* (Paris: Les Éditions Karthala, 2013) 41, 90.

[92] Peter McCormick, "Waiting for Globalization: An Empirical Study of the McLachlin Court's Foreign Judicial Citations" (2009) 41 *Ottawa L Rev* 209, 225.

adopts methods (e.g., proportionality) applied elsewhere, and as the Canadian justices exert influence on foreign court deliberations.[93]

18.4. REGRETS?

One gets the sense that there was real disappointment with the opinion in *Quebec* v. *Canada*, particularly among constitutional scholars from within Quebec. Drawing upon the idea of federalism, key to generating autonomy, security and continuity for the largest French-speaking community in North America, the Supreme Court was urged to generate new rules that would govern the federation. The hope was that the Court would embrace something akin to the German principle of federal loyalty as an element of unwritten principles rather than having *rapport de forces* determine outcomes. In addition to unwritten principles, these scholars could rely on a judicial record in which unilateralism, at both federal and provincial levels, was discouraged.[94] The federal government's insistence on destroying data was an instance of unilateralism worthy of judicial condemnation.

Quebec-based scholars were particularly insistent upon moving the law of federalism in a direction that would constrain unilateral exercises of power that would hinder freely made policy choices issuing out of the other jurisdiction. The idea of federal solidarity, Hugo Cyr maintained, is internal to the logic of cooperative federalism. It flows "from the commitment of federal partners to belong to a common body politic."[95] Drawing on the continental idea, Cyr argued that partners to the federation should forgo self-interest in favor of a disposition that respects the jurisdictional space of each other. It "entails a certain benevolence towards the others that is clearly not limited to one's formal *obligations*."[96] In the context of the destruction of gun registry data, courts were entitled to step in to ensure that Parliamentary authority was not abused. Cyr concluded that the federal law, though formally valid, should be inapplicable to those provinces seeking data collected on the basis of the principle of cooperation.[97]

---

[93] Adam Liptak, "U.S. Court, a Longtime Beacon, Is Now Guiding Fewer Nations" *The New York Times* (17 September 2008) A1 and MacCharles, Supra note 87 (note 86).
[94] David Schneiderman, "Making Waves: The Supreme Court of Canada Confronts Stephen Harper's Brand of Federalism" in Anita Anand (ed.), *What's Next for Canada? Securities Regulation after the Reference* (Toronto: Irwin Law Inc, 2012) 85–6.
[95] Hugo Cyr, "Autonomy, Subsidiarity, Solidarity: Foundations of Cooperative Federalism" (2014) 23(4) *Constitutional Forum* 20, 30.
[96] Ibid. (italics in original).
[97] Ibid., 34.

Drawing upon the comparative federal experience, Jean-Francois Gaudreault-Desbiens argued that the principle of federal loyalty generates a political morality that can guide federal–provincial relations.[98] In the case of the dispute over firearms registry data, "loyalty should be explicitly acknowledged as consubstantial to the constitutional principle of federalism."[99] Though the Supreme Court has not endorsed such a duty in federal–provincial relations, there are intimations of it in some of the Court's opinions. Gaudreault-Desbiens, for instance, points to the constitutional duty to negotiate in the Secession Reference as an example in addition to the "duty to consult" in circumstances where government acts in ways that undermine pending Aboriginal rights claims as performing similar functions. In the context of the firearms registry dispute, writing before the Supreme Court issued its reasons, Gaudreault-Desbiens called upon the Court to adopt the "bold" attitude that "the federal government has a duty to help the province exercise its jurisdiction over property and civil rights by not destroying and transferring data already collected."[100]

Among the handful of cases that Gaudreault-Desbiens associates with the principle of federal loyalty is *Reference re Securities Act*.[101] There, the Court struck down yet another Harper government initiative, on this occasion the establishment of a federal securities regulator, proposed over the objections of several provinces. Courts of Appeal in both Alberta and Quebec had concluded that there was no federal authority under "general trade and commerce" to establish a national regulatory body. The scholarly consensus, in both official languages, suggested otherwise. The Supreme Court of Canada, to the surprise of many including the Harper government, concluded that the scheme was beyond federal authority.[102] A national securities regulator could be established, but only with the cooperation of the provinces and without trespassing on traditional provincial jurisdiction. Though the Supreme Court appeared merely to be enforcing the division of powers as laid down in the Constitution and subsequently interpreted by the Court, the principle of federalism played a modest role in the ruling. It seems to have been deployed principally as a means of moving out of the ensuing impasse.[103] The Court

[98] Gaudreault-Desbiens describes the method as trans-systemic in his "Underlying Principles and the Migration of Reasoning Templates", Supra note 91, 203.
[99] Jean-François Gaudreault-Desbiens, "Cooperative Federalism in Search of Normative Justification: Considering the Principle of Federal Loyalty" (2014) 23(4) *Constitutional Forum* 1, 9.
[100] Ibid., 15.
[101] [2011] 3 SCR 837.
[102] See discussion in Schneiderman, Supra note 92.
[103] This is a strategy the Judicial Committee of the Privy Council had recourse to in some its controversial Canadian rulings.

noted that the appropriate way to resolve "complex governance problems" in a federation such as Canada's was "by seeking cooperative solutions that meet the needs of the country as a whole as well as its constituent parts." This approach, the Court continued, "is supported by Canadian constitutional principles" which "respect" the constitutional authority of each level of government.[104] "Cooperation is the animating force," the Court wrote: "The federalism principle upon which Canada's constitutional framework rests demands nothing less."[105]

From this, Gaudreault-Desbiens describes the principle of federalism as having played "a crucial role in the court's reasoning."[106] This does not seem a fair reading of the case. The Court's decision was driven primarily by its prior interpretation of the textual division of powers (in GMC).[107] Most surprising about the Securities Act Reference was the Court's return to policing the division of powers. This was a function the Court, up till now, appears to have abandoned.[108] It is reminiscent of the period associated with classical legal federalism of the late nineteenth and early twentieth centuries, when the Judicial Committee of the Privy Council invoked a "watertight compartments" metaphor to describe the law of Canadian federalism. Rather than succumbing to the modern discourse of inevitable overlap (or "double aspect"), the Court vindicated traditional provincial authority over property and civil rights as Quebec, Alberta and others had argued before the Court. Again, text and precedent mostly persevered.

Which is not to say that there was no political context for the constitutional dispute. Karazavin and Gaudreault-Desbiens claim, for instance, that the Court's legitimacy hung in the balance. So long as the Court issued reasons having "genuine normative stringency," its legitimacy would be preserved. That is, so long as the Court applied the tests for federal trade and commerce authority persuasively, legitimacy concerns were less likely to arise. That the Court need only apply precedent persuasively was an implicit acknowledgment that the stakes in the Securities Act Reference were not so high.[109] Having sought judicial rulings from provincial courts of appeal as a means of halting the federal scheme it could hardly be a source of complaint for the

---

[104] *Reference re Securities Act* (note 87), paras 132–3.
[105] Ibid.
[106] Gaudreault-Desbiens, Supra note 99, 14.
[107] *General Motors of Canada Ltd. v. City National Leasing* [1989] 1 S.C.R. 641.
[108] Bruce Ryder, "Equal Autonomy in Canadian Federalism: The Continuing Search for Balance in the Interpretation of the Division of Powers" (2011) 54 *Sup Ct L Rev* (2d) 565.
[109] Noura Karazivan and Jean-François Gaudreault-Desbiens, "On Polyphony and Paradoxes in the Regulation of Securities within the Canadian Federation" (2010) 40 *Can Bus LJ* 1, 38–9.

Quebec government to have the Supreme Court of Canada assume the task of authoritatively resolving the dispute.

To the extent that an unwritten principle of federalism played a role in the Securities Act Reference, it served, in the reading offered here, merely to smooth ruffled feathers. It was a rhetorical aid – a strategic device, one could say – a means by which the Court could convince its various audiences that it was doing the right thing.[110] Particularly ironic is the fact that the Harper government was espousing a version of classical legal federalism and the restoration of "constitutional balance" in the federation, namely, withdrawal of the federal government from provincial jurisdictional space, in its campaign platforms.[111] There was no need to make mention of unwritten constitutional principles in Conservative campaign discourse, just as it was unnecessary in the Securities Act Reference. The Court, from this perspective, acted consistently with the expectations of many of the relevant political actors, though at odds with the federal government's attempted power grab in this instance.

18.5. CONCLUSION

If the argument in this chapter has been that the identification of unwritten constitutional principles is best explained by the Supreme Court's strategic behavior, this does not mean that unwritten principles will not evolve into something more legally robust having precedential value. Legal concepts have an ability to live well beyond the reasons for their initial prompting, and can take on a life of their own.[112] As the personnel on the Court changes, and as law students are schooled in their utility, the Supreme Court may become more receptive to unwritten constitutional principles. Some Justices, like Louis LeBel, who did not sit on the Secession Reference bench and joined in the minority opinion in *Quebec v. Canada*, have exhibited less timidity in this regard.[113] There is no reason to think that unwritten principles will not have more of a

---

[110] Such a rhetorically minded approach to constitutional review was inaugurated, in Canada, by Marc Gold and expounded by Andrée Lajoie. See e.g., Marc Gold, "The Mask of Objectivity: Politics and Rhetoric in the Supreme Court of Canada" (1985) *Supreme Court L Rev* 455, and Andrée Lajoie, *Jugements des valeur* (Paris: Presses Universitaires de France, 1997).

[111] Schneiderman, Supra note 94, 89–93.

[112] Karl Renner, *The Institutions of Private Law and their Social Functions* trans. Agnes Schwarzschild (London: Routledge and Kegan Paul, 1949) 57.

[113] Justice Lebel, who co-wrote the dissent in *Quebec v. Canada*, is now retired. See discussion of his views in Mark Walters, "Federalism in its Biggest Sense: Justice Louis LeBel and the Federal Idea in Canadian Constitutional Law" in Dwight Newman and Malcolm Thorburn (eds.), *The Dignity of Law: The Legacy of Justice Louis LeBel* (Markham, ON: Lexis Nexis, 2015).

role to play, for these reasons, in future constitutional litigation. The worry is that it provides easy cover for contestable constitutional maneuvers, imposing a rule of political morality where there may be little consensus.

The contestable nature of unwritten principles, I surmise, helps to explain the Court's reluctance to robustly endorse them since the Secession Reference. The justices, instead, are aware that there is much work that legal federalism can do (as in the Securities Act Reference). The Court can answer constitutional questions with some jurisprudential specificity using more conventional resources.

When it departs from its more traditional methods and refers to unwritten principles, this signals the Court is being attentive to the institutional context in which it operates. Though this context will be present in many cases, overt departures from conventional legal methods entail risks for the Court. Presumably, the justices will embark on such a course only when other traditional legal methods fail to generate reasons consistent with their preferred outcomes. With its reputation hanging in the balance, the members of the Court were willing to take such a risk in the high stakes Secession Reference so as to generate an unwritten constitutional duty to negotiate. No such reputational risk was at play in *Quebec* v. *Canada*, and so nothing more was required. The majority of the justices could proceed along a more conventional path even though the outcome threatened to unleash a backlash, of a sort, from Quebec elite opinion. Then again, that opinion could have been attentive to the fact that an unwritten principle of federal loyalty worked in both directions – that it could hamper the Quebec National Assembly should it disrespect its federal partner sometime in the future. Sticking to conventional judicial methods turns out to have been the shrewder, and more cautious, course of action. Canada's unwritten constitution could safely be cabined until the next occasion when members of the Court need to get creative.

19

Lost in Transition

Invisible Constitutionalism in Hungary

Gábor Attila Tóth

In its first landmark judgment, in 1990, the Constitutional Court of Hungary abolished the death penalty.[1] The interpretation on human dignity, both a moral value and a constitutional right, served as an example for the Ukrainian, Lithuanian, Albanian, and South African constitutional courts.[2] But this is not the only reason why the judgment has been echoed in a number of studies and judgments. Chief Justice Sólyom expressed in *obiter dicta* that he was applying the invisible constitution:

> The Constitutional Court must continue its effort to explain the theoretical bases of the Constitution and the rights included in it and to form a coherent system with its decisions in order to provide a reliable standard of constitutionality – an "invisible Constitution" – beyond the Constitution, which is often amended nowadays by current political interests; and because of this "invisible Constitution" probably will not conflict with the new Constitution to be established or with future Constitutions. The Constitutional Court enjoys freedom in this process as long as it remains within the framework of the concept of constitutionality.[3]

On the face of it, the early message about the Hungarian variety of invisible constitution may appear to correspond to the renowned concept from Laurence Tribe. The fact is, however, that this innovation did not exert influence on Tribe's book in any way. Indeed, the notion of the invisible constitution has never been adopted explicitly *per curiam* in Hungary. In spite of

---

[1] Judgment 23/1990 (X. 31.) HCC.
[2] *The State v. T. Makwanyane and M. Mchunu*, CCT/3/94, Judgment of June 6, 1995. Lithuania, Case No. 2/98. Judgment of December 9, 1998; Albania, Case No. 65. Judgment of December 10, 1999; Ukraine, Case No. 11-rp/99. Judgment of December 29, 1999.
[3] Judgment 23/1990 (X. 31.) HCC, concurring opinion by Chief Justice Sólyom.

this, it emerged from the status of personal revelation of the Chief Justice to become the benchmark of Hungarian constitutionalism after the democratic transition, thanks to some leading judgments under Sólyom's name.[4]

In this chapter I would like to contribute to the analysis of the rise and fall of the Hungarian constitutionalism and rule of law. I focus particularly on the dichotomy between visible and invisible constitutions in order to better understand the nature of regime changes, as well as the competing judicial and scholarly positions. I first summarize briefly the attributes of, as mentioned above, the "often emended" 1989 Constitution. Then I turn to its correlative by offering an explanation regarding the "theoretical bases" of the invisible constitution. The question is thus whether it really served as a "coherent system" and "reliable standard" or not. The second part addresses the new Constitution, officially the 2011 Fundamental Law. I describe how and why the prediction that "the invisible Constitution probably will not conflict with the new Constitution" did not come true.

What I argue for is twofold: although the previous system based upon the 1989 Constitution was – despite its imperfections – a constitutional democracy, and while the new regime based upon the 2011 Fundamental Law can be seen as a form of incomplete authoritarianism, the notion of the invisible constitution could not fully justify democratic and liberal constitutionalism because of its aristocratic aura, religious commitment, and incoherent judicial application.[5]

19.1. THE 1989 CONSTITUTION: SUBSTANCE OVER FORM

After the Second World War, Stalinist dictatorships emerged in East Central Europe. In 1949 the communist-dominated Hungarian Parliament adopted a constitution – the first charter constitution to enter into force in the country – which closely followed the Soviet Stalinist Constitution of 1936. The regime based on legal and extra-legal repression occurred mainly in its first years and after the failure of the 1956 Revolution. Although the political system became

---

[4] The Constitutional Court of the Republic of Moldova asserted mistakenly that the *per curiam* theory of "invisible constitution" follows the German constitutional jurisdiction: judgment of December 5, 2013, No. 8b/2013, 41b/2013, [77].
[5] For a different, praiseful summary, see K. L. Scheppele, "On the Unconstitutionality of Constitutional Change: An Essay in Honor of László Sólyom," in Z. Csehi, B. Schanda and P. Sonnevend (eds.) *Viva Vox Iuris Civilis. Tanulmányok Sólyom László 70. születésnapja alkalmából* (Budapest: Szent István Társulat, 2012), 302–10; for a critical analysis, see A. Sajó, "Reading the Invisible Constitution: Judicial Review in Hungary" (1995) 15 *Oxford Journal of Legal Studies* 253.

gradually more consolidated, rule of law and constitutionalism were alien to the soft dictatorship, and the numerous constitutional changes that occurred during the communist period made little difference in this regard.

Like other communist constitutions, the provisions of the 1949 Constitution served purely ideological purposes; in other words, as a semantic constitution it was a political declaration and was never intended to serve as normative guidance in the actual use of political power, which was determined by the interests and whims of the Communist Party leadership. The formal constitutional system did not aim to provide genuine protection of fundamental rights at all, since the 1949 Constitution could not be invoked in court.

The historical turning point for the transformation from authoritarian regime to democracy was the autumn of 1989. Departing from both the tradition of revolutionary constitution-making and the models of merely reformatory processes, the peaceful, negotiated regime changes in East Central Europe – along with the previous Spanish and Portuguese experiences – established a new type of constitution making, labeled "coordinated transition."[6] This means that, with the exception of Romania, the single or dominant party systems collapsed through a series of roundtable negotiations between the old regime and the democratic opposition.

The 1989 roundtables were meant to regulate the transition from the old regime to a new one, but they did not have a mandate for constitution making. In order for their decisions to take legal effect, those decisions needed to be sent for enactment to the old legislature. The roundtables left the completion of the process to an assembly with the democratic mandate they were lacking.[7] This constitution-making profile can be characterized as consisting of two stages. In the first stage, a roundtable agreement determines the ground rules of preparing and holding free elections. The second stage takes place when a

---

[6] J. Kis, "Between Reform and Revolution: Three Hypotheses about the Nature of Regime Change" (1995) 1 *Constellations* 399; A. Arato, "Post-Sovereign Constitution-Making in Hungary: After Success, Partial Failure, and Now What?" (2010) 26 *South African Journal on Human Rights: Constitution-Making as a Learning Process* 19.

[7] Kis characterizes the coordinated transition as an interruption of legitimacy, but continuity of legality. Kis, Supra note 6, 317. See also critical reflections of the legitimacy of the 1989 Constitution: A. Arato, "Dilemmas Arising from the Power to Create Constitutions in Eastern Europe," in M. Rosenfeld (ed.) *Constitutionalism, Difference, Identity, and Legitimacy* (Durham: Duke University Press, 1994), 165–94; J. Kis, "Introduction: From the 1989 Constitution to the 2011 Fundamental Law," in G. A. Tóth (ed.) *Constitution for a Disunited Nation: On Hungary's 2011 Fundamental Law* (Budapest; New York, NY: Central European University Press, 2012), 1–23.

body of freely elected representatives adopts, in the sovereign people's name, a new constitution.[8]

Consequently, in formal terms, the 1989 Constitution was a mere modification of the 1949 Constitution. In substantive terms, however, the 1989 political transition breathed new life into the Hungarian Constitution. Since the models of the reshaped Constitution were international human rights instruments, as were the more recent Western constitutions, they were written in the language of modern constitutionalism: rules for free and fair elections, representative government, a parliamentary system, an independent judiciary, ombudspersons to guard fundamental rights, and a Constitutional Court to review the laws for their constitutionality.[9] Like other East Central European democracies, Hungary followed Western European traditions in establishing a parliamentary system instead of importing a US presidential architecture.[10] A 1990 constitutional amendment made it clear that the Prime Minister heads the executive and the Government is the supreme body of that branch, responsible to Parliament.

Unlike the other postcommunist countries, however, Hungary omitted the second step, as it did not formally adopt a new constitution prior to 2011. Although the 1989 Constitution was amended several times – for example, to qualify Hungary to join the European Convention of Human Rights, NATO, and the European Union – the country did not accomplish the symbolic mission: it failed to adopt a constitution, a step which would have demonstrated a successful completion of the democratic transition.

This failure may seem unexpected, because compared to those of other European states the 1989 Hungarian Constitution was easy to amend. Despite the fact that the Constitution could not be modified or amended by the ordinary lawmaking procedure according to a simple majority rule, it was regarded as relatively flexible rather than rigid, in the sense that it did not render any provision or principle unamendable, and it required only the votes of two-thirds

---

[8] In the aftermath of the Polish Round Table Agreement, the old constitution was amended in April 1989, and the first democratic parliament then reshaped the relations between the legislative and executive branches of the state ("Small Constitution"). The reformed constitution was finally replaced in 1997 by a completely new constitution for Poland. The old constitution of Czechoslovakia was also amended in 1989. The Charter of Fundamental Rights and Basic Freedoms was incorporated in 1991. After the dissolution of the federal state, the Czech Republic and the Slovak Republic each adopted a new constitution in 1992. In Bulgaria and Romania, the second step was taken in 1991.

[9] In more detail, see G. A. Tóth, "Hungary," in L. Besselink et al. (eds.) *Constitutional Law of the E.U. Member States* (Deventer: Kluwer, 2014), 775–9.

[10] L. Garlicki, "Democracy and International Influences," in G. Nolte (ed.) *European and U.S. Constitutionalism* (Cambridge: Cambridge University Press, 2005), 264.

of the members of the one-chamber legislative body. Neither a referendum, nor any other form of ratification (e.g., approval by the subsequent parliament) was required for the adoption of a new constitution or a constitutional amendment. However, the increasingly hostile political environment and the divergent, often diffuse constitutional conceptions prevented a consensus, or even compromises on a formally new constitution.[11]

19.2. READING THE 1989 CONSTITUTION: AN UNPRECEDENTED JUDICIAL VENTURE

Judicial protection of the Constitution was also closer to the centralized German model than to the United States judicial review.[12] This meant that the Constitutional Court was institutionally separated from the ordinary court system and had unique, *erga omnes* constitutional interpretative authority. One of the main reasons for this was that the transition was characterized by a deep mistrust of the judiciary among the new elites and the masses, as it was considered to be a means of oppression from the previous regime.[13]

As member of the third generation of European constitutional courts, the Hungarian institution embodied how modern constitutional practice emerges from democratic change.[14] Famously, the Austrian, German, and Italian constitutional courts were (re)established after the fall of totalitarian regimes, in the late 1940s and the early 1950s, then the Spanish and Portuguese courts were set up after the fall of the regimes of Franco and Salazar in the late 1970s; these were followed by the constitutional courts of post-Soviet democracies,

---

[11] A. Arato, "The Constitution-Making Endgame in Hungary" (1996) 4 *East European Constitutional Review* 31.
[12] From a theoretical and critical point of view, see W. Sadurski, *Rights before Courts: A Study of Constitutional Courts in Post-Communist States of Central and Eastern Europe* (Dordrecht: Springer, 2005). See also H. Schwartz, *The Struggle for Constitutional Justice in Post-Communist Europe* (Chicago, IL: University of Chicago Press, 2000).
[13] A. Sajó, "Contemporary Problems of the Judiciary in Hungary," in K. Rokumoto (ed.) *The Social Role of the Legal Profession* (Tokyo: International Centre for Comparative Law and Politics, University of Tokyo, 1993).
[14] Originally, Favoreau distinguished "three waves" of constitutional justice, starting with the Austrian and Czechoslovak constitutional courts from the 1920s, then the re-establishment of the Austrian court together with setting up the German court, finally, the Spanish, Portuguese, and East-Central European courts: Louis Favoreu, *Les Cours Constitutionnelles* (Paris: Presses Universitaires de France, 1986). See also L. Favoreu and W. Mastor, *Les cours constitutionnelles. Connaissance du droit* (Paris: Dalloz, 2011). As for the first three generations of constitutional courts, see L. Sólyom, "The Role of Constitutional Courts in the Transition of Democracy: with Special Reference to Hungary" (2003) 18 *International Sociology* 133.

along with the postapartheid South African Constitutional Court, from the early 1990s.[15]

In Hungary, the 1990 starting point for constitutional jurisdiction meant, on the one hand, that neither domestic precedents nor a doctrinal framework elaborated by academics guided the Court; on the other, the Chief Justice, based on his distinguished expertise and striking judicial ambition, had a chance to dominate the inceptive period of the adjudication. The declaration on the invisible constitution can be seen as the best manifestation of his credo.

As another presentation of the strong belief in the groundbreaking mission, a *per curiam* judgment expressed that the Court

> has to fulfill its task embedded in history. The Constitutional Court is the repository of the paradox of the "revolution under the rule of law": in the process of the peaceful transition, beginning with the new Constitution, the Constitutional Court must, within its competences, in all cases unconditionally guarantee the conformity of the legislative power with the Constitution.[16]

19.2.1. *Imported Universal Standards*

The Court seemed to be the most important institutional guarantee of constitutionalism, on account of its decisions favoring human rights and principles of the rule of law.[17] The Sólyom-lead court promptly realized that constitutional principles of freedom and equality are interpretive concepts. They are at the core of the text of the Constitution, and the basis of the jurisdiction of the Court. The way in which the case law of the Court affects the meaning of the phrases of the Constitution is determined by values and principles that explain why interpretation should have that role. With only mild exaggeration, we could say that under the guidelines of the invisible constitution, the early reading of the text of the Constitution gave rise to applied theories of justice and dignity in Hungarian constitutional jurisdiction.

---

[15] For the case of Hungary, see C. Dupré, *Importing the Law in Post-Communist Transitions: The Hungarian Constitutional Court and the Right to Human Dignity* (Portland, OR: Hart Publishing, 2003) and L. Sólyom and G. Brunner, *Constitutional Judiciary in a New Democracy: The Hungarian Constitutional Court* (Ann Arbor, MI: The University of Michigan Press, 2000).

[16] Judgment 11/1992 (III. 5.) HCC. See also G. A. Tóth, "The Bitter Pills of Political Transition," in A. Jakab, P. Takács and A. Tatham (eds.) *The Transformation of the Hungarian Legal Order 1985–2005* (Alphen aan de Rijn: Kluwer Law International, 2007), 281–6.

[17] S. Zifcak, "Hungary's Remarkable, Radical, Constitutional Court" (1996) 3 *Journal of Constitutional Law in Eastern and Central Europe* 1; Dupré, Supra note 15.

As Dworkinian and some other conceptions advise, the Court placed human dignity at the center of its judicature. In the Capital Punishment Case, the Chief Justice emphasized that the constitutional concept of human dignity is more than a declaration of moral value; it is a value *a priori* and beyond law, a source of rights; therefore the Court's task is to transform many of its aspects into a true right. The reasoning went on with the idea that

> [t]he right to human dignity has two functions. On the one hand, it means that there is an absolute limit which may not be transgressed either by the State or by the coercive power of other people – i.e., it is a seed of autonomy and individual self-determination withdrawn from the control of anybody else by virtue of which, according to the classical wording, man may remain an individual and will not be changed into a tool or object ... The other function of the right to dignity is to ensure equality.[18]

As to the latter function, under the human dignity-based conception of equality, everyone has a right to equal respect and treatment (as Dworkin said, "treatment as an equal"). The Court elaborated its standard of prohibition of discrimination according to which all people must be treated as equal, as persons with equal dignity; the right to human dignity may not be impaired by law; and the criteria for the distribution of the entitlements and benefits shall be determined with the same respect and prudence, and with the same degree of consideration of individual interests.[19] We can call this a comparative standard: individuals and members of particular groups have certain rights because others, in a comparative situation, also enjoy them.

The Court connected the requirement of preferential treatment to this principle. The right to equal personal dignity requires that goods and opportunities must be distributed with equal concern to everyone. If, however, a just social purpose may only be achieved if equality in the narrower sense cannot be realized, then a preferential treatment shall not be declared unconstitutional. The limitation upon preferential treatment is either the prohibition of discrimination in its broader meaning, i.e., respecting equal dignity, or the protection of the fundamental rights expressed in the Constitution (Family Protection Case).[20]

As to the former, the counterpart of the dignity-based conception of equality, dignity-based individual freedom means that the scope of rights is independent

---

[18] Judgment 23/1990 (X. 31.) HCC, concurring opinion by Chief Justice Sólyom.
[19] Judgment 9/1990 (IV. 25.) HCC.
[20] Judgment 9/1990 (IV. 25.) HCC. For the theoretical foundation, see R. Dworkin, *Sovereign Virtue, the Theory and Practice of Equality* (Cambridge, MA: Harvard University Press, 2000).

of egalitarian, distributive principles. Individuals have fundamental rights and freedoms not because others, in a comparative situation, enjoy them, but because as human beings they deserve certain treatment.

In its initial landmark decisions, the Court established that from freedom of speech to the right to privacy, each liberty right originates from the notion of human dignity. As an example, the Court clarified all the relevant notions concerning personal freedom of religion. "The individual freedom of conscience and religion acknowledges that the person's conviction, and, within this, in a given case, religion, is a part of human dignity, so their freedom is a pre-condition for the free development of personality."[21]

In general, a not far from Rawlsian conception of justice was echoed in giving priority to each person's equal right to basic liberties, including liberty of conscience compatible with the similar liberty of others. The relationship between basic liberties and equality of opportunity was also read through the lens of Rawls.[22] In addition to this, the Court's concept concerning the neutrality of the state originates from the notion of equal liberty of conscience. The requirement of religious neutrality of the state means separation of the state from churches. This separation means that the state must not be institutionally attached to any church or churches; that the state must not identify itself with the teachings of any church; that it must not interfere with the internal working of any church, and especially that it must not take a stance in matters of religious truth. From this it follows that the state must treat all churches equally (Churches Case I).[23]

Beyond principles borrowed from theories, the Sólyom Court also took international and foreign standards of judicial review as precedents. The Court protected fundamental rights effectively with the help of the proportionality principle, and the *allgemeine Handlungsfreiheit* imported from Strasbourg and Karlsruhe (General Personality Right Case),[24] as well as the *clear and present danger* scrutiny derived from the United States constitutional adjudication (Hate Speech Case I).[25]

It may seem reasonable to conclude that the strong aspiration of the Chief Justice and the majority that took shape around him has been fulfilled: the "invisible constitution" provided the theoretical bases for the 1989 constitution. The Court took a decisive part in developing a coherent constitutional

---

[21] Judgment 4/1993 (II. 12.) HCC.
[22] J. Rawls, *A Theory of Justice* (Cambridge, MA: The Belknap Press of Harvard University Press, 1971), 60–1.
[23] Judgment 4/1993 (II. 12.) HCC. Rawls, Supra note 22, 205–11.
[24] Judgment 8/1990 (IV. 23.) HCC.
[25] Judgment 30/1992 (V. 26.) HCC.

system and fundamental rights included in it on the basis of the invisible constitution. This extra-textual constitutional framework, at first glance, may seem to be close to a Dworkinian account of constitutional law. *Substantively*, as introduced above, the Court initiated to create from case to case a coherent system of fundamental rights. *Methodologically*, as Sólyom acknowledged in one of his interviews, the Court undertook the moral reading of the underlying principles of the Constitution. Reading the invisible constitution contributed to explicating the internal relations of constitutional values and phrases.

In all likelihood the leading role of the Court in democratic transition, as well as some of its landmark judgments on fundamental rights stemming from Rawlsian and Dworkinian theoretical roots, led to the widespread understanding that the Court could be characterized ideologically as liberal. As a current example, Bojan Bugarič and Tom Ginsburg refer to the initial achievements in terms of how the Court "under the strong leadership of liberal Chief Justice Sólyom, issued a series of decisions that established its reputation as the key protector of political and social rights in Hungary."[26]

I think, however, neither Dworkinism nor liberalism is the best explanation of the invisible constitution doctrine of the early Hungarian Constitutional Court.

19.2.2. Methodology: Critical, Hierarchical, Aristocratic

The lack of a new constitution increased the responsibilities of the Constitutional Court as the ultimate interpreter of constitutional principles and fundamental rights, and the most crucial constitutional check on the powers of Parliament. Importantly, the famous metaphor of the invisible constitution was applied not only to developing the underlying principles that articulate and justify the text of the constitution, as advised by the Dworkinian moral reading, but also to critically *revising* the text of the Constitution by invoking the idea of constitutionalism.[27]

According to the statement on the invisible constitution, the amendments to the text of the 1989 Constitution were a matter of "current political interests," while the invisible constitution was above and beyond the text, and the only limit on the Court's activity was the framework of constitutionalism. In this way, disrespecting the constitutional text, the Court might ground some of its decisions on the invisible constitution *rather than* on the written one.

---

[26] B. Bugarič and T. Ginsburg, "The Assault on Postcommunist Courts" (2016) 27 *Journal of Democracy* 69.
[27] J. Kis, *Constitutional Democracy* (Budapest: Central European University Press, 2003), 253–9.

In short, the doctrine was understood as a tool for implicitly amending the text of the constitution in the name of constitutional ideas, as happened in the Capital Punishment Case: the reasoning implied that the Court opposed the text of the Article 54(1) that prohibited the "arbitrary deprivation" of one's life and dignity, and logically, did not exclude the possibility that someone may be deprived of life and human dignity in a nonarbitrary way. The Court deduced, however, that any deprivation of them was conceptually "arbitrary."

This is a clear departure from a moral reading that also presupposes that the bases of the constitutional norms are moral principles that justify them. In this respect the Dworkinian approach is in line with the famous phrase from Chief Justice Marshall that it must never be forgotten that it is the Constitution that judges are expounding.[28] It is hard to imagine a constructive and coherent application of the constitution without commitment to principles and rules of the visible constitutional text.

A further attribute of the invisible constitution doctrine is its *hierarchical* nature, with an aristocratic flavor. The centralized model of constitutional adjudication, the separation from the ordinary court system, and the *erga omnes* constitutional interpretative authority can certainly be associated with hierarchy. Similarly to the Kelsenian hierarchy of legal norms, with the constitution at its peak, in the field of institutions the constitutional court is the highest in rank. However, the concurring opinion of the Chief Justice named – or perhaps better to say degraded – the Parliament, the constitution-making authority, as being motivated by actual political interests. Thus, not only direct, popular forms of democratic decision-making, but also indirect, representative forms were regarded with ambiguity. Sólyom himself believed that the symbolic completion of the democratic transition with a brand new constitution was unnecessary because the Court, as the highest-ranking constitutional body, could replace the constitution-making authority by its principled judgments.[29]

As regards the legitimacy of this kind of judicial attitude, many advocates of a powerful constitutional court engaged in endless debates with those scholars, e.g., Bruce Ackerman, who were doubtful about the initial achievements

---

[28] *McCulloch v. Maryland*, 17 U.S. 316, 408 (1819).
[29] See a debate on this between Scheppele and Arato: K. L. Scheppele, "Constitutional Negotiations: Political Contexts of Judicial Activism in Post-Soviet Europe," in S. A. Arjomand (ed.) *Constitutionalism and Political Reconstruction* (Leiden: Brill, 2007); A. Arato, *Post Sovereign Constitution Making: Learning and Legitimacy* (Oxford: Oxford University Press, 2016), 86, 173–5.

of the court because of its weak democratic justification.[30] Although it also touched on the very nature of East Central European coordinated transitions, this discussion can be placed within the general debates on the final guardians of the constitution. The main question was supposedly which organ possesses the "final word" in matters of constitutional justice. In this way the rival scholars were revolving judicial interpretive authority, as well as its mandate to review the constitutionality of legislative acts.

It is noteworthy that Sólyom's approach vindicated even the status of a substitute constitution-making authority, much beyond the role of final constitutional arbitrator, as opposed to the Dworkinian theory, which argues for constitutional review only by saying that democracy does not insist on judges having the last word in constitutional issues, but it does not insist that they must not have it.[31]

We may say that anti-parliamentarian sentiments from the constitution-interpreting authority in an emerging parliamentary democracy seem paradoxical. Unfortunately, the fight over "who has the final say" overshadowed those pluralistic and cooperative approaches, highlighting that parliament and constitutional court may mutually react to each other's activity.

As regards to methods of interpretation of constitutional rights, we also find a special hierarchy. By explaining the invisible constitution, the Chief Justice and his fellow justices declared that human life and dignity have the greatest value in the constitutional order. Furthermore, "the rights to human life and human dignity form an indivisible and unrestrainable fundamental right which is the source of and the condition for several additional fundamental rights."[32] Subsequently the Court added that the freedom of expression, the so-called "mother right" of fundamental rights of communication (freedom of the press and all media, as well as freedom of information), also takes a special place in the hierarchy of rights. Although this privileged place does not mean that this right may not be restricted – unlike the right to life or human dignity – it nonetheless necessarily implies that the freedom of expression must only give way to a few rights; that is, the laws restricting this freedom must be strictly construed.[33] Finally in this line, the Court stated further that this second-best

---

[30] B. Ackerman, *The Future of the Liberal Revolution* (New Haven, CT: Yale University Press, 1992), Ch. 6. See also S. Holmes, "Back to the Drawing Board" (1993) 2 *East European Constitutional Review* 21; S. Holmes and C. R. Sunstein, "The Politics of Constitutional Revision in Eastern Europe," in S. Levinson (ed.) *Responding to Imperfection: Theory and Practice of Constitutional Amendment* (Princeton, NJ: Princeton University Press, 1995), 300.
[31] R. Dworkin, *Freedom's Law: The Moral Reading of the American Constitution* (Oxford: Oxford University Press, 2005), 7.
[32] Judgment 23/1990 (X. 31.) HCC.
[33] Judgment 30/1992 (V. 26.) HCC.

status in the hierarchy of rights also applies to the freedom of religion, because "in a certain sense, religion is part of human dignity."[34]

Contrary to the critical review of the constitutional text and the aristocratic self-image, which had a direct effect on the decision-making, the hierarchy of the fundamental rights served mainly as a symbol: in any given case the Court never reached a conclusion based only on the hierarchical ranks of the competing rights, nor did the case law classify a whole system of rights in a hierarchical order.

Adjudication in constitutional courts is elite-driven in the sense that it is decision-making by the highest-ranking judges. The hierarchical and aristocratic methodologies of the invisible constitution doctrine may be linked with elitism, to be sure, but we should bear in mind the dissimilarities too. The Court demonstrated a superior attitude associated with the political elite, that is to say that representative government was the target of devaluing judicial assessments. This means that the Court as a privileged legal unit of the establishment expressed ambivalent, antiestablishment attitudes toward the political elite. We may say that this phenomenon is an atypical, descending theme of antielitism, as opposed to the widespread, ascending antielitism stemming from depressed social groups.

Moreover, under the 1989 Constitution, the methods and procedures of the Court were not per se elitist. Anyone was entitled to bring an action without limitation; there were no deadlines to be observed, nor was the applicant required to show any impact or other legally protected interest due to the procedural rules of *actio popularis*. In the first two decades, the great majority of the proceedings fell in this category. This mechanism made it possible to eliminate many unconstitutional laws, the death penalty included, from the legal order. In sum, if we intend to label the invisible constitution doctrine as elitist, it is worth adding that that is an aristocratic variant of elitism.

19.2.3. Substance: Partial Application of the Principles

Despite the flourishing clarification of dignity-based constitutional freedoms and equality, the Court had a Janus-faced constitutional adjudicatory role, especially when it was not able to escape from inappropriate political expectations or rigid social attitudes.

The Court never declared unconstitutionality based upon suspect classification or special needs of vulnerable groups for protection. It did not clash

---

[34] Judgment 4/1993 (II. 12.) HCC.

with the legislature in order to support women's rights. It found gender-based discrimination affecting mostly men.[35] In a similar fashion, the Court slightly preferred a *pro-life* approach in abortion cases. Although, not going against the rather pro-choice public opinion, it maintained in practice an intermediate regulation between the conflicting alternatives, the Sólyom-led Court recommended the Parliament introducing criminal sanctions against those women who terminate their pregnancies even in the first trimester (Abortion Case II).[36] The reasoning envisaged that the extension of human rights protection to the embryo and fetus "would be comparable only with the abolition of slavery, or would be greater than that" (Abortion Case I).[37]

As to same-sex couples, the landmark judgment implicitly established the category of *separate and unequal*. Even though the decision required legal recognition of same-sex partnerships, it emphasized that same-sex couples might not get married; moreover, when it comes to regulating their partnership the differences between such relationships and marriage, flowing from "nature" as well as from traditions, was to be maintained.

It is well known that many hundreds of thousands of Roma living in Hungary have to face social difficulties, prejudice, and segregation. Despite several petitions, however, the problems relating to the exclusion and discrimination of Roma remained absolutely hidden.[38] In one case, the petitioner argued that in the course of employment she found herself in an unfavorable situation due to the fact that her name revealed her mother's Roma origin. The Chief Justice of the Court dismissed her petition on procedural grounds since she did not question explicitly a specific legal rule, but only the application of a legal provision in a concrete case. According to the procedural order that dismissed the claim, the law on changing names "has no relevant constitutional relationship with the right to work and non-discrimination clauses" of the Constitution.[39] Thus, the discriminatory nature behind the, on the surface of it, neutral law could not be unveiled.

In another case a nongovernmental organization protecting minorities, the Otherness Foundation, challenged a local government resolution, which provided: the local representative body "with respect to the future declares those people *persona non grata* who do not fit in the life of the community, violating and endangering the public security and in the future, with all legal

[35] K. Kovács, "Think Positive, Preferential Treatment in Hungary" (2008) 5 *Fundamentum* 48.
[36] 48/1998 (XI. 23.) HCC.
[37] 64/1991 (XII. 17.) HCC.
[38] In detail, see G. A. Tóth, "Unequal Protection: Historical Churches and Roma People in the Hungarian Constitutional Jurisprudence" (2010) 51 *Acta Juridica Hungarica* 122.
[39] Order 924/I/1996 HCC.

instruments it will make every effort to make these persons leave the town." The judges concluded that the decree had neither individual, nor normative nature: it expresses "intent" and "general will" to solve local social problems and counts as "the autonomous and democratic administration of local public affairs."[40] In this way the Court indirectly, but unintentionally, legitimized local governmental aspirations to hidden or indirect racism. With stronger terms, under the veil of the invisible constitution the Court not only remained color-blind, but wholly blind and mute.

Thus, the Court applied neither the concept of dignity-based equality, nor that of preferential treatment, nor yet the principles of liberty rights in cases of vulnerable groups; yet it qualified another group, historical churches, to be subject to preferential treatment.

By implementing the principle of separation of church and state, the Court concluded that this does not mean that the state must disregard the special characteristics of religion and church in its legislation. Additionally, "treating the churches equally does not exclude taking the actual social roles of the individual churches into account."[41] According to this interpretation, it became possible to treat preferably those churches that had been operating for a long period of time.

Thus, numerous cases addressing the communist past and laying the foundations for the future ended with an exceptionally (mostly from a financial perspective) favorable outcome for historical churches. Within the scheme of reprivatization, only historical churches were returned some of their real estate in the course of property compensation. Other institutions were given only very limited compensation for their nationalized real estate. Following this, the Court declared it constitutional that churches are exempted from the general statutory ban on acquiring land.[42] The Court upheld that "obligatory lustration (exclusion of persons from the former regime) extends, besides state leaders and professional politicians, to persons who carry out public-opinion-forming tasks." However, contrary to journalists, for example, a decision exempted church leaders from lustration.[43] Similarly, practicing clergymen did not have to serve mandatory military service because this so-called "positive discrimination" ensured the believers' free exercise of religion.[44] In order

---

[40] Order 949/B/1997 HCC.
[41] Judgment 4/1993 (II. 12.) HCC.
[42] Judgment 4/1993 (II. 12.) HCC; Judgment 35/1994 (VI. 24.) HCC.
[43] Judgment 31/2003 (VI. 4.) HCC. This decision overruled a former one that stated: certain organization of churches and their representatives "surely take part in forming the public opinion." Judgment 60/1994 (XII. 24.) HCC.
[44] Judgment 46/1994 (X. 21.) HCC. Mandatory military service ceased to exist in 2005 by constitutional amendment.

to fulfill their role emanating from the free exercise of religion, "positive discrimination" is to be secured for church-run schools and kindergartens as compared to not-for-profit public education institutions run by foundations or associations. As a result, only church-run schools have the right to an auxiliary subsidy above the normative state allowance.[45]

One of the leading judgments on church status explicitly and purposively provided preferential treatment for historical churches vis-à-vis other churches, religious groups and communities.[46] Following the *ratio decidendi*, the Court declared constitutional the governmental decree on army chaplain service, a decree which provided for the free exercise of religion and spiritual care only for members of the four "historical churches (Catholic, Calvinist, Lutheran, Jewish)." The Court came to the conclusion that the privileges of historical churches are not unconstitutional, but "refer to the real historical role and social significance of such churches." (The empirical findings did not show the degree of exercise of religion, but only the formal affiliation with churches.)[47]

We can see that, in the cases of historical churches, the judges applied the concept of preferential treatment, but it is not clear what type of inequality can be found at the starting point. The Court accepted the – possibly counterfactual – premise that historical churches have outstanding social weight, and that they have a crucial role in the field of spiritual care, and also socially and culturally. At the same time, with its decisions the Court influenced communal practice in such a way that historical churches were granted exceptionally favorable conditions for their spiritual and other activities. Here tradition appears in the strong sense, meaning that tradition is an unconditionally obligatory norm. This type of traditionalism supports maintaining the tradition, even if it violates the principles of equal dignity.

19.2.4. *Catholic Natural Law*

Now we may understand better the reason behind the Janus-faced constitutional adjudication. The interpretation based upon the invisible constitution can be called a variety of moral reading that is not, in itself, either a liberal or a conservative scheme. If it were argued that the Court determined the abstract principle of dignity in a Kantian or Dworkinian way, the conclusion

---

[45] Judgment 22/1997 (IV. 25.) HCC.
[46] András Sajó argued that the 1989 Constitution provided for the separation of the state and church, however, the Court's judgment treated other countries' (e.g., Austria, Germany) century-old compromises as models: A. Sajó, "A 'kisegyház' mint alkotmányjogi képtelenség [the 'small church' as constitutional nonsense]" (1999) 3(2) *Fundamentum* 96.
[47] Judgment 970/B/1994 HCC. For a critical account, see Kis, Supra note 27, 282.

after case studies would be that the system is self-contradictory. It is far from both coherence and reliable standard, because in many individual cases the Court tendentiously reached a conclusion opposite to that which should have come from the proper meaning of the abstract principles.

The theoretical basis of the invisible constitution doctrine lies elsewhere. The interpretive practice of the Sólyom Court was determined by a Christian moral and political worldview; specifically, an alternative conception of the Second Vatican Council, a progressive but non-secular Catholic view. This is what – of course not entirely – but most closely explains the judicial tendencies of the first Hungarian Constitutional Court.[48]

To sum up, establishment of a human dignity-based constitutional concept of freedom and equality, acknowledgment of the separation of state and church, respect for freedom of speech, religion and other liberty rights on the one hand; and conservative views on the social role of women and families, protecting zealously the life of the embryo and the early fetus, denying equal respect to same-sex couples, while privileging traditional marriage and churches on the other, can be easily associated with the teaching of the post-Second Vatican Council Catholic Church.

Probably the most illuminating element of this link can be found in the concurring opinion to the Capital Punishment Judgment, which not only revealed the idea of the invisible constitution, but also elucidated its "image of human being" in order to define the relationship between the right to life and dignity. Justice Sólyom argued that at the present time a dual approach is predominant: a secularized view of the status of body and soul. "Bodily" or biological-physical rights, such as the right to life, are separated from the "soul," the right to dignity. According to Sólyom, the Court is free to reject the dualism of life and dignity by adopting a uniform and indivisible image of a human being that is to view personality in the unity of its life and dignity.

> Accordingly, only the unity of the subjective right to life and to dignity will provide the status that is specifically related to the concrete individual: it is the untouchability and equality contained in the right to human dignity that results in man's right to life being a specific right to human life (over and above animals' and artificial subjects' right to being); on the other hand, dignity as a fundamental right does not have meaning for the individual if he or she is dead.[49]

---

[48] Kis, Supra note 27, 295. See also Tóth, Supra note 38.
[49] Judgment 23/1990 (X. 31.) HCC, concurring opinion by Chief Justice Sólyom.

This view fully corresponds to the understanding of the Catholic Church according to which human beings consist of the physical body and the soul, and the two are inseparably joined. I think the reasoning would hardly survive the test either of the separation principle, or that of the religious neutrality of the state and of the ban on religious discrimination.

It is worth adding that, as the concurring opinion's wording expressed, "beyond the Constitution" we found a natural law concept of constitutionalism, which is an obvious difference between the conceptions of Sólyom and Tribe. In his *Invisible Constitution*, Tribe argues that there are principles and requirements (e.g., rule of law, prohibition of torture, judicial review, and anti-secession principles) which cannot be said to follow from the very text of the United States Constitution. For him, these principles constituting the invisible constitution "are far too historically contingent and institutionally specialized to count as serious candidates for 'natural law' canonization."[50] Antje Wiener also uses the phrase "invisible constitution" in a different sense. According to her, the constitution also entails an informal dimension, organizational, cultural, social practices, and these remain institutionally invisible by definition.[51]

Finally, I add two remarks on the extension of this theory. First, the judicature was far from coherent also in the sense that in cases of transitional justice – specifically the retroactive punishment of previous political crimes – the Court positioned itself as strictly positivist. A famous phrase from the leading judgment says: "Legal certainty based on formal and objective principles [of the rule of law] is more important than necessarily partial and subjective justice."[52] With the help of an entirely formalistic concept of rule of law, the Court was presumably trying to prevent a political and legal witch-hunt. From a comparative perspective, it did not adopt the German Constitutional Court's reception of the Radbruch Formula (in cases connected to Nazi crimes), which says, in short, that "legal norms lose their legal validity when they are extremely unjust." In this way the Court preferred the apparently value-neutral category of the rule of law to justice as a matter of value judgment. This approach, however crucial and advantageous it was during the early years of the rule of law in Hungary, did not fit the objectivism that the Court constituted in most of its other leading judgments.

---

[50] L. H. Tribe, *The Invisible Constitution* (Oxford: Oxford University Press, 2008), 30.
[51] A. Wiener, *The Invisible Constitution of Politics: Contested Norms and International Encounters* (Cambridge: Cambridge University Press, 2008), 16.
[52] Judgment 11/1992 (III. 5).

Second, after the initial three or four years of its jurisdiction, the Court became much more self-restrained.[53] The period when it was willing to extend the scope of fundamental rights in the name of human dignity was over after a short time. The Court became very active again between 2006 and 2010, almost paralyzing the legislature by declaring an unprecedented number of newly adopted acts unconstitutional and void. During this period the Head of the State (László Sólyom) vetoed as many acts as his predecessors did in the previous one-and-a-half decades. As an apparent result, citizens witnessed a constitutional system which did not work at all. This period saw the downfall of constitutional democracy based upon the 1989 Constitution.

19.3. 2011 FUNDAMENTAL LAW: A SEMANTIC CONSTRUCTION ALONG WITH A MYTHICAL CONSTITUTION

The judicial approach performed in the name of the invisible constitution by the Court during its inceptive years faced two substantive rivals. One of them also favored the equal dignity-based judicial activity, but insisted on secular foundations. Moreover, this rival approach did not welcome the Court's role as substitute constitution maker, and advised the symbolic completion of the democratic transition by a new constitution instead.

The other rival attitude can be called reactionary: it drew a dark picture of fragile constitutional democracy in Hungary, arguing that the political transition was unfinished or had not even started, because conventional moral values expressing religious and national prominence appeared neither in the 1989 Constitution, nor the case law of the Court preferring individual rights and freedoms. This side envisaged a new constitution that would not be a symbolic fulfillment of the democratic transition started in 1989; rather it appealed for a recovery of national sovereignty, priority of national interests to cosmopolitanism, for the rule of "real people" instead of the legalistic elite; denounced "juristocracy," both constitutional adjudication at national level and human rights justice at supranational level; and required traditional religious values rather than "empty," neutral principles.

In the 2010 general elections, the then-opposition party Fidesz won a landslide majority of 68 percent of the seats with 53 percent of the votes. It was a majority sufficiently large enough to amend the Constitution or rewrite it totally. In the first one-and-a-half years of its term, the ruling party adopted a range of amendments to the 1989 Constitution regulating inter alia the

---

[53] Bruce Ackerman foresaw this: Ackerman, Supra note 30, 110.

representative bodies, judiciary, media, and civil liberties. As many reports have chronicled, the Court was among the first subjects of the rapid transformation.[54] The new Parliament reformed the nomination and election process so that the parliamentary majority alone would choose candidates. It enlarged the Court's membership from eleven to fifteen, adding up to four justices to the bench. (In sum, due to vacancies seven new justices were elected within one year.) It limited the competence of the Court by banning the annulment of unconstitutional tax and financial measures.[55]

In the name of a "winner-take-all" conception of constitutional politics, on the first anniversary of the election victory, the Parliament adopted the 2011 Fundamental Law as a new constitution which proclaimed the 1989 Constitution invalid, and repeated the previously introduced limitations on the Court. What is more, after the Court, using its preceding judgments, took some hesitant steps as a check and balance of the ruling majority, the Parliament adopted several amendments to the Fundamental Law, one of which stated: "Decisions of the Constitutional Court delivered prior to the entering into force of the Fundamental Law become void." In this way, the whole influential work of the Sólyom-led Court became a constitutional past.

Some scholars argue that the determining factor is legal continuity: since the former legal order remained valid, and a democratically elected parliament adopted the Fundamental Law in conformity with the 1989 Constitution's two-thirds rule, the new system is both legal and legitimate.[56] The new system receives favorable reviews, because reportedly the Fundamental Law and its governmental enforcement replace judicial supremacy with parliamentary sovereignty. The representative government of Hungary gives the majority of people what they want instead of the former rule of "juristocracy," i.e., the counter-majoritarian activity, indeed, time-to-time zealotry, of the unelected, elitist, aristocratic Constitutional Court.[57]

According to many opposing views, however, this has nothing to do with the formally continuous legality, because the Fundamental Law and its subsequent amendments are in conflict with the basic normative features of

---

[54] K. Kovács and G. A. Tóth, "Hungary's Constitutional Transformation" (2011) 7 *European Constitutional Law Review* 183; Tóth (ed.) *Constitution for a Disunited Nation: On Hungary's 2011 Fundamental Law*; Tóth, Supra note 9.

[55] Venice Commission, Opinion No. 614/2011, [10].

[56] A. Jakab and P. Sonnevend, "Kontinuität mit Mängeln: Das neue ungarische Grundgesetz" (2012) 72 *Zeitschrift für ausländisches öffentliches Recht und Völkerrecht* 79–102.

[57] See generally M. Tushnet, *Taking the Constitution away from the Courts* (Princeton, NJ: Princeton University Press, 1999); R. Hirschl, *Towards Juristocracy: The Origins and Consequences of the New Constitutionalism* (Cambridge, MA: Harvard University Press, 2007).

constitutional legitimacy.[58] Although, on the face of it, the Fundamental Law upholds the rule of law, the primary status of human rights, and parliamentary architecture with constitutional constraints, the way the text was drafted, and the content of the text are far from constitutional values and principles.

Political theorists also face difficulties when they attempt to label the new Hungarian constitutional system. In formal terms it still belongs to constitutional democracies, but according to various views the Hungarian democracy is majoritarian rather than consensual, populist instead of elitist, nationalist as opposed to cosmopolitan, religious and not neutral. In sum, it is based upon realist considerations in place of idealist theories. The term "illiberal democracy" is also applied to Hungary because political power is based upon repetitive elections, but the power-holders systematically violate the freedoms of the people they represent.[59]

In my view, the new constitutional system – between constitutional democracy and totalitarianism – belongs to modern *authoritarianism*;[60] it establishes the entire set of formal institutions associated with constitutional democracy, yet these serve as either a tool of authoritarian imposition, or a façade of representation. Hungary, like other modern authoritarian systems, does not reject multiparty elections; on the contrary, the regime legitimizes itself as a "democracy" through elections. However, voting practice is hegemonic in its nature. In other words, there is no separation between the ruling party and the state. As a result, the head of government may keep the process and outcome of the vote under control. Importantly, though the ruling party gained power democratically in 2010, the subsequent elections in 2014 were unfair.[61]

From this perspective, the Fundamental Law can be seen as an example of paper constitutions called semantic camouflage, or a façade constitution. As regards key legislative, executive, and judicial bodies, it does not serve as a normative benchmark; it is only a descriptive map of formal powers. Moreover, formal and actual powers are different. All political power resides with the leader and a leading clique of the ruling party. Formal governmental dominance is subordinate to informal party dominance.

---

[58] M. Bánkuti, G. Halmai and K. L. Scheppele, "From Separation of Powers to a Government without Checks," in G. A. Tóth (ed.) *Constitution for a Disunited Nation: On Hungary 2011 Fundamental Law* (Budapest; New York, NY: Central European University Press, 2012), 237–68.
[59] F. Zakaria, "The rise of Illiberal Democracy" (1997) 76 *Foreign Affairs* 22.
[60] G. A. Tóth, "Authoritarianism," in R. Grote, F. Lachenmann, R. Wolfrum (eds.) *Max Planck Encyclopedia of Comparative Constitutional Law* (Oxford: Oxford University Press, 2017).
[61] OSCE/ODIHR Limited Election Observation Mission Final Report, Hungary Parliamentary Elections April 6, 2014, Warsaw, July 11, 2014.

Distinctively, the text of the Fundamental Law does not call itself a "constitution," rather lending this word to the "historical constitution" only. The Preamble of the text, called "National Avowal" states that:

> We honor the achievements of our historical constitution and we honor the Holy Crown, which embodies the constitutional continuity of Hungary's statehood and the unity of the nation. We do not recognize the suspension of our historical constitution due to foreign occupations.

The Fundamental Law also lays down as a principle that its provisions shall be interpreted in accordance with, inter alia, the achievements of the historical constitution. Since there is no clear definition what the "achievements of the historical constitution" are, this concept, used both in the National Avowal and in Article R, brings a certain vagueness into constitutional interpretation. The Venice Commission characterized this as a "lack of clarity and consistency" among the elements of principles of constitutional interpretation.[62]

The Fundamental Law suggests that the historical constitution is coupled with the Holy Crown. The holy crown doctrine was introduced by the scholar and theologian István Werbőczy, who retrospectively codified it in his work *Tripartitum* (1517), which was a de facto law-book until 1848. According to his teaching, the king and the equal noblemen were somehow united in the holy crown. Thus, the holy crown was the symbol of the community of nobles. During the nineteenth century the holy crown doctrine served as a protector of the Throne and the Altar, thus becoming a targeted notion by reformists and revolutionaries. Late nineteenth-century legal historicism breathed new life into the doctrine. What law historians declared to be an ancient Hungarian idea was mostly their intellectual creation: a romantic, nationalist, self-defensive ideology of the noblemen. In addition, the holy crown doctrine allowed for "a kingdom without a king," which legitimized governor Miklós Horthy's authoritarian regime between 1920 and 1944. This period added revisionist significance to the crown, after the Trianon peace treaty reduced the territory of Hungary to one-third of what it was previously. Consequently, the holy crown doctrine prefers a mystic "membership" of the ancient territory of the Hungarian Kingdom to the current borders of the state, and noble privileges to the republican traditions of 1946 and 1989.

The nation, the very subject of the constitution, is identified in the Preamble as an "intellectual and spiritual" community. The text insists that there is "one single Hungarian nation that belongs together," a nation including all

---

[62] Venice Commission, Opinion No. 621/2011, [28].

ethnic Hungarians regardless of their habitual residence and effective link to the state. At the same time, those resident Hungarian citizens who belong to national minorities are not included in the category of nation. This concept of the nation diverges from those European constitutional standards that admit that modern nation states are multiethnic societies, and thus require the identification of people with citizens as subjects of the same legal system.

According to the Preamble, the country was, on the one hand, a hero fighting in the defense of Europe over the centuries. On the other hand, the country was a victim of the occupying German and Soviet forces during and after the Second World War. Nevertheless, the text does not mention the republican traditions or look back on the tragic failures of the nation. In the sense of the Preamble, 1989 was a beginning of confusion, and the real revolutionary year was 2010, because of the results of the parliamentary elections. What can be read in the text is, as Adam Michnik would put it, that historical narratives are replaced by myths, ideological agendas, and a sense of victimization.[63]

As opposed to the invisible constitution doctrine, the Fundamental Law refers explicitly to religious foundations. The Preamble reads as follows: "We are proud that one thousand years ago, our King Saint Stephen established the Hungarian State on solid foundations, and led our country to become part of Christian Europe" and "we acknowledge the nation-preserving role of the Christian faith." It is noteworthy that the declaration does not simply remember the historical role of Christianity in founding the state, but expresses that the constitutionalism present is based upon traditional Christian faith. Consequently, it identifies itself with the moral and political foundations of a certain faith, in spite of the fact that Hungarian citizens, like other political communities in Europe, are divided by ethical and religious disagreements.

In conformity with the premise that the new system is authoritarian, we can also say that the Court, as the highest interpreting authority, plays a legitimizing role instead of fulfilling the task of final guardian of fundamental rights. Decisions of the constitutional justices, elected according to the will of the authoritarian leader, contribute to the reinforcement of the regime. Here Hungary follows Russia, where the altered but not abolished court serves as a tool of authoritarian imposition.

I think much scholarly research is still needed to understand better the Hungarian case – and similar systems – where not only the Constitution has become invisible, but also the Constitutional Court and the constitutional justice in total.

---

[63] A. Michnik, in Irena Grudzinska Gross (ed.) *The Trouble with History: Morality, Revolution, and Counterrevolution* (New Haven, CT: Yale University Press, 2014), 80–86.

Index

abandonment, 439, 447, 449, 528
Abas, Mohamad Salleh, 383
Aboriginals Ordinance, 348
abortion, 22, 41, 437, 438, 439, 553
Abortion Information Bill, 431, 437, 439, 440, 442, 446, 447, 449, 453
absurdity, 116, 117, 118, 441
abuse, 23, 24, 33, 42, 69, 76, 202, 204, 212, 334
acceptance, 185, 198, 345, 362, 374, 437
accountability, 190, 308, 423, 424
Ackerman, Bruce, 7, 498, 550, 551, 558
acquisitions, 131, 360
Act of Settlement, 322
Act on Election Procedure, 185
activism, 262, 298, 319, 395, 457, 505, 524, 550
additive judgments, 13, 457, 459, 464, 465, 471, 472, 473, 475, 476, 478, 479, 480, 481
additive performance judgments, 473, 475
additive sentences, 464, 471, 479
adjudication, 40, 149, 199, 200, 202, 205, 206, 235, 243, 247, 249, 250, 251, 254, 260, 271, 274, 327, 335, 336, 376, 421, 447, 454, 498, 546
administrative law, 237, 241, 252, 254, 255, 263, 275, 470
Advocates Law case, 302, 303, 316
affirmative action, 40
Affordable Care Act (ACA), 43, 55, 56, 57
Africa, 4, 18, 28, 67, 169, 173, 174, 178, 179, 180, 181, 182, 183, 189, 278, 279, 441

agglomeration, 76, 86
Albania, 169, 173, 174, 179, 181, 188, 189, 541
aliens, 115, 116, 226, 348
Alliance Party, 379, 380
Amar, Akhil Reed, 7, 36, 62, 94, 95, 97, 101, 517
ambiguity, 54, 75, 76, 77, 78, 90, 91, 92, 93, 102, 107, 111, 115, 279, 450, 456, 550
ambiguous terms, 116
American Convention on Human Rights, 214
ancestry, 57, 58
apostasy, 382, 385, 395
appeals, 120, 141, 162, 163, 244, 246, 247, 254, 255, 265, 317, 349, 395, 522, 523
Arab states, 173, 272
Arato, Andrew, 168, 169, 174, 184, 190, 543, 545, 550
Aristotle, 168, 173
Arizona State Legislature v. Arizona Independent Redistricting Commission, 27
Arizona, 27, 28, 43
Army, 59, 176, 274
Articles of Confederation, 25, 26, 30, 37, 42, 63, 67, 79, 80
artistic endeavour, 21
Ashwander v. Tennessee Valley Authority, 53
Asia, 18, 237, 239, 328, 391
Asia-Pacific region, 18
assumptions, 5, 41, 122, 126, 128, 129, 131, 132, 133, 134, 135, 140, 145, 161, 165, 270, 285, 431, 486, 527, 528, 530
attitudinal model, 520, 521

Australia, 8, 17, 64, 118, 120, 126, 136, 160, 162, 264, 284, 343, 344, 345, 346, 347, 348, 349, 350, 351, 353, 355, 356, 357, 359, 360, 362, 363, 364, 366, 367, 368, 369, 370, 371, 373, 374, 375, 399, 497
Australian Capital Television v. Commonwealth (ACTV case), 134, 137, 353, 361, 363, 364, 365, 370
Australian Capital Territory, 368
Australian constitutional law, 343, 345, 346, 357, 364
authoritarianism, 299, 307, 309, 542, 560
authorization, 13, 26, 199, 233, 275, 343, 356
autonomy, 14, 186, 195, 199, 201, 202, 208, 232, 235, 246, 250, 282, 325, 352, 403, 415, 416, 417, 418, 419, 420, 421, 422, 423, 424, 425, 426, 432, 435, 447, 450, 451, 452, 453, 454, 455, 527, 532, 536, 547
axiomatic systems, 153, 157

Bach, Kent, 113, 114
Baird v. State Bar of Arizona, 48
Bali bombing case, 301, 303
Balkin, Jack, 70, 397
Barak, Aharon, 140, 141, 142, 143, 144, 270, 274, 277, 278, 279, 280, 281, 282, 283, 286, 289, 290, 292, 293, 294, 295, 296, 485
Bari, Abdul Aziz, 382, 395
Barisan Nasional, 379, 381, 398
Basic Law, 8, 269
  German, 15, 175
  Hong Kong, 17, 20, 235
  Israeli, 14
  of the Macau SAR, 230, 231, 234–237, 246–255, 256–257, 260–266
  of Special Administration Regions, 407
basic rights, 296, 309, 485, 501, 507, 510, 511, 513, 514
Beijing, 10, 232, 233, 242, 243, 248, 249, 261, 422, 423, 425, 427
Bentham, Jeremy, 441, 443
Benthamite, 441
Benz, Arthur, 175
Berlin, 29, 253, 325, 424
Bickel, Alexander, 55, 498
Bill of Rights
  American, 141
  Australia's partial, 359–360, 364, 373
  Basic Laws and, 280, 283, 289
  Hong Kong, 4, 196, 239–242, 262
  Malaysia, 381, 394
  in South Africa, 179
  statutory, 368–369
binding effect, 29, 47, 177, 181, 185, 186, 204, 206, 209, 216, 223, 233, 251, 254, 261, 262, 265, 305, 306, 368, 457
Black, Hugo 22
Black, Justice, 22, 30, 31, 32, 45, 67
Blasphemy Law, 312
Bobbitt, Philip, 94, 103
bodily integrity, 275, 435
Boilermakers' principle, 343, 347, 348
Bokhary PJ, 206, 215
Book Banning case, 305
Bork, Robert H., 45
breaches, 303, 314, 315, 368
Brennan CJ, 136, 358
Brennan Committee, 370
bribery, 300
Britain, 195, 208, 232, 264, 378, 441, 522
British Crown, 211, 237, 322, 561
British Empire, 232, 238
British Parliament, 238, 381, 517
broadcasts, 304
Brown v. Board of Education, 102, 105
Buddhism, 313, 390
Budelli, Mpfariseni, 180
Bulgaria, 544
burden, 161, 177, 178, 197, 308, 354, 371, 415, 473, 475
Burdick, William L., 495
Bureau of Identity Establishment, 253
Burke, Edmund, 499
Burmeister case, 249, 254, 262, 265
Burton v. Honan, 372
Bush v. Gore, 27, 28
Butt, Simon, 8, 298, 306, 308, 316

campaigns, 313, 339
Canada, 10, 18, 20, 38, 240, 278, 279, 369, 372, 497, 517, 518, 519, 520, 521, 522, 524, 525, 526, 527, 528, 529, 530, 531, 532, 533, 534, 535, 536, 537, 538, 539, 540

Canadian Charter of Rights and Freedoms, 4, 240, 264, 275, 522
Canadian Senate, 529, 531
Canas, Vitalino, 247, 253
canons, 112, 118
Canotilho, Gomes, 250, 252
Capital Punishment case, 547, 550
Capital Relocation case, 12
capitalist system, 210, 232, 235
Capoccia, Giovanni, 177
Cardinal, Paulo, 246, 247, 248, 253, 424
Carolan, Eoin, 9, 431, 449, 454
case law, 136, 198, 237, 239, 241, 263, 281, 432, 438, 442, 445, 447, 449, 451, 452, 453, 460, 471, 481, 491, 492, 508, 520, 546, 552
Casper, Gerhard, 484, 505
Castellucci, Ignazio, 231
Catholic Church, 216, 387, 388, 434, 446, 556, 557
Catholics, 14
Central Authorities, 199, 236
Central People's Government (China), 200, 205, 207, 208, 235, 236, 238, 243, 245, 246, 412, 423
Chamber of the National Legislature (Sudan), 189
Chan, Johannes, 5, 10, 14, 200, 202, 239, 240, 243
charity, 13, 438, 444, 448, 449
Charlesworth, Hilary, 371
Charter of Fundamental Rights and Basic Freedoms (Czechoslovakia), 544
Chaskalson, Matthew, 179
Che Omar, 383, 389, 392, 393, 396
Chemical Weapons Convention, 53, 54
Chen, Albert H. Y., 9, 200, 201, 215, 230, 237, 238, 403, 424
Cheung, Eric, 206, 208
Chief Executive, 206, 211, 212, 217, 218, 235, 250, 251, 261, 421, 423, 424, 425, 427
Chief Justices, 16
children, 23, 33, 40, 122, 128, 129, 202, 224, 309, 348, 358, 386, 387
China, 9, 14, 194, 195, 201, 205, 208, 209, 228, 230, 232, 233, 234, 235, 238, 247, 248, 249, 261, 265, 401, 402, 403, 404, 406, 407, 408, 409, 410, 411, 412, 415, 416, 417, 418, 419, 420, 421, 422, 423, 426, 493
Chong Fung Yuen v. Director of Immigration, 203
Christian, 385, 435, 437, 439, 441, 442, 445, 447, 448, 449, 453, 454, 512, 556, 562
Christianity, 388, 390, 437, 445, 448, 562
citizenship, 286, 288, 379, 436
civil code, 253, 299, 467, 469, 483, 484, 486, 490, 493, 494, 495, 496, 500, 501, 507, 508, 512
civil law cases, 15
civil law tradition, 299, 307, 483, 484, 485, 486, 487, 489, 490, 492, 493, 495, 496, 499, 500, 501, 502, 503, 505, 506, 508, 511, 512, 513, 516
civil rights, 15, 16, 58, 194, 195, 217, 220, 221, 225, 227, 228, 232, 234, 238, 252, 257, 262, 265, 275, 299, 306, 307, 316, 329, 377, 380, 384, 385, 386, 387, 389, 391, 392, 393, 395, 399, 407, 424, 483, 484, 485, 486, 487, 488, 489, 490, 491, 492, 493, 494, 495, 496, 497, 499, 500, 501, 502, 503, 505, 506, 508, 510, 511, 512, 513, 514, 516, 529, 535, 537, 538, 559
Civil War, 37, 71, 523
civilian tradition, 20, 493, 502, 535
claims, 48, 57, 144, 168, 177, 190, 306, 310, 316, 321, 344, 357, 383, 387, 404, 436, 442, 445, 458, 499, 532, 537
classes, 44, 471, 472, 518
classification test, 199, 200, 201
Code of Administrative Litigation, 255
Code of Administrative Procedure, 248, 254
Code of Criminal Procedure, 317, 464
codification, 493, 495, 501, 506, 508, 509
colonial government, 237, 238
Colonial Laws Validity Act, 237, 238
Colonial Regulations, 211
colonial rule, 195, 217, 218, 234, 237, 238, 239, 240, 262, 272, 352, 377, 378, 408, 421, 441, 489, 508
colour, 201, 223, 245
commentaries, 31, 83, 97, 101
Commerce Clause, 26, 43, 51, 55, 56, 65, 80

commerce, 25, 26, 56, 57, 65, 117, 118, 123, 371, 537, 538
Committee Against Torture, 198
Committee on Economic, Social and Cultural Rights, 222
common law system, 14, 17, 135, 194, 195, 196, 199, 202, 204, 208, 209, 228, 422, 498
common law tradition, 483, 485, 486, 487, 489, 490, 491, 492, 496, 498, 500, 502, 504, 506
Commonwealth of Australia, 49, 110, 115, 116, 117, 118, 120, 123, 124, 125, 126, 131, 136, 137, 162, 163, 343, 346, 347, 348, 350, 351, 352, 353, 354, 355, 356, 357, 358, 359, 360, 362, 363, 364, 365, 366, 368, 369, 370, 372, 378
communicative content, 11, 62, 64, 66, 67, 68, 69, 70, 71, 72, 73, 74, 77, 78, 81, 82, 83, 84, 85, 86, 87, 88, 90, 91, 92, 94, 95, 98, 99, 100, 103, 104, 105, 106, 107, 108
communis opinio, 303
Communist Party, 232, 305, 543
communists, 48, 174, 175, 184, 185, 195, 232, 305, 411, 542, 543, 544, 545, 546, 554
community, 5, 11, 59, 115, 141, 142, 147, 197, 210, 215, 231, 241, 265, 267, 272, 273, 278, 279, 301, 302, 303, 314, 358, 363, 370, 383, 388, 390, 392, 536, 553, 561
Community Protection Act, 349
compositionality, 65
Comprehensive Social Welfare Assistance (CSSA), 212, 224
The Concept of Law, 77, 148, 150, 153
Congo, 10, 18, 174, 176, 179, 180, 194, 201, 202, 205, 207, 208
Congo case, 10, 18
Congress of the United States, 81
Conservative Party, 531, 532
Constituent Assembly, 181, 187, 272, 458
Constitution in Parliament, 381
Constitution of the People's Republic of China, 204, 261, 403
Constitution of the Commonwealth of Australia, 8, 17, 115, 116, 117, 120, 122, 123, 129, 130, 140, 161, 162, 346, 359, 360, 364, 370, 374, 375
Constitution of the Confederate States of America, 65
Constitution of the Transition (Democratic Republic of the Congo), 174, 179
Constitution of the United States of America, 3, 23, 63, 65, 66, 67, 70, 77, 79, 81, 89, 91, 97, 101, 108, 122, 123, 124, 159, 171, 257, 259, 323, 397, 517, 557
Constitutional Act, 174, 175, 176, 178
constitutional actors, 4, 7, 16, 71, 79, 103, 172, 327, 341
constitutional addition, 466
constitutional adjudication, 231, 261, 262, 271, 289, 292, 296, 327, 328, 336, 342, 377, 394, 395, 399, 432, 436, 439, 440, 443, 445, 446, 448, 449, 451, 452, 454, 455, 456, 548, 550, 555, 558
constitutional amendment, 19, 37, 122, 123, 181, 188, 189, 190, 292, 296, 311, 341, 368, 397, 398, 432, 434, 508, 523, 544, 545, 554
constitutional arrangements, 7, 177, 324, 330, 341, 348, 421
Constitutional Assembly, 176, 179
constitutional claim, 343
Constitutional Commission (Democratic Republic of the Congo), 175, 368, 369, 378, 379, 380
constitutional communication, 67, 68, 70, 71, 76, 77, 90, 92, 93, 96, 102, 103, 104, 106
constitutional construction, 5, 68, 81, 82, 83, 84, 85, 86, 90, 92, 93, 94, 97, 98, 103, 105, 106, 107, 108, 326, 330, 344, 394
Constitutional Court of Korea. *See* Korean Constitutional Court (KCC)
constitutional democracies, 324, 327, 336, 338, 373, 497, 560
constitutional doctrine, 46, 64, 68, 69, 71, 72, 73, 79, 82, 84, 91, 92, 99, 101, 103, 104, 105, 106, 107, 108, 291, 366, 500, 520, 534
constitutional documents, 6, 14
constitutional features, 172, 177, 182
constitutional fundamentals, 193, 229, 377

constitutional ideals, 9, 17
constitutional implications, 11, 13, 14, 16, 17, 85, 86, 89, 92, 98, 110, 140, 144, 326, 344, 345, 346, 357, 359, 363, 365, 374, 375, 389, 401, 426
constitutional justice, 326, 457, 459, 460, 481, 483, 545, 551, 562
constitutional norm, 12, 14, 15, 40, 124, 283, 325, 443, 447
constitutional order, 146, 153, 158, 159, 164, 183, 186, 230, 231, 335, 359, 374, 376, 383, 384, 388, 389, 390, 402, 431, 432, 446, 448, 449, 453, 454, 455, 456, 486, 506, 518, 519, 527, 551
constitutional powers, 139, 199, 337, 352, 353
constitutional practice, 6, 7, 9, 10, 16, 61, 62, 69, 72, 74, 82, 98, 103, 104, 105, 108, 109, 147, 325, 331, 344, 345, 375, 397, 406, 431, 545
constitutional principles, 4, 9, 10, 17, 18, 20, 26, 109, 140, 167, 178, 181, 186, 194, 229, 253, 286, 288, 323, 330, 331, 339, 354, 404, 463, 477, 517, 518, 519, 520, 523, 524, 526, 527, 528, 529, 531, 534, 538, 539, 546, 549
constitutional protection, 22, 28, 40, 48, 215, 216, 263, 279, 347, 350, 355, 367, 371, 450, 451, 475, 507, 514
constitutional provisions, 24, 25, 31, 32, 34, 35, 46, 48, 69, 70, 71, 78, 90, 94, 97, 106, 107, 135, 141, 149, 178, 180, 249, 291, 296, 318, 325, 332, 377, 389, 393, 397, 398, 399, 404, 468, 507, 530
constitutional reasoning, 331, 363, 436, 440, 447, 453
constitutional review, 175, 179, 198, 218, 225, 228, 230, 231, 243, 244, 248, 249, 298, 300, 328, 334, 336, 422, 460, 461, 466, 487, 500, 539, 551
constitutional rights, 34, 35, 49, 62, 85, 124, 198, 217, 244, 254, 269, 270, 288, 290, 292, 295, 298, 299, 300, 302, 303, 308, 311, 312, 314, 315, 316, 317, 318, 325, 329, 332, 340, 343, 344, 345, 357, 358, 360, 361, 364, 371, 385, 386, 388, 389, 394, 395, 439, 441, 475, 483, 529, 541, 551
constitutional roles, 219, 221
constitutional scholarship, 7, 18, 401, 406, 409, 426, 510
constitutional silence, 24, 26, 41, 43, 326, 402, 410
constitutional sources, 3, 4, 5, 7, 8, 12, 262, 370, 376, 389
constitutional systems, 4, 14, 284, 290, 292
constitutional text, 5, 8, 19, 47, 62, 63, 64, 67, 69, 71, 72, 73, 77, 78, 79, 81, 82, 83, 85, 88, 94, 97, 99, 100, 102, 103, 104, 105, 106, 107, 108, 140, 148, 149, 158, 161, 164, 165, 167, 168, 170, 171, 176, 180, 193, 259, 269, 270, 271, 280, 284, 285, 287, 291, 292, 293, 294, 296, 297, 324, 331, 345, 346, 354, 358, 362, 365, 366, 372, 374, 394, 400, 435, 438, 444, 448, 453, 454, 457, 458, 460, 486, 499, 510, 518, 527, 549, 550, 552
constitutional theory, 61, 63, 64, 69, 74, 75, 101, 108, 250, 290, 315, 486, 508
constitutional tradition, 6, 147, 282
Constitutional Tribunal (Poland), 180, 185, 186
Constitutional Tribunal Act (Poland), 186
Constitutional, Legislative and Judicial Committee (Israel), 273
constitutionalism, 3, 10, 18, 19, 62, 95, 124, 178, 186, 269, 271, 286, 288, 290, 292, 293, 296, 297, 321, 324, 325, 327, 329, 367, 370, 374, 402, 407, 409, 410, 454, 483, 484, 485, 492, 496, 497, 498, 499, 501, 509, 514, 516, 526, 528, 541, 542, 543, 544, 546, 549, 557, 562
constitutionalists, 71, 82, 409
constitutionality appeal, 248
Constraint as Consistency, 72, 73, 84, 99
Constraint Principle, 62, 64, 69, 71, 72, 73, 74, 82, 83, 84, 85, 92, 93, 94, 99, 100, 101, 103, 104, 105, 106, 107, 108
contextual enrichment, 11, 67, 68, 70, 78, 86, 89, 90, 92, 98, 99, 100, 102, 103, 104, 113, 114, 119, 134, 145
Continental Congress, 30, 67, 81
contract law, 137, 484

568   Index

controversial issues, 178, 300
controversy, 8, 16, 28, 52, 90, 251, 262, 317,
    364, 371, 382, 385, 387, 393, 431, 438,
    487, 512
conventions, 65, 68, 79, 107, 109, 113, 114,
    132, 170, 236, 322, 323, 326, 401, 406,
    407
conviction, 60, 219, 300, 303, 385, 432, 434,
    465, 489, 548
corruption, 13, 127, 299, 300, 306, 307, 308,
    311, 334
Corwin, Edward S., 30
cosmopolitanism, 499, 558
Court of Appeal of Victoria, 119
Court of Final Appeal (CFA) (Hong King),
    14, 15, 17, 18, 20, 194, 197, 198, 199,
    200, 201, 202, 203, 204, 205, 206, 208,
    209, 212, 213, 214, 215, 216, 218, 220,
    221, 222, 223, 224, 225, 227, 228, 236,
    241, 243, 244, 245, 247, 248, 249, 250,
    254, 261, 262, 264, 423
Covenant, 196, 222, 236, 239
cover both sides principle, 304
criminal activity, 53
Criminal Assets Recovery Act, 349
criminal code, 299, 469, 471, 472
criminal law, 468, 471, 472, 484, 495, 503,
    535
criminal penalties, 302, 305, 312, 479
criticism, 135, 141, 225, 340, 354, 365, 366,
    404, 408, 510, 514
Cultural Revolution, 195, 196
culture, 10, 21, 51, 80, 93, 161, 165, 171, 177,
    231, 265, 267, 271, 288, 321, 343, 345,
    362, 369, 370, 373, 374, 375, 397, 400,
    418, 483, 484, 485, 486, 487, 492, 493,
    494, 495, 496, 500, 501, 505, 510, 512,
    515, 516
custody, 60, 348, 386, 387
customs, 171, 331, 372, 386, 411, 483, 493
Czech Republic, 28, 38, 544
Czechoslovakia, 38, 544

Dangerous Drugs Ordinance (Hong Kong),
    240
death penalty, 99, 183, 184, 383, 432, 541,
    552

debts, 278, 352
decentralisation, 403, 410, 411, 412, 419, 426
Declaration of Independence, 63, 79, 80, 101,
    102, 272, 273
defamation, 277, 471
defeasibility, 72, 92, 106
Defence Housing Authority, 353
democracy, 10, 12, 17, 18, 61, 126, 141, 143,
    145, 148, 182, 185, 217, 238, 258, 278,
    279, 286, 293, 294, 299, 309, 323, 324,
    325, 326, 327, 328, 330, 331, 333, 336,
    339, 340, 341, 342, 343, 345, 346, 353,
    357, 359, 361, 363, 365, 367, 373, 421,
    425, 457, 497, 505, 524, 542, 543, 545,
    551, 558, 560
demonstration, 198, 225
    right of, 198, 252, 253, 255
dependencies, 167, 169
desecration law, 198, 244
detention, 60, 348, 349, 350, 469
Dicey, Albert Venn, 321
Dietrich, Thomas, 483
dignity, 10, 14, 40, 41, 61, 183, 245, 275, 277,
    282, 286, 288, 290, 325, 344, 360, 432,
    434, 435, 447, 448, 449, 450, 451, 452,
    453, 454, 464, 506, 513, 541, 546, 547,
    548, 550, 551, 552, 554, 555, 556, 558
disability, 130, 380, 470
discretion, 54, 226, 243, 254, 255, 260, 335,
    368, 372, 417, 439, 445, 453, 468, 469,
    470, 474, 476, 485, 512, 513, 514, 517,
    530
discrimination, 39, 40, 58, 59, 126, 130, 131,
    223, 226, 244, 264, 352, 357, 359, 369,
    374, 494, 547, 553, 554, 557
disputes, 44, 63, 73, 141, 199, 249, 268, 299,
    300, 348, 386, 426, 445, 478, 485, 487,
    491, 512, 520, 523, 528
divorce, 152, 277, 386, 391, 468
Dixon CJ, 110, 372
Dixon J., 351, 352, 353, 363
Dixon, Rosalind, 3, 8, 10, 16, 19, 170, 176,
    343, 344, 367, 368, 369, 370, 373, 458,
    517
doctrines, 4, 8, 9, 16, 25, 42, 54, 64, 65, 68,
    69, 72, 84, 85, 100, 106, 126, 290, 296,
    343, 351, 353, 356, 362, 406, 446

domestic law, 196, 221, 225, 233, 239
double jeopardy, 303
Douglas, Justice, 45, 58
drafting, 10, 17, 20, 28, 38, 67, 70, 71, 110, 111, 112, 167, 175, 176, 178, 180, 181, 187, 188, 189, 190, 233, 272, 349, 379, 383, 392, 396, 413, 445
DRC, 176, 179
drug trafficking, 383
dualism, 344, 375, 534, 556
due process, 13, 14, 16, 24, 40, 59, 95, 186, 198, 213, 275, 283, 302, 304, 305, 306, 307, 309, 311, 312, 316, 317, 318, 350, 360, 361, 500
Dupré, Catherine, 174, 175, 184, 546
Dworkin, Ronald, 73, 130, 141, 147, 148, 152, 210, 271, 344, 484, 547, 551
Dworkinian model, 146, 547, 549, 550, 551, 555

eavesdropping, 22, 29, 30, 31
Ebrahim, Hassen, 182
economic policies, 215, 222, 223, 224, 233, 245, 264
economic rights, 15, 194, 215, 220, 222, 223, 224, 225, 227, 228
education, 39, 210, 215, 216, 228, 283, 293, 352, 384, 390, 418, 527, 555
efficacy, 105, 111, 137, 138, 150, 505
Eighth Amendment, 24, 99
Ekins, Richard, 114, 142, 143
elections, 39, 61, 128, 130, 132, 180, 197, 227, 272, 274, 299, 300, 305, 328, 329, 333, 334, 336, 337, 338, 339, 341, 355, 398, 529, 530, 532, 543, 544, 558, 559, 560, 562
Electoral Independence Commission (EIC), 179
eligibility, 213, 214, 215, 224
elites, 231, 267, 341, 344, 369, 370, 371, 373, 526, 545
ellipses, 116, 117, 118, 119, 134, 145
emergency, 59, 398
Emerton, Patrick, 5, 109, 115, 132, 146, 162
employees, 352, 467
Engineers' case, 344, 345, 359

English, 17, 66, 68, 74, 81, 90, 92, 93, 121, 136, 158, 180, 198, 231, 232, 237, 240, 241, 255, 264, 268, 273, 274, 286, 303, 330, 331, 332, 406, 441, 443, 489, 491, 493, 494, 495, 508, 520, 535
entrenchment, 9, 168, 178, 274
enumeration, 46, 91, 92, 95, 100, 119, 120, 123
equality, 10, 13, 40, 41, 58, 124, 126, 140, 141, 198, 244, 252, 253, 256, 264, 275, 276, 277, 282, 295, 303, 309, 310, 311, 312, 318, 337, 338, 339, 341, 344, 347, 357, 360, 362, 374, 394, 465, 466, 467, 470, 473, 474, 484, 499, 513, 527, 546, 547, 548, 552, 554
erga omnes, 261, 462, 477, 481, 545, 550
errors, 111, 255
ethnicity, 300, 420
ethos, 63, 80, 81, 94, 103, 399, 448, 511
euphemisms, 122, 136
Europe, 10, 18, 147, 184, 262, 315, 372, 492, 497, 506, 542, 543, 545, 546, 550, 551, 562
European Convention on Human Rights, 186, 478, 544
European Court of Human Rights, 198, 478
European Union, 38, 503, 544
evolution, 69, 73, 189, 231, 247, 266, 339, 409, 411, 412, 415, 426, 431, 447, 449, 474
ex hypothesi, 142, 155
ex parte hearings, 349
executive government, 116, 217, 221, 227
executive power, 343, 346, 355, 356, 374, 509
executive practices, 4, 8
expert panel, 359, 360, 369
explanatory burden, 308
express meaning, 113, 114, 117, 121, 122, 129, 132, 142, 145
expressio unius, 12, 122, 123, 126, 138
expressio unius est exclusio alterius, 122
expression, 23, 47, 75, 83, 122, 132, 133, 136, 204, 244, 261, 331, 357, 405, 415, 451, 452, 463, 469, 480, 488, 496, 511, 527, 551
extra-constitutional sources, 4, 12, 108, 170, 391

extratextual sources, 63, 64, 73, 78, 79, 81, 82, 83, 84, 85, 106, 108, 517

fabricated implications, 135, 138, 142, 145
fair hearing, 210, 226
fair trial, 14, 221, 275, 302, 303, 304, 317, 394
   five pillars of, 315
   right to, 303
fairness, 131, 207, 347, 453, 499
Fallon, Richard H., 4, 5, 14, 32, 58, 500
family law, 384, 386, 387, 484
Federal Constitution (Malaysia), 376, 378, 381, 383, 386, 388, 393, 394, 398, 400
Federal Constitutional Court (Germany), 16, 289, 482, 484, 485, 487, 501, 504, 505, 512, 515, 557
Federal Court (Australia), 347
Federal Court (Malaysia) 383, 386, 387, 388, 389, 392, 393
Federal Court of Justice (Germany), 500, 512
federal courts, 26, 47, 53, 54, 95, 118, 119, 349, 487, 506
federal loyalty, 520, 534, 536, 537, 540
Federal Magistrates Court (Australia), 347
federalism, 17, 18, 38, 42, 50, 53, 93, 145, 343, 346, 351, 355, 357, 358, 370, 374, 403, 411, 412, 500, 514, 519, 520, 526, 527, 528, 532, 533, 534, 536, 537, 538, 539, 540
The Federalist, 26, 54, 79, 102
Federalist Papers, 79, 80, 81, 101
federal-state relations, 50
Federation of Malaya Independence Bill, 381
Fernando, Joseph M., 378, 379, 380, 395
Fifteenth Amendment, 39
Fifth Amendment, 24, 58
Finance Ministry, 412, 413, 414
Financial Constitution, 507
fines, 131, 302
First Amendment, 23, 24, 33, 35, 45, 48, 49, 67, 68, 82, 93, 95, 355
Fisher, Louis, 29
Fixation Thesis, 62, 64, 69, 70, 71, 73, 74, 94, 101, 104
Fok Chun-wa v. Hospital Authority, 215, 222, 226
foreign affairs, 199, 205, 206, 208, 358, 421

foreign policy, 205, 484
formalism, 103, 271, 289, 407, 483, 485, 487, 496, 500, 501, 502, 504, 516
Fourteenth Amendment, 24, 34, 39, 58, 65, 74, 84, 91, 141, 339
Fourth Amendment, 22, 29, 31, 33, 34, 35, 36, 42, 48, 77, 508
framers, 22, 31, 42, 67, 69, 70, 73, 125, 126, 139, 344, 361, 371, 382, 384, 392, 393, 394, 395, 396, 397, 487
framing, 30, 63, 80, 179, 182, 184
France, 119, 120, 490, 495, 509, 545
franchise, 197, 343, 346, 355, 374
Franco, Francisco (General), 545
Frankfurter, Felix, 67, 113
free speech, 65, 67, 68, 82, 222, 277, 282
freedom of communication, 353, 354
freedom of expression, 23, 83, 223, 241, 244, 277, 306, 314, 395, 472, 511, 551
Freedom of Information Act, 49
freedom of movement, 357, 360, 398
freedom of speech, 33, 49, 65, 67, 68, 81, 82, 83, 91, 93, 95, 184, 275, 282, 290, 398, 471, 548, 556
freedoms, 49, 129, 162, 179, 182, 196, 220, 221, 235, 236, 305, 306, 307, 313, 324, 357, 369, 370, 448, 548, 552, 558, 560
freestanding principle, 11, 12, 98, 99, 100, 101, 357
Fundamental Law, 169, 174, 185, 529, 542, 543, 558, 559, 560, 561, 562
fundamental rights, 182, 195, 196, 197, 220, 221, 222, 223, 226, 235, 253, 278, 310, 377, 394, 396, 409, 433, 436, 438, 442, 447, 475, 479, 485, 515, 543, 544, 547, 548, 549, 551, 552, 558, 562

GA v. Director of Immigration, 225, 226
Gadamer, Hans-Georg, 96, 97
Gageler J, 347, 373
Gale, Susan Gaylord, 495
Gandhi, Indira 15, 386, 387
Gardner, John, 149, 171
Garlicka, Zofia, 179
Garlicki, Lech, 179
Gaudreault-Desbiens, Jean-Francois, 524, 534, 535, 537, 538

Gavison, Ruth, 276, 509
gender, 40, 41, 43, 245, 484, 553
German Constitution, 482
Germany, 9, 16, 175, 271, 278, 279, 288, 289, 433, 441, 482, 483, 484, 485, 486, 487, 488, 489, 490, 491, 492, 493, 494, 496, 497, 500, 501, 502, 503, 504, 505, 506, 507, 508, 510, 512, 515, 516, 520, 555
Ghai, Yash, 200, 202, 232, 238, 239, 246, 247, 261
Ginsburg, Tom, 16, 19, 176, 189, 268, 549
Gleeson CJ, 136, 355
Glenn, H. Patrick, 482, 488
Gloppen, Siri, 181
God, 277, 313, 387, 432, 433, 436, 437, 449
Goldberg, Justice, 46, 47
Goldsworthy, Jeffrey, 5, 11, 64, 90, 75, 109, 111, 114, 124, 126, 127, 130, 132, 134, 135, 136, 137, 138, 139, 140, 143, 149, 160, 172, 344, 371, 499
Goss, Caitlin, 9, 14, 16, 167
government power, 33, 42, 314, 345
grammar, 65, 75, 106, 113, 163, 455
Great Britain, 38
Green, Andrew, 521, 522
Greene, Jamal, 397, 399, 400
Grice, H. P., 117, 121
Gricean theory, 118, 133, 144
Griswold v. Connecticut, 21, 32, 41, 45, 46, 124
Grudzinska-Gross, Irena, 186
Grutter v. Bollinger, 39
guarantees, 212, 233, 239, 286, 288, 309, 317, 343, 344, 346, 350, 355, 360, 368, 371, 377, 381, 436, 451, 452, 460, 476, 527
gun registry, 532, 536

Habeas Corpus Acts, 322
Hamid, Abdul, 380, 384
Hamilton, Alexander, 26, 173, 259
Hammer v. Dagenhart, 26, 30
Hamzah, Chandra Muhammad, 306
Han Chinese, 233, 420
Harari case, 272, 273, 281
Harper government, 532, 537, 539
Harrison, Robert Pogue, 27
Hartmann J, 212, 219, 222

Harvard Law School, 29, 60, 320
Havel, Vaclav, 38
Hawking, Stephen, 51
Hayek, Frederik, 6
Hayward, Steven F., 46
health services, 222
Henchy J., 447, 451
heritage, 286, 288, 418, 489, 495
hierarchy of laws, 314
High Court of Australia (HCA), 17, 118, 162, 344–375
High Court of Ireland, 424–450
High Court of Malaysia, 386–393
Himes, Geoffrey, 21
Hindu, 387, 391, 489
Hinduism, 313, 385, 390
Hirschl, Ran, 18
historical practice, 78, 80, 106, 107, 108
historicism, 377, 388, 394, 395, 397, 495, 561
holism, 94, 95, 96, 97, 98
Holmes, Oliver Wendell, 259, 491
homogenisation, 157, 165, 166
homosexual, 198, 447, 469
Hong Kong Basic Law (HKBL), 17, 20, 235
Hong Kong Bill of Rights Ordinance, 4, 196, 239, 240, 241, 242, 262
Hong Kong Court of Appeal, 240
Hong Kong Law Journal, 198, 206, 208, 209, 214, 215, 225, 237, 238, 240, 403, 407
Hong Kong, 4, 9, 10, 14, 15, 16, 17, 20, 193, 194, 195, 196, 197, 198, 199, 200, 201, 202, 203, 204, 205, 206, 207, 208, 209, 210, 213, 214, 215, 216, 217, 218, 220, 221, 222, 225, 226, 228, 229, 230, 231, 232, 233, 234, 235, 236, 237, 238, 239, 240, 241, 242, 243, 244, 245, 247, 248, 249, 253, 257, 260, 261, 262, 263, 264, 265, 266, 403, 407, 421, 422, 423, 424, 425, 426
Hong Kong SAR (HKSAR), 195, 196, 197, 198, 199, 201, 202, 203, 204, 211, 212, 213, 215, 217, 218, 221, 222, 223, 230, 231, 233, 234, 235, 236, 237, 238, 240, 241, 242, 243, 257, 260, 261, 262, 264, 266, 421, 422, 423, 424, 425, 427
H.P. Hood & Sons, Inc. v. Du Mond, 26

human dignity, 282, 283, 286, 288, 547, 548, 550, 551, 556
human rights, 111, 139, 180, 182, 183, 184, 232, 238, 239, 240, 241, 244, 257, 263, 264, 271, 275, 278, 279, 294, 295, 296, 300, 302, 309, 310, 311, 312, 313, 314, 327, 334, 341, 358, 360, 361, 366, 368, 369, 370, 394, 407, 436, 443, 448, 509, 544, 546, 558, 560
Human Rights Act 1998 (UK), 111, 264, 368
Human Rights Committee, 198, 213
Human Rights Law (Indonesia), 317
Hume, David, 6, 360, 365
Hungarian Constitutional Court, 170, 174, 175, 183, 184, 185, 546, 549, 556
Hungary, 10, 61, 169, 174, 181, 184, 185, 190, 497, 541, 542, 543, 544, 545, 546, 549, 553, 557, 558, 559, 560, 561, 562

ICCPR, 196, 197, 198, 220, 225, 236, 239, 241, 242, 244, 262, 266, 313
idealism, 58, 287, 295
Immigration Ordinance, 226
immigration, 225, 347, 348, 358, 420
immunity, 95, 202, 205, 206, 207, 208, 353, 362
impeachment, 9, 13, 95, 300, 328, 334, 335, 336, 337, 340, 341, 424
Implementation Act, 54
implicature, 11, 86, 87, 89, 90, 91, 92, 93, 99, 102, 108, 116, 121, 122, 123, 124, 126, 133, 134, 138, 142, 145
implicit assumption, 126, 133, 134, 138, 139, 140, 142, 145
implied meaning, 113, 119, 145
implied rights, 298, 301, 316, 317, 318, 319, 361, 364, 365, 440
implied rights cases, 301
implying rights, 298, 299, 315, 316, 318
imprisonment, 219, 221, 275, 302, 312, 385
in bonam partem, 471, 472
in malam partem, 471, 479
incompatibility, 58, 349, 365, 469, 470
incompleteness, 118, 455
inconsistency, 111, 135, 180, 184, 205, 243, 248, 257, 260, 266, 283, 332, 378

Independence Constitution (Malaysia), 378, 379
indexicals, 66, 115, 145
India, 18, 489
Indira Gandhi case, 15
individual rights, 17, 42, 44, 92, 197, 198, 343, 344, 345, 350, 355, 357, 359, 361, 367, 370, 371, 372, 374, 375, 394, 395, 483, 558
Indonesia, 13, 14, 16, 298, 299, 300, 301, 302, 305, 306, 307, 308, 309, 310, 311, 312, 313, 314, 316, 317, 318
Indonesian Constitution, 8, 16, 313, 316
Indonesian Constitutional Court, 13, 298, 318
inexplicit content, 114, 134, 144, 145
Inland Revenue Board (Hong Kong), 216
innocence, 223, 240, 303, 304, 306, 307, 317
institutional practices, 4, 81, 106
intentionalism, 114, 145, 397
intentions, 69, 73, 112, 113, 114, 115, 118, 129, 132, 141, 142, 143, 144, 145, 160, 161, 162, 163, 282, 381, 397
inter alia, 145, 240, 261, 432, 457, 472, 506, 558, 561
Inter-American Court of Human Rights, 198, 214
Interim Constitution of the Republic of South Africa 1993, 173
interim constitutions, 16, 167, 168, 169, 171, 172, 173, 174, 175, 176, 177, 178, 179, 180, 181, 183, 187, 188, 189, 190
interim texts, 167, 176, 177, 189, 190
International Court of Justice, 198, 525
International Covenant on Economic, Social and Cultural Rights, 196, 220, 222, 225, 236
interpretation, 4, 5, 7, 8, 9, 10, 14, 15, 16, 19, 20, 28, 29, 35, 49, 57, 62, 63, 64, 65, 74, 75, 76, 77, 79, 81, 82, 83, 85, 91, 94, 95, 98, 101, 102, 103, 104, 106, 107, 108, 109, 110, 111, 112, 113, 117, 118, 123, 124, 125, 128, 129, 130, 134, 135, 137, 141, 143, 145, 152, 156, 160, 161, 165, 170, 182, 183, 184, 185, 187, 188, 193, 194, 196, 197, 199, 200, 201, 202, 203, 204, 205, 206, 207, 208, 209, 210, 212,

217, 218, 220, 231, 236, 237, 238, 242,
243, 249, 250, 252, 258, 259, 260, 265,
268, 271, 275, 278, 281, 282, 285, 286,
289, 290, 291, 292, 297, 319, 327, 331,
346, 359, 362, 363, 365, 366, 368, 375,
376, 389, 390, 393, 394, 396, 397, 399,
401, 404, 406, 413, 423, 424, 425, 435,
438, 444, 445, 446, 457, 459, 481, 485,
487, 496, 498, 503, 510, 512, 513, 519,
530, 538, 541, 546, 551, 554, 555, 561
  clarifying, 112
  creative, 112
  rectifying, 112
  supplementing, 112
interpretation-construction, 74, 75, 76, 91,
  103, 104, 106
interpretive principles, 110, 112, 121, 135,
  361
interpretivism, 62, 73, 96, 97
intervention, 40, 212, 217, 241, 255, 300, 334,
  468, 471, 472, 476, 477, 478, 481
intimacy, 34, 47
intratextualism, 96, 97, 98
invalidity, 111, 533
invasion, 36, 48, 116, 212, 260
invisibility, 3, 4, 5, 6, 7, 8, 11, 16, 146, 150,
  151, 159, 172, 320, 322, 376, 436, 439,
  454, 455, 456, 458
invisible constitution, 3, 4, 6, 7, 9, 10, 11, 13,
  14, 15, 16, 18, 19, 20, 32, 37, 61, 62, 63,
  78, 85, 108, 117, 123, 134, 146, 148, 150,
  151, 167, 168, 169, 170, 172, 177, 180,
  181, 183, 184, 188, 189, 190, 193, 229,
  266, 320, 321, 323, 324, 325, 328, 331,
  333, 336, 344, 367, 374, 375, 376, 401,
  402, 404, 405, 406, 410, 426, 431, 446,
  447, 451, 453, 517, 541, 542, 546, 548,
  549, 550, 551, 552, 554, 555, 556, 557,
  558, 562
invisible constitutional principle, 210, 220
Ireland, 13, 240, 431, 432, 433, 434, 436, 439,
  440, 441, 442, 445, 447, 449, 450, 453,
  454, 455
Irish Constitution, 9, 14, 438, 440, 442, 449
Islam, 313, 376, 377, 379, 380, 381, 382, 383,
  384, 385, 386, 387, 388, 389, 390, 391,
  392, 393, 395, 396, 399, 400

Israel, 8, 9, 20, 44, 268, 269, 271, 272, 274,
  275, 276, 277, 278, 279, 280, 281, 282,
  284, 296, 297
Israeli Basic Law, 14
Israeli Supreme Court, 277, 284, 291
Italian Constitution, 13, 457, 458, 479
Italian Constitutional Court, 13, 457, 459,
  460, 461, 462
Italy, 8, 278, 279, 457, 458, 460, 473
ius receptum, 480

Jackson, Robert, 26, 58
Jackson, Vicki C., 5, 8, 38, 61, 168, 169, 372,
  514, 518
Jarvis, Christopher, 189
Jefferson, Thomas, 173
Jewish states, 29, 272, 276, 277, 555
Jones, John Paul, 188
Joy, Lina, 15, 382, 385, 386, 389, 390, 392,
  393, 395, 396
judges, 9, 10, 11, 17, 20, 51, 80, 84, 94, 100,
  105, 107, 111, 112, 126, 129, 131, 135,
  136, 138, 139, 140, 141, 142, 143, 151,
  186, 190, 198, 210, 247, 248, 259, 261,
  262, 264, 265, 268, 270, 281, 291, 292,
  296, 298, 300, 314, 315, 317, 319, 320,
  327, 350, 353, 356, 363, 364, 366, 369,
  370, 377, 391, 392, 394, 395, 439, 444,
  445, 446, 448, 450, 452, 460, 461, 478,
  481, 487, 492, 496, 497, 498, 499, 503,
  512, 517, 518, 520, 521, 522, 534, 550,
  551, 552, 554, 555
Judicial Committee of the Privy Council, 137,
  238, 243, 523, 537, 538
judicial decision-making, 19, 310, 505, 521,
  523
judicial decisions, 4, 8, 16, 63, 64, 80, 170,
  177, 229, 247, 254, 278, 292, 307, 312,
  319, 327, 373, 398, 425, 491, 492, 512
judicial discretion, 15, 289, 336, 373,
  496
judicial hierarchy, 152, 162, 317
judicial independence, 206, 208, 261, 300,
  311, 312, 423, 425, 518, 529, 531
judicial interpretation, 167, 170, 271, 346,
  376
judicial opinion, 59, 103, 254, 255

judicial power, 54, 94, 98, 100, 118, 162, 163, 164, 217, 235, 243, 247, 260, 261, 262, 266, 284, 312, 343, 345, 346, 347, 349, 350, 398, 422, 433, 504, 509, 513
judicial proceedings, 223, 249, 350
judicial review, 25, 51, 60, 161, 180, 189, 190, 218, 220, 227, 228, 231, 235, 237, 238, 239, 240, 241, 242, 243, 249, 250, 253, 255, 256, 257, 258, 259, 260, 262, 263, 264, 266, 269, 275, 280, 281, 285, 286, 288, 289, 293, 294, 295, 298, 315, 317, 325, 338, 344, 345, 355, 367, 368, 369, 370, 371, 373, 374, 378, 401, 409, 421, 422, 442, 460, 487, 497, 499, 500, 504, 506, 542, 545, 548, 557
judicial review power, 242, 298, 317, 442
judicial system, 238, 246, 247, 265, 299, 306, 349, 417
jurisdiction, 4, 7, 9, 18, 25, 53, 97, 118, 120, 162, 163, 187, 193, 199, 202, 205, 206, 207, 208, 217, 219, 220, 236, 237, 242, 243, 246, 247, 248, 255, 260, 262, 298, 316, 317, 319, 338, 345, 350, 382, 385, 387, 391, 395, 398, 423, 433, 460, 486, 487, 491, 500, 504, 505, 512, 518, 525, 533, 536, 537, 542, 546, 558
jurisprudence, 10, 13, 14, 15, 17, 20, 32, 47, 52, 56, 146, 180, 182, 185, 186, 198, 231, 237, 239, 251, 257, 262, 263, 264, 265, 266, 271, 275, 284, 288, 289, 291, 298, 301, 304, 316, 318, 345, 352, 364, 365, 372, 374, 389, 395, 396, 397, 431, 434, 439, 440, 442, 445, 446, 449, 451, 452, 453, 463, 494, 498, 502, 504, 509, 514, 533, 535, 553
juristocracy, 558, 559
just terms, 131, 360, 368
justification, 12, 22, 58, 83, 84, 94, 101, 106, 156, 188, 197, 204, 222, 223, 224, 240, 245, 256, 258, 264, 271, 292, 293, 330, 331, 334, 382, 410, 435, 436, 450, 455, 467, 498, 551
justification test, 244, 245, 264

Kable principle, 163, 343, 348, 349, 350, 365, 366
Kahn, Ronald, 523, 524

Kantian model, 285, 555
Kartinyeri, 358, 359, 366
Katz, 22, 23, 30, 32, 33, 34, 508
Katz v. United States, 22, 30, 33
Kelemen, R. Daniel, 177
Kempton Park, 183
Kennedy C.J., 432, 433
Kim, Jongcheol, 8, 325, 328, 336, 339
King Jr., Martin Luther, 60
Kirby J, 136, 138, 353, 359, 366
Kirk principle, 120, 126, 136, 137, 163, 350
Knesset, 8, 268, 269, 272, 273, 274, 275, 276, 277, 278, 279, 281, 282, 283, 285, 292, 294
Kommers, Donald P., 175, 484, 485
Kong Yunming, 194, 198, 212, 215, 223, 224, 225, 227, 245
Korea, 8, 9, 12, 320, 324, 325, 328, 329, 331, 336, 337, 339, 341
Korean Constitutional Court (KCC), 9, 319, 325, 326, 328, 329, 330, 331, 332, 333, 334, 335, 336, 337, 338, 339, 340, 341
Korematsu v. United States, 57, 58, 59, 60
Kovács, K., 553, 559
Kowloon Peninsula, 232
Kruger case, 136, 348, 357, 358, 374
Krygier, Martin, 14, 147, 148
Kyllo v. United States, 34

land law, 299
Lange, 138, 160, 162, 345, 353, 354, 357, 365, 373
Laor case, 292, 293
Latin America, 18
law enforcement, 212, 306, 314, 519
Law of Regional National Autonomy (LRNA), 417, 418
Law on the Major Constitutional Provisions (Albania) 1991, 173
lawmakers, 112, 115, 118, 135, 138, 139, 142, 143, 144, 145, 160, 161, 162, 163, 164, 314
Law-making Law of the PRC, 414, 426
lawmaking, 28, 32, 144, 313, 314, 500
Learned Hand, Judge, 139, 259, 260
Lee, Jimoon, 339
Leeth case, 124, 125, 126, 357, 374

legal aid, 302, 316
legal certainty, 212, 305, 314, 318, 504
legal content, 64, 68, 69, 71, 72, 74, 78, 79, 81, 82, 84, 86, 91, 101, 104, 105, 106, 107, 108, 159, 160, 161
legal continuity, 17, 559
legal inference, 152, 154, 155, 156, 157, 158, 165
legal interest, 15, 254
legal meaning, 112, 145, 147
legal norms, 109, 249, 521
legal principles, 17, 182, 322, 384, 409, 499, 512
legal protection, 311, 443
legal status, 3, 149, 152, 170, 422, 444, 445
legal texts, 65, 66, 86, 90, 110, 112, 122, 135, 136, 146, 147, 148, 150, 160, 165, 453, 463
legal tradition, 16, 261, 262, 482, 486, 489, 493, 496, 498, 515
legality, 148, 152, 194, 212, 218, 219, 220, 221, 228, 252, 310, 314, 348, 414, 437, 471, 499, 543, 559
Legislative Council (Hong Kong), 217, 218, 219, 220, 224, 228, 237, 238, 251, 423, 424, 425
legislative omission, 463, 464, 478
legislative policy, 344, 347, 370, 371, 372
legislative powers, 123, 124, 237, 372
legislative provision, 218, 257, 261, 262, 266, 490
legislature, 27, 28, 194, 211, 214, 215, 217, 221, 226, 228
legitimacy, 11, 13, 18, 19, 34, 38, 79, 89, 108, 118, 129, 136, 190, 258, 270, 272, 285, 293, 294, 307, 315, 336, 365, 372, 398, 404, 406, 407, 451, 455, 460, 466, 468, 477, 480, 489, 509, 524, 526, 528, 531, 538, 543, 550, 560
Legrand, Pierre, 486, 489, 496
Letters Patent, 211, 237, 238, 239, 240, 262
Leung Kwok Hung v. Clerk to the Legislative, 219
Leung Kwok Hung v. HKSAR, 197, 198, 212, 218, 219, 220, 241, 243, 263
Levinson, Sanford, 7, 38
Lewis Carroll, 154, 157

liberal, 10, 15, 17, 226, 265, 276, 282, 284, 286, 299, 394, 494, 542, 549, 555
liberalism, 196, 500, 549
liberals, 276, 394, 395
liberty, 17, 24, 40, 41, 42, 59, 139, 195, 196, 239, 275, 277, 282, 355, 360, 362, 371, 386, 387, 388, 389, 390, 392, 500, 508, 512, 548, 554, 556
linguistic meaning, 64, 69, 78, 81, 104, 112, 132
linguistics, 66, 67, 75, 86, 88, 112, 144
Lisbon, 38, 246, 253
literal meaning, 66, 67, 87, 113, 114, 117, 118, 121, 144, 145, 309
litigation, 117, 201, 210, 249, 256, 293, 382, 395, 435, 437, 444, 446, 478, 540
living conditions, 283
Lochner v. New York, 30
Long Gun Registry Act (Canada), 532

Maastricht Treaty, 38
Mabo case, 370
Macau SAR, 4, 9, 15, 17, 20, 230–237, 246–257, 260–266, 421, 424
MacKinnon LJ, 133
Magistrates, 347, 349, 350
Makwanyane case, 182, 183, 541
Malanjum, Richard, 386, 393
Malaysia, 15, 16, 376, 377, 378, 379, 380, 381, 382, 383, 384, 385, 387, 388, 390, 392, 393, 394, 395, 396, 398, 399, 400
Malaysian Constitution, 376, 382, 383, 384, 394, 395, 397, 399, 400
Mangu, André Mbata B, 179
Marbury v. Madison, 25, 243, 260, 505, 506
margin of appreciation, 215, 218, 221, 223, 227, 245
Market Misconduct Board (Hong Kong), 216
Marmor, Andrei, 114, 127, 134, 135, 160, 257, 258, 260
marriage, 15, 40, 41, 152, 277, 299, 325, 385, 391, 435, 553, 556
  same-sex, 41
Marshall Islands, 28
Marshall, John, 25, 47
Marshall, Justice, 22, 30, 36, 550
Martins, Alberto, 247

Mason CJ, 131, 134, 137
Mason, Sir Anthony, 197, 198, 242, 262, 363, 371
maxims, 112, 118, 321
MBL. *See* Basic Law: of the Macau SAR
McConnell, Michael W., 32, 105
McCulloch v. Maryland, 25, 30, 33, 37, 47, 127, 550
McGee v. Attorney General, 436
McHugh J, 131, 353, 354, 357, 361, 366, 367, 372, 373
Medellin v. Texas, 43
media, 49, 197, 318, 354, 427, 528, 532, 551, 559
Melbourne Corporation principle, 343, 351, 353
Merdeka, 377, 378
methodology, 6, 163, 164, 165, 184, 257, 345, 374, 397, 404, 406, 451
  originalist, 12
Mikhail, John, 100, 124
Miklósi, Zoltán, 174, 184
military, 57, 58, 59, 60, 299, 310, 354, 362, 402, 408, 421, 432, 507, 554
Miller, Russell A., 9, 175, 482, 484, 485, 488, 493, 503, 504
Miners, Norman, 237
Ming dynasty, 233
mini-constitutions, 230
minimalist view, 73, 402, 455, 461
Ministry of Foreign Affairs, 206
minorities, 25, 374, 379, 383, 416, 419, 420, 526, 527, 553, 562
Mizrahi Bank case, 268, 277, 278, 280, 281, 282, 283, 284, 286, 289
Mochtar, Akil, 300, 308
modulation, 11, 86, 88, 89, 462
Mohamad, Mahathir, 382
monarch, 378, 421, 517
Moore, Michael, 62, 285, 295
moral contestation, 13, 450, 454
morality, 9, 79, 80, 84, 99, 100, 107, 322, 323, 384, 436, 450, 454, 495, 537, 540
morals, 77, 266
Moreira, Vital, 252
mothers, 222, 477
MSAR. *See* Basic Law: of the Macau SAR
Mureinik, Etienne, 179

Murphy, Lionel, 364
Murphy, Walter, 497
Muslims, 299, 313, 380, 384, 385, 386, 387, 392, 393
Myers v. United States, 44
mythical constitution, 558

Napoleon, 76, 509
NASA, 34, 35, 36, 48, 51, 52
NASA v. Nelson, 34, 48, 51, 52
National Assembly, 326, 328, 330, 333, 334, 337, 338, 339, 340, 341, 540
National Avowal, 561
National Front, 379, 398
national legislatures, 117, 298, 299, 319
national parliaments, 298, 299, 316, 319
National People's Congress (NPC) of China, 233, 234, 261, 406, 412, 413, 418, 422, 424, 425
national security, 57, 266, 324
nationalism, 382, 383, 391, 441
Nationwide News case, 353, 370
NATO, 544
natural law, 9, 13, 14, 285, 290, 291, 295, 431, 432, 433, 434, 435, 436, 437, 438, 439, 440, 441, 442, 443, 444, 445, 446, 447, 448, 449, 450, 451, 452, 453, 454, 504, 557
  Catholic, 555
natural rights, 93, 101, 119, 290, 437, 441, 442, 443, 444, 446
Nazis, 29, 433, 441, 501, 502, 557
Necessary and Proper Clause, 37, 55, 100
necessity test, 137, 199, 200, 201, 202, 204
Negara Hukum, 301–315, 317–319
negotiation, 73, 190, 229, 233, 420
Nepal, 174, 175, 181, 187, 189
neutrality, 334, 548, 557
New Administrative Capital Act (PR Korea), 328, 329, 334, 340
New Deal, 53, 67, 105
New Order (PR Korea), 310
New South Wales (NSW), 110, 118, 120, 136, 160, 163, 348, 349, 353, 354, 363, 373
New Zealand, 7, 172, 264, 369, 373
news, 186, 277, 304, 305, 360, 369, 373, 382, 385, 387, 388, 421, 425, 482

NFIB v. Sebelius, 43, 55
Ng Ka Ling v. Director of Immigration, 18, 197, 200, 201, 202, 203, 207, 218, 243, 261, 423
Ninth Amendment, 45, 46, 47, 48, 50, 62, 68, 84, 88, 89, 91, 92, 93, 94, 95, 99, 119, 120, 123, 133
NLRB v. Jones & Laughlin Steel Corp., 30
non-textual features, 167, 180, 182, 183, 186
normative principles, 13, 451, 454, 455
normativism, 407
norms, 8, 12, 19, 64, 65, 79, 80, 81, 84, 101, 103, 109, 110, 188, 189, 190, 247, 248, 249, 250, 251, 252, 257, 260, 262, 264, 315, 367, 369, 376, 389, 426, 432, 437, 445, 446, 448, 449, 450, 453, 454, 455, 457, 459, 464, 479, 491, 493, 498, 500, 501, 521, 550, 555
North America, 18, 536
Northwest Ordinance, 63, 102

oath, 54, 219, 425
Obama, President, 55
obedience, 441, 444, 504
Obergefell case, 40, 41, 47, 325
objective rights, 286, 290
objective value order, 286, 287, 288, 289
obviousness, 133, 134, 135, 137, 138, 139
Office of the Commissioner for Ministry of Foreign Affairs, ('OCMFA'), 206, 207
officers, 35, 211, 317, 350, 352, 354
omissions, 27, 35, 37, 47, 480
One Country, Two Systems, 194, 195, 196, 228, 230, 232, 253, 407, 421, 422, 424, 427
'one person, one vote' rule, 337, 338
'one vote, one value' rule, 337
One-Way Permit System, 225
open texture, 76, 77, 78, 82
Opium War, 232
Ordolli, Stiliano, 188
organized crime, 347, 348, 350
originalism, 32, 61, 62, 63, 64, 69, 70, 71, 72, 73, 74, 78, 83, 84, 85, 86, 94, 98, 99, 101, 103, 104, 105, 106, 108, 111, 115, 145, 290, 394, 395, 397, 399, 400

originalist theory, 62, 69, 74, 83, 85, 89, 94, 103, 134, 397
originalists, 12, 61, 62, 64, 71, 73, 74, 79, 81, 82, 84, 85, 92, 93, 94, 95, 96, 98, 100, 101, 102, 103, 104, 105, 106, 107

Palestine, 272
Pan-Malaysian Islamic Party (PAS), 381, 382
Parliament of the Commonwealth of Australia, 344, 367
partnership, 467, 525, 534, 553
Pascal, 28
patterns, 15, 65, 407, 408, 521
Pearl Harbor, 58
Pearson, Noel, 359, 369
Peking, 232, 233, 408, 409, 413
peninjauan kembali, 317
People's Liberation Army, 421
People's Republic of China (PRC), 195, 196, 197, 199, 204, 205, 206, 208, 209, 228, 230, 231, 232, 233, 234, 250, 261, 265, 267, 403, 406, 414, 420
perception, 151, 215, 224, 287, 291, 400
permanency, 168, 173, 178
permissions, 129, 161
perpetual Union, 37
personal rights, 357, 434, 435, 448
phenomena, 8, 68, 70, 76, 86, 93, 125, 133, 146, 147, 150, 151, 162, 163, 164, 165, 285, 287, 295, 377, 382, 395, 476, 486, 488, 552
Philadelphia, 68, 79, 102, 107, 173
philosophy, 66, 75, 82, 83, 86, 106, 112, 121, 124, 144, 146, 153, 160, 271, 286, 290, 292, 295, 309, 319, 371, 431, 434, 441, 443, 452, 498
Planned Parenthood case, 41, 47
Plato, 27, 285, 286, 287, 295
Platonic conception, 270, 271, 280, 285, 288, 289, 290, 291, 292, 293, 294, 295, 297, 452
Platonic Conception of the Constitution, 270
pluralism, 454, 484
Poland, 169, 174, 175, 176, 178, 179, 181, 185, 497, 544
Polish Round Table Agreement, 544
political change, 341, 373

political communication, 137, 343, 346, 353, 355, 357, 361, 363, 364, 372, 374
political context, 5, 146, 148, 164, 165, 379, 383, 391, 409, 532, 538
political power, 328, 369, 543, 560
political rights, 196, 220, 225, 227, 236, 239, 306, 345, 355, 357, 362, 374
political system, 217, 228, 277, 283, 284, 285, 339, 352, 374, 421, 424, 542
political-cultural issues, 344, 345, 367, 375
politics, 10, 30, 40, 80, 96, 163, 164, 181, 184, 189, 190, 239, 245, 262, 284, 299, 310, 322, 328, 353, 376, 401, 403, 407, 421, 484, 487, 498, 499, 502, 505, 509, 512, 516, 519, 520, 551, 559
polity, 8, 95, 177, 189, 484, 489, 499
poll tax, 39
Poole, Thomas, 496, 499
population policies, 225
Porat, Iddo, 8, 9, 14, 19, 268, 271, 289, 372, 373, 452
Portugal, 233, 234, 246, 247, 250, 253, 262
Positive Law, 290, 291
positivism, 114, 146, 148, 150, 153, 439, 441, 445, 453, 483, 485, 487, 496, 500, 501, 502, 504, 516
post-war agreements, 169, 458, 483, 484, 485, 486, 487, 497, 500, 501, 502, 505, 506
pragmatics, 67, 73, 113, 114, 117, 144
precedents, 15, 47, 78, 94, 103, 104, 105, 261, 307, 389, 393, 395, 405, 439, 441, 491, 499, 512, 515, 519, 520, 538
predictability, 107, 373, 496, 526
prejudice, 206, 250, 489, 497, 553
presence of absence, 29
press, 49, 50, 67, 81, 95, 334, 471, 511, 551
presumptions, 112, 118
presupposition, 86, 88, 90, 92, 93, 99, 100, 119, 120, 134, 143
Primus, Richard, 40, 100, 399
principle of proportionality, 254, 336
principle of quantity, 118, 122, 133
prisoners, 287, 355
privacy, 22, 23, 30, 34, 35, 36, 40, 42, 45, 46, 48, 51, 124, 198, 212, 275, 277, 282, 325, 435, 436, 447, 448, 508, 548
private citizens, 22, 318, 461

privilege, 18, 335, 357, 394, 397, 474, 492, 530
probes, 35, 48
process-based theory, 373
procession
  right of, 241, 253
process-related rights, 316, 317
prohibition, 24, 33, 34, 39, 46, 131, 186, 227, 256, 302, 303, 325, 436, 447, 503, 547, 557
proof, 41, 206, 405
proportionality, 9, 15, 16, 17, 194, 197, 213, 220, 221, 224, 227, 230, 231, 237, 239, 240, 241, 242, 244, 245, 248, 254, 255, 257, 263, 264, 266, 296, 335, 336, 344, 348, 354, 371, 372, 485, 511, 514, 536, 548
proportionality test, 213, 221, 227, 240, 244, 245, 255, 257, 264, 372
propositions, 3, 57, 80, 110, 116, 153, 156, 157, 320, 341, 437
protections, 17, 42, 275, 343, 350, 353, 355, 359, 361, 364, 367, 371, 407, 501, 505
provision test, 200, 201, 202
prudence, 94, 438, 444, 449, 498, 547
public discourse, 181, 382, 395
public funds, 222, 223, 245
public health, 226, 266, 418
public meaning, 12, 62, 69, 71, 73, 74, 81, 83, 91, 92, 96, 98, 101, 102, 104, 108, 396, 397
public opinion, 120, 465, 553, 554
public order, 266, 306, 471, 472
public reason, 13, 454, 455
public service, 211
purposes, 12, 15, 28, 30, 31, 32, 34, 36, 39, 59, 64, 67, 76, 79, 83, 88, 89, 101, 111, 123, 125, 129, 135, 137, 138, 139, 140, 141, 142, 143, 144, 145, 155, 169, 197, 242, 244, 248, 261, 283, 286, 287, 310, 348, 357, 382, 437, 519, 527, 543
purposivism, 141

Qing Imperial Court, 232, 233
qualifications, 72, 126, 128, 129, 130, 135, 210, 337

quasi-constitutional, 170, 176, 265, 293, 367, 368
Quebec, 10, 18, 38, 518, 519, 520, 522, 524, 525, 526, 527, 528, 529, 531, 532, 533, 534, 535, 536, 537, 538, 539, 540
Queensland, 109, 131, 151, 348, 349, 350, 352, 354

race, 39, 58, 126, 223, 245, 358, 359, 369, 381
Radbruch Formula, 557
Radbruch, Gustav, 314, 502
Rahman, Tunku Abdul, 378, 380
ratifiers, 67, 69, 70, 73
ratio decidendi, 465, 555
rationality, 15, 197, 237, 495, 509, 514
Raz, Joseph, 77, 168
Reagan, President, 46
reasonableness, 15, 30, 222, 245, 254, 256, 264, 355, 468, 469, 470
rebellions, 70, 76
Recess Appointments Clause, 89
Rechtsstaat principle, 185, 186, 310, 314, 336
Reconstruction Amendments, 71
referendum, 12, 28, 227, 329, 332, 334, 340, 366, 367, 368, 437, 438, 440, 442, 525, 532, 545
Regulation of Urban Ethnic Affairs (China), 420
regulation, 26, 55, 68, 250, 252, 275, 339, 353, 356, 476, 477, 553
Reid Commission, 379
Reid Report, 378, 379, 380, 384
religion, 15, 67, 245, 275, 276, 277, 290, 300, 312, 313, 360, 368, 376, 377, 379, 380, 381, 382, 383, 384, 385, 386, 388, 389, 390, 392, 394, 395, 399, 400, 548, 552, 554, 555, 556
religious conversion, 15, 387, 392
religious courts, 299, 385, 387, 395
religious freedom, 282, 376, 382, 385, 386, 387, 389, 390, 393, 395, 527
remuneration, 347, 349
representative government, 218, 353, 355, 357, 544, 552, 559
residence requirement, 212, 215, 224, 225
Residential Tenancies Act (Australia), 353

resistance, 265, 344, 345, 357, 359, 370, 371, 372, 374, 483, 500, 514
responsible government, 343, 346, 353, 354, 355, 356, 357, 361, 362, 365, 373
restriction, 197, 213, 214, 215, 220, 221, 223, 224, 227, 239, 244, 245, 252, 255, 264, 325, 349, 354, 358
restrictive immunity, 205, 206, 207, 208, 209
retained rights, 92, 93, 95, 99
retirement, 247, 253
revenues, 67, 411, 414, 420, 507
revisionists, 395
revolution, 238, 269, 278, 279, 284, 285, 286, 289, 292, 293, 299, 310, 341, 425, 480, 494, 543, 546
Richmond Newspapers, Inc. v. Virginia, 49
right to property, 221, 278, 329, 360
right to work, 225, 226, 553
rime obbligate, 465, 468, 469, 470, 480, 481
riots, 70, 76
RNA (regional), 403, 415, 416, 417, 418
Roe v. Wade, 22, 41, 47
Roma, 553
Roman ideas, 387, 388, 490, 491, 492, 493, 495
Romania, 543, 544
Roosevelt, Kermit, 404, 406
roundtables, 174, 370, 543
Roux, Theunis, 363
rule of construction, 45, 46, 48, 49, 50, 89, 91, 92, 94, 103, 120
rule of law principle, 4, 13, 14, 18, 28, 72, 83, 86, 107, 108, 143, 145, 147, 148, 202, 228, 262, 294, 298, 299, 301, 303, 305, 307, 308, 309, 310, 311, 312, 313, 314, 315, 321, 324, 336, 337, 404, 413, 423, 472, 504, 505, 526, 527, 528, 529, 531, 542, 543, 546, 557, 560
rules of interpretation, 45
rules of recognition, 148, 149, 150
Russell, Bertrand, 51
Russia, 29, 562

safety, 212, 225, 266, 467
Sajó, A., 542, 545, 555
Salazar, António de Oliveira, 545
same-sex couples, 41, 47, 553

Saunders, Cheryl, 346
Scalia, Antonin, 32, 62, 105
Schneiderman, David, 10, 17, 20, 517, 522, 524, 525, 526, 528, 530, 531, 536, 539
scholars, 5, 7, 10, 20, 136, 168, 174, 261, 268, 269, 284, 310, 393, 399, 404, 406, 407, 408, 409, 410, 413, 426, 490, 510, 513, 520, 524, 528, 536, 550, 559
schools, 216, 249, 356, 393, 555
searches, 22, 29, 31, 34
Secession Reference Case, 18, 519, 520, 523, 524, 525, 529, 531, 532, 534, 535, 537, 539, 540
Secretary for Justice (Hong Kong), 198, 206, 208, 215, 216, 217, 244
secular framework, 377, 392
secular law, 384, 391
Securities Act Reference case, 533, 537, 538, 539, 540
seizures, 22, 29, 31, 34
semantic meanings, 65, 66, 81, 107, 116
semantics, 66, 73, 113, 114, 116, 163, 295
Senate Reform, 529, 530
Seoul, 12, 329, 332, 333, 340
separation of judicial power, 346
separation of powers, 17, 42, 94, 145, 194, 196, 218, 219, 220, 224, 226, 227, 228, 265, 310, 330, 343, 357, 370, 374, 504, 560
1787 Constitution, 26, 29, 30
Seventeenth Amendment, 39, 86
sex, 21, 34, 39, 41, 43, 47, 128, 223, 325, 553, 556
sexual orientation, 40, 223, 244, 245
shadow constitution, 14, 20, 60, 182, 262, 270, 287, 289, 367, 437, 443, 449
Sharia, 385, 386, 387, 391
Shigong, Jiang, 406, 407
silences, 21, 26, 27, 28, 29, 31, 32, 35, 36, 37, 38, 41, 42, 43, 45, 51, 60
  in the Constitution, 45
Sino-British Joint Declaration (SBJD), 195, 233, 234, 235
Sino-Portuguese Joint Declaration on the Question of Macau ('SPJD'), 234, 235, 246

Siracusa Principles, 198
slavery, 37, 39, 122, 484, 553
Slovakia, 38
Small Constitution (Poland), 175, 178, 544
Smith, Adam, 6
social acceptance, 454, 455
social norms, 4, 79, 84
social order, 94, 434, 447, 451, 452
social security, 212, 283, 470, 474
social services, 245, 264
social welfare, 194, 210, 212, 213, 214, 215, 222, 224, 225, 228, 245, 264, 420
socialism, 194, 196, 232, 235, 261, 262, 265, 402
society, 5, 14, 59, 113, 127, 141, 147, 150, 151, 165, 193, 221, 245, 262, 263, 274, 284, 285, 292, 340, 341, 371, 379, 383, 398, 399, 402, 408, 436, 443, 444, 448, 453, 458, 485, 489, 494, 495, 499, 509
Socrates, 27
Soeharto, 299, 300, 309, 310, 311
Solicitor General (HKSAR), 242
Solicitor General (USA), 21, 57
solidarity, 473, 536
Solum, Larry, 3, 4, 5, 11, 61, 62, 64, 69, 70, 73, 74, 75, 96, 101, 103, 111, 117, 123, 134, 172, 295, 344
Sólyom, Chief Justice, 170, 183, 184, 541, 542, 545, 546, 547, 548, 549, 550, 551, 553, 556, 557, 558, 559
South Africa, 178, 181, 183, 441
South African Interim Constitution (SA-IC), 181
sovereignty, 83, 84, 93, 103, 194, 195, 205, 206, 208, 209, 219, 220, 228, 232, 272, 293, 311, 324, 331, 333, 409, 421, 438, 457, 525, 532, 533, 558, 559
Soviet Stalinist Constitution, 542
Special administrative regions (SAR)
  Hong Kong SAR, 195–199, 201–204, 211–213, 215, 217–218, 221–223, 230–231, 233–238, 240–243, 257, 260–262, 264, 266, 421–425, 427
  Macau SAR, 4, 9, 15, 17, 20, 230–237, 246–257, 260–266, 421, 424
Spiewak, Pawel, 179

Spitz, Richard, 179
stability, 13, 105, 107, 168, 454, 455, 456, 505, 509
standards, 4, 149, 186, 303, 358, 360, 366, 372, 453, 478, 498, 501, 515, 546, 548, 562
Standing Committee, 194, 196, 199, 204, 236, 402, 413, 418, 422, 424, 425
Standing Committee of the National People's Congress (NPCSC), 10, 14, 199, 200, 201, 202, 203, 204, 205, 206, 207, 208, 209, 210, 236, 240, 242, 243, 251, 262
Starski, Paulina, 186
State Council, 413, 414, 415, 418, 420, 427
state courts, 51, 162, 163, 343, 348, 350
state governments, 351, 352
state immunity, 205, 208, 209
state institutions, 300, 317
state law, 45, 47, 120, 150, 350, 354
state parliaments (Australia), 123, 130
statutory provisions, 193, 243, 300
statutory rights, 317, 344, 367, 370
Stone, Adrienne, 3, 19, 170, 346, 357, 372, 458, 517
Story, Joseph, 97
Strauss, David A., 7, 32, 498
structure–rights dualism, 343, 345
subjective rights, 286, 290
substance, 162, 200, 213, 214, 226, 251, 287, 290, 348, 406, 508, 511, 530, 531, 542
successor constitutions, 171, 177
Sudan, 173, 174, 176, 181, 189
suicide, 106, 450, 452
suitability, 372
Sullivan, Barry, 49
Sunstein, Cass R., 29, 40, 406, 455, 456
superannuation, 352
supremacy, 114, 168, 185, 237, 239, 257, 258, 259, 260, 301, 309, 318, 324, 352, 367, 370, 376, 378, 382, 383, 384, 386, 388, 390, 400, 415, 433, 441, 443, 460, 479, 486, 505, 512, 525, 559
Supreme Court of Canada (SCC), 18, 20, 518, 520, 521, 535, 539
supreme law, 258, 323, 378, 527
sustainability, 222, 224
Sweet, Alec Stone, 315, 372

syllogism, 62, 86, 261
syntax, 65, 75, 106, 113

Tai, Benny, 206, 218
tax legislation, 413, 414
tax reform, 414, 415
tax revenue, 414, 415, 507
tax, 39, 55, 56, 57, 117, 352, 411, 412, 413, 414, 415, 507, 559
taxation, 117, 131, 413
television, 277, 525
Tenth Amendment, 50, 51
tenure, 347, 363, 364, 530
terminology, 74, 86, 97, 103, 135, 158, 159, 182, 328, 337, 432, 446, 447
terrorism, 299, 303, 347
tertium comparationis, 465, 466, 467, 474
Texas v. White, 37
textual recognition, 12, 359
textualism, 62, 95, 97, 406
Thatcher, Margaret, 232
Theophanous, 361, 362, 373
Tian Lei, 408
Tibet AR, 416, 420
tobacco, 471, 529
Toohey JJ, 124, 126
torture, 225, 226, 325, 557
Tóth, G. A., 10, 543, 544, 546, 553, 556, 559, 560
trade, 37, 99, 117, 123, 199, 371, 419, 537, 538
traditions, 3, 8, 9, 14, 15, 231, 261, 267, 370, 399, 400, 418, 482, 486, 487, 488, 489, 490, 492, 500, 516, 517, 535, 544, 553, 561, 562
transgender, 40
Transitional Administrative Law (Iraq), 176
transitional constitutions, 168
transparency, 13, 190, 202, 203, 308
travel, 71, 242, 244, 306, 437
Treaty of Paris, 79, 80
trial, 49, 221, 303, 307, 316, 340, 355, 360, 368, 371, 386, 389, 402, 434, 514, 533
Tribe, Laurence H., 3, 22, 23, 26, 27, 32, 37, 40, 44, 50, 55, 56, 61, 170, 320, 404, 405, 410, 541

Tribunal de Ultima Instancia (Macau), 247, 248, 249, 250, 251, 252, 253, 254, 255, 256, 257, 260, 261, 262, 264, 265
Trudeau, Pierre, 38, 522
Tushnet, Mark, 449

UK, 7, 19, 111, 176, 197, 214, 239, 264, 368, 369, 421
ultra vires doctrine, 237, 238, 413, 533, 534
UN Convention on Restrictive Immunity, 206, 209
unconstitutionality, 185, 292, 316, 462, 463, 464, 467, 469, 471, 472, 474, 476, 477, 478, 479, 542, 552
under-determinacy thesis, 114
unenumerated rights, 84, 92, 103, 282, 434, 435, 438, 439, 445, 448, 449, 450, 451
unexpressed law, 152
Unilateral Declaration of Independence (UDI), 525, 526, 528, 532
unilateralism, 536
unitary system, 401, 402, 403, 407, 410, 412, 414, 415, 416, 421, 425, 426
United Kingdom, 63, 87, 150, 171, 240, 264, 356, 378, 437, 518, 527
United Malays National Organization (UMNO), 379, 381, 382
United States Constitution. *See* Constitution of the United States of America
United States Supreme Court, 104, 307, 491, 505, 506, 513, 515, 521
unreasonableness standard, 30, 225, 237, 241, 255, 256, 263, 264, 470
unwritten constitution, 5, 7, 20, 61, 62, 63, 73, 78, 94, 268, 329, 330, 332, 333, 334, 388, 397, 399, 404, 405, 406, 407, 408, 410, 531, 540
unwritten law, 149, 171, 322
USSR, 38
utterance, 11, 65, 66, 68, 70, 71, 74, 87, 113, 114, 115, 116, 117, 119, 131, 132, 134, 279

vagueness, 75, 76, 77, 78, 90, 111, 135, 423, 561
Valcke, Catherine, 495
validation, 151, 152, 155, 156, 157, 158, 159, 165

Vallejos v. Commission of Registration, 204
values, 4, 5, 7, 13, 14, 17, 34, 48, 50, 61, 79, 83, 84, 103, 107, 125, 135, 140, 141, 142, 144, 145, 170, 193, 223, 231, 245, 265, 267, 275, 289, 309, 313, 323, 335, 361, 370, 409, 432, 435, 437, 438, 439, 441, 442, 443, 445, 447, 448, 449, 450, 451, 452, 454, 455, 479, 485, 496, 499, 500, 501, 507, 509, 546, 549, 558, 560
Varol, Ozan, 177, 399
Vatican Council, 556
Velvet Revolution, 38
Venice, 561
Vermeule, Adrian, 62, 499
Victorian charter of Rights and Responsibilities, 368
violence, 69, 70, 76, 116
Virginia, 49, 103, 118, 124, 173, 355
visible constitution, 61, 108, 170, 172, 320, 325, 346, 375, 453
vocabulary, 63, 86, 110, 286

Wall Shooting case, 504
wars, 54, 395
Wednesbury standard, 224, 237, 241, 255, 263, 264
welfare, 194, 213, 214, 215, 224, 225, 245, 324, 348, 388, 470
Westminster, 272, 353, 378
White Australian Policy, 371
will of the people, 294, 315, 327, 330, 333
Williams case, 89, 90, 92, 120, 123, 133, 134, 348, 355, 356, 360, 361, 362, 363, 365, 367, 369, 370
Windeyer J, 136, 363
women, 47, 152, 277, 391, 450, 477, 532, 553, 556
Wong, Thomas, 225
Working Party, 380
World War II, 29, 195, 286, 299, 484, 542, 562
written constitution, 3, 4, 5, 19, 20, 38, 75, 90, 109, 145, 149, 151, 161, 171, 172, 176, 193, 238, 257, 258, 260, 262, 323, 324, 329, 330, 331, 332, 333, 339, 371, 401, 405, 406, 407, 410, 426, 452, 533

Xiao Weiyun, 249
Xiaoping, Deng, 232, 234, 409
Xu Jian, 413

Yap, Po Jen, 208
Yau, Yuk Lung, 244
Yongkun, Zhou, 407
Young, Simon, 214, 247

Youngstown Sheet & Tube Co. v. Sawyer, 43
Youngstown, 43, 44

Zhai, Han, 9, 14
Zhiyong, Zhai, 407
Zimmermann, Reinhard, 493
Zivotofsky v. Kerry, 43, 44
Zoll, Andrzej, 185, 186

Lightning Source UK Ltd.
Milton Keynes UK
UKHW021813100822
407098UK00020B/357